PENGUIN CLASSICS

KURMA PURANA

Bibek Debroy was a renowned economist, scholar and translator. He has worked in universities, research institutes, industry and for the government. He has widely published books, papers and articles on economics. As a translator, he is best known for his magnificent rendition of the Mahabharata in ten volumes, the three-volume translation of the Valmiki Ramayana and the *Shiva Purana*, along with the *Harivamsha*, *Bhagavata Purana*, *Markandeya Purana*, *Brahma Purana*, *Vishnu Purana* and *Brahmanda Purana*, published to wide acclaim by Penguin Classics. He is also the author of *Sarama and Her Children*, which splices his interest in Hinduism with his love for dogs.

PRAISE FOR *SHIVA PURANA*

'Bibek Debroy's translation of the *Shiva Purana* is written in an easy-to-understand language, with copious footnotes, and marked by scrupulous attention to consistency in the use of terms. The greater use of Sanskrit terms that do not have an exact or reasonably accurate translation in English is eased for the reader through the use of explanatory footnotes'— News18

PRAISE FOR *THE BHAGAVATA PURANA*

'An exhaustive but accessible translation of a crucial mythological text'—*Indian Express*

'The beauty of recounting these stories lies in the manner in which the cosmic significance and the temporal implications are intermingled. Debroy's easy translation makes that experience even more sublime'—*Business Standard*

'The Puranas are 18 volumes with more than four lakh *shloka*s, and all in Sanskrit—the language of our ancestors and the sages, which only a few can speak and read today and only a handful have the mastery to translate. Bibek Debroy is one such master translator, who wears the twin title of economist and Sanskrit scholar, doing equal justice to both'—*Outlook*

PRAISE FOR *MARKANDEYA PURANA*

'[The] *Markandeya Purana* is a marvellous amalgam of mythology and metaphysics that unfolds a series of conversations in which sage Markandeya is asked to answer some deeper questions raised by the events in the Mahabharata'—*Indian Express*

'Bibek Debroy's translation of the *Markandeya Purana* presents the English reader with an opportunity to read the unabridged version in English. As he writes in the introduction, "*But all said and done, there is no substitute to reading these texts in the original Sanskrit.*" If you cannot read the original in Sanskrit, this is perhaps the next best thing'—Abhinav Agarwal

PRAISE FOR *VISHNU PURANA*

'Bibek Debroy's unabridged translation brings his trademark felicity of prose. Copious footnotes, numbering over a thousand, and scrupulous attention to keeping this a translation and not an interpretation, make this a much-needed and valuable text'—Firstpost

'Like the others, this *Purana* captures ancient and medieval stories, and concepts of Hinduism in a range and complexity that no other Sanskrit texts offer . . . or the *Vishnu Purana* ends on a sombre note, but not without offering hope that those who chant Vishnu's name can still reclaim dharma'—*Business Standard*

'Immense credit to the translator for keeping the flow as light and engaging as the original may allow and for capturing and conveying intact the soul of the *Vishnu Purana* . . . In essence, this text functions as a concise encyclopaedia of perhaps the most evolved research and thought of the time and a 360-degree portrayal of Lord Vishnu in myriad forms aggregated from various oral or lost sources and tales . . . A treasure trove; a slow-paced perusal of the text is an eye-opener, an education in itself'—*New Indian Express*

PRAISE FOR *THE BRAHMA PURANA*

'In two volumes and over 1000 pages, Mr Debroy's translation of what is called the Adi Purana (or the original Purana) brings alive the many myths and legends surrounding Hindu gods, traditions, customs and ways of living'—*Business Standard*

KURMA PURANA

Translated by

BIBEK DEBROY

PENGUIN BOOKS

An imprint of Penguin Random House

PENGUIN BOOKS

Penguin Books is an imprint of the Penguin Random House group of companies
whose addresses can be found at global.penguinrandomhouse.com

Published by Penguin Random House India.Pvt. Ltd
4th Floor, Capital Tower 1, MG Road,
Gurugram 122 002, Haryana, India

First published in Penguin Books by Penguin Random House India 2025

Translation copyright © Bibek Debroy 2025

10 9 8 7 6 5 4 3 2 1

Please note that no part of this book may be used or reproduced in any manner for
the purpose of training artificial intelligence technologies or systems.

ISBN 9780143469582

Typeset in Sabon LT Std by Manipal Technologies Limited, Manipal
Printed at Replika Press Pvt. Ltd, India

www.penguin.co.in

Dedicated to Pradhan Mantri ji Sri Narendra Modi ji

In December 2014, My late husband, Dr Bibek Debroy presented Prime Minister Modi the first set of ten volumes of his Mahabharata translation, a gesture of deep respect for a leader who shared his passion for India's heritage. Ten years later, I his wife, Suparna Banerjee dedicates one of his final translation, the *Kurma Purana*, to the PM—drawing a heartfelt parallel to the Kurma avatar, who balanced the churning ocean to reveal its treasures, just as the PM's steady leadership has guided India through its challenges to uncover its true potential.

—Suparna Banerjee, December 2024

Contents

Introduction

The word 'Purana' means old, ancient. The Puranas are old texts, usually referred to in conjunction with Itihasa (the Ramayana and the Mahabharata).[1] Whether Itihasa originally meant only the Mahabharata, with the Ramayana being added to that expression later, is a proposition on which there has been some discussion. But that's not relevant to our purposes. In the Chandogya Upanishad, there is an instance of the sage Narada approaching the sage Sanatkumara for instruction. Asked about what he already knows, Narada says he knows Itihasa and Purana, the Fifth Veda.[2] In other words, Itihasa–Purana possessed an elevated status. This by no means implies that the word 'Purana', as used in these two Upanishads and other texts too, is to be understood in the sense of the word being applied to a set of texts known as the Puranas today. The Valmiki Ramayana is believed to have been composed by Valmiki and the Mahabharata by Krishna Dvaipayana Vedavyasa. After composing the Mahabharata, Krishna Dvaipayana Vedavyasa is believed to have composed the Puranas. The use of the word composed immediately indicates that

---

[1] For example, *shloka*s 2.4.10, 4.1.2 and 4.5.11 of the Brihadaranyaka Upanishad use the two expressions together.
[2] Chandogya Upanishad, 7.1.2.

Itihasa–Purana are 'smriti' texts, with a human origin. They are not 'shruti' texts, with a divine origin. Composition does not mean these texts were rendered into writing. Instead, there was a process of oral transmission, with inevitable noise in the transmission and distribution process. Writing came much later.

Pargiter's book on the Puranas is still one of the best introductions to this corpus.[3] To explain the composition and transmission process, one can do no better than to quote him. 'The Vayu and Padma Puranas tell us how ancient genealogies, tales and ballads were preserved, namely, by the *suta*s,[4] and they describe the *suta*'s duty . . . The Vayu, Brahmanda and Visnu give an account, how the original Purana came into existence . . . Those three Puranas say—Krsna Dvaipayana divided the single Veda into four and arranged them, and so was called Vyasa. He entrusted them to his four disciples, one to each, namely Paila, Vaisampayana, Jaimini and Sumantu. Then with tales, anecdotes, songs and lore that had come down from the ages, he compiled a Purana and taught it and the Itihasa to his fifth disciple, the suta Romaharsana or Lomaharsana . . . After that he composed the Mahabharata. The epic itself implies that the Purana preceded it . . . As explained above, the *suta*s had from remote times preserved the genealogies of gods, rishis and kings, and traditions and ballads about celebrated men, that is, exactly the material—tales, songs and ancient lore—out of which the Purana was constructed. Whether or not Vyasa composed the original Purana or superintended its compilation, is immaterial for the present purpose . . . After the original Purana was composed, by

---

[3] *Ancient Indian Historical Tradition*, F.E. Pargiter, Oxford University Press, London, 1922.

[4] *Suta*s were bards, minstrels, raconteurs.

Vyasa as is said, his disciple Romaharsana taught it to his son Ugrasravas, and Ugrasravas the sauti appears as the reciter in some of the present Puranas; and the sutas still retained the right to recite it for their livelihood. But, as stated above, Romaharsana taught it to his six disciples, at least five of whom were brahmans. It thus passed into the hands of brahmans, and their appropriation and development of it increased in the course of time, as the Purana grew into many Puranas, as Sanskrit learning became peculiarly the province of the brahmans, and as new and frankly sectarian Puranas were composed.' Pargiter cited reasons for his belief that the Mahabharata was composed after the original Purana, though that runs contrary to the popular perception about the Mahabharata having been composed before the Puranas. That popular and linear perception is too simplistic since texts evolved in parallel, not necessarily sequentially.

In popular perception, Krishna Dvaipayana Vedavyasa composed the Mahabharata. He then composed the Puranas. Alternatively, he composed an original core Purana text, which has been lost, and others embellished it through additions. The adjective 'Purana', meaning 'ancient', became a proper noun, signifying a specific text. To be classified as a Purana, a Purana has to possess five attributes—*pancha lakshmana*. That is, five topics must be discussed—*sarga, pratisarga, vamsha, manvantara* and *vamshanucharita*. The clearest statement of this is in the Matsya Purana. Unlike the Ramayana and the Mahabharata, there is no Critical Edition of the Puranas.[5]

---

[5] The Critical Edition of the Valmiki Ramayana was brought out by the Baroda Oriental Institute, now part of the Maharaja Sayajirao University of Baroda. The Critical Edition of the Mahabharata was brought out by the Bhandarkar Oriental Research Institute, Pune. For a few Puranas, work on Critical Editions has started.

Therefore, citing chapter and verse from a Purana text is somewhat more difficult, since verse, if not chapter, may vary from text to text. With that caveat, the relevant *shloka* (verse) should be in the fifty-third chapter of the Matysa Purana. *Sarga* means the original or primary creation. The converse of *sarga* is universal destruction and dissolution, or *pralaya*. That period of *sarga* lasts for one of Brahma's days, known as *kalpa*. When Brahma sleeps, during his night, there is universal destruction.

In measuring time, there is the notion of a *yuga* (era) and there are four *yugas*—*satya yuga* (also known as *krita yuga*), *treta yuga*, *dvapara yuga* and *kali yuga*. *Satya yuga* lasts for 4000 years, *treta yuga* for 3000 years, *dvapara yuga* for 2000 years and *kali yuga* for 1000 years. However, all these are not human years. The Gods have a different time scale, and these are the years of the gods. As one progressively moves from *satya yuga* to *kali yuga*, virtue (*dharma*) declines. But at the end of *kali yuga*, the cycle begins afresh, with *satya yuga*. An entire cycle, from *satya yuga* to *kali yuga*, is known as a *mahayuga* (great era). However, a *mahayuga* is not just 10,000 years. There is a further complication. At the beginning and the end of every *yuga*, there are some additional years. These additional years are 400 for *satya yuga*, 300 for *treta yuga*, 200 for *dvapara yuga* and 100 for *kali yuga*. A *mahayuga* thus has 12,000 years, adding years both at the beginning and at the end. A thousand *mahayuga*s make up one *kalpa* (eon), a single day for Brahma. A *kalpa* is also divided into fourteen *manvantara*s, a *manvantara* being a period during which a Manu presides and rules over creation. Therefore, there are 71.4 *mahayuga*s in a *manvantara*. Our present *kalpa* is known as the Shveta Varaha Kalpa. Within that, six Manus have come and gone. Their names

are: (1) Svayambhuva Manu, (2) Svarochisha Manu,
(3) Uttama Manu, (4) Tapasa Manu, (5) Raivata Manu
and (6) Chakshusha Manu. The present Manu is known
as Vaivasvata Manu. Vivasvat, also written as Vivasvan,
is the name of Surya, the Sun God. Vaivasvata Manu has
that name because he is Surya's son. Not only do Manus
change from one *manvantara* to another. So do the gods,
the ruler of the gods and the seven great sages, known as
the *saptarshi*s (seven *rishi*s). Indra is the title of the ruler
of the gods. It is not a proper name. The present Indra is
Purandara. However, in a different *manvantara*, someone
else will hold the title. In the present seventh *manvantara*,
known as Vaivasvata *manvantara*, there will also be 71.4
*mahayuga*s. We are in the twenty-eighth of these. Since
a different Vedavyasa performs that task of classifying
and collating the Vedas in every *mahayuga*, Krishna
Dvaipayana Vedavyasa is the twenty-eighth in that series.
Just so that it is clear, Vedavyasa isn't a proper name. It is
a title conferred on someone who collates and classifies the
Vedas. There have been twenty-seven who have held the
title of Vedavyasa before him, and he is the twenty-eighth.
His proper name is Krishna Dvaipayana, Krishna because
he was dark and Dvaipayana because he was born on an
island (*dvipa*). This gives us an idea of what the topic of
manvantara is about. This still leaves *pratisarga*, *vamsha*
and *vamshanucharita*. The two famous dynasties/lineages
were the solar dynasty (*survya vamsha*) and lunar dynasty
(*chandra vamsha*), and all the famous kings belonged to
one or other of these two dynasties. *Vamshanucharita* is
about these lineages and the conduct of these kings. There
were the gods and sages (*rishi*s) too, not always born
through a process of physical procreation. Their lineages
are described under the heading of *vamsha*. Finally, within

that cycle of primary creation and destruction, there are smaller and secondary cycles of creation and destruction. That's the domain of *pratisarga*. To a greater or lesser degree, all the Puranas cover these five topics, some more than the others. The Purana which strictly adheres to this five-topic classification is the *Vishnu Purana*.

There are many types of Puranas. Some are known as Sthala Puranas, describing the greatness and sanctity of a specific geographical place. Some are known as Upa-Puranas, minor Puranas. The listing of Upa-Puranas has regional variations and there is no country-wide consensus about the list of Upa-Puranas, though it is often accepted there are eighteen. The Puranas we have in mind are known as Maha-Puranas, major Puranas. Henceforth, when we use the word Puranas, we mean Maha-Puranas. There is consensus that there are eighteen Maha-Puranas, though it is not obvious that this number of eighteen existed right from the beginning. The names are mentioned in several of these texts, including a *shloka* that follows the *shloka* cited from the Matsya Purana. Thus, the eighteen Puranas are: (1) Agni (15,400); (2) Bhagavata (18,000); (3) Brahma (10,000); (4) Brahmanda (12,000); (5) Brahmavaivarta (18,000); (6) Garuda (19,000); (7) Kurma (17,000); (8) Linga (11,000); (9) Markandeya (9000); (10) Matsya (14,000); (11) Narada (25,000); (12) Padma (55,000); (13) Shiva (24,000); (14) Skanda (81,100); (15) Vamana (10,000); (16) Varaha (24,000); (17) Vayu (24,000); and (18) Vishnu (23,000).

A few additional points about this list: First, the Harivamsha is sometimes loosely described as a Purana, but strictly speaking, it is not a Purana. It is more like an addendum to the Mahabharata. Second, Bhavishya (14,500) is sometimes mentioned, with Vayu excised from

the list. However, the Vayu Purana exhibits many more
Purana characteristics than the Bhavishya Purana does.
There are references to a Bhavishyat Purana that existed,
but that may not necessarily be the Bhavishya Purana
as we know it today. That's true of some other Puranas
too. Texts have been completely restructured hundreds of
years later. Third, it is not just a question of Bhavishya
Purana and Vayu Purana. In the lists given in some
Puranas, Vayu is part of the eighteen, but Agni is knocked
out. In some others, Narasimha and Vayu are included,
but Brahmanda and Garuda are knocked out. Fourth,
when a list is given, the order also indicates some notion
of priority or importance. Since that varies from text to
text, our listing is simply alphabetical, according to the
English alphabet. Fifth, when one uses the term Bhagavata,
does one mean Bhagavata Purana or does one mean Devi
Bhagavata Purana? The numbers within brackets indicate
the number of *shloka*s each of these Puranas has or is
believed to have. The range is from 9000 in Markandeya to
a mammoth 81,100 in Skanda. The aggregate is a colossal
4,09,500 *shloka*s. To convey a rough idea of the orders
of magnitude, the Mahabharata has or is believed to have
1,00,000 *shloka*s. It's a bit difficult to convert a *shloka*
into word counts in English, especially because Sanskrit
words have a slightly different structure. However, as a
very crude approximation, one *shloka* is roughly twenty
words. Thus, 1,00,000 *shloka*s become two million
words and 4,00,000 *shloka*s, four times the size of the
Mahabharata, amounts to eight million words. There is
a reason for using the expression 'is believed to have',
as opposed to 'has'. Rendering into writing is of a later
vintage, the initial process was one of oral transmission.
In the process, many texts have been lost or are retained in

imperfect condition. This is true of texts in general and is also specifically true of Itihasa and Puranas. The Critical Edition of the Mahabharata, mentioned earlier, no longer possesses 1,00,000 *shloka*s. Including the Harivamsha, there are around 80,000 *shloka*s. The Critical Edition of the Mahabharata has of course deliberately excised some *shloka*s. For the Puranas, there is no counterpart to Critical Editions, though work has started on a few. However, whichever edition of the Puranas one chooses, the number of *shloka*s in that specific Purana will generally be smaller than the numbers given above. Either those many *shloka*s did not originally exist, or they have been lost. This is the right place to mention that a reading of the Puranas assumes a basic degree of familiarity with the Valmiki Ramayana and the Mahabharata, more the latter than the former. Without that familiarity, one will often fail to appreciate the context completely. More than passing familiarity with the Bhagavat Gita, strictly speaking, a part of the Mahabharata, helps.[6]

Other than the five attributes, the Puranas have a considerable amount of information on geography and even geological changes (changes in the courses of rivers) and astronomy. Therefore, those five attributes shouldn't suggest the Puranas have nothing more. They do, and they have therefore been described as encyclopedias. Bharatavarsha is vast and heterogeneous, and each Purana may very well have originated in one particular part of the

---

[6] The Bhagavat Gita translation was published in 2006 and reprinted in 2019, the translation of the Critical Edition of the Mahabharata in 10 volumes between 2010 and 2014 (with a box set in 2015) and the translation of the Critical Edition of the Valmiki Ramayana in 2017. The translations are by Bibek Debroy, and in each case, the publisher is Penguin.

country. Accordingly, within that broad compass of an overall geographical description, the extent of geographical information varies from Purana to Purana. Some are more familiar with one part of the country than with another. Though not explicitly mentioned in the five attributes, the Puranas are also about pursuing *dharma, artha, kama* and *moksha*, the four objectives of human existence, and about the four *varna*s and the four *ashrama*s. The general understanding and practice of *dharma* is based much more on the Puranas than on the *Veda*s. Culture, notions of law, rituals, architecture and iconography are based on the Puranas. There is beautiful poetry too.

Perhaps one should mention that there are two ways these eighteen Puranas are classified. The trinity has Brahma as the creator, Vishnu as the preserver and Shiva as the destroyer. Therefore, Puranas where creation themes feature prominently are identified with Brahma (Brahma, Brahmanda, Brahmavaivarta, Markandeya). Puranas where Vishnu features prominently are identified as Vaishnava Puranas (Bhagavata, Garuda, Kurma, Matysa, Narada, Padma, Vamana, Varaha, Vishnu). Puranas where Shiva features prominently are identified as Shaiva Puranas (Agni, Linga, Shiva, Skanda, Vayu). While there is a grain of truth in this, Brahma, Vishnu and Shiva are all important and all three feature in every Purana. Therefore, beyond the relative superiority of Vishnu vis-à-vis Shiva, the taxonomy probably doesn't serve much purpose. The second classification is even more tenuous and is based on the three *guna*s of *sattva* (purity), *rajas* (passion) and *tamas* (ignorance). For example, the Uttara Khanda of the Padma Purana has a few *shloka*s along these lines, recited by Shiva to Parvati. With a caveat similar to the one mentioned earlier, this should be in the 236th chapter of Uttara

Khanda. According to this, the Puranas characterized by *sattva* are Bhagavata, Garuda, Narada, Padma, Varaha and Vishnu. Those characterized by *rajas* are Bhavishya, Brahma, Brahmanda, Brahmavaivarta, Markandeya and Vamana. Those characterized by *tamas* are Agni, Kurma, Linga, Matysa, Skanda and Shiva.

Within a specific Purana text, there are earlier sections, as well as later ones. That makes it difficult to date a Purana, except as a range. Across Purana texts, there are older Puranas, as well as later ones. Extremely speculatively, the dating will be something like the following. (1) Agni (800–1100 CE); (2) Bhagavata (500–1000 CE); (3) Brahma (700–1500 CE); (4) Brahmanda (400–600 CE); (5) Brahmavaivarta (700–1500 CE); (6) Garuda (800–1100 CE); (7) Kurma (600–900 CE); (8) Linga (500–1000 CE); (9) Markandeya (250–700 CE); (10) Matsya (200–500 CE); (11) Narada (900–1600 CE); (12) Padma (400–1600 CE); (13) Shiva (1000–1400 CE); (14) Skanda (600–1200 CE); (15) Vamana (450–900 CE); (16) Varaha (1000–1200 CE); (17) Vayu (350–550 CE); (18) Vishnu (300 BCE to 450 CE); and (19) Bhavishya (500–1900 CE). Reiterating once again that there is no great precision in these ranges, by this reckoning, the *Vishnu Purana* is the oldest and some parts of the Bhavishya Purana are as recent as the nineteeth century. To state the obvious, within the same Purana, there may be older sections and newer ones.

As mentioned earlier, there is no critical edition for the Puranas. Therefore, one has to choose a Sanskrit text one is going to translate from. If one is going to translate all the Puranas, it is preferable, though not essential, that one opts for a common source for all the Purana texts. In all the Purana translations, as a common source, I have used and will use, the ones brought out by Nag Publishers, with funding from the Ministry of Human Resource Development.[7] To the best of my knowledge, other than this translation, there are two other unabridged translations of the Brahmanda Purana in English. For the first, G.V. Tagare was the translator, published under the 'Ancient Indian Tradition and Mythology Series'.[8] In the course of this translation, extensive comparisons have been made with the Tagare translation. The Sanskrit texts used for the two translations are similar, but not always identical. However, the differences are minor. More importantly, the discerning reader, who compares the two, will find that we have sometimes differed in interpreting words and sentences. The second is by Shanti Lal Nagar and K.L. Joshi.[9]

In the second half of the nineteenth century, the contribution of Calcutta and Bengal towards preserving the Itihasa–Purana legacy was remarkable. Consider the following: (1) Kaliprasanna Singha's unabridged translation of the Mahabharata in Bengali; (2) the Sanskrit and unabridged Bengali translation of the Burdwan edition of the Mahabharata; (3) the unabridged Bengali translation of the Mahabharata, published by Pratap Chandra Roy; (4) the unabridged English translation of the Valmiki Ramayana by William Carey and Joshua Marshman; (5) Hemachandra Bhattacharya's unabridged translation of the Valmiki Ramayana in Bengali; (6) Ganga Prasad Mukhopadhyaya's verse translation of the Valmiki

---

[7] *The Kurmamahapuranam*, Nag Publishers, Delhi, 1983.

[8] *The Kurma Purana*, translated and annotated by G.V. Tagare, two volumes, Motilal Banarsidass Publishers, Delhi, 1981 and 1982.

[9] *Kurma Mahapurana: An Exhaustive Introduction, Sanskrit Text, English Translation and Scholarly Notes*, Shanti Lal Nagar and K.L. Joshi, Parimal Books, 2008.

Ramayana; (7) Panchanan Tarkaratna's Sanskrit editions
and Bengali translations of Valmiki Ramayana, Adhyatma
Ramayana and several Puranas; (8) unabridged translations
of the Mahabharata in English by Kisari Mohan Ganguli
and Manmatha Nath Dutt; (9) the Asiatic Society's[10]
Bibliotheca Indica Sanskrit editions of Agni Purana,
Brihad Dharma Purana, Brihad Naradiya Purana, Kurma
Purana, Varaha Purana and Vayu Purana; and (10) F.E.
Pargiter's unabridged English translation of Markandeya
Purana. (11) And most important of all, Horace Hayman's
Wilson translation of the Vishnu Purana, in five volumes,
between 1864 and 1870.[11] Though Wilson's translation
wasn't part of the Bibliotheca Indica corpus, it was part
of the same broad tradition. Wilson's work was almost
certainly the first unabridged translation of any Purana
into English, and the scholarship was remarkable. An act
of research and scholarship still needs to be undertaken,
cross-referencing names, genealogies and incidents across
Itihasa and Purana texts. Often, when the same incident
is narrated in different Purana texts, there are differences
in nuances and details. Since ours is a translation, we have
deliberately refrained from undertaking such an exercise.
But the Horace Hayman Wilson translation did seek to
do that. Before that work can be undertaken, the Purana
corpus has to be translated, meaning translation into
English. More often than not, practices of *dharma* are
based on the Itihasa–Purana corpus. The Purana project,
published by Penguin, is part of that translation endeavour.

[10] The Asiatic Society went through several name changes, but
it can simply be called the Asiatic Society.
[11] *The Vishnu Purana: A System of Hindu Mythology and
Tradition*, Horace Hayman Wilson, Trubner & Company, London,
1864–1870.

Translations of *Bhagavata Purana*, *Markandeya Purana*, *Brahma Purana*, *Vishnu Purana*, *Shiva Purana* and *Brahmanda Purana* have already been published and *Kurma Purana* is the seventh.

As has been mentioned earlier, the composition of Kurma Purana is dated to between 600 to 900 CE. It is not a very early Purana, nor one too late, somewhere in the middle. R.C. Hazra's dissertation is still one of the best introductions to the Purana corpus, for all the Puranas.[12] He devoted several pages to Kurma Purana, highlighting its importance. To quote from Hazra, 'The Kurma-p. informs us that the entire Purana of this title consisted of four Samhitas, viz. Brahmi, Bhagavati, Sauri and Vaisnavi, and that the copy of the Purana which is now available is only a part named Brahmi Samhita . . ..The present Kurma-p. betrays the two main stages through which it passed to attain its present form . . . We have now sufficient reason to hold that the extant Kurma-p. was originally a Pancaratra document. It was afterwards recast so successfully by the Pasupatas that its Visnuite character was obscured almost totally.' With today's text, it is impossible to separate these two elements. Suffice to say, throughout Kurma Purana, there is the overwhelming presence of Shiva, synthesized and identified with Vishnu, Surya and Brahma.

A quote from Wilson's preface[13] will add to what has already been said. 'The name, being that of an Avatara of Vishnu, might lead us to expect a Vaishnava work: but it is always, and correctly, classified with the Saiva Puranas;

[12] *Studies in the Puranic Records on Hindu Rites and Customs,* R.C. Hazra, University of Dacca, 1940. This has since been reprinted several times, by different publishers.
[13] *Op.cit.*

the greater portion of it inculcating the worship of Siva and Durga.' Every Purana satisfies the *pancha lakshmana* characteristics and Kurma Purana is no different. When reading one Purana and comparing it to another, there is often the feeling that accounts are repetitive. This is partly true, but there is more to it than that. Even when the same incident is narrated, each Purana has its twists and nuances. Having said that and having covered that familiar terrain, each Purana has something special, something that is specific and incremental to it. For Kurma Purana that will be the sections on Devi, Ishvara Gita and Vyasa Gita, the last covering topics usually identified with the *dharmashastra*s. In all Puranas, some chapters are almost verbatim reproductions of sections from the Mahabharata, Hari Vamsha and other Puranas. One should not deduce that a specific Purana text has been copied from another since these various texts might have had a common origin. That apart, even when the *shloka*s seem to be virtually identical, there are interesting changes in words and nuances. This has a bearing on the Hazra and Wilson arguments. Today, given the texts we possess, it is impossible to unambiguously establish the original text. Who can determine which preceded which? After all, each Purana evolved and was added to.

In terms of its present structure and attributes, the Kurma Purana displays all the characteristics of a Maha Purana. It covers the five topics and is divided into two parts, the first part (*purvarddha*) and the second part (*uttararddha*). The Kurma Purana is supposed to have 17,000 *shloka*s. As the table at the beginning of the translation indicates, this text possesses 5896 *shloka*s, divided into 3195 *shloka*s for the first part and 2701 *shloka*s for the second part. There are ninety-nine chapters, divided into fifty-three for the first part and forty-six for the second part. The reason for this gap is that the Brahmi Samhita alone remains, the Bhagavati, Souri and Vaishnavi Samhitas having been lost. A word about the numbering we have followed for the chapters, such as Chapter 57(2)(4). The first number is a consecutive numbering of chapters of the entire Kurma Purana, while the second number indicates the part, the first or the second as the case might be. The number within the next bracket indicates a consecutive numbering of chapters within that part. As with many Purana texts, the chapters have no headings. If there is a colophon, the chapter heading is based on the colophon. If there is no colophon, the chapter heading is based on what the chapter is about.

As with every Purana, there are layers within layers, and the account is not recited by a single person. The basic template is of course the standard one of the Suta reciting the Purana to sages who have assembled for a sacrifice in Naimisha Forest. But there is a core template that is behind this, that of Kurma reciting the Purana to Indradyumna. Right at the end of the text, we are given lines of transmission, from Narayana to the sages, from Brahma to Panchashikha and from Sanatkumara to Suta.

In the translations of the Bhagavat Gita, the Mahabharata, the Hari Vamsha, the Valmiki Ramayana, the *Bhagavata Purana*, the *Markandeya Purana*, the *Brahma Purana*, the *Vishnu Purana*, the *Shiva Purana* and the *Brahmanda Purana*,[14] we followed the principle of not using diacritical marks. The use of diacritical

---

[14] *The Bhagavata Purana,* Volumes 1–3, Penguin Books, 2018. *The Markandeya Purana*, Penguin Books, 2019. *The Brahma Purana*, Volumes 1–2, Penguin Books 2021. The *Vishnu Purana*, Penguin Books, 2022. *The Shiva Purana*, Volumes 1-3, Penguin Books, 2023.

marks (effectively the international alphabet of Sanskrit transliteration) makes the pronunciation and rendering more accurate, but also tends to put off readers who are less academically inclined. Since diacritical marks are not being used, there is a challenge in rendering Sanskrit names in English. Sanskrit is a phonetic language and we have used that principle as a basis. Applied consistently, this means that words are rendered in ways that may seem unfamiliar. Hence, Gautama will appear as Goutama here. This is true of proper names, and, in a few rare cases, of geographical names. The absence of diacritical marks causes some minor problems. How does one distinguish Mahadeva Shiva from Parvati Shivaa? Often, the context will make the difference clear. If not, we have written Mahadeva as Shiva and Parvati as Shivaa. This is especially the case when names of feminine divinities might give rise to confusion. In translating, the attempt has been to provide a word-for-word translation, so that if one were to hold up the Sanskrit text, there would be a perfect match. In the process, the English is not as smooth as it might have been, deliberately so.

The intention is to offer a translation, not an interpretation. That sounds like a simple principle to adopt, and for the most part, is easy to follow. However, there is a thin dividing line between translation and interpretation. In some instances, it is impossible to translate without bringing in a little bit of interpretation. Inevitably, interpretation is subjective. We have tried to minimize the problem by (a) reducing interpretation; (b) relegating interpretation to footnotes and (c) when there are alternative interpretations, pointing this out to the reader through those footnotes. But all said and done, there is no substitute for reading these texts in the original Sanskrit.

Finally, the Kurma Purana is not an easy Purana to translate, read and understand. That has a lot to do with the text. Unlike Puranas that are read all the time, like Bhagavata Purana, the text of Kurma Purana is not that clean and is full of typos. Inevitably, until there are Critical Editions, there are problems in interpretation and translation. In the specific Sanskrit text we have used, alternative readings are sometimes given as notes. In some instances, we have used these alternative readings instead of the main text. When one has had to take liberties to make the meaning clear, this has been indicated, so that the reader is warned.

The Kurma Purana

	Chapter	Number of *shlokas*
Purvarddha **(the first part)**		
1(1)(1)	Indradyumna's salvation	131
2(1)(2)	Description of *varnas* and *ashramas*	111
3(1)(3)	Description of *ashramas*	28
4(1)(4)	Prakrita creation	66
5(1)(5)	Enumeration of time	26
6(1)(6)	Varaha saves the earth	25
7(1)(7)	Description of creation	70
8(1)(8)	Mukhya and other creations	30
9(1)(9)	Brahma's origin	87
10(1)(10)	Creation by Rudra	90
11(1)(11)	Devi's *avatara*	16
12(1)(12)	Devi's greatness	325
13(1)(13)	Lineage of Daksha's daughters	24
14(1)(14)	Svayambhuva Manu's lineage	65
15(1)(15)	Destruction of Daksha's sacrifice	99

	Chapter	Number of *shloka*s
16(1)(16)	Lineages of Daksha's daughters	238
17(1)(17)	Trivikrama's conduct	69
18(1)(18)	Description of lineages	19
19(1)(19)	Lineages of *rishi*s	28
20(1)(20)	Description of royal lineages	76
21(1)(21)	The Ikshvaku lineage	61
22(1)(22)	Description of Soma *vamsha*	87
23(1)(23)	Lineage of kings	47
24(1)(24)	Description of Yadu's lineage	86
25(1)(25)	Krishna's austerities	92
26(1)(26)	Origin of the *lingam*	110
27(1)(27)	Krishna's departure	22
28(1)(28)	Partha meets Vyasa	7
29(1)(29)	Description of *yuga*s	51
30(1)(30)	Description of *kali yuga*	69
31(1)(31)	Varanasi's greatness	80
32(1)(32)	Varanasi's greatness continued	29
33(1)(33)	Greatness of Kapardishvara	53
34(1)(34)	Greatness of Madhyameshvara	31
35(1)(35)	Different *tirtha*s	33
36(1)(36)	Greatness of Prayaga	48
37(1)(37)	Rules for visiting *tirtha*s	39
38(1)(38)	More on *tirtha*s	16
39(1)(39)	More on *tirtha*s	18
40(1)(40)	Description of the world	48
41(1)(41)	Locations of luminous bodies	45

	Chapter	Number of *shlokas*
42(1)(42)	Twelve Adityas	27
43(1)(43)	The earth's sphere	46
44(1)(44)	The *loka*s	29
45(1)(45)	*Dvipa*s and mountains	41
46(1)(46)	Guardians of the worlds	40
47(1)(47)	Ketumala and other *varsha*s	47
48(1)(48)	Description of Jambudvipa	62
49(1)(49)	Plaksha and other *dvipa*s	72
50(1)(50)	Pushkara-dvipa	26
51(1)(51)	*Manvantara*s and Vishnu's greatness	50
52(1)(52)	Branches of *Veda*s	26
53(1)(53)	Shiva's incarnations	34
Total in *Purvarddha*	53	3195
Uttararddha (the second part)		
54(2)(1)	Conversation between *rishi*s	51
55(2)(2)	Ishvara's *yoga* – Ishvara Gita	56
56(2)(3)	Purusha and Prakriti	23
57(2)(4)	Greatness of Shiva	34
58(2)(5)	The sages praise Shiva	46
59(2)(6)	Shiva's glory	52
60(2)(7)	Shiva's powers	32
61(2)(8)	Crossing over *samsara*	18
62(2)(9)	Shiva's *nishkala* form	20
63(2)(10)	Shiva as the supreme *brahman*	17
64(2)(11)	The path of *yoga*	147

	Chapter	Number of shlokas
65(2)(12)	Duties of *brahmacharis* – Vyasa Gita	65
66(2)(13)	Virtuous conduct for *achamana*	45
67(2)(14)	*Dharma* for *brahmacharis*	91
68(2)(15)	*Dharma* for householders	42
69(2)(16)	Good conduct for householders	96
70(2)(17)	Permissible and prohibited food	44
71(2)(18)	*Nitya* rites for a householder	119
72(2)(19)	Rules for eating	32
73(2)(20)	*Shraddha* rites	47
74(2)(21)	Rules for a *shraddha*	47
75(2)(22)	Rules for a *shraddha* continued	107
76(2)(23)	Impurities of birth and death	83
77(2)(24)	*Agnihotra* and other rites	21
78(2)(25)	A *dvija*'s subsistence	21
79(2)(26)	*Danadharma*	78
80(2)(27)	*Dharma* of *vanaprastha*	39
81(2)(28)	*Dharma* of *yatis*	31
82(2)(29)	*Dharma* of *yatis* continued	47
83(2)(30)	Rules of *prayashchitta*	26
84(2)(31)	Kapalamochana *tirtha*	108
85(2)(32)	Description of *prayashchitta*	24
86(2)(33)	Description of *prayashchitta* continued	39

	Chapter	Number of *shlokas*
87(2)(34)	Description of *prayashchitta* continued	152
88(2)(35)	Gaya and other *tirthas*	76
89(2)(36)	Destruction of Kala	38
90(2)(37)	Description of *tirthas*	61
91(2)(38)	Devadaru-vana	83
92(2)(39)	Entry into Devadaru-vana	80
93(2)(40)	Greatness of Narmada	40
94(2)(41)	Greatness of Narmada continued	107
95(2)(42)	Greatness of Narmada continued	42
96(2)(43)	Greatness of Japyeshvara	42
97(2)(44)	Greatness of *tirthas*	24
98(2)(45)	Types of *pralaya*	61
99(2)(46)	Prakrita *pralaya* and subsidiary creation	147
Total in *Uttararddha*	46	2701
Total in Kurma Purana	99	5896

Chapter 1(1)(1)
(Indradyumna's salvation)

The Kurma Purana starts. This is a description of Indradyumna's salvation. OUM. I prostrate myself before the immeasurable Vishnu, who assumed the form of Kurma.[1] I will narrate the Purana recited by the origin of the universe. At the end of the sacrifice, the *maharshis*[2] in Naimisha asked the unblemished Suta, Romaharshana, about the sacred Purana Samhita.[3] 'O immensely intelligent Suta! O illustrious one! You know about the *brahman*. For the sake of Itihasa Purana, you served Vyasa properly. Since Dvaipayana's words delighted you and made all your body hair stand up, you became Romaharshana. In earlier times, the illustrious lord, Vyasa, himself asked you to speak about Purana Samhita to the sages. At the time of Svayambhu's long sacrifice, when the *soma* juice was extracted, to speak about the Samhita, through his

---

[1] Kurma means tortoise/turtle, and this is a reference to Vishnu's Kurma *avatara* (incarnation).

[2] Great sages.

[3] *Suta*s were bards and raconteurs and also charioteers. Romaharshana, equivalently Lomaharshana, obtained his name because his recitals made the body hair of his listeners stand up. Alternatively, his body hair stood up. *Samhita* means a collection. Here, it refers to Kurma Purana.

portion, Purushottama manifested himself in your form.[4]
Therefore, we are asking you about the excellent Kurma
Purana. You are accomplished in the meanings of the
Puranas, and you should tell us about it.' Hearing the
words of the sages, Suta, supreme among those who knew
the Puranas, mentally prostrated himself before his *guru*,
Satyavati's son[5] and spoke.

Romaharshana said, 'I prostrate myself before Hari,[6]
the origin of the universe, who assumed the form of Kurma.
I will narrate the divine account of the Purana, which
destroys sins. If he hears this, an evil doer will also proceed
to the supreme destination. This account of the Purana must
never be spoken about to a non-believer.[7] It must be narrated
to the devout and the serene, *dvija*s[8] who are devoted to
dharma. One should speak about this account, narrated
by Narayana[9] himself. The five signs of a Purana are *sarga*,
pratisarga, *vamsha*, *manvantara* and *vamshanucharita*.
Brahma Purana is the first. Padma and Vishnu are next.
Then there are Shiva, Bhagavata, Bhavishya and Naradiya.
After this, there are Markandeya, Agni, Brahmavaivarta,
Linga, Varaha, Skanda and Vamana. Then, there are
Kurma, Matsya, Garuda and Vayaviya. It is said that

---

[4] Svayambhu, the one who created himself, is Brahma.
Purushottama, the excellent being, is Vishnu.

[5] Vedavyasa was the son of Satyavati.

[6] Vishnu.

[7] The text uses the word *nastika*, meaning non-believer, rather
than atheist.

[8] A *dvija* is a person with a second birth, the second birth
referring to the sacred thread ceremony. Sometimes, the word *dvija*
is used for a *brahmana*. However, more generally, it applies to the
first three *varna*s.

[9] Vishnu.

the eighteenth is known as Brahmanda.[10] The sages have
spoken about other Upapuranas.[11] O *brahmana*s! Briefly,
it has been heard that they are the following. The first is
Sanatkumara. Narasimha is next. The third is known to
be Skanda and it is said that this was recited by Kumara
himself.[12] The fourth is known as Shivadharma, recited by
Nandisha himself. Thereafter, there is the wonderful one
narrated by Durvasa, followed by Naradiya. There are
Kapila, Vamana, the one narrated by Ushanas, Brahmanda,
Varuna, the one known as Kalika, Maheshvara, Samba
and Soura, which has the essence of everything. Finally,
there are the ones narrated by Parashara, Maricha and the
one known as Bhargava.'

'The excellent Kurma Purana is said to be the fifteenth.
This sacred account is divided into four Samhitas. These
are said to be Brahmi, Bhagavati, Souri and Vaishnavi.
These four sacred Samhitas bestow *dharma*, *artha*, *kama*
and *moksha*.[13] Of these, Brahmi Samhita is as revered
as the four *Veda*s. It is said that there are six thousand
*shloka*s in it. O lords among sages! It describes everything
about the greatness of *dharma*, *artha*, *kama* and *moksha*.
Parameshvara,[14] the *brahman*, is known through this. In

---

[10] Because of what was said in the Introduction, nineteen
Mahapuranas are listed here.

[11] Minor Puranas.

[12] Skanda Purana figures in both lists, Mahapuranas and
Upapuranas. Kumara is Skanda/Karitkeya. Naradiya is also
repeated, as is Brahmanda.

[13] These are the four *purushartha*s or objectives of human
existence. *Dharrma* has multiple meanings, *artha* is the pursuit
of wealth/prosperity, *kama* is the pursuit of sensual pleasures
and *moksha* is the pursuit of liberation from the cycle of human
existence (*samsara*).

[14] The supreme lord.

connection with this divine and sacred account, *sarga*,
pratisarga, *vamsha*, *manvantara* and *vamshanucharita*
are described. *Brahmana*s and others who are devoted
to *dharma*, those who are accomplished in the *Veda*s,
should retain it. I will describe what Vyasa narrated in
earlier times.'

'Earlier, for the sake of *amrita*, the *daitya*s and *danava*s
churned the ocean of milk, along with the *deva*s.[15] Mount
Mandara was made the churning rod. Desiring the welfare
of the *deva*s, when the churning took place, in the form
of Kurma, the divinity Janardana,[16] bore Mandara on his
back. *Deva*s and Narada and other *maharshi*s praised the
divinity. They saw that the imperishable Vishnu, the witness,
had assumed the form of Kurma. Shri, loved by Narayana,
emerged from within.[17] Bhagavan Vishnu Purushottama
accepted her. Narada and the other *maharshi*s were
deluded by the energy of Vishnu, who is not manifest. For
the sake of their welfare, along with Shakra,[18] they spoke
these words. "O Bhagavan! O divinity! O lord of *deva*s!
O Narayana! O one who pervades the universe! Who is
this Devi Vishalakshi?[19] We are asking you. Please tell us."
Hearing their words, Vishnu, who crushes *danava*s, glanced
towards Devi and replied to Narada and the others, who

[15] The *deva*s are also known as *sura*s or Adityas, since they
were the sons of the sage Kashyapa and Aditi. The antithesis of
*sura*s is *asura*s, with *daitya*s and *danava*s sometimes used as
synonyms. However, *daitya*s were the sons of Kashyapa and Diti,
while *danava*s were the sons of Kashyapa and Danu.
[16] Vishnu.
[17] From within the ocean, as a result of the churning. Shri is
Lakshmi, the goddess of prosperity.
[18] Indra.
[19] Literally, the one with the large eyes.

were unblemished, "This is supreme Shakti, and she is in me. Her form is that of the *brahman*. She is *maya*.[20] She is my beloved. She is the one who holds up the universe. O best among *brahmanas*! Through her, I delude, devour and create the entire universe, with all the *devas*, *asuras* and humans. Those who look towards their *atmans* possess the knowledge to understand origin, dissolution and coming and going. They can cross over this extensive *maya*. O gods! Basing themselves on her, Brahma, Ishana[21] and all the others obtain their powers. She is all my Shakti. The entire universe originates from her. She is Prakriti, with the three *gunas* in her.[22] In an earlier *kalpa*, Shri, who resides on a lotus, originated from me. She possesses four arms and holds a conch shell, a *chakra* and a lotus in her hands. She is garlanded. She resembles the radiance of one crore suns. She is Mohini, who deludes all those with bodies. The *devas*, the ancestors, humans and Vasava[23] and others cannot overcome her *maya*, not to speak of others on earth who possess bodies." Addressed thus by Vasudeva, the sages spoke to Vishnu. "O Pundarikaksha![24] When time decays, please tell us what is left." Hrishikesha,[25] worshipped by large numbers of sages, replied to the sages.'

Hrishikesha said, 'It has been heard that there was a supreme *dvija*, Indradyumna. In an earlier birth, he was a king and Shankara[26] and the others found him to be

[20] Illusion.
[21] Shiva.
[22] The three *gunas* of *sattva* (purity), *rajas* (passion) and *tamas* (darkness).
[23] Indra.
[24] With eyes like a lotus, Vishnu.
[25] Vishnu.
[26] Shiva.

unassailable. He saw me in my form as Kurma and in
front of the lords among sages, heard the divine Purana
Samhita directly from my mouth. He understood that the
Shaktis of Brahma, Mahadeva and the other *deva*s are
established in my Shakti. Therefore, he sought refuge in
me. To accomplish his objective, I told him, "You will be
born as a *brahmana*. You will be known as Indradyumna.
When you are born, you will remember your former birth.
O unblemished one! I will speak to you about the greatest
secret, unknown not only to all creatures but even to *deva*s.
I will impart that *jnana* to you.[27] Having obtained this
jnana from me, in the end, you will enter me. In a different
portion, remain there on earth and withdraw yourself
well. When Vaivasvata *manvantara* is over, for the sake
of accomplishing a task, you will enter me." Prostrating
himself before me, he went to his city and ruled over the
earth. He followed the *dharma* of time.[28] After some time, in
Shvetadvipa, along with me, he enjoyed all the Vaishnava[29]
objects of pleasure, ones that even *yogi*s find impossible to
obtain. O best among sages! Following my command, he
was born again, in a lineage of *brahmana*s. He knew that I
am known as Vaasudeva, in whom the imperishable *vidya*
and *avidya* are hidden.[30] Mysterious in form, I am known
as the supreme *brahman*. He worshipped Parameshvara,[31]
the refuge of all beings, through vows, fasting, rules,

---

[27] *Jnana* is knowledge/learning. The words *jnana* and *vijnana*
are often used as synonyms. When a distinction is drawn, *jnana* is
what is learned from a teacher and sacred texts. *Vijnana* is acquired
through self-reflection and contemplation.

[28] In due course, he died.

[29] Related to Vishnu.

[30] *Vidya* is knowledge and *avidya* is ignorance.

[31] The supreme lord.

offering of oblations and the satisfaction of *brahmana*s. He prostrated himself before the lord, with devotion and attentiveness to him. He worshipped the great divinity who is lodged in the hearts of *yogi*s. On one occasion, while he was engaged in doing this, the supreme portion, originating from Vishnu, displayed her own divine form to him. On beholding Bhagavan Vishnu's beloved, he lowered his head and prostrated himself before her.'

'He joined his hands in salutation and addressed and praised her, using different kinds of *stotram*s.[32] Indradyumna asked, "O auspicious Devi! O one with large eyes! Who are you? You are marked with Vishnu's signs. Please tell me the truth about your precise nature now." Hearing his words, the extremely auspicious one was greatly pleased. She smiled, remembered Vishnu and addressed the beloved *brahmana* in these words. Shri said, "The sages and the *deva*s, with Shakra at the forefront, cannot see me. I am the supreme *maya* in Narayana's *atman*. He is full of me. If one reflects on this properly, there is no difference between me and Narayana. The supreme *brahman*, Vishnu Parameshvara, is full of me. In this world, I have no power over those who worship Purushottama, the refuge of beings, through the *yoga* of *jnana* and *karma*. He is without beginning and without destruction. Therefore, by devoting yourself to *karma yoga* and through *jnana*, worship Ananta.[33] Yoo will thereby obtain *moksha*."'

Romaharshana continued, 'O best among sages! The immensely intelligent Indradyumna was addressed in this way. He lowered his head and prostrated himself before

---

[32] Hymns of praise.
[33] The infinite one, Vishnu.

Devi. He joined his hands in salutation and spoke again.
Indradyumna asked, "Bhagavan Isha is eternal. Achyuta is
nishkala.[34] O Devi! O Parameshvari![35] Please tell me. How
can one know him?" Asked in this way by the *brahmana*,
Devi, who resides on a lotus, replied. "O sage! Narayana
himself will bestow that *jnana* on you." As the sage
prostrated himself before her, she touched him with both
her hands. Remembering Vishnu, who is greater than the
greatest, she vanished from the spot. To see Narayana, he
immersed himself in supreme *samadhi*.[36] He worshipped
Hrishikesha, who removes the afflictions of those who
prostrate themselves before him. A long period of time
passed. The great *yogi*, Narayana, who pervades the
universe, manifested himself, attired in yellow garments.
He saw the divinity, Vishnu, whose *atman* is imperishable,
approach. He sank on his knees on the ground and praised
the one who had Garuda on his banner. Indradyumna
said, "O lord of sacrifices! O Achyuta! O Govinda! O
Madhava! O Ananta! O Keshava! O Krishna! O Vishnu! O
Hrishikesha! I prostrate myself before the one whose *atman*
is in the universe. O Hari! O ancient one! Your form is
the universe. I prostrate myself before you. O cause behind
creation, preservation and destruction! O one infinite in

[34] Achyuta is the one without decay, Vishnu. *Nishkala* means
without parts, names and forms. *Sakala* means with names and
forms.
[35] Feminine of Parameshvara.
[36] *Samadhi* is deep meditation. *Yoga* has eight limbs and
is known as *ashtanga yoga*. These are *yama* (control), *niyama*
(observance of rules), *asana* (posture), *pranayama* (control of the
breath of life), *pratyahara* (withdrawal), *dharana* (concentration),
dhyana (meditation) and *samadhi* (deep meditation and absorption
in the supreme).

powers! O *nirguna*![37] I prostrate myself before you. O
nishkala! I prostrate myself before you. I bow down. O
Purusha! I prostrate myself before you. O one whose form
is the universe! I prostrate myself before you. O Vaasudeva!
O Vishnu! O origin of the universe! I prostrate myself before
you. O one who lacks a beginning, a middle and an end!
O one who can be approached through *jnana*! I prostrate
myself before you. I prostrate myself before the one who is
without transformations. I prostrate myself before the one
who is beyond *prapancha*.[38] I prostrate myself before the
one who lacks both differences and absence of differences.
You are the one whose form is bliss. I prostrate myself
before the one who saves. You are the serene one. I prostrate
myself before the one whose *atman* faces no impediments.
You are infinite in form. You are without form. I prostrate
myself before you. I bow. I prostrate myself before the
supreme objective. I prostrate myself before the one who
is beyond *maya*. I prostrate myself before Paramesha,[39] the
brahman, the *paramatman*. I prostrate myself before the
one who is exceedingly subtle. I prostrate myself before
the great divinity. I prostrate myself before the auspicious
and pure one. I prostrate myself before Parameshthi.[40] You
have created everything. You are the supreme objective.
You are the father of all beings. O Purushottama! You
are the mother. You are imperishable and the supreme
abode. You are consciousness alone. You are space. You
are *nishkala*. You are the support for everything. You are
unmanifest and infinite. You are beyond darkness. The

[37] Without the *guna*s of *sattva* (purity), *rajas* (passion) and
tamas (darkness). *Saguna* is with *guna*s.
[38] *Prapancha* is the visible universe.
[39] The same as Parameshvara.
[40] The great lord.

paramatman can only be seen with the lamp of *jnana*. I seek refuge in your form. You are Vishnu, the supreme objective." Bhagavan, who is in the *atman*s of all beings and is the creator of all beings, was praised in this way. As he touched him with both his hands, he seemed to smile. As soon as he was touched by Bhagavan Vishnu, through his favours, the bull among sages got to know the supreme truth.'

'Delighted in his mind, he prostrated himself before Janardana. He spoke to Achyuta, who was attired in yellow garments and whose eyes were like blooming lotuses. "O Purushottama! Through your favours, doubts have been dispelled. I have obtained *jnana* about the subject of the absolute *brahman*. This bestows success and supreme bliss. O Bhagavan! O Vaasudeva! O creator! I prostrate myself before you. O lord of *yoga*! O one who pervades the universe! Please tell me what I should do." Hearing this, Madhava Narayana addressed Indradyumna in these words. For the welfare of all the worlds, he smiled and spoke these words. Shri Bhagavan said, "Men should worship the divinity, the great lord, by observing *varna*s and *ashrama*s.[41] The worship must be undertaken through *jnana* and *bhakti yoga*, not through any other means. Know the supreme truth, the power and cause and effect. Know my conduct. In pursuit of *moksha*, worship Ishvara. Cast aside every kind of association. Know that this world is full of *maya*. With a sense of *advaita*[42] in your mind, see Parameshvara. O *brahmana*! Understand that I am spoken

[41] The four *varna*s are *brahmana*s, *kshatriya*s, *vaishya*s and *shudra*s. The four *ashrama*s are *brahmacharya*, *garhasthya*, *vanaprastha* and *sannyasa*.

[42] Non-duality, unity between the *jivatman* (individual *atman*) and the *paramatman*. Duality is *dvaita*.

about with three kinds of inclinations. The first is fixed on me as an object. The second depends on a manifest form. The third kind of inclination is known as Brahmi, and it is beyond the *guna*s. A learned person will depend on one of these inclinations. According to the *shruti* texts, the *Veda*s, those incapable should resort to the first. In this case, one should make every possible effort to be devoted and attentive. If you worship the lord of the universe in this way, you will obtain *moksha*." Indradyumna asked, "What is the supreme truth! O Janardana! What is that power? What is cause and what is effect? What is the nature of your conduct?" Shri Bhagavan replied, "The truth, greater than the greatest, is the supreme and *brahman*, without decay. This is full of constant bliss. This is imperishable illumination, beyond darkness. That eternal prosperity is spoken of as *vibhuti*.[43] The effect is the universe. The cause is unmanifest, pure and imperishable. I am instated in the inner recesses of all beings. My conduct is spoken of as the acts of creation, preservation and destruction. O *brahmana*! Use your inclinations to comprehend all this. After this, use *karma yoga* to properly worship the eternal one." Indradyumna asked, "In the *varna*s and *ashrama*s, what conduct should be used to worship the supreme one? What is the nature of *jnana*? What is the divine, on which, the three kinds of inclinations are based? How did creation occur earlier? How will withdrawal take place? How many creations are there in the worlds? What is the number of *vamsha*s and *manvantara*s? What are their dimensions? What are pure vows? What are the *tirtha*s?[44]

[43] Glory.
[44] *Tirtha*s and *kshetra*s are sacred places of pilgrimage. Typically, in a *tirtha*, there will be water one descends into.

What is the location of the sun and other entities? What are the dimensions of the earth? How many *dvipas*,[45] oceans, mountains, large rivers and small rivers are there? O Pundarikaksha! Now, please tell me accurately about all this." Shri Kurma said, "Thus addressed, I wished to be compassionate towards my devotee. O bulls among sages! I told him everything, exactly and accurately. I explained everything that the *brahmana* had asked me about. Having shown my favours to the *brahmana*, I vanished from the spot. O excellent *brahmana*s! He followed the rules I had spoken about. Controlled and with pure sentiments, he worshipped the supreme. He gave up affection towards sons and other things. He freed himself of the opposite pairs of sentiments.[46] He was without possessions. He renounced all *karma* and sought refuge in non-attachment. He looked towards the *atman* within his own *atman*.[47] He saw his *atman* in the entire world. First meditating on the imperishable *brahman*, he achieved the supreme inclinations. Achieving supreme *yoga*, he saw the absolute alone. This is the *moksha* Indras among *yogi*s seek, conquering sleep and their breath. Only rarely are they able to see the imperishable *brahman*. Following the instructions of Aditya,[48] he then went to the mountain that is to the north of Manasa.[49] As a result of the power and prosperity of his *yoga*, this Indra among *brahmana*s travelled through the sky. An excellent *vimana*,[50] resembling the sun, appeared. This was followed by a large number

---

[45] Continents.
[46] Happiness and unhappiness, hot and cold, and so on.
[47] *Paramatman* in the *jivatman*.
[48] Surya, the Sun God.
[49] That is, Meru.
[50] Celestial vehicle. The word also means a mansion.

of *deva*s and a large number of *gandharva*s and *apsara*s.[51] *Siddha*s and *brahmarshi*s saw that Indra among *yogi*s and followed him along the route. Worshipped by the gods, he reached the mountain and entered. This was a place full of *yogi*s. The supreme being resided there. He reached that supreme region, as resplendent as ten thousand suns. He entered inside the residence, a place that was difficult for even *deva*s to reach. He thought of the supreme, the refuge of all those with bodies. This was the grandfather, the lord of *deva*s, without a beginning and without an end. At this, an extremely wonderful radiance appeared. In its centre, he saw the first Purusha, the supreme objective. This was a mass of great energy, impossible for those who hate Brahma to reach. He possessed four faces and extensive limbs. His beautiful form was surrounded by rays. He saw the *yogi*, who was present there, prostrating himself. The divinity, the *atman* of the universe, himself advanced and embraced him. When he was embraced by the divinity, a great beam of moonlight emerged from the body of the Indra among *brahmana*s and entered the solar disc. This was the sacred and unblemished destination, known as *Rig*, *Sama* and *Yajur*. Bhagavan Hiranyagarbha, who enjoys *havya* and *kavya*, is present there.[52] This is the first door for *yogi*s who are established in Vedanta. This is the prosperous energy of the *brahman*, seen by those who are learned. Bhagavan Brahma, surrounded by the rays, looked at the sage, and he was Ishvara's energy, serene and auspicious, going

[51] *Gandharva*s are celestial musicians and singers. *Apsara*s are celestial dancers. *Siddha*s are those who have achieved *siddhi* (success). In the hierarchy of *rishi*s (sages), *brahmarshi*s are above *maharshi*s and *maharshi*s are above *rishi*s.

[52] *Havya* is oblations offered to the gods and *kavya* is oblations offered to the ancestors.

everywhere. He saw his own *atman* in the imperishable
space that is Vishnu's supreme destination. This is the place
for the *brahman*. This is Parameshvara, full of unwavering
bliss. Established in this great wonder, he saw his own
atman in all beings. He obtained the undecaying abode for
the *atman*, known as *moksha*. Therefore, one should make
every effort to follow the rules for *varna*s and *ashrama*s. A
learned person must resort to ultimate sentiments and pass
beyond *maya* and Lakshmi." Hari told Narada and the
other *maharshi*s this.'

'Along with Shakra, all of them questioned the one with
Garuda seated on his standard. The *rishi*s said, "O lord
of *deva*s! O Hrishikesha! O lord! O Narayana, without
decay! Please tell us everything that you had spoken about
earlier, to convey *jnana* about *dharma* and other things
to the *brahmana* Indradyumna. O one who pervades the
world! Your friend, Shakra, wishes to hear too." In the
form of Kurma, who had gone down to Rasatala,[53] the
divinity, Bhagavan Vishnu Janardana, told Narada and
the other *maharshi*s all that they had asked him about and
narrated the excellent Kurma Purana. I will tell you what
he narrated, in the presence of the king of *deva*s. This is
sacred and blessed and bestows fame, a long lifespan and
moksha on men. O *brahmana*s! Hearing this Purana and
in particular, narrating it, are excellent. Even if one hears a
single chapter, one is freed from all sins. Even if one hears

---

[53] There are seven nether regions. Patala is often a generic
term for all of them together. Though the list varies a bit, the usual
listing of these seven is Atala, Sutala, Vitala, Gabhastala, Mahatala,
Shritala and Patala. To support Mandara as the churning rod when
the ocean was churned, Kurma *avatara* had descended to the nether
regions.

a single *upakhyana*,[54] one obtains greatness in Brahma's world. This supreme Kurma Purana was narrated by the lord of *deva*s himself, in his form as Kurma. Dvijas must regard it with reverence.'

Chapter 2(1)(2)
(Description of *varna*s and *ashrama*s)

Kurma said, 'O *rishi*s! For the welfare of the universe, all of you listen to what you have asked me about. I will tell you everything that I told Indradyumna. This extensive Purana has accounts about the past, the present and the future. It describes *moksha dharma* and bestows the auspicious on men. In the beginning, I, the divinity Narayana, alone existed. There was no one else. On a couch made from the serpent,[55] I lay in deep sleep. When the night was over, I woke up and thought about creation again.[56] O bulls among sages! At this, I was suddenly filled with great pleasure. Brahma, the grandfather of the worlds, possessing four faces, was born. Meanwhile, for some reason, anger was generated in me. O tigers among sages! From me, the divinity Maheshvara was created. Rudra was born from this rage. He possessed three eyes and wielded

[54] A short account that is repeated.

[55] Shesha *naga*.

[56] When it is Brahma's day, creation takes place. When it is Brahma's night, there is destruction. But this is during the secondary cycle of creation and dissolution (*pratisarga*). Brahma has a lifespan of one hundred years. What is being described is the original creation (*sarga*), when Brahma had to manifest himself. Everything had been reduced to a single mass of water and Narayana slept on that.

a trident in his hand. His energy resembled that of the
sun, and he seemed to burn down the three worlds. At the
time, Devi Shri appeared, with large eyes that were like
lotuses. She was exceedingly beautiful, with a pleasant
face. She was capable of deluding all those with bodies.
Her smile was sweet, and she was exceedingly pleased. She
was auspicious and a store of greatness. Her beauty was
divine, and she was adorned with divine garlands. This was
Narayani Mahamaya, known as primordial Prakriti. She
filled up everything and approached my side, her abode.
On seeing her, Bhagavan Brahma spoke to me, the lord
of the universe. "Please engage this exceedingly beautiful
one to delude all beings. O Madhava! That way, my great
creation will flourish." I agreed to this and smiled as I
spoke to Devi Shri. "O Devi! Following my instructions,
delude this entire universe, consisting of *deva*s, *asura*s and
humans. Hurl them into *samsara*. But maintain a distance
and avoid those who follow *jnana yoga*, are controlled,
are devoted to the *brahman*, those who speak about
the *brahman*, lack in rage and are devoted to the truth.
Maintain a distance and avoid those who are engaged in
dhyana,[57] lack a sense of "mine", are serene and devoted to
dharma, are accomplished in the *Veda*s, those who perform
sacrifices and are ascetics. Maintain a distance and avoid
*brahmana*s who are devoted to great sacrifices, those who
worship Maheshvara, the lord of *deva*s, through *japa* and
oblations.[58] Make efforts to avoid from a distance, those
who engage in self-study and offer oblations of *ghee*,
those who are full of *bhakti yoga* and have surrendered
their minds to Ishvara. Maintain a distance and avoid

---

[57] Meditation.
[58] *Japa* is the silent chanting of a *mantra* and related meditation.

those who are devoted to *pranayama* and such things,
those whose minds are attached to Pranava[59] and those
who are devoted to performing *japa* on Rudra. Avoid
those who know *dharma* and are knowledgeable about
Atharvashirsha.[60] What is the need to speak a lot? Do not
delude and distract those who follow their own *dharma*
and are engaged in worshipping Ishvara." In this way I
sent Mahamaya, Hari's beloved. She did as she had been
asked to. Therefore, one should worship Lakshmi. When
Bhagavan's wife is worshipped, she bestows extensive
prosperity, nourishment, intelligence, fame and strength.
Therefore, Lakshmi should be worshipped.'

'After this, Bhagavan Brahma, the grandfather of the
worlds, started creation. Following my instructions, he
created mobile and immobile entities, as they had existed
earlier.[61] Through his knowledge of *yoga*, he created
Marichi, Bhrigu, Angiras, Pulastya, Pulaha, Kratu, Daksha,
Atri and Vasishtha. These nine *brahmana*s, Brahma's
sons, were excellent *brahmana*s. Marichi and the others
were *sadhaka*s[62] and spoke about the *brahman*. The lord,
the grandfather, created *brahmana*s from his mouth and
*kshatriya*s from his arms. The divinity created *vaishya*s
from his thighs and *shudra*s from his feet. Except for
*shudra*s, the others were created for undertaking sacrifices.
Through them, for the sake of protecting the *deva*s, Yajna[63]
emerged. So did the *Rig*, *Yajur*, *Sama* and *Atharva Veda*s.
Brahma's natural form is always in the form of Shakti.

[59] OUMKARA, the sound of OUM.
[60] A group of *mantra*s, usually used for Shiva's worship.
[61] Before the dissolution, in the earlier *kalpa*.
[62] *Sadhaka* is a person who strives for *siddhi*. *Sadhana* is the means/method.
[63] The personified form of the sacrifice.

Speech[64] is divine and is without a beginning and without an end. However, it was created by Svayambhu.[65] In the beginning, this had the form of the *Veda*s and all activities flow from this. They led to many other sacred texts on earth. However, an intelligent person finds no delight in these. It is only the learned heretic who is delighted with these. In ancient times, the sages have laid down in the *smriti* texts tasks that conform with the meanings of the *Veda*s. The excellent follow this. This should be known as supreme *dharma*, not that which depends on other sacred texts. There are *smriti* texts that are outside the pale of the *Veda*s. These have a wicked vision. After death, these are futile in every possible way. They are said to be based on darkness.'[66]

'In the earlier *kalpa*, the *praja*s who were born did not suffer from any kind of obstruction. All of them were internally pure and followed their own *dharma*. After this, succumbing to time, attached and aversion appeared. O tigers among sages! In following one's own *dharma*, *adharma* is an impediment. As a consequence, their natural *siddhi* was no longer available easily. The *siddhi* that they could then obtain was based on the quality of *rajas*. With the progress of time, this was also completely exhausted. Without that *siddhi*, as a means of subsistence, they had to resort to tasks involving the use of the hand.[67] Therefore, for them, the lord Brahma arranged that work was needed for survival. Svayambhuva Manu, who could see everything,

---

[64] *Vak*.

[65] Speech can't be created, strictly speaking. Brahma made it manifest.

[66] Of ignorance.

[67] Agriculture, trade, artisanship.

had spoken about *dharma* earlier.[68] O *dvija*s! He was
created by Brahma in the form of Prajapati himself. Bhrigu
and the others heard about this *dharma* from his mouth.
O excellent *dvija*s! A *brahmana* can engage in six tasks—
performing sacrifices, officiating at the sacrifices of others,
donations, receiving, studying and teaching. *Dharma* for
*kshatriya*s and *vaishya*s lies in donating, studying and
performing sacrifices. *Kshatriya*s will punish and fight,
while agriculture is praised for *vaishya*s. For *shudra*s,
dharma can be pursued by serving *dvija*s. For subsistence,
they can become artisans. For them, *paka-yajna* is also in
accordance with *dharma*.[69] With the *varna*s established,
the *ashrama*s were established—*garhasthya*, *vanaprastha*,
the state of being a mendicant and *brahmacharya*.[70] O
bulls among sages! Tending to the fire, serving an *atithi*,[71]
performing sacrifices, giving donations and worshipping
the gods—in brief, this is *dharma* for a householder.
Oblations, surviving on roots and fruits, studying and
sharing properly[72]—this is *dharma* for a person who
resides in the forest. Surviving on what has been begged,

---

[68] Since that was in a different *kalpa*.

[69] *Paka-yajna* has many different meanings. Literally, the word
means cooking for a sacrifice, that is, cooked food is distributed.
The idea is of a domestic sacrifice, where *mantra*s are not used, and
the text suggests that *shudra*s can undertake such sacrifices.

[70] In the due order, the first is *brahmacharya*, when one is a
celibate student. The second is *garhasthya*, the state of being a
householder. The third is *vanaprastha*, when one leaves for the
forest. The fourth is the state of renunciation or *sannyasa*. The
text refers to this as the stage of being a *bhikshuka*, when one is a
mendicant who begs for alms.

[71] An *atithi* is not just an ordinary guest. An expected and invited
guest is not *atithi*. An *atithi* is a guest who turns up unexpectedly.

[72] With others.

maintaining silence, austerities, *dhyana* in particular, the pursuit of proper *jnana* and non-attachment—this is held to be *dharma* for a *bhikshuka*. Surviving on what has been begged, service to the *guru*, studying, *sandhya* rites and rites for the fire—this is *dharma* for a *brahmachari*. The one who originated from the lotus has said that, in general, celibacy must be observed by those in *brahmacharya* and *vanaprastha* and those who are *bhikshuka*s. At the time of her season, a householder should approach his wife and no one else. He must avoid *parva* days.[73] For a person in *garhasthya*, it is said that this is as good as celibacy. O Indras among *brahmana*s! Out of distraction, if he does not undertake this task of conception, he suffers the sin of killing a foetus. According to capacity, a householder's supreme *dharma* is to study the *Veda*s, perform *shraddha*s,[74] worship *atithi*s, worship *deva*s and follow the rules and maintain the sacred fire ignited at the time of marriage in the morning and in the evening. He need not do this if his wife is dead, or if he has gone to a different country. The householder is said to be the support for the other three *ashrama*s. The others obtain their subsistence through him. Therefore, the householder is the best. The instructions of the *shruti* texts have said the single *ashrama* of being a householder encapsulates all four. Hence, *garhasthya* is alone known to be the *sadhana* for *dharma*. *Artha* and *kama* are devoid of *dharma* and must be avoided. If an act of *dharma* is against all the world, it should not be followed. *Artha* results from *dharma*. *Kama* also results from *dharma*. *Dharma* enables liberation from *samsara*. Hence, one should resort to *dharma*. It is held that the three categories of *dharma*,

[73] *Parva* days are special auspicious days for rites and festivals.
[74] Funeral rites for the ancestors.

artha and *kama* reflect the three *guna*s of *sattva*, *rajas* and *tamas*. Hence, one should resort to *dharma*. Those based on *sattva* proceed upwards. Those based on *rajas* remain in the middle. The conduct and qualities of those based on *tamas* are inferior and they proceed downwards.[75] If a person is based on *dharma* and pursues *artha* and *kama*, he obtains happiness in this world. After death, it is thought that he obtains the infinite. *Moksha* originates from *dharma* and *kama* is the result of *artha*. These are indicated as the four objectives, the *sadhana* and the *sadhya*.[76] If a man knows about the greatness of *dharma*, *artha*, *kama* and *moksha* and pursues them, it is thought that he is entitled to the infinite. Therefore, renouncing *artha* and *kama*, one should depend on *dharma*. Those who speak about the *brahman* have said that everything results from *dharma*. Everything in the world, mobile and immobile, is sustained by *dharma*. O excellent *dvija*s! Such is Brahma's Shakti, which is without a beginning and without an end. There is no doubt that *dharma* can be achieved through *karma* and *jnana*. Hence, using *jnana*, one should resort to *karma yoga*. According to the *Veda*s, there are two types of *karma*—based on *pravritti* and *nivritti*.[77] Action with *jnana* is based on *nivritti*. Anything else is based on *pravritti*. A person who practices *nivritti* proceeds to the

---

[75] This *shloka* is a verbatim restatement of *Bhagavat Gita* 14.18. Proceed upwards means to go to heaven or be born as a *deva*. Middle means to be born on earth as human. Downwards means to go to hell or be born as the member of an inferior species.

[76] *Sadhya* means the objective.

[77] In *nivritti*, one renounces the fruits of the action. Action is not undertaken for fruits. In *pravritti*, action is undertaken for fruits.

supreme destination. Hence, one should follow *nivritti*.
Otherwise, one will return to *samsara* again.'

'Manu has said that, in brief, *dharma* for the four
*varna*s consists of forgiveness, self-control, compassion,
donations, lack of avarice, renunciation, uprightness, lack
of envy, frequenting of *tirtha*s, truthfulness, contentment,
being an *astika*,[78] faith, restraint of the senses, worship of
*deva*s, worship of *brahmana*s in particular, non-violence,
pleasantness in speech, avoidance of calumny and lack of
taints. It is said that *brahmana*s who follow the rites obtain
Prajapati's world. *Kshatriya*s who do not run away from the
field of battle obtain Indra's world. *Vaishya*s who follow
their own *dharma* obtain the world of the Maruts. Those
who are born as *shudra*s and practice servitude obtain the
world of the *gandharva*s. There are eighty-eight thousand
*rishi*s who have held up their seed. It is said that this location
is for those who reside with their *guru*s. It is said that the
world of the *saptarshi*s is for those who are in *vanaprastha*.[79]
Svayambhu has said that householders obtain Prajapati's
world. There are mendicants who have conquered their
senses. They have renounced and held up their seed. They
obtain Hiranyagarbha's world and there is no return[80] from
there. The immortal region for *yogi*s is known as Vyoma. It
is supreme and without decay. It is Ishvara's abode, full of
bliss. It is the ultimate. It is the supreme objective.'

---

[78] Being a believer. *Nastika* is non-believer, not atheist. Atheist
is *nirishvaravadi*.

[79] *Saptarshi* means the seven (*sapta*) great sages (*rishi*). The
list changes from *manvantara* to *manvantara*. In the present one,
the usual list is Marichi, Atri, Angiras, Pulastya, Pulaha, Kratu
and Vasishtha. In the sky, *saptarshi* means the constellation Ursa
Majoris (Great Bear).

[80] No rebirth in *samsara*.

'The *rishi*s asked, "O Bhagavan! O one who slays the enemies of *deva*s! O destroyer of Hiranyaksha! There are said to be four *ashrama*s. Why have you mentioned *yogi*s as a separate category?"

'Kurma replied, "If a *yogi* is immobile, has renounced all *karma* and is unwaveringly fixed in *samadhi*, this is the fifth stage of being a *sannyasi*.[81] The *shruti* texts have instructed that all the *ashrama*s have two types. A person in *brahamacharya* can be *upakurvana*, or *naishthika*, devoted to the *brahman*. Having studied the *Veda*s in the proper way, if a person proceeds to the stage of *garhasthya*, he is known as *upakurvana*. *Naishthika* is a person who pursues the objective till death. A person in *garhasthya* is of two types, *udasina* and *sadhaka*. A householder who strives to ensure subsistence for his family is a *sadhaka*. Having repaid the three debts,[82] if a person renounces his wife and other things, roaming around alone, searching for *moksha*, he is *udasina*. If a person torments himself through austerities in the forest, performing sacrifices and offering oblations to *deva*s and engaged in studying, such a person, in *vanaprastha*, is considered *tapasa*.[83] In the *ashrama* of *vanaprastha*, if a person suffers excessive hardships through austerities and is supremely devoted to *dhyana*, he is known to be in *sannyasa*. If a person is constantly devoted to the practice of *yoga*, if he strives to ascend by conquering his senses and if he pursues *jnana*, such a *bhikshuka* is known as *parameshthika*. If a person is constantly content with his own *atman* and if he

---

[81] This will be qualified later.

[82] To ancestors through having sons, to sages through studies and to *deva*s through sacrifices.

[83] An ascetic, engaged in *tapasya*.

possesses correct insight, such a *bhikshuka* is said to be
a great sage and a *yogi*. There are said to be three types
of *parameshthika*s. Some *sannyasi*s pursue *jnana*. Others
renounce the *Veda*s.[84] Still, others renounce *karma*. It is
known that there are three types of *yogi*s. The first two are
bhoutika and *samkhya*. The third is known as *ashrami* and
consists of those who devote themselves to excellent *yoga*.
The first focus on meditation. The second, *samkhya*, focus
on meditation on the imperishable. The third, known as the
ultimate, meditate on Parameshvari. O *dvija*s! Such are the
four *ashrama*s. In all the *Veda*s and the sacred texts, there
is no mention of a fifth. In this way, the spotless lord of the
*deva*s created the *varna*s and the *ashrama*s. The one whose
atman is in the universe told Daksha and the others, "Create
many types of *praja*s." O excellent sages! The sons, Daksha
and the others, followed Brahma's words and created all
the *praja*s, starting with *deva*s and humans. In this way,
Bhagavan Brahma engaged himself in the task of creation.
I preserve this and the wielder of the trident takes away.
These are spoken of as the three forms, Brahma, Vishnu
and Maheshvara. They possess *sattva*, *rajas* and *tamas* and
are manifestations of the supreme *paramatman*. They are
devoted to each other and depend on each other. In their
pastimes, these Parameshvaras prostrate themselves before
each other. O *dvija*s! There are three kinds of meditation—
Brahmi, Maheshvari and meditation on the imperishable.
The Maheshvari meditation on the imperishable exists in
Rudra. All three, including meditation on the imperishable,
exist in me. Meditation on the imperishable is said to be
the same as Brahmi meditation. The supreme truth is that
there is no difference between me and Mahadeva. Ishvara

---

[84] Since they no longer need them.

is established inside and, according to his wishes, divided his *atman*. He wished to create the three worlds, with *deva*s, *asura*s and humans. Purusha is supreme and is not manifest but assumed the form of Brahma. Thus, Brahma is Mahadeva. Vishnu is the supreme Vishveshvara. All three are known to be manifestations of the one, engaged in different tasks for the Lord. Therefore, one should make every effort to respect and, in particular, worship them. Without delay, if one desires to obtain the imperishable state known as *moksha*, one must lovingly follow the *dharma* indicated by the *varna*s and the *ashrama*s. As long as one lives, one should pledge to respectfully perform the worship. O *dvija*s! This is what is said about the rules for the *varna*s and the *ashrama*s. There are three *ashrama*s, named after Vishnu, Brahma and Hara.[85] If a person wears the respective *lingam*s,[86] the devotees are always affectionate towards him. A person who is devoted to knowledge about the *brahman* should worship them and perform *dhyana* on them. For all devotees, Shambhu's *lingam* is supreme. Using white *bhasma*, one should draw the *tripundraka* mark on the forehead.[87] If a person has sought refuge with the supreme destination of the divinity Narayana, using fragrances mixed with water, he should always wear the mark of a trident on his forehead. If a person seeks refuge with Brahma Parameshthi, the seed of the universe, he

---

[85] Shiva. Shambhu is also Shiva's name.

[86] *Lingam* means sign.

[87] The *tripundraka* mark, consisting of three horizontal lines, is for Shiva's devotees and is drawn with white ashes (*bhasma*). The word used in the text is *shula*, meaning trident. This is for Vishnu's devotees and consists of three vertical lines, usually drawn with sandalwood paste and water. A *tilaka* is for Brahma's devotees and the text suggest this should be circular in shape.

should always wear a *tilaka* on his forehead. This is like wearing the essence of *bhutadi*, with time in his *atman*.[88] When one wears *tripundraka*, with lines above and below, this is like wearing Pradhana,[89] with the three *guna*s of Brahma, Vishnu and Shiva. There is no doubt that this is also the case when the trident is worn. When the *tilaka* is worn, this is like wearing Ishvara, with Brahma's energy within a white solar disc. Hence, one should wear the mark of a trident or the auspicious *tilaka*. Worn in the proper way, all three bestow long lifespans on devotees. A person should perform sacrifices, offer oblations into the fire, perform *japa*, donate, conquer his senses, be serene and controlled and know about the rules for *varna*s and *ashrama*s. He should control himself and, as long as he lives, worship *deva*s. Within a short span of time, he will then obtain a permanent and beneficial region.'

Chapter 3(1)(3) (Description of *ashrama*s)

The *rishi*s said, 'O Bhagavan! You have told us about the *varna*s and the four *ashrama*s. O lord! Please tell us now about the order of the *ashrama*s.'

Kurma replied, 'The order of the *ashrama*s is said to be *brahmachari*, *grihastha*, *vanaprastha* and *yati*.[90] But

---

[88] *Bhutadi* means the first among beings, or the origin of beings. In *samkhya*, it means *ahamkara*. Here, the sense is that wearing the *tilaka* is like wearing Brahma on the forehead.

[89] The primary source of the material world, the cosmic intellect.

[90] *Brahmachari* is one in *brahmacharya*, *grihastha* is one in *garhasthya* and *yati* is mendicant (one in *sannyasa*). Across the text, the word used for one in *sannyasa* varies.

there are also reasons for it to be otherwise. Even after *brahmacharya*, if *jnana* and *vijnana* have appeared and if a person is filled with supreme non-attachment, if a person desires the supreme destination, he can become a mendicant. A person should take a wife in the proper way, perform the different types of sacrifices and have sons. However, if he is non-attached, he should take to *sannyasa*. An intelligent *brahmana* will not renounce his home and the state of being a householder, taking to *sannyasa*, unless he has performed different sacrifices and has had sons. But the force of non-attachment may be so strong that he is not interested in the home. Such a learned and excellent *dvija* can take to *sannyasa*. Nevertheless, one should normally perform the different kinds of sacrifices and then take to the forest, tormenting oneself through austerities. When austerities and *yoga* lead to non-attachment, it is then that one should take to *sannyasa*. Having entered the *ashrama* of *vanaprastha*, one should not become a householder again. Nor should a person in *sannyasa* turn to *vanaprastha*. A *sadhaka*[91] must not become a *brahmachari*. A learned *dvija* must perform the sacrifice known as Prajapatya or Agneyi[92] and then become a mendicant. A householder will first move to *vanaprastha* and then become a mendicant. This is the instruction of the *shruti* texts. If a person is incapable of offering oblations, performing sacrifices and rites, if he is blind or lame, or if he is poor and non-attached, such a *dvija* can take to *sannyasa*. For everyone, non-attachment is recommended before *sannyasa*. If a person wishes to

[91] Meaning, a householder.
[92] While there are different kinds of Prajapatya sacrifices, in one kind, one uses the sacrifice to donate all one's possessions, before becoming an ascetic. Agneyi (a sacrifice to Agni) seems to be similar.

take to *sannyasa* without being non-attached, he will
face a downfall. But there may be a devout person who
desires to properly remain in a single *ashrama* until death.
It is thought that such a person deserves immortality. If a
person earns wealth through lawful means, is serene and
devoted to knowledge about the *brahman* and if he always
follows his own *dharma*, it is thought that such a person
deserves to be united with the *brahman*. If a person offers
up all *karma* to the *brahman*, if he is devoid of attachment
and desire and if he does everything with a pleased mind,
he also proceeds to that destination. It is the *brahman*
that gives what deserves to be given, what is given is the
brahman, the means of giving is the *brahman* and it is to
the supreme *brahman* that everything is rendered.[93] "I am
not the one who does anything. It is the *brahman* that
acts." The *rishi*s who possess insight into the truth have
said that this means rendering everything to the *brahman*.
"May the eternal Bhagavan Isha be pleased with this
karma." When a person acts, if his intelligence is always
like this, he renders everything to the supreme *brahman*.
The renouncing of the fruits of *karma* and offering them
to Parameshvara is said to be the excellent act of rendering
everything to the *brahman*. If a learned person carries out
his tasks, controlling himself and giving up all attachment,
the *karma* undertaken bestows *moksha*. Alternatively, if a
dvija carries out the *nitya karma*,[94] without renouncing the
fruits, those fruits bind him down. Therefore, every effort
must be undertaken to renounce the fruits that result from

----

[93] This echoes *Bhagavat Gita* 4.24.
[94] *Nitya karma* is tasks/rites carried out every day, *naimittika karma* is for special occasions, *kamya karma* is for specific desired fruits.

karma. Doing this, even an ignorant person can obtain the destination through his *karma*, after some time. *Karma* destroys sins, from this birth and earlier ones. In this way, a man obtains happiness of mind and gets to know the *brahman*. When *karma* is combined with *jnana*, proper *yoga* results. When *jnana* is combined with *karma*, there are no sins. Therefore, in whichever *ashrama* a person is in, he must make every effort to satisfy Ishvara with his *karma*. He then obtains a state of *naishkarma*.[95] Having obtained supreme *jnana* and *naishkarma* through the favours,[96] he is alone and serene, without a sense of ownership. Even when alive, he is liberated. He sees the supreme *paramatman*, the *brahman* Maheshvara. He is full of constant bliss. He dissolves into the one who is not manifest. Therefore, with a pleased mind, one must always practice *karma yoga*. When Paramesha is satisfied, one proceeds to the eternal destination. I have told you everything about the four excellent *ashrama*s. If a man transgresses them, he cannot obtain *siddhi*.'

Chapter 4(1)(4) (Prakrita creation)

Suta said, 'Hearing everything about the rules for the *ashrama*s, the minds of the *rishi*s were delighted. Prostrating themselves before Hrishikesha, they again spoke to him in the following words. The sages said, "You have told us everything about the four excellent *ashrama*s. We now wish to hear how the universe was created. From where did this entire universe originate? Into what will it

---

[95] When *karma* is no longer needed.
[96] Of Ishvara.

be dissolved? Who controls it? O Purushottama! Please tell us everything." Hearing the words spoken by the *rishi*s, Narayana, the undecaying origin of all beings, who was in the form of Kurma, addressed them in a deep voice.'

Kurma said, 'Maheshvara is eternal and unmanifest. He is supreme and has four *vyuha*s.[97] He is infinite and immeasurable. He is the controller who faces every direction. Those who have thought of the truth have spoken of him[98] as the unmanifest cause, the eternal one who has both existence and non-existence in his *atman*. He is spoken of as Pradhana and Prakriti. He is devoid of smell, colour and taste. He is devoid of sound and touch. He is without decay and constant. He is not diminished and exists eternally in his own *atman*. He is the great element, the origin of the universe. He is the supreme and eternal *brahman*. His form exists in all beings. His *atman* pervades Mahat.[99] He is without a beginning and without an end. He is without birth and subtle. He possesses the three *guna*s and is the source of creation. He is not only for the present. He cannot be known, and he existed before Brahma. When there is equilibrium between the *guna*s, Purusha is established in his own *atman*. Until the universe evolves again, that period is known as Prakrita dissolution. This period is spoken of as Brahma's night. The period of creation is spoken of as his day. But actually, there is no night or day for him. It is merely thought of in that way. When the night is over, the origin of the universe, who is himself without a beginning, wakes up. This is supreme

[97] A *vyuha* is a manifestation. For Narayana, they are Vaasudeva, Samkarshana, Pradyumna and Aniruddha. For Shiva, these would be Sadyojata, Vamadeva, Tatpurusha and Aghora.

[98] There is no gender in the text, so one could have used 'it'.

[99] Mahat is the intellect, the primordial principle.

Ishvara, who exists inside all beings. He is not manifest. Maheshvara quickly enters Prakriti and Purusha. Through his supreme *yoga*, Parameshvara agitates them. This is like the breeze in spring intoxicating men and women. In that way, the embodied form of *yoga* enters and agitates them. O *brahmana*s! Parameshvara is the one who agitates, and he is also the one who is agitated. To expand and contract, he is established in his state of Pradhana. When the ancient Purusha is agitated by Pradhana, the seed of Mahat appears, consisting of the essence of both Pradhana and Purusha. It is said that Mahat, the *atman*, intelligence, Brahma, understanding, discrimination, Ishvara, wisdom, fortitude, memory and knowledge originated from this. There were three types of *bhutadi*—*vaikarika*, *taijasa* and *tamasa*.[100] These three types of *ahamkara* evolved from Mahat. *Ahamkara* is said to be the pride and thought of being the doer. This sense of "I" being supreme exists in *jivatman*s and drives all action. From *ahamkara*, the *tanmatra*s of the five subtle elements were born. This resulted in all the senses and everything in the universe. The mind[101] is said to have originated from the unmanifest. It is spoken of as the first transformation. When it is born, it thinks of itself as the doer and glances at the *bhutadi*s. The creation that resulted from *vaikarika ahamkara* was *vaikarika*. The senses resulted from *taijasa ahamkara* and the ten divinities who preside over them are the *vaikarika*s.[102] The mind is the eleventh and possesses its own qualities of both perception and action. O *dvija*s! This creation of the

---

[100] Respectively associated with *sattva*, *rajas* and *tamas*.

[101] *Manas*.

[102] Five senses of perception (ears, skin, eyes, tongue, nose) and five senses of action (anus, genital organs, hands, feet, speech).

*tanmatra*s of the elements emerged from *bhutadi*. When
bhutadi was transformed, the *tanmatra* of sound was
created. Space originated from this and it is held that the
quality of space is sound. When space was transformed,
the *tanmatra* of touch was created. Wind evolved from this
and the learned know that the quality of wind is touch.
When wind was transformed, the *tanmatra* of form was
created. Fire resulted from wind and its quality is said to
be form. When fire was transformed, the *tanmatra* of taste
resulted. Water originated from this and it is a store of
taste. When water was agitated, the *tanmatra* of smell was
created. The mass of earth resulted from this and it is held
that the quality of earth is smell. Space only possesses the
tanmatra of sound, but it is surrounded by the *tanmatra* of
touch. Wind possesses double the qualities, of both sound
and touch. These two qualities of sound and touch enter
form. Therefore, fire possesses three qualities of sound,
touch and form. Sound, touch and form enter the *tanmatra*
of taste. Therefore, water, which possesses the essence of
taste, is known to possess four qualities. Sound, touch, form
and taste entered smell. Thus, earth possesses five qualities
and among the elements, is said to be the most gross.'

'Serenity, being terrible and dumbness are said to be their
special characteristics. They enter each other and sustain
each other. These seven great-souled ones[103] depended on
each other. However, without coming together completely,
they were incapable of creating *prajas*.[104] Purusha presided
over them and the unmanifest[105] showed favours. In this

---

[103] The five elements, *manas* and *ahamkara*.
[104] Beings, offspring, descendants.
[105] Prakriti.

way, starting with Mahat and ending with Vishesha,[106] the cosmic egg was created. Just as bubbles simultaneously emerge in water, the egg emerged from Vishesha. It was gigantic and lay down in the water. The egg originated from Prakriti and Parameshthi became successful in the objective and the means. Brahma is described as *kshetrajna*.[107] He is spoken of as Purusha, the first one with a body. He is the first creator of beings. Brahma is the one who existed first. He is known as Purusha and Hamsa, stationed beyond Pradhana. He is Hiranyagarbha and Kapila. He is eternal and the *chhandas*[108] are his body. The sac that surrounded the embryo became Meru. The outer skin of the embryo became the mountains. *Paramatman*'s foetal fluid became the oceans. The entire universe, with *deva*s, *asura*s and humans, emerged from inside the egg. This was also true of the sun, the moon, the *nakshatra*s, the *graha*s and the wind.[109] On the outside, the egg was surrounded by water that was ten times the size. On the outside, the water was surrounded by fire that was ten times the size. On the outside, the fire was surrounded by wind that was ten times the size. Wind was surrounded by space and space was surrounded by *bhutadi*. *Bhutadi* was surrounded by Mahat and Mahat was surrounded by the unmanifest. These are the worlds and all the great-souled ones, proud because they know the truth, reside in them. Their *atman*s are established in Purusha. They are lords who know about

[106] The specific, with differences.

[107] *Kshetra* is the field or material/physical body and the one who knows the *kshetra* (the *atman*) is *kshetrajna*.

[108] Metres.

[109] *Nakshatra*s are asterisms. Some are constellations, not stars. There are twenty-seven along the circle of the Zodiac, twenty-eight with Abhijit added. *Graha*s (those that seize/attract) are planets.

the *dharma* of *yoga*. There are others who contemplate the truth. They are omniscient and their *rajas* has been quietened. They are always happy in their minds. The egg is surrounded by these seven sheaths that evolved from Prakriti.[110] O *dvijas*! Since the *maya* is deep, one is only capable of speaking this much. I spoke of a seed and that is the working of Pradhana. The *shruti* texts of the *Veda*s say that is Prajapati's first supreme body. The cosmic egg possesses the strength of all seven worlds.[111] The divinity's second body is that of Parameshthi. From the golden eggs, Bhagavan Brahma emerged as Hiranyagarbha.[112] Those who know the meanings of the *Veda*s say that this is the illustrious one's third body. The intelligent one possesses another body that has the *guna* of *rajas*. This is Bhagavan with the four faces, who embarks on the task of creating the universe. With his *atman* in the universe and with his face in every direction, Vishnu, the lord of the universe, depending on the *guna* of *sattva*, protects everything that has been created. In the end, the divinity Parameshvara, who is in all *atman*s, depends on the *guna* of *tamas* and as Rudra, withdraws the universe. Mahadeva is one but is established in three kinds of forms. He is *nirguna* and without blemish. However, for creation, preservation and dissolution, he assumes *guna*s. He assumes one, two, three or many *guna*s. He is Yogeshvara[113] and creates, and takes away, bodies of many different forms. In his own pastimes, he assumes tasks and forms. For the welfare of

---

[110] Water, fire, wind, space, *bhutadi*, Mahat and the unmanifest.

[111] While this can refer to the seven sheaths, it can also mean the seven upper regions of Bhuloka, Bhuvarloka, Svarloka, Maharloka, Janaloka, Tapoloka and Satyaloka (Brahmaloka).

[112] With a golden womb.

[113] Lord of *yoga*.

devotees, he devours again. He divides his *atman* into three
and functions in the three worlds. In particular, he creates,
devours and looks on. He shows favours and creates and
then devours *praja*s again. He assumes *guna*s in the three
periods of time but is spoken of as one. In the beginning,
the eternal one manifested himself as Hiranyagarbha. Since
he was the first one, he is known as Adideva. Since he is not
born, he is described as Aja. Since he saves all the *praja*s,
he is described as Prajapati.[114] Among all *deva*s, he is the
great divinity. Therefore, he is described as Mahadeva.
Since he is large, he is said to be Brahma.[115] Since he is
supreme, he is Parameshvara. Since he controls, but is not
controlled by anyone, he is described as Ishvara.[116] Since he
goes everywhere, he is Rishi.[117] Since he takes everything
away, he is Hari.[118] Since he was the first and was not
generated, he is Svayambhu. Since he is the refuge of men,
he is Narayana.[119] Since he takes *samsara* away, he is Hara.
As a result of his lordship, he is spoken of as Vishnu.[120] He
is Bhagavan because he possesses every kind of *vijnana*.[121]
Since he protects, he is OUM.[122] Since he possesses every
kind of *vijnana*, he is Sarvajna.[123] Since he is in everything,

[114] Lord of *praja*s. *Praja*s are offspring, beings, descendants.
[115] With a root in *brih*, meaning to increase.
[116] From a root meaning capable.
[117] From the verbal root meaning to go or move.
[118] From the verbal root meaning to take away.
[119] *Ayana* means abode or dwelling-place. *Naara* is water and
Nara is man. Since Vishnu lies down in the water, he is Narayana.
That is the standard derivation. This derivation is based on refuge
of men.
[120] Based on a root that means someone who enters everywhere.
[121] *Bhaga* means knowledge, a meaning used to derive this.
[122] Derived from *avana*, protection.
[123] The omniscient one.

he is Sarva. Since he is sparkling, he is Shiva.[124] Since he goes everywhere, he is Vibhu.[125] Since he saves from every kind of misery, he is spoken of as Taraka.[126] What is the need to speak a lot? Everything in the universe is full of the *brahman*. Dividing himself into many kinds of differences, Parameshvara sports. I have described Prakrita creation briefly. O *brahmanas*! Now hear about the creation that occurred before intelligence[127] manifested itself.'

Chapter 5(1)(5) (Enumeration of time)

Kurma said, 'Since he does not emerge from any prior entity, he is described as Svayambhu. Since he is the refuge of men, he is said to be Narayana. Since he takes away *samsara*, he is Hara. Because of his lordship, he is spoken of as Vishnu. Since he possesses every kind of *vijnana*, he is Bhagavan. Since he protects, he is described as OUM. Since he possesses every kind of *vijnana*, he is Sarvajna. Since he is everywhere, he is Sarva.'[128]

'O supreme *dvijas*! Since Svayambhu, the enumeration of time started. But even he is incapable of enumerating it, even if he tries for many years. Briefly, the enumeration of time is conceived of as consisting of two *parardhas*. This is the ultimate measurement of time. After this, creation starts afresh. According to his measurement of time, his

---

[124] The auspicious one.

[125] Based on a root that means to penetrate/pervade.

[126] From a root that means the one who saves and enables a person to cross over difficulties.

[127] That is, Mahat.

[128] These repetitions exist in the text.

lifespan is said to be one hundred years. Some say that this is a *parardha*. Others say that half of this is a *parardha*. O excellent *dvijas*! Fifteen *nimeshas*[129] are said to amount to one *kashtha*. Thirty *kashtha*s are one *kalaa* and when thirty *kalaa*s have passed, there is one *muhurta*. A human day and night consist of that number of *muhurta*s.[130] That number of days and nights amounts to one month, divided into two *paksha*s. Six months are one *ayana* and two *ayana*s, *dakshinayana* and *uttarayana*, constitute a year. *Dakshinayana* is the night for *deva*s and *uttarayana* is their day. The four *yuga*s, *krita*, *treta* and the others, are measured as twelve thousand divine years. Understand the division. *Krita yuga* is said to consist of four thousand years. *Sandhya* and *sandhyamsha* for *krita yuga* are four hundred years.[131] Progressively, *sandhya* and *sandhyamsha* for the other *yuga*s become three hundred, two hundred and one hundred years. If one doesn't include the *sandhyamsha* of *krita yuga*, all the *sandhyamsha*s thus amount to six hundred years. Without *sandhya* and *sandhyamsha*, the duration is three thousand, two thousand and one thousand years. For those who know about time, this is described as the duration of *dvapara*, *treta* and *tishya*.[132] The aggregate is thus thought to be more than twelve thousand years.[133] A *manvantara* is

---

[129] The time taken for the blinking of an eye.

[130] That is, there are thirty *muhurta*s, fifteen during the day and fifteen at night.

[131] *Sandhya* and *sandhyamsha* are both intervening periods between two *yuga*s, *sandhya* at the beginning of a *yuga* and *sandhyamsha* at the end.

[132] *Tishya* is the same as *kali*.

[133] Probably recognizing the difference between a lunar year and a solar year.

said to consist of seventy-one *mahayuga*s.[134] O *brahmana*s!
In one of Brahma's days, there are fourteen *manvantara*s.
These are Svayambhuva and the others and Savarni and
the others.[135] This entire earth consists of seven *dvipa*s[136]
and mountains. Earlier, lords among men protected it for a
full thousand years.[137] When one *manvantara* is described,
all the other *manvantara*s are similar. There is no doubt
that when one *kalpa* is described, all the other *kalpa*s are
similar. One of Brahma's days is a *kalpa* and his night is of
the same duration. The learned have said that one thousand
*mahayuga*s amount to one *kalpa*. O excellent *dvija*s! Three
hundred and sixty *kalpa*s amount to one of Brahma's years.
Those who know, say this. O excellent *dvija*s! It is known
that one hundred times that number is a *parardha*. At the
end of this period, all living beings collectively get dissolved
into Prakriti. The virtuous speak of this as a Prakrita
withdrawal. Brahma, Narayana and Isha, these three are
also subject to Prakrita dissolution. It is said that when the
time is right, they manifest themselves again. In this way,
Brahma, Vaasudeva, Shankara and the elements are created
in the course of time and are devoured again. Bhagavan
Kala is without a beginning. He is infinite. He does not

[134] A *mahayuga* is a cycle of *satya*, *treta*, *dvapara* and *kali*, with
*sandhya*s and *sandhyamsha*s added. There are 1000 *mahayuga*s in
one of Brahma's days. There are also 14 *manvantara*s in one of
Brahma's days. Therefore, each *manvantara* has 1000/14 = 71.4
*mahayuga*s.

[135] We are in Vaivasvata *manvantara* and the past six are
Svayambhuva, Svarochisha, Outtama, Tamasa, Raivata and
Chakshusha. The names of the future seven *manvantara*s are not
consistently given across texts, but they generally have the qualifier
Savarni.

[136] *Dvipa* is a continent, the word also means an island.

[137] Each king ruled that long.

suffer from old age and death. He goes everywhere and is autonomous. Maheshvara is in all *atman*s. There have been many Brahmas, Rudras, Narayanas and others. However, the wise Bhagavan Kala, Isha, is one. So say the *shruti* texts. O *dvija*s! Brahma's first *parardha* is over now. It is now the second *parardha* and the first *kalpa*. The learned know the *kalpa* that has immediately been over as Padma *kalpa*. It is Varaha *kalpa* now and I will describe it in detail.'

Chapter 6(1)(6) (Varaha saves the earth)

Kurma said, 'There was a single undifferentiated and terrible ocean and everything was covered in darkness. The wind and other things were pacified. Nothing could be discerned. In that single ocean, all mobile and immobile entities had been destroyed. At the time, Brahma originated, with one thousand eyes and one thousand feet. He was Purusha, with one thousand heads. He was golden in complexion, beyond the grasp of the senses. At the time, Brahma, known as Narayana, slept on the water. In this connection, a *shloka* is cited about Narayana. "The divinity is the *brahman*'s own form. He is the one who creates and destroys the universe. Water is known as *naara*, and water is known as this because it is the descendant of *nara*.[138] Since he lay down there, he is described as Narayana. He slept during the night, with a duration equal to one thousand *mahayuga*s. At the end of the night, for the sake of creation, he assumed the form of Brahma. He understood that the earth was submerged

---

[138] *Nara* means man, in this context, the cosmic man. Descended from him, water became *naara*.

inside the water. Having determined this, Prajapati wished
to raise it. To sport in the water, he assumed the form of
a beautiful Varaha.[139] This was a form of the *brahman*,
impossible to comprehend through thoughts or speech. To
raise the earth, he entered Rasatala. The one who holds up
the earth, the one who is his own support, raised it with
his tusks. Famous for his virility, the earth was spread out
on the tips of his tusks. On seeing this, the *siddha*s and
*brahmarshi*s, who were in Janaloka, praised Hari.'[140]

The *rishi*s said, 'I prostrate myself before the lord
of *deva*s, Brahma Parameshthi. You are the ancient and
eternal Purusha, the victorious one. I prostrate myself
before Svayambhu, the creator who knows the meaning
of everything. I prostrate myself before the creator
Hiranyagarbha, the *paramatman*. I prostrate myself before
Vaasudeva Vishnu, the origin of the universe. You are the
divinity Narayana, who does what is good for *deva*s. I
prostrate myself before the one with the four faces, the one
who holds the Sharnga bow, the *chakra* and the sword. You
are in the *atman*s of all beings. I prostrate myself before
you. You are the hidden one. I bow down. I prostrate
myself before the one who is the mystery of the *Veda*s. I
prostrate myself before the one who is the source of the
*Veda*s. I prostrate myself before the pure and enlightened
one. I prostrate myself before the one who is the form of
jnana. I prostrate myself before the one who is the form
of bliss. I prostrate myself before the one who is a witness
to the worlds. You are the infinite and immeasurable one,

---

[139] Boar, Vishnu's Varaha incarnation. In some versions, the
earth was taken down to the nether regions by Hiranyaksha,
Hiranyakashipu's twin brother.

[140] The upper worlds aren't destroyed at the end of a *kalpa*.

the cause and the effect. I prostrate myself before the one who is the five elements. I prostrate myself before the one whose *atman* is in the five elements. I prostrate myself before the one who is primordial Prakriti. I prostrate myself before the one whose form is *maya*. I prostrate myself before Varaha. I prostrate myself before the one who has the form of Matsya.[141] I prostrate myself before the one who can be approached through *yoga*. I prostrate myself before Samkarshana.[142] I prostrate myself before the one with three forms, with three abodes, divine in energy. I prostrate myself before the one who is Siddha, the one who is worshipped, the one who divides the *guna*s into three. I prostrate myself before the one who has a form as Aditya. I prostrate myself before the one who originated from the lotus. I prostrate myself before the one who has no form, the one who has form. I prostrate myself before Madhava. You are the one who has created everything. Everything is established in you. You are the one who protects and saves everything in the universe. You are the refuge and the destination.'

Kurma continued, 'In this way, Sanaka and the others praised Bhagavan Vishnu.[143] In his form as Varaha, Ishvara showed them his favours. The one who holds up the earth conveyed the earth to its own place. The one who holds up the earth then discarded the form he had conceived through his mind. Like a giant boat, the earth was stationed on that ocean of water. Because its expanse was huge, it did not sink. He levelled the earth and gathered together the

---

[141] Vishnu's incarnation in the form of a fish.

[142] The one who attracts, also Balarama's name.

[143] Through the powers of his mind, Brahma had four sages as sons—Sanaka, Sanandana, Sanatana and Sanatkumara. Later in the text, Kratu is added to the usual list of four.

mountains on earth. Everything in the former creation had
been burnt down. His mind turned to creating again.'

Chapter 7(1)(7) (Description of creation)

Kurma said, 'At the beginning of the *kalpa*, he thought
of creating, just as it had existed earlier. A creation
that was not based on intellect appeared and it was full
of darkness. From the great-souled one, five kinds of
darkness emerged, known as—Tamas, Moha, Mahamoha,
Andhatamisra and Avidya as the fifth.[144] As he meditated
and identified with it, there were these five kinds of creation.
Like seeds covered inside a pot, they were enveloped in
darkness. Inside and outside, there was no illumination.
It was stupefied, with no association. Since mountains are
said to have been the chief, this is described as Mukhya
Sarga.[145] The lord saw that this would not serve the purpose
and thought of another creation. As he reflected on this,
the Tiryaka-Strotas Sarga resulted.[146] Since the conduct
was diagonal and sideways, this is described as Tiryaka-
Srotas. O *dvija*s! These are known as animals and other
such entities that follow contrary paths. Realizing that
this would not serve the purpose, he thought of another
creation. This creation is known as Urdhva-Srotas.[147] This

---

[144] Respectively, darkness, delusion, great delusion, blinding
darkness and negation of knowledge.

[145] *Sarga* means creation and *mukhya* means first/foremost. This
creation had immobile entities like mountains and trees and was
insentient.

[146] *Tiryaka* means diagonally and sideways. This led to the
creation of inferior species, like animals and birds.

[147] One that flows upwards.

is the creation of *deva*s, who possess *sattva* in them. They are full of happiness and pleasure. Inside and outside, they are not covered.[148] Since inside and outside, their nature is that of illumination, they are known as *deva*s.[149] After this, he meditated again, his meditation permeated by the truth. A creation known as Arvaka-Srotas[150] was formed, and this would accomplish the purpose. This possessed a lot of illumination but was contaminated by an excess of *tamas* and *rajas*. Therefore, though possessing *sattva*, they suffered from terrible miseries and are described as humans. Seeing them, Bhagavan Aja[151] thought of another creation. As he meditated on this creation, the creation of *bhutas*[152] and others appeared. All of them received possessions and all of them divided them again. All of them devoured and possessed bad conduct. This is described as the creation of *bhuta*s and others. O bulls among *dvija*s! These are the five kinds of creation that are described. Brahma's first creation is known as that which flowed from Mahat. The second creation is described as that of *bhuta*s, the *tanmatra*s.[153] The third creation is described as *vaikarika*, that of the senses. After these Prakrita creations, there was creation with the use of intelligence. The fourth creation is described as Mukhya Sarga, immobile entities being the foremost. Tiryaka-Strotas, the one that flowed sideways, is described as the fifth. Urdhva-Srotas, the creation of *deva*s, is described as the sixth. The seventh creation was Arvaka-

---

[148] In the sense of being constrained.

[149] The word *deva* means the shining one.

[150] One that flows downwards.

[151] One without birth, Brahma.

[152] We have deliberately not translated *bhuta* here. It means beings, as well as elements.

[153] Here, *bhuta*s mean subtle elements.

Srotas, that of humans. The eighth creation is described as Bhoutika Sarga, that of *bhuta*s and others. The ninth is that of Kumaras.[154] The earlier creations[155] were Prakrita and Vaikrita. The first three creations were Prakrita, without the use of intelligence. O bulls among sages! Starting with Mukhya, the rest were with the use of intelligence.'

'Initially, through the powers of his mind, Brahma Prajapati created sons who were his equals—Sanaka, Sanatana, Sanandana, Kratu and Sanatkumara. O *brahmana*s! These five were *yogi*s, supremely devoted to non-attachment. Their minds were devoted to Ishvara. They were not interested in creation. On seeing that they were not interested in creating the worlds, Prajapati was instantly deluded by the *maya* of Parameshthi, who is full of *maya*, and lost his senses. Narayana is a great sage and great *yogi*, who delights the minds of *yogi*s. The universe is full of his *maya,* and he woke him up. Having been woken up, the one whose *atman* is in the universe tormented himself through supreme austerities. Though Bhagavan scorched himself, nothing was obtained. After a long period of time, he was filled with grief and rage. When he was overwhelmed by anger, teardrops fell from his eyes. Parameshthi's forehead was furrowed in a frown. Mahadeva Nilalohita, the refuge, originated from this. Bhagavan Isha is eternal and is a mass of energy. Those who are learned can see this Parameshvara within their own *atman*s. Bhagavan Brahma remembered OUMKARA and joined his hands in salutation. Prostrating himself, he said, "Create many kinds of *praja*s." Hearing Bhagavan's words, Shiva Shankara, whose mount is *dharma*, used the

[154] Sanaka and the others.
[155] Till the eighth.

powers of his mind to create Rudras who were just like him. They possessed matted hair and were fearless. They had three eyes and had a bluish red complexion. Bhagavan Brahma told him, "Create *praja*s who will experience birth and death." Isha replied, "I will not create *praja*s who experience birth and death. O Bhagavan! If you wish, you create such inauspicious *praja*s." At this, the one born from the lotus restrained Rudra and started to create himself.'

'Listen and understand about those positions and those who took pride in those positions[156]—water, fire, space, heaven, wind, earth, rivers, oceans, mountains, trees, creepers, *lava*s,[157] *kashtha*s, *kalaa*s, *muhurta*s, days, nights, half-months, months, *ayana*s, years, *yuga*s and so on. After creating those who took pride in these positions, he created *sadhaka*s—Marichi, Bhrigu, Angiras, Pulastya, Pulaha, Kratu, Daksha, Atri, Vasishtha, Dharma and Sankalpa. Brahma created Daksha from his breath of life and Marichi from his eyes. The divinity created Angiras from his head and Bhrigu from his heart. He created Atri from his eyes and Dharma from his conduct. The grandfather of the worlds created Sankalpa from his resolution.[158] He created Pulastya from *udana* and the sage Pulaha from *vyana*. He comfortably created Kratu from *apana* and Vasishtha from *samana*.[159] Brahma created

---

[156] The presiding deities of those positions.

[157] *Lava* is a measure of time, smaller than a *nimesha* and not consistently defined.

[158] The word *sankalpa* means resolution.

[159] *Prana* is the breath of life. It has five aspects—*udana* (ascends and circulates above the heart), *prana* (inward moving, circulates throughout the body), *samana* (above the navel, uniting the upward and the downward), *apana* (downward moving, lower part of the body) and *vyana* (nerve channels, integrating all the others).

these *sadhaka*s who were householders. Assuming human forms, they went about establishing *dharma*. After this, wishing to create the four categories of *deva*s, *asura*s, ancestors and humans, Bhagavan Isha invoked his own *atman*. When Prajapati invoked his *atman*, there was an excess of *tamas*. Initially, from his loins, *asura*s were born as his sons. After creating *asura*s, Purushottama cast aside that body. When he cast aside the body, the night was instantly created from it. Since it has an excess of *tamas*, *praja*s sleep during that period. The divinity then accepted another body, primarily consisting of *sattva*. Thus, *deva*s were born from his shining mouth. When he cast aside that body, day, generally consisting of *sattva*, was generated from it. Therefore, those who observe *dharma* worship *deva*s during the day. He accepted another body, primarily consisting of *sattva*. The ancestors, who regarded him like a father, were born from this. After creating ancestors, the witness to the universe cast aside this body too. *Sandhya* was immediately created from the body that was cast aside.[160] Hence, day is for *deva*s and night is for those who hate the *deva*s. Between the two, the form of the glorious *sandhya* is for the ancestors. Therefore, all the *deva*s, *asura*s, sages and humans always attentively worship the form that is between day and night. Brahma created another body, possessing an excess of *rajas*. Humans, who are full of *rajas*, were born as sons from this. Thereafter, Prajapati quickly cast aside this body. O *brahmana*s! The period before *sandhya*, known as *jyotsna*,[161] resulted from this. O bulls among *brahmana*s! Bhagavan Brahma again assumed a revered form that was generally full of *tamas* and *rajas*. In

[160] *Sandhya* means joint, in this context, the joint between day and night. Thus, *sandhya* means dawn and dusk. Sometimes, midday is also mentioned as a third *sandhya*.
[161] Meaning moonlight.

the darkness, *rakshasa*s, who suffered from hunger, were born from this. They were powerful sons, generally full of *tamas* and *rajas*. They were *nishachara*s.[162] In this way, *sarpa*s, *bhuta*s and *gandharva*s were also born.[163] The lord created another body, full of *rajas* and *tamas*. Birds were created from his lifespan and sheep from his chest. Others, like goats, were created from his mouth. Cattle were fashioned out of his stomach. Horses, elephants, donkeys, *gavaya*s and *mriga*s were created from his feet.[164] Prajapati created camels and mules from his forearms. Herbs, roots and fruits were created from his body hair. From his first face, he created the *gayatri*, *rik*s, *trivritstoma*, *rathantara* and *agnishtoma* sacrifices. From his face to the south, he created *yajus*, *trishtubh chhanda*, *panchadasha stoma*, *brihatsama* and *uktha*. From the mouth to the west, he created *saman*, *jagati chhanda*, *saptadasha stoma*, *vairupa* and *atiratra*. From his mouth to the north, he created *ekavimsha*, *atharva*, *aptoryama*, *anushtubh* and *vairaja*.[165]

[162] Those who roam around in the night.

[163] *Sarpa*s are snakes. They are distinct from *nagas/uragas/pannagas*. *Naga*s possess semi-divine traits, have worlds of their own and can assume any form at will. *Bhuta*s are beings who are spirits and demons, often described as Shiva's companions. *Gandharva*s are semi-divine and are celestial musicians.

[164] *Gavaya* is a wild ox. *Mriga* is usually deer, but also means any wild animal that is hunted. When *mriga* is used in the sense of wild animal, *pashu* is used in the sense of domestic animal, especially one that is sacrificed.

[165] Brahma possesses four faces. The first face is to the east and then one goes around, clockwise. From each face, five different objects were created—a *chhanda* or metre (*gayatri, trishtubh, jagati, anushtubh*), a verse from *Rig, Yajur, Sama* and *Atharva Veda* (*rik, yajus, saman, atharva*), a *stoma* or hymn of praise (*trivritstoma, panchadasha stoma, saptadasha stoma, ekavimsha*), a specific *sama* hymn (*rathantara, brihatsama, vairupa, vairaja*) and a sacrifice (*agnishtoma, uktha, atiratra, aptoryama*).

Superior and inferior beings were created from his body.
In this way, Brahma Prajapati embarked on the task of
creating *praja*s. He created the four categories of beings,
*yaksha*s, *pishacha*s, *gandharva*s and auspicious *apsara*s,
*deva*s, *rishi*s, ancestors and humans.[166] He created all
the mobile and immobile entities—humans, *kinnara*s,
*rakshasa*s, birds, *pashu*s, *mriga*s and *uraga*s. There were
both those that decayed and those that did not decay, the
mobile and the immobile. In the former creation, they
possessed different kinds of *karma*. They are repeatedly
created, possessing that. There are the violent and the non-
violent, the mild and the cruel, those who follow *dharma*
and those who follow *adharma*, the true and the false.
They were all conceived according to whatever appealed
to them. There were many kinds of great elements, the
objects of the senses and forms. The creator himself
determined and engaged the beings. He gave names
and forms, in accordance with the visible universe of
Prakriti.[167] Maheshvara created them as they were earlier,
in conformity with the words of the *Veda*s. In accordance
with the *Veda*s, the *rishi*s were also created and given
names. At the end of the night, they were thus created,
and Aja gave them names. Until the end, each of them
progresses according to the respective signs and forms.
They are seen to possess the sentiments they harboured at
the onset of the *mahayuga*s.'

[166] *Yaksha*s are semi-divine, companions of Kubera. *Apsara*s are
celestial dancers, often described in association with *gandharva*s.
*Pishacha*s are demons that feed on flesh. *Kinnara*s (also known as
*kimpurusha*s) are also semin-divine.

[167] *Prapancha* means the visible universe.

Chapter 8(1)(8) (Mukhya and other creations)

Kurma said, 'In this way, mobile and immobile entities were created. However, the intelligent one saw that the *praja*s that he had created did not increase. Brahma was enveloped in *tamas* and grieved miserably. He used his intelligence to determine what was going on. When he glanced at his own *atman*, he saw that the excess of *tamas* was controlling everything, though *rajas* and *sattva* also existed. Following his own *dharma*, he withdrew and cast aside the *tamas*, along with the *sattva* and *rajas*. A couple was born from that rejected *tamas*. O *brahmana*s! The male was Adharmacharana and the female, with inauspicious signs, was Himsaa.[168] Brahma then cast aside his radiant body. He divided this body into two. Half became a man and half became a woman. The lord created the man, Virat. He created the woman known as Shatarupa. She was an auspicious *yogini*.[169] She remained established there, pervading heaven and earth with her greatness. She possessed the strength and prosperity of *yoga*. She possessed *jnana* and *vijnana*. A son was born from the man, Virat, who was born from the unmanifest. This man was the *deva*, Svayambhuva Manu, who was a sage. The *devi*, known as Shatarupa, performed extremely difficult austerities. She obtained Manu, blazing in his fame, as a husband. Through him, Shatarupa gave birth to two sons, Priyavrata and Uttanapada. There were two excellent daughters too. Manu bestowed his daughter, Prasuti, on Daksha. Ruchi Prajapati was born through Brahma's mental powers, and

---

[168] Adharmacharana means conduct of *adharma*, Himsaa means violence.

[169] *Yogini* is the feminine of *yogi*.

he accepted the daughter, Akuti. Through Ruchi, born through mental powers, Akuti gave birth to auspicious twins. They were Yajna and Dakshinaa and the world flourishes through them.[170] Through Dakshinaa, Yajna had twelve sons. They were the Yamas, known as *deva*s during Svayambhuva *manvantara*.'[171]

'Through Prasuti, Daksha had twenty-four daughters. Listen accurately to their names. They were Shraddhaa, Lakshmi, Dhriti, Tushti, Pushti, Medhaa, Kriyaa, Buddhi, Lajjaa, Vapu, Shanti, Siddhi and Kirti as the thirteenth.[172] Dharma accepted these auspicious daughters of Daksha as wives. There were eleven younger ones. They were virtuous and possessed excellent eyes. They were Khyati, Sati, Sambhuti, Smriti, Priti, Kshamaa, Santati, Anasuyaa, Urjaa, Svahaa and Svadhaa.[173] In the due order, excellent sages who possessed *jnana* accepted these daughters as wives—respectively, Bhrigu, Bhava, Marichi, the sage Angiras, Pulastya, Pulaha, Kratu who knew about supreme *dharma*, Atri, Vasishtha, Vahni[174] and the ancestors. Shraddhaa's son was Kama and Lakshmi's son is said to have been Darpa.[175] Dhriti's son was Niyama and Tushti's

---

[170] Yajna is the personified form of a sacrifice and Dakshinaa is the personified form of donations/fees given at sacrifices.

[171] From one *manvantara* to another *manvantara*, *deva*s, *saptarshi*s and Indra change.

[172] Respectively meaning faith, prosperity, fortitude, contentment, nourishment, mental vigour, activity, intelligence, modesty, form, peace, achievement and deeds.

[173] Respectively meaning fame, virtue, origin, memory, affection, forgiveness, progeny, lack of envy, energy, exclamation made when offering oblations to gods and exclamation made when offering oblations to ancestors.

[174] Agni.

[175] Kama means desire and Darpa means insolence.

son is said to have been Santosha.[176] Pushti's son was Labha and Medhaa's son was Shama.[177] Kriyaa's sons were Danda and Naya.[178] Buddhi had the sons Bodha and Apramada.[179] Lajjaa's son was Vinaya and Vapu's son was Vyavasaya.[180] Shanti's son was Kshema and Siddhi gave birth to Siddha.[181] Kirti's son was Yasha.[182] These were Dharma's sons. Kama's son was Harsha and Harsha's son was Ananda.[183] Dharma's descendants, who brought happiness, have thus been described. Through Adharma, Himsaa had the sons Nikriti and Anrita.[184] Nikriti's offspring were Bhaya and Naraka and the twins Mayaa and Vedanaa.[185] Through Bhaya, Mayaa had Mrityu, who takes away beings, as a son.[186] Through Rourava, Vedanaa had Duhkha as a son.[187] Mrityu's offspring were Vyadhi, Jaraa, Shoka, Trishnaa and Krodha.[188] All of these possess signs of *adharma* and are described as those who give rise to great grief. All of them held up their seed and did not have wives and sons. This is Tamasa Sarga and Dharma

[176] Niyama means restraint/rules and Santosha means satisfaction.

[177] Labha means gain and Shama means self-control.

[178] Danda means punishment and Naya means good policy.

[179] Bodha is understanding and Apramada is lack of distraction.

[180] Vinaya is humility and Vyavasaya means endeavour.

[181] Kshema means well-being and Siddha is someone who has achieved success.

[182] Yasha means fame.

[183] Harsha is delight and Ananda is joy.

[184] Nikriti is wickedness and Anrita is falsehood.

[185] Bhaya is fear, Naraka is hell and Vedanaa is pain.

[186] Mrityu means death.

[187] Rourava is the name of a hell (perhaps being used for Naraka here) and Duhkha is unhappiness.

[188] Vyadhi is ailment, Jaraa is old age, Shoka is grief, Trishnaa is thirst and Krodha is rage.

was born in this way. O bulls among sages! I have briefly
spoken about this secondary creation.'

Chapter 9(1)(9) (Brahma's origin)

Suta said, 'Hearing these words, Narada and the other
*maharshi*s prostrated themselves before Vishnu, the one
who bestows boons. However, full of doubts, they asked.'

The sages asked, 'O Janardana! You have spoken
about Mukhya and the other creations. But we have a
doubt, and you should dispel it now. Bhagavan Isha, the
wielder of Pinaka,[189] was older. How did Shambhu become
the son of Brahma, whose birth is not manifest? How was
Bhagavan Brahma, the grandfather of the worlds, born
from the cosmic egg? O lord of the universe! You should
tell us about this.'

Kurma replied, 'O all the *rishi*s! Hear about how the
infinitely energetic Shankara became the son of Brahma and
about how Brahma originated from a lotus. When the past
kalpa ended, the three worlds were covered in darkness.
There was a single terrible ocean. There were no *deva*s
or *rishi*s. In that desolate deluge, the divinity Narayana
Purushottma happily slept on Shesha *naga*. He[190] possessed
one thousand heads, one thousand eyes, one thousand feet
and one thousand arms. He is the omniscient one. Learned
ones think about him in their *atman*s. His garments were
yellow, and his eyes were large. His complexion resembled
that of a blue cloud. He possesses powers and *yoga* in

[189] Pinaka is the name of Shiva's bow and trident and Shiva's
name is Pinaki.
[190] Narayana.

his *atman* and is compassionate towards *yogi*s. On one occasion, while he slept, in his pastimes, a wonderful, divine and sparkling lotus, representing the essence of the three worlds, emerged from his navel. It extended for one hundred *yojana*s and resembled the rising sun.[191] It was sacred, with divine fragrances. It possessed pericarp and filaments. The wielder of the Sharnga bow remained thus, for a very long period of time. Bhagavan Hiranyagarbha[192] arrived at that place. The one whose *atman* is in the universe used his hand to wake up the eternal one. Confounded by his *maya*, he addressed him in sweet words. "This terrible ocean is desolate and is enveloped in darkness. O bull among men! You are alone. Please tell me who you are." Hearing his words, the one with Garuda on his standard laughed.[193] He addressed the divinity Brahma in a deep voice that rumbled like clouds. "I am the divinity Narayana, the cause behind the creation and destruction of the universe. I am the great lord of *yoga*. Know me to be Purushottama. O grandfather of the worlds! Behold. The entire universe is inside me. The mountains and the great *dvipa*s are there, surrounded by the seven oceans." Having addressed him in this way, Hari, the great *yogi* whose *atman* is in the universe, questioned the being, the creator, though he knew the answer. "Who are you?" At this, Bhagavan Brahma, the lord who is a store of the *Veda*s, laughed. He smiled and addressed the lotus-eyed one in gentle words. "I am Dhatri and Vidhatri.[194] I am Svayambhu, the great-grandfather. The universe is established in me. I am Brahma, who faces

---

[191] *Yojana* is a measure of distance, between 8 and 9 miles. It is the distance that can be travelled through a single yoking.

[192] Brahma.

[193] Vishnu has Garuda on his standard.

[194] Dhatri is the creator, and Vidhatri is the one who ordains.

every direction." Hearing these words, Bhagavan Vishnu, for whom truth is valour, took his permission. Using *yoga*, he entered Brahma's body. He saw all three worlds, with *deva*s, *asura*s and humans, inside the divinity's stomach and was filled with wonder. The one whose abode is the Indra among *pannaga*s emerged through the mouth. Bhagavan Vishnu addressed the grandfather. "O eternal one! Now you also enter my stomach. O bull among beings! Enter and see the wonderful worlds." Hearing Shripati's delightful words, Kushadhvaja entered his stomach.[195] Truthful in valour, he saw those worlds in the womb. He wandered around inside the divinity but could not find Hari's end. The great-souled Janardana had closed all the exit points. Finally, he found a door in the navel. Using the strength of his *yoga*, the one who was born from the golden egg entered this. The one with the four faces manifested himself through the form of the lotus. As resplendent as the inside of a lotus, he was radiant, seated on the lotus. Bhagavan Svayambhu Brahma is the grandfather who is the origin of the universe. He thought himself to be the lord and *atman* of the universe, the supreme destination. He addressed Purusha Vishnu in a deep voice that rumbled like the clouds. "Desiring your own victory, what have you done now? I am the only one who is powerful. No one is capable of assailing me." Narayana attentively heard the words spoken by Brahma. Hari addressed him in sweet words of conciliation. "You are Dhatri and Vidhatri. You are Svayambhu, the great-grandfather. It was not because of malice that I closed the exit points. I did that in my pastimes. There was no desire to constrain you. Who is

---

[195] Shripati is Shri's (Lakshmi's) consort, Vishnu. Kushadhvaja (with *kusha* grass on his standard) is Brahma's name.

capable of impeding the grandfather, the lord of *deva*s?
O Brahma! You are incapable of being restricted. You are
revered in every possible way. O fortunate one! If I have
offended you in any way, please pardon me. O Brahma!
Because of this reason, you should become my son. O one
who pervades the universe! Do this to bring me pleasure.
You will be known as Padmayoni."[196] At this, the divinity,
Bhagavan, bestowed that boon on Kiriti.'

'Filled with great delight, he spoke to Vishnu again.
"You are in all *atman*s. You are infinite. For everyone,
you are the supreme Ishvara. You are in the *atman*s of all
beings. You are the eternal and supreme *brahman*. I am
Maheshvara, the illumination. All the worlds are in my
atman. Everything is pervaded by me. I am the *brahman*,
the supreme Purusha. Barring the two of us, there is no
other Parameshvara in the worlds. We, Narayana and the
grandfather, are one, but have divided ourselves into two
forms." Addressed in this way by Brahma, Vaasudeva
replied. "This pledge of yours will lead to your destruction.
With *yoga*, can you not see the imperishable one who is
Brahma's lord? He is Ishana, the lord of Pradhana and
Purusha. I know that Parameshvara. Indras among *yogi*s and
practitioners of *samkhya*[197] cannot perceive Maheshvara.
He is without a beginning and an end. O Brahma! Seek
refuge with him." At this, Brahma became angry and
replied to the lotus-eyed Keshava. "O Bhagavan! I know
myself to be the supreme and imperishable one. I am the
brahman and the universe is in my *atman* alone. I am the

---

[196] Padmayoni means one who originated from a lotus. Kiriti is
one with a crown, Vishnu's name.

[197] One of the six *darshana*s (schools of philosophy), associated
with the name of the sage Kapila.

supreme destination. Barring the two of us, there is no other Parameshvara in the worlds. Cast aside this extensive sleep and look towards your own *atman*." The lord heard these words, resulting from anger and said, "O fortunate one! Do not speak in this way and abuse the great-souled one. O Brahma! Nothing is unknown to me and I do not say anything that is contrary. O Brahma! However, the infinite Parameshvari causes delusion. This is the specific *maya* of the infinite one and arises from his *atman* for this reason alone." Saying this, Bhagavan Vishnu was silent. The lord of gods knew the supreme truth and his own *atman*.'

'Hara's *atman* is immeasurable. For all beings, he is Parameshvara. Wishing to show a favour to Brahma, he manifested himself. The divinity had a mass of matted hair and an eye in the centre of his forehead. Bhagavan was a store of great energy and carried a trident in his hand. He wore an extraordinary garland that hung all the way down to his feet. It had been wrought with divine skills and incorporated the moon, the stars and the planets. Seeing the divinity Ishana, Brahma, the grandfather of the worlds, was exceedingly deluded by *maya* and addressed the one attired in yellow garments.[198] "Who is this blue being, with three eyes and with a trident in his hand? O Janardana! He is a mass of energy and, immeasurable in his *atman*, is advancing." Hearing his words, Vishnu, the crusher of *danava*s, looked at the divinity, Ishvara, who blazed against the sparkling water. He knew the supreme sentiments of Ishvara, who had conceived Brahma. He stood up and spoke to Bhagavan, the grandfather who was the lord of *deva*s. "This is the eternal divinity, Mahadeva, who is self-resplendent. He is without a beginning and

---

[198] That is, Vishnu.

an end. He cannot be thought of. He is the great lord of the worlds. He is Shankara, Shambhu, Ishana. He is the Parameshvara who is in the *atman*s of all beings. He is the lord of *bhuta*s. He is the *yogi* Mahesha. He is sparkling Shiva. He is Dhatri and Vidhatri. He is the foremost lord, who does not decay. Mendicants, who immerse themselves in the *brahman* and meditate, see him. He is the one who creates the entire universe. He preserves and destroys. Mahadeva alone is the one who becomes Kala. He is Nishkala Shiva.[199] Earlier, the eternal one created you, Brahma, and gave you the *Veda*s. It is Shankara who is approaching. O great grandfather! He is the eternal origin of the universe and know that I, known as Vaasudeva, to be one of his other forms. Can you not see the lord of *yoga*, Brahma's imperishable lord? May you possess divine eyes, so that you are able to see the supreme one." The grandfather of the worlds obtained such eyes from Vishnu. He understood that supreme *jnana* was standing in front of him. The grandfather obtained supreme *jnana* about Ishvara. He then sought refuge with the divinity Shiva, his father. He remembered OUMKARA and fixed his mind in his own *atman*. He joined his hands in salutation and used *Atharvashirsha* to praise the divinity.'

'Parameshvara was praised by Bhagavan Brahma. He was filled with great joy and seemed to smile as he spoke. "O child! There is no doubt that you are my devotee, and you are thus my equal. Earlier, for the creation of the worlds, I created you as the one without decay. You are the *atman*, the primordial Purusha who evolved from my body. O one whose *atman* is in the universe! O unblemished one! I am

---

[199] Nishkala means without form or parts. Kala has various meanings—time, destiny, destroyer.

the one who bestows boons. Ask for a boon." The one born
from the lotus heard the words spoken by the lord of *deva*s.
He glanced towards Purusha Vishnu. Prostrating himself,
he spoke to Shankara. "O Bhagavan! O lord of the past and
the future! O Mahadeva! O Ambikaa's lord![200] I wish that
you, or someone like you, should be my son. O Mahadeva!
I was deluded by your subtle *maya*. O Shiva! I did not
know the true nature of your inclinations. O divinity! For
your devotees, you are the mother, the father, the brother
and the well-wisher. Be pleased. I prostrate myself before
your lotus-feet and seek refuge with you." Hearing his
words, Vrishadhvaja,[201] the lord of the universe, glanced at
Janardana and spoke to his son. "O Bhagavan! O son! I will
do what you have asked for. O unblemished one! Divine
vijnana about Ishvara will manifest itself in you. You are
hereby engaged as the original creator of all beings. O lord
of *deva*s! O grandfather of the worlds! Use your *maya* for
them. This Narayana originated from me. He is my other
form. O Ishana![202] Hari will bestow *yoga* and *kshema*."[203]
Pleased, Parameshvara extended his hands and touched
the divinity, Brahma, with them. He then addressed Hari
in these words. "O one who pervades the universe! Since
you have always been my devotee, I am pleased with you.
Though it is the supreme truth that there is no difference
between the two of us, please ask for a boon." Vishnu, who
pervades the universe, heard his words. Pleased, he glanced
towards his face and spoke these words. "This alone is a
praiseworthy boon that I am able to see Parameshvara. May

[200] Ambikaa is one of Parvati's names.
[201] One with a bull on his standard, Shiva's name.
[202] Meaning Brahma.
[203] *Yoga* is to obtain what is not possessed, *kshema* is to preserve what is already possessed.

I always have devotion towards you, the *paramatman*."
Agreeing to this, Mahadeva again spoke to Vishnu. "I am
the overlord, but you will be the doer for all tasks. There is
no doubt that everything will be full of you and full of me.
You are the moon and I am the sun. You are night and I am
day. You are unmanifest Prakriti and I am Purusha. You
are *jnana* and I am the one who knows. You are the Shakti
that exists in knowledge and I am Ishvara, the one who has
that Shakti. I am the Nishkala divinity and you are Lord
Narayana. *Yogi*s, who speak about the *brahman*, see us as
one. O one whose *atman* is in the universe! A *yogi* who does
not seek refuge with you, will not obtain me. Protect the
entire universe, with *deva*s, *asura*s and humans." Bhagavan
has no beginning and deludes and divides all beings with his
own *maya*. He is infinite in his powers. Saying this, he left
for his abode, which is not manifest and is devoid of birth,
growth and destruction.'

Chapter 10(1)(10) (Creation by Rudra)

Kurma said, 'When the divinity Maheshvara had left,
the grandfather again returned to the radiant and great
lotus that arose from the navel. After a long period of time,
two great *asura*s, unmatched in manliness, arrived there.
These were the two brothers, Madhu and Kaitabha. They
were full of great rage and their bodies were like gigantic
mountains. They had emerged from inside the ears of the
lord of *deva*s, the one who wields the Sharnga bow.[204] On

[204] They emerged from the wax in Vishnu's ears. In more
common renderings, Madhu and Kaitabha were killed by Vishnu
Narayana.

seeing them advance, the lord Aja spoke to Narayana. "These two *asura*s are like thorns for the three worlds and you should kill them." Hearing his words, Lord Narayana Hari instructed two beings that they should be killed. O *dvijas*! At this command, a great battle commenced between those two *asura*s. Jishnu defeated Kaitabha and Vishnu vanquished Madhu. The grandfather, the lord of the universe, was seated on the lotus. His mind full of affection, Hari addressed him in sweet words. "I have been bearing you. But I am unable to do so any longer. Your energy is too heavy for me to tolerate. Please get down from the lotus." At this, the one whose *atman* is in the universe descended and entered the body of the one who wields the *chakra*. He became one with Vishnu and succumbed to Vishnu's sleep. He entered and became one with the one who holds a conch shell, a *chakra* and a mace. At the time, Brahma became known as Narayana and slept in the water. The *paramatman* experienced bliss for a long period of time. He was without a beginning and without an end and possessed no second. He was within his own *atman*, known as the *brahman*. When it was morning, the one with *yoga* in his *atman* became the divinity with four faces. Assuming the inclinations of Vishnu, he created those who were similar in forms. Initially, the divinity created Sananda, Sanaka, Ribhu, Sanatkumara and the eldest, Sanatana. They were free from delusion and the opposite pair of sentiments.[205] They were filled with supreme non-attachment. Having understood the nature of supreme inclinations, they turned their minds towards *jnana*. They were thus indifferent towards creating the worlds. Because

---

[205] Heat and cold, joy and misery and so on.

of Parameshthi's *maya*, the grandfather lost his senses.[206]
At this, the ancient Purusha, whose eternal form is in
the universe, spoke to his own son, so as to destroy the
delusion suffered by the one who originated from the lotus.
Vishnu asked, "Have you forgotten what, in earlier times,
you requested the eternal divinity who wields the trident in
his hand? You asked Shambhu Shankara to be your son.
Shankara had told you that he would become your son
through your mental powers." Thanks to Govinda, the
grandfather, who was born from the lotus, regained his
senses. Making up his mind to create *praja*s, he performed
extremely difficult austerities.'

'However, though he tormented himself, nothing
happened. After a long period of time, he was filled
with grief and rage. When he was overwhelmed by rage,
teardrops fell from his two eyes. *Bhuta*s and *preta*s arose
from these.[207] On seeing all of these in front of him, Brahma
censured himself. Overwhelmed by anger, Bhagavan
Prajapati gave up his breath of life. Full of the breath of
life, Rudra manifested himself from the lord's mouth. He
resembled one thousand suns together and could burn
down, like the fire that comes at the end of a *yuga*. This
was the lord of *deva*s, Shiva, himself and he wept in a
loud and terrible voice. Since he was crying, Brahma told
him, "Do not cry. Since you wept, you will be famous in
the world as Rudra."[208] The grandfather of the worlds
gave him seven other names, wives, eternal sons and
eight places to reside in. These seven names were Bhava,
Sharva, Ishana, Pashupati, Bhima, Ugra and Mahadeva.

---

[206] He did not know what to do.
[207] A *preta* is a ghost, the spirit of a dead person.
[208] *Rud* means to cry/weep.

The eight forms[209] were the sun, water, the earth, fire, the
wind, space, initiated *brahmana*s and the moon. If people
prostrate themselves before Rudra in these locations, these
eight forms of divinity bestow the supreme destination.
The wives were Suvarchalaa, Umaa, Vikeshi, Shivaa,
Svahaa, Dishah, Dikshaa and Rohini. The sons are said to
have been Shanaishchara, Shukra, Lohitanga, Manojava,
Skanda, Sarga, Santana and Budha.[210] Such was the nature
of Bhagavan Mahadeva, the lord of *deva*s. He cast aside the
dharma of desire and created *praja*s and resorted to non-
attachment. With inclinations of Ishvara, he meditated on
the *atman* within his own *atman*. He drank the eternal and
supreme *amrita* that is the imperishable *brahman*. However,
Brahma instructed Nilalohita to create *praja*s. Through the
powers of his mind, Shiva created Rudras who were just
like his own self. They were fearless and had matted hair.
Their throats were blue, and they wielded Pinakas. There
were several, with tridents in their hands. They possessed
three eyes and were always full of bliss. They did not suffer
from old age or death and their mounts were large bulls.
They were devoid of attachment and omniscient. The lord
created crores and hundreds of crores that were like this.
The preceptor saw many kinds of sparking Rudras. These
Nilalohitas did not suffer from old age or death. He told
Hara, "O divinity! You should not wish to create such
*praja*s, who do not suffer from death. O lord of *bhuta*s!
Create others, those who suffer from birth and death."
Bhagavan Kapardi, who chastised Kama, replied.[211]

[209] The eight places to reside in.
[210] Shanaishchara is Saturn, Shukra is Venus, Lohitanga is Mars
and Budha is Mercury.
[211] Kapardi, meaning one with matted hair, is Shiva's name.
Shiva burnt down Kama, the god of love.

"I will not create in this way. You create different types of *praja*s." Since then, the divinity no longer created such auspicious *praja*s. He remained there, withdrawing himself from creating Rudras who were like his own self. The lord of *deva*s, the wielder of the trident, became Sthanu.[212] There are eight imperishable attributes that always exist in Shankara—*jnana*, non-attachment, powers, austerities, truth, forgiveness, forbearance, insight about the *atman*, understanding and the quality of presiding. Such is Pinaki Shankara, the Parameshvara himself.'

'Bhagavan Brahma glanced at the three-eyed divinity and at the Rudras who had been created through his mental powers. His eyes dilated in joy. Through the insight of *jnana*, he got to know about Ishvara's supreme inclinations. He bowed his head down, joined his hands in salutation and praised the lord of the universe. Brahma said, "I prostrate myself before Mahadeva. I prostrate myself before Parameshvara. I prostrate myself before the divinity Shiva. I prostrate myself before the one whose form is the *brahman*. I prostrate myself before Mahesha. I prostrate myself before the serene cause. I prostrate myself before the lord of Pradhana and Purusha, the lord of *yoga*. I prostrate myself before Kala Rudra, the one with the trident, the one who is the great devourer. I prostrate myself before the one who holds Pinaka in his hand. I prostrate myself before the three-eyed one. I bow down. I prostrate myself before the one with three forms. You are Brahma's father. You are the lord of knowledge about the *brahman*. You are the one who bestows knowledge about the *brahman*. I prostrate myself before

---

[212] Sthanu means the immobile/stationary one and is Shiva's name.

the one who is the mystery of the *Veda*s. I prostrate
myself before the destroyer of Kala. I prostrate myself
before the one who is the core essence of *Vedanta*, one
whose *atman* is a form of the *Veda*s. I prostrate myself
before Rudra, understanding incarnate. I prostrate myself
before the *guru* of *deva*s. You are surrounded by many
kinds of *bhuta*s and are devoid of all miseries. I prostrate
myself before the divinity who is fond of *brahmana*s. I
prostrate myself before Brahma's lord. I prostrate myself
before Parameshthi, the three-eyed primordial divinity.
I prostrate myself before you, who wears the directions
as a garment.[213] I prostrate myself before the one with
the shaven head, before the one who holds a staff. You
are without a beginning and without blemish. I prostrate
myself before the one who can be known through *jnana*.
I prostrate myself before the *tirtha*, the one who enables
a person to cross over.[214] I prostrate myself before the
cause behind the prosperity of *yoga*. I prostrate myself
before the one who can be approached through *dharma*
and other means. I prostrate myself before the one who
can be approached through *yoga*. I prostrate myself
before the one who is beyond *prapancha*. I prostrate
myself before the one who is beyond illumination. I
prostrate myself before the *brahman paramatman*. The
universe is your form. You have created everything.
Everything is established in you. O one who pervades
the universe! Starting with Pradhana, you are the one
who draws in the universe. You are Ishvara Mahadeva.
You are Maheshvara, the supreme *brahman*. You are
serene Shiva Parameshthi, *nishkala* Purusha Hara. You

---

[213] That is, is naked.
[214] Cross over *samsara*.

are the supreme refulgence that is without decay. You are Kala Parameshvara. You are the infinite Purusha, Pradhana and Prakriti. You are earth, water, fire, wind, space and *ahamkara*. I prostrate myself before the form that is described as the *brahman*. Your head is heaven. Your feet are the earth. The directions are your arms. The firmament is your stomach. I prostrate myself before the radiant one. You are the one who always scorches, illuminating the directions with your own radiance. You are the *brahman*, full of energy. The sun is in your *atman*. I prostrate myself before the universe. Your terrible body is full of energy and always bears *havya*. The fire is in your *atman*. I prostrate myself before the one who bears *kavya* to the large number of ancestors. You are the one whom the entire universe always invokes with the words "*svadha*".[215] A large number of *deva*s drink you. I prostrate myself before the one who has the moon in his *atman*. Your power always roams around in all the beings. The wind is in your *atman*. I prostrate myself before Maheshvari Shakti. I prostrate myself before the one with the wind in his *atman*. You are the one who creates everyone, in accordance with their own *karma*. I prostrate myself before the one who is established in all *atman*s, with the one with the four faces[216] in the *atman*. You are the one who lies down on the couch of Shesha, shrouding the universe in your *maya*. You are the one with the power of *yoga* in your *atman*. I prostrate myself before the one who has Vishnu in his *atman*. I prostrate

---

[215] *Svadha* is the exclamation used when oblations are offered to the ancestors. *Svaha* is the exclamation used when oblations are offered to the gods.

[216] Brahma.

myself before the power of the one who has Shesha, who
is always the support and holds up the fourteen worlds
and the entire cosmic egg on his hood, in his *atman*.
When everything is over, you drink the supreme bliss and
Devi alone is your witness, as you dance in your infinite
greatness. I prostrate myself before the one who has
Rudra in his *atman*. You are inside all beings. You are
established as the Ishvara who controls. The clouds are
your hair. The rivers are the joints in all your limbs. The
four oceans are your stomach. I prostrate myself before
the one who has water in his *atman*. O divinity who is a
witness to everything! I prostrate myself before the one
whose form is the universe. Those engaged in *yoga* go
without sleep and conquer their breath. They are content
and impartial in outlook. They are the ones who see that
radiance. I prostrate myself before the one who has *yoga*
in his *atman*. A *yogi* who has destroyed his sins is able
to cross over that *maya*, limitless and without bounds.
I prostrate myself before the one who has knowledge in
his *atman*. He is the radiant one, whose resplendence
shines beyond the great darkness. I seek refuge with that
supreme truth, the form of Parameshvara. He is eternal
bliss. He is without support. He is the supreme *nishkala*
Shiva. I seek refuge with the *paramatman*. You are
Parameshvara." Having praised Mahadeva in this way,
Brahma was pervaded by him. Brahma joined his hands
in salutation and remained there, prostrating himself
before the eternal one.'

'Out of affection for Brahma, Hara Mahadeva bestowed
Ishvara's divine and excellent *yoga* on him, conferring
non-attachment. He takes away the afflictions of those
who prostrate themselves and he touches him with his
soft hands. He showed his favours to the grandfather and

seemed to smile, as he spoke. "O Brahma! You requested that I should become your son. I will do all that. Create many kinds of worlds. O Brahma! I will divide myself into three and be known as Brahma, Vishnu and Hara. For the sake of creation, preservation and dissolution, *nishkala* Parameshvara will possess *guna*s. You are my eldest son, fashioned for the sake of creation. You have originated from the right side of my body, Purushottama[217] from the left. Rudra evolved from the region around the heart of Shambhu, the supreme lord of *deva*s. I am his other form. O Brahma! Brahma, Vishnu and Shiva are for the purposes of creation, preservation and destruction. Though Shankara is established as one, it is out of his own will that he has divided himself. In this way, using my *maya*, I have other forms too. Mahadeva's nature is that he is self-assured, absolute and without form. His supreme form is beyond the forms of these three divinities. The three-eyed Maheshvari always bestows peace on *yogi*s. O grandfather! Her supreme form is also mine. I possess eternal powers, *vijnana*, energy and *yoga*. Established in the *guna* of *tamas*, I devour everything. I become Kala. No one can assail me, not even in the mind. O one born from the lotus! O unblemished one! Whenever you constantly think about me, at that time, you will obtain my presence." Saying this, *guru* Hara honoured Brahma. Along with the sons born through his mental powers,[218] he instantly vanished from the spot. Resorting to *yoga*, he[219] created many kinds of worlds. Bhagavan Prajapati, known as Narayana, created them, as they had existed earlier. Using the knowledge

---

[217] Vishnu.
[218] The Rudras.
[219] Brahma.

of *yoga*, he created Marichi, Bhrigu, Angiras, Pulastya, Pulaha, Kratu, Daksha, Atri and Vasishtha. It is the certain determination of the Puranas that these are the nine *brahmana*s. All of them are Brahma's equals. They are *sadhaka*s who speak about the *brahman*. Earlier, I have already described everything about Sankalpa, *dharma*, the *dharma* of *yuga*s, the eternal positions and those who take pride in those.'

Chapter 11(1)(11) (Devi's *avatara*)

Kurma said, 'In this way, the grandfather, the lord of *deva*s, created Marichi and the others. Along with the sons born through mental powers, he tormented himself through supreme austerities. When he scorched himself, Rudra, resembling the fire of destruction, emerged from his mouth. With a trident in his hand, the three-eyed Ishana manifested himself. Half of his body was male, and half was female. He was extremely terrible and impossible to behold. "Divide yourself." Saying this, because of his fright, he vanished. Thus addressed, he divided himself into two, male and female. The male again divided himself into eleven parts. These are known as the eleven Rudras and they are the lords of the three worlds. O *brahmana*s! These Kapalishas and others are engaged in the tasks of the *deva*s. The lord and divinity also divided his own female form into many parts, amiable and fierce, serene and turbulent, fair and dark. O *brahmana*s! These potencies are famous as Shaktis on earth. In the forms of Lakshmi and the others, Shankari pervades the universe. O *dvija*s! Then, Ishani divided herself into many portions again. Engaged by Mahadeva, she went and presented herself before the grandfather. Bhagavan Brahma told her, "Become Daksha's daughter." Requested, she manifested herself as Prajapati's[220] daughter. Asked by Brahma, he bestowed Devi Sati on Rudra. Rudra, the wielder of the trident, accepted Daksha's daughter as his own. Following Prajapati's instruction, after some time, Parameshvari Ishani again separated herself from Lord Shankara.[221] Thereafter, Sati became the daughter of Himalaya and Menaa. O *dvija*s! For the welfare of all the *deva*s, the three worlds and his own self, the excellent mountain bestowed Parvati on Rudra. Thus, Devi Maheshvari became half of Shankara's body. *Sura*s and *asura*s prostrate themselves before Shivaa Sati Haimavati.[222] Her powers are unmatched. All the *deva*s, along with Vasava, and the sages say this. But only Shankara and Hari himself know her. O *brahmana*s! I have thus told you how the infinitely energetic Shankara became the son of Brahma Parameshthi, who originated from the lotus.'

Chapter 12(1)(12) (Devi's greatness)

Suta said, 'The sages heard what Vishnu said in the form of Kurma. Prostrating themselves, they again asked Hari. The *rishi*s asked, "Who is Bhagavati Devi, who is half of Shankara's body? We are asking you. Please tell us accurately about Shivaa Sati Haimavati." Hearing the

---

[220] Daksha was a Prajapati.
[221] This seems to refer to Daksha insulting Shiva, after which, Sati gave up her body.
[222] Haimavati, Himalaya's daughter, is Parvati's name.

words of the sages, the great *yogi*, Purushottma, meditated
on his own supreme state and replied.'

Kurma answered, 'Earlier, on the extremely beautiful
slopes of Meru, the grandfather spoke about this.
This *vijnana* is especially secret and mysterious. This is
supreme *samkhya* for the followers of *samkhya*. This is
excellent *vijnana* about the *brahman*. This alone frees
beings who are submerged in the ocean of *samsara*. She is
Maheshvari Shakti, in the form of the *jnana* one hankers
for exceedingly. Haimavati is described as the firmament.
She is held to be the supreme point. Shivaa is infinite and
goes everywhere. She is beyond the *guna*s. She is *nishkala*.
She is one but has many divisions. Her form is that of
great hankering for *jnana*. She is *nishkala* and without a
parallel. In her own energy, she is established in the truth.
She is the natural foundation, and her sparkling radiance is
like that of the sun. Maheshvari Shakti is one, but she has
many appellations. In his presence, she sports in superior
and inferior forms. She does everything. This universe is
the result of her action. The wise say that Ishvara has no
task, nor is he the instrument. Within her, four of Devi's
Shaktis exist in their own forms. O bulls among sages!
They exist because of her. Hear about them. They are said
to be Shanti, Vidyaa, Pratishthaa and Nivritti.[223] Hence,
the divinity Parameshvara is described as possessing four
*vyuha*s. Through this means, the divinity enjoys supreme
bliss in his own *atman*. The four *Veda*s are Maheshvara's
four forms. Her great potency is unmatched, and her
achievement is without a beginning. Because of her
association with Rudra, the *paramatman*, she is infinite.
Devi Ishvari is the one who makes all beings function.

---

[223] Respectively, peace, knowledge, stability and renunciation.

Bhagavan Hari Maheshvara is spoken of as Kala and *prana*. Everything in the entire universe is woven into him, like warp and woof. Those who speak about the *Veda*s sing of him as the divinity Hara, the fire of destruction. Kala creates beings. Kala destroys *prajas*. Everything is under the subjugation of Kala. Kala is not under the subjugation of anyone. Pradhana, the *tattva* Purusha, Mahat, the *atman* and *ahamkara* and other *tattva*s are permeated by Kala, the *yogi*. His form is everywhere in the universe and his Shakti is known as *maya*. Isha Purushottama uses his *maya* to whirl everything around. This Shakti, in the form of *maya*, is eternal and assumes every kind of form. It always manifests Mahesha's form as the universe. There are other foremost Shaktis, fashioned by the divinity. These three are *jnana* Shakti, *kriya*[224] Shakti and *prana* Shakti. O Indras among *brahmana*s! Using his *maya*, the powerful one, who is without a beginning and without destruction, has fashioned these Shaktis. *Maya* is in all the Shaktis. It is impossible to counter and impossible to cross. The possessor of *maya* is the lord of all these Shaktis. The lord Kala is the one who brings about destruction. Kala is the one who acts. Kala is the one who destroys everything. Kala establishes the universe. This universe is subjugated by Kala. *Maya* obtained the presence of Parameshthi, the overlord of *deva*s. He is infinite and is the lord of everything. The lord Shambhu has Kala in his *atman*. Having done this, *maya* assumed the forms of Pradhana and Purusha. She is one, goes everywhere and is infinite. She is absolute. She is *nishkala* Shivaa. Shakti is one. Shiva is one. Shiva is spoken of as the one who possesses Shaktis. However, from the Shaktis, other Shaktis and those who possess

[224]Kriya is action/activity.

these Shaktis, evolved. Those who know the supreme
truth say that there is a difference between Shaktis and the
possessor of Shaktis. But *yogi*s who have thought about
the truth do not see any difference between them. These
Shaktis are Devi, the mountain's daughter. Shankara is the
one who possesses the Shaktis. Those who speak about
the *brahman* mention this special difference in the Purana.
Vishveshvari Devi, devoted to her husband, Maheshvara,
is described as the one who is enjoyed. Bhagavan Kapardi
Nilalohita is said to be the one who enjoys. The divinity,
Vishveshvara Shankara, the destroyer of Manmatha,[225]
is the one who thinks. Those who reflect speak of Ishani
as intellect and the object to be thought. O *brahmana*s!
Everything in this universe originated from Shaktis and
the possessor of Shaktis. Sages with insight about the
truth have said this in all the *Veda*s. This is the supreme
and divine greatness of Devi that has been manifested.
Those who speak about the *brahman* have determined
this in all the discussions of *Vedanta*. She is one and goes
everywhere. She is subtle and hidden. She does not move
and is eternal. *Yogi*s have perceived this supreme state of
Mahadevi. She is imperishable bliss. She is the absolute
brahman. She is supreme and *nishkala*. *Yogi*s have
perceived Mahadevi's supreme state. She is greater than
the greatest. She is the eternal truth. She is auspicious and
does not decay. She dissolves into infinite Prakriti. Such is
Devi's supreme state. It is auspicious and without blemish.
It is pure and devoid of *guna*s and devoid of duality. Devi's
supreme state can be obtained through the realization of
the *atman*. She is Dhatri and she is Vidhatri. For those
who desire supreme bliss, with the support of Ishvara,

---

[225] Manmatha is Kama, the god of love, destroyed by Shiva.

she destroys all the torments of *samsara*. Therefore, if one wishes for liberation, one should seek refuge with Parvati Parameshvari. Shivaa's *atman* is in the *atman*s of all beings.'

'The lord of mountains tormented himself through extremely difficult austerities and obtained Sharvani[226] as his daughter. Along with his wife, he sought refuge with Parvati Parameshvari. The one with the beautiful face was born out of her own will. When she was this, Menaa, Himalaya's wife, spoke to him. Menaa said, "O king! Behold this child. Her face resembles a lotus. Because of our austerities, she has been born for the welfare of all beings." He also saw Devi, with a complexion like that of the rising sun. She possessed matted hair and four faces. She had three eyes and was extremely eager. She possessed eight hands and her eyes were large. The moon was her ornament. She was *nirguna* and *saguna*. She was herself existence and non-existence and was devoid of any notion of manifestation. Greatly agitated because of her energy, he prostrated his head on the ground. Terrified, he joined his hands in salutation and spoke to Parameshvari. Himalaya asked, "O large-eyed Devi! Who are you? Your body is decorated with the moon. O child! I do not know who you are. Please tell me accurately what I have asked you." Hearing the words spoken by the Indra among mountains, Parameshvari, who bestows freedom from fear to *yogi*s, replied to the great mountain. Shri Devi answered, "Know me to be the supreme Shakti, who finds a refuge in Maheshvara. I am no different from him and am without decay. I am the absolute one. Those who desire *moksha*, see me. I am the one whose *atman*

---

[226] Shivaa.

is in every kind of conception. I am Shivaa, present in all *atman*s. I am the eternal power. *Vijnana* is my form. I am the one behind every kind of activity. I am infinite and my greatness is infinite. I enable the crossing over of the ocean of *samsara*. I will bestow divine sight on you. Behold the form of my powers."[227] Saying this, she herself bestowed *vijnana* on Himalaya. She showed him her divine form, associated with Parameshvara. It resembled one crore suns. There was a serene orb of energy. There were thousands of garlands of blazing flames, resembling one hundred fires of destruction. There were cruel teeth, impossible to assail. The form was ornamented by a mass of matted hair. It wore a crown and held a mace in its hand. It held a conch shell and a *chakra*. There was an excellent trident in the hand. It was a terrible and fearful form. But the face was also serene and amiable, possessing infinite powers. One hundred thousand moons decorated the body, and the dazzle was like that of one crore moons. There was a crown and a mace in the hand. The form was adorned with anklets. There were divine garlands and garments, smeared with divine fragrances and unguents.[228] The hands held a conch shell and a *chakra*. The desirable form was three-eyed and was clad in a hide.[229] It was located inside the cosmic egg and outside it. Everything was inside and outside this form. It possessed every kind of Shakti and was pure. It was eternal and possessed every kind of form. Brahma, Indra, Upendra[230] and Indras among *yogi*s worshipped the lotus feet. There were hands

[227] Reminiscent of 11.8 of *Bhagavat Gita*.
[228] Identical to 11.11 of *Bhagavat Gita*.
[229] *Krittivasa*, specifically, the hide of an elephant. Krittivasa is Shiva's name.
[230] Indra's younger brother, Vishnu's name.

and feet in every direction. There were eyes, heads and
faces in every direction. He saw Parameshvari established
there, enveloping everything. On seeing Devi's supreme
Maheshvara form, the king was overwhelmed by fear but
was also delighted in his mind.'

'He fixed himself on his *atman* and remembered
OUMKARA within his own *atman*. He praised Parameshvari
with one thousand and eight names. Himalaya said,[231]
"(1) Shivaa; (2) Umaa; (3) Paramaa;[232] (4) Shakti; (5)
Anantaa;[233] (6) Nishkalaa; (7) Amalaa;[234] (8) Shantaa;[235]
(9) Maheshvari; (10) Nityaa;[236] (11) Shashvati;[237] (12)
Paramaksharaa;[238] (13) Achintyaa;[239] (14) Kevalaa;[240] (15)
Ananyaa;[241] (16) Shivatmaa;[242] (17) Paramatmikaa;[243]

---

[231] Naturally, the numbering doesn't exist in the text. We have
added that for convenience. Some names have more than one
meaning. As listed, there are 998 names, but one shouldn't read
too much into this number. With words combined in Sanskrit, it is
sometimes difficult to decide what is a combined name and what
are individual names. It is also difficult to distinguish an adjective
from a name. A few names are also repeated. There are a few typos
in the text. But, sometimes, the text also gives alternative versions
in footnotes. In a few cases, we have opted for these alternative
versions, rather than the main text.

[232] Supreme one.

[233] Infinite one.

[234] Unblemished one.

[235] Tranquil one.

[236] Everlasting one.

[237] Eternal one.

[238] The one who is supremely imperishable.

[239] One who cannot be thought of.

[240] Absolute one.

[241] Without a second.

[242] With Shiva in the *atman*.

[243] With the *paramatman* in the *atman*.

(18) Anadi;[244] (19) Avyayaa;[245] (20) Shuddhaa;[246]
(21) Devatmaa;[247] (22) Sarvagaa;[248] (23) Achalaa;[249]
(24) Ekaneka-vibhagasthaa;[250] (25) Mayatitaa;[251] (26)
Sunirmalaa;[252] (27) Maha-Maheshvari; (28) Satyaa;[253]
(29) Mahadevi; (30) Niranjanaa;[254] (31) Kashthaa;[255]
(32) Sarvantarasthachalaa;[256] (33) Chicchakti;[257] (34)
Atilalasaa;[258] (35) Nandaa;[259] (36) Sarvatmikaa;[260]
(37) Vidyaa;[261] (38) Jyotirupaa;[262] (39) Amritaa;[263]
(40) Aksharaa;[264] (41) Shanti;[265] (42) Pratishthaa;[266]
(43) Sarvesham-nivritti;[267] (44) Amritapradaa;[268] (46)

---

[244] Without a beginning.
[245] Without decay.
[246] Pure one.
[247] With an *atman* in the *deva*s.
[248] One who goes everywhere.
[249] One who does not move.
[250] Though one, established in many divisions.
[251] Beyond *maya*.
[252] Extremely pure.
[253] Truth.
[254] Without taints.
[255] Ultimate.
[256] Unmoving inside everyone.
[257] Shakti of consciousness.
[258] Extremely eager.
[259] Charming one.
[260] Inside every *atman*.
[261] Learning.
[262] With a form as radiance.
[263] Immortal.
[264] Without decay.
[265] Peace.
[266] Stability.
[267] Bestowing *nivritti* on everyone.
[268] One who bestows immortality.

Vyomamurti;[269] (47) Vyomalayaa;[270] (48) Vyomadharaa;[271] (49) Achyutaa;[272] (50) Amaraa;[273] (51) Anadinidhanaa;[274] (52) Amoghaa;[275] (53) Karanatmaa;[276] (54) Akulakulaa;[277] (55) Svatah-prathamajaa;[278] (56) Nabhiramritasya;[279] (57) Atmasamsrayaa;[280] (58) Praneshvara-priyaa;[281] (59) Mataa;[282] (60) Mahamahisha-vasini;[283] (61) Praneshvari;[284] (62) Pranarupaa;[285] (63) Pradhana-purusheshvari;[286] (64) Mahamayaa;[287] (65) Sudushpuraa;[288] (66) Mula-prakritirishvari;[289] (67) Sarvashakti;[290] (68) Kalakaraa;[291]

[269] With space as a form.
[270] One who dissolves into space.
[271] One who supports space.
[272] One who is not dislodged.
[273] Immortal one.
[274] Without beginning and destruction.
[275] Infallible one.
[276] With cause in the *atman*.
[277] With a family and without a family.
[278] Born first, of her own accord.
[279] Navel of immortality.
[280] One who supports herself.
[281] Loved by her beloved.
[282] Mother.
[283] One who resides on the great Mahisha (buffalo), a reference to Devi killing Mahishasura. *Ghatini* (slayer) instead of *vasini* sounds better.
[284] Ishvari of *prana*, beloved one.
[285] With a form as *prana*.
[286] Ishvari of Pradhana and Purusha.
[287] The great *maya*.
[288] Extremely difficult to fill.
[289] Ishvari of primordial Prakriti.
[290] With all the Shaktis.
[291] One who brings about the *kalaa*s.

(69) Jyotsnaa;[292] (70) Dyou;[293] (71) Mahimaspadaa;[294] (72) Sarva-kaya-niynatri;[295] (73) Sarva-bhuteshvareshvari;[296] (74) Samsara-yoni;[297] (75) Sakalaa;[298] (76) Sarva-shakti-samudbhavaa;[299] (77) Samsara-potaa;[300] (78) Durvaraa;[301] (79) Durnirikshyaa;[302] (80) Durasadaa;[303] (81) Pranashakti;[304] (82) Pranavidyaa;[305] (83) Yogini; (84) Paramakalaa;[306] (85) Mahavibhuti;[307] (86) Durdharshaa;[308] (87) Mula-prakriti-sambhavaa;[309] (88) Anadyananta-vibhavaa;[310] (89) Paramadyaa;[311] (90) Apakarshini;[312] (91) Sarga-sthityanta-karani;[313] (91) Sudurvachyaa;[314] (92) Duratyayaa;[315] (93) Shabdayoni;[316] (94) Shabdamayi;[317]

[292] Moonlight.
[293] Firmament.
[294] Possessing grandeur.
[295] Controller of all bodies.
[296] Ishvari of the Ishvara who is in all *bhuta*s.
[297] Womb of *samsara*.
[298] With all the digits.
[299] Born from all the Shaktis.
[300] Boat for crossing *samsara*.
[301] Impossible to counter.
[302] Impossible to behold.
[303] Impossible to approach.
[304] Shakti of *prana*.
[305] Knowledge of *prana*.
[306] Supreme part.
[307] Great power.
[308] Impossible to assail.
[309] Originating from primordial Prakriti.
[310] With no beginning or end to the prosperity.
[311] Supreme and first one.
[312] One who takes away.
[313] One who brings about creation, preservation and destruction.
[314] Extremely difficult to describe.
[315] Difficult to cross.
[316] Source of sound.
[317] Full of sound.

(95) Nadakhyaa;[318] (96) Nadavigrahaa;[319] (97) Anadi;[320] (98) Avyaktagunaa;[321] (99) Mahanandaa;[322] (100) Sanatani;"[323]

"(101) Akashayoni;[324] (102) Yogasthaa;[325] (103) Maha-yogeshvareshvari;[326] (104) Mahamayaa;[327] (105) Sudushparaa;[328] (106) Mula-prakritirishvari;[329] (107) Pradhana-purushatitaa;[330] (108) Pradhana-purushatmikaa;[331] (109) Puranaa;[332] (110) Chinmayi;[333] (111) Pumasamadi;[334] (112) Purusharupini;[335] (113) Bhutantarasthaa;[336] (114) Kutasthaa;[337] (115) Mahapurusha-samjnitaa;[338] (116) Janma-mrityu-jaratitaa;[339] (117) Sarva-shakti-samanvitaa;[340]

[318] Described as sound.
[319] With a form as sound.
[320] Without a beginning.
[321] One whose gunas are not manifest.
[322] Great joy.
[323] Eternal one.
[324] Source of space.
[325] Established in yoga.
[326] Ishvari of the great lord of yoga.
[327] Great maya.
[328] One whose limit is extremely difficult to find.
[329] Ishvari of primordial Prakriti.
[330] Beyond Pradhana and Purusha.
[331] With Pradhana and Purusha in the atman.
[332] Ancient one.
[333] With a form as consciousness.
[334] Origin of men.
[335] With a form as Purusha.
[336] Established inside bhutas.
[337] Hidden deep inside.
[338] Described as the great Purusha.
[339] Beyond birth, death and old age.
[340] Possessing all the Shaktis.

(118)   Vyapini;[341]   (119)   Anavacchinnaa;[342]   (120)
Pradhanaupraveshini;[343] (121) Kshetrajna-shakti;[344] (122)
Avyaktalakshmanaa;[345]   (123)   Malavarjitaa;[346]   (124)
Anadimaya-sambhinaa;[347]   (125)   Tritattvaa;[348]   (126)
Prakritigrahaa;[349]   (127)   Mahamaya-samutpannaa;[350]
(128) Tamasi;[351] (129) Pourushi;[352] (130) Dhruvaa;[353]
(131) Vyaktavyaktatmikaa;[354] (132) Krishnaa;[355] (133)
Raktaa;[356] (134) Shuklaa;[357] (135) Prasutikaa;[358] (136)
Akaryaa;[359] (137) Karya-janani;[360] (138) Nityam-prasava-
dharmini;[361]   (139)   Sarga-pralaya-nirmuktaa;[362]   (140)
Srishti-sthityanta-dharmini;[363]   (141)   Brahmagarbhaa;[364]

[341] One who pervades.
[342] Without any breaks.
[343] One who enters Pradhana.
[344] Shakti of *kshetrajna*.
[345] With signs that are not manifest.
[346] Devoid of impurities.
[347] Distinct from primordial *maya*.
[348] With three *tattva*s.
[349] One who seizes Prakriti.
[350] Originating from great *maya*.
[351] Possessing *tamas*.
[352] Possessing virility.
[353] Fixed one.
[354] With the manifest and the unmanifest in the *atman*.
[355] Dark one.
[356] Red one.
[357] White one.
[358] One who gives birth.
[359] Without any tasks.
[360] Mother of tasks.
[361] With the *dharma* of constantly giving birth.
[362] Free from creation and dissolution.
[363] Following the *dharma* of creation, preservation and destruction.
[364] With Brahma in the womb.

(142) Chaturvimshaa;[365] (143) Padmanabhaa;[366] (144)
Achyutatmikaa;[367] (145) Vaidyuti;[368] (146) Shashvati;[369]
(147) Yoni;[370] (148) Jaganmataa;[371] (149) Ishvarapriyaa;[372]
(150) Sarvadharaa;[373] (151) Maharupaa;[374] (152)
Sarvaishvarya-samanvitaa;[375] (153) Vishvarupaa;[376] (154)
Mahagarbhaa;[377] (155) Vishveshecchanuvartini;[378] (156)
Mahiyasi;[379] (157) Brahmayoni;[380] (158) Mahalakshmi-
samudhbhavaa;[381] (159) Maha-vimana-madhyasthaa;[382]
(160) Mahanidraa;[383] (161) Atmahetukaa;[384] (162)
Sarvasadharani;[385] (163) Sukshmaa;[386] (164) Avidyaa;[387]
(165) Paramarthikaa;[388] (166) Anantarupaa;[389] (167)

[365] With twenty-four, a reference to samkhya's 24 principles.
[366] With a lotus in the navel.
[367] With Achyuta in the atman.
[368] Possessing lightning.
[369] Eternal one.
[370] Womb.
[371] Mother of the universe.
[372] Ishvara's beloved.
[373] Support for everything.
[374] With a great form.
[375] Possessing every kind of prosperity.
[376] With the universe as a form.
[377] With a great womb.
[378] One who follows the wishes of the lord of the universe.
[379] Possessing greatness.
[380] Brahma's origin.
[381] Originating from Mahalakshmi.
[382] Established in the centre of a great vimana.
[383] Great slumber.
[384] Cause behind the atman.
[385] Common to everyone.
[386] Subtle one.
[387] Ignorance.
[388] Supreme truth.
[389] With infinite forms.

Anantasthaa;[390] (168) Devi; (169) Purshamohini;[391] (170) Anekakara-samsthaa;[392] (171) Kalatraya-vivarjitaa;[393] (172) Brahmajanmaa;[394] (173) Harermurti;[395] (174) Brahma-Vishnu-Shivatmikaa;[396] (175) Brahmesha-Vishnu-janani;[397] (176) Brahmakhyaa;[398] (177) Brahma-samshrayaa;[399] (178) Vyaktaa;[400] (179) Prathamajaa;[401] (180) Brahmi; (181) Mahati;[402] (182) Brahmarupini;[403] (183) Vairagyaishvarya-dharmatmaaa;[404] (184) Brahmamurti;[405] (185) Hridisthitaa;[406] (186) Apamyoni;[407] (187) Svayambhuti;[408] (188) Manasi;[409] (189) Tattva-sambhavaa;[410] (190) Ishvarani; (191) Sharvani; (192) Shankararddha-sharini;[411] (193) Bhavani; (194) Rudrani; (195) Mahalakshmi; (196) Ambikaa; (197) Maheshvara-

---

[390] Established in the infinite.
[391] One who charms Purusha.
[392] Established in many kinds of forms.
[393] Devoid of the three periods of time.
[394] One who gave birth to Brahma.
[395] With a form as Hari.
[396] With Brahma, Vishnu and Shiva in the *atman*.
[397] Mother of Brahma, Isha and Vishnu.
[398] Described as the *brahman*.
[399] Established in the *brahman*.
[400] Manifest one.
[401] Born first.
[402] Great one.
[403] The form of the *brahman*.
[404] With the *dharma* and prosperity of non-attachment in the *atman*.
[405] The form of the *brahman*.
[406] Established in the heart.
[407] Source of water.
[408] Self-born.
[409] In the mind.
[410] Origin of the *tattva*s.
[411] Half of Shankara's body.

samutpannaa;[412]   (198)   Bhukti-mukti-phala-pradaa;[413]
(199) Sarvershvari;[414] (200) Sarva-vandhyaa;"[415]

"(201)   Nitaym-mudita-manasaa;[416]
(202)   Brahmendropendra-namitaa;[417]   (203)
Shankarecchanuvartini;[418]   (204)   Ishvararddhasana-
gataa;[419]   (205)   Maheshvara-pativrataa;[420]   (206)
Sakridvibhataa;[421] (207) Sarvarti-samdura-parishoshini;[422]
(208)Parvati;[423](209)Himavatputri;[424](210)Paramananda-
dayini;[425] (211) Gunadhyaa;[426] (212) Yogajaa;[427] (213)
Yogyaa;[428] (214) Jnanamurti;[429] (215) Vikasini;[430] (216)
Savitri; (217) Kamalaa; (218) Lakshmi; (219) Shri; (220)
Anantorasi-sthitaa;[431]   (221)   Sarojanilayaa;[432]   (222)

[412] Originating from Maheshvara.

[413] One who bestows objects of pleasure and emancipation as fruits.

[414] Ishvari of everyone.

[415] Deserving worship by everyone.

[416] Always delighted in the mind.

[417] One before whom Brahma, Indra and Upendra prostrate themselves.

[418] One who follows Shankara's wishes.

[419] One who occupies half of Ishvara's seat.

[420] Devoted to Maheshvara as a husband.

[421] One who dawns once.

[422] One who dries up the ocean of every kind of affliction.

[423] Mountain's daughter.

[424] Himalaya's daughter.

[425] One who bestows supreme bliss.

[426] Possessing excellent quaslities.

[427] Born from *yoga*.

[428] Worthy one.

[429] With a form as *jnana*.

[430] One who causes development.

[431] Established on Ananta's chest.

[432] With a lotus as abode.

Gangaa; (223) Yoganidraa; (224) Asurardini;[433] (225) Sarasvati; (226) Sarvavidyaa;[434] (227) Jagajjyeshthaa;[435] (228) Sumangalaa;[436] (229) Vagdevi;[437] (230) Varadaa;[438] (231) Avachyaa;[439] (232) Kirti;[440] (233) Sarvartha-sadhikaa;[441] (234) Yogishvari;[442] (235) Brahmavidyaa;[443] (236) Mahavidyaa;[444] (237) Sushobhanaa;[445] (238) Guhyavidyaa;[446] (239) Atmavidyaa;[447] (240) Dharmavidyaa;[448] (241) Atmabhavitaa;[449] (242) Svahaa; (243) Vishvambharaa;[450] (244) Siddhi; (245) Svadhaa; (246) Medhaa;[451] (247) Dhriti;[452] (248) Shruti;[453] (249) Niti;[454] (250) Suniti;[455] (251) Sukriti;[456] (252) Madhavi;

[433] One who afflicts asuras.
[434] Every kind of learning.
[435] Eldest in the universe.
[436] Extremely auspicious.
[437] Goddess of speech.
[438] One who bestows boons.
[439] One who is impossible to speak about.
[440] Fame.
[441] One who accomplishes every objective.
[442] Ishvari of yogis.
[443] Knowledge about the brahman.
[444] Great knowledge.
[445] Extremely beautiful.
[446] Secret knowledge.
[447] Knowledge about the atman.
[448] Knowledge about dharma.
[449] Cleansed by the atman.
[450] One who sustains the universe, earth.
[451] Intellect.
[452] Fortitude.
[453] Learning.
[454] Policy.
[455] Excellent policy.
[456] Good deeds.

(253) Naravahini;[457] (254) Pujyaa;[458] (255) Vibhavati;[459] (256) Soumyaa;[460] (257) Bhogini;[461] (258) Bhoga-shayini;[462] (259) Shobhaa;[463] (260) Shankari; (261) Lolaa;[464] (262) Malini;[465] (263) Parameshthini; (264) Trailokya-sundari;[466] (265) Namyaa;[467] (266) Sundari;[468] (267) Kamacharini;[469] (268) Mahanubhavaa;[470] (269) Sattvasthaa;[471] (270) Maha-mahisha-mardini;[472] (271) Padmanabhaa; (272) Papaharaa;[473] (273) Vichitra-mukutangadaa;[474] (274) Kantaa;[475] (275) Chitrambara-dharaa;[476] (276) Divyabharana-bhushitaa;[477] (277) Hamsakhyaa;[478] (278) Vyomanilayaa;[479] (279) Jagatsrishti-vivardhini;[480]

[457] With men as a mount. Naravahana is Kubera's name.
[458] Worthy of being worshipped.
[459] Radiant one.
[460] Amiable one.
[461] One who enjoys.
[462] One who lies down on a serpent.
[463] Beauty.
[464] The tremulous one.
[465] One who is garlanded.
[466] Most beautiful in the three worlds.
[467] One worthy of being bowed down to.
[468] Beautiful one.
[469] One who roams around as she wishes.
[470] Glorious one.
[471] Established in *sattva*.
[472] One who crushed the great Mahisha.
[473] One who dispels sins.
[474] With a wonderful crown and armlets.
[475] Desired one.
[476] With wonderful garments.
[477] Adorned with divine ornaments.
[478] One described as Hamsa.
[479] With an abode in space.
[480] One who enhances the creation of the universe.

(280) Niyantri;[481] (281) Yantramadhyasthaa;[482] (282) Nandini;[483] (283) Bhadrakalikaa; (284) Adityavarnaa;[484] (285) Kouberi;[485] (286) Mayura-vara-vahanaa;[486] (287) Vrishasanagataa;[487] (288) Gouri;[488] (289) Mahakali; (290) Surarchitaa;[489] (291) Aditi; (292) Niyataa;[490] (293) Roudraa;[491] (294) Padmagarbhaa;[492] (295) Vivahanaa;[493] (296) Virupakshi;[494] (297) Lelihanaa;[495] (298) Mahasura-vinashini;[496] (299) Mahaphalaa;[497] (300) Anavadyangi;[498] (301) Kamarupaa;[499] (302) Vibhavari;[500] (303) Vichitra-ratna-mukutaa;[501]   (304)   Pranatarti-prabhanjani;[502]

[481] One who controls.
[482] Established in the centre of a *yantra*.
[483] One who delights.
[484] With the complexion of the sun.
[485] Feminine divinity associated with Kubera.
[486] With an excellent peacock as a mount.
[487] One who moves with a bull as a mount.
[488] Fair one.
[489] Worshipped by gods.
[490] Restrained one.
[491] Fierce one.
[492] With a lotus as a womb.
[493] This can be interpreted in different ways, without a mount, or with a horse or bird as mount.
[494] With malformed eyes.
[495] With a tongue that licks.
[496] Destroyer of the great *asura*.
[497] One who bestows great fruits.
[498] With unblemished limbs.
[499] One who can assume any form at will.
[500] Night.
[501] With a wonderful bejewelled crown.
[502] One who destroys the afflictions of those who prostrate themselves.

(305) Koushiki; (306) Karshani;[503] (307) Ratri;[504] (308) Tridasharti-vinashini;[505] (309) Bahurupaa;[506] (310) Svarupaa;[507] (311) Virupaa;[508] (312) Rupavarjitaa;[509] (313) Bhaktarti-shamani;[510] (314) Bhavyaa;[511] (315) Bhavatapa-vinashini;[512] (316) Nirgunaa;[513] (317) Nitya-vibhavaa;[514] (318) Nihsaraa;[515] (319) Nirapatrapaa;[516] (320) Tapasvini;[517] (321) Samagiti;[518] (322) Bhavanka-nilayalayaa;[519] (323) Dikshaa;[520] (324) Vidyadhari;[521] (325) Diptaa;[522] (326) Mahendra-vinipatini;[523] (327) Sarvatishayini;[524] (328) Vishvaa;[525] (329) Sarva-siddhi-pradayini;[526] (330) Sarveshvara-priyabharyaa;[527] (331)

[503] One who drags.
[504] Night.
[505] Destroyer of afflictions of gods.
[506] With many forms.
[507] With her own form.
[508] Malformed.
[509] Devoid of form.
[510] One who pacifies the afflictions of devotees.
[511] Fortunate one.
[512] One who destroys the torments of the world.
[513] Devoid of *guna*s.
[514] With perpetual prosperity.
[515] One who goes forth.
[516] Devoid of shame.
[517] Ascetic.
[518] Songs of *Sama Veda*.
[519] One who dissolves into her abode on Bhava's (Shiva's) lap.
[520] Initiation/consecration.
[521] One who possesses learning.
[522] Blazing one.
[523] One who brought down the great Indra.
[524] One who surpasses everyone.
[525] Universe.
[526] One who bestows every kind of *siddhi*.
[527] Sarveshvara's beloved wife.

Samudrantara-vasini;[528]   (332)   Akalankaa;[529]   (333)
Niradharaa;[530] (334) Nityasiddhaa;[531] (335) Niramayaa;[532]
(336) Kamadhenu;[533] (337) Dhimati;[534] (338) Moha-
nashini;[535] (339) Nihsankalpaa;[536] (340) Niratankaa;[537]
(341) Vinayaa;[538] (342) Vinayapriyaa;[539] (343) Jvala-mala-
sahasradhyaa;[540] (344) Devadevi;[541] (345) Manomayi;[542]
(346) Maha-bhagavati;[543] (347) Bhargaa;[544] (348) Vasudeva-
samudbhavaa;[545] (349) Mahendropendra-bhagini;[546] (350)
Bhaktigamyaa;[547] (351) Paravaraa;[548] (352) Jnana-jneyaa;[549]
(353) Jaratitaa;[550] (354) Vedanta-vishayaa;[551] (355) Gati;[552]

[528] One who resides inside the ocean.
[529] Without taint.
[530] Without support.
[531] Always successful.
[532] Without ailment.
[533] The cow that yields everything desired.
[534] Intelligent one.
[535] One who destroys delusion.
[536] Devoid of resolution.
[537] Without fear.
[538] Possessing humility.
[539] One who loves humility.
[540] With thousands of excellent garlands of flames.
[541] Devi of *deva*s.
[542] One who urges the mind.
[543] Immensely illustrious one.
[544] Resplendent one.
[545] One who originated from Vasudeva.
[546] Sister of the great Indra and Upendra (Vishnu).
[547] One who can be reached through devotion.
[548] The most excellent among the supreme.
[549] *Jnana* and the one who is to be known.
[550] Beyond old age.
[551] The subject of *Vedanta*.
[552] Destination.

(356) Dakshinaa;[553] (357) Dahati;[554] (358) Dirghaa;[555] (359) Sarvabhuta-namaskritaa;[556] (360) Yogamayaa; (361) Vibhagajnaa;[557] (362) Mahamohaa;[558] (363) Gariyasi;[559] (364) Sandhyaa; (365) Sarva-samudbhuti;[560] (366) Brahma-vidyashrayaa;[561] (367) Bijankura-samudbhuti;[562] (368) Mahashakti; (369) Mahamati;[563] (370) Kshanti;[564] (371) Prajnaa;[565] (372) Chiti;[566] (373) Sacchit;[567] (374) Mahabhogindra-shayini;[568] (375) Vikriti;[569] (376) Shankari;[570] (377) Shasti;[571] (378) Gana-gandhrava-sevitaa;[572] (379) Vaishvanari;[573] (380) Mahashalaa;[574] (381) Mahasenaa;[575] (382) Guhapriyaa;[576] (383) Maharatri;[577]

[553] Dexterous one.
[554] One who immolates herself.
[555] Long one.
[556] One before whom all beings prostratel
[557] One who knows about divisions.
[558] Great delusion.
[559] Greater one.
[560] Cause behind the origin of everything.
[561] Refuge of learning about the *brahman*.
[562] Cause behind the origin of seeds and shoots.
[563] Great intellect.
[564] Forgiveness.
[565] Wisdom.
[566] Consciousness.
[567] Existence and consciousness.
[568] One who lies down on the large Indra among serpents.
[569] Aberration.
[570] One who bestows what is auspicious.
[571] One who chastises.
[572] Served by *gana*s and *gandharva*s.
[573] Universal fire.
[574] Great householder.
[575] Great army, also Guha's wife.
[576] Guha's beloved.
[577] Great night.

(384) Shivanandaa;[578] (385) Shachi-duhsvapna-nashini;[579]
(386) Ijyaa;[580] (387) Pujyaa;[581] (388) Jagaddhatri;[582]
(389) Durvijneyaa;[583] (390) Surupini;[584] (391) Tapasvini;
(392) Samadhishthaa;[585] (393) Trinetraa;[586] (394) Divi-
samsthitaa;[587] (395) Guhambikaa;[588] (396) Gunotpatti;[589]
(397) Mahapithaa;[590] (398) Marutsutaa;[591] (399) Havya-
vahantaragadi;[592] (400) Havya-vaha-samudbhavaa;"[593]

"(401) Jagadyoni;[594] (402) Jaganmataa; (403) Janma-
mrityu-jaratigaa;[595]   (404)   Buddhi;[596]   (405)   Maha-
buddhimati;[597]   (406)   Purushantara-vasini;[598]   (407)
Tarasvini;[599] (408) Samadhisthaa; (409) Trinetraa; (410)
Divi-samsthitaa; (411) Sarveindriya-manomataa;[600] (412)

---

[578] One who gives happiness to Shiva.
[579] One who destroys Shachi's (Indra's wife) nighmares.
[580] Sacrifice.
[581] Worthy of being worshipped.
[582] Mother of the universe.
[583] One who is difficult to understand.
[584] Extremely beautiful.
[585] Immersed in *samadhi*.
[586] With three eyes.
[587] Established in heaven.
[588] Guha's mother.
[589] Origin of *guna*s.
[590] Possessing a great seat.
[591] Daughter of the wind.
[592] With a fondness for the one who bears *havya*.
[593] One who arose from the fire that bears *havya*.
[594] Origin of the universe.
[595] Beyond birth, death and old age.
[596] Intelligence.
[597] Possessing great intelligence.
[598] Residing inside Purusha.
[599] Spirited one.
[600] Mother of all the senses and the mind.

Sarva-bhuta-hridisthitaa;[601] (413) Samsara-tarini;[602] (414)
Vidyaa; (415) Brahmavadi-manolayaa;[603] (416) Brahmani;
(417) Brihati;[604] (418) Brahmi; (419) Brahmabhutaa;[605]
(420) Bhavarani;[606] (421) Hiranmayi;[607] (422) Maharatri;
(423) Samsara-parivartikaa;[608] (424) Sumalini;[609] (425)
Surupaa;[610] (426) Bhavini;[611] (427) Harini;[612] (428)
Prabhaa;[613] (429) Unmilani;[614] (430) Sarva-sahaa;[615] (431)
Sarva-pratyaya-sakshini;[616] (432) Susoumyaa;[617] (433)
Chandra-vadanaa;[618] (434) Tandavasakta-manasaa;[619] (435)
Satttva-suddhikari;[620] (436) Suddhi;[621] (437) Malatraya-
vinashini;[622] (438) Jagatpriyaa;[623] (439) Jaganmurti;[624] (440)

[601] Established in the hearts of all beings.
[602] One who enables the crossing of *samsara*.
[603] One whose abode is in the minds of those who speak about
the *brahman*.
[604] Large one.
[605] One who originated from the *brahman*.
[606] Kindling-stick (*arani*) of the world.
[607] Golden one.
[608] One who transforms *samsara*.
[609] With excellent garlands.
[610] Beautiful in form.
[611] Cleansed one.
[612] One who takes away.
[613] Radiance.
[614] One who makes the eyes open.
[615] One who tolerates everything.
[616] One who is a witness to everything that is evident.
[617] Extremely amiable.
[618] With a face like the moon.
[619] One whose mind is attached to the *tandava* dance.
[620] One who purifies with the truth.
[621] Purification.
[622] One who destroys the three kinds of impurities.
[623] Loved by the world.
[624] One whose form is the world.

Trimurti;[625] (441) Amritashrayaa;[626] (442) Nirashrayaa;[627]
(443) Niraharaa;[628] (444) Nirankushapadodbhavaa;[629]
(446) Chandrhastaa;[630] (447) Vichitrangi;[631] (448)
Sragvini;[632] (449) Padmadharini;[633] (450) Paravara-
vidhanajnaa;[634] (451) Mahapurusha-purvajaa;[635]
(452) Vishveshvara-priyaa;[636] (453) Vidyut;[637] (454)
Vidyujjihvaa;[638] (455) Jitashramaa;[639] (456) Vidyamayi;[640]
(457) Sahasrakshi;[641] (458) Sahasra-vadanatmajaa;[642] (459)
Sahasra-rashmi;[643] (460) Sattvasthaa;[644] (461) Maheshvara-
padashrayaa;[645] (462) Kshalini;[646] (463) Mrinmayi;[647] (464)
Vyaptaa;[648] (465) Taijasi; [649] (466) Padma-bodhikaa;[650]

[625] With three forms.
[626] Refuge of *amrita*.
[627] Without support.
[628] Without food.
[629] Originating from a place that has no impediments.
[630] With the moon in the hand.
[631] With wonderful limbs.
[632] With garlands.
[633] Holding a lotus.
[634] Possessing knowledge about superior and inferior rules.
[635] Born before the great Purusha.
[636] Loved by Vishveshvara.
[637] Lightning.
[638] With lightning as a tongue.
[639] One who has conquered exhaustion.
[640] Full of learning.
[641] With one thousand eyes.
[642] Daughter of the one with one thousand faces.
[643] With one thousand rays.
[644] Established in *sattva*.
[645] With a refuge at Maheshvara's feet.
[646] One who washes.
[647] Made of earth.
[648] One who is pervaded.
[649] Energetic one.
[650] One who makes lotuses wake up.

(467) Mahamayashrayaa;[651] (468) Manyaa;[652] (469) Mahadeva-manoramaa;[653] (470) Vyomalakshmi;[654] (471) Simharathaa;[655] (472) Chekitanaa;[656] (473) Amitaprabhaa;[657] (474) Vireshvari;[658] (475) Vimanasthaa;[659] (476) Vishokaa;[660] (477) Shokanashini;[661] (478) Anahataa;[662] (479) Kundalini;[663] (480) Nalini;[664] (481) Padmabhasini;[665] (482) Sadanandaa;[666] (483) Sadakirti; [667] (484) Sarva-bhutashraya-sthitaa;[668] (485) Vagdevataa;[669] (486) Brahmakalaa;[670] (487) Kalatitaa;[671] (488) Kalarani;[672] (489) Brahmashri;[673] (490) Brahmahridayaa;[674] (491) Brahma-Vishnu-Shiva-priyaa;[675] (492) Vyomashakti;[676]

[651] One who resorts to great *maya*.
[652] Worthy of reverence.
[653] One who pleases Mahadeva's mind.
[654] Splendour of space.
[655] With a lion as a chariot.
[656] Intelligent one.
[657] Infinite in radiance.
[658] Ishvari of heroes.
[659] Stationed in a *vimana*.
[660] Bereft of grief.
[661] Destroyer of grief.
[662] One who has not been struck.
[663] With ear-rings, but there is also the *kundalini* of *yoga*.
[664] Lotus.
[665] Ass radiant as a lotus.
[666] Constantly full of happiness.
[667] With perpetual fame.
[668] One who is established in the refuge for every being.
[669] Goddess of speech.
[670] Part of the *brahman*.
[671] Beyond time.
[672] *Arani* for the arts.
[673] Prosperity of the *brahman*.
[674] Brahma's heart.
[675] Loved by Brahma, Vishnu and Shiva.
[676] Shakti of space.

(493) Kriyashakti;[677] (494) Jnanashakti;[678] (495) Paragati;[679] (496) Kshobhikaa;[680] (497) Bandhikaa;[681] (498) Bhedyaa;[682] (499) Bhedabheda-vivarjitaa;[683] (500) Abhinnaa;[684] (501) Bhinna-samsthanaa;[685] (502) Vashini;[686] (503) Vamsha-harini;[687] (504) Guhyashakti;[688] (505) Gunatitaa;[689] (506) Sarvadaa;[690] (507) Sarvatomukhi;[691] (508) Bhagini;[692] (509) Bhagavatpatni;[693] (510) Sakalaa;[694] (511) Kalaharini;[695] (512) Sarvavit;[696] (513) Sarvatobhadraa;[697] (514) Guhyatitaa;[698] (515) Guhavali;[699] (516) Prakriyaa;[700] (517) Yogamataa;[701] (518) Gangaa; (519) Vishveshvareshvari; (520) Kalilaa;[702]

[677] Shakti of *kriya*.
[678] Shakti of *jnana*.
[679] Supreme objective.
[680] One who agitates.
[681] One who binds.
[682] One who can be differentiated.
[683] One devoid of any notion of difference or non-difference.
[684] Not different.
[685] With different abodes.
[686] One who is subjugated.
[687] One who takes away the lineage.
[688] The hidden Shakti.
[689] Beyond *guna*s.
[690] One who bestows everything.
[691] One who faces every direction.
[692] Fortunate one.
[693] Bhagavan's wife.
[694] With all the parts.
[695] One who takes away time.
[696] One who knows everything.
[697] One who provides welfare in every direction.
[698] Beyond what is hidden.
[699] Collection of what is hidden.
[700] Procedure.
[701] Mother of *yoga*.
[702] Impenetrable one.

(521) Kapilaa;[703] (522) Kantaa; (523) Kamalabhaa;[704]
(524) Kalantaraa;[705] (525) Punyaa;[706] (526) Pushkarini;[707]
(527) Bhoktri;[708] (528) Purandara-purassaraa;[709] (529)
Poshini;[710] (530) Paramaishvarya-bhutidaa;[711] (531)
Bhutibhushanaa;[712] (532) Panchabrahma-samutpatti;[713]
(533) Paramarthartha-vigrahaa;[714] (534) Dharmodayaa;[715]
(535) Bhanumati;[716] (536) Yogijneyaa;[717] (537)
Manojavaa;[718] (538) Manoramaa;[719] (539) Mahorasyaa;[720]
(540) Tapasi;[721] (541) Vedarupini;[722] (542) Vedashakti;[723]
(543) Vedamataa;[724] (544) Vedavidya-prakashini;[725] (545)
Yogeshvareshvari;[726] (546) Mataa; (547) Mahashakti; (548)

[703] Tawny one.
[704] With the complexion of a lotus.
[705] With the arts inside.
[706] Sacred one.
[707] Full of lotuses.
[708] One who enjoys.
[709] One ahead of Purandara (Indra).
[710] One who nourishes.
[711] One who bestows supreme power and prosperity.
[712] With ashes as ornament.
[713] Originating from the five *brahmana*s (Ganesha, Surya, Shiva, Vishnu and Shakti).
[714] One whose body consists of the supreme meaning.
[715] One who makes *dharma* rise.
[716] With radiant rays.
[717] Known to *yogi*s.
[718] With the speed of the mind (thought).
[719] One who delights the mind.
[720] With a large face.
[721] Ascetic.
[722] The form of the *Veda*s.
[723] Shakti of *Veda*s.
[724] Mother of *Veda*s.
[725] One who reveals the knowledge of the *Veda*s.
[726] Ishvari of the lords of *yoga*.

Manomayi; (549) Visvavasthaa;[727] (550) Viyanmurti;[728] (551) Vidyunmalaa;[729] (552) Vihayasi;[730] (553) Kinnari; (554) Surabhi;[731] (555) Vidyaa; (556) Nandini; (557) Nandi-vallabhaa;[732] (558) Bharati;[733] (559) Paramanandaa; (560) Parapara-vibhedikaa;[734] (561) Sarva-praharanopetaa;[735] (562) Kamyaa; (563) Kameshvareshvari;[736] (564) Achintyaa; (565) Ananta-vibhavaa;[737] (566) Bhulekhaa;[738] (567) Kanakaprabhaa; (568) Kushmandi; (569) Dhana-ratnadhyaa;[739] (570) Sugandhaa; (571) Gandhadayini;[740] (572) Trivikrama-padodbhutaa;[741] (573) Dhanushpani;[742] (574) Shivodayaa;[743] (575) Sudurlabhaa;[744] (576) Dhanadhyakshaa;[745] (577) Dhanyaa;[746] (578) Pingala-lochanaa;[747] (579) Shanti; (580) Prabhavati;[748] (581)

[727] Established in the universe.
[728] With the sky as a form.
[729] With a garland of lightning.
[730] The sky.
[731] Fragrant one.
[732] Loved by Nandi.
[733] Goddess of speech.
[734] One who differentiates between the superior and the inferior.
[735] Possessing every kind of weapon.
[736] Ishvari of Kameshvara.
[737] Infinite in prosperity.
[738] The line on the ground.
[739] With excellent riches and jewels.
[740] One who bestows fragrances.
[741] Originating from Trivikrama's (Vishnu's) feet.
[742] With a bow in the hand.
[743] Causing the rise of the auspicious.
[744] Extremely difficult to obtain.
[745] Divinity who controls riches.
[746] Blessed one.
[747] With tawny eyes.
[748] Possessing radiance.

Dipti;[749] (582) Pankajayata-lochanaa;[750] (583) Adyaa;[751] (584) Bhuh;[752] (585) Kamalodbhutaa;[753] (586) Gavam-mataa;[754] (587) Ranapriyaa;[755] (588) Satkriyaa;[756] (589) Girishaa;[757] (590) Shuddhi;[758] (591) Nityapushtaa;[759] (592) Nirantaraa;[760] (593) Durgaa; (594) Katyayani; (595) Chandi; (596) Charchitangi;[761] (597) Suvigrahaa;[762] (598) Hiranyavarnaa;[763] (599) Jagati;[764] (600) Jagadyantra-pravartikaa;"[765]

"(601) Mandaradri-nivasaa;[766] (602) Sharadaa; (603) Svarnamalini;[767] (604) Ratnamalaa;[768] (605) Ratnagarbhaa;[769] (606) Prithvi-vishva-pramathini;[770] (607) Padmanabhaa; (608) Padmanibhaa;[771] (609)

---

[749] Illumination.
[750] With eyes as wide as lotuses.
[751] First one.
[752] Earth.
[753] One who originated from a lotus.
[754] Mother of cows.
[755] One who loves battles.
[756] Virtuous rites.
[757] Girisha's (Shiva's) wife.
[758] Purification.
[759] Always nourished.
[760] Without any gaps.
[761] With smeared limbs.
[762] With an excellent form.
[763] With a golden complexion.
[764] The world, or the metre.
[765] One who makes the *yantra* of the world function.
[766] One who resides on Mount Mandara.
[767] Garlanded in gold.
[768] With a garland of jewels.
[769] Origin of jewels.
[770] One who crushes the earth and the universe.
[771] Resembling a lotus.

Nityarushtaa;[772](610)Amritodbhavaa;[773](611)Dhunvati;[774] (612) Dushprakampaa;[775] (613) Suryamataa;[776] (614) Drishadvati; (615) Mahendra-bhagini;[777] (616) Soumyaa; (617) Varenyaa;[778] (618) Varadayikaa;[779] (619) Kalyani;[780] (620) Kamalavasaa;[781] (621) Panchachudaa;[782] (622) Varapradaa;[783] (623) Vachyaa;[784] (624) Amareshvari;[785] (625) Vidyaa; (626) Durjayaa;[786] (627) Duratikramaa;[787] (628) Kalaratri;[788] (629) Mahavegaa;[789] (630) Virabhadra-priyaa;[790] (631) Hitaa;[791] (632) Bhadrakali; (633) Jaganmataa; (634) Bhaktanam-bhadra-dayini;[792] (635) Karalaa;[793] (636) Pingalakaraa;[794] (637) Kamabhedaa;[795]

[772] Always enraged.
[773] Arising out of *amrita*.
[774] One who causes trembling.
[775] One who cannot be made to tremble.
[776] Surya's mother.
[777] The great Indra's sister.
[778] Worthy of being worshipped.
[779] One who bestows boons.
[780] Fortunate one.
[781] With an abode in a lotus.
[782] With five tufts of hair.
[783] One who bestows boons.
[784] One who is spoken about.
[785] Ishvari of the immortals.
[786] Impossible to defeat.
[787] Impossible to cross.
[788] Night of destruction.
[789] With great speed.
[790] Loved by Virabhadra.
[791] Beneficial one.
[792] One who bestows good fortune on devotees.
[793] Cruel one.
[794] With a tawny form.
[795] With differences in desire.

(638) Mahasvanaa;[796]   (639) Yashasvini;[797]   (640)
Yashodaa;[798] (641) Shadadhva-parivartikaa;[799] (642)
Shankhini;[800] (643) Padmini;[801] (644) Sankhyaa[802] (645)
Samkhya-yoga-pravartikaa;[803]   (646) Chaitraa; (647)
Samvatsararudha;[804] (648) Jagatasampurani;[805] (649)
Dhvajaa;[806] (650) Shumbhari;[807] (651) Khechari;[808] (652)
Svasthaa;[809] (653) Kambugrivaa;[810] (654) Kalipriyaa;[811]
(655)Khagadhvajaa;[812](656)Khagarudhaa;[813](657)Varahi;
(658) Pugamalini;[814] (659) Aishvarya-padma-nilayaa;[815]
(660) Viraktaa;[816] (661) Garudasanaa;[817] (662) Jayanti;[818]

[796] With a great sound.
[797] Illustrious one.
[798] One who bestows fame.
[799] One who causes transformations in the six vices of kama (desire), krodha (anger), lobha (greed), moha (delusion), mada (insolence) and matsarya (envy).
[800] With a conch shell.
[801] With a lotus.
[802] Enumeration.
[803] One who brought about the practice of samkhya and yoga.
[804] One astride the year.
[805] One who fills up the universe.
[806] With a standard.
[807] Shumbha's enemy.
[808] One who travels in the sky.
[809] One established in her own self.
[810] With a neck like a conch shell.
[811] Loved by Kali.
[812] With a bird on the standard.
[813] Astride a bird.
[814] With a garland of betel nuts.
[815] With an abode in the lotus of prosperity.
[816] Without attachment.
[817] Seated on Garuda.
[818] Victorious one.

(663)   Hridguhagamyaa;[819]   (664)   Gahvershthaa;[820]
(665) Ganagrani;[821] (666) Sankalpa-siddhaa;[822] (667)
Samyasthaa;[823] (668) Sarva-vijnana-dayini;[824] (669) Kali-
kalka-vihantri;[825] (670) Guhyopanishaduttamaa;[826] (671)
Nishthaa;[827] (672) Drishti;[828] (673) Smriti;[829] (674) Vyapti;[830]
(675) Pushti;[831] (676) Tushti;[832] (677) Kriyavati;[833] (678)
Vishvamareshvareshanaa;[834] (679) Bhuktirmukti;[835] (680)
Shivamritaa;[836] (681) Lohitaa;[837] (682) Sarpamalaa;[838] (683)
Bhishani;[839] (684) Vanamalini;[840] (685) Anantashayanaa;[841]
(686) Anantaa; (687) Nara-Narayanodbhavaa;[842] (688)
Nrisimhi; (689) Daityamathini;[843] (690) Shankha-chakra-

[819] One who goes to the inner recesses of the heart.
[820] Established in a cavity.
[821] Foremost among the *gana*s.
[822] One who ensures resolutions are successful.
[823] Established in equilibrium.
[824] One who bestows every kind of *vijnana*.
[825] One who destroys the impurities of Kali.
[826] Supreme among the secret *Upanishad*s.
[827] Devotion.
[828] Sight.
[829] Memory.
[830] Pervasiveness.
[831] Nourishment.
[832] Contentment.
[833] One who performs the rites.
[834] One who rules over the immortal lords in the universe.
[835] Objects of pleasure and emancipation.
[836] Immortal and auspicious.
[837] Red one.
[838] With a garland of snakes.
[839] Terrible one.
[840] With a garland of wild flowers.
[841] One who lies down on Ananta.
[842] One who originated from Nara and Naryana.
[843] One who crushes *daitya*s.

gada-dharaa;[844] (691) Samkarshini;[845] (692) Samputpatti;[846] (693) Ambikaa-pada-samshrayaa;[847] (694) Mahajvalaa;[848] (695) Mahabhuti;[849] (696) Sumurti;[850] (697) Sarva-kama-dhuk;[851] (698) Shubhraa;[852] (699) Sustanaa;[853] (700) Souri; (701) Dharma-kamartha-mokshadaa;[854] (702) Bhrumadhya-nilayaa;[855] (703) Purvaa;[856] (704) Purana-Purusharani;[857] (705) Maha-vibhutidaa;[858] (706) Madhyaa;[859] (707) Saroja-nayanaa;[860] (708) Samaa;[861] (709) Ashtadasha-bhujaa;[862] (710) Anadyaa;[863] (711) Nilotpala-dala-prabhaa;[864] (712) Sarva-Shaktyasanarudhaa;[865] (713) Dharmadharma-vivarjitaa;[866] (714) Vairagya-

[844] Holding a conch-shell, a *chakra* and a mace.
[845] The one who drags.
[846] Origin.
[847] One who seeks refuge at Ambikaa's feet.
[848] Great blaze.
[849] Great prosperity.
[850] With an excellent form.
[851] One who satisfies every desire.
[852] Fair one.
[853] With excellent breasts.
[854] One who grants *dharma*, *artha*, *kama* and *moksha*.
[855] One who resides between the eye-brows.
[856] First one.
[857] With the ancient Purusha as *arani*.
[858] One who bestows great prosperity.
[859] In the middle.
[860] With eyes like lotuses.
[861] Level.
[862] With eighteen arms.
[863] Without a beginning.
[864] With a radiance like the petals of a blue lotus.
[865] Astride a seat that consists of all the Shaktis.
[866] Devoid of notions of *dharma* and *adharma*.

jnana-nirataa;[867] (715) Niralokaa;[868] (716) Nirindriyaa;[869] (717) Vichitra-gahanadharaa;[870] (718) Shashvata-sthana-vasini;[871] (719) Sthaneshvari;[872] (720) Niranandaa;[873] (721) Trishula-vara-dharini;[874] (722) Ashesha-devata-murti;[875] (723) Devata-vara-devataa;[876] (724) Ganambikaa;[877] (725) Gireh-putri;[878] (726) Nishumbha-vinipatini;[879] (727) Avarnaa;[880] (728) Varna-rahitaa;[881] (729) Trivarnaa;[882] (730) Jiva-sambhavaa;[883] (731) Ananta-varnaa;[884] (732) Ananyasthaa;[885] (733) Shankari; (734) Shanta-manasaa;[886] (735) Agotraa;[887] (736) Gomati;[888] (737) Goptri;[889] (738) Guhyarupaa;[890] (739) Gunottaraa;[891] (740) Gouh;[892]

---

[867] Devoted to the *jnana* of non-attachment.
[868] Devoid of illumination.
[869] Devoid of senses.
[870] Foundation of the wonderful and the mysterious.
[871] One who resides in an eternal place.
[872] Ishvari of the place.
[873] Devoid of happiness.
[874] Holding an excellent trident.
[875] With a form that consists of all the *deva*s.
[876] Supreme divinity among the *deva*s.
[877] Mother of *gana*s.
[878] Mountain's daughter.
[879] One who brought down Nishumbha.
[880] Devoid of complexion.
[881] Devoid of *varna*s.
[882] With three *varna*s.
[883] Origin of living beings.
[884] With infinite complexions.
[885] Not established anywhere else.
[886] Peaceful in mind.
[887] Without a *gotra*.
[888] Possessing cattle.
[889] One who protects.
[890] With a hidden form.
[891] Beyond *guna*s.
[892] Cow.

(741) Gih;[893] (742) Gavyapriyaa;[894] (743) Gouni;[895] (744) Ganeshvara-namaskritaa;[896] (745) Satyabhamaa; (746) Satyasandhaa;[897] (747) Trisandhyaa;[898] (748) Sandhi-vivarjitaa;[899] (749) Sarva-vadashrayaa;[900] (750) Sankhya; (751) Samkhya-yoga-samudbhavaa;[901] (752) Asankhyeyaprameyakhyaa;[902] (753) Shunyaa;[903] (754) Shuddh-kulodbhavaa;[904] (755) Bindu-nada-samutpatti;[905] (756) Shambhu-vamaa;[906] (757) Shashi-prabhaa;[907] (758) Pishangaa;[908] (759) Bheda-rahitaa;[909] (760) Manojnaa;[910] (761) Madhusudani;[911] (762) Mahashri;[912] (763) Shri-samutpatti;[913] (764) Tamah-pare-pratishthitaa;[914] (765) Tritattva-mataa;[915] (766) Trividhaa;[916] (767) Susukshma-

[893] Word.
[894] One who loves products from cows.
[895] Possessing qualities.
[896] One before whom Ganeshvaras prostrate themselves.
[897] Devoted to the truth.
[898] Three *sandhya*s.
[899] Devoid of joints.
[900] One who is the subject of all debates.
[901] One who emerged from *samkhya* and *yoga*.
[902] With immeasurable and innumerable names.
[903] Empty.
[904] Born in a pure lineage.
[905] Origin of *bindu* and *nada*.
[906] Shambhu's wife.
[907] With the radiance of the moon.
[908] Tawny.
[909] Devoid of differences.
[910] Charming one.
[911] Slayer of Madhu.
[912] The great Shri.
[913] Origin of Shri.
[914] Established beyond darkness.
[915] Mother of the three *tattva*s.
[916] With three types.

pada-samshrayaa;[917] (768) Shantaa; (769) Bhitaa;[918] (770) Malatitaa;[919] (771) Nirvikaraa;[920] (772) Shivashrayaa;[921] (773) Shivakhyaa;[922] (774) Chitta-nilayaa;[923] (775) Shivajnana-svarupini;[924] (776) Daitya-danava-nirmathi;[925] (777) Kashyapi; (778) Kalakarnikaa;[926] (779) Shastrayoni;[927] (780) Kriyamurti;[928] (781) Chaturvarga-pradarshikaa;[929] (782) Narayani; (783) Narotpatti;[930] (784) Koumudi; (785) Lingadharini;[931] (786) Kamuki;[932] (787) Kalitabhavaa;[933] (788) Paravara-vibhutidaa;[934] (789) Paranga-jata-mahimaa;[935] (790) Badava;[936] (791) Vamalochanaa;[937] (792) Subhadraa; (793) Devaki; (794) Sitaa; (795) Veda-vedanga-paragaa;[938] (796) Manasvini;[939] (797)

[917] Seeking refuge with the extremely subtle state.
[918] Scared one.
[919] Beyond dirt.
[920] Without transformations.
[921] Seeking a refuge with Shiva.
[922] One known as Shivaa.
[923] One who resides in the consciousness.
[924] One whose form is *jnana* about Shiva.
[925] One who crushes *daitya*s and *danava*s.
[926] Pericarp of Kala.
[927] Womb of the sacred texts.
[928] With *kriya* as form.
[929] One who shows the four *varga*s (*dharma*, *artha*, *kama*, *moksha*).
[930] Origin of Nara.
[931] One who wears *linga*s (signs).
[932] One who desires.
[933] With sentiments gathered together.
[934] One who bestows superior and inferior prosperity.
[935] With greatness originating from supreme limbs.
[936] Mare, also spelt as Vadava.
[937] With beautiful eyes.
[938] Accomplished in *Veda*s and *Vedanga*s.
[939] Spirited one.

Manyumataa;[940]   (798)   Maha-manyu-samudbhavaa;[941]
(799) Amanyu;[942] (800) Amritasvadaa;"[943]

"(801) Puruhutaa;[944] (802) Purushtutaa;[945] (803)
Ashochyaa;[946] (804) Bhinna-vishayaa;[947] (805) Hiranya-
rajata-priyaa;[948] (806) Hiranya-rajani;[949] (807) Haimaa;[950]
(808) Hemabharana-bhushitaa;[951] (809) Vibhrajamanaa;[952]
(810) Durjneyaa;[953] (811) Jyotishtoma-phala-pradaa;[954]
(812) Mahanidra-samudbhuti;[955] (813) Anidraa;[956] (814)
Satya-devataa;[957] (815) Dirghaa; (816) Kakudmini;[958] (817)
Hridyaa;[959] (818) Shantidaa;[960] (819) Shanti-varddhini;[961]
(820) Lakshmyadi-shakti-janani;[962] (821) Shakti-chakra-

[940] Mother of rage.
[941] Born from great rage.
[942] Without rage.
[943] With the taste of *amrita*.
[944] One offered oblations first.
[945] One praised first
[946] One not grieved about.
[947] With different subjects.
[948] One who loves gold and silver.
[949] Golden night.
[950] Golden.
[951] Adorned in golden ornaments.
[952] Radiant.
[953] Impossible to know.
[954] One who bestows the fruits of a *jyotishtoma* sacrifice.
[955] Originating from great slumber.
[956] Devoid of sleep.
[957] Divinity of truth.
[958] With a hump, lofty.
[959] Delightful one.
[960] One who bestows peace.
[961] One who enhances peace.
[962] Mother of Lakshmi and other Shaktis.

pravartikaa;[963] (822) Trishakti-janani;[964] (823) Janyaa;[965] (824) Shadurmi-parivarjitaa;[966] (825) Sudhoutaa;[967] (826) Karmakarani;[968] (827) Yuganta-dahanatmikaa;[969] (828) Samkarshani;[970] (829) Jagaddhatri; (830) Kamayoni;[971] (831) Kiritini;[972] (832) Aindri; (833) Trailokya-namitaa;[973] (834) Vaishnavi; (835) Parameshvari; (836) Pradyumna-dayitaa;[974] (837) Datri;[975] (838) Yugma-drishti;[976] (839) Trilochanaa;[977] (840) Madotkataa;[978] (841) Hamsagati;[979] (842) Prachandaa;[980] (843) Chanda-vikramaa;[981] (844) Vrishaveshaa;[982] (845) Viyanmataa;[983] (846) Vindhya-parvata-vasini;[984]   (847)   Himavanmeru-nilayaa;[985] (848)   Kailasa-giri-nivasini;[986]   (849)   Chanurahantri-

---

[963] One who makes the wheel of Shaktis move.
[964] Mother of the three Shaktis.
[965] Pleasure.
[966] Devoid of the six waves (vices).
[967] Washed well.
[968] One who performs karma.
[969] The scorching fire at the end of a yuga in her atman.
[970] One who drags.
[971] Origin of Kama.
[972] Wearing a crown.
[973] One before whom the three worlds bow down.
[974] Loved by Pradyumna.
[975] One who gives.
[976] With double vision.
[977] With three eyes.
[978] Insolent with pride.
[979] With the gait of a swan.
[980] Terrible one.
[981] Terrible in valour.
[982] One who enters the best.
[983] Mother of the sky.
[984] One who resides on Mount Vindhya.
[985] With an abode in Himalaya and Meru.
[986] With a residence in Mount Kailasa.

tanayaa;[987] (850) Nitijnaa;[988] (851) Kamarupini;[989] (852) Vedavidyaa;[990] (853) Vratasnataa;[991] (854) Brahma-shaila-nivasini;[992] (855) Virabhadra-prajaa;[993] (856) Viraa;[994] (857) Mahakama-samudbhavaa;[995] (858) Vidyadhara-priyaa;[996] (859) Siddhaa;[997] (860) Vidyadhara-nirakriti;[998] (861) Apyayani;[999] (862) Haranti;[1000] (863) Pavani;[1001] (864) Poshani;[1002] (865) Kalaa;[1003] (866) Matrikaa;[1004] (867) Manmathodbhutaa;[1005] (868) Varijaa;[1006] (869) Vahanapriyaa;[1007] (870) Karishini;[1008] (871) Sudhavani;[1009] (872) Veena-vadana-tatparaa;[1010] (873) Sevitaa;[1011] (874)

[987] Daughter of the one who killed Chanura.
[988] One who knows about good policy.
[989] One who assumes any form at will.
[990] Knowledge of the *Vedas*.
[991] One who has bathed after *vrata*s.
[992] One who resides in Mount Brahma.
[993] Virabhadra's offspring.
[994] Brave one.
[995] Originating from the great Kama.
[996] Loved by *vidyadhara*s.
[997] With *siddhi*.
[998] One who repulses *vidyadhara*s.
[999] One who welcomes.
[1000] One who takes away.
[1001] One who purifies.
[1002] One who nourishes.
[1003] The arts.
[1004] Mother.
[1005] Originating from Manmatha (Kama).
[1006] Born from water.
[1007] One who loves mounts/vehicles.
[1008] Goddess of wealth.
[1009] Sweet speech.
[1010] Devoted to playing the *veena*.
[1011] One who is served.

Sevikaa;[1012] (875) Sevyaa;[1013] (876) Sinivali;[1014] (877)
Garutmati;[1015] (878) Arundhati; (879) Hiranyakshi;[1016]
(880) Mrigankaa;[1017] (881) Mana-dayini;[1018] (882)
Vasupradaa;[1019] (883) Vasumati;[1020] (884) Vasurddharaa;[1021]
(885) Vasundharaa;[1022] (886) Dharadharaa;[1023] (887)
Vararohaa;[1024] (888) Paravasa-sahasradaa;[1025] (889)
Shriphalaa;[1026] (890) Shrimati;[1027] (891) Shrishaa;[1028] (892)
Shrinivasaa;[1029] (893) Shiva-priyaa;[1030] (894) Shridharaa;[1031]
(895) Shrikari;[1032] (896) Kalyaa;[1033] (897) Shridhararddha-
sharirini;[1034] (898) Anantadrishti;[1035] (899) Akshudraa;[1036]

[1012] One who serves.
[1013] One worthy of being served.
[1014] Night of new moon.
[1015] With Garuda.
[1016] With golden eyes.
[1017] Marked with signs of deer.
[1018] One who bestows honour.
[1019] One who bestows wealth.
[1020] Possessing wealth, the earth.
[1021] Flow of wealth.
[1022] One who holds up wealth, the earth.
[1023] One who holds up the flow.
[1024] With beautiful hips.
[1025] One who bestows one thousand excellent residences.
[1026] Bestowing prosperity as fruit.
[1027] Possessing prosperity.
[1028] Goddess of prosperity.
[1029] Abode of prosperity.
[1030] Loved by Shiva.
[1031] One who supports prosperity.
[1032] One who acts for prosperity.
[1033] Vigorous one.
[1034] Half of Shridhara's body.
[1035] With infinite vision.
[1036] Not inferior.

(900) Dhatrishaa;[1037] (901) Dhanada-priyaa;[1038] (902) Nihantri-daitya-sanghanam;[1039] (903) Simhikaa;[1040] (904) Simha-vahanaa;[1041] (905) Suvarchalaa;[1042] (906) Sushroni;[1043] (907) Sukirti;[1044] (908) Chinnasamshayaa;[1045] (909) Rasajnaa;[1046] (910) Rasadaa;[1047] (911) Ramaa;[1048] (912) Lelihanaa; (913) Amritashravaa;[1049] (914) Nityoditaa;[1050] (915) Svayamjyoti;[1051] (916) Utsukaa;[1052] (917) Mritajivanaa;[1053] (918) Vajra-dandaa;[1054] (919) Vajra-jihvaa;[1055] (920) Vaidehi; (921) Vajra-vigrahaa;[1056] (922) Mangalyaa;[1057] (923) Mangala-malaa;[1058] (924) Nirmalaa;[1059] (925) Malaharini;[1060] (926) Gandharvi;

[1037] Goddess of the earth.
[1038] Loved by Dhanada (Kubera).
[1039] One who slays hordes of *daitya*s.
[1040] Lioness.
[1041] With a lion as a mount.
[1042] Extremely radiant.
[1043] With excellent hips.
[1044] With excellent deeds.
[1045] With doubts dispelled.
[1046] One who knows about tastes.
[1047] One who bestows tastes.
[1048] Beautiful one.
[1049] One who exudes *amrita*.
[1050] One who rises constantly.
[1051] Self-luminous.
[1052] One who is eager.
[1053] One who brings the dead back to life.
[1054] With the *vajra* as a staff.
[1055] With a tongue like the *vajra*.
[1056] With a body like the *vajra*.
[1057] Auspicious one.
[1058] With an auspicious garland.
[1059] Devoid of impurities.
[1060] One who takes away impurities.

(927) Karukaa;[1061] (928) Chandri; (929) Kambalashvatara-priyaa;[1062] (930) Soudamini;[1063] (931) Jananandaa;[1064] (932) Bhrukuti-kutilananaa;[1065] (933) Karnikara-karaa;[1066] (934) Tryakshaa;[1067] (935) Kamsa-pranapaharini;[1068] (936) Yugandharaa;[1069] (937) Yugavartaa;[1070] (938) Trisandhyaa; (939) Harshavardhini;[1071] (940) Pratyaksha-devataa;[1072] (941) Divyaa;[1073] (942) Divyagandhaa;[1074] (943) Divahparaa;[1075] (944) Shakrasana-gataa;[1076] (945) Shakri; (946) Sadhyaa;[1077] (947) Charu-sharasanaa;[1078] (948) Ishtaa;[1079] (949) Vishishtaa;[1080] (950) Shishteshtaa;[1081] (951) Shishtashishta-prapujitaa;[1082] (952) Shatarupaa;[1083] (953)

[1061] Artisan.
[1062] Loved by Kambala and Ashvatara, both are *naga*s.
[1063] Lightning.
[1064] One who delights people.
[1065] One whose face has frowning eye-brows.
[1066] With a *karnikara* flower in the hand. *Karnikara* is usually identified as *Cassia fistula*.
[1067] Three-eyed.
[1068] One who took away Kamsa's life.
[1069] One who holds up the *yuga*s.
[1070] The whirlpool of *yuga*s.
[1071] One who enhances delight.
[1072] Divinity who is directly manifest.
[1073] Divine.
[1074] With a divine fragrance.
[1075] Beyond heaven.
[1076] One seated on Shakra's (Indra's) seat.
[1077] Objective.
[1078] With a beautiful bow.
[1079] Desired.
[1080] Special.
[1081] Desired by the virtuous.
[1082] Worshipped by the virtuous and the wicked.
[1083] With a hundred forms.

Shatavartaa;[1084] (954) Vinataa;[1085] (955) Surabhi; (956)
Suraa;[1086] (957) Surendra-mataa;[1087] (958) Sudyumnaa;[1088]
(959) Sushumnaa; (960) Surya-samsthitaa;[1089] (961)
Samikshyaa;[1090] (962) Satpratishthaa;[1091] (963)
Nivritti-jnana-paragaa;[1092] (964) Dharma-shastrartha-
kushalaa;[1093] (965) Dharmajnaa;[1094] (966) Dharma-
vahanaa;[1095] (967) Dharmadharma-vinirmatri;[1096] (968)
Dharmikanam-shivapradaa;[1097] (969) Dharmashakti;[1098]
(970) Dharmamayi;[1099] (971) Vidharmaa;[1100] (972)
Vishvadharmini;[1101] (973) Dharmantaraa;[1102] (974)
Dharmamayi; (975) Dharmapurvaa;[1103] (976)
Dhanavahaa;[1104] (977) Dharmopadeshtri;[1105] (978)

[1084] With a hundred eddies.
[1085] Humble.
[1086] Liquor.
[1087] Mother of Indra of the gods.
[1088] With excellent splendour.
[1089] Established in the sun.
[1090] Examination.
[1091] Established in the truth.
[1092] Accomplished in *jnana* about *nivritti*.
[1093] Accomplished in the meaning of sacred texts on *dharma*.
[1094] One who knows about *dharma*.
[1095] With *dharma* as a vehicle.
[1096] One who fashions *dharma* and *adharma*.
[1097] One who bestows the auspicious on those who follow
dharma.
[1098] Shakti of *dharma*.
[1099] Full of *dharma*.
[1100] With special *dharma*.
[1101] With universal *dharma*.
[1102] With a different *dharma*.
[1103] Before *dharma*.
[1104] One who brings wealth.
[1105] One who instructs about the state of *dharma*.

Dharmatmaa;[1106]   (979)   Dharmagamyaa;[1107]   (980)
Dharadharaa; (981) Kapali;[1108] (982) Shakalaa;[1109] (983)
Murti;[1110](984)Kala-kalita-vigrahaa;[1111](985)Sarva-shakti-
vinirmuktaa;[1112]   (986)   Sarva-shaktyashrayashrayaa;[1113]
(987) Sarvaa;[1114] (988) Sarveshvari; (989) Sukshmaa;
(990) Sukshma-jnana-svarupini;[1115] (991) Pradhana-
purusheshaa;[1116] (992) Ishaa; (993) Mahadevi; (994)
Ekasakshini;[1117] (995) Sadashivaa;[1118] (996) Viyanmurti;
(997) Vedamurti; (998) Amurtikaa.'[1119]

Suta continued, 'In this way, Mount Himalaya praised
her with these one thousand names. Scared in his heart, he
prostrated himself again. Joining his hands in salutation, he
spoke the following words. "O Parameshvari! This potent
form of yours is terrible. I am terrified at having seen this.
Please show me some other form now." Thus addressed by
the mountain, Devi Parvati withdrew that from and again
showed him a different form. The complexion resembled
the petals of a blue lotus. The fragrance was that of a blue
lotus. There were two eyes and two arms. The amiable
form was adorned with blue-black hair. The soles of the

[1106] With *dharma* in the *atman*.
[1107] One who can be reached through *dharma*.
[1108] One who holds a skull.
[1109] A part.
[1110] Image.
[1111] With a body that consists of the parts.
[1112] Free from all the Shaktis.
[1113] Refuge of refuges of all the Shaktis.
[1114] Everything.
[1115] With a form that consists of subtle *jnana*.
[1116] Goddess of Pradhana and Purusha.
[1117] The single witness.
[1118] Always auspicious.
[1119] Without an image.

feet were like red lotuses. The palms were like sprouts
and were extremely red. The handsome and proud form
was playful. A *tilaka* blazed on the forehead. All the limbs
were extremely delicate and were adorned with beautiful
ornaments. A large garland, made out of gold, hung atop
the breasts. The lips, which were like *bimba* fruit,[1120]
seemed to smile a little. The anklets tinkled. The face was
pleasant and filled with divine and infinite greatness. The
excellent mountain saw her own form, which was like this.
He cast aside his fear. Pleased in his mind, he spoke to
Parameshvari.'

Himalaya said, 'Today, my birth has been rendered
successful. Today, my austerities have been rendered
successful. The unmanifest refuge has directly come within
my range of vision. You created the universe. Starting with
Pradhana, everything is established in you. O Devi! It is
into you that it is dissolved. Indeed, you are the supreme
destination. Some speak of you as Prakriti, or as beyond
Prakriti. Others, who know about the supreme meaning,
speak of you as Shivaa, with Shiva as a refuge. You are
Pradhana and Purusha, Mahat, Brahma and Ishvara. You
are ignorance. You are the *maya* that controls. You are *kalaa*
and the hundreds of parts. You are supreme Shakti. You
are infinite Parameshthini. You are free from every kind of
difference. You are the refuge that every kind of difference
depends on. O Yogeshi! O Mahadevi! Maheshvara is
established in you. Starting with Pradhana, you make
everything in the universe function and cease to function.
It is in association with you that the divinity enjoys bliss
in his own *atman*. You are supreme bliss. You are the one
who bestows bliss. You are supreme and without decay.

[1120] A fruit that is scarlet when ripe.

You are space. You are the great illumination. You are
without blemish. You are auspicious. You go everywhere.
You are subtle. You are the eternal and supreme *brahman*.
Among all the *deva*s, you are Shakra. Among those who
know about the *brahman*, you are Brahma. You are
Vayu among the strong. O Devi! Among *yogi*s, you are
Kumaraka.[1121] Among *rishi*s, you are Vasishtha. Among
those who know the *Veda*s, you are Vyasa. O Devi. You
are Kapila among those who follow *samkhya*. Among the
Rudras, you are Shankara. You are Upendra among the
Adityas.[1122] Among the Vasus, you are Pavaka.[1123] Among
the *Veda*s, you are *Sama Veda*. Among the *chhanda*s
of *Sama Veda*, you are *gayatri*.[1124] Among all kinds of
knowledge, you are knowledge about *adhyatma*.[1125] You are
the supreme objective among all objectives. Among every
kind of Shakti, you are *maya*. Among those who control,
you are Kala.[1126] Among everything that is secret, you are
OUMKARA. Among *varna*s, you are the excellent *dvija*.
Among *ashrama*s, you are *garhasthya*. You are Maheshvara
among Ishvaras. Among men, you alone are Purusha. You
are established in the heart of every being. O Devi! Among
all Upanishads, you speak about the secret Upanishad.
You are Ishana among all the *kalpa*s.[1127] Among *yuga*s,
you are *krita*. You are Aditya among all those who follow

[1121] Probably meaning Sanatkumara.

[1122] There are twelve Adityas and Upendra (Vishnu) is one.

[1123] There are eight Vasus and one of these is Agni (Pavaka).

[1124] *Chhanda* is metre and one of the seven main metres is
gayatri.

[1125] *Adhyatma* is transcendental knowledge, knowledge about
the *jivatman* and the *paramatman*.

[1126] As in, time/destiny.

[1127] In some lists of *kalpa*s, Ishana *kalpa* is the tenth.

paths. Among all speeches, you are Devi Sarasvati. Among all those who are beautiful in form, you are Lakshmi. You are Vishnu among those who possess *maya*. Among faithful wives, you are Arundhati. You are Suparna among the birds. Among *suktam*s, you are Purusha *suktam*.[1128] Among *sama* hymns, you are Jyeshthasama.[1129] Among those mantras used to perform *japa*, you are Savitri.[1130] Among hymns of the *Yajur Veda*, you are Shatarudriya.[1131] You are the great Meru among mountains. You are Ananta among serpents. Among everything, you are the supreme *brahman*. Everything is permeated by you. Your entire form is devoid of all transformations. Your sparkling and single form cannot be perceived. There is no beginning, no middle and no end. You are infinite and primordial. I prostrate myself before the truth that is beyond darkness. Those who possess *vijnana* about *Vedanta* have determined the meaning and have seen the origin of the universe. You are bliss alone and are known as Pranava. I seek refuge with that form. This form is hidden inside all beings and is the cause behind the union and separation of Pradhana and Purusha. It is full of energy and is devoid of birth and destruction. I prostrate myself before the form that is known as *prana*. You are without a beginning and an end. The universe is a form of your *atman*. Existing in different forms, you are beyond Prakriti. Your form is hidden and not manifest. I prostrate myself before the form that is known as Purusha. You are the refuge for everything. You arrange for the entire universe. You go everywhere. You

[1128] *Suktam* (literally, well-said) is a hymn of praise. Purusha *suktam* is from *Rig Veda*, 10.90.

[1129] A specific *suktam* from *Sama Veda*.

[1130] The *savitri mantra*, usually known as *gayatri mantra*.

[1131] A *mantra* to Rudra, from Vajasaneyi Samhita.

are devoid of birth and destruction. You are subtle and
wonderful, with the three *guna*s. I prostrate myself before
the form Pradhana, with different types of forms. You
are the primordial and great one, known as Purusha and
established in Prakriti, carrying the seed of the three *guna*s
in the *atman*. This is full of contrary kinds of *dharma*,
with prosperity and *vijnana*. O Devi! I prostrate myself
before that form. As you were established in the water, the
fourteen worlds, with their wonderful differences, were in
your *atman*. You are the absolute Purusha, the lord. There
are many types of different entities that reside in those. I
prostrate myself before the form that is described as the
cosmic egg. You alone are the primordial one, with all the
*Veda*s in your *atman*. In truth, it is your energy that fills the
worlds with differences. You are the cause behind the three
periods of time.[1132] I prostrate myself before the form that is
established in the solar disc and is known as Parameshthi.
You are the ancient Purusha, with one thousand arms and
one thousand heads, infinite in powers. At the end, you lie
down in the waters. I prostrate myself before the form that
is known as Narayana. Your form possesses cruel teeth
and brings about the fire of destruction that comes at the
end of a *yuga*. You are worshipped by the gods. You are
the cause behind the destruction of all the eggs, with the
beings inside. I prostrate myself before the form known as
Kala. You are worshipped as the foremost Indra among
serpents, with one thousand shining hoods spread out.
Janardana sleeps, astride that form of yours. I prostrate
myself before your form, known as Shesha. Your form,
with the odd number of eyes, is unimpeded in its prosperity.
It is described as the only one that knows the immortal

[1132] Past, present and future.

bliss of the *brahman*. At the end of all the *yuga*s, it dances in the firmament. I prostrate myself before your form, known as Rudra. You are devoid of grief. You are devoid of forms. Your lotus-feet are worshipped by gods and *asura*s. O Devi! You are radiant and extremely delicate. O Bhavani! I prostrate myself before your fair form. OUM! O Mahadevi! I prostrate myself before you. O Parameshvari! I prostrate myself before you. O Bhagavati! O Ishani! I prostrate myself before you. O Shivaa! I prostrate myself before you. I bow down. I am pervaded by you. You are my support. You are my destination. I seek refuge with you. O Parameshvari! Be pleased. There is no one who is equal to me in the worlds, not even among *deva*s and *danava*s. Because of my austerities, the mother of the universe has manifested herself as my daughter. O Devi! This Menaa, the daughter of the ancestors, has become your mother. Blessed am I. The mother of the universe has granted me this sacred glory. O Ishani! Along with Menaa, always save me. I prostrate myself before your lotus-feet. I seek refuge with Shiva. How wonderful is my great good fortune. Mahadevi has arrived. O Mahadevi! O Shankari! Please command me. What shall I do?'

Suta continued, 'The snow-clad lord of mountains spoke to her in these words. Standing by Girijaa's[1133] side, he joined his hands in salutation and glanced at her. The *arani* of the universe heard his words. Remembering Pashupati,[1134] she smiled and spoke to her father.'

Shri Devi said, 'First listen to this secret about Ishvara, who cannot be perceived. O best among mountains! This

---

[1133] Girijaa means the daughter of the mountain and is Parvati's name.

[1134] The lord of *pashu*s, Shiva's name.

is the instruction followed by those who speak about the
brahman. You have directly seen my wonderful form,
which is that of Ishvara. It is infinite and is full of all the
Shaktis. It is the supreme entity that urges. Be faithful and
seek refuge with that supreme form, controlled and
tranquil in mind, devoid of any sense of pride and ego. O
father! With single-minded devotion, seek refuge in my
supreme sentiments. Always worship it, with every kind
of sacrifice, austerities and donations. Behold it in your
mind. Meditate on it and worship it. O unblemished one!
If you follow my instructions, I will destroy *samsara* for
you. When you are full of supreme devotion, I will
establish you in Ishvara's *yoga*. Within a short period of
time, I will raise you from this ocean of *samsara*. O best
among mountains! You can obtain me through *dhyana*,
karma yoga, *bhakti* and *jnana*, not through crores of
other kinds of *karma*.[1135] The *shruti* and *smriti* texts have
spoken about proper *karma*, incorporating *varna*s and
*ashrama*s. For liberation, always act accordingly,
combining it with *jnana* about *adhyatma*. *Bhakti* is
generated through *dharma*. It is through *bhakti* that one
obtains the supreme. It is held that *dharma* consists of
sacrifices and other things, spoken about in the *shruti* and
smriti texts. Nothing else results in *dharma*. *Dharma*
flows from the *Veda*s. Thus, those who seek the objectives
of *dharma* and *moksha* resort to the *Veda*s, which are my
form. My ancient and supreme Shakti is known as the
*Veda*s. From the beginning of creation, this continued in
the form of the *Rig*, *Yajur* and *Sama* hymns. To protect
the *Veda*s, Bhagavan Aja[1136] created *brahmana*s and

[1135] *Dhyana* is meditation and *bhakti* is devotion.
[1136] Aja, the one without birth, is Brahma's name.

others and engaged them in their own respective *karma*.
For those who do not follow this *dharma*, Brahma devised
the lower regions of hell, Tamisra and the others. There is
no sacred text other than the *Veda*s that lays down what
is known as *dharma*. Those who take delight in other
things should not be known as *dvija*s. Many kinds of
sacred texts are seen in the worlds. Some are against the
*shruti*s and *smriti*s. Devotion to them is *tamas* in nature.
Kapala, Bhairava, Yamala, Vama and Arhata – there are
others like this, for purposes of creating delusion. The
application of these wicked *shastra*s serves to delude
humans. In another existence, I created such *shastra*s, to
delude. To cause me pleasure, excellent men who know
the meanings of the *Veda*s should make efforts to follow
the *karma* of the *Veda*s, as stated in *smriti* texts. Engaged
by me, out of compassion for the *varna*s, the great
Svayambhuva Manu himself enunciated this *dharma*,
stated by the sages earlier. Other sages heard about this
excellent *dharma* from his mouth. To establish *dharma*,
they composed the *dharmashastra*s. At the end of a *yuga*,
these disappear. Following Brahma's words, from one
yuga to another *yuga*, the *maharshi*s compose them again.
Initially, Vyasa and others spoke about eighteen Puranas.
O king! This is because they were engaged by Brahma
and *dharma* is established in them. There are other Upa
Puranas that his *shishya*s[1137] have spoken about. From
one *yuga* to another *yuga*, those who know about the
*dharmashastra*s have done this. *Shiksha, kalpa, vyakarana,
nirukta, chhanda, jyotisha* and *nyayashastra*, all these

[1137]Vyasa's disciples.

kinds of knowledge are for enhancement.[1138] O excellent
dvijas![1139] There are thus fourteen of these. Taken with
the four *Veda*s, no other *dharma* exists. Following my
instructions, Manu, Vyasa and others established this
dharma of the grandfather. It has existed till now and will
remain till the deluge of beings. At that time, along with
Brahma, all of them will be subject to withdrawal. Having
immersed their *atman*s in the supreme, they will enter the
supreme destination. Therefore, every effort must be
made to pursue the *dharma* and *artha*, dependent on the
*Veda*s. When *dharma* is united with *jnana*, the supreme
brahman is revealed. There are those who cast aside all
association and seek refuge with me. Basing themselves
on Ishvara's *yoga*, they constantly worship me, devoutly.
They are compassionate towards all beings. They are
peaceful and self-controlled, devoid of malice. They are
intelligent and lack pride. They are ascetics, firm in their
vows. Their minds are on me. Their breath of life is in me.
They are devoted to speaking about my *jnana*. They are
those in *brahmacharya*, *garhasthya*, *vanaprastha* and
sannyasa. Since they are steadfast, I destroy all the
darkness of *maya* that arises in them. Within a short
period of time, this is done with the lamp of *jnana*. When

[1138] *Vedanga*s are six ancillary branches of learning needed
to understand the *Veda*s. These are *shiksha* (phonetics), *kalpa*
(rituals), *vyakarana* (grammar), *nirukta* (etymology), *chhanda*
(prosody) and *jyotisha* (astronomy). While the *nyaya* school of
philosophy (*darshana*) is about logic, here *nyayashastra* is the same
as *nitishastra*, meaning good policy.

[1139] Since this is spoken by Devi and not by Suta, there is an
inconsistency. The fourteen include the four *Veda*s and the six
*Vedanga*s. The other four are not consistently stated, but are usually
from *ayurveda* (medicine), *dhanurveda* (art of fighting), *gandharva-
veda* (music), *dharmashastra*, *nitishastra*, *arthashastra* and Puranas.

that darkness has been blown away, with *jnana* alone, they are immersed in me. They experience eternal bliss and are not repeatedly born in *samsara*. Therefore, using every possible means, one should be faithful to me and devoted to me. I must be worshipped everywhere. The mind must seek refuge with me. If you are incapable of performing *dhyana* on my imperishable form as Ishvara, then seek refuge with my supreme form, which starts with Kala. O father! My real nature will then be perceived by your mind. Be attentive and devoted to you. Worship it attentively. My *nishkala* and auspicious form consists of consciousness alone. It is beyond all names. It is supreme, infinite and immortal. That supreme form can only be obtained through hardships, through *jnana* alone. Using *jnana*, those who see it, enter me. When the mind is fixed on it, when one is devoted to it and when it is established in the *atman*, *jnana* destroys sins and one goes to the place, from where there is no return. With me as the supreme refuge, one obtains the sparkling destination of *nirvana*.[1140] O Indra among kings! It cannot be obtained otherwise. Therefore, seek refuge in me. O lord of the earth! Worship me as one, or as separate or in either way. You will proceed to the objective. My truth is naturally auspicious and sparkling. Without seeking refuge in me, it cannot be known. O Indra among kings! Therefore, seek refuge in me. This is the eternal and imperishable form. This is the form of Ishvara. Therefore, make efforts to worship it. You will then cast aside the blindness. In thoughts, words, deeds and sentiments, worship Shiva everywhere, all the time. You will then proceed to that

---

[1140] *Nirvana* means a state where everything is extinguished. It is a state of liberation.

destination. Those deluded by my *maya* cannot reach that divinity. Shiva Maheshvara is without birth. He is supreme, without a beginning and without an end. He is established in the *atman*s of all beings. He is without blemish and is the support for everything. He is in constant bliss, without indications. He is *nirguna*. He is beyond the darkness. He is the non-dual and immoveable *brahman*. He is *nishkala* and beyond *prapancha*. He is the one who knows himself. He is the one who cannot be known. He is the supreme one who is established in space. There are those who are constantly enveloped by the darkness of my subtle *maya*. They are repeatedly born in this terrible ocean that is *samsara*. O king! To counter the bonds of birth, one should use single-minded devotion and proper *jnana* to search out that *brahman*. One should renounce *ahamkara*,[1141] malice, desire, anger and attachment to *adharma*. One must depend on non-attachment. One should see one's own *atman* in all beings and all beings in one's own *atman*. A person who sees the *paramatman* in the *jivatman* is thought to be worthy of merging into the *brahman*. A person who merges into the *brahman* finds delight in his own *atman*. He does not cause fear to any being. He does not think of anything else and obtains supreme devotion and prosperity. He beholds the supreme truth. This is Ishvara, *nishkala brahman*. He becomes free of everything in *samsara* and is established in the *brahman*. Shiva, supreme among the supreme, is what the *brahman* is established in. There is no other. He alone is imperishable. Maheshvara is the one who supports the *atman*. O king! To free yourself of everything in *samsara*, use *jnana*, *karma yoga* and *bhakti yoga* to seek refuge

[1141] *Ahamakra* is ego, the sense that one is the doer.

with Ishvara. O lord of mountains! I have thus imparted this secret instruction to you. Examining all this, you should do what you wish to. I originated from Parameshvara and was entreated by the *deva*s. Therefore, since he criticized Parameshvara, I censured my father, Daksha. To establish *dharma* and because of your worship, I have now been born from Menaa's body, with you as my father. Engaged by the divinity Brahma, the *paramatman*, in a *svayamvara*,[1142] bestow me on Rudra. O king! As a result of this alliance, all the *deva*s, along with Vasava,[1143] will bow down before you. O father! Shankara will also be pleased. Therefore, make an effort to recognize me as Ishvara, who cannot be perceived. Worship the divinity Ishana, the one with whom one should seek refuge. Seek refuge with him.'

Suta continued, 'Himalaya, the lord of the mountains, was addressed in this way by Devi, the goddess of the *deva*s. He prostrated his head before Devi. Joining his hands in salutation, he spoke again. "O Maheshani! Please tell me in detail about *jnana* of the *atman*, the means of *yoga*, supreme *jnana* and the excellent *yoga* about the *atman*." Ishaa described the details to him accurately. From her lotus-mouth, the Indra among mountains, worshipped by the worlds, heard this. Hearing about this supreme *jnana* from the mother of the worlds, he again became attached to *yoga*. Thanks to his great good fortune, urged by Brahma and in the presence of the *deva*s, he bestowed the virtuous Parvati on Mahesha. In Shiva's presence, if a person, full of devotion and pure sentiments, reads

---

[1142]In a *svayamvara* marriage, the bride chooses her groom from the assembled suitors.
[1143]Indra.

this chapter, which describes Devi's greatness, he is freed from all sins and obtains divine *yoga*. Passing over Brahma's world, he obtains Devi's abode. If a person controls his mind and reads this *stotram* in the presence of *brahmana*s, he is also freed from all sins. If a person knows and chants Devi's one thousand and eight names, invoking Parameshvari, he proceeds to the solar disc. Full of *bhakti yoga*, she should be worshipped with fragrances, flowers and other things. With supreme sentiments, one should remember Devi and Maheshvara as an objective. A *dvija* should be single-minded and constantly perform *japa*, until death. At the time of death, he will then regain his memory[1144] and obtain the supreme *brahman* as a destination. Alternatively, the *brahmana* will be born in a pure *brahmana* lineage. As a result of the great prior cleansing he has been through, he will obtain knowledge about the *brahman*. He will obtain supreme *yoga* and divine Parameshvara. Serene and controlled, he will obtain *sayujya*[1145] with Shiva. At the time of the three *savana*s,[1146] if one offers oblations with each of these names, one is freed from taints associated with epidemics and taints associated with planets. If one desires prosperity, one should follow the rules and attentively worship Devi Parvati for an entire year, constantly performing *japa* every day. Full of devotion, along her side, one should worship the three-eyed Shambhu. Through Mahadeva's favours, one will then obtain great prosperity. Therefore, to free oneself of all sins, *dvija*s must make an effort to

[1144]Presumably of past lives.

[1145]Union.

[1146]The three times a day one bathes, at the time of the three *sandhya*s.

perform this *japa* with Devi's one thousand names. O *brahmana*s! In this connection, Devi's excellent greatness has been described. After this, hear about the creation of *praja*s by Bhrigu and others.'

Chapter 13(1)(13) (Lineage of Daksha's daughters)

Suta said, 'Through Khyati, Bhrigu gave birth to Lakshmi, loved by Narayana. The *deva*s, Dhatri and Vidhatri, were the auspicious sons-in-law of Meru. The great-souled Meru had the daughters, Ayati and Niyati. Through Dhatri and Vidhatri, these two gave birth to two sons. They were Prana and Mrikandu and Mrikandu's son was Markandeya. Prana had a resplendent son, named Vedashira. Through Sambhuti, Marichi had Purnamasa as a son. She also had four daughters, who possessed all the auspicious signs. Tushti was the eldest and the others were Vrishti, Krishti and Apachiti. Purnamasa's two sons were Virajas and Parvata. Through Prajapati Pulaha, Kshamaa gave birth to sons. Kardama was the eldest and Sahishnu was an excellent sage. The youngest among them cleansed all sins through austerities. Through Atri, Anasuya gave birth to sons who were without blemishes. They were Soma, Durvasa and the *yogi*, Dattatreya. Through Anigras, Smriti gave birth to daughters who possessed all the signs. They were Sinivali, Kuhu, Raka and Anumati. Through Priti, the illustrious lord, Pulastya, had Dambhoji as a son. In an earlier birth, in Svayambhuva *manvantara*, he was known as Agastya. He[1147] also had Devabahu as a son and a

---

[1147]Pulastya.

daughter named Dvitiya. Through Santati, Kratu had sixty
thousand sons. All of them held up their seed and were
known as *valakhilya*s. Through Urjaa, Vasishtha had seven
sons. There was also a daughter named Pundarikakshaa,
who possessed every kind of beauty. The seven extremely
energetic sons were Raja, Matra, Urddhabahu, Savana,
Anaga, Sutapa and Shukra. O *dvija*s! Vahni was Brahma's
son and had Rudra in his *atman*. Through Svahaa, he had
three sons who were extensive and great in their energy.
They were Pavaka, Pavamana and Shuchi and they were
Agni's forms. The fire that is churned is Pavamana and
that in lightning is described as Pavaka. The fire that exists
in the sun and scorches is said to be Shuchi. These had
forty-five descendants. Along with Pavamana, Pavaka and
Shuchi and their father, these are described as the forty-
nine fires. All of them are said to be ascetics and all of them
have shares in sacrifices. All of them are said to have Rudra
in their *atman*s, with *tripundraka* marked on their heads.
The ancestors, Ayajvana and Yajvana,[1148] were Brahma's
sons. These two categories are respectively established as
Agnishvattas and Barhishads. Through them, Svadhaa had
the daughters Menaa and Dharini. O best among sages!
Both spoke about the *brahman* and both were *yogini*s.
Menaa gave birth to Mainaka and his younger brother
was Krouncha. Gangaa, who purifies all the worlds, was
born from the Himalaya. Through the strength of the
fire of his own *yoga*, he obtained Devi Maheshvari as a
daughter. Devi's excellent greatness has been accurately
described earlier. Dharini, whose face was like a lotus, was
the wife of King Meru. The *deva*s, Dhatri and Vidhatri,

[1148] Respectively, those who did not perform sacrifices and those
who performed sacrifices.

were Meru's sons-in-law. Thus, I have described the sons
and descendants of Daksha's daughters. Now hear about
Manu's creation.'

Chapter 14(1)(14) (Svayambhuva Manu's lineage)

Suta said, 'Through Shatatrupaa, Svayambhuva Manu
had two sons, Priyavrata and Uttanapada. They were
extremely valiant and devoted to *dharma*. Uttanapada
had a son named Dhruva. As a result of his devotion to
the divinity Narayana, he obtained an excellent place.
Dhruva's sons were Shishti and Bhavya and Bhavya's son
was Shambhu. Through Succhayaa, Shishti had five sons
who were spotless. As a result of Vasishtha's words, that
lady had tormented herself through extremely difficult
austerities. In Shalagrama,[1149] she had worshipped Purusha
Vishnu Janardana. They were Ripua, Ripunjaya, Vipra,
Kapila and Vrishatejas. They were pure and devoted to
Narayana, observing their own *dharma*. Ripu's queen
gave birth to Chakshusha, who possessed every kind of
energy. Through Pushkarini, the daughter of the great-
souled Virana Prajapati, he had the extremely handsome
Chakshusha Manu as a son. Through Vairaja Prajapati's
daughter, Manu had ten extremely energetic and extremely
valiant sons. They were Uru, Puru, Shatadyumna, Tapasvi,
Satyavak, Shuchi, Agnishut, Atiratra, Sudyumna and
Abhimanyu. Through Agneyi, Uru had six extremely
strong sons. They were Anga, Sumanas, Khyati, Kratu,
Angiras and Shiva. Later, Anga's son was Vena and Vena's

[1149]Place where river Gandaki originates. *Shalagrama* stones,
found in the river, are Vishnu's images.

son was Vainya. This immensely strong lord of subjects became famous as Prithu. Earlier, desiring the welfare of *prajas*, he had milked the earth. He had done this when urged by Brahma, along with the immensely energetic Indra of *devas*. Earlier, when Vena's son conducted an extensive sacrifice to the grandfather, Suta, who knew about the Puranas, was born. He was the form of Hari himself, born through *maya*. He knew about *dharma* and was devoted to his *guru*. He recounted all the sacred texts. O best among sages! Know that I am he, the eternal one who was born earlier. In this *manvantara*, he[1150] himself became Vyasa Krishna Dvaipayana. The ancient Purusha, Hari, lovingly made me hear those. Other *sutas* were born in my lineage, denied access to the *Vedas*. They were instructed that they should adopt the narration of the Puranas as a means of subsistence.'

'The intelligent Prithu Vainya was devoted to the truth. He conquered his senses. He was a universal emperor who was greatly energetic. He protected his own *dharma*. Since his childhood, he possessed devotion towards Narayana. Reaching Mount Govardhana, he conquered his senses and tormented himself through austerities. Bhagavan, who holds a conch shell, a *chakra* and a mace, was pleased at his austerities. The divinity, Damodara[1151] himself, arrived and spoke to the king. "Through my favours, there is no doubt that two sons will be born to you. They will be handsome and devoted to *dharma*. They will be excellent in wielding every kind of weapon." Saying this, Hrishikesha merged into his own nature. Vainya possessed unwavering devotion and followed the rules of the *Vedas*.

[1150] Hari.
[1151] Vishnu's (Krishna's) name.

Thinking about Madhusudana, he ruled over his own kingdom. Through Antardhanaa, his slender-limbed wife who possessed beautiful smiles, he soon had two sons, Shikhandin and Havirdhana.'

'Shikhandin had a son who was famous as Sushila. He was handsome and devoted to *dharma*. He was accomplished in the *Veda*s and the *Vedanga*s. Established in austerities, he studied the *dharma* of the *Veda*s properly. He knew about *dharma*. Such was his fortune, that his mind turned towards renunciation. Established in austerities and self-studies, he visited the *tirtha*s. On one occasion, he visited the slopes of the Himalayas, frequented by *siddha*s. There was a forest named Dharmavana there, which bestowed *siddhi* in *dharma*. Only *yogi*s could go there and see it. Those who hated *brahmana*s found it impossible to reach. The extremely sacred and sparkling river, named Mandakini, was there. It was decorated with groves and clumps of lotuses and blue lotuses, with the hermitages of *siddha*s. On the southern bank, he saw an extremely sacred and beautiful hermitage, frequented by Indras among sages and *yogi*s. He was filled with joy. He bathed in the waters of Mandakini and satisfied *deva*s and ancestors. With flowers, lotuses and blue lotuses, he worshipped Mahadeva. He meditated on Ishana, established in the sun. He raised his hands above his head in salutation. He glanced at the radiant sun and praised Parameshvara. He studied about Rudra and the conduct of Girisha Rudra. Using many other *stotram*s from the *Veda*s, he praised Shambhu. Meanwhile, he saw a great sage arrive. He was named Shvetashvatara and he was supreme among Pashupati's great devotees. His limbs were smeared with ashes, and he was only covered with a loincloth. He had emaciated himself through austerities and he wore a white

sacred thread. He completed Shambhu's praise. His eyes
were dimmed with tears of joy. He lowered his head and
worshipped his feet. Joining his hands in salutation, he
addressed him in these words. "O lord among sages! O
lord of *yoga*! O supreme among those who know about
yoga! O illustrious one! I am blessed and favoured that I
have seen you directly. How wonderful is my great good
fortune! My austerities have been rendered successful. O
unblemished one! I am your *shishya*. What will I do? Please
protect me." He showed his favours to King Sushila, who
possessed good conduct. Since his austerities had destroyed
his sins, he accepted him as a *shishya*. The discriminating
one made him perform all the rites appropriate for a
sannyasi. He bestowed *jnana* about Ishvara on him and
the recommended vows for his own branch. He gave him
the entire essence of the *Veda*s, required to free a *pashu* of
the bonds.[1152] This is famous as the last *ashrama*, followed
by Brahma and others. He glanced at all his *shishya*s, who
resided in that hermitage. There were *brahmana*s, *kshatriya*s
and *vaishya*s, all following *brahmacharya*. He said, "*Yogi*s
should study the branch I have propounded. Briefly, they
should perform *dhyana* on Mahadeva, the Ishvara of the
universe. Here, the divinity Mahadeva amuses himself
with Umaa. Desiring to show compassion for devotees,
Bhagavan Isha is present here. Narayana is the creator
of the universe. Earlier, for the welfare of the worlds, he
himself worshipped Mahadeva here. It is here that *deva*s
and *danava*s worshipped the divinity Ishana, the lord of
the *deva*s, and obtained great *siddhi*. Through the strength
of their austerities, it is here that Marichi and all the other

---

[1152] A *pashu* is an animal; also, humans. Tied by bonds (*pasha*),
a being is known as *pashu*.

sages obtained the universal *jnana* about Maheshvara. O
Indra among kings! Therefore, full of austerities and *yoga*,
you should constantly remain here with me. You will then
obtain *siddhi*." Saying this, the Indra among *brahmana*s
meditated on the divinity Pinaki. He told him accurately
about the great *mantra* that bestows every kind of *siddhi*. It
has the essence of the *Veda*s and destroys all sins. It grants
liberation. About Agni and other things,[1153] it is sacred
and has been practised by the *rishi*s. Full of devotion, King
Sushila acted in accordance with these words. He followed
Pashupati and followed the *Veda*s. He smeared his limbs
with ashes and survived on tubers, roots and fruits. He was
serene and controlled, conquering rage. He followed the
rules of *sannyasa*.'

'Through Agneyi, Havirdhana had a son named
Prachinabarhi. He was accomplished in *dhanurveda*. The
illustrious Prachinabarhi was supreme among those who
wielded every kind of weapon. Through the daughter
of the ocean, he had ten sons. They were known as the
Pranchetas and they were kings famous for their energy.
Devoted to Narayana, they studied their own branches
of the *Veda*s. The immensely fortunate Prajapati Daksha,
who had earlier been Brahma's son, was born as the son
of the ten Prachetas and Marishaa. Daksha had a dispute
with the intelligent Mahesha Rudra. Cursed by Rudra,
he was born as the son of the Prachetas. On seeing that
Daksha was coming to his house, along with Devi, Hara
Mahadeva himself offered Daksha the honours that were
due to him. However, at the time, Brahma's son was
enveloped in excessive *tamas*. Thinking that he had not
been shown the worship he deserved, he angrily left for

[1153]This is not enough to identify the specific *mantra*.

his own house. On one occasion, Sati arrived at his house
and the extremely evil-minded Daksha rebuked her and
angrily censured her husband. "My other sons-in-law are
superior to your husband, Pinaki. You are worse than my
other daughters. Leave my house and return to wherever
you have come from." Devi, loved by Shankara, heard his
words. She prostrated herself before Pashupati Krittivasa,
her husband. She reprimanded her father and used her
atman to burn herself down. Satisfied by Himalaya's
austerities, she became his daughter. Bhagavan Rudra Hara,
who takes away the afflictions of those who seek refuge,
got to know about her. He arrived at Daksha's house and
angrily cursed him. "Give up this body you obtained from
Brahma and be born in a lineage of *kshatriya*s. You will
be foolish in your mind and will have a son through your
own daughter."[1154] Saying this, Mahadeva left for Mount
Kailasa. At the time of Svayambhuva Manu, Daksha was
born as the son of the Prachetas. I have thus described
everything about Svayambhuva Manu's creation, up to
Daksha. If one hears this, sins are destroyed.'

Chapter 15(1)(15)
(Destruction of Daksha's sacrifice)

The residents of Naimisha said, 'O Sura! Please tell us in
detail about the origin of *deva*s, *danava*s, *gandharva*s,
*uraga*s and *rakshasa*s in Vaivasvata *manvantara*. King
Daksha, the son of the Prachetas, was formerly cursed by

[1154]There doesn't seem to be any account about this.

Shambhu. What did he do? O immensely intelligent one! We wish to hear about that now.'

Suta answered, 'I will describe this in connection with the earlier *kalpa*, as stated by Narayana. This is about the three periods of time, and it destroys sins. I will speak about the creation of *prajas* in detail. Earlier, King Daksha, the son of the Prachetas, was cursed by Shambhu. He censured him and because of this earlier enmity, performed a sacrifice in Gangadvara.[1155] All the *devas*, along with Vishnu, were invited for their shares. O bulls among sages! All of them arrived, along with the sages. Seeing that all the lineages of the *devas* had arrived, without Shankara, the *brahmana rishi* named Dadhicha spoke to the son of the Prachetas. Dadhicha said, "Starting with Brahma and ending with *pishachas*, everyone follows his bidding. In accordance with the norms, why is that divinity Rudra not being worshipped now? Daksha replied, "In any sacrifice, no share has been planned for him. There are no *mantras* for him. That is the reason Shankara, along with his wife, is not worshipped." The great sage, who was himself full of every kind of *jnana*, laughed at Daksha's words. While all the *devas* heard, he angrily replied. Dadhicha said, "His *atman* is in the universe, and everything flows from him. He is Parameshvara. All those who know about sacrifices worship him. Why is Shankara not here?" Daksha replied, "He is not Shankara.[1156] He is Rudra, the destroyer. He is Hara, full of *tamas*. He is known as the naked Kapali.[1157] He is not someone whose *atman* is in the universe. The

---

[1155] Gangadvara (door of the Ganga) is the place where the Ganga enters the plains. Identified as Haridvara.

[1156] Shankara means someone who brings about the auspicious.

[1157] Kapali is someone who holds a skull.

lord, Ishvara Narayana Hari, is the creator of the universe.
Bhagavan has *sattva* in his *atman* and is worshipped in all
rites." Dadhicha asked, "Can you not see the illustrious
one, with the one thousand rays? He alone is the one who
destroys all the worlds. He is Parameshvara, with Kala in
his *atman*. Learned ones, who know about *dharma* and
speak about the *brahman*, chant about him. With his
terrible rays, he is the witness. With Kala in his *atman*,
he has assumed this body as Shankara. This is Rudra
Mahadeva Kapali, the compassionate Hara. He is the
illustrious Aditya Surya. He is Nilagriva Vilohita.[1158] Those
who know the *Sama* hymns, *adhvaryu*s and *hotri*s, praise
him as the one with one thousand rays.[1159] Can you not
see the creator of the universe? The three exist in Rudra's
form." Daksha replied, "The twelve Adityas have come
here, to accept their shares in the sacrifice. All of them are
known as Suryas. There is no other Ravi."[1160] When he
said this, the sages who had come there, to see the sacrifice
and help Daksha, agreed with him. Since their minds were
overwhelmed by *tamas*, they could not see Vrishadhvaja.
There were many hundreds and thousands of them. They
criticized the *mantra*s of the *Veda*s and Hara, the lord of all
beings. As a result of Daksha's words and confounded by
Vishnu's *maya*, they did not worship him. Vasava and all

[1158]Nilagriva is one who is blue in the throat. Vilohita is one
who is very red.
[1159]There are four types of officiating priests—*hotri* (one who
recites from the *Rig Veda*), *udgatri* (one who recites from the
Sama Veda), *adhvaryu* (one who recites from the *Yajur Veda*)
and *brahmana* (one who recites from the *Atharva Veda*). But this
classification has varied over time.
[1160]Ravi is another name for Surya. Surya has twelve different
forms (the twelve Adityas) in the twelve months.

the other *deva*s arrived there, for their shares in the sacrifice. But with the exception of Narayana Hari, they did not see the divinity, Ishana. Bhagavan Hiranyagarbha Brahma is supreme among those who know about the *brahman*. While all of them looked on, he instantly vanished. When Bhagavan vanished, Daksha sought refuge with the divinity Narayana Hari, the protector of the universe. The fearless Daksha resumed the sacrifice.'

'Bhagavan Vishnu, the preserver, is the one with whom one seeks refuge and he had become the protector. The illustrious *rishi*, Dadhicha, saw that a large number of *rishi*s and all the *deva*s hated Rudra. He spoke to Daksha again. "If a person who should not be worshipped is worshipped, or if a person who should be worshipped is not worshipped, there is no doubt that a man commits a great sin. When the wicked are honoured and the virtuous are dishonoured, the terrible staff of destiny suddenly descends." Saying this, the *brahmana rishi* cursed all the *brahmana*s who had arrived to help Daksha and who hated Ishvara. "Since you have kept Parameshvara outside the purview of the *Veda*s and since you have censured Mahadeva Shankara, worshipped by the worlds, all of you hate Ishvara and will be kept outside the pale of the three.[1161] You have criticized Ishvara's path and your minds are attracted to wicked texts. Your studies and conduct will be false. Your knowledge and conversations will be false. When the terrible *kali yuga* arrives, you will suffer on account of your taints. Abandoning all the strength of your austerities, you will go to hell again. Though you have sought refuge with Hrishikesha, he will turn away from you." Saying this,

---

[1161] The three *Veda*s.

the *brahmana rishi*, the store of austerities, stopped. In his mind, he sought refuge with Rudra, who destroys all sins.'

'Meanwhile, Devi, who witnesses everything, got to know this. She spoke to her husband, the divinity Mahadeva Maheshvara Pashupati. Shri Devi said, "In an earlier life, my father, Daksha, performed a sacrifice. O Shankara! He criticized you and your *atman*. To help him, the *deva*s and *maharshi*s have assembled there. Quickly destroy that sacrifice. This is the boon I seek from you." Devi requested the supreme lord, the lord of *deva*s, this. Wishing to destroy Daksha's sacrifice, he suddenly created Rudra. He was enraged and possessed one thousand heads. He had one thousand eyes and was mighty-armed. With one thousand hands, he was invincible. He resembled the fire that rises at the end of a *yuga*. His teeth were cruel, and he was impossible to behold. The lord held a conch shell and a *chakra*. He held a staff in his hand and roared. He held the Sharnga bow, and his ornaments were ashes. He was known as Virabhadra and lords among *deva*s were with him. As soon as he was born, he joined his hands in salutation and presented himself before the lord of *deva*s. He told him, "May all be well with you. Destroy Daksha's sacrifice. O *ganeshvara*![1162] Criticizing me, he is performing a sacrifice in Gangadvara." Like a single lion that has been released from bondage, Virabhadra playfully left, to destroy Daksha's sacrifice. In her rage, Umaa created Maheshvari Bhadrakali. Along with her, the *gana* left, astride a bull. To assist him, from his body hair, the intelligent one created thousands of others, known as Rudras. They held tridents, spears, clubs, staffs and boulders in their hands.

[1162] *Ganeshvara* is a leader of *gana*s. *Ganesha* has the same meaning.

They resembled the Rudra who is the fire of destruction
and they roared in ten directions. All of them were astride
bulls and their extremely terrible wives were with them.
Surrounding the best among ganas, they proceeded towards
Daksha's sacrifice. All of them reached that region, famous
as Gangadvara. They saw the region where the infinitely
energetic Daksha was performing his sacrifice. There were
thousands of excellent celestial women there and there were
sounds of apsaras singing. There were the excellent sounds
of flutes and veenas and the place resounded with chanting
from the Vedas. They saw the rishis and devas seated, along
with Prajapati.[1163] Virabhadra, loved by Rudra, seemed to
smile as he spoke. "All of us are followers of the infinitely
energetic Sharva. We have come here, desiring our shares.
Please give us our desired shares. O supreme and excellent
sages! Please tell us if someone's delusion has led to the
decision that shares are to be given to you, but not to us.
Please inform the one who has commanded you. Let us
get to know from him." Thus addressed by ganesha, with
Prajapati at the forefront, the devas replied. The devas said,
"We do not know of any mantras that prove the lord is
entitled to shares." The mantras responded, "O gods! Your
minds are shrouded by the darkness of ignorance. You are
not worshipped Maheshvara, the king of sacrifices. He is
the lord of all beings. The bodies of all devas are in Hara.
Those who desire the accomplishment of all siddhi, worship
him in all sacrifices." Though they were addressed in this
way, their intelligence was destroyed by Mahesha's maya
and they paid no heed. Therefore, the mantras left the devas
and returned to their own abodes. Along with his wife and
the ganeshvaras, the illustrious Virabhadra touched the

[1163] Meaning Daksha.

brahmana rishi, Dadicha, with his hands. The destroyer
of *deva*s spoke. "Since your strength made you insolent,
you did not accept the proof of the *mantra*s. Since you are
proud and insolent, I will destroy you now." Saying this,
the bull among *gana*s burnt down the sacrificial pavilion.
The enraged *ganeshvara*s uprooted the sacrificial posts
and flung them away. All the terrible *ganeshvara*s seized
the sacrificial horse, the *hotri*s and the subsidiary chanters
and flung them into the flows of the Ganga. When Shakra
raised his hand, proud and spirited, Virabhadra paralyzed
his hand and he did the same to the other residents of
heaven. Wit the tips of his nails, he playfully plucked out
Bhaga's eyes. He struck Pushan's teeth with a blow of his
fist and uprooted them. Smiling, the powerful *ganeshvara*
toyed with the *deva* Chandra and kicked him with his toe.
Playfully, he severed Vahni's hands and plucked out his
tongue. He kicked sages and lords among sages on their
heads with his feet. The immensely strong Vishnu arrived,
astride Garuda. He pierced him with sharp arrows and
stupefied Sudarshana *chakra*. Garuda saw the mighty-armed
gana and advanced. Roaring like the ocean, he violently
struck him with his wings. However, Rudra himself created
thousands of Garudas. They were superior to the Garuda
who was Vinataa's son and made him run away. On seeing
them, the intelligent Garuda fled with great speed. That he
abandoned Madhava with great speed was extraordinary.'

'When Vinataa's son disappeared, Bhagavan, born
from the lotus, arrived and restrained Virabhadra and
Keshava. He placated and praised Bhagavan Isha. To
honour Parameshthi, Shambhu himself arrived there. On
seeing the lord of *deva*s, along with Umaa, surrounded
by all the qualities, Bhagavan Brahma, Daksha and all
the residents of heaven praised him and especially praised

Devi Parvati, who was half of Ishvara's body. Daksha
used many kinds of *stotram*s. He prostrated himself and
joined his hands in salutation. Bhagavati Devi smiled at
Maheshvara. Pleased in her mind, she addressed Rudra,
the ocean of compassion, in these words. "You are the
one who created the universe. You are the one who rules
and protects. O Bhagavan! Please show your favours to
Daksha and the residents of heaven. Bhagavan Kapardi
Nilalohita smiled. Hara spoke to the *deva*s and the son
of Prachetas, who had prostrated themselves. "O *deva*s!
All of you can go. I am pleased. I should be worshipped
in all sacrifices. In particular, I should not be criticized. O
Daksha! Listen to my words. These will protect everyone.
Give up everything desired in the worlds and make efforts
to become my devotee. At the end of a *kalpa*, as a result
of my favours, you will become a *ganesha*. Arise. Till then,
follow my command and refrain from anything that is not
your entitlement." Telling this to the infinitely energetic
Daksha, along with his wife and his followers, Bhagavan
vanished from his sight. When Mahadeva Shankara
vanished, the one born from the lotus, himself addressed
Daksha in words that were for the welfare of the entire
worlds. Brahma said, "When Vrishadhvaja is pleased with
you, why should you suffer from delusion? Parameshvara
is in the heart of all beings. The divinity constantly protects,
attentively. Learned ones, who speak about the *Veda*s and
have merged into the *brahman*, see him. He is the *atman*
of all beings. He is the seed and the supreme destination.
Maheshvara, the lord of the *deva*s, is praised in the *mantra*s
of the *Veda*s. The eternal Rudra is worshipped within one's
own *atman*. Those who are full of his sentiments, proceed to
the supreme destination. Therefore, Parameshvara should
be known as one who is without a beginning, without a

middle and without an end. One should attentively make
efforts to worship him in thoughts, words and deeds. One
should carefully make efforts to avoid criticizing him. That
only destroys one's own self. The rites of a person who
criticizes suffer from every kind of taint. The great *yogi*,
the imperishable Vishnu, is the one who protects. But
there is no doubt that he is the divinity Bhagavan Rudra
Mahadeva. Those who think that Vishnu, the origin of the
universe, is different from Ishvara, are men who suffer from
delusion and go to hell. They do not abide by the *Veda*s.
Following the *Veda*s, Rudra is the divinity Narayana.
Those who see them as one deserve to be liberated. "The
one who is Vishnu, is Rudra himself. The one who is
Rudra, is Janardana." If one worships the divinity with
this view, one proceeds to the supreme destination. Vishnu
creates the entire world; Ishvara looks at it and establishes
it. In this way, the entire universe originates from Rudra
and Narayana. Therefore, abandon all criticism of Hari.
Fix your mind on Hari. Seek refuge with Mahadeva, the
refuge of those who speak about the *brahman*." Prajapati
heard Virinchi's[1164] words. He sought refuge with the
divinity Gopati[1165] Krittivasa. There were *maharshi*s who
had been burnt down by the fire of Dadhicha's curse since
they had been deluded and had hated the divinity. They
were born in *kali yuga* in the families of *brahmana*s, but
gave up the strength of their austerities. This was because
of Brahma's words and because of the greatness of their
former purification. At the end of the *kalpa*, they will be
freed from all the curses, Rourava and other things, where
they had fallen. In the course of time, they will become as
radiant as the sun. As instructed by Svayambhu Brahma,

[1164]Virinchi is Brahma's name.
[1165]Gopati (lord of cows) is Vishnu's name.

they will worship Ishana, the lord of the universe and the lord of gods, through austerities, *yoga* and other things. Through Shankara's favours, they will become as they had been earlier. I have thus told you everything about the destruction of Daksha's sacrifice. Now hear about the offspring of all of Daksha's daughters.'

Chapter 16(1)(16) (Lineages of Daksha's daughters)

Suta said, 'Earlier, Syamambhu instructed Daksha to create *prajas*. He created *devas*, *gandharvas*, *rishis*, *asuras* and *uragas*. However, the *prajas* created earlier did not multiply. Therefore, henceforth, he created beings based on physical intercourse. Through Ashikni, Virana Prajapati's daughter who was devoted to *dharma*, he had one thousand sons.[1166] Through Virana Prajapati's daughter, Daksha had sixty sons. He bestowed ten on Dharma, thirteen on Kashyapa, twenty-seven on Soma, four on Arishtanemi, two on Bahuputra, two on the intelligent Krishashva and two on Angiras. I will describe their lineages in detail.'

'Dharma's ten wives were Marutvati, Vasu, Yami Lambaa, Bhanu, Arundhati, Sankalpaa, Muhurtaa, Sadhyaa and the beautiful Vishvaa. Hear about their sons. Vishvaa gave birth to the Vishvadevas and Sadhyaa gave birth to the Sadhyas. Marutvati's sons were Marutvantas and Vasu's sons were Vasus. Bhanu's sons were Bhanus

---

[1166]But these sons were destroyed through Narada's *maya*. Elsewhere, Virana Prajapati's daughter is referred to as Asikini. These sons were known as Haryashvas. Narada asked them to determine the dimensions of the world before creating and they never returned. This also happened with another set of sons, not mentioned in this text, known as Shabalashvas.

and Muhurtaa's sons were Muhurtas. Lambaa gave birth
to Ghosha and Yami to Nagavithis. Arundhati gave birth
to everything associated with the earth. Sankalpaa gave
birth to Sankalpa. Ten of Dharma's sons have wealth as
their breath of life. These are *deva*s who are foremost
among luminous bodies. I will describe these eight Vasus in
detail. They are Apa, Dhruva, Soma, Dhara, Anala, Anila,
Pratyusha and Prabhasa. These are described as the eight
Vasus. Apa's sons were Vaitandya, Shrama, Shanta and
Dhvani. Dhruva's son was the illustrious Kala, who makes
the world manifest. Soma's son was the illustrious Varcha
and Dhara's son was Dravina. Anila's sons were Manojava
and Avijnatagati. Anala's son was Kumara, described as
Senapati.[1167] Pratyusha had the illustrious *yogi*, Devala,
as a son. Prabhasa's son was Prajapati Vishvakarma, the
creator of works of art.'

'Kashyapa's   thirteen   wives   were   Aditi,   Diti,
Danu, Arishtaa, Surasaa, Surabhi, Vinataa, Tamraa,
Krodhavashaa, Iraa, Kadru, Muni and Dharmajnaa. Hear
about their sons. Aditi's sons were Amsha, Dhatri, Bhaga,
Tvashta, Mitra, Varuna, Aryama, Vivasvan, Savitar,
Pushan, Amshuman and Vishnu. In the earlier Chakshusha
manvantara, they were named the Tushitas. In Vaivasvata
manvantara, they are described as Adityas.'

'Through Kashyapa, Diti obtained two sons who
were proud of their strength. Hiranyakashipu was the
eldest and Hiranyaksha was his younger brother. *Daitya*
Hiranyakashipu was immensely strong and valiant.
Through austerities, he worshipped the supreme lord and
divinity, Brahma. Praising him with many kinds of hymns,
he saw him and obtained divine boons. As a result of

[1167]Since Kumara became the commander of the *deva* forces.

his strength, all the *deva*s and *maharshi*s were impeded. Oppressed, they went to the grandfather, the lord of *deva*s. They went and sought refuge with the divinity who is a worthy refuge. He pervades the universe and provides welfare. Brahma is the creator of the worlds. He is the supreme being and the saviour. Mysterious, he alone is the supreme and ancient being in the universe. O lords among sages! The supreme *deva*s and sages entreated him. The sages, Indra and the immortals prostrated themselves and praised him. For the welfare of all the *deva*s, the one who is seated on the lotus went to the northern shores of the ocean of milk, where Ishvara Hari was. He saw the divinity, Vishnu, the origin of the universe and the auspicious *guru* of the universe. He prostrated his head at his feet. Joining his hand in salutation, he spoke. Brahma said, "For all beings, you are the destination. You are infinite. Your *atman* is in everything. You pervade every sacrifice. You are the eternal and great *yogi*. Your *atman* is in all beings. You are beyond Pradhana and Prakriti. You are attached to non-attachment and prosperity. You are beyond speech and without blemish. You are the creator, and you are the one who sustains. You are the one who slays the enemies of the gods. O infinite lord! You should save. O supreme lord! You are the saviour." Thus awoken by Brahma, Bhagavan Vishnu, whose eyes were like a blossoming lotus and who was attired in yellow garments, spoke. "O gods worshipped by *dvija*s! You are extremely valiant. O gods! With Prajapati, why have you come to this region? What task can I perform for you?" The *deva*s replied, "O Bhagavan! There is a *daitya* named Hiranyakashipu. He is insolent because of a boon obtained from Brahma. He is impeding all the *deva*s and *rishi*s. O Purushottama! With your exception, he cannot be killed by any other being. O one who pervades the universe! You should kill him and save everyone." Hearing the words spoken by the *deva*s, for the slaying of the foremost *daitya*, Vishnu, the one who conceives the worlds, created a being who was just like he himself. His body was as large as Mount Meru. His form was terrible and fearsome. He held a conch shell, a *chakra* and a mace in his hand. Garudadhvaja told him, "You must kill Hiranyakashipu, the king of *daitya*s, again.[1168] Having used your manliness to quickly slay him, you should return to this place." Hearing Vishnu's words, he prostrated himself before Purushottama, the unmanifest and great Purusha.'

'He left for the great city of the *daitya*s. Wielding a conch shell, a *chakra* and a mace, he emitted a horrible roar. The divinity was astride Garuda, who resembled another gigantic Meru. The foremost *daitya*s heard this roar, resembling the thunder of large clouds. Scared of the lord of *daitya*s, they also roared equally loudly. The *asura*s said, "Urged by the *deva*s, a great being is arriving. He is emitting a horrible roar. We know he is Janardana." Along with supreme *asura*s and sons like Prahlada, Hiranyakashipu armoured himself and seized his weapons. They saw the being astride Garuda, with the resplendence of one crore suns. He was like a mountain and like another Narayana. Some fled. With fear in their eyes, others spoke. "This is the divinity Narayana, the protector of the *deva*s and our enemy. The imperishable one has come, or perhaps it is his son." Saying this, they released showers of weapons towards the being. Unharmed by those, the

---

[1168] Garudadhvaja is the one with Garuda on his standard, that is, Vishnu. The "again" probably refers to the fact that Hiranyakashipu is killed in birth after birth.

divinity playfully destroyed them. Hiranyakashipu had four
sons who were famous for their energy. Thundering like
clouds, they fought against the son who had arisen from
Narayana. They were Prahlada, Anuhlada, Samhlada and
Hlada.[1169] Prahlada used the Brahma weapon, Anuhlada the
Vaishnava weapon, Samhlada the Koumara weapon and
Hlada the Agneya weapon.[1170] The four weapons reached
the being born from Vishnu. But they were incapable of
moving Vishnu Vasudeva, who remained as he was. The
mighty-armed and immensely strong one used his hands
to seize the four sons by their feet. He flung them away
and roared. When the sons were released, Hiranyakashipu
himself kicked the strong one forcefully on the chest with
his foot. Suffering excessively on account of this, Garuda
and the follower became invisible. They quickly returned
to the place where Lord Narayana was. Having gone
there, they reported to him everything that had happened.
The unblemished divinity, who does not suffer from any
ailments and possesses every kind of *jnana*, thought about
this in his mind. He created a being with a body that was
half-man and half-lion. In this form of Nrisimha,[1171] the
unmanifest one suddenly arrived in Hiranyakashipu's city
and confounded the *daitya*s and *danava*s. His fangs were
cruel. With *yoga* in his *atman*, he resembled the fire that
comes at the end of a *yuga*. He was astride his own Shakti,
responsible for the destruction of everything. Ananta
Narayana was as resplendent as the midday sun. The *asura*
saw the being Narasimha and sent his eldest son, Prahlada,

[1169] Equivalently, Prahrada, Anuhrada, Samhrada and Hrada.
[1170] Divine weapons respectively named after Brahma, Vishnu,
Kumara and Agni.
[1171] Also Narasimha, half-man and half-lion.

to kill Nrisimha. "This being, Nrisimha, is inferior in strength, compared to the earlier ones. Despatched by me, along with all your younger brothers, quickly destroy him." Engaged by the *asura*, Prahlada made every effort to fight the imperishable Vishnu. But he was defeated by Narasimha. Urged by the *daitya*, Hiranyaksha, the younger brother, meditated on the Pashupata weapon. He released it and roared. Vishnu, the overlord of the *deva*s, is infinite in his energy. The weapon of the divinity who wields the trident couldn't harm him at all.[1172] When he saw that the weapon was repulsed, as a result of his great good fortune, Prahlada thought that the eternal divinity, Vasudeva, was in all *atman*s. With his mind full of *sattva*, he cast aside all weapons. He prostrated his head before the divinity who is established in the hearts of *yogi*s. He praised Narayana with *stotram*s from the *Rig*, *Yajur* and *Sama Veda*s. He restrained his father, brothers and Hiranyaksha and said, "This is the eternal Ananta Narayana. He is Bhagavan Aja. He is the ancient Purusha. He is the divinity and great *yogi* who pervades the universe. He is Dhatri and Vidhatri. He is self-luminous and is without blemish. He is described as the *tattva* behind Pradhana, Purusha and primordial Prakriti. He is Ishvara, who is inside all beings. He is beyond *guna*s. Go and seek refuge with the imperishable and unmanifest Vishnu." When he said this, the extremely evil-minded Hiranyakashipu was himself exceedingly confounded by Vishnu's *maya* and spoke to his son. "This Nrisimha is limited in valour. Using every possible means, he must be killed. Urged by death, he has now arrived in our residence." The immensely intelligent son laughed at his father's words. "Do not abuse the imperishable lord.

[1172]Pashupata is Pashupati's (Shiva's) weapon.

He alone controls beings. This divinity, the great divinity, is eternal and is devoid of Kala. How can Death slay Vishnu? He assumes the form of Kala and has Kala in his *atman*." However, the narrow-minded Suvarnakashipu[1173] was goaded by destiny. Though restrained by his son, he fought against the imperishable Hari. Ananta's eyes reddened with rage. While Prahlada looked on, he used his nails to tear apart Hiranyanayana's elder brother. When Hiranyakashipu was killed, the immensely strong Hiranyaksha abandoned his son,[1174] Prahlada and fled, agitated by fear. The lions that emerged from Nrisimha's body conveyed Anuhlada and the other sons and hundreds of other *asura*s to Yama's abode. The lord, Hari Narayana, then withdrew that form. He assumed his own supreme form, known as that of Narayana.'

'When Narayana had left, the *daitya* Prahlada, the excellent *asura*, consecrated and instated Hiranyaksha. He constrained the gods in battle and defeated the sages. Having performed austerities and worshipped Shankara, he obtained a great son, Andhaka. He[1175] conquered the *deva*s and Indra of the *deva*s. He agitated the earth and took it down to Rasatala. The *Veda*s lost their sheen. Prosperity faded from the faces of Brahma and the *deva*s. They went to Hari's residence and informed Vishnu about this. The one without decay, whose *atman* is in the universe, thought about a means for slaying him. He first assumed the fair form of Varaha, with all the *deva*s inside him. At the beginning of the *kalpa*, Purushottama went

[1173] Means the same as Hiranyakashipu. Hiranyanayana is the same as Hiranyaksha.

[1174] By extrapolation.

[1175] Hiranyaksha.

and killed Hiranyanayana. He then raised the earth on his tusks. After establishing the enemies of the gods in their proper places, he gave up his form as Varaha and left the spot. He assumed his own divine nature and merged into Vishnu, the supreme destination. When the two enemies of the immortals had been killed, Prahlada became devoted to Vishnu. He cast aside all *asura* sentiments and ruled over his own kingdom. In the proper way, he performed sacrifices to *deva*s and was engaged in worshipping Vishnu. As a result of Vishnu's powers, his kingdom was always without a rival. On one occasion, a *brahmana* happened to visit him in his home. As a result of divine *maya*, the *asura* did not speak to him in the proper way. As a result of delusion, he dishonoured the ascetic, who cursed the king of *asura*s, eyes red with rage. "Depending on your strength, you have dishonoured a *brahmana*. That divine Vaishnavi Shakti will be destroyed." Saying this, the *dvija* swiftly left Prahlada's house. He was deluded and attached to his kingdom. Because of the strength of the curse, he impeded Indras among *brahmana*s. He did not know Janardana. Remembering his father's death, he was full of rage towards Hari. There was an extremely terrible battle between the divinity Narayana and Prahlada, the enemy of the immortals. It made the body hair stand up. Having fought that extremely great battle, he was defeated by Vishnu. As a consequence of the greatness of his former purification, he obtained *vijnana* about Hari and he sought refuge with Purusha, the one with whom one should seek refuge. Since then, the Indra among *daitya*s nurtured unwavering devotion towards Narayana Purushottama and attained great *yoga*. The mind of Hiranyakashipu's son became attached to *yoga*. In this way, that great kingdom was obtained by Andhaka, a bull among *asura*s.

Though born from Shambhu's body on Mandara, he was Hiranyanetra's son. He was the son of Devi Umaa, the mountain's daughter.'

'In earlier times, thousands of sages who were householders worshipped Ishvara in sacred Daruvana.[1176] They performed austerities. On one occasion, because of the great misfortune that is impossible to cross, there was an extremely fierce drought. This led to the destruction of beings. All the sages approached Goutama, a store of austerities. Overwhelmed by hunger, they asked him for food, so that they could sustain their lives.[1177] The learned one gave them many kinds of sweet food. Without any suspicion in their minds, all the *brahmana*s ate this. Twelve years were over and it was as if the end of the *kalpa* had passed. There was a great shower of auspicious rain and the world became exactly as it had been before. All the excellent sages consulted among themselves. They told *maharshi* Goutama, "We will swiftly leave." He restrained them. "O learned ones! Reside happily in my house for some more time. After that, you will certainly leave." All of them constructed a black cow that was made out of *maya* and placed her near the great-souled Goutama. He saw her, and full of compassion, was eager to save her. He tied her to the cow pen. But as soon as he tied her, she

[1176] Also known as Darukavana, a forest of *devadaru* (cedar) trees. But later, the text draws a distinction between these two.

[1177] The text glosses over a vital part of the story. Goutama's hermitage had water, since Varuna had been satisfied with his austerities. The wives of the other sages were jealous of Ahalya (Goutama's wife) on this account. Goaded by their wives, the sages plotted against Goutama. Eventually, Goutama worshipped Shiva and brought down Godavari. This story is narrated in other Puranas, like Shiva Purana.

died. Tormented by grief, the great sage did not know what
should be done and what should not be done. The sages
immediately spoke to the *rishi*. "O best among *dvija*s! As
long as this sin of killing a cow adheres to your body,
your food should not be eaten. We will leave." Allowed
by him, since they were suffering from the sin, they went
to the auspicious Devadaruvana, to perform austerities,
as they had done earlier. Sage Goutama got to know, that
for some reason, the killing of the cow had been caused
by their *maya*. Full of great rage, he cursed them. "You
are the equals of those who commit great sins and will be
outside the pale of the three.[1178] As a result of this curse,
you will be born again and again." The sages became like
left-over food. All of them approached Shankara, lord of
*deva*s, and the imperishable Vishnu. They praised those
two omnipresent ones with common *stotram*s.[1179] "O
lords of *deva*s! O great divinities! O ones who destroy
the afflictions of devotees! O great *yogi*s! You should
save us from the sin we committed because of desire."
Vrishadhvaja glanced at Vishnu, who was standing next
to him. He asked, "What should those who desire good
merits, do?" Bhagavan Vishnu is the one with whom one
should seek refuge. He is affectionate towards his devotees.
Hari glanced at the prostrated Indras among *brahmana*s
and spoke to Gopati.[1180] "O Shankara! If a man is outside
the pale of the *Veda*s, there is not the least bit of good
merit in him. O Mahadeva! Resplendent *dharma* emerges
from the *Veda*s. O Maheshvara! However, since we are
affectionate towards our devotees, they must be saved

[1178]The three *Veda*s.
[1179]Since they could no longer use *stotram*s from the *Veda*s.
[1180]In this case, meaning Shiva.

by us. Otherwise, they will go to hell. O Vrishadhvaja!
Therefore, to confound and save sinners who are outside
the pale of the *Veda*s, we will compose sacred texts."
Rudra was thus addressed by Madhava Murari. He
composed these confusing sacred texts. Urged by Shiva,
Keshava did the same. They were Kapala, Nakula, Vama,
Bhairava, Purva-Pashchima, Pancharatra, Pashupata and
thousands of others.[1181] Having created these, he[1182] said,
"O those who are without the *Veda*s! Act in accordance
with what these sacred texts say. For many *kalpa*s, you
will repeatedly descend into terrible hells. When your sins
have been cooked and have decayed, you will be born in
the world of humans. Through the strength of worshipping
Ishvara, you will proceed to the destination obtained by
those with virtuous deeds. Through my favours, this will
happen. There is no other means of salvation for you."
Ishvara and Vishnu urged the *maharshi*s in this way. They
acted in accordance with the commands of Shiva and the
enemy of *asura*s. Engaged in this way, they themselves
composed many other sacred texts. They showed their
*shishya*s the fruits and taught them these. To cause more
delusion, Shankara himself descended on earth. With the
welfare of the *dvija*s in mind, he begged, along with them.
His ornament was a garland of skulls. He covered himself
with ashes from dead bodies. He decorated himself with
a mass of matted hair. All this was done to delude the
world. At the time, he entrusted Devi Parvati to the care
of the infinitely energetic Vishnu. To chastise the wicked,
Bhagavan Rudra engaged Bhairava. He also entrusted

[1181] These are different sects and cults, not part of the mainstream.
[1182] In the singular, though both Shiva and Vishnu said this.

Devi's son,[1183] the delight of the lineage, to Narayana.
He instated Indra of the *deva*s there, as the foremost
among *gana*s. Having done this, Mahadeva left. Vishnu,
whose body is the universe, himself assumed the form of
a woman and constantly served Maheshvari. Brahma,
Hutashana,[1184] Shakra, Yama and other bulls among gods
also served Mahadevi, assuming the forms of beautiful
women. Bhagavan Shambhu loved Nandishvara a lot.
As was the case earlier, this controller of *gana*s instated
himself at the gate.'

'Meanwhile, there was the evil-minded *daitya*,
named Andhaka. Desiring to abduct Girijaa, he arrived
in Mandara. Hara, whose *atman* is immeasurable, had
assumed the form of Kala. Seeing that he had come,
Shankara Kalabhairava restrained Andhaka. There was an
extremely terrible battle between them, and it made the
body hair stand up. Vrishadhvaja struck the *daitya* on the
chest with his trident. But thousands of *daitya*s, known
as Sahasrandhakas, arrived. Nandishvara and others
were defeated by these *daitya*s and Andhaka. These were
Ghantakarna, Meghanada, Chandesha, Chandatapana,
Vinayaka, Meghavaha, Somanandi and Vaidyuta. Thanks
to Andhaka, supreme among *daitya*s, all of them were
extremely strong. They fought with tridents, spears,
swords, peaks of mountains and battle axes. These Indras
among *daitya*s were extremely strong. They used their
hands to seize their adversaries by the feet, whirled them
around, and flung them hundreds of *yojana*s away. In this
way, Andhaka created hundreds and thousands. They
resembled the sun that rises at the time of destruction and

[1183] It is not clear who this means.
[1184] One who devours oblations, Agni.

advanced against Bhairava. There were extremely great and
fearful sounds of lamentation. Seizing a terrible trident, the
deva Bhairava fought. But he saw that Andhaka's excellent
army was invincible. Defeated, Hara went and sought
refuge with the lord and divinity, Vasudeva Aja. Bhagavan
Vishnu created one hundred excellent *devi*s. To ensure the
destruction of the enemies of the gods, the divinity himself
remained by Devi's side. In the field of battle, thanks to
Keshava's greatness, the *devi*s playfully conveyed those
thousands of Andhakas to Yama's abode. The great *asura*,
Andhaka, saw that his soldiers had been vanquished. He
withdrew from the field of battle and fled with great speed.'

'Mahadeva completed his pastimes, which had lasted
for twelve years and which he had undertaken for the
welfare of devotees in the world. He returned to Mandara.
All the *ganeshvara*s got to know that Ishvara had returned.
They assembled and stood there, like *dvija*s before the sun.
He entered his auspicious residence, impossible for those
without *yoga* to reach. Shiva saw *deva* Nandi, Bhairava
and Keshava. When Nandi prostrated himself, the divinity
showed him his favours. Full of love, Ishana first embraced
Keshava. He saw Devi Mahadevi, her eyes widened in
love. She prostrated her head at Ishvara's feet. Shankari
informed Shankara about the victory. With Bhairava by
his side, he heard about Vishnu's greatness. Shambhu
heard about Keshava's valour and victory. With Devi,
Bhagavan Isha sat down on an excellent seat. All the large
number of *deva*s and *dvija*s, Marichi being the foremost,
came to Mandara to see the three-eyed lord of *deva*s. There
were the one hundred excellent *devi*s, who had defeated
the assembled *daitya* soldiers earlier. They arrived, desiring
to see Isha. They saw him seated on the excellent seat with
Devi, with the moon as his ornament. Extremely eager,

those *devi*s lovingly prostrated themselves and sang. They
prostrated themselves before Devi Girijaa, who was on
Pinaki's left. In their minds, they saw Narayana seated on
that divine seat, along with Devi. They saw that Narayana
seemed to be seated on the throne, along with Devi.
Prostrating themselves before the divinity Ishana, those
beautiful women questioned him. The maidens asked, "O
radiant one! Who are you? Who is this beautiful woman, as
radiant as the sun? Who is this one, with the radiant body
and with large eyes like a lotus?" Hearing their words, the
great *yogi*, the imperishable overlord of *bhuta*s, with an
excellent Indra among bulls as his mount, replied. "This
is the eternal Narayana. This is Gouri, the mother of the
universe. The divinity Ishvara divides his *atman* in many
kinds of ways and is established here. The *maharshi*s do
not know my supreme truth or that of Devi's. This is only
known by the one whose *atman* is in the universe,[1185] by
Bhavani, and by Vishnu. I am without desire and serene.
I am absolute and without possessions. I am known as
Keshava and Devi Ambikaa is known as Lakshmi. He is
Dhatri and Vidhatri. He is the cause and the action. Vishnu
is the one who acts and makes others act. He is the one who
bestows objects of pleasure and emancipation as fruits. He
is the immeasurable being who enjoys. In the form of Kala,
he is the one who destroys. Vasudeva is the creator and
the one who preserves. His *atman* is in the universe and he
faces every direction. He is mysterious and imperishable.
He is the *yogi* who pervades. Narayana has no decay. He
is Purusha, who enables one to cross over. His *atman* is
the sole supreme destination. This is Maheshvari Gouri,
my Shakti, who is without blemish. She is serene. She is

[1185] Shiva.

truth. She is constant bliss. The *shruti* texts say that she is the supreme destination. Everything originates from her and dissolves into her. She is the destination for all beings. She is the supreme objective. I am absolute, supreme and *nishkala*. However, uniting with Devi, I perceive everything, including the *paramatman*, without decay. Thus, there is no duality between the *atman* of Vishnu and Ishvara. Know us as one. You will then attain *nivritti*. Full of devotion, there are those who think of Vishnu as the unmanifest *atman*. However, those who worship Ishana, perceiving the two to be different, are not dear to me. Those who hate the creator of the world are deluded. They are cooked in Rourava and other places. They are not freed for hundreds of crores of *kalpa*s. Vishnu, without decay, is the one who protects all beings. Knowing that this is the truth, one should always meditate on the lord." Hearing Bhagavan's words, all the *devi*s and all the *ganeshvara*s prostrated themselves before the divinity, Narayana, and Devi, Himalaya's daughter. They prayed that they might be full of devotion towards Ishana, loved by devotees, and towards the feet of Bhavani and Narayana's lotus feet. After this, the *ganesha*s and the *matrika*s[1186] could no longer see the creator of the universe. It was extraordinary.'

'Meanwhile, Andhaka, the great *daitya*, became blind with desire. He was charmed by Girijaa and arrived at the mountain, to abduct her. The unblemished and handsome Narayana is a *yogi*. His form is infinite. So as to fight with the *daitya*s, Purushottama arrived there. With Vishnu, the foremost among *gana*s, Shilada's son[1187] and the *matrika*s by his side, the divinity, Bhagavan Isha and Kalarudra,

[1186] Mother goddesses, the *devi*s.
[1187] Nandi.

advanced to fight. The lord of *deva*s advanced in front,
seizing a trident that resembled fire. He was followed
by arrays of kings among *gana*s. The divinity with one
thousand arms also advanced.[1188] With the complexion of
lotus petals, Bhagavan was radiant amidst the gods, astride
his mount. Bhagavan, who cannot be described in words,
resembled the sun, glancing at the three worlds from the
summit of Meru. This was the immeasurable and victorious
Bhagavan, without a beginning. Hara was as radiant as the
one with one thousand rays. He roared, with the trident in
his hand. From the sky, *deva*s showered flowers on him.
The enemy of the *deva*s[1189] saw him advance, surrounded
by kings among *ganesha*s, and *ganesha*s. He fought against
Shakra, the *matrika*s, all the *gana*s and the foremost
immortals. With the strength of his arms, he defeated all
of them in the battle. Without any distress in his mind,
astride his *vimana*, he then approached Shambhu's infinite
abode, where Kalarudra was. Bhagavan Garudadhvaja
saw that Andhaka was advancing. He spoke to Mahadeva
Bhairava, adorned in ashes. "You should kill *daitya*
Andhaka, the thorn of the worlds. O Bhagavan! Barring
you, there is no one else who is capable of killing him. You
are the one who destroys all the worlds. Your *atman* has
Kala and your body is Ishvara. Discriminating ones who
know the *Veda*s praise you with many kinds of *mantra*s."
Bhagavan Hara heard Vasudeva's words. Making up his
mind to kill the Indra among *daitya*s, he glanced towards
Vishnu. He approached the army of the *deva*s and this
increased the delight of the *gana*s. "Victory to the infinite
and eternal Mahadeva, with Kala as his form. You are

[1188] Vishnu.
[1189] The text says enemy of the *daitya*s. We have corrected it.

Agni. You are established inside every kind of sentiment. You go everywhere. You are the creator and destroyer of the worlds. You are Dhatri, the imperishable Hari. You are Brahma. You are Mahadeva. You are the refuge and the supreme destination. OUMKARA is your form. *Yoga* is in your *atman*. O three-eyed one! The three are your eyes. You are great in your powers. You are the lord of the universe. O infinite lord of the universe! Victory to you." Ishvara Rudra, who was like the fire of destruction, seized Andhaka. The destination of the virtuous pierced Andhaka with the tip of his trident and started to dance. A large number of *deva*s and the grandfather saw that Andhaka had been impaled by the trident. They prostrated themselves before the divinity Ishvara Bhairava, who frees one from the world. Sages and *siddha*s praised him. *Gandharva*s and *kinnara*s sang. Large numbers of charming *apsara*s danced in the firmament.'

'Impaled on the tip of the trident, Andhaka's sins were burnt away. Every kind of *vijnana* was generated and he praised Parameshvara. Andhaka said, "I control myself and prostrate my head before the sole Bhagavan. His truth is known as Isha. He is ancient and sacred, infinite in form. He is Kala. He is the wise one, the cause behind union and separation. With his terrible teeth, he is dancing in the firmament. His mouth is like fire. His form is like that of the blazing sun. You possess one thousand feet, eyes and heads. You are the sole one. I prostrate myself before that Rudra. Victory to the primordial divinity. The immortals worship your feet. You are devoid of divisions. Your form is the unblemished truth. You alone are Agni, worshipped in many kinds of ways. Despite external differences, your form exists within all *atman*s. You alone are spoken of as the ancient Purusha. Your complexion is like that of the

sun, beyond darkness. You behold and protect many. You
are the destroyer, served by large numbers of *yogi*s. Inside
the *atman*, you are one. But you are instated in many kinds
of bodies, devoid of any characteristics associated with
bodies. You are the truth about the *atman*. When the word
paramatman is used, you are spoken about. Some speak
of you as Shiva. You are the imperishable and supreme
brahman. You are sacred, with bliss as your form. Your
name is Pranava. For those who know the *Veda*s, you are
famous as Ishvara. You are Svayambhu, devoid of any
special difference. Your form is Indra. You are Varuna.
Your form is Agni. You are Hamsa. You are the breath of
life. You are death and destruction. You are the sacrifice.
You are Prajapati. You are Bhagavan, with many forms.
Those who know the *Veda*s praise you as the one with
the blue throat. You are Narayana, without a beginning,
the cause behind the universe. You are the grandfather
and the great-grandfather. You are the secret in *Vedanta*
and the *Upanishad*s. You are sung about as Sadashiva.
You are Parameshvara. I prostrate myself before the one
who is beyond darkness. You are supreme. You are the
paramatman, established inside the fourteen.[1190] You are
beyond the three Shaktis. You are without blemish. You
are established on a seat with one thousand Shaktis. You
have three forms. Your own form is the infinite destination.
You reside in the universe, and you pervade the universe.
I prostrate myself before the one who is established in the
hearts of people. I prostrate myself before the one who wears
an Indra among serpents as a necklace. Your lotus feet are
worshipped by Indras among sages and *siddha*s. You are
established in a seat of prosperity and *dharma*. I prostrate

[1190]The fourteen worlds, seven above and seven below.

myself before the one who is beyond the ultimate. You are the cause behind the world. One thousand moons and suns are your one thousand forms. I prostrate myself before the one who is with the slender-waisted Umaa. I prostrate myself before the golden-armed divinity. I prostrate myself before the one whose eyes are the fire, the moon and the sun. I prostrate myself before Mrida,[1191] Ambikaa's husband. I prostrated myself before the secret one, secreted within cavities. He has been determined through *Vedanta* and *vijnana*. You are devoid of the three notions of time. Your unblemished abode is the refuge. I prostrate myself before Mahesha. I prostrate myself before Shiva." In this way, from the tip of the trident, he praised Bhagavan. Pleased, Parameshvara touched him with his hands and spoke. "O *daitya*! In every possible way, I am now pleased with your praise. Become a *ganapati*[1192] and always reside near me. You will be without ailments. You will be devoid of doubts. You will be worshipped by the *deva*s. You will be Nandishvara's follower and will be devoid of every kind of misery." As soon as the lord of *deva*s said this, the *deva*s saw that the great *daitya*, Andhaka, had become a *ganeshvara* and was near the divinity. He possessed three eyes and resembled one thousand suns. He was marked with the sign of the moon. His throat was blue, and he had a mass of matted hair on his head. He held a trident in his large hand. Filled with great wonder, they praised the *daitya*. Bhagavan Vishnu seemed to smile, as he spoke to the lord of *deva*s. "O Mahadeva! This being has obtained this position because of your great powers. You do not consider birth or taints. You only accept the good

---

[1191] Shiva's name.
[1192] Leader of *gana*s.

qualities." When this was said, Bhairava, a bull among
*deva*s and leader of *gana*s, approached near Shankara,
along with Keshava and Andhaka.'

'Shankara saw the *deva* approach, along with Andhaka
and Madhava, and with the *matrika*s. Hara was filled
with satisfaction. Ishvara grasped Hiranyalochana's son
by the hand and went to the place where Isha's beloved,
the daughter of the mountain, was, near her *vimana*. She
saw her husband, who removes the afflictions of the world,
arrive with Andhaka. Pleased with Andhaka, she said, "O
Andhaka! I am happy." Andhaka saw Maheshvari by
the divinity's side. He fell like a rod on the ground and
prostrated himself before her lotus feet. "I prostrate myself
before the mountain's daughter, loved by the divinity. You
are without a beginning. Pradhana and Purusha flow from
you. You destroy the entire universe. Along with Shiva,
you are radiant on the auspicious, golden and sparkling
seat. You are without change. I prostrate myself before the
daughter of the snow-clad mountain. The entire universe
is within you. The universe merges into dissolution within
you. I prostrate myself before Umaa, who is devoid of all
taints. Umaa is not born. She is not subject to increase or
decrease. I prostrate myself before Umaa, the mountain's
daughter, who is beyond *guna*s. O Devi! O daughter
of a mountain! Please pardon whatever I have done in
my delusion. I prostrate myself before your lotus feet,
worshipped by gods and *asura*s." Bhagavati Devi Parvati
was thus praised by the lord of *daitya*s who prostrated
himself in devotion. She accepted Andhaka as her son.'

'Following Shambhu's instructions, the great lord,
Bhairava, who had originated from Rudra, went to Patala,
along with the *matrika*s. Vishnu's *tamas* form, which causes
destruction, exists there. Ishvara Hari, who is not manifest,

is established there as Nrisimha. Shambhu is there, in
his form as Ananta, worshipped by Shesha. Bhagavan
Kalagni Rudra's *atman* is united with the supreme *atman*.
When the divinity was engaged in *yoga* in this way, all
the hungry *matrika*s prostrated themselves before the
three-eyed Mahadeva. The *matrika*s said, "O Mahadeva!
We are hungry. You should permit us. Unless we devour
the three worlds, we will not be satisfied." The *matrika*s,
who had originated from Vishnu, addressed him in these
words. They devoured the three worlds, with all the mobile
and immobile entities. The divinity, Bhairava, meditated
on Hari, in his form as Nrisimha. He joined his hands
in salutation and prostrated himself before the divinity,
Narayana. As soon as he knew that Umaa's lord had
thought of him, Hari instantly manifested himself. He was
told, "These *matrika*s are devouring the three worlds. O
Bhagavan! They originated from you. Please restrain them
immediately." When they were remembered by Vishnu, in
his form as Nrisimha, these *devi*s again appeared before the
great divinity, who was in the form of Narasimha. Having
reached Vishnu's presence, these ones, who destroyed
everything, bestowed their powers on Shambhu and the
infinitely energetic Bhairava. The *matrika*s saw that the
extremely terrible Nrisimha, the origin of the universe, and
Shesha, were instantly united. Hrishikesha said, "Every
effort must be made to protect the devotees of the wielder
of the trident and those who remember me. My unmatched
form, which destroys everything, has originated from
Maheshvara's limbs. It bestows objects of pleasure and
emancipation. Ananta Bhagavan Kala and the one with
the four faces, the lord of *deva*s, are my two aspects, based
on *tamas* and *rajas*. I am the invincible divinity, Kala, who
destroys the worlds. At the end of the *kalpa*, as Rudra, I

devour the entire universe. My charming form is known as Narayana. Established in an excess of *sattva*, it always establishes the entire universe. Vishnu is the supreme *brahman*, the *paramatman*, the supreme destination. This is the unmanifest and primordial Prakriti, described as eternal bliss." Thus, Vishnu kindled understanding in the *devi*s, the *matrika*s born from Vishnu. They sought refuge in the supreme and great divinity. I have thus told you everything about the slaying of Andhaka and about the greatness of the lord of *deva*s and the infinitely energetic Bhairava.'

Chapter 17(1)(17) (Trivikrama's conduct)

Suta said, 'When Andhaka was restrained, the great-souled Prahlada's powerful son, named Virochana, became the king. He defeated the *deva*s and Indra of the *deva*s. For many years, the great *asura* ruled over the three worlds, with their mobile and immobile entities, in accordance with *dharma*. While this was going on, on one occasion, the illustrious and great sage, Sanatkumara, was urged by Vishnu and arrived in his city. When Brahma's son reached, the great *asura* arose from his throne. He bowed his head down. Joining his hands in salutation, he spoke these words. "I am blessed. You have shown me a great favour by coming to my excellent city. O illustrious one! You are a lord of *yoga*. You know about the *brahman*. O *brahmana*! You are like the divinity, the grandfather, himself. Why have you come now? O Brahma's son! Please tell me what task I can perform for you." The illustrious *deva* spoke to the great *asura*, who was full of *dharma*.

"You are fortunate. I have come here to see you. O excellent *daitya*! Good policy is extremely rare among the *daitya*s. Indeed, in the three worlds, there is no one else who is your equal in devotion to *dharma*." Thus addressed, the king of *asura*s spoke to the great sage again. "O supreme among those who know about the *brahman*! Among different kinds of *dharma*, please tell me about supreme *dharma*." The illustrious *yogi* told the great-souled Indra among *daitya*s about the most secret *dharma*, the excellent *jnana* about the *atman*. Having obtained this supreme *jnana*, he gave his *guru* the *dakshina*.[1193] He entrusted the kingdom to his son and devoted himself to the practice of *yoga*.'

'His son was the great and intelligent *asura* named Bali. He was exceedingly devoted to *dharma* and *brahmana*s. He defeated Purandara. Surrounded by all the immortals, Shakra fought a great battle against him. However, defeated, he went and sought refuge with the divinity, Vishnu Achyuta. Meanwhile, *devi* Aditi, the mother of the *deva*s, was extremely miserable. "So that the Indra among *daitya*s can be killed, let me have a son." She tormented herself through a mass of extremely terrible austerities. She sought refuge with the unmanifest Vishnu Hari, the one with whom one should seek refuge. In the filament of the lotus of her heart, she thought of the *nishkala* supreme objective, Vishnu who is without a beginning and without an end, who is only space, full of bliss. Bhagavan Vishnu, who holds the conch shell, *chakra* and mace, was pleased. Hari, who has *yoga* in his *atman*, appeared in front of the mother of the *deva*s. Aditi, full of devotion, saw that Vishnu had arrived. Thinking that she

---

[1193]The fee paid by a *shishya* to a *guru* after the successful completion of studies.

had been successful in her objective, she satisfied Keshava.
Aditi said, "Victory to the one who alone is the cause
behind the destruction of torrents of sins. Victory to the
infinitely great one, who is full of *yoga*. Victory to the one
who is without a beginning, a middle and an end, the one
whose form is *vijnana*. Victory to the one who is like the
sky, with a form consisting of unsullied bliss. I prostrate
myself before Vishnu, whose form is Kala. I prostrate
myself before Narasimha and Shesha. I prostrate myself
before Kalarudra, the cause behind destruction. I prostrate
myself before Vasudeva. I prostrate myself before the one
who arranges for *maya* in the universe. I prostrate myself
before the one who can be reached through *yoga*, the
truth. I prostrate myself before the one who is established
in *dharma* and *vijnana*. I prostrate myself before Varaha.
I repeatedly bow down. I prostrate myself before the one
whose form is one thousand suns and moons. I prostrate
myself before the one who can be reached through the
*Veda*s, *vijnana* and *dharma*. I prostrate myself before the
immeasurable one who holds up the earth. I prostrate
myself before the lord who is the origin of the universe.
I bow down again. I prostrate myself before Shambhu,
established in truth. I prostrate myself before the cause,
the one whose form is the universe. I prostrate myself
before the one who is inside the pedestal of *yoga*. I again
prostrate myself before the single one, whose form is that
of auspiciousness." In this way, Bhagavan Vishnu, who
pervades the universe, was satisfied by the mother of the
*deva*s. He seemed to smile, as he asked her to choose a
boon. She prostrated her head on the ground and asked
for an excellent boon. "For the welfare of the *deva*s, I ask
for the boon that you should become my son." Bhagavan,
who is affectionate towards those who seek refuge, agreed.

The immeasurable one granted her the boon and vanished from the spot.'

'Many days passed after this. Bhagavan Janardana Narayana himself entered the womb of the mother of the *deva*s. Hrishikesha entered the womb of the mother of the *deva*s. There were terrible evil portents in the city of Bali, Virochana's son. The Indra among *daitya*s witnessed all these omens and was agitated by fear. He prostrated himself before the aged *asura*, his grandfather Prahlada. Bali said, "O grandfather! O immensely wise one! What are these evil portents that can be seen in the city? What is the reason and what should we do?" Hearing these words, the great *asura* meditated for a long time. Prostrating himself before Hrishikesha, he spoke these words. Prahlada replied, "Vishnu is worshipped through sacrifices. This entire universe is his. For the destruction of *asura*s, the mother of gods has conceived him. Though he has no differences, every difference originates from him. Vasudeva has entered the body of the mother of the *deva*s. The *deva*s do not know the truth about his own supreme form. But that Vishnu has willingly entered Aditi's body. Beings originate from him and dissolve into him. The great *yogi*, the ancient Purusha Hari, has incarnated himself. Conceptions of name, birth and other things do not apply to him. His *atman* only has the form of existence alone. Vishnu has been born through one of his portions. The mother of the universe, who holds up *dharma*, is his power. Bhagavti Lakshmi is full of *maya*. That Janardana has incarnated himself. His *tamas* form is that of Shankara. His *rajas* body is that of Brahma. Vishnu, who holds up *sattva*, was born through one of his portions. With your mind prostrated in devotion, think of Govinda. Seek refuge with him. That is how you will attain *nivritti*." Following Prahlada's words, Bali, Virochana's son, who knew about *dharma*, sought refuge with Hari and ruled over the world.'

'When the time arrived, Mahavishnu was himself born as the son of Kashyapa and Aditi, the mother of the *deva*s, thus increasing the delight of the *deva*s. He possessed four arms and large eyes and his chest was marked with the Srivatsa sign.[1194] He resembled a blue cloud and was radiant, surrounded by prosperity. All the gods, *siddha*s, Sadhyas, *charana*s,[1195] Indra and the others and Brahma, surrounded by large numbers of *rishi*s, presented themselves before Upendra. After *upanayana*[1196] was performed, Bhagavan Hari studied the *Veda*s and good conduct from Bharadvaja, so as to instruct the three worlds. The lord thus displayed the customary path followed by the world. Whatever he establishes as the norm, is followed by the worlds.[1197] After some time, the intelligent Bali, Virochana's son, himself performed a sacrifice dedicated to the lord of sacrifices. He worshipped Vishnu, who goes everywhere. He worshipped *brahmana*s and gave them a lot of wealth. *Brahmarshi*s arrived at the great-souled one's sacrificial arena.'

'Bhagavan Vishnu got to know about this. Urged by Bharadvaja, he assumed the form of Vamana[1198] and arrived at the place where the sacrifice was being held. His radiant limbs were covered with black antelope skin and a sacred

[1194]Shrivatsa is the place where Shri (Lakshmi) resides, on Vishnu's chest. It is marked by the twirl of hair.

[1195]Celestial bards.

[1196]The rite of being invested with the sacred thread.

[1197]A verbatim reproduction of the second half of *Bhagavat Gita* 3.21.

[1198]Vishnu's *vamana* (dwarf) *avatara*.

thread, and he held a staff made of *palasha* wood.[1199] The extremely radiant one was in the form of a *brahmana* with matted hair, chanting the *Veda*s. Hari arrived before the king of *asura*s in the form of a mendicant seeking alms. He asked Bali for land that could be covered in three of his steps. Bali's sentiments were full of Vishnu, and he washed his feet, performing *achamana* with the water.[1200] He picked up a golden vessel and said, "I will give you what can be covered in three of your steps. May the divinity Hari, whose form is not manifest, be pleased." Thinking this, he poured the extremely cool water on the divinity's hands, which were like sprouts. The lord of *daitya*s wished to seek refuge with him. Wishing to take away all attachment from him, the primordial divinity covered the earth, the sky and heaven in three of his steps. Covering the three worlds in his three steps, from Prajapati's world, he reached Brahma's world. Adityas and other foremost among gods and *siddha*s who resided there, prostrated themselves before him. Bhagavan, the grandfather who is without a beginning, arrived and satisfied Vishnu. Using his staff, adorned in divine ornaments, he[1201] shattered the upper shell of the cosmic egg and left. When the shell was broken, a great flow of cool water, resorted to by the virtuous, resulted. This became the excellent river established in the firmament, named Ganga by Brahma. After having passed Mahat, Prakriti and Pradhana, the sole Purusha who is the *brahman* and the origin of the

---

[1199]Palasha is *Butea frondosa*. This staff, known as *ashadha*, is carried by a *brahmachari* or ascetic.

[1200]*Achamana* is the act of rinsing the mouth with water, an act of purification before any rite or pledge. One touches water before making a pledge.

[1201]Vishnu.

universe, reached Isha's imperishable destination. On seeing him, the *deva*s praised him at every such place. Full of *bhakti yoga* towards Vishnu, Bali saw the great Purusha, whose form is the universe. In his mind, he prostrated himself before the absolute and imperishable Narayana, before whom, the *Veda*s prostrate themselves. Having assumed the form of Vamana again, Bhagavan Vasudeva, the original creator, spoke. "O lord of *daitya*s! You have now thought of handing over the three worlds to me." The *daitya* prostrated his head down again. Taking water on the tip of his hand, he said, "O one with an infinite abode! You are Trivikrama, infinite in valour.[1202] I grant them to you." The one with the conch shell in his hand accepted what had been given by the son of Prahlada's son. The one whose *atman* is inside the universe told the *daitya*, "Go and enter the lowest part of Patala. Having reached there, always enjoy objects of pleasure that even the *deva*s find difficult to obtain. Through *bhakti yoga*, I constantly meditate on myself. When the *kalpa* is over, you will enter me again." Vishnu, for whom truth is his valour, told the lion among *daitya*s this. Jishnu Urukrama[1203] gave Purandara the three worlds. *Siddha*s, *devarshi*s, *kinnara*s, Brahma, Shakra, Bhagavan Rudra, the Adityas and large numbers of Maruts praised the great *yogi*. Assuming the form of Vamana, Vishnu performed his wonderful deet. While everyone looked on, he vanished from the spot. Urged by Prahlada and other supreme *asura*s and full of devotion towards Vishnu, the prosperous and excellent *daitya* went to Patala. He asked Prahlada about Vishnu's greatness, excellent *bhakti yoga* and the means of worship.

[1202] Trivikrama means the one with three valiant strides.
[1203] Both Jishnu and Urukrama are Vishnu's names.

He acted in accordance with what he was told. He sought refuge with the one who holds a *chakra* and a conch shell in his hand, the immeasurable lord whose eyes are like lotuses. With his sentiments full of *yoga* and love, he followed *karma yoga*. O *brahmana*s! I have thus described Vamana's valour. Purushottama always performs tasks for the *devas*.'

Chapter 18(1)(18) (Description of lineages)

Suta said, 'Bali had one hundred sons who were extremely strong and valiant. Foremost among them was the radiant one, named Bana. He was extremely powerful. Extremely devoted to Shankara, this king ruled over his kingdom. He brought the three worlds under his subjugation and constrained Vasava. Shakra and the other *deva*s went and spoke to Krittivasa. "The great *asura*, Bana, is devoted to you and is oppressing us." Thus, addressed by the *deva*s, Maheshvara, the lord of all the *deva*s, playfully burnt down Bana's city with a single arrow. When the city was burnt, Bana went and sought refuge with Rudra Ishana Nilalohita, Ganga's lord and the wielder of the trident. Devoid of all attachment, he bore Shambhu's *lingam* on his head. He emerged from the city and praised Parameshvara. When Bhagavan Isha Shankara Nilalohita was praised in this way, he lovingly engaged Bana as a *ganapati*. In that way, Danu had extremely terrible sons, Tara and others. The foremost among them are described as Tara, Shambara, Kapila, Shanchara, Svarbhanu and Vrishaparva. O *dvija*s! Surasaa gave birth to one thousand *sarpa*s. These great-souled ones had many heads and travelled through the sky.

Arishtaa gave birth to one thousand *gandharva*s. Kadru's sons are described as Ananta and other great *naga*s. O bulls among *dvija*s! Tamraa had six daughters—Shuki, Shyeni, Bhasi, Sugrivaa, Granthikaa and Shuchi. Surabhi gave birth to cows and buffaloes. Iraa gave birth to trees, creepers, climbing vines and everything that is in the nature of grass. Muni's offspring were *yaksha*s, *rakshasa*s and *apsara*s. O excellent ones! Krodhavashaa gave birth to large numbers of *rakshasa*s. Vinataa had two sons, famous as Garuda and Aruna. Of the two, the intelligent Garuda performed extremely difficult austerities. Through the favours of the one who wields the trident, he obtained the status of becoming Hari's mount. In that way, Aruna used austerities to worship the divinity Mahadeva. Earlier, pleased by this, Shambhu thought of him as Arka's charioteer.[1204] Thus, Kashyapa's descendants have been described, mobile and immobile, born during Vaivasvata *manvantara*. If one hears this, that is destructive of sins. Soma's wives, excellent in vows, are said to number twenty-seven. Arishtanemi's wives had many children. The learned Bahuputra had four sons, who are said to be different kinds of lightning. The sons of Angiras were excellent *rishi*s who were revered. *Devarshi* Krishashva's son was lord Praharana. At the end of one thousand *mahayuga*s, these will be born again. In different *manvantara*s, their tasks and names are always similar.'

Chapter 19(1)(19) (Lineages of *rishi*s)

Suta said, 'After having these sons, so as to ensure that *praja*s and offspring continued, desiring sons, Kashyapa performed extremely difficult austerities. As he

---

[1204] Arka is Surya and Aruna is Surya's charioteer.

tormented himself excessively, two sons appeared. These
were Vatasara and Asita and spoke about the *brahman*.
Vatsara gave birth to Naidhurva and Raibhya and they
were extremely famous. Raibhya's sons were *vaidya*s,[1205]
supreme among learned ones. Chyavana's daughter,
Sumedhaa, was the great-souled Naidhruva's wife. She
gave birth to sons known as Kundapayins. Asita and
Ekaparnaa had a son who was devoted to the *brahman*.
This son's name was Devala. He was a great ascetic and
a teacher of *yoga*. Shandilya was extremely handsome.[1206]
He was pure and knew the truth about everything.
Through the favours of Parvati's lord, he attained
supreme *yoga*. O *brahmana*s! These three descendants of
Kashyapa, Shandilya, Naidhruva and Raibhya, possessed
human natures.'

'I will tell you about Pulastya's descendants. O
*brahmana*s! Trinabindu had a daughter, famous under the
name of Ailavilaa. The *rajarshi* bestowed this daughter on
Pulastya. Ailavilaa gave birth to *rishi* Vishrava. He had
four wives who extended Pulastya's lineage. They were
Pushpotkataa, Vakaa, Kaikasi and Devavarnini. They
possessed beauty and charm. Hear about their offspring.
Devavarnini gave birth to the eldest son, Vaishravana.[1207]
Kaikasi's children were Ravana, lord of *rakshasa*s,
Kumbhakarna, Shurpanakhaa and Vibhishana. Through
Vishrava, Pushpotkataa gave birth to auspicious sons.
Vakaa had sons, Mahodara, Prahasta, Mahaparshva,
Khara and a daughter, Kumbhinasi. Other sons were

[1205] Physicians.
[1206] There were many Shandilyas. This Shandilya was the son of
Asita and Ekaparnaa.
[1207] Kubera.

Trishira, Dushana and Vidyujjihva. These ten *rakshasas*[1208]
were Pulastya's sons and were cruel in deeds. All of them
possess the strength of austerities. They were extremely
terrible and were Rudra's devotees.'

'Pulaha's sons were *mriga*s, all the serpents, fanged
animals, *bhuta*s, *pishacha*s, bears, pigs and elephants. It
is said that in Vaivasvata *manvantara*, Kratu did not have
offspring. Kashyapa was Marichi's son and was himself a
Prajapati. Bhrigu's son was Shukra, the great ascetic and
preceptor of the *daitya*s. He was devoted to studies and
yoga. The immensely radiant one was devoted to Hara.
Atri's son was Vahni and his brother was Naidhruva.[1209]
We have heard that, through Ghritachi, the *brahmana
rishi*, Krishashva, had sons. These were the greatly
energetic Svastyatreyas. They were devoted to the *Veda*s
and Vedangas and destroyed their sins through austerities.
Narada bestowed *devi* Arundhati on Vasishtha.[1210] As a
result of Daksha's curse, Narada held up his seed. This was
because the Haryashvas were destroyed through Narada's
maya. His eyes red with rage, Daksha cursed Narada. "O
brahmana! All my sons have been destroyed because of
your *maya*. Therefore, you will never have offspring."
Through Arundhati, Vasishtha had Shakti as a son. Shakti's
son was the prosperous Parashara, who knew everything
and was supreme among those who undertook austerities.
He worshipped Isha, the lord of *deva*s and the destroyer
of Tripura. Thereby, he obtained an unmatched son, the
lord Krishna Dvaipayana. Through his own portion,

[1208]Ravana, Kumbhakarna, Mahodara, Prahasta, Mahaparshva,
Khara, Trishira, Dushana and Vidyujjhiva adds up to nine. So
Vibhishasana must be part of the list.
[1209]A different Naidhruva.
[1210]According to one account, Arundhati was Narada's sister.

Bhagavan Shankara was born as Shuka, Dvaipayana's son. He incarnated himself and obtained his own supreme destination. Shuka had five sons who were great ascetics. They were Bhurishrava, Prabhu, Shambhu, Krishna and Goura as the fifth. He also had a daughter, Kirtimati. She was firm in her vows and was the mother of *yoga*. Brahma spoke about Atri's lineage, consisting of those who spoke about the *brahman*. After this, hear about the kings born through Kashyapa.'

Chapter 20(1)(20) (Description of royal lineages)

Suta said, 'Through Kashyapa, Aditi gave birth to the lord Aditya. Aditya had four wives—Samjnaa, Rajni, Prabhaa and Chhayaa. Hear about their sons. Through Surya, Samjnaa, Tvashta's daughter, gave birth to the excellent Manu, Yama and Yamunaa. Rajni gave birth to Revanta. Through Aditya, Prabhaa gave birth to Prabhata. In the due order, Chhayaa's children were Savarni, Shani, Tapati and Vishti. The first Manu[1211] had nine extremely energetic sons, who were his equals. They were Ikshvaku, Nabhaga, Dhrishta, Sharyati, Narishyanta, Nabhaga, Arishta, Karusha and Prishadhra. They resembled Shakra. Ilaa was the eldest and best. She extended Soma's lineage. She went to the residence of Budha, Soma's son, and united with him. Through Soma's son, this lady gave birth to the excellent Pururava. We have heard that Budha's son caused the ancestors to be satisfied. He had a sparking son,

---

[1211]Svayambhuva Manu was the first Manu. But this clearly means Vaivasvata Manu. Nabhaga is repeated here. Lists in other Puranas mention ten sons, with Nriga and Pranshu added.

famous as Sudyumna.[1212] Having had three sons, Utkala, Gaya and Vinata, he went back to being a woman, Ilaa. These excellent sons were unmatched and sought refuge with the one who originated from the lotus. Ikshvaku's son was the brave king named Vikukshi. He was the eldest and he had fifteen sons. The eldest of these was Kakutstha and Kakutstha's son was Suyodhana. Suyodhana's son was the prosperous Prithu and Prithu's son was Vishvaka. Vishvaka's son was the intelligent Ardraka and Ardraka's son was Yuvanashva.'

'The powerful Yuvanashva reached Gokarna. He saw the *brahmana* Goutama, whose austerities were as resplendent as the fire. Desiring a son, the lord of the earth prostrated himself like a rod on the ground. He asked, "Through what *karma* can one obtain a son devoted to *dharma*?" Goutama replied, "Worship the primordial Purusha, Narayana, who is free from ailments. He is without a beginning and without an end. You will then obtain a son who is devoted to *dharma*. The primordial lord, Krishna, had Brahma himself as a son and Nilalohita as a grandson. By worshipping him, one can obtain a son. Bhagavan Brahma does not know the truth about his powers. Therefore, worship Hrishikesha and you will obtain a son who is devoted to *dharma*." Hearing Goutama's words, Yuvanashva, the lord of the earth, worshipped the eternal Hrishikesha Vasudeva. His son was the brave and famous Shravasti. In the region of Gouda, he built the great city

---

[1212] The text is confusing. Vaivasvata Manu had this son, known as Ila or Sudyumna. As a man, he had the sons Utkala, Gaya and Vinata. He was then cursed that he would become a woman and, as Ilaa, gave birth to Pururava. As stated in the text, after having the sons Utkala, Gaya and Vinata, Ila went back to being a woman, Ilaa.

of Shravasti. His son was Brihadhashva and Brihadashva's son was Kuvalayashva. Having killed the great *asura*, Dhundhu, he became known as Dhundhumara. O excellent *dvija*s! It is said that Dhundhumara had three sons— Dridhashva, Dandashva and Kapilashva. Dridhasvha's son was Pramoda and Pramoda's son was Haryashva. Haryashva's son was Nikumbha and Nikumbha's son was Samhitashva. Samhitashva had two sons, Kritashva and Ranashva. Ranashva's son was Yuvanashva[1213]. In a battle, his strength was equal to that of Shakra. Through the favours of the *rishi*s, he performed a sacrifice to Varuna. He then obtained an excellent and unmatched son who was devoted to Vishnu. This was the immensely wise Mandhata, supreme among those who wielded every kind of weapon. Mandhata's sons were Purukutsa, the valiant Ambarisha and Muchukunda, who was pure in his *atman*. All of them were Shakra's equals in a battle. Ambarisha's son is said to have been another Yuvanashva. Yuvanashva's son was Harita and Harita's son was Haarita. Purukutsa's heir was the immensely illustrious Trasadasyu. Through Narmadaa, he had a son known as Sambhuti. Sambhuti's son was Vishnuvriddha and Vishnuvriddha's son was Anaranya. Anaranya's son was Brihadashva and Brihadashva's son was Haryashva. This king was extremely devoted to *dharma*. Through the favours of Kardama Prajapati, he obtained a son who was devoted to *dharma* and devoted to Surya. This king was Vasumana. He worshipped Surya and obtained an unmatched and auspicious son, Tridhanva, the scorcher of enemies. O excellent *dvija*s! After defeating enemies, he performed a horse sacrifice. He

---

[1213]There was more than one king with the same name.

studied, possessed good conduct and donated. Wishing to cross over, he was greatly devoted to *dharma*.'

'The *rishi*s assembled at the great-souled one's sacrificial arena. Vasishtha and Kashyapa were the foremost among them. With Indra at the forefront, the *deva*s were also there. Having completed the sacrifice in the proper way, the great king, full of humility, prostrated himself before Vasishtha and the other excellent *dvija*s and questioned them. Vasumana asked, "O bulls among *brahmana*s! What is best in this world, sacrifices, austerities or *sannyasa*? O ones who know everything! Please tell me." Vasishtha said, "One should attentively study the *Veda*s in the proper way and have sons. One should worship the lord of sacrifices through sacrifices. After this, one should leave for the forest and realize the *atman*." Pulastya said, "A *yogi* should worship the divinity Parameshvara through austerities and the excellent gods through sacrifices. Having done this in the proper way, he should leave for the forest." Pulaha said, "The single ancient Purusha is Parameshvara. He is the one with one thousand rays. If one worships him through austerities, one will obtain *moksha*." Jamadagni said, "He is without birth. He is the creator of the universe. He is the eternal seed of the universe. He is inside all beings. That divinity must be worshipped through austerities." Vishvamitra said, "The infinite Agni is inside all *atman*s. He creates himself and he faces all directions. That Rudra must be worshipped through fierce austerities and not through any other sacrifices." Bharadvaja said, "The eternal divinity, Vasudeva, is worshipped through sacrifices. All the *deva*s are in his body, and he must be worshipped." Atri said, "Everything has originated from him and Prajapati is his son. That Maheshvara must be worshipped through extremely great austerities." Goutama said, "Pradhana and Purusha originate from him. All the power in the universe is his. That eternal lord of *deva*s must be worshipped through austerities." Kashyapa said, "The divinity with one thousand eyes is the witness, Shambhu Prajapati. The great *yogi* must be worshipped and pleased through supreme austerities." Kratu said, "Having studied, performed sacrifices and obtained sons, there is nothing other than austerities. That is what is seen in the *dharmashastra*s." Delighted in his mind, the royal sage prostrated himself before them. He worshipped them and took his leave from them. He told Tridhanva, "I will use austerities to worship the divinity described in the single *akshara*.[1214] He is *prana*, the great Purusha, established inside Aditya. Always be devoted to *dharma* and rule attentively over the entire earth, full of the four *varna*s." Saying this, the king entrusted the kingdom to him. To torment himself through supreme austerities, the unblemished one left for the forest.'

'On the beautiful summit of Himalaya, he sought refuge in a *devadaru* forest. He performed sacrifices to the gods and subsisted on tubers, roots and fruits. Observing austerities for more than one hundred years, he cleansed his sins. In his mind, he performed *japa* on *devi* Savitri, the mother of the *Veda*s.[1215] While he was performing austerities in this way, the divinity Svayambhu Parameshvara Hiranyagarbha, whose *atman* is in the universe, himself arrived at the spot. He saw the divinity Brahma, who faces every direction, arrive. He prostrated

[1214] *Akshara* is a syllable with a single vowel sound. Here, it means OUM.

[1215] The *savitri mantra*, commonly known as the *gayatri mantra*. *Gayatri* is actually the metre.

his head at his feet and chanted his names. "I prostrate
myself before Brahma, the *paramatman*, the divinity who
is the lord of the *deva*s. Your form is golden. You are the
creator, with one thousand eyes. I prostrate myself before
Dhatri and Vidhatri. I prostrate myself before the one
who has all the *deva*s in his form. You can be reached
through *samkhya* and *yoga*. I prostrate myself before the
one whose form is *jnana*. I prostrate myself before the one
who has the three forms. You are Tvashta, who knows
the meaning of everything. I prostrate myself before the
ancient Purusha, the *guru* of *yogi*s." At this, Bhagavan
Virinchi, who conceived the universe, was pleased. He told
him, "O fortunate one! I am the one who bestows boons.
Ask for a boon." The king replied, "O divinity! O lord of
*deva*s! I wish to perform *japa* with Gayatri, the mother of
the *Veda*s, for more than one hundred years again. Please
grant me the requisite lifespan." The one whose *atman*
is in the universe glanced at the lord of men and agreed
to this. Extremely happy, he touched him with his hands
and vanished. Having obtained the boon, the prosperous
one was pleased in his mind and performed the *japa*. He
was serene, bathed at the time of the three *savana*s and
ate tubers, roots and fruits. When one hundred years were
over, Bhagavan, the great *yogi* with the fierce rays, who is
established in Bhanu's disc,[1216] appeared. He saw the eternal
one who is established in the disc, his form consisting of
the *Veda*s. He possessed four faces, eight hands and three
eyes and there was a mass of matted hair on his head. This
was Hara, with a body that was half man and half woman,
marked with the handsome body of the moon. Nilakantha
illuminated the entire world with his own rays. His

[1216]Bhanu is Surya's name.

complexion was red, and he was attired in red garments. He was decorated with red garlands and unguents. On seeing him, he was imbibed with supreme sentiments and filled with great devotion towards him. Using the *savitri mantra*, he prostrated his head before Rudra. "I prostrate myself before the radiant Nilakantha Parameshthi. The three are in you. You are Rudra, with a form like Kala. You are the cause." Pleased in his mind, Mahadeva replied to the king. "O unblemished one! Hear my secret names. They are sung about in all the *Veda*s, and they pacify *samsara*. O king! Purify yourself and always worship with these names. Study Shatarudriya, said to represent the essence of *Yajur* hymns. O king! With single-minded attention and with your mind immersed in me, perform *japa* with this. Observe *brahmacharya* and fast. Control yourself and use *bhasma*. If a person performs *japa* to Rudra until death, he proceeds to the supreme destination." Desiring to show compassion towards a devotee, Bhagavan Rudra said this. He also conceived of an additional lifespan of one hundred years for the king. Parameshvara granted him supreme *jnana* about non-attachment. Then, in an instant, Rudra vanished. It was wonderful. With single-minded attention, the king performed austerities and *japa* on Rudra. Controlled and serene, he covered himself with *bhasma* and bathed at the time of the three *savana*s. For an additional one hundred years, the king performed *japa*. In the course of time, his inclinations turned towards *yoga,* and in the course of time, he obtained the supreme destination. He entered Parameshthi's abode, the essence of the *Veda*s. He reached the sparkling solar disc and then reached Maheshvara. If a person hears or reads about the king's excellent conduct, he is freed from all sins and obtains greatness in Brahma's world.'

Chapter 21(1)(21) (The Ikshvaku lineage)

Suta said, 'The prince, Tridhanva, ruled over the earth in accordance with *dharma*. He had a learned son, known as Trayyaruna. He had an extremely strong son, named Satyavrata. His wife was named Satyadhanaa and she gave birth to Harishchandra. Harishchandra had a valiant son named Rohita. Rohita's son was Vrika and Vrika's son was Bahu. Harita was Rohita's son and Harita's son was Dhundhu. Dhundhu had two sons, Vijaya and Sudeva. Vijaya had a valiant son, named Karuka. His son was Sagara, and this king was extremely devoted to *dharma*. Sagara had two wives, Prabhaa and Bhanumati. They worshipped Vahni and he granted each of them an excellent boon. Bhanumati accepted the boon of a single son, Asamanjasa. The auspicious Prabhaa accepted the boon of sixty thousand sons.[1217] Asamanjasa's son was the king named Amshuman. Amshuman's son was Dilipa and Dilipa's son was Bhagiratha. He performed austerities and brought down Ganga, in the form of Bhagirathi. This was because of the favours of the intelligent divinity, the lord of *deva*s, Mahadeva. The divinity Hara's mind was pleased with Bhagiratha's austerities. With Soma[1218] as his ornament, he bore Ganga on his head, near Soma. Bhagiratha had a son named Shruta. His heir was Nabhaga and Nabhaga's son was Sindhudvipa. Sindhudvipa's son was Ayutayu and Ayutayu's son was the immensely

---

[1217] In other variants of the story, the boon is granted by Bhrigu, not Agni. The two wives were given a choice, between sixty thousand sons who wouldn't survive and a single son who would survive, but be wicked.

[1218] Chandra, the moon.

strong Rituparna. Rituparna's son was Sudasa, and he was devoted to *dharma*. His son was Soudasa, famous as Kalmashapada. In Kalmashapada's *kshetra*, the immensely energetic Vasishtha had a son named Ashmaka, who was a standard for the Ikshvaku lineage.[1219] Through Utakalla, Ashmaka had the king named Nakula as a son. Scared of Rama,[1220] the king was extremely miserable and left for the forest. He used women as his armour and had Shataratha as a son. Shataratha's son was Bilibili and Bilibili's son was the prosperous Vriddhasharma. Vriddhasharma's son was Vishvasaha and Vishvasaha's son was the famous Khatvanga. Khatvanga's son was Dirghabahu and Dirghabahu's son was Raghu. Raghu's son was Aja and Aja's son was King Dasharatha.'

'Dasharatha's son was the valiant Rama, who knew about *dharma* and was famous in the worlds. The others were Bharata, Lakshmana and the immensely strong Shatrughna. All of them possessed Vishnu's powers and were like Shakra in a battle. For the destruction of Ravana, Vishnu, who enjoys the universe, was born through his portion. Rama's wife was the extremely fortunate and auspicious daughter of Janaka. She was famous in the three worlds as Sitaa and she possessed the qualities of good conduct and generosity. Janaka satisfied Devi, the daughter of the Indra among mountains, through his austerities. She gave him Janaki Sitaa and her support was Rama, her husband. Pleased, Bhagavan Isha Nilalohita,

---

[1219]In different versions of the story, Soudasa was cursed and became Kalmashapada. Soudasa was also cursed that he would die if he had intercourse with his queen. *Kshetra* means field, in this case, wife. Hence, through Kalmashapada's wife, Vasishtha had a son.

[1220]Parashurama.

who wields the trident, gave Janaka a wonderful bow, for the destruction of his enemies. The intelligent King Janaka wished to bestow his daughter. O bulls among *dvija*s! The destroyer of enemies announced in the world, "If anyone in the three worlds is capable of wielding this bow, even if he happens to be a *deva* or a *danava*, he deserves to obtain Sitaa." Knowing this, the powerful Lord Rama went to Janaka's residence. As if toying, he seized the bow and broke it. Rama was supremely devoted to *dharma*. Like Shankara marrying Parvati and Shanmukha marrying Senaa,[1221] he married his daughter. After many days passed, King Dasharatha himself started to make arrangements to instate his brave eldest son as the king. His wife was the extremely beautiful Kaikeyi, possessing beautiful smiles. Scared in her mind, she restrained her husband and spoke to him. "You should make my brave son, Bharata, the king. You had earlier granted me two boons."[1222] Hearing her words, the king's mind was dejected. However, he agreed to these words. The undecaying Rama knew about *dharma*. He prostrated himself at his father's feet and took a pledge. Along with Lakshmana and his wife, he left for the forest. The immensely strong one took this pledge for fourteen years. The illustrious lord resided there, along with Lakshmana. On one occasion, while they were in the forest, in the disguise of a mendicant, *rakshasa* Ravana abducted Sitaa and took her to his own city. Unable to see Sitaa, the senses of Lakshmana and Rama were agitated.

[1221]Shanmukha, the one with the six faces, is Skanda or Kartikeya. Skanda's wife is Senaa or Mahasenaa.

[1222]In a battle, Kaikeyi had saved Dasharatha's life and he had granted her two boons, which she had said she would ask for later. The first boon was that Rama be exiled and the second that Bharata be made the king.

Those two scorchers of enemies were tormented by misery and grief. O excellent *dvija*s! On one occasion, Rama, unblemished in deeds, had an alliance with the *kapi* Sugriva and the *vanara*s.[1223] Sugriva's follower was the brave *vanara* named Hanuman. This extremely energetic one was Vayu's son and was always loved by Rama. Firm in his fortitude, he resolved before Rama, "I will bring Sitaa back." Saying this, intent on finding Sitaa, he traversed the earth, right up to the frontier of the ocean. He went to Ravana's city of Lanka, located in the ocean. In a desolate spot there, he saw the one with beautiful smiles at the foot of a tree. The unblemished Sitaa was surrounded by *rakshasi*s.[1224] The eyes of the unblemished one were full of tears. In her heart, she remembered Rama, who was as dark as a blue lotus, and Lakshmana, who was in control of his *atman*. In private, the lord[1225] informed Sitaa about himself. To allay her suspicions, he gave her Rama's ring. Sitaa saw her husband's extremely beautiful ring. She thought that Rama had himself come and her eyes widened in joy. Seeing Sitaa, the mighty-armed one comforted her and said, "I will take you to Rama's presence." He then went back to Rama again. In control over his *atman*, he told Rama that he had seen Sitaa. While he stood before them, Rama and Lakshmana honoured him. Along with Hanuman himself and Lakshmana, the powerful Rama made up his mind to fight against the *rakshasa*. So as to kill Ravana, supremely devoted to *dharma*, the lord made hundreds of *vanara*s build a bridge across the great ocean,

---

[1223] We have deliberately not translated *kapi* or *vanara* as monkey.

[1224] *Rakshasi* is the feminine of *rakshasa*.

[1225] Hanuman.

as a route to Lanka. The scorcher of enemies killed him,
along with his wife, his sons and his brothers. With Vayu's
son as his aide, he brought Sitaa back. In the centre of the
bridge, Raghava established a *lingam* of Mahadeva Ishana
Krittivasa and worshipped it. The divinity, Bhagavan
Mahadeva Shankara directly appeared before him, along
with Parvati, and granted him an excellent boon. "If
*dvija*s see the *lingam* you have established, their sins will
be destroyed, even if they happen to be grave sins. If one
sees the *lingam* and bathes in the great ocean, there is no
doubt that all other sins will be destroyed. As long as the
mountains remain, as long as the earth exists and as long
as the bridge exists, I will remain here, in invisible form.
Bathing, donations, austerities, *shraddha*s and everything
else performed here will lead to ever-lasting merits. Even if
the *lingam* is remembered, sins will be destroyed." Saying
this, Bhagavan Shambhu embraced Raghava. Along with
Nandi and the *gana*s, Rudra then vanished from the spot.
Devoted to *dharma*, Rama ruled over the kingdom. He
was instated as the king by the immensely energetic and
immensely strong Bharata. In particular, he[1226] honoured
all the *brahmana*s and worshipped Ishvara. Through a
horse sacrifice, he worshipped Shankara, the destroyer of
the sacrifice.'[1227]

'Rama had a son, famous as Kusha. He also had the
extremely fortunate and intelligent Lava, who knew the
truth about everything, as a son. Kusha's son was Atithi
and Atithi's son was Nishadha. Nishadha's son was Nala
and Nala's son was Nabhas. Pundarikaksha was the son
of Nabhas and Pundarikaksha's son was Kshemadhanva.

[1226]Rama.
[1227]Daksha's sacrifice.

Kshemadhanva's son was the valiant and powerful Devanika. Devanika's son was Ahinagu and Ahinagu's son was Mahasvan. Mahasvan's son was Chandravaloka and Chandravaloka's son was Taradhisha. Taradhisha's son was Chandragiri and Chandragiri's son was Bhanuvitta. Bhanuvitta's son was Shrutayu. O excellent *dvija*s! All these were the foremost kings of the Ikshvaku lineage, and they have been described briefly. If a person constantly hears about this excellent lineage of Ikshvaku, he is freed from all sins and obtains greatness in the world of the *deva*s.'

Chapter 22(1)(22) (Description of Soma *vamsha*)

Suta said, 'Aila Pururava became the king and ruled over the kingdom. He had six sons whose energy was like that of Indra's. They were Ayu, Mayu, Amayu, the valiant Vishvayu, Shatayu and Shrutayu. They were the sons of the divine Urvashi. We have heard that Ayu had five brave and extremely energetic sons, born through Prabhaa, Svarbhanu's daughter. Nahusha was the first among them. He was devoted to *dharma* and famous in the world. Nahusha had five heirs, and their energy was like that of Indra's. These immensely strong ones were born through Virajaa, the daughter of the ancestors. They were Yati, Yayati, Samyati, Ayati and Ashvaka as the fifth. Among these five, Yayati was extremely strong and valiant. He obtained Devayani, the daughter of Ushanas, as a wife. His other wife was Sharmishtha, the daughter of the *asura* Vrishaparva. Devayani's sons were Yadu and Turvasu. Sharmishtha gave birth to Druhyu, Anu and Puru. He passed over the unblemished and eldest Yadu and instated the youngest, Puru, since he carried out his father's words.[1228] He instructed his son, Turvasu, to rule over the south-east direction. The king appointed the eldest son, Yadu, over the south-west direction. Druhyu was appointed over the west and Anu over the north. All of them followed *dharma* and ruled over the earth. With his wife, the immensely illustrious king also went to the forest.'

'Yadu had five sons who were like sons of *deva*s. The eldest among them was Sahasrajit. The others were Kroshtu, Nila, Jina and Raghu. Sahasrajit's son was the king named Shatajit. Shatajit had three sons who were greatly devoted to *dharma*. They were Haihaya, Haya and King Venuhaya. Haihaya had a son, known as Dharma. O *brahmana*s! His son was the powerful Dharmanetra. Dharmanetra's son was Kirti and Kirti's son was Sanjita. Sanjita's son was Mahishma and Mahishma's descendant was Bhadrashrenya. Bhadrashrenya's heir was the king named Durdama. Durdama's intelligent and valiant son was named Andhaka. Andhaka had four heirs who were revered by the worlds. They were Kritavirya, Kritagni and Kritavarma and the fourth son was Kritouja. Kritavirya's son was Kartavirya Arjuna. He possessed one thousand arms and was resplendent. He was supreme among those who knew about *dhanurveda*. He died at the hands Janardana, in the form of Rama, Jamadagni's son. He had one hundred sons. Five were *maharatha*s.[1229] They were strong and accomplished in the use of weapons. They

---

[1228] Among the five, Puru was the only one who accepted (temporarily) Yayati's old age, handing over his youth. The other sons were made kings in the frontier regions.

[1229] In gradations of warriors, *maharatha*s were greater than *ratha*s and *atiratha*s were greater than *maharatha*s. A *maharatha*, apart from knowing about divine weapons, could fight against 10,000 warriors simultaneously.

were brave and spirited, with *dharma* in their *atman*s. They were Shura, Shurasena, Krishna and Dhrishna. There was also the powerful king, Jayadhvaja, who was devoted to Narayana.'

'The other four, Shurasena and the others, were famous for their energy. These great-souled ones were Rudra's devotees and worshipped Shankara. The intelligent Jayadhvaja sought refuge with the divinity, Vishnu Narayana Hari. His destiny was such that he was devoted to *dharma*. The other sons told him, "O unblemished one! This is not *dharma*. It has been heard that our father was intent on worshipping Ishvara." The immensely energetic one told them, "This is my supreme *dharma*. All the kings on earth have originated as Vishnu's portions. It is certainly Bhagavan Purushottama who protects a kingdom. The unvanquished Vishnu must be worshipped. Hari protects the worlds. The lord himself has three forms of *sattva*, *rajas* and *tamas*. It is said that this is for reasons of creation, preservation and destruction. With *sattva* in his *atman*, Bhagavan Vishnu always establishes. Brahma, the *rajas* form, creates. Hara, the *tamas* form, destroys. Therefore, Bhagavan Vishnu Keshava, the one who crushed Keshi, must be worshipped by kings who protect their kingdoms." Hearing his words, the other four spirited brothers replied, "Those who desire liberation should worship Rudra, the destroyer. Bhagavan Rudra is everything. This entire universe is Shiva. Resorting to the *guna* of *tamas*, when the time is over, the lord destroys. This most terrible form is full of supreme energy. The wielder of the trident first withdraws knowledge and then *samsara*." Thinking about this, King Jayadhvaja told them, "A being is freed through *sattva*. Bhagavan Hari has *sattva* in his *atman*." His brothers replied, "People who are full of *sattva* serve

Rudra. Those full of *sattva* are then liberated. Hara must always be worshipped." Prince Jayadhvaja seemed to laugh as he answered. "Liberation occurs through the practice of one's own *dharma*. The sages have said that there is no other way. Vishnu's Shakti always supports kings. Therefore, worship of the infinitely energetic Murari is supreme *dharma*." King Krishna, supreme among intelligent ones, told him, "Our father, Arjuna, is the one who followed *dharma*." While this debate was going on, Shurasena spoke these words. "The *rishi*s are the proof. They must say what is true." At this, all those agitated tigers among kings went to the hermitage of the *saptarshi*s and questioned those who spoke about the *brahman*. Vasishtha and the other sages told them the truth. "A divinity is whoever a man takes him to be. However, if a divinity is worshipped for a specific purpose, men obtain what is wished for. There is always specific worship. O kings! Without deviation, that is the rule. Divinities for kings are Vishnu, Isha and Purandara. Divinities for *brahmana*s are Agni, Aditya, Brahma and the wielder of Pinaka. The divinity for *deva*s is Vishnu. The divinity for *danava*s is the wielder of the trident. Soma is said to be the divinity for *gandharva*s and *yaksha*s. Vagdevi[1230] is the divinity for *vidyadhara*s. For *siddha*s, it is Bhagavan Hari. For *rakshasa*s, it is Shankara Rudra. For *kinnara*s, it is Parvati. For *rishi*s, it is Bhagavan Brahma and Mahadeva, the wielder of the trident. For women, Umaa Devi, Vishnu, Isha and Bhaskara[1231] must be revered. All these are for householders. For *brahmachari*s, it is Brahma. For

---

[1230] The goddess of speech.
[1231] Surya.

vaikhanasas, it is Arka and for yatis, it is Maheshvara.[1232]
For bhutas, it is Bhagavan Rudra. For kushmandas,[1233] it is
Vinayaka. For everyone, it is Bhagavan Prajapati Brahma,
the lord of devas. The divinity, Bhagavan Brahma, has
himself said all this. Therefore, it is indeed the case that
Jayadhvaja should worship Vishnu. However, men should
worship Hari after understanding that his atman is the
same as that of Rudra's. Otherwise, Hari will not destroy
a king's enemies." Prostrating themselves, they returned to
their extremely beautiful city. Having conquered the entire
earth in battles, they ruled over it.'

'O Indras among brahmanas! There was a danava
named Videha, terrifying to all beings. On one occasion,
he came to their city. His teeth were cruel, and he blazed,
like the fire at the end of a yuga. He seized a spear that
resembled the sun and roared in ten directions. On hearing
this, those who resided there, died. Others, who remained
alive, were agitated by fear and fled. The five immensely
strong kings who were Kartavirya's sons, Shurasena and
the others, prepared themselves. They fought against the
danava, using spears, summits of mountains and bludgeons.
O Indras among brahmanas! He laughed as he warded all
these off with his spear. Full of intolerance, they rushed
against Videha, to fight against him. Shura unleashed
Rudra's weapon, Shurasena Varuna's. Krishna invoked
Prajapati's weapon and Dhrishna Vayu's. Jayadhvaja used
the weapons of Kubera, Indra and Agni. Using his spear,
the danava shattered these weapons. At this, the immensely

[1232] Vaikhanasa is a hermit who lives in isolation, yati is an
ascetic who has conquered his senses.
[1233] The word kushmanda has different meanings. Here, it can
be taken in the sense of spirit.

valiant Krishna seized a terrible club. He touched it, hurled
it with force and roared. That club struck Videha's chest,
which was like a rock. But it was incapable of making the
danava, who resembled the Destroyer, move. Witnessing
his great manliness, they were struck with extreme fear and
fled. The intelligent Jayadhvaja remembered the lord of the
universe, the victorious Vishnu, the immeasurable origin
of the worlds, the one who is without ailments. He is the
primordial Purusha, the saviour, Shripati, attired in yellow
garments. At this, the *chakra* manifested itself, resembling
ten thousand suns in radiance. Vasudeva, who shows
favours to his devotees, instructed it. The king remembered
Narayana, the origin of the universe, and grasped it. Like
Hari using it against *danava*s, he hurled it towards Videha.
The terrible Sudarshana *chakra* struck him in the region
around the shoulder. It severed his head, which resembled
the peak of a mountain, and brought it down to the ground.
Earlier, Vishnu had obtained this *chakra* after worshipping
Shankara through austerities. Therefore, it was capable of
destroying *asura*s. When the enemy of the *deva*s was killed,
the kings, Shura and the other brothers returned to their
beautiful city. They honoured their brother.'

'Hearing about Jayadhvaa's valour, the illustrious and
great sage, Vishvamitra, arrived to see Kartavirya's son. On
seeing him come, the king's eyes were filled with respect.
When he was seated on a beautiful seat, he respectfully
worshipped him. He said, "O illustrious one! It is because
of your favours that the *asura* and lord of *danava*s, Videha,
has been brought down by me. Your words dispelled my
doubts about Vishnu, for whom truth is valour. Through
your favours, I performed the auspicious act of seeking
refuge with him. I will worship the supreme lord Vishnu,
whose eyes are like the petals of a lotus. How is lord Hari

worshipped; through what rules? O one excellent in vows! Who is the divinity Narayana and what are his powers? Please tell me everything. I am filled with great curiosity." Hearing Jayadhvaja's words and witnessing his supreme devotion towards Hari, the tranquil sage, Vishvamitra, replied. Vishvamitra said, "All beings originate in him and the entire universe ends in him. He is Vishnu, who is in the *atman*s of all beings. Those who seek refuge in him are liberated. He is without decay. He is greater than the greatest. He is described as the one who is in the cavity of the heart. He is supreme bliss. Narayana is described as space. He rises all the time. He is without an alternative. He is in constant bliss. He is without blemish. Though Vishnu is himself said to be without *vyuha*s, he assumes the form of the four *vyuha*s. He is *paramatman*, the supreme destination. He is the supreme space and the supreme objective. Those who speak about the *brahman* describe him as the *brahman*, with his three feet in the *akshara*.[1234] He is Vasudeva, whose *atman* is in the universe. He is Purushottama, with *yoga* in his *atman*. Brahma and Parameshvara Rudra originated as his portions. Depending on the *dharma* of his own *varna* and *ashrama*, a man should worship Purushottama as part of his vow, with no desire in mind. There is no other way." Saying this, the illustrious *brahmana*, the great ascetic Vishvamitra, was worshipped by Shura and the others and returned to his own hermitage. Shura and the others worshipped the divinity Maheshvara. Without any desire in mind, they used sacrifices to worship the imperishable Rudra, who can only be reached through sacrifices. The illustrious Vasishtha, who knew about *dharma*, officiated at the sacrifice. Goutama, Agasti and

[1234] That is, OUM.

Atri also worshipped Rudra's valour. The illustrious
Vishvamitra made Jayadhvaja, the destroyer of enemies,
perform a sacrifice to Janardana, the primordial divinity
who is the origin of beings. At this sacrifice, the divinity
and great *yogi*, Hari, himself appeared. That Bhagavan
should manifest himself was extraordinary. Jayadhvaja
understood everything, that Vishnu was Rudra's supreme
body. He attentively worshipped Achyuta. If a person
constantly hears about Jayadhvaja's valour, he is freed
from all sins and goes to Vishnu's world.'

Chapter 23(1)(23) (Lineage of kings)

Suta said, 'Jayadhvaja is said to have had Talajangha as a
son. He had one hundred sons, known as Talajanghas.
The eldest among them was the immensely valiant king,
Vitihotra. There were Vrisha and other Yadavas, auspicious
in deeds. In Vrisha's lineage, his son was Madhu. Madhu
had one hundred sons, but only Vrishana continued the
lineage. Vitithotra's son was the famous Ananta. Ananta's
son was Durjaya, who was accomplished in all weapons.
His wife was beautiful and was ornamented with all the
qualities. She was devoted to her husband and followed
her *dharma* and that of her husband.'

'On one occasion, the great king was on the banks of
the Kalindi.[1235] He saw the divine Urvashi, who was singing
in a sweet voice.He approached her, his mind overwhelmed
with desire. He said, "O divine one! For a long period of
time, you should enjoy yourself with me." The divine one

[1235]Yamuna.

saw that the king possessed beauty and charm. Since he
was like another Kama, she enjoyed herself with him, for
a long period of time. When the king understood that a
long period of time had elapsed, he spoke to the beautiful
Urvashi. "I will go to my beautiful city." She laughed and
spoke these words. "O handsome king! I am not yet satisfied
with the enjoyment. To my delight, you should remain with
me for one more year." The intelligent one replied, "I will
quickly go to my city and return again. You should allow
me." The immensely fortunate one said, "O lord of the
earth! Do that. However, you should not engage in sexual
intercourse with any other *apsara*." Agreeing to this, he
quickly went to his extremely beautiful city. Having gone
there, he saw his wife, who was devoted to her husband and
was scared. His wife possessed qualities and was devoted
to her husband. Possessing heavy breasts, she addressed
him in these words. "O husband! Why are you scared? I
am pleased with you. What is the reason for this fear that
has come over you now? Please tell me the truth. This does
not enhance a king's fame." Hearing her words, his mind
was overcome with shame. The king did not say anything
in reply. But with her insight of *jnana*, she got to know
and said, "O king! You need not be frightened. However,
you must perform the task of atoning for your sin. O great
king! If you are scared, your kingdom will be destroyed."
At this, the radiant king emerged from his city again. He
went to Kanva's sacred hermitage and saw the great sage
there. From Kanva's mouth, he heard about the auspicious
rites for *prayashchitta*.[1236] As instructed, the immensely
strong one went to the slopes of the Himalaya. The Indra
among kings saw a supreme and excellent *gandharva* there.

[1236] Rite of atonement.

He was radiant and resplendent in the sky, adorned with
a celestial garland. On seeing the garland, the destroyer
of enemies remembered the excellent *apsara*, Urvashi. The
thought came to his mind that she deserved this garland.
Full of great desire, the king fought a great battle with the
gandharva, so as to seize the garland. O *dvijas*! Durjaya
defeated him in the battle and seized the garland. Wishing
to see the *apsara*, he lovingly went to Kalindi. However, he
could not see the *apsara* there and suffered from Kama's
arrows. He travelled over the entire earth, with its seven
*dvipa*s. Eager to see Urvashi, he crossed over the flanks
of the Himalayas. It is heard that he went to Hemakuta,
supreme among mountains. Here and there, noble *apsara*s
saw him, terrible in his valour, like a lion. He was adorned
in that wonderful garland, and they were smitten with
desire. However, he remembered Urvashi's words and his
mind was only attached to her. Though he climbed the
peaks of all the mountains, he did not see her. Unable to
see the divine *apsara*, he suffered from desire. Like a *deva*
in his valour, he went to the great Meru, in the world of
the *deva*s. There is a lake named Manasa there, famous
in the three worlds. With the strength of his own arms,
he climbed over the summit and reached there. He saw
the one with the unblemished limbs wandering around
there. He gave her the garland and was again filled with
great desire. When he saw the divine lady adorned with
the garland, he was charmed. He thought that he had
become successful in his objective and enjoyed himself
with her for a very long time. At the end of the intercourse,
Urvashi addressed the noble king in these words. "O brave
king! After going to your city, what did you do?" He told
her everything that his wife had said, about his meeting
Kanva and about seizing the garland. Hearing what had

happened, desiring his welfare, she said, "Kanva will curse
me and so will your beloved. You should leave." Though
she addressed him in this way, the great king was deluded
by desire. His mind was so attached to her that he did not
act by her words. At this, Urvashi, who could assume any
form at will, showed the king her hideous form. She always
showed him this form, tawny-eyed and covered with hair.
His mind was disenchanted with her, and he remembered
what Kanva had said. "Shame on me." He made up his
mind to perform austerities. He did this for twelve years,
surviving on tubers, roots and fruits. For another twelve
years, the king survived only on air. Terrified, he then
went to Kanva's hermitage and reported everything to him,
how he resided with the *apsara* and performed supreme
austerities thereafter. Seeing the tiger among kings, the
illustrious *rishi* was pleased. Wishing to remove the seeds
of desire, he addressed him in these words. Kanva said,
"Go to the divine city of Varanasi, where Ishvara resides.
To liberate the world, the divinity Maheshvara is present
there. Bathe in the proper way in the Ganga and satisfy the
*deva*s and ancestors. When you see Vishveshvara's *lingam*,
your sins will be instantly destroyed." Prostrating his head
down, Durjaya took his leave from Kanva. He saw Hara in
Varanasi and was freed from his sins. He went to his own
sparkling city and ruled over the earth. He performed a
sacrifice and out of compassion, the sage Kanva officiated
at the sacrifice.'

'Durjaya's son is said to have been the intelligent
Supratika. As soon as he was born, it was evident that
he would be the king. Through Urvashi, he[1237] had seven
immensely valiant sons, who were like the sons of *deva*s. O

[1237]This should mean Durjaya.

*dvija*s! All of them accepted the daughters of *gandharva*s
as their beloved wives. Thus, I have properly described to
you the excellent lineage of Sahasrajit, which destroys the
sins of men. Now hear about Kroshtu.'

Chapter 24(1)(24) (Description of Yadu's lineage)

Suta said, 'Kroshtu had one son, known as Vajravan.
Vajravan's son was Shanti and Shanti's son was
Kushika. Kushika had a powerful son, named Chitraratha.
Chitraratha's son was known in the world as Shashabindu.
Shashabindu's son was Prithuyasha, a king who was
devoted to *dharma*. Prithuyasha's son was Prithukarma
and Prithukarma's son was Prithujaya. Prithujaya's
son was Prithukirti, Prithukirti's son was Prithudana,
Prithudana's son was Prithushrava and Prithushrava's
son was Prithusattama. Prithusattama's son was Ushanas,
and the son of Ushanas was Shateshu. Shateshu's son was
Rukmakavacha and Rukmakavacha's son was Paravritta.
Paravritta's son was Yamagha, who was famous in the
world. Yamagha's son was Vidarbha and Vidarbha's sons
were Kratha and Koushika. The king had a third son,
Lomapada. Lomapada's son was Dhriti and Dhriti's son
was Shveta. Shveta had a strong son, known under the
name of Vishvasaha. Vishvasaha's son is said to have been
the powerful and extremely valiant Koushika. Koushika
had an intelligent son, Sumanta. Sumanta's son was
Anala. Anala's son was Shveni. Shveni had many other
sons. Chief among them was Dyutiman and Dyutiman's
son was Vapushman. Vapushman's son was Brihanmedha
and Brihanmedha's son was Shrideva. O *brahmana*s!
Shrideva's son was the immensely strong Vitaratha, who

was Rudra's devotee. Kratha's son was Kunti and Kunti's son was Vrishni.'

'Vrishni had an extremely strong son, named Navaratha. O bulls among sages! On one occasion, he went on a hunt. Seeing an energetic *rakshasa*, he was filled with great fear and fled. The extremely strong and angry *rakshasa* pursued him. He resembled fire and was impossible to fight against. He held a spear in his large hand. King Navaratha was terrified. Not far away, he saw Sarasvati's supreme spot, which was protected well. With great speed, the intelligent king reached that place. On seeing Devi Sarasvati herself, he lowered his head and worshipped her. The conqueror of enemies joined his hands in salutation and praised her with excellent words. He prostrated himself like a rod on the ground and said, "I seek refuge with you. I prostrate myself before Mahadevi, Devi Sarasvati herself. You are the goddess of speech. You are without a beginning and without an end. You are Ishvari. You are a *brahmacharini*.[1238] I prostrate myself before the origin of the universe. You are a *yogini*. You are the supreme part. You originated from Hiranyagarbha. You are three-eyed and have the moon on your crest. I prostrate myself before the supreme bliss. You are a portion that is consciousness. You are the form of the *brahman*. O supreme Ishani! Please save me. I am scared and seek refuge." Meanwhile, wishing to kill the king, the angry lord of *rakshasa*s arrived at the spot where Devi Sarasvati was. Insolent about his strength, he entered, raising his spear. This was the place of the mother of the three worlds, resembling the moon and the sun. At the time, a great being arose, resembling the sun that rises at the end of a *yuga*. He used a spear to shatter the

---

[1238]Feminine of *brahmachari*.

rakshasa's chest and brought him down to the ground. He
said, "O great king! Leave quickly. Now that the *rakshasa*
has been killed, you can be fearless and need not remain
here any longer." Delighted in his mind, King Navaratha
prostrated himself. O Indras among *brahmana*s! He went
to his supreme city, which was like Purandara's city. Full
of devotion, he instated Deveshi there. With many kinds
of oblations and sacrifices, he worshipped Devi Sarasvati.
Navaratha's son was Dasharatha, extremely devoted to
dharma. He was extremely energetic and devoted to Devi.
Shakuni was his son. Shakuni's son was Karambha and
Karambha's son was Devarata, who performed a horse
sacrifice. Devarata's son was Devakshatra. Devakshatra's
heir was Madhu and Madhu's son was Kuru. Kuru had
two sons, Sutrama and Anu. Anu's son was Priyagotra and
Priyagotra's successor was Amshu.'

'Amshu had a powerful son named Andhaka, who was
devoted to Vishnu. He was great-souled and devoted to
donating. He was supreme among those who knew about
dhanurveda. Following Narada's words, he was engaged
in worshipping Vasudeva. He propounded the sacred texts,
known as *kundagola* and others.[1239] The beautiful and
famous Satvata texts are named after him. For the welfare
of *kunda*s and others, he propounded these great sacred
texts. Andhaka's son was Satvata, accomplished in all the
sacred texts. Because of what he propounded this great king
was famous for his sacred deeds. Koushalya[1240] had the
Satvatas as sons and they possessed the quality of *sattva*—

[1239]*Kunda* is a son born through one's own wife, through
adultery. *Gola* is a son born to a widow. But *kundagola* is a class
of *tantra* texts that worship Devi, often not regarded as part of
mainstream texts.
[1240]Satvata's wife.

Andhaka, Mahabhoja, Vrishni and King Devavridha. The eldest was known as Bhajamana and he was supreme among those who knew about *dhanurveda*. Among them, King Devavridha performed supreme austerities. The lord thought, "Let me have a son who possesses all the qualities." He thus had Babhru as a son, a king who was famous for his deeds. He possessed beauty and was devoted to *dharma*. He was always engaged in the pursuit of true *jnana*. Bhajamana's sons were Bhajamanas, who worshipped the divine Shri. The foremost and famous among them were Nimi and Krikana. Bhojas and Vaimatrikas were born in Mahabhoja's lineage. Vrishni's sons were the powerful Sumitra, Anamitra and Timi. Anamitra's son was Nighna. Nighna had two sons, the immensely fortunate Prasena and an excellent one, named Satrajit. Anamitra's son was Sini, the youngest among Vrishni's descendants. He was truthful in speech and devoted to the truth. Sini's son was Satyaka and Satyaka's son was Satyaki Yuyudhana. Yuyudhana's son was Asanga. Asanga's son was Kuni and Kuni's son was the intelligent Yugandhara. Through Madri, Vrishni had Vrishni as a son[1241] and he was a delight of the Yadu lineage. Vrishni had two sons, Shvaphalka and Chitraka. Shvaphalka obtained the daughter of the king of Kashi as a wife. Through her, he had a son named Akrura, who was devoted to *dharma*. He also had many other sons, Upamangu, Mangu and others. It is said that Akrura's sons were the famous Devavan and Upadeva, who had the *deva*s in his *atman*. Upadeva's sons were Vishva and Pramathin. Chitraka's sons were Prithu, Viprithu, Ashvagriva, Subahu, Sudhashvaka and Gavekeshaka. Through Andhaka's daughter, he has four sons—Kukura,

---

[1241] Father and son had the same name.

Bhajamana, Shamika and Balagarvita. Kukura's son was Vrishni and Vrishni's son was the famous Kapotaroma, whose son was Vilomaka.'

'Vilomaka's son was the learned Tama, who was Tumburu's[1242] friend. Tama had Anakadundubhi as a son. He went to Govardhana and tormented himself through extensive austerities. Brahma, the great lord of the worlds, granted him a boon. His lineage would obtain imperishable fame. He would obtain excellent *jnana* and *yoga*. O *brahmana*s! He would surpass his *guru* and be able to assume any form at will. Having obtained these excellent boons, using songs, he worshipped Sthanu, whose mount is a bull, who deserves to be worshipped and is worshipped by the gods. While he was singing in this way, Bhagavan, Ambikaa's husband, gave him a jewel among maidens, impossible for even the gods to obtain. Along with her, the king engaged in the practice of excellent singing. The slayer of enemies taught his beloved, who possessed tremulous eyes, this. Through her, he had a beautiful son, named Subhuja. He also had Hrimati, who possessed beauty and charm, as a daughter. While they were still children, in the proper way, the mother taught the beautiful son and the daughter knowledge about singing. After upanayana, he[1243] studied the *Veda*s in the proper way from a *guru*. He married Manasi, a daughter of the *gandharva*s. Through her, he had five excellent sons. They possessed knowledge about playing the *veena* and were accomplished in the art of singing. The king was accomplished in singing. Along with his sons, grandsons and wife, he used songs to worship the divinity who destroyed Tripura. Hrimati was

[1242] Tumburu is a *gandharva*.
[1243] Subhuja.

beautiful in her limbs. She was charming, with large eyes. A *gandharva* named Subahu abducted her and took her to his city. Through the extremely energetic *gandharva*, she had Sushena, Dhira, Sugriva, Subhojana and Naravahana as sons. Anakadundubhi had the valiant Abhijit as a son. Abhijit's son was Punarvasu. Subsequently, Ahuka was born as a son. O excellent *dvija*s! Ahuka's sons were Ugrasena and Devaka. Devaka's brave sons were the equals of the gods. They were Devavan, Upadeva, Sudeva and Devarakshita. They had seven sisters, who were bestowed on Vasudeva. They were Dhritadevaa, Upadevaa, Devarakshitaa, Shridevaa, Shantidevaa, Sahadevaa, excellent in vows, and Devaki. Among them, the slender-waisted Devaki was the best. Ugrasena's sons were Nyagrodha and Kamsa. There were also Subhumi, Rashtrapala, Tushtiman and Shanku. The famous Viduratha was the son of Bhajamana. Viduratha's son was Surasama and Surasama's son was Pratikshatra. Pratikshatra's son was Svayambhoja and Svayambhoja's son was Dhatrika, the scorcher of enemies. Dhatrika's sons were Kritavarma and Shurasena. Vasudeva was also his son, and he was always devoted to *dharma*.'

'Vasudeva's son was the mighty-armed Vaasudeva, the *guru* of the universe. Entreated by the *deva*s, Hari became Devaki's son. The beautiful and immensely fortunate Rohini was Vasudeva's wife. She gave birth to his eldest son, Samkarshana Rama, whose weapon was a plough. Vaasudeva, who pervades the universe, is the *paramatman*. The lord Samkarshana, with the plough as his weapon, is Shesha himself. As a result of Bhrigu's curse, he had to assume a human body.[1244] Madhava thus manifested himself through Devaki and Rohini. Koushiki

---

[1244]Since Vishnu killed Kavyamataa, Bhrigu's wife.

Yoganidraa originated from Umaa's body. Engaged by
Vaasudeva, she became Yashodaa's daughter. Vasudeva
had other sons, older than Vaasudeva. O excellent sages!
Earlier, all of them had been killed by Kamsa. They were
Sushena, Dayi, Bhadrasena, Mahabala, Vajradambha,
Bhadrasena and the revered Kirtiman. When all of them
had been killed, through Vasudeva, Rohini gave birth
to Balabhadra Rama, the lord of the worlds, with the
plough as his weapon. After Rama was born, Devaki
gave birth to Achyuta Krishna, the first among *deva*s,
with the Shrivatsa mark on his chest. Rama's wife was
named Revati, and she possessed excellent qualities.
Through her, he had two sons, Nishita and Ulmuka.
Krishna, unblemished in deeds, had sixteen thousand
wives and hundreds and thousands of sons. Through
Rukmini, Vaasudeva had immensely strong and valiant
sons—Charudeshna, Sucharu, Charuvesha, Yashodhara,
Charushrava, Charuyasha, Pradyumna and Samba.[1245]
These sons were the best among all his sons. On seeing
these brave sons, born to Janardana through Rukmini,
Jambavati, Krishna's wife with sweet smiles, spoke to
him. "O Pundarikaksha! O slayer of *danava*s! Please
grant me a son who will be distinctive in superior
qualities, one who will be revered by lords among gods."
Hearing Jambavati's words, Hari Jagannatha, scorcher
of enemies and store of austerities, himself started to
perform austerities. O best among sages! Hear about how
Devaki's son tormented himself through fierce and great
austerities, saw Rudra and obtained a son.'

[1245] As stated, there are inconsistencies. Samba was Jambavati's
son.

Chapter 25(1)(25) (Krishna's austerities)

Suta said, 'For the sake of a son, the divinity, Bhagavan Hrishikesha Purushottama, tormented himself through terrible austerities. Having taken an *avatara*, the creator of the universe, did what needed to be done. Though he knew his root was Parameshvara, he acted according to his nature.[1246] He went to the hermitage of the great-souled Upamanyu, Indra among sages. It was full of *yogis* and frequented by many kinds of birds. He mounted the infinitely energetic Suparna,[1247] the king of birds. The conch shell, *chakra* and mace were in his hands. He was marked by the sign of Shrivatsa. There were many kinds of trees and creepers there. The place was adorned by many kinds of flowers. There were the hermitages of *rishis*, echoing with the sounds of the *Vedas* being chanted. The place was full of lions, bears, *sharabhas*, tigers and elephants.[1248] The place was adorned with beautiful lakes, with sparkling and tasty water. There were different types of pleasure groves and auspicious temples to *devas*. There were *rishis*, sons of *rishis* and large numbers of great sages. They were engaged in studying the *Vedas*, and there were those who performed *agnihotra* rites. There were *yogis* engaged in *dhyana*, their eyes fixed on the tips of their noses. In every direction, there were sacred ones, pursuing *jnana* and insight about the truth. On every side, there were rivers, frequented by those who spoke about the *brahman* and performed *japa*. There were sacred ascetics, intent on worshipping Isha.

[1246] That is, he behaved like a human.

[1247] Garuda.

[1248] *Sharabha* is an eight-legged creature that feeds on lions. However, the word also means a camel, or a young elephant.

They were tranquil and truthful in resolution, devoid
of grief and devoid of obstructions. With all their limbs
covered with *bhasma*, they were engaged in *japa* on
Rudra. Their heads were shaved or covered with matted
hair. There were other pure ones, with tufts of hair in
the matted hair. The place was always served by ascetics,
who pursued *jnana* and spoke about the *brahman*. That
beautiful and excellent hermitage was adorned with the
hermitages of *siddha*s. The illustrious Ganga, the destroyed
or sins, always flowed there. The one whose *atman* is in the
universe saw the place, full of ascetics who were devoid
of taints. Madhava prostrated himself and worshipped
them with his words. They saw the origin of the universe,
holding the conch shell, the *chakra* and the mace. Full of
devotion, they prostrated themselves before the *yogi* who
was the supreme *guru*. With the eternal one in their hearts,
they praised him with *mantra*s from the *Veda*s. They told
each other, "This is the unmanifest and original divinity,
the great sage. This is the sole Bhagavan, Narayana, the
supreme witness. The divinity, the foremost Purusha, has
himself come here now. He is the one without decay. He is
the one who creates, preserves and destroys. He is without
a form. But he has assumed a form and has come here
to see the Indras among sages. He is Dhatri and Vidhatri.
He goes everywhere and has come here. He is without a
beginning and without decay. He is infinite. He is the great
being and the great lord." Hari, who is beyond words,
heard and understood their words. Govinda quickly
went to the great-souled one's[1249] place. In each *tirtha*,
with appropriate sentiments, Yadava touched the water.
Devaki's son offered oblations to *deva*s, *rishi*s and ancestors.

[1249]Upamanyu's.

Along the banks of the rivers, the lords among sages had instated *lingam*s of the infinitely energetic Shambhu. He worshipped these. Wherever the residents saw Janardana arrive, they worshipped him with flowers and *akshata*.[1250] They saw Vasudeva, holding the Sharnga bow, the conch shell and a sword. With auspicious limbs and controlled minds, all of them remained immobile. There were those whose minds wished to ascend upwards to Janardana. When they saw him, they emerged, controlled themselves and stood before Hari.'

'He immersed himself in the Ganga and offered oblations to *deva*s and *rishi*s. Collecting excellent flowers, he then entered the home of the Indra among sages. He saw the best among *yogi*s, his body smeared with *bhasma*. His hair was matted and he was clad in bark. He was serene. He prostrated his head before the sage. The one who knew the truth saw Krishna arrive and worshipped him. He made the foremost *atithi* of *yogi*s sit on a seat. He told the origin of words, "We know that you are the supreme destination. You are Vishnu, whose abode is not manifest. We are instated here, in our positions as *shishya*s. O Hrishikesha! Welcome. All our austerities have been rendered successful. Vishnu, whose *atman* is in the universe, has himself come to my home. Even though they endeavour, sages and *yogi*s cannot see you. Such a person has arrived here. What is the reason for your arrival?" Hearing Upamanyu's words, the great *yogi*, Bhagavan, Devaki's son, was pleased and prostrated himself before replying. Krishna said, "O illustrious one! I wish to see Girisha Krittivasa. Eager to see Bhagavan, I have come to your place. How can Bhagavan

---

[1250]This can mean grain of any kind. But it is specifically used for threshed and winnowed rice that has not been dehusked.

Isha, supreme among those who know about *yoga*, be
seen? Without any delay, where can I see Umaa's consort?"
The illustrious one replied, "Bhagavan Parameshvara can
only be seen through intense devotion. Therefore, control
yourself and perform austerities. Here, Indras among
sages who speak about the *brahman*, perform *dhyana*
on Ishvara, the lord of *deva*s. *Yogi*s and ascetics worship
him. Surrounded by diverse *bhuta*s and *yogi*s, the divinity,
Bhagavan Vrishadhvaja sports here, along with his wife.
Earlier, in this hermitage, the illustrious *rishi*, Vasishtha,
worshipped Rudra by tormenting himself with extremely
terrible austerities and obtained *yoga* from Maheshvara.
It is here that the illustrious Krishna Dvaipayana Vyasa
himself saw Paramesha and obtained *jnana* about Ishvara.
In this beautiful hermitage, full of devotion, learned ones
tormented themselves through austerities dedicated to
Kapardi and obtained sons from Rudra. It is here that *deva*s
praised Mahadevi Bhavani Maheshvari and Mahadeva
and obtained freedom from fear and *nivritti*. Savarni,
the supreme ascetic, worshipped Mahadeva here.[1251] He
obtained supreme *yoga* and became an excellent composer
of texts. For the virtuous, he propounded an auspicious
Samhita. It is here that Kapeya of the Shamshapayana *gotra*
saw Mahadeva and composed a Purana at his bidding.[1252]
O Purushottama! This had twelve thousand *shloka*s. The
sacred Purana named Vayaviyottara, in conformity with
the *Veda*s, with more than sixteen thousand *shloka*s, was
propounded here. For excellent *dvija*s, through his favour,

[1251]Savarni was Romaharshana's *shishya* and composed his
own Purana Samhita.

[1252]There is a gross error in the text and we have corrected it.
The text says, Kama Shashipayina. This makes no sense. We have
amended Kama to Kapeya and Shashipayina to Shamshapayana.

the *dvija* propounded the sacred Purana. It is here that Vaishampayana's *shishya*s described what he narrated. Through austerities, the great *yogi*, Yajnavalkya, saw Hara here. Engaged by him, he composed an excellent sacred text on *yoga*. Earlier, it was here that Bhrigu tormented himself through great austerities. From Maheshvara, he obtained as a son Shukra, supreme among those who know about *yoga*. Therefore, torment yourself through extremely difficult austerities, dedicated to the lord of *deva*s, if you wish to see the fierce and terrible Kapardi, the lord of the universe." Saying this, the great sage Upamanyu gave Krishna, unblemished in deeds, the *jnana* about Pashupata *yoga* and *vrata*.'

'As instructed by the noble sage, the lord Madhusudana worshipped the divinity Rudra there, using austerities. He smeared all his limbs with *bhasma*. He shaved his head and wore bark. With his mind fixed only on Shiva, he incessantly performed *japa* on Rudra. After many days had passed, Mahadeva Maheshvara showed himself in the sky, with the half-moon as his ornament and with Devi Umaa. He wore a diadem and held a mace. He wore a colourful garland. The lord of *deva*s held Pinaka and a trident. His limbs were covered in a garment made out of tiger skin. He saw Mahadeva, along with Devi. The ancient lord, Purusha, was in front of him. This was the eternal lord of *yogi*s. Smaller than the smallest, he was infinite in his powers. He saw Shambhu, the lord of *prana*. He was three-eyed and there was a battle axe in his hand. His limbs were covered in *bhasma* and the hide of Nrisimha.[1253] He was gigantic and was chanting Pranava. He saw him, resembling one thousand suns. He saw Rudra, the primordial *deva* in

[1253] As in man-lion, whom Shiva killed.

front of him. Even today, *deva*s, the grandfather, Indra,
Agni, Varuna and Death are incapable of speaking about
his powers. On Girisha's left, he saw himself, with an
unmanifest and infinite form. Using many kinds of words,
he was praising Isha, whose hands held a conch shell, a
sword and a *chakra*. To the right of the lord of gods, he
saw a being, his hands joined in salutation and astride a
swan. Stationed in heaven, the grandfather, the *guru* of the
worlds, was praising Isha's supreme powers. There were
*ganeshvara*s resembling one thousand suns. There were
Nandishvara and others, infinite in powers. In front of
the lord of the three worlds, he saw Kumara, resembling a
fire, and Ganesha. He saw Marichi, Atri, Pulaha, Pulastya,
Prachetas, Daksha, Kanva and Parashara, and beyond
them, Vasishtha and Svayambhuva Manu.'

'Vishnu, pervasive in his intelligence, joined his hands
in salutation and used *mantra*s to praise the foremost
among immortals. He thought of his *atman* within his
own *atman* and full of devotion, prostrated himself before
Girisha and Devi. Krishna said, "O eternal one! I prostrate
myself before you. O one with every kind of *yoga*! Brahma
and the rishis speak of you as *tamas*, *sattva* and *rajas*.
They speak the truth about all three existing in you. O
Rudra! You are Brahma and Hari. You are the creator of
the universe and the destroyer. You reside in the solar disc.
You are *prana*. You are the bearer of oblations, Vasava
and all the different entities are you alone. I seek refuge
with the lord of *deva*s. Those who follow *samkhya* say that
you are the single one, devoid of *guna*s. Those who follow
yoga constantly worship you in their hearts. The *Veda*s
speak of you as Rudra, who is to be worshipped. I seek
refuge with the single one, the lord of *deva*s. If one offers
a flower or a single leaf at your feet, one is freed from the

bonds of the universe. Large numbers of *siddha*s and *yogi*s remember your two feet and through your favours, all their sins are destroyed. You are devoid of any differences. Unblemished, you are established inside the heart. You are the infinite origin. You alone are immobile. You are the supreme truth. You go everywhere. You are spoken of as the place that has no beginning, no middle and no end. You are the eternal origin from which all this is generated. O Vishveshvara! O Shiva! You are spoken of as truth in your powers. OUM! I prostrate myself before the swift and three-eyed Nilakantha. I constantly prostrate myself before Mahadeva. I prostrate myself before Ishana. I prostrate myself before Pinaki. I prostrate myself before the one with the shaven head, the one with the staff. I prostrate myself before the one who has the *vajra* in his hand, Kapardi, who wears the directions as a garment. I prostrate myself before the one whose roar is terrible, the one who is fanged in the form of Kala. I prostrate myself before the one whose sacred thread is a serpent, whose seed is the fire. I prostrate myself before Girisha. I prostrate myself before the one who is the sound of *svaha*. I prostrate myself before the one who laughs uproariously. I prostrate myself before the terrible one. I bow down. I prostrate myself before the one who destroyed Kama. I prostrate myself before the one who crushed Kala. I prostrate myself before the one who has the garb of Bhairava, Hara, who holds the bow. I prostrate myself before Tryambaka.[1254] I prostrate myself before Krittivasa. I prostrate myself before Ambikaa's lord. I prostrate myself before Pashupati. I prostrate myself before the one who has a form as space. I prostrate myself before the lord of space. You are the one with a body as a man

---

[1254] One with three eyes.

and a woman. You are the exponent of *samkhya* and *yoga*.
I prostrate myself before Bhairava's lord. Your *lingam* is
followed by the *deva*s. I prostrate myself before Kumara's
guru, the lord of *deva*s. I prostrate myself before the lord
of sacrifices. I prostrate myself before the one who is a
brahmachari. You are the great hunter of deer. I prostrate
myself before Brahma's lord. I prostrate myself before
Hamsa. I prostrate myself before the one who confounds
the universe. I bow down. You are a *yogi*, who can be
reached through *yoga*. I prostrate myself before the one
who is the *maya* of *yoga*. I prostrate myself before the one
who protects *prana*, the one who loves the sound of bells.
I prostrate myself before Kapali. I prostrate myself before
the lord of luminous bodies. I prostrate myself before you.
I bow down. I prostrate myself before you again. I bow
down. O Parameshvara! Please grant me every desire that
there is in my mind." In this way, Madhava devoutly
praised the lord of *deva*s. O *brahmana*s! Like a rod, he fell
at the feet of the divinity and Devi.'

'Along with Umaa, Bhagavan raised Krishna, the slayer
of Keshi. He addressed him in sweet words, with a sound
resembling the rumbling of clouds. "O Pundarikaksha!
Why are you tormenting yourself through these austerities?
You are the one who grants everyone desires and *karma* in
this world. Indeed, you are my supreme form, known as
Narayana. O Purushottama! Without you, nothing in the
universe can exist. O Narayana! O Keshava! Through your
own *yoga*, you know the infinite *atman*, Parameshvara
Mahadeva, the great *yogi*." Hearing his words, Krishna
glanced towards Vrishadhvaja, the lord of the universe,
and Devi, the daughter of the mountain. He smiled and
said, "O Shankara! Through your own *yoga*, you know
everything. O Shankara! I desire a son who is my equal.

Please grant this to a devotee." Pleased in his mind, Hara, whose *atman* is in the universe, agreed to this. He glanced towards Devi Girijaa and embraced Keshava. Devi, the daughter of the snow-clad Indra among mountains, the mother of the universe who is half of Shankara's body, spoke to Hrishikesha. "O infinite one! O Achyuta! O Keshava! I know that you always possess single-minded devotion towards Ishvara and me, not towards anyone else. You are Narayana Purushottama, who is directly in all *atman*s. Since the *deva*s requested you earlier, you have been born as Devaki's son. Now behold your *atman* in the *atman* and in my *atman*. There is no difference between us. The wise see us as one. O Keshava! Accept these desired boons from me—knowledge of everything, prosperity and *jnana* about Parameshvara. You will possess unwavering devotion towards Ishvara and supreme strength." Mahadevi spoke to Krishna Janardana in this way. He lowered his head and accepted Devi's command. Ishvara also agreed to this. Along with Devi, Bhagavan Isha, the lord of the *deva*s, grasped Krishna by the hand. Worshipped by sages and lords among gods, Girisha took him to Mount Kailasa.'

Chapter 26(1)(26) (Origin of the *lingam*)

Suta said, 'Along with Umaa and Keshava, Bhagavan Maheshvara entered the golden-hued Kailasa, on Meru's summit, and sported there. The residents of Mount Kailasa saw the great-souled one. They worshipped Achyuta Krishna like the lord of the *deva*s. He possessed four arms and large limbs. His sheen was like that of a dark

cloud. He wore a crown and the Sharnga bow was in his
hand. The Shrivatsa mark was on his chest. His arms were
long, and his eyes were large. Achyuta was clad in yellow
garments. On his chest, there was an excellent Vaijayanti
garland.[1255] Along with Devi Shri, he was radiant. He was
young and extremely delicate. His feet were like lotuses.
His eyes were like lotuses. He smiled and was the one who
bestowed a virtuous destination.'

'On one occasion, the one who enhanced Devaki's
lineage was sporting in the caves in the mountain. Along
with Shri, Krishna wandered around, radiant. On seeing
the one who pervades the universe, *gandharva*s, *apsara*s,
all the foremost daughters of *naga*s, *siddha*s, *yaksha*s and
*deva*s were filled with great wonder. Their eyes dilated
in joy. They showered down flowers on the great-souled
one's head. Daughters of *gandharva*s and divine supreme
*apsara*s, wearing pure ornaments, glanced at Krishna and
praised him. Some, accomplished in singing, sang many
kinds of songs. They glanced at Devaki's handsomeness
and were overwhelmed with desire. Seeking to entice him,
many danced in front of him. Some glanced at his smiling
face and drank the *amrita* from there. Some maidens took
off the excellent ornaments from their own limbs and
offered these ornaments to Krishna, who was an ornament
of the worlds. Some took the excellent ornaments from his
limbs and adorned themselves with these. Some adorned
Madhava with their own ornaments. Full of desire, one
approached near Krishna. Charmed, with eyes like those
of a doe, she kissed his lotus-face. Another was deluded
by the *maya* of the origin of the worlds. She clasped

[1255] Vishnu's necklace/garland, made out of pearls, rubies,
emeralds, blue sapphires and diamonds.

Govinda by the hand and took him to her own house.
Assuming many kinds of forms, Bhagavan, the lotus-eyed
Krishna, playfully satisfied all their desires. In this way, the
handsome Hari Narayana, who deludes the universe with
his *maya*, amused himself for a long period of time in the
city of the lord of *deva*s.'

'When many days passed, the residents of Dvaravati[1256]
suffered. Separated from Govinda, the people were scared.
Suparna had forcefully been released earlier. Searching
for Krishna's trail, he went to Mount Himalaya. Unable
to see Govinda there, he prostrated his head before sage
Upamanyu and returned to the city of Dvaravati again.
Meanwhile, great *daitya*s and extremely terrible *rakshasa*s
arrived at the fair city of Dvaraka in thousands and
caused terror. Suparna was strong, Krishna's equal in
valour. He killed them in a great battle and protected the
fair city. Meanwhile, the illustrious *rishi*, Narada, went
to the summit of Kailasa and saw Krishna there. When
rishi Narada went to Dvaravati, all the residents saw him
and asked, "Where is our protector, Bhagavan Narayana
Hari?" He told them, "The great *yogi*, Bhagavan Hari is
now amusing himself on the summit of Kailasa. I have
come here after seeing him there." O *brahmana*s! Hearing
his words, Suparna, the excellent bird, travelled to Kailasa,
the excellent mountain, through the sky. He saw Devaki's
son in a residence studded with jewels and saw Govinda
Hari seated on a seat, near the lord of the *deva*s. In every
direction, immortals and divine women were worshipping
him. He was surrounded by Mahadeva's *gana*s, *siddha*s
and *yogi*s. Like a rod on the ground, Suparna prostrated
himself before Shankara Shiva. He informed Hari about

[1256]Also known as Dvaraka.

what was happening in the city of Dvaraka. Prostrating
his head before Shankara Nilalohita, Krishna took Hara's
permission and ascending Kashyapa's son,[1257] left for the
city. He was honoured by large numbers of women and
Madhusudana honoured them back in words that were as
sweet as *amrita*. The best among *gandharva*s and *apsara*s
saw that the slayer of enemies was leaving. They followed
the great *yogi*, the one who holds a conch shell a *chakra*
and a mace. Hari, whose *atman* is in the universe, took his
leave of the women.'

'Govinda quickly went to the divine city of Dvaravati.
O lords among sages! When the divinity, the enemy of the
*asura*s, left, the women faded, like the night without the
moon. Hearing the excellent news about Krishna's return,
the residents quickly decorated the divine and auspicious
city of Dvaravati. There were large flags and inside and
outside, they arranged for standards. The people adorned
the beautiful city with garlands. They played sweet tones
on many kinds of musical instruments. Thousands of conch
shells were blown and *veena*s were sounded. As soon as
Govinda entered the auspicious city of Dvaravati, the
women, adorned with youth, sang sweet songs. Standing on
the tops of mansions, they saw the lord and danced. They
showered down flowers on Vasudeva's son. To the sound
of auspicious benedictions, Bhagavan Krishna entered.
Attended by the queens, the great *yogi* was resplendent on
an excellent seat. In an extremely beautiful and sparkling
pavilion, he was surrounded by Shankha and others.[1258]
He was surrounded by his sons and thousands of foremost

[1257] Garuda.
[1258] It is not clear who this Shankha is, probably the *rishi* who
was *rishi* Likhita's brother.

women. On that beautiful and excellent seat, Achyuta was
with Jambavati. He was as radiant as the divinity, when he
is with Devi Umaa. O *dvija*s! To see the undecaying cause
of the worlds, *deva*s, *gandharva*s and *maharshi*s arrived
there. There were also Markandeya and others, those
who had been born earlier. When Bhagavan Krishna saw
Markandeya arrive, he lowered his head in prostration.
Hari offered him his own seat. Along with his followers, he
honoured and prostrated himself before the large number
of *rishi*s. Hari gave them whatever they wished for and
took his leave from them.'

'It was midday. Hari, the lord of *deva*s, bathed and
wore white garments. He joined his hands in salutation
and worshipped Bhanu. Using many kinds of *mantra*s, he
glanced towards Divakara[1259] and performed *japa*. The
lord of *deva*s offered oblations to *deva*s, large numbers of
ancestors and sages. Along with Markandeya, he entered
the divinity's residence.[1260] He worshipped the *lingam* of
the lord of *bhuta*s, whose ornaments are *bhasma*. The
one who controls men controlled himself and observed
all the *niyama*s. He fed the excellent sage and worshipped
*brahmana*s. O Indras among *brahmana*s! He himself
performed *yoga*. Surrounded by his sons and along with
Markandeya, Achyuta conversed about the sacred accounts
of the Puranas. The great sage, Markandeya, saw all the
rites that he had completed. Smiling, he addressed Krishna
in sweet words. Markandeya asked, "Through these
auspicious rites, which divinity did you worship? Please
tell me. You are the one who is worshipped through rites.
*Yogi*s meditated on you. You are the supreme *brahman*,

[1259] The maker of the day, Surya.
[1260] That is, the temple.

the unblemished destination of *nirvana*. O lord! For the sake of reducing the earth's burden, you have been born in the Vrishni lineage." At this, the mighty-armed Krishna, supreme among those who know about the *brahman*, replied.'

'While all his sons heard, he seemed to smile as he spoke. Shri Bhagavan said, "There is no doubt that everything you have said is the truth. Nevertheless, I worship the eternal divinity, Ishana. O *brahmana*s! No task exists for him. Nor is there anything I need to obtain.[1261] Nevertheless, since I know the supreme Shiva, I worship Isha. People who are deluded by *maya* do not see the divinity. Therefore, I worship Isha, indicating that he is the root cause behind me. There is nothing as sacred in the world as worshipping the *lingam*. It destroys calamities. Those who desire the welfare of the worlds must worship Shiva in the form of the *lingam*. People who know about the utterances of the *Veda*s say that the *lingam* is my form. Therefore, when I worship Ishana, it is as if I am worshipping myself. I am his supreme form. There is no doubt that I permeate him. The *Veda*s state that there is certainly no difference between the two of us. Those who are sacred of *samsara* should know that the *lingam* is Maheshvara. The divinity, Mahadeva, must always be worshipped through sacrifices. He must be worshipped and revered." Markandeya asked, "O best among gods! What is the *lingam*? Who is worshipped in the form of the *lingam*? O Krishna! O large-eyed one! Please tell us about this excellent mystery."'

'Shri Bhagavan replied, "The *lingam* is spoken of as the unmanifest. This is bliss and imperishable illumination. The *Veda*s speak of the imperishable divinity, Maheshvara,

---

[1261] Reminiscent of parts of *Bhagavat Gita* 3.22.

as the one who has a *lingam*. Earlier, everything mobile
and immobile was destroyed in a terrible single ocean
of water. To kindle understanding in Brahma and me,
the great Shiva manifested himself. Since that time,
desiring the welfare of the worlds, Brahma and I have
constantly worshipped Mahadeva." Markandeya asked,
"Earlier, to kindle understanding, how did Ishvara, the
supreme destination, manifest himself in the form of the
lingam? O Krishna! You should speak about it now."
Shri Bhagavan replied, "There was a single and terrible
ocean of water. There were no divisions, and it was full
of darkness. I was there, in that single ocean of water,
holding a conch shell a *chakra* and a mace. I possessed
one thousand heads, one thousand eyes, one thousand feet
and one thousand hands. I was the eternal Purusha, who
was lying down. At the time, not very far away, I saw a
Purusha who was infinite in radiance. He was resplendent,
surrounded by prosperity, and resembled one crore suns.
He had four faces. This was the great *yogi* and lord, the
cause. The divinity was clad in black antelope-skin and
Rig, *Yajur* and *Sama* hymns praised him. In an instant,
the best among those who know about *yoga*, reached me.
The immensely radiant Brahma smiled and spoke to me.
"Who are you? Where have you come from? Why are you
stationed here? O lord! Please tell me. I am Svayambhu,
the great grandfather and the creator of the worlds."
Thus addressed by Brahma, I answered him in these
words. "Repeatedly, I am the creator and destroyer of
the worlds." Because of Parameshthi's *maya*, the debate
continued. To kindle understanding, the supreme *lingam*,
with Shiva in the *atman*, manifested itself. It dazzled like
the fire of destruction. There were garlands of flames. It
was devoid of increase or decrease. It was devoid of a

beginning, a middle and an end. Bhagavan Aja told me,
"You quickly go downwards. I will go upwards. Let us
know its limits." Having contracted this agreement, we
swiftly went downwards and upwards. But the grandfather
and I could not ascertain the limits. We assembled again.
We were overwhelmed by wonder and fear, deluded
by the *maya* of the divinity who wields the trident. We
performed *dhyana* on the lord of the universe. We loudly
chanted OUMKARA, the supreme *akshara*. We joined our
hands in salutation and praised the supreme Shambhu.
Brahma and Vishnu said, "O Shambhu! You are without
a beginning and without a cause. You are the physician for
the disease of *samsara*. I prostrate myself before the serene
Shiva, the *brahman* who has the form of the *lingam*. You
are established in this ocean of dissolution. You are the
cause behind dissolution and creation. I prostrate myself
before the serene Shiva, the *brahman* who has the form
of the *lingam*. You resemble a garland of flames. You
are in the form of a blazing column. I prostrate myself
before the serene Shiva, the *brahman* who has the form of
the *lingam*. You are devoid of a beginning, a middle and
an end. Your natural form is that of sparkling radiance.
I prostrate myself before the infinite Shiva, the *brahman*
who has the form of the *lingam*. You are the lord of
Pradhana and Purusha. You are the creator, in the form
of space. I prostrate myself before the serene Shiva, the
brahman who has the form of the *lingam*. You are without
transformations. You are truth. You are always unmatched
in energy. Your form is the essence of *Vedanta*. I prostrate
myself before the one whose form is Kala. I prostrate
myself before the serene Shiva, the *brahman* who has the
form of the *lingam*." Praised in this way, Maheshvara
manifested himself. The shining divinity, the great *yogi*,

was as resplendent as one crore suns. Thousands of crores of mouths seemed to devour up the sky. There were one thousand hands and one thousand feet. The sun, the moon and the fire were his eyes. Bhagavan held Pinaka in his hand. Krittivasa wielded the trident. A serpent constituted his sacred thread. His voice resembled that of the cloud, or a drum. Mahadeva said, "O excellent gods! I am pleased. Look at me, Mahadeva, and be free of all your fears. Earlier, you two, eternal ones, originated from my limbs. Brahma, the grandfather of the worlds, is my right flank. Vishnu, the preserver, is my left flank. Hara is in my heart. I am pleased with the two of you. I will grant you the proper boons you desire." Saying this, Mahadeva Shiva himself embraced me, the divinity, and Brahma, the divinity. He glanced at us with favourable eyes. Delighted in our minds, we prostrated ourselves before Maheshvara. Narayana and the grandfather glanced towards his face and spoke. "O divinity Maheshvara! If you are pleased with us and if we deserved to be granted boons, let it be such that we always possess devotion towards you." At this, Bhagavan Isha smiled. Delighted and with a cheerful mind, Parameshvara Mahadeva spoke to me. The lord of *deva*s said, "O lord of the earth! You are the cause behind creation, preservation and dissolution. O child! O child Hari! Preserve the universe, with the mobile and immobile entities. O Vishnu! I am divided into three parts and am known as Brahma, Vishnu and Hara. I am *nirguna* and without blemish, but assume *guna*s for creation, preservation and dissolution. O Vishnu! Cast aside this delusion and protect the grandfather. This eternal Bhagavan will become your son. At the beginning of the *kalpa*, I will assume the form of a god and will emerge from your face, with a trident in my hand.[1262] I will become your son, originating from your rage." O excellent sage! Mahadeva spoke to Brahma in this way. Showing his favours to me and the divinity, he vanished from the spot. Since then, the worship of the *lingam* has been properly established in the worlds. O *brahmana*! This is known as *lingam*, because it is the supreme form of the *brahman*. O unblemished one! I have thus spoken to you about the greatness of the *lingam*. Those who know about *yoga* understand this, but not *deva*s and *danava*s. This is supreme and unmanifest *jnana*, described as Shiva. Those with the insight of *jnana* can see the subtle and unthinkable one. Therefore, we always prostrate ourselves before Bhagavan. He is the divinity Mahadeva, the lord of *deva*s and of Bhringi. I prostrate myself before the secret of the *Veda*s. I prostrate myself before Nilakantha. I prostrate myself before the terrible one, the serene one, before the cause, Sthanu. He is the *brahman*. He is Vamadeva. He is three-eyed and the greatest. You should constantly prostrate your before Shankara, Mahesha, Girisha, Shiva and perform *dhyana* on Maheshvara. Within a short period of time, you will then be raised up from this ocean of *samsara*." In this way, the bull among sages was instructed by Vaasudeva. In his mind, he approached the divinity Ishana, who faces every direction. The great sage prostrated his head and took his leave from Krishna. He then went to his desired Shambhu, the lord of the *deva*s who wields the trident.'

'If a person constantly makes heard this excellent chapter about the *lingam*, if he hears or reads it, he is freed from all sins. O Indras among *brahmana*s! Even if he hears it only once, the good merits are like those of Vaasudeva

---

[1262]This is addressed to Brahma.

performing excellent austerities. Such a man is freed from sins. If a person constantly performs *japa* with this night and day, he obtains greatness in Brahma's world. The great *yogi*, the lord Krishna Dvaipayana, said this.'

Chapter 27(1)(27) (Krishna's departure)

Suta said, 'Krishna obtained a boon from Maheshvara and through Jambavati, had the great-souled Samba as a son, who was the best among his sons. The immensely strong Aniruddha was Pradyumna's son. Both possessed qualities and both were like two other Krishnas. Having killed Kamsa, Naraka and hundreds of *asura*s, having defeated Shakra in his pastimes, having conquered the great *asura* Bana and having established eternal *dharma* in the world and the entire universe, Narayana's excellent intelligence made up his mind to return to his own abode. Meanwhile, *brahmana*s, Bhrigu and others, came to Dvaraka to see the eternal lord Krishna, who had accomplished his objective. The one whose *atman* is in the universe prostrated himself and worshipped them. Seated comfortably on a seat, along with Rama, the intelligent one spoke to them. "I will go to my own supreme abode, described as that of Vishnu. I have accomplished all tasks. O lords among sages! Be pleased and allow me. The terrible and inauspicious *kali yuga* has now presented itself. All the people will follow sin. You should propagate *vijnana* among the ignorant, so that it is beneficial for them. O excellent *dvija*s! That way, they will be freed from the sins caused by *kali*. If people who are devoted to Purushottama remember me, the lord, even once during *kali*, their sins are destroyed. *Dvija*s who constantly and devoutly worship me during *kali yuga*, following the rules indicated in the *Veda*s, they proceed to that destination. Thousands of *brahmana*s will be born in your lineages. In *kali yuga*, they will possess devotion towards Narayana. People who are devoted to Narayana reach the greater than the greatest. Those who hate Maheshvara do not go there. For those who criticize Maheshvara, their *dhyana*, *yoga*, tormenting through austerities, *jnana* and sacrifices and other rites are swiftly destroyed. If a person single-mindedly worships me constantly, full of unwavering sentiments, but criticizes the divinity Ishana, he goes to hell for ten thousand years. O *dvija*s! Therefore, criticism of Pashupati must be avoided. My devotee should make every effort to do this, in thoughts, words and deeds. O excellent *dvija*s! There were those who were cursed by Dadhicha at the time of Daksha's sacrifice. When they are born in *kali yoga*, devotees must make efforts to shun them. There are those who hated the divinity Ishana and have been born in your lineages on earth. They were cursed by Goutama. Excellent *dvija*s must not converse with them." Thus addressed by Krishna, all the *maharshi*s said, "OUM". Those excellent ones swiftly left for their own abodes. Narayana Krishna pervades the universe. In his pastimes, he completely withdrew his own lineage and proceeded to the supreme destination. The lineage of kings has been properly described, briefly. It is impossible to describe it in detail. What else do you wish to hear? If a person reads or hears this auspicious narration of lineages, he is freed from all sins and obtains greatness in the world of heaven.'

Chapter 28(1)(28) (Partha meets Vyasa)

The *rishi*s said, 'O Suta! The four *yuga*s are *krita*, *treta*, *dvapara* and *kali*. Please tell us briefly about their powers.'

Suta answered, 'Narayana Krishna left for his own supreme destination. Pandava Partha, the scorcher of enemies who was extremely devoted to *dharma*, was engulfed by great grief and performed the subsequent rites.[1263] As he was proceeding, he saw the sage, Krishna Dvaipayana. The one who spoke about the *brahman* was surrounded by his *shishya*s and by disciples of the *shishya*s. Abandoning his grief, Arjuna prostrated himself like a rod on the ground. Full of great joy, he asked, "O great sage! Where have you come from now? O lord! Towards what region are you proceeding in a hurry? On seeing you, my extensive grief has gone away. O one with eyes like a lotus! Please tell me what I should do now." The great *yogi* and sage, Krishna Dvaipayana, sat down on the banks of a river. Surrounded by his *shishya*s, he spoke.'

Chapter 29(1)(29) (Description of *yuga*s)

Vyasa said, 'O Pandu's descendant! The terrible *kali yuga* has now presented itself. Therefore, I am going to the divinity's auspicious city, Varanasi. In this terrible *kali yuga*, people will follow sin. O mighty-armed one! They will be devoid of *varna*s and *ashrama*s. In *kali yuga*, I do

---

[1263] Since everyone else had died, Arjuna performed Krishna's funeral rites.

not see any *prayashchitta* and any means for creatures to pacify all sins other than liberation in the city of Varanasi. In each of *krita*, *treta* and *dvapara*, there are great-souled ones who are devoted to *dharma* and are truthful in speech. You are famous in the worlds for your fortitude and are loved by people. Now observe your own supreme *dharma* and you will be freed from fear.'

Suta continued, 'Partha, the conqueror of enemy cities, was addressed by the illustrious one in this way. O excellent *dvija*s! He prostrated himself and asked about the *dharma* of *yuga*s. The sage, Satyavati's son, told him everything about the eternal *dharma* of *yuga*s, after prostrating himself before the divinity, Ishana.'

Vyasa said, 'O lord of men! I will briefly describe the *dharma* of *yuga*s. O king! I am incapable of describing it in detail. The learned say that the first *yuga* is known as *krita yuga*. After that, there is *treta yuga*. O Partha! The third is *dvapara* and the fourth is said to be *kali*. For *krita yuga*, there is said to be *dhyana* and austerities. For *treta*, it is said to be *jnana*. In *dvapara*, it is said to be sacrifices. In *kali yuga*, it is donations alone. Brahma is the divinity for *krita yuga*. For *treta*, it is Bhagavan Ravi. For *dvapara*, the divinity is Vishnu. For *kali*, the divinity is Maheshvara. Brahma, Vishnu and Surya—all these are worshipped in *kali* too. Bhagavan Rudra, the wielder of Pinaka, is worshipped in all four. In the first *yuga* of *krita*, *dharma* is said to possess four feet. There are three feet in *treta yuga* and only two feet remain in *dvapara*. Devoid of three feet, only the bare essence remains in *kali*. In *krita yuga*, beings originated through couples, but without any direct desire in mind. All the *praja*s were always content. They enjoyed every kind of happiness. O conqueror of cities! There were no distinctions between them, no inferior or superior.

In *krita yuga*, they were equal in happiness, beauty and lifespans. They were devoid of grief and generally devoted to the truth. In general, they preferred solitude. They were devoted to *dhyana* and devoted to austerities. They were devoted to Mahadeva. The conduct was bereft of desire, and they were always cheerful in their minds. O scorcher of enemies! They resided in mountains and oceans and were without any fixed abodes.'

'O *dvija*s![1264] With the progress of time, in the *yuga* known as *treta*, taste and pleasure were destroyed. When that kind of *siddhi* was destroyed, another kind of *siddhi* resulted. The happiness that resulted from the flow of waters was obstructed. However, it started to flow from clouds. With the thundering of clouds, rain was generated. Even when it rained once on the surface of the earth, trees materialized from it, and these were known as homes.[1265] Everything that they needed was generated from the trees. At the onset of *treta yuga*, this was how *praja*s maintained themselves. After a long period of time, they faced a catastrophe. Suddenly, their sentiments were overwhelmed by anger and avarice. As a result of time, there was an aberration in sentiments. All the trees, described as homes, were destroyed. When these were destroyed, those who originated through copulation were bewildered. They meditated on *siddhi* and meditated on the truth. At this, the trees, described as homes, appeared again. These yielded garments, fruits and ornaments. It was from these that honey, not resulting from bees, was generated in every cup. It possessed fragrance, colour and taste and was full

---

[1264]This doesn't belong, since Arjuna is being addressed. But the entire conversation is being repeated by the Suta.
[1265]Humans lived on trees.

of great energy. At the onset of *treta yuga*, *praja*s subsisted
on this. They were happy and content. Because of this
siddhi, all of them were devoid of anxiety. After some time
had elapsed, they were again overcome with greed. They
forcibly seized honey from trees and from bees. As a result
of their wicked conduct and since they were again overcome
by avarice, here and there, some *kalpavriksha*[1266] were
destroyed, along with the honey. They suffered terribly
from cold, rain and heat and were extremely miserable.
Suffering from the opposite pairs of sentiments,[1267] they
devised coverings for themselves. Having countered the
opposite pairs of sentiments, they thought of a means
of subsistence. At the time, the *kalpavriksha*s had been
destroyed, along with the honey. In *treta yuga*, another
kind of *siddhi* again presented itself. There was another
kind of means of subsistence. It rained, without wishing
for it. The rainwater flowed downwards and resulted in
rivers. In different places, the rain led to flows of water
that proceeded downwards. When there was a lot of water,
there was food on the surface of the earth. When water
came into contact with the ground, herbs resulted. Without
being tilled and without being sown, fourteen types of
village and forest crops resulted.[1268] Seasonal flowers and
fruits and trees and shrubs originated. But at the time, anger
and avarice resulted everywhere. This was the inevitable

[1266] A *kalpavriksha* is a tree that bestows everything desired.

[1267] In this context, heat and cold.

[1268] The usual list of seven village crops is paddy, barley,
wheat, millet, sesamum, saffron and fine pulses. The usual list of
seven forest/wild crops is *shyamaka*, wild paddy, wild sesamum,
gavedhuka, *kuruvinda*, *markataka* and bamboo. *Shyamaka* and
markataka are kinds of grain, *gavedhuka* and *kuruvinda* are species
of grass.

consequence, as they came under the subjugation of *treta yuga*. Therefore, they seized rivers, fields and mountains. According to strength, they seized trees, shrubs and herbs. Because of this transgression, the herbs entered the earth. Engaged by the grandfather, Prithu milked the earth. But, senseless with rage, they seized all these from each other. As a result of this use of force and because of the force of time, good conduct was destroyed. Knowing this, Bhagavan Aja wanted to establish ordinances for the welfare of *brahmana*s. Brahma created *kshatriya*s. In *treta*, the lord created the system of *varna*s and *ashrama*s. He instituted a system of sacrifices, but without violence being caused to animals.'

'In *dvapara*, among men, there were differences in views. As a result of anger and greed, they made up their minds to fight. The single *Veda*, with four parts, was thought of as being divided into three. At the beginning of every *dvapara yuga*, Vedavyases classify the *Veda*s into four. Because of confusion in insight, sons of *rishi*s again divide the *Veda*s. They classify *mantra*s and Brahmanas,[1269] with changes in sounds and letters. The supreme *rishi*s speak about the *Rig*, *Yajur* and *Sama Veda*s. O one excellent in vows! Here and there, as a result of general differences in insight, *Brahmana*s, *kalpasutra*s,[1270] sayings about the *brahman*, Itihasa, Puranas and *dharmashastra*s resulted. There were drought, death and other calamities. As a result of taints in thoughts, words and deeds, indifference resulted among men. Because of this indifference, they reflected on liberation from miseries. The reflection led to non-attachment and non-attachment led to insight about

[1269] The Brahmana texts.
[1270] Texts on rituals for sacrifices.

taints. Insight about taints led to the generation of *jnana* in *dvapara*. O *dvijas*![1271] Conduct in *dvapara* was full of *rajas* and *tamas*. In the beginning, *dharma* existed in *krita* and it continued in *treta*. It became agitated in *dvapara* and was destroyed in *kali yuga*.'

Chapter 30(1)(30) (Description of *kali yuga*)

Vyasa said, 'In *tishya*, men are constantly agitated by *tamas*. Suffering from *maya* and jealousy, they bring about the deaths of ascetics. In *kali*, diseases become epidemics and there is the constant fear of hunger. There is the terrible fear of drought and countries are devastated. People follow *adharma* and suffer from lack of food. They are extremely prone to rage and limited in energy. They utter falsehoods. Those born in *tishya* are greedy and bad *prajas*. The sacrifices are bad. The studies are bad. The conduct is bad. The *agama* texts are bad.[1272] Because of defects in rites performed by *brahmanas*, the subjects who are born are full of fear. *Dvijas* do not study the *Vedas*, nor do they perform sacrifices. Those who are limited in intelligence perform sacrifices and read the *Vedas*. *Shudras* utter *mantras* and have associations and alliances with *brahmanas*. In *kali yuga*, they lie down, eat and are seated together. Kings are generally *shudras* and obstruct *brahmanas*. Among kings, there will be the practice of foeticide and the slaying of heroes. *Dvijas* no longer undertake bathing, oblations, *japa*, donations, worship of

[1271] Suta is repeating the conversation.
[1272] *Nigama* texts are texts associated with the *Vedas*. *Agama* texts are traditional texts that are parallel to the *Vedas*.

*deva*s and other such rites. In *kali yuga*, people criticize Mahadeva, *brahmana*s, Purushottama, sacred traditions, *dharmashastra*s and Puranas. They undertake many rites not indicated in the *Veda*s. Among *brahmana*s, no interest is generated in their own *dharma*. People are wicked in conduct and are surrounded by futile heretics. People repeatedly seek from each other. When it is *kali yuga*, food is sold in habitations. Auspicious objects are sold at the crossroads. Women sell their hair. There are those known as *jina*s,[1273] displaying white teeth. They shave their heads and wear ochre garments. When the end of the *mahayuga* presents itself, *shudra*s practice *dharma*. There are those who steal the crops of others, even those who steal the garments of others. Thieves steal from thieves. Those who seize have their possessions seized. Others kill them. There is plenty of misery. Lifespans are short. Because of disease, bodies suffer. It is said that in *kali yuga*, conduct is immersed in *tamas* and is based on devotion to *adharma*. There are those clad in ochre and *nirgrantha*s and *kapalika*s.[1274] There are others who sell the *Veda*s and still others who sell *tirtha*s. Seeing *dvija*s seated, those who are limited in intelligence dislodge them. *Shudra*s, who earn their living from kings, strike Indras among *dvija*s. O scorcher of enemies! Amidst *dvija*s, *shudra*s occupy the higher seats. In *kali yuga*, because of their strength, kings dishonour *dvija*s. *Dvija*s are limited in learning, fortune and strength. They use flowers, ornaments and other auspicious objects to serve *shudra*s. O king! *Shudra*s do not even glance at excellent *dvija*s who deserve worship. Instead, they glance

[1273] A reference to Buddhism and Jainism.
[1274] *Nirgrantha* (unbound one) is a reference to Jain monks, *kapalika* is a reference to the outlier sect that bears skulls.

at *dvija*s stationed at the door, waiting to serve. *Brahmana*s serve and earn a living from *shudra*s. In *kali*, they praise and laud *shudra*s, seated on mounts and seats. Earning a living from *shudra*s, they teach *shudra*s the *Veda*s. In this way, when the *Veda*s lose meaning, they resort to terrible atheism.[1275] Excellent *dvija*s sell austerities, sacrifices and arts. There are hundreds and thousands of mendicants. They destroy their *dharma* and do not proceed to the destination. O lord of men! They sing ordinary songs to the *deva*s. In *kali yuga*, *brahmana*s and *kshatriya*s pursue left-handed paths and *pashupata* and *pancharatra* rites. When *jnana* and *karma* vanish in the world, there are no rites. Insects, rats and snakes harass humans. Earlier, at the time of Daksha's sacrifice, *dvija*s were burnt down by Devi's curse. They take birth in the families of *brahmana*s. Their minds are overwhelmed by darkness and they criticize Mahadeva. In *kali yuga*, at the end of the *mahayuga*, their pursuit of *dharma* is in vain. Amongst their own kin, *brahmana*s and all the others are regarded as heroes. There were others who were burnt down by the great-souled Goutama's curse. All of them are born in the wombs of *brahmana*s. They censure Hrishikesha and *brahmana*s who speak about the *brahman*. Vows that are outside the pale of the *Veda*s are observed. There is evil conduct and exertions are in vain. By indicating the fruits, all the people are deluded. With minds overwhelmed by darkness, worst among people follow the vows of cats.'[1276]

'In *kali*, Rudra Mahadeva is the supreme Ishvara for people. The lord of *deva*s is the means for men. For the

---

[1275] The word used is *nastikya*, which is non-belief rather than atheism.

[1276] Meaning, they are crooked and deceitful.

sake of establishing *shruti* and *smriti dharma* and desiring
the welfare of devotees, Shankara Nilalohita assumes
*avatara*s. He instructs *shishya*s about *jnana*, described
as the *brahman*. This is the essence of all *Vedanta*,
indicated in the *dharma* of the *Veda*s. These instructions,
instructions about their own *dharma*, are for all the
*varna*s. Pleased, they serve him in whatever way they can.
In this way, they conquer the taints of *kali* and proceed to
the supreme destination. *Kali* is tainted by many defects,
but has one great quality. With a little bit of effort, a
man can accumulate great good merits. Therefore, every
effort must be made to achieve unity with Maheshvara.
This is especially true of *brahmana*s. One should seek
refuge with Rudra Ishana. If a person prostrates himself
before Virupaksha Ishana Krittivasa, with a cheerful
mind, he proceeds to a supreme destination with Rudra.
If one prostrates oneself before Rudra, it is certain that
everything desired is obtained as fruits. If one prostrates
oneself before any other *deva*, only that specific fruit is
obtained. This is the way to cleanse the taints of *kali*. The
shruti texts have said that one should prostrate oneself
before Mahadeva and practice *dhyana* and donations.
Therefore, if one desires the supreme destination, one
should abandon all other *deva*s and seek refuge with
the divinity Maheshvara Virupaksha. For those who do
not worship Rudra Shiva, worshipped by the gods, their
donations, austerities and sacrifices, and even their lives,
are in vain. I prostrate myself before the great Rudra, the
lord of *deva*s, the one with the trident. I prostrate myself
before the three-eyed Tryambaka, the *guru* of *yogi*s. I
prostrate myself before Mahadeva the creator, the lord
of *deva*s, the eternal Shambhu Sthanu Shiva Parameshthi.
Along with Umaa, I prostrate myself before Rudra, the

great devourer, the cause. I seek refuge with Virupaksha, the refuge of *brahmacharis*. Mahadeva Ishana, Ambikaa's husband, is the great *yogi*. He is enveloped in the *maya* of *yoga*. He is the one who bestows *yoga* on *yogis*. He is the *guru* and *acharya* for *yogis*. Pinaki can be reached through *yoga*. Rudra is the one who enables one to cross over *samsara*. He is Brahma and he is Brahma's lord. He is eternal. He is serene and goes everywhere. He is devoted to *brahmanas* and is loved by *brahmanas*. Parameshvara Kapardi is without a form but has a form as Kala. He has a single form and a great form. The lord of the firmament can be known through the *Veda*s. He is Nilakantha, with the universe as his form. The seed of the universe pervades. He is the fire of destruction. He is the Kala that burns down. He bestows wishes. He is Kama's destroyer. I prostrate myself before the divinity Girisha, ornamented with the body of the moon. Parameshthi is extremely red, like the sun with a flickering tongue. He is the fierce and terrible Pashupati. He is Bhaskara. He is the supreme one who scorches.'

'Thus, the characteristics of the *yuga*s have been briefly described, for the past and the future, as long as the *manvantara*s remain. What is described as true of one *manvantara* is true of all the *manvantara*s. There is no doubt that this is true, from one *kalpa* to another *kalpa*. In all *manvantara*s, past and present, all those who take pride in their names and forms are similar.'

Suta continued, 'The illustrious one addressed Kiriti Shvetavahana in this way.[1277] He developed supreme and unwavering devotion towards Ishana. He prostrated

---

[1277] Kiriti (with the crown) and Shvetavahana (with white horses) are Arjuna's names.

himself before the *rishi*, the lord Krishna Dvaipayana, who knew everything and was directly established as a form of Vishnu, who undertakes everything. As Partha, the conqueror of enemy cities prostrated himself, the sage touched him with his hands. Vyasa spoke again. "You are blessed. There is no one else who has been as favoured as you. O conqueror of enemy cities! Indeed, in the three worlds, Shankara has no other devotee like you. You have seen the divinity whose eye is in every direction and who faces every direction. You alone, among everyone else, has seen Rudra who pervades everything in the universe. You have accurately understood the divine *jnana* about Ishvara. Cheerfully, the eternal Hrishikesha himself recounted that to you. Depart. Go to your own place. You should not grieve. With great devotion, seek refuge with Shiva, the refuge." Saying this, the illustrious lord showed his favours to Arjuna. So as to worship Bhava, he went to Shankara's city. Following his words, Pandava sought refuge with Shiva. Knowing about the supreme, he abandoned all other rites. There has not been, nor will there be, anyone equal to him in devotion and worship of Shambhu. Satyavati's son and Krishna, Devaki's son, said this. One should always prostrate oneself before the serene, intelligent and illustrious Vyasa, the infinitely energetic sage who was Parashara's son. Krishna Dvaipayana was the eternal Vishnu himself. Who else could know the truth about Rudra Parameshvara? Prostrate yourself before the *rishi* Krishna, Satyavati's son, the great-souled and undecaying Vishnu, the *yogi* who was Parashara's son. All the sages controlled themselves and heard this. They prostrated themselves before the great-souled Vyasa, Satyavati's son.'

Chapter 31(1)(31) (Varanasi's greatness)

The *rishi*s asked, 'After reaching the divine Varanasi, what did the immensely intelligent sage, Krishna Dvaipayana, wish to do? We are curious about that.'

Suta replied, 'Having reached the divine Varanasi, the great sage touched the water of Jahnavi and worshipped the divinity, Vishveshvara Shiva. On seeing that the sage had come, the sages who resided there worshipped Vyasa, bull among sages. All of them prostrated themselves and asked him about Mahadeva's sacred abode, which destroys sins, and about eternal *moksha dharma*. The illustrious rishi, who was omniscient, told them about the greatness of the lord of *deva*s and about the *dharma* indicated in the *Veda*s. In the midst of those Indras among sages, Vyasa's *shishya*, the great sage Jaimini, asked Vyasa about the mysterious meaning of what is eternal.'

Jaimini said, 'O illustrious one! O one who knows everything! You should dispel a doubt. Nothing is unknown to a supreme *rishi* like you. Some praise *dhyana*. Other people praise *dharma*. Others praise *samkhya* and *yoga*. Still other *maharshi*s praise austerities. Indeed, there are other *maharshi*s who speak about *brahmacharya*. Others praise non-violence and truth. Other learned ones praise *sannyasa*. Some praise compassion, donations and studying. Others praise visiting the *tirtha*s and restraint of the senses. O bull among sages! Please describe what is the best among these. If there is anything else that is a secret, you should speak about that too.'

Suta continued, 'Hearing Jaimini's words, the sage Krishna Dvaipayana prostrated himself before the one who has a bull on his banner and replied in a deep voice.'

The illustrious one replied, 'O immensely fortunate one! O sage! You have asked a praiseworthy question. I will describe the greatest secret among secrets. The other *maharshi*s can also listen. Earlier, Ishvara spoke about this eternal *jnana*. This secret is hated by those who aren't wise but loved by those who possess subtle insight. It should not be imparted to those who lack devotion, or to those who aren't Parameshthi's devotees. This excellent *jnana*, the best among all kinds of *jnana*, should not be imparted to those who do not know the *Veda*s. On the summit of Meru, Devi was seated on her divine seat and asked Mahadeva Ishana, Tripura's enemy. This is what she asked Mahadeva. Shri Devi said, "O lord of *deva*s! O Mahadeva! O one who destroys the afflictions of devotees! O divinity! Without any delay, how can a man see you? Is it *samkhya*, *yoga*, austerities, *dhyana*, *karma yoga*, or the *Veda*s? O Shankara! There are many other means, said to be easy and difficult. What is that through which the subtle Bhagavan can be seen by all those with bodies, whether their minds are confused, or whether they are *yogi*s who possess *vijnana*? This *jnana* is the greatest secret among secrets and is followed by Brahma and others. O one who destroyed Kama's limbs! For the welfare of all devotees, please describe it."'

Ishvara answered, 'This secret truth should not be spoken about to the ignorant, those who are outside the pale of *jnana*. I will tell you the exact truth, as stated by supreme *rishi*s. My city of Varanasi is a supreme and secret *kshetra*. It enables all beings to cross over the ocean of *samsara*. O Mahadevi! My great-souled devotees, those who resort to my *vrata*s and follow supreme *niyama*s, reside there. It is an excellent place and is the best among all *tirtha*s. This excellent *jnana* is *jnana* about my supreme

Avimukta.[1278] There are other sacred *tirtha*s and temples in other places, in heaven and on earth. All of them are present in this *shmashana*. My abode in the firmament is not in contact with the earth. Those who are not free cannot see it. Those who are free in their minds can see it. This famous place is described as *shmashana* and Avimukta. O beautiful one! Becoming Kala, it is from here that I destroy the universe. O Devi! This most secret of places is loved by me the most. When my devotees go there, they enter me. Donations, *japa*, oblations, sacrifices, tormenting through austerities, *dhyana*, studying, *jnana*—all these become imperishable there. There are thousands of sins committed in earlier births. As soon as one enters Avimukta, all those are destroyed. O one with the beautiful face! In the course of time, *brahmana*s, *kshatriya*s, *vaishya*s, *shudra*s, mixed *varna*s, women, *mleccha*s,[1279] those of inferior birth, those born as wicked species, insects, ants and other animals and birds may die in Avimukta. O Devi! Those who die in the city of the three-eyed Shiva, with the moon on the crest and the great bull as a mount, are born as humans. A sinner who dies in Avimukta never goes to hell. Thanks to Ishvara's favours, all of them proceed to the supreme destination. Knowing that it is very difficult to obtain *moksha* in this extremely terrible *samsara*, a man should strike his feet with stone[1280] and reside in Varanasi. O Parameshvari! It is extremely difficult for a being to achieve austerities. But for those who suffer, this is a place that frees from *samsara*. O daughter of the Indra among mountains!

[1278] Avimukta is another name for Kashi/Varanasi. *Smashana* means cremation-ground.

[1279] Barbarians, those who do not speak Sanskrit.

[1280] So that he cannot move.

This is because this place has my favours. Ignorant ones, those who are deluded by my *maya*, cannot see it. Foolish ones, enveloped in darkness, cannot see Avimukta. They repeatedly enter, in the midst of urine, excrement and semen.[1281] O Devi! Even if a person is struck by hundreds of impediments, once he enters there, he proceeds to the supreme destination. Having gone there, a person does not grieve. He goes to Shiva's supreme abode, free from birth, death and old age. This is the destination for those who desire *moksha*, for those who do not want to die again. A learned person thinks that having reached it, he has accomplished every objective. Through donations, austerities, sacrifices and learning, one does not obtain the best destination, obtained through Avimukta. The learned know that Avimukta is the best medication and the best atonement for those of different *varna*s, for those without *varna*s, *chandala*s[1282] and other condemned ones and for those whose bodies are full of sin. Avimukta is supreme *jnana*. Avimukta is the supreme destination. Avimukta is the supreme truth. Avimukta is the supreme Shiva. For faithful ones, who initiate themselves into the vow of residing in Avimukta, at the end, I grant them supreme *jnana* and the supreme destination. There are these sacred places that are famous in the three worlds—Prayaga, the sacred Naimisha, Shrishaila, Himalaya, Kedara, Bhadrakarna, Gaya, Pushkara, Kurukshetra, Rudrakoti, Narmada, Hatakeshvara, Shaligrama, Pushpagra, Vamsha, Kokamukha, Prabhasa, Vijayeshana, Gokarna and

---

[1281] That is, they are repeatedly born again and again.

[1282] *Chandala* has different nuances and a *chandala* is not necessarily a *shudra*. A *chandala* is also of mixed parentage, with a *shudra* father and a *brahmana* mother. More generally, *chandala*s are outcastes, while *shudra*s are within the caste fold.

Shankukarna. But those who die in Varanasi proceed to
the supreme *moksha*. In particular, Ganga has three flows
in Varanasi. As soon as one immerses oneself there, sins
committed in hundreds of births are destroyed. Elsewhere,
it is easy to bathe in the Ganga and perform *shraddha*s,
donations, *japa* and *vrata*s. But it is extremely rare that one
gets the opportunity to do these in Varanasi. Residing in
Varanasi, a man must always perform sacrifices, constantly
offer oblations, worship others and subsist on air. Even if
a man is a sinner, a deceitful person or one who is devoted
to *adharma*, once he reaches Varanasi, he purifies three
generations of his lineage. It is known that those who
praise and worship Mahadeva there are freed from all sins
and become *ganeshvara*s. Those who perform sacrifices,
pursue *jnana* or use *sannyasa* and other means in other
places and attain the supreme destination after thousands
of births. However, devotees who reside in the city of Isha,
the lord of *deva*s, obtain ultimate *moksha* in a single birth.
One need not go to any other hermitage. If one reaches
Avimukta, *yoga*, *jnana* and liberation are obtained in a
single birth. It is known as Avimukta because I have not
abandoned it.[1283] This is the greatest of all secrets. When
one knows this, one is liberated. O one with the excellent
eyebrows! There are those devoted to *jnana* and *dhyana*,
desiring supreme bliss. The destination determined for
them is obtained by a person who dies in Avimukta.
*Deva*s constantly speak about many other places that yield
liberation. However, the city of Varanasi is more auspicious
than all those places. When one gives up one's body there,
the imperishable Mahadeva Ishvara himself instructs about

[1283]The word *mukta* has several meanings. One of these is
abandoned. Since Shiva has not abandoned it, it is Avimukta.

taraka-brahman.[1284] That is the reason it is Avimukta. O Devi! There is a truth that is greater than the greatest. It is said that this is obtained in a single birth in Varanasi. That is the reason it is Avimukta. Avimukta is located between the eyebrows, the centre of the navel, the heart, the head and the sun.[1285] In that way, it is established in Varanasi. The city of Varanasi is between the rivers Varana and Asi. The truth of Avimukta is constantly established there. There has not been, nor will there be, a place that is superior to Varanasi. The divinity Narayana, Mahadeva, the lord of the firmament,[1286] *deva*s, *gandharva*s, *yaksha*s, *uraga*s and *rakshasa*s reside there. The grandfather, the lord of *deva*s, constantly worships me there. There are those who commit great sins and sinners who are even worse. Once they reach Varanasi, they attain the supreme destination. Therefore, those who desire liberation should constantly reside there, until death. O Mahadevi! Having obtained *jnana* in Varanasi, one is liberated. However, if the mind is overwhelmed by sins, there will be obstacles. Hence, one should not commit sins, in thoughts, words and deeds. O excellent *dvija*s![1287] This is the secret of the *Veda*s and the Puranas. Avimukta is the place for *jnana*. I do not know of anything that is superior.'

Suta continued, 'While *deva*s, *rishi*s and Parameshthi heard, the divinity told Devi this. It destroys all sins. Narayana Purushottama is the best among *deva*s. Girisha is the best among lords. Like that, this is the most excellent of places. Those who have worshipped Rudra in former

[1284] The *brahman* that enables one to cross over.
[1285] Here, the word Avimukta is being used in the sense of a focal point for liberation.
[1286] Surya.
[1287] Being repeated by Suta.

lives, obtain this supreme *kshetra* of Avimukta, Shiva's abode. Those whose minds suffer from the taints caused by *kali* are incapable of seeing Parameshthi's place. Those who constantly remember Kala attain this city. Their sins, in this world and in the next world, are swiftly destroyed. If those who make their homes here commit sins, in his form as Kala, Shiva destroys all of them. Those who desire liberation and come and reside in this place, once they die, they no longer suffer from birth and immersion in this ocean that is the world. Therefore, a man must make every effort to reside in Varanasi, whether he is a *yogi* or not a *yogi*, whether he has committed sins or performed auspicious deeds. If the mind turns towards a destination in Avimukta, the words of people or parents, or the words spoken by a *guru*, should not become a deterrent.' Saying this, the illustrious Vyasa, supreme among those who know the *Veda*s, went to Varanasi, with the best of his *shishya*s.

Chapter 32(1)(32) (Varanasi's greatness continued)

Suta said, 'Surrounded by his *shishya*s, the intelligent *guru*, the sage Dvaipayana, went to the large *lingam* of Omkara, which bestows emancipation.[1288] Along with his *shishya*s, the great sage worshipped Mahadeva there. He spoke about its greatness to the sages who had cleansed their *atman*s. "This sparkling and beautiful *lingam* is named Omkara. As soon as one remembers it, one is freed from all sins. Here, in Varanasi, who bestows liberation, the sages have always worshipped the excellent

[1288]This Omkareshvara *lingam* is in Varanasi, in the locality known as Machhodari (Matsyodari).

Panchayatana, the supreme *jnana*.[1289] Mahadeva is himself present in his five forms here. To bestow liberation on beings, Bhagavan Rudra sports here. Pashupata *jnana* is said to consist of five truths. All of these are established in the sparkling *lingam* of Omkara. These are *shantyatita*, *para-shanti*, *vidya*, *pratishtha* and *nivritti*. These are the five truths of Ishvara's *lingam*. The five *deva*s, Brahma and the others, find refuge here. It is said that one should understand the Omkara *lingam* to be Panchayatana. If one remembers Ishvara's undecaying Panchayatana *lingam*, after death, one enters supreme radiance and bliss. Earlier, *devarshi*s, *siddha*s and *brahmarshi*s worshipped the divinity Ishana here and obtained the supreme destination. This is an auspicious, sacred and most secret of places, on the banks of Matsyodari. O Indras among *brahmana*s! This is Ishvara's excellent Omkara *lingam*, only the size of a cow's hide. O excellent *dvija*s! The secret *lingam*s in Varanasi are the *lingam* of Krittivaseshvara, the excellent Madhyameshvara, Vishveshvara, Omkara and the excellent Kapardishvara." Saying this, Krishna, the great sage who was Parashara's son, went to see the divinity, the wielder of the trident, in Krittivaseshvara *lingam*.[1290] Along with his *shishya*s, he worshipped it. The illustrious one, supreme among those who know about the *brahman*, told the *brahmana*s about the greatness of Krittivasa. "Earlier,

---

[1289]Panchayatana is another name for the Omkareshvara *lingam*, where Shiva exists in his five (*pancha*) forms—*shantyatita* (beyond tranquillity), *para-shanti* (supreme tranquillity), *vidya* (knowledge), *pratishtha* (stability) and *nivritti*. The five *deva*s are Shiva, Parvati, Vishnu, Brahma and Surya.

[1290]This is now in the Daranagar area of Varanasi and the *lingam* is said to consist of the demon Gajasura's body. Gajasura is *asura* in the form of a *gaja* (elephant).

in this place, a *daitya* assumed the form of an elephant and
approached Bhava. He approached to kill the *brahmana*s
who always performed worship here. O best among *dvija*s!
Affectionate towards his devotees, to protect his devotees,
the three-eyed Mahadeva manifested himself from the
lingam. Toying, Hara used his trident to kill the *daitya*
in the form of an elephant. He used the hide to fashion
a garment for himself and thus became Krittivaseshvara.
O bulls among sages! Sages have obtained supreme *siddhi*
here. In their own physical bodies, they reached the
supreme destination. Those who are described as Vidyaas,
Vidyeshvaras, Rudras and Shivaas are always established
here, surrounding Krittivaseshvara *lingam*. There are
people who know that *kali yuga* is full of terrible and great
adharma. They do not leave Krittivasa and there is no
doubt that they are successful in their objectives. Liberation
may or may not be obtained in one thousand births. But
in Krittivasa, one obtains liberation in a single birth. It is
said that this place is the residence of all the *siddha*s. It is
protected by Mahadeva Shambhu, the lord of *deva*s. From
one *yuga* to another *yuga*, self-controlled *brahmana*s,
accomplished in the *Veda*s, have worshipped Mahadeva
here and performed *japa* with Shatarudriya. They have
constantly praised the divinity, Tryambaka Mahadeva. In
their hearts, they have constantly performed *dhyana* on
Sthanu Shiva, who is inside everyone. *Siddha*s have sung
songs about *brahmana*s who reside in Varanasi. Those who
sought refuge with Krittivasa have obtained emancipation
in a single birth. Birth in a family of *brahmana*s is desired
and is extremely rare in this world. Having obtained it,
mendicants have performed *dhyana* and *japa* on Rudra. In
their hearts, they have meditated on Mahesha. In the centre
of Varanasi, Indras among sages have worshipped the lord

Isha, the saviour. Devoid of desire, they have performed sacrifices and prostrating themselves before Shambhu, have praised Rudra. I prostrate myself before Bhava, the abode of unsullied sentiments. I seek refuge with the ancient Sthanu Girisha. I remember Rudra, established in my heart. I know that Mahadeva has many forms.'''

Chapter 33(1)(33) (Greatness of Kapardishvara)

Suta said, 'Having addressed the sages, the intelligent one went to see the undecaying Kapardishvara *lingam* of the lord of *deva*s, the wielder of the trident.[1291] O *dvija*s! Following the norms, he bathed in Pishachamochana *tirtha*, satisfied the ancestors and worshipped the wielder of the trident. Along with their *guru*, the sages witnessed a wonder there. Taking this to be indicative of the *kshetra*'s greatness, they prostrated themselves before Girisha Hara. A tiger, terrible in form, approached the excellent Kapardishvara, so as to devour a doe. Terrified in its heart, it performed *pradakshina*.[1292] Running around and extremely scared, it succumbed to the tiger. The extremely strong tiger tore it apart with its sharp claws. However, on seeing the lords among sages, it left for a desolate spot. The young doe fell dead, in front of Kapardishvara. They saw a great blaze in the firmament, like the sun in radiance. The radiance possessed three eyes and was blue

---

[1291] Kapardishvara *lingam* is in Pishachamochana *tirtha*, where a *pishacha* worshipped Shiva and was cleansed of his sins.

[1292] *Pradakshina* is much more specific than a mere act of circling. This circling or circumambulation has to be done in a specific way, so that the right side (*dakshina*) always faces what is being circled.

in the throat. He was marked by the moon on the crest.
He was astride a bull and was surrounded by men who
were just like him in appearance. From the sky, flowers
were showered down on his head. This was Ganeshvara
himself. But in a short instant, he could no longer be
seen. Witnessing this great wonder, the disciples, Jaimini
being the foremost, asked their undecaying *guru* about the
greatness of Kapardishvara. Seated in front of the divinity
and prostrating himself before Vrishadhvaja, the illustrious
one told them about the greatness of Kapardishvara.'

Vyasa said, 'If one resides in Varanasi and remembers
and worships Kapardishvara, torrents of sins, taints
like desire and anger and all kinds of impediments are
swiftly destroyed. Therefore, one should see the excellent
Kapardishvara. This is the divinity's excellent *lingam* of
Kapardishvara. One must make every effort to worship it
and praise it with hymns from the *Veda*s. If *yogi*s, serene
in their minds, constantly perform *dhyana* here, there is
no doubt that within six months, they obtain *siddhi* in
yoga. If one bathes in the pond of Pishachamochana and
performs worship here, sins like the killing of a *brahmana*
are destroyed. O *brahmana*s! Earlier, in this *kshetra*, there
was an ascetic who was firm in his vows. He was known
as Shankukarna and he worshipped the wielder of the
trident. With Pranava, which is Rudra's form, night and
day, he performed *japa* to Rudra. He used flowers, incense,
*stotram*s, prostrations and *pradakshina*. With *yoga* in his
atman, he faithfully initiated himself and resided there. On
one occasion, he saw that a hungry *preta* arrived there. His
emaciated limbs consisted of skin and bones and he was
sighing repeatedly. On seeing him, the best among sages
was filled with great compassion. He asked, "Who are you?
From what region have you come to his region?" Suffering

from hunger, the *pishacha* addressed him in these words. "In my earlier birth, I was a *brahmana* and possessed wealth and grain. I had sons and grandsons and was eager to maintain my family. I never worshipped *deva*s, cows or guests. I never performed a deed with merits, not even one that was a trifle. On one occasion, I saw Bhagavan Rudra, Ishvara Vishveshavara who rides on a bull, in Varanasi. I touched him and prostrated myself. Within a short period of time, I died. O sage! However, I did not see Yama's extremely terrible face. Instead, I obtained this kind of *pishacha* birth, where I suffer from hunger and thirst. I do not know what is beneficial and what is not. O lord! If you see any means of uplifting me, please do that. I prostrate myself before you. I seek refuge with you." Thus addressed, Shankukarna replied to the *pishacha*. "In this world, there is no one who has performed an excellent meritorious deed like you. You have already seen Bhagavan Vishveshvara Shiva. You have touched him and worshipped him. Who on earth is your equal? As a result of committing that pure act, you have come to this place. Control yourself and quickly bathe in that pond. You will then swiftly abandon this condemned birth." Thus addressed by the compassionate sage, the *pishacha* fixed his mind on the three-eyed Kapardishvara, the three-eyed Ishvara who is supreme among *deva*s and is the saviour. He immersed himself. When he immersed himself, he died in the sage's presence. He was seen in a *vimana* that resembled the sun, clad in divine ornaments and with a beautiful crest marked by the sign of the moon. He rose in the firmament, resplendent and surrounded by Rudras and immeasurable *yogi*s. He was like the *deva* Bhanu, the ultimate *deva*, when he rises surrounded by *valakhilya*s and others.[1293] In the firmament, *siddha*s and groups of *deva*s praised him and beautiful divine *apsara*s danced. *Gandharva*s, *vidyadhara*s, *kinnara*s and others showered down flowers, with bees buzzing around them. He obtained understanding through Bhagavan's favours and was praised by large numbers of Indras among sages. He entered the foremost disc,[1294] where Rudra, full of the three, is radiant. On seeing that the *pishacha* had been liberated, the sage was pleased in his mind. He thought of Mahesha Rudra, the best among the wise. He prostrated himself and praised Kapardi. Shankukarna said, "I constantly prostrate myself before the one who is greater than the greatest, the single ancient Purusha who is the protector. I seek refuge with Isha, the lord of *yoga*, the saviour, Aditya Agni, who is astride that large impenetrable mass. You are beyond the *brahman*. You are golden. You are without a beginning. You are established in the hearts of *yogi*s. I seek refuge with Rudra, the sacred and great sage, the supreme *brahman* who is in the firmament. You possess one thousand feet, eyes and heads. You possess one thousand arms and are beyond darkness. I prostrate myself before the three-eyed Shambhu, the lord of Hiranyagarbha, who is beyond the *brahman*. The universe originated in you. O Shiva! Everything will dissolve into you. O Bhagavan Isha! You are beyond the *brahman*. I constantly prostrate myself and seek refuge with you. You are without a *lingam*. You are without illumination. You are without a form. You are yourself the lord of consciousness. You are the single and unmatched

---

[1293]There are 60,000 *valakhilya rishi*s and they are as small as the thumb. They surround the sun's chariot.
[1294]The solar disc.

Rudra. I prostrate myself before Parameshvara, who is beyond Brahma. There is no one other than you. *Yogi*s who give up *sabija yoga* and achieve *samadhi*, merge with the *paramatman*.[1295] They see the divinity who is beyond the *brahman*. I constantly prostrate myself before that form of yours. There are no names there. There is no special kind of contentment. One is established like your own form, which is beyond the *brahman*. O Svayambhu! I constantly prostrate myself before you. I seek refuge with you. Those who are devoted to the *Veda*s and possess *vijnana* about the *brahman* know that form to be without differences. It is single and without a form. They perceive your single form alone, beyond the *brahman*. I constantly prostrate myself before that. I prostrate myself before your resplendent and great form as Kala, the ancient form from which Pradhana and Purusha emerged, and before which, the *deva*s prostrate themselves. I constantly seek refuge with Mahesha. I seek refuge with the ancient Sthanu Girshia. I seek refuge with Shiva Hara, with the moon on the crest. I seek refuge with Pinaki." Shankukarna praised Bhagavan Kapardin. He prostrated himself like a rod on the ground and uttered the auspicious Pranava. At that instant, the supreme *lingam*, with Shiva in it, manifested itself. This was without duality and was in the form of *jnana* and bliss. It resembled one crore fires of destruction. The sage Shankukarna's entire *atman* became spotless, and he merged into the sparkling *lingam*. It was extraordinary. I have described the mystery and greatness of Kapardi. Those immersed in *tamas* do not know it and even the learned are deluded. If a devotee constantly hears this account, which destroys sins, he is

---

[1295] *Sabija yoga* is *dhyana* with the support of a *bija* (seed) *mantra*. When this *bija* is no longer necessary, it becomes *nirbija*.

freed from sins and obtains Rudra's proximity. If a pure man constantly reads this great praise of the one who is beyond the *brahman*, in the morning, at mid-day and in the evening, he attains *yoga*. We will constantly reside here and see Kapardi, lord of *deva*s. We will constantly worship the three-eyed divinity.'

Suta concluded, 'Having said this, the immensely radiant and illustrious Vyasa resided there with his *shishya*s, engaged in *yoga* and worshipping Kapardi.'

Chapter 34(1)(34) (Greatness of Madhyameshvara)

Suta said, 'After residing near Kapardisha for a large number of years, the illustrious lord went to see Madhyamesha. The sacred Mandakini is there, frequented by a large number of *rishi*s. The sparkling water of the river was fit to be drunk. On seeing this, the sage was delighted. Along with the sages, the lord Dvaipayana, whose sentiments and *atman* were pure, glanced at it. He knew about the rules for bathing and bathed there. Satyavati's son worshipped Bhava, the origin of the worlds, with many kinds of flowers. Along with the foremost *shishya*s, he entered. In the proper way, he satisfied *deva*s, *rishi*s and a large number of ancestors. He worshipped Ishana Madhyameshvara, the wielder of the trident. There were serene followers of the Pashupata vow there, their limbs covered with *bhasma*. They had come to see Rudra Ishvara Madhyameshvara. Their minds were fixed on OUMKARA. They were devoted to studying the *Veda*s. They had matted hair, or shaven heads. Their sacred threads were pure. Some wore loincloths as garments. There were others without garments. They were devoted to *brahmacharya*. They were tranquil and self-controlled, devoted to *jnana*. On seeing Dvaipayana and his *shishya*s, the *brahmana*s, they surrounded the sage. They honoured him in the proper way and addressed him in these words. "O great sage! Who are you and where have you come from, along with your *shishya*s?" With their minds full of *dharma*, Paila and the other *shishya*s spoke to those *rishi*s. "This is Satyavati's son, the lord Krishna Dvaipayana. This is Vyasa, Hrishikesha himself. He is the one who separated the *Veda*s. This is the lord for whom the divinity Mahadeva, the wielder of the trident, became a son in his portion, named Shuka. In every possible sentiment, he is like Mahadeva Shankara himself. Full of great devotion, he obtained *jnana* about Ishvara." At this, the body hair of all those who followed the Pashupata vow stood up in joy. Eager in their minds, they spoke to Vyasa, Satyavati's son. "O illustrious one! You possess *vijnana* about Parameshthi. Through the favours of the lord of *deva*s, you obtained that supreme knowledge about Maheshvara. We are eager to hear about this excellent mystery and secret from your illustrious mouth so that we can quickly see the divinity." At this, he released the *shishya*s, of whom Sumantu was the foremost.[1296] The one whose knowledge about *yoga* was excellent spoke to the *yogi*s about supreme *jnana*. At that instant, a sparkling and excellent illumination manifested itself. In an instant, the *brahmana*s vanished inside this.'

'The illustrious one, who knew about the *brahman*, then called his *shishya*s back. With Paila as the foremost, he spoke to them about the greatness of Madhyamesha.

[1296] It is not clear why Vyasa temporarily dismissed his disciples and called them back later. One can speculate that he didn't want his disciples to also vanish.

"In this place, surrounded by Rudras, the divinity, Bhagavan Maheshvara, sports with Devi. Earlier, Krishna Hrishikesha, Devaki's son whose *atman* is in the universe, lived here for a year, always surrounded by those who followed the Pashupata vow. With all his limbs covered with *bhasma*, he was intent on worshipping Rudra. Following the Pashupata vow, Hari worshipped Shambhu. There were many of his *shishya*s, devoted to *brahmacharya*. Following his words, they obtained *jnana* and saw Maheshvara. The divinity, Bhagavan Mahadeva Nilalohita, the bestower of boons, showed himself directly and gave Krishna an excellent boon. "O one who pervades the universe! If my devotees follow the rules and worship Govinda, they will obtain *jnana* about Ishvara. You are Isha. Because of my favours, there is no doubt that those who are my devotees, *dvija*s, will worship you and perform *dhyana* on you." Those who see the lord of *deva*s and performed *dhyana* on the divinity Pinaki, their sins, like the killing of a *brahmana*, are swiftly destroyed. *Brahmana*s who give up their lives here, even if they have committed sins, proceed to the supreme destination. There is no need to reflect on this. O *brahmana*s! Those who bathe in the waters of Mandakini and worship Mahadeva as the excellent Madhyameshvara are blessed. O *brahmana*s! Even if one of bathing, donations, austerities, *shraddha* and offering of *pinda*s[1297] is done here, seven generations of the lineage are purified. When Rahu devours the sun,[1298] if water is touched here, the fruits obtained by a mortal become ten times as large." Saying this, the lord, the great *yogi*,

---

[1297] *Pinda* is a funeral cake, a ball of rice offered to ancestors.
[1298] At the time of a solar eclipse.

resided near Madhyamesha for a long period of time and worshipped Maheshvara.'

Chapter 35(1)(35) (Different *tirtha*s)

Suta said, "There are all the other secret *tirtha*s. Surrounded by them, Jaimini being the foremost, the illustrious Vyasa went to those. Prayaga is a supreme *tirtha*. The *tirtha* of Vishvarupa is more auspicious than Prayaga. There is the excellent Kalatirtha. There is the great tirtha known as Akasha and the supreme *tirtha* of Anusha. There is the great *tirtha* of Svarllina and the excellent Gouritirtha. Prajapatya is a supreme *tirtha* and there is also Svargadvara. There is the place known as Jambukeshvara and the excellent *tirtha* known as Charma. Gayatirtha is a great *tirtha* and Mahanadi is also a *tirtha*. There is the supreme *tirtha* of Narayana and the excellent Vayutirtha. Jnanatirtha is extremely secret and Varahatirtha is excellent. Yamatirtha is an extremely sacred *tirtha* and there is Samvartaka. O best among *dvija*s! There is Agnitirtha and the excellent Kalakeshvara. There are also Nagatirtha, Somatirtha and Suryatirtha. There is the extremely sacred place known as Parvata and the excellent Manikarna. There is the supreme *tirtha* of Ghatotkacha, Shritirtha and that of the grandfather. There is Gangatirtha and the excellent *tirtha* of Devesha. There are Kapila, Somesha and the excellent Brahmatirtha. There, Brahma arrived and went to take a bath. Meanwhile, Vishnu established Ishvara's *lingam* there, a *lingam* that should be worshipped. Having returned after taking his bath, Brahma spoke to Hari. "I brought this *lingam*. Why did you instate it?" Vishnu replied, "My

devotion towards Rudra is firmer than yours. That is the
reason I established the *lingam*, though it will be named
after you." O excellent *dvija*s! There are Bhuteshvara
tirtha, the *tirtha* of Dharma-sambudbhava, the extremely
auspicious Gandharvatirtha, the excellent *tirtha* of Vahni,
Dourvasika, Homatirtha, Chandratirtha, the sacred
Chitrangadeshvara, the sacred Vidyadhareshvara, the
foremost *tirtha* known as Kedara, the excellent Kalanjara,
Sarasvata, Prabhasa, Khetakarna, the auspicious *tirtha*
to Hara, the great *tirtha* known as Loukika, the *tirtha*
of Himalaya, Hiranyagarbha, Goprakhya, the *tirtha*
of Vrishadhvaja, Upashanta, Shiva, the excellent
Vyaghreshvara, the great *tirtha* of Trilochana, Lolarka,
the place known as Uttara, Kapalamochana *tirtha*, which
destroys the sin of killing a *brahmana*,, the extremely
sacred Shukreshvara and the excellent Anandapura. I
have described the main *tirtha*s. O excellent *dvija*s! I am
incapable of describing the enumeration of *tirtha*s in detail.
The great sage, Parashara's son, bathed in all these *tirtha*s
and worshipped the eternal one. He fasted and satisfied
ancestors and *deva*s. He offered *pinda*s. He then again
went to the place where Vishveshvara Shiva was. Along
with his *shishya*s, the great sage bathed and worshipped
the great *lingam*. The one with *dharma* in his *atman* told
his *shishya*s, "Go wherever you wish." Paila and the other
*dvija*s prostrated themselves before the great-souled one
and left. He controlled himself and resided in Varanasi.
He was tranquil and restrained, bathing thrice a day. He
worshipped Pinaki. He survived by begging for alms. He
was pure in his *atman* and devoted to *brahmacharya*. O
excellent *dvija*s! On one occasion, while the infinitely
energetic Vyasa resided there, though he wandered
around, he did not receive any alms. Rage permeating

his body, he said, "I will create obstacles for men who dwell here. All their *siddhi* will be diminished." At that instant, Mahadevi, who constitutes half of Shankara's body, was filled with affection and manifested herself, in the garb of a human. "O Vyasa! O immensely intelligent one! You should not curse the city. Accept alms from me." Saying this, Shivaa gave him alms. Mahadevi spoke again. "O sage! Since you are prone to rage, you should not reside in this *kshetra*. You are always ungrateful." Thus addressed, the illustrious one got to know through his *dhyana* that this was the supreme Shivaa. Prostrating himself, he praised her through excellent hymns and said, "O Shankari! Please allow me to enter on *ashtami* and *chaturdashi*."[1299] Granting this, Devi vanished. Since the illustrious, ancient and great *yogi*, Vyasa, resided there, everyone got to know about the qualities of the *kshetra* and lived by his side. Knowing that Vyasa resided there, learned ones frequented the *kshetra*. Therefore, a man must make every possible effort to live in Varanasi. If a person reads or hears about Avimukta's greatness, or if he makes it heard to serene *dvija*s, he proceeds to the supreme destination. O *dvija*s! This should be done at the time of *shraddha*s, rites connected with *deva*s, in the night and during the day, along the banks of rivers and in temples to *deva*s. Knowing this, if a person controls his mind, gets rid of desire and anger and prostrating himself, performs *japa* to Isha, he proceeds to the supreme destination."

[1299] *Asthami* is the eighth lunar *tithi* and *chaturdashi* is the fourteenth lunar *tithi*.

Chapter 36(1)(36) (Greatness of Prayaga)

The *rishi*s said, "O one excellent in vows! You have accurately described the greatness of Avimukta. Please tell us now about the greatness of Prayaga. There are famous and great *tirtha*s there. O Suta! You know the meaning of everything. Please tell us about those now."

Suta replied, "O *rishi*s! All of you listen. I will describe Prayaga's greatness in detail. The divinity, Brahma, is there. Markandeya described this to the great-souled Kounteya Yudhishthira. I will tell you about it. When the Kouravas were killed, along with all his brothers, the king was overwhelmed by great grief. Yudhishthira was deluded. Within a short period of time, Markandeya, the great ascetic, reached Hastinapura and waited at the royal gate. Seeing him there, the gatekeeper quickly informed the king about this. "Wishing to see you, the sage Markandeya is waiting at the gate." Swiftly, Dharma's son reached the gate. Having reached the gate, he said, "O great sage! Welcome. Today, my birth has been rendered successful. Today, I have saved my lineage. O sage! When you are satisfied today, my ancestors will be content." He made him sit on the throne and worshipped him with *padya* and other things.[1300] The great-souled Yudhishthira worshipped the sage. Questioned, Markandeya spoke to Yudhishthira. "Why are you deluded? Getting to know all this, I have come." At this, King Yudhishthira prostrated his head and said, "Briefly, please tell me how I can cleanse myself of my sins. In connection with our battle with the Kouravas, we have killed many innocent men. O excellent

---

[1300] *Padya* is water to wash the feet. A guest is offered *padya*, *achamaniya* (water to rinse the mouth), a seat and *arghya* (a gift).

sage! Sins committed through violence are carried across other births. You should now tell us how we can cleanse ourselves of this sin." Markandeya replied, "O king! O immensely fortunate one! O Bharata! Hear what you have asked me about. For destroying sins, it is best for men to go to Prayaga. O lord of men! The divinity Mahadeva Rudra reside there. Along with the *deva*s, Bhagavan Svayambhu Brahma is there." Yudhishthira said, "O illustrious one! I wish to hear about the fruits of going to Prayaga. What is the destination for those who die there? What are the fruits from bathing there? Please tell us the fruits of those who reside in Prayaga. You know this. Please describe it. I prostrate myself before you."'

Markandeya answered, 'O child! I will describe to you the fruits of bathing in Prayaga. Earlier, when the *maharshi*s conversed about this, I heard it properly. This is Prajapati's *ksehtra*, famous in the three worlds. If one bathes here, one goes to heaven. If one dies here, one is not born on earth again. Brahma and the other *deva*s assemble there and protect. There are many other *tirtha*s there, which take away all sins. I am incapable of describing them, in many hundreds of years. I will briefly describe what is recited about Prayaga. It extends for sixty thousand bow-lengths and protects Jahnavi. Savitar,[1301] with the seven horses, always protects Yamuna. In particular, Vasava himself dwells in Prayaga. Hari protects this circle, revered by all the *deva*s. Maheshvara, with the trident in his hand, always protects the *nyagrodha* tree.[1302] The *deva*s protect this place, which takes away every kind of sin. People who are enveloped by their own *karma* can never go to that

[1301] Surya.
[1302] The sacred fig tree.

destination. O lord of men! Whatever slightest sin a person
may have committed, as soon as Prayaga is remembered,
all those head towards destruction. Through seeing it,
through chanting the name of the *tirtha*, or by applying
mud from that place, a man is freed from sin. O Indra
among kings! There are five pools there and Jahnavi flows
through their centre. As soon as a man enters Prayaga, sin
is instantly destroyed. If a man remembers Ganga from a
distance of one thousand yojanas, even if he has committed
evil deeds, he obtains the supreme destination. A person
who chants about it is freed from sins. A person who sees
it obtains good fortune. O Indra among kings! If a person
touches the water there, he obtains greatness in the world
of the gods. Even if a man is diseased, dejected or angry,
all his sins are destroyed, and he saves his ancestors. If a
person resides in Prayaga, he crosses over the ocean that
is the world. Bulls among sages say that if a person makes
efforts to give up his life between Ganga and Yamuna, he
obtains everything that he desires. He is on *vimana*s with
the blazing complexion of the sun, studded with every
kind of divine jewel and adorned with many flags. These
follow the sun. Auspicious in signs, he enjoys himself with
many beautiful women. When he sleeps, he is woken up
by singing and the sounds of musical instruments. Until he
remembers his birth, he obtains greatness in heaven. After
that, when his good merits are exhausted, that excellent
man is dislodged from heaven. He is born into a prosperous
lineage that possesses gold and jewels. As soon as he
remembers the *tirtha*, he goes there. Whether it is in one's
land, in the forest, in a foreign land or at home, if a person
remembers Prayaga and gives up his life, bulls among sages
say that he obtains Brahma's world. The ground there is
golden, and trees yield everything desired as fruits. The

place has *rishi*s, sages and *siddha*s. He goes to that world. As a result of the deeds he has himself undertaken, on the beautiful and auspicious banks of Mandakini, along with the sages, he enjoys himself with thousands of women. He is worshipped by *siddha*s, *charana*s, *gandharva*s, *deva*s and *danava*s. When he is dislodged from heaven, he becomes the lord of Jambudvipa. After this, he repeatedly remembers his auspicious deeds. We have heard that he therefore possesses qualities and good conduct. In thoughts, words and deeds, he is established in true *dharma*. In connection with his own rite, rites of the ancestors, or studying at the *tirtha* that is in between Ganga and Yamuna, if a man enjoys a village, gold, pearl or any other possession offered to him, his intention to obtain fruits from the *tirtha* are rendered unsuccessful. Therefore, in the *tirtha* or in sacred habitations, one should not accept anything. A *dvija* must never be distracted by all these kinds of causes. O excellent one! If a man donates a brown tawny or black milk-yielding cow, its horns covered with gold, its hooves with silver and its ears with cloth, he obtains greatness in Rudra's world for as many thousands of years as there are body hair on the cow's limbs.'

Chapter 37(1)(37) (Rules for visiting *tirtha*s)

Markandeya said, 'O child! I will describe to you the rules and order for visiting *tirtha*s, as I have seen and as I have heard. *Rishi*s have laid down these rules. A man desiring to visit the *tirtha* of Prayaga may, on some occasion, proceed mounted on a bull. Hear about the fruits that result. He resides in terrible hell for as many years as there are in one hundred thousand *kalpa*s.

When he returns from there, he faces the extremely
terrible anger of cattle. If a being casts aside his infant
sons, without any food to eat, his ancestors do not accept
water offered by him. Everything, even he himself, must
be offered to *brahmana*s.[1303] Because of prosperity, greed
or delusion, a man should not proceed on a vehicle. A
vehicle must be avoided. Otherwise, his visit to the *tirtha*
will be futile. Depending on his prosperity, in between
Ganga and Yamuna, if a person bestows his daughter
according to the *arsha* form of marriage, as a result of
this deed, he does not see a terrible hell.[1304] If a man goes
to Uttara Kuru and gives up his life at the foot of the
vata tree[1305] there, he enjoys himself for an eternal period
of time. Passing over the world of heaven, he goes to
Rudra's world. Brahma and the other *deva*s and the lords
of directions and sub-directions are there. The guardians
of the worlds and all the ancestors are established in
that world. The *brahmarshis* are there, Sanatkumara
being the foremost. They are always worshipped by
*naga*s, Suparnas and *siddha*s. Bhagavan Hari is there,
worshipped by Prajapati. O tiger among kings! The region
between Ganga and Yamuna is described as the earth's
loin. Prayaga is famous in the three worlds. Firm in vows,
if a person performs *abhisheka*[1306] at this confluence, the
fruits obtained are equal to those obtained from a royal or

[1303] Before proceeding on a journey to *tirtha*s.

[1304] Strictly speaking, in an *arsha* form of marriage, a daughter
was bestowed on a *rishi*, in exchange for two cows. This was not
regarded as one of the better forms of marriage. Hence, the text
may not have intended *arsha* in its strict sense.

[1305] Banyan, the large Indian fig tree.

[1306] Initiation or consecration, involving ablutions or ritualistic
sprinkling of water on the head.

horse sacrifice. O son! If a person has made up his mind
to go to Prayaga, the words of a mother or the words
of people should not dissuade him. O descendant of the
Kuru lineage! There are sixty thousand *tirtha*s and sixty
crore other *tirtha*s in its vicinity. If a person gives up his
life at the confluence of Ganga and Yamuna, the learned
have said that the destination obtained by him is the same
as the destination obtained by a *sannyasi* engaged in *yoga*.
O Yudhisthira! People who live here and there and do not
go to Prayaga, do not really live. In the three worlds, they
are deceived. Having seen the supreme destination and
tirtha of Prayaga, one is freed from all sins, like the moon
from Rahu. The two *naga*s, Kambala and Ashvatara, are
on the southern banks of Yamuna. If one bathes there
and drinks the water, one is freed from all sins. Having
gone to Mahadeva's place, if an intelligent person bathes
there, he saves ten generations of his ancestors and ten
generations of his descendants. If a man undertakes
abhishekha, he obtains the fruits of a horse sacrifice.
Until the onset of the deluge, he obtains the world of
heaven. On the eastern bank of Ganga, there is a hole in
the ground. This is Sarva-Samudra, famous in the three
worlds. There is also the famous Pratishthana. If a man
goes there and, conquering his anger, remains there are a
brahmachari for three nights, he is cleansed from all sins
and obtains the fruits of a horse sacrifice. To the north
of Pratishthana and left of Bhagirathi, there is the *tirtha*
named Hamsa-prapatana, famous in the three worlds. As
soon as one remembers it, the fruits of a horse sacrifice
are generated. As long as the sun and the moon last, he
obtains greatness in heaven. There is the beautiful and
large Urvashi-pulina, as white as swans. Hear about the
fruits if one gives up one's life there. O lord of men! Along

with the ancestors, he remains in the world of heaven for sixty-six thousand years. In the beautiful Sandhyavata, if a *brahmachari* is pure and performs worship, that man obtains Brahma's world. If a person reaches Koti-tirtha and gives up his life, he obtains greatness in the world of heaven for one thousand crore years. The immensely fortunate Ganga has many *tirtha*s and hermitages. Therefore, this is known as *siddha-kshetra*.[1307] There is no need to think about this. She is known as Tripathaa[1308] because she saves mortals on earth, *naga*s in the nether regions and *deva*s in heaven. As long as a man's bones remain in the Ganga, he obtains greatness in the world of heaven for that many thousands of years. This *tirtha* is supreme among *tirtha*s. This river is supreme among rivers. For all beings, she grants liberation, even those who have committed great sins. Everywhere, Ganga can easily be reached. But there are three places where Ganga is difficult to reach—Gangadvara, Prayaga and the confluence of Ganga with the ocean. For all beings, even if their minds are overwhelmed by sin, there is no destination equal to the destination Ganga ensures. She is the most sacred among everything sacred. She is the most auspicious among everything auspicious. The auspicious one was dislodged from Maheshvara and dispels all sins. Naimisha *tirtha* is distinguished in *krita*, Pushkara is best in *treta*, Kurukshetra in *dvapara* and Ganga in *kali*. People live near Ganga, especially in Prayaga. O king! Against the terrible *kali yuga*, there is no other medication. Whether willingly or inadvertently, if a person dies near Ganga, he goes to heaven and does not see hell.'

[1307] A place where one obtains *siddhi*.
[1308] One with three courses/flows.

Chapter 38(1)(38) (More on *tirtha*s)

Markandeya said, 'In the month of Magha,[1309] sixty-six thousand *tirtha*s go to the confluence of Ganga and Yamuna. In the month of Magha, if a person bathes in Prayaga for three days, the fruits obtained are the same as those obtained from the proper donation of one hundred thousand cows. O lord of the earth! If a man possesses all his limbs, is without disease and possesses the five senses and if he accomplishes *karishagni*[1310] in between Ganga and Yamuna, he obtains greatness in the world of heaven for as many thousands of years as there are body hair on his body. After this, he is dislodged from heaven and becomes the lord of Jambudvipa. Having enjoyed extensive objects of pleasure, he goes to that *tirtha* again. If a man enters the water[1311] at this confluence, famous in the worlds, like Soma freed from Rahu, he is freed from all sins. He obtains Soma's world and enjoys himself with Soma for sixty-six thousand years. From heaven, he goes to Shakra's world, served by sages and *gandharva*s. O Indra among kings! When he is dislodged from there, he is born in a prosperous lineage. If a man hangs feet upwards and head downwards and drinks from the flow,[1312] he obtains greatness in the world of heaven for seven thousand years. O Indra among men! When he is dislodged from there, he becomes a man who observes *agnihotra* sacrifices. After enjoying extensive objects of pleasure, he goes to that *tirtha* again.

[1309] January–February.
[1310] *Karishagni* means a fire kindled with dried cow dung. However, accomplishing *karishagni* means committing self-immolation in such a fire.
[1311] That is, kills himself by submerging himself in the water.
[1312] That is, Ganga's water.

Hear about the fruits obtained by a person who slices off his limbs and offers them to birds, thus being devoured by birds. He obtains greatness in Soma's world for one hundred thousand years. When he is dislodged from there, he becomes a king who is devoted to *dharma*. He possesses qualities and beauty. He is learned and pleasant in speech. Having enjoyed objects of pleasure and donated, he goes to that *tirtha* again. On the northern bank of Yamuna and to the south of Prayaga, there is the *tirtha* named Rina-pramochana.[1313] This is described as supreme. Even if a person resides there for one night and bathes, he is freed from debts. He obtains the world of heaven and is always free of debt.'

Chapter 39(1)(39) (More on *tirtha*s)

Markandeya said, 'The *devi* who is Tapana's daughter is famous in the three worlds.[1314] The immensely fortunate river, Yamuna, reaches there. Yamuna flows the same way Ganga does, for thousands of *yojana*s. She is sung about as the one who destroys sins. If one bathes or drinks at the place where Yamuna flows downwards, one is freed from all sins and purifies seven generations of the lineage. If a person gives up his life there, he achieves the supreme destination. On Yamuna's southern bank, there is the famous Agnitirtha. To the west is Dharmaraja's[1315] *tirtha*, described as Anaraka.[1316] If a person bathes there,

---

[1313] Where one is freed (*pramochana*) from debt (*rina*).
[1314] Tapana is Surya and Surya's daughter means Yamuna.
[1315] Meaning, Yama's.
[1316] Without *naraka* (hell).

he goes to heaven. Those who die there, are not born again. If a person purifies himself and on *chaturdashi* of *krishnapaksha* bathes and satisfies Dharmaraja, there is no doubt that he is freed from great sins. The learned have said that there are ten crores and ten thousand *tirtha*s in Prayaga. Vayu has spoken about three and a half crore *tirtha*s in heaven, the firmament and earth. All of them are said to exist in Jahnavi. Where the immensely fortunate Ganga exists, that region is a hermitage. The region along the banks of Ganga is known as *siddha-kshetra*. The divinity Mahadeva Maheshvara is there, along with Madhava. The lord of *deva*s is always present in that *tirtha*, which is like a hermitage. With *japa*, this truth must be imparted into the ears of *dvija*s, virtuous people, sons, well-wishers and devoted *shishya*s. "This is blessed. This is fortunate. This is sacred and auspicious. This is holy. This is beautiful and purifying. This is excellent *dharma*. This is a secret known to *maharshi*s. It frees from all sins. A *dvija* who studies a chapter here, becomes sparkling. If a person constantly purifies himself and constantly hears about this sacred *tirtha*, he remembers his past life and enjoys himself in the vault of heaven."[1317] These *tirtha*s are visited by the virtuous, those who instruct those with good behaviour. O Kouravya! Do not have perverse intelligence. Bathe in those *tirtha*s.'

Suta concluded, 'The illustrious and great sage, Markandeya, said this. He described all the *tirtha*s on earth. Having been asked, he described everything about the location of the earth and oceans, the establishment of planets and luminous bodies. After this, the sage left. If a

---

[1317] The quote seems to end here, though not clearly indicated.

person gets up in the morning and reads or hears this, he is freed from all sins and goes to Rudra's world.'

Chapter 40(1)(40) (Description of the world)

Thus addressed, the sages in Naimisha asked the great sage, Suta more, about the determination of the earth and other things.

The *rishi*s said, 'You have described Svayambhuva Manu's auspicious creation. We now wish to hear about the globes of the three worlds. You should tell us briefly about the extent of oceans and *dvipa*s, *varsha*s, mountains, forests, rivers, the location of Surya and the planets, the support for everything that exists and the kings who have existed in earlier times."

Suta replied, 'I prostrate myself before the powerful Vishnu, the Vishnu who is the lord of the *deva*s and is immeasurable. After this, I will describe what that intelligent one narrated. Earlier, it had been said that Priyavrata was the son of Svayambhuva Manu. He had ten sons who were the equal of Prajapatis. They were Agnidhra, Agnibahu, Vapushman, Dyutiman, Medha, Medhatithi, Havya, Savana, Putra. The tenth, Jyotishman, was immensely strong and valiant. He was devoted to *dharma* and devoted to donating. He was compassionate towards all beings. Medha, Agnibahu and Putra—these three were devoted to *yoga*. These immensely fortunate ones remembered their past lives and their minds were not interested in the kingdom. Priyavrata instated the seven other sons in the seven *dvipa*s. The king made his son, Agnidhra, the lord of Jambu-dvipa. Medhatithi was made the lord of Plaksha-dvipa. Vapushman was instated as the lord and king of

Shalmali-dvipa. The lord made Jyotishman the king of Kusha-dvipa. He instructed that Dyutiman should be the king of Krouncha-dvipa. Priyavrata made Havya the lord of Shaka-dvipa. The Prajapati instated Savana as the lord of Pushkara-dvipa.'

'The lord of Pushkara was supreme among those who have excellent sons. He had two sons, Mahadvita and Dhataki. The great-souled one's *varsha* is said to have been Mahavita.[1318] Dhataki's region is said to have been named after Dhataki. Havya, the lord of Shaka-dvipa, had the sons Jalada, Kumara, Sukumara, Manichaka, Kushottara, Modaki and Mahadruma as the seventh. The first *varsha* is said to be Jalada, named after Jalada. Kumara's is named after Kumara and the third after Sukumara. Manichaka is the fourth and Kushottara the fifth. Modaka[1319] is said to have been the sixth and the seventh is Mahadruma. Dyutiman, the lord of Krouncha-dvipa had sons. Kushala was the first, Manohara was the second, Ushna is said to have been the third and Pivara is described as the fourth. The others were Andhakara, Muni and Dundubhi. These were the seven. The auspicious regions of Krouncha-dvipa were named after their names. Jyotishman of Kusha-dvipa had seven immensely energetic sons. They were Udbheda, Venuman, Ashvaratha, Lambana, Dhriti, Prabhakara as the sixth and Kapila is said to have been the seventh. O ones excellent in vows! The *varsha*s were marked by their names. It should be known that in the other *dvipa*s, the principles followed were the same. Vapushman, the lord

---

[1318] The earth is divided into seven *dvipa*s (continents). Each *dvipa* is sub-divided into sub-continents, known as *varsha*s. The *varsha*s were named after the sons.

[1319] Modaka, not Modaki.

of Shalmali-dvipa, had the sons Shveta, Harita, Jimuta, Rohita, Vaidyuta, Manasa and the seventh is said to have been Suprabha. Medhatithi, the lord of Plaksha-dvipa, had seven sons. The eldest was Shantamaya. The others were Shishira, Sukhodaya, Ananda, Shiva, Kshemaka and Dhruva. It should be known that, starting with Plaksha-dvipa and ending with Shaka-dvipa, it is held that the path to liberation is to follow one's own *dharma*, in accordance with the division of *varna*s.'

'O best among *dvija*s! Agnidhra, the lord of Jambu-dvipa, had immensely strong sons. Hear their names. They were Nabhi, Kimpurusha, Hari, Ilavrita, Ramya, Hiranvan, Kuru, Bhadrashva and Ketumalaka. Agnidhra, the immensely intelligent lord and king of Jambu-dvipa, did what is proper. He divided it into nine parts and handed over these regions. The father gave Nabhi the southern *varsha*, known as Hima. He gave Kimpurusha the *varsha* of Hemakuta. The father bestowed the third *varsha*, Naishadha, on Hari. Ilavrita, located in the centre of Meru, was given to Ilavrita. The father gave Ramya the *varsha* around Mount Nila. The father gave the northern *varsha* of Shveta to Hiranvan. The *varsha* to the north of Mount Shringavan was given to Kuru. The *varsha* to Meru's east was given to Bhadrashva. Gandhamadana *varsha* was given to Ketumala.[1320] The lord of men instated his sons in these *varsha*s. Knowing that *samsara* has no essence, he left for the forest, to torment himself through austerities. The great-souled Nabhi obtained the *varsha* known as Hima. Through Merudevi, he had an extremely radiant son, Rishabha. Rishabha had one hundred sons. The eldest was the valiant Bharata. Rishabha instated his

---

[1320]The same as Ketumalaka.

son Bharata as the lord of the earth and left for the *ashrama* of *vanaprastha*, to follow the rules and torment himself through austerities. Through austerities, undertaken day and night, he emaciated himself excessively. Devoted to *jnana* and *yoga*, he followed the great Pashupata vow. Bharata had a son named Sumati, who was extremely devoted to *dharma*. Sumati's son was Taijasa and Taijasa's son was the immensely radiant Indradyumna. Indradyumna's son was Parameshthi and Pratihara followed him. Pratihara had a son who was famous as Pratiharta. Pratiharta's son was Bhava and Bhava's son was Udgitha. Udgitha's son was Prastavi. Prastavi's son was Prithu, Prithu's son was Nakta, Nakta's son is said to have been Gaya, Gaya's son was Nara and Nara's son was Viraj. Viraj's son was Mahavirya and Mahavirya's son was Dhiman. Dhiman's son was Rouvana and Rouvana's son was Tvashtri. Tvashtri's son was Viraja and Viraja's son was Raja. Raja's son was Shatajit and Shatajit's son was Rathajit. O *dvijas*! Rathajit had one hundred sons. Among them, Vishvajyoti is said to have been the strongest and most important. He worshipped the divinity Brahma and obtained a son named Kshemaka, who knew about *dharma*. This king was mighty-armed and a conqueror of enemies. In earlier times, kings possessed great spirits and great energy. Earlier, born in these lineages, they enjoyed the earth.'

Chapter 41(1)(41) (Locations of luminous bodies)

Suta said, 'O excellent *dvijas*! After this, I will briefly describe the dimensions of the three worlds. I am incapable of describing it in detail. The worlds that emerged from the cosmic egg are Bhurloka, Bhuvarloka, Svarloka, Maharloka, Janaloka, Tapoloka and Satyaloka. O bulls among *dvija*s! In the Puranas, the extent that is illuminated by the rays of the sun and the moon is described as Bhurloka. Bhuvarloka has the same dimensions, diameter and circumference as Bhurloka and extends up to Bhaskara's circle. Above this circle, the space till the location of Dhruva is known as Svarloka. Vayu's fellies are there. Avaha, Pravaha, Anuvaha, Samvaha, Vivaha, Paravaha above that, and Parivaha—these are Vayu's seven fellies.[1321] Bhanu's circle is located one hundred thousand *yojana*s above the earth. The moon's circle is said to be located one hundred thousand *yojana*s from Divakara. The circle of *nakshatra*s provides illumination one hundred thousand *yojana*s from this. O *brahmana*s! Budha is two hundred thousand *yojana*s from the circle of *nakshatra*s. The division is such that Ushanas[1322] is located at the same distance from Budha. Angaraka[1323] is located at the same distance from Shukra. The priest of the *deva*s is located two hundred thousand *yojana*s from Bhouma.[1324] Souri is located two hundred thousand *yojana*s from Guru's circle.[1325] The circle of *saptarshi*s provides illumination at a distance of one hundred thousand *yojana*s from that. Dhruva[1326] is located above the circle of *rishi*s, at a distance of one hundred thousand *yojana*s. Bhagavan Vishnu Narayana,

[1321] These are Vayu's (the wind's) seven flows.
[1322] Shukra, Venus.
[1323] Mangala, Mars.
[1324] Bhouma is another name for Mangala and the priest of the *deva*s means Brihaspati (Jupiter).
[1325] Guru is Brihapasti and Souri is Surya's sun, that is, Saturn.
[1326] The Pole Star.

who is *dharma*, is established there. Savitar's[1327] diameter
is said to be nine thousand *yojana*s. The dimensions of
the circumference are said to be three times that.[1328] The
moon's expanse is said to be double that of the sun. When
Svarbhanu[1329] approaches them, he assumes a dimension
that is equal to them in size. Having taken away the earth's
shadow, he assumes that circular form. Svarbhanu has
a third large location, and it is full of darkness.[1330] It is
such that Bhargava[1331] is one-sixteenth Chandra's size. It
should be known that Brihaspati is one-quarter smaller,
compared to Bhargava. Bhouma and Soura[1332] are both
one-quarter smaller, compared to Brihaspati. Compared to
these two, in size and circumference, Budha is one-quarter
smaller. The forms of *tara*s[1333] and *nakshatra*s amount to
a body that, in size and circumference, is equal to that
of Budha's. Vis-à-vis each other, the forms of *tara*s and
*nakshatra*s are smaller by five hundred, four hundred, three
hundred and two hundred *yojana*s. The sizes of *taraka*s are
progressively drawn up in this way. The distance between
them is not less than half a *yojana*. The three *graha*s that
are above move a great distance away. It should be known
that Soura, Angira and Vakra have slow and retrograde
movements.[1334] There are four other great *graha*s that are
below them. Surya, Soma, Budha and Bhargava move

[1327] The sun's.
[1328] With an implied Pi value of 3.
[1329] Rahu, who swallows them up at the time of eclipses.
[1330] The other two being at the time of eclipses.
[1331] Shukra.
[1332] The same as Souri, Saturn.
[1333] Stars. Also known as *taraka*s.
[1334] Vakra is another name for Angaraka. Angira is a rare way
of referring to Brhispati.

swiftly. When Surya, the one with the rays, travels along the *dakshinayana* path,[1335] he moves below the *graha*s that have been mentioned earlier. With an extensive circle, the moon moves above this. The entire circle of *nakshatra*s moves above Soma. Budha is above the *nakshatra*s and Bhargava is above Budha. Vakra is above Bhargava and Brihaspati is above Vakra. Shanaishchara is above that and the circle of *saptarshi*s is above Saturn. Dhruva is located above the seven *rishi*s.'

'O excellent *dvija*s! Bhaskara's chariot is nine thousand *yojana*s long. The length of the axle-poles is twice as much. The axle measures more than one and a half crores and seven hundred *yojana*s and the wheel is fixed to this. The entire wheel of time consists of one year, twenty-one naves, five spokes and six rims. O excellent *dvija*s! There is a second axle that is established with a length of forty-five thousand and five hundred *yojana*s. The length of both axles is half those of the yokes. The short axle and yoke of the chariot depend on Dhruva for support. The second axle of the wheel is fixed on Mount Manasa. Hear about the names of the seven *chhanda*s, which are the horses. They are *gayatri*, *brihati*, *ushnik*, *jagati*, *pankti*, *anushtup* and *trishtup*. These *chhanda*s are said to be the sun's horses. Above Manasa and in the eastern direction, there is the great Indra's great city. To the south is Yama's and to the west is Varuna's. To the north is Soma's. Hear about their names. They are respectively Amaravati, Samyamani, Sukha and Vibhavari. Seizing the circle of luminous bodies, the grandfather, the

---

[1335] *Dakshinayana* is when the sun moves south of the equator, from summer solstice to winter solstice. *Uttarayana* is when the sun moves north of the equator, from winter solstice to summer solstice.

lord of *deva*s,[1336] moves swiftly towards the south, like an arrow that has been shot. O Indras among *brahmana*s! In each of the seven *dvipa*s and at all times, the position of the sun at mid-day is directly opposite the position of the sun at midnight. O Indras among *brahmana*s! At all times, sunrise and sunset are directly opposite each other, in directions and sub-directions. The lord seems to move like a potter's wheel. O *dvija*s! When he leaves the earth, he creates night. Divakara fills up the three worlds. O bulls among sages! The virtuous have spoken about these three worlds to people. There is no doubt that Aditya is the cause behind all three worlds. The entire universe, with *deva*s, *asura*s and humans, results from this. The radiant one conquered all the resplendent worlds of Rudra, Upendra, Chandra, Indras among *brahmana*s and residents of heaven. He is in all *atman*s. He is the lord of all the worlds. He is Mahadeva Prajapati. Surya is the cause of the worlds and the supreme divinity. There are twelve other Adityas who have rights to be *deva*s and carry out their tasks. They are said to be Vishnu's portions and forms. Everyone, *gandharva*s, *yaksha*s, *uraga*s, *kinnara*s and others, bows down before the one with one thousand arms. Indras among sages worship the ancient one, who is full of the *brahman* and full of *chhanda*s, with many kinds of sacrifices.'

Chapter 42(1)(42) (Twelve Adityas)

Suta said, 'He is established on his chariot, accompanied by *deva*s, Adityas, sages, *gandharva*s, *apsara*s,

---

[1336] Here, these expressions refer to Surya.

*gramani*s,[1337] *sarpa*s and *rakshasa*s. The twelve Adityas
who are Divakaras are Dhatri, Aryama, Mitra, Varuna,
Shakra, Vivasvan, Pushan, Parjanya, Amshu, Bhaga,
Tvashta and Vishnu.[1338] In Vasanta and the other seasons,
in due order, Bhanu approaches them. The sages who speak
about the brahman are Pulastya, Pulaha, Atri, Vasishtha,
Angiras, Bhrigu, Bharadvaja, Goutama, Kashyapa, Kratu,
Jamadagni and Koushika. In the due order, they praise
the divinity with many kinds of *chhanda*s. The *gramani*s
who gather the reins of the lord of *deva*s are Rathakrit,
Rathouja, Rathachitra, Subahuka, Rathasvana, Varuna,
Sushena, Senajit, Tarkshya, Arishtanemi, Kritajit and
Satyajit. O Indras among *brahmana*s! In the due order, the
foremost *rakshasa*s who proceed in front are Heti, Praheti,
Pourusheya, Vadha, Sarpa, Vyaghra, Apa, Vata, Vidyut,
Divakara, Brahmopeta and Yajnopeta. O *dvija*s! In the
due order, the *sarpa*s who bear him are Vasuki, Kankanila,
Takshaka, Sarpapungava, Elapatra, Shankhapala, the one
known as Airavata, Dhananjaya, Mahapadma, Karkotaka,
Kambala and Ashvatara. O excellent *dvija*s! The twelve
*gandharva*s, excellent singers, are Tumburu, Narada,
Haha, Huhu, Vishvavasu, Ugrasena, Suruchi, Arvavasu,
Chitrasena, Urnayu, Dhritarashtra and Suryavarcha. In
the due order, using *shadaja* and others,[1339] they sing many
kinds of songs to Bhanu. O excellent *dvija*s! The *apsara*s

[1337] In this context, *gramani*s are celestial beings who are on
Surya's chariot.

[1338] One Aditya for each month. Each Aditya is accompanied
by a set of sages, *gramani*s, *rakshasa*s, *sarpa*s, *gandharva*s, *apsara*s
and *deva*s. *Gramani*s are equated with *yaksha*s. Similarly, the word
*yatudhana*s means *rakshasa*s.

[1339] *Shadaja, rishabha, gandhara, madhyama, panchama,
dhaivata* and *nishadaka, sa-re-ga-ma-pa-dha-ni.*

are Ritusthala, supreme among *apsara*s, Punjikasthala, Menaka, Sahajanya, Pramlocha, Anumlocha, Vishvachi, Ghritachi, Urvashi, Purvachitti, Rambha and Tilottama. In Vasanta and the other seasons, in the due order, they use *tandava*[1340] and many other forms of dance to satisfy the great divinity, Bhanu, whose *atman* is imperishable. Similarly, in the due order, *deva*s reside for two months each. They use their energy to nourish Surya, the store of energy. The sages use collections of words to praise Ravi. *Gandharva*s and *apsara*s worship him with singing and dancing. *Gramani*s, *yaksha*s and *bhuta*s gather the reins. *Sarpa*s bear the lord of *deva*s and *yatudhana*s advance in front. From sunrise to sunset, the *valakhilya*s surround the sun. These are described as the ones who heat, shower down, shine, blow, create and take away the inauspicious deeds committed by beings. Along with the ones who follow Bhanu, Surya traverses the firmament. They are always seated on a *vimana* that is as swift as the wind and can go wherever it wishes. In the due order, following the order of the *yuga*s, they shower down, heat, delight and protect all beings. The lord heats, according to the vigour and austerities of these *deva*s and according to their *yoga* and spirits. Prajapati is the reason behind the separation of day and night. Ravi always nourishes ancestors, *deva*s, humans and others. The radiant divinity is Mahadeva Maheshvara himself. For those who know the *Veda*s, the eternal Nilagriva is the one who shines. This divinity is Bhagavan Parameshthi Prajapati. Those who know the *Veda*s know Aditya's position and know that his forms are the *Veda*s.'

[1340] A type of frantic dance created by Tandu, after receiving instructions from Shiva.

Chapter 43(1)(43) (The earth's sphere)

Suta said, 'In this way, the grandfather, Mahadeva, the lord of the *deva*s, controls time. In his form as Ishvara, he has Kala in his *atman*. He loves his rays, which provide illumination to all the worlds. Among these, seven rays are the best and they are the source of origin for *graha*s. These seven are described as Sushumna,[1341] Harikesha, Vishvakarma, Vishvashrava, Samyadvasu, Arvavasu and Svaraka. Surya's ray, Sushumna, nourishes the one with the cool radiance.[1342] It is read that Sushumna's movement is sideways and upwards. The ray Harikesha is said to nourish *nakshatra*s. The ray Vishvakarma always nourishes Budha. The ray Vishvashrava always nourishes Shukra. The one known as Samyadvasu nourishes Lohita.[1343] The lord uses the ray Aryavasu to nourish Brihaspati. The seventh, Svaraka, nourishes Shanaishchara. In this way, through Surya's powers, all the *nakshatra*s and *taraka*s are always developed. Thus developed, they always nourish the divine, those on earth and those in the night. With his energy, since he constantly takes away darkness, he is Aditya.[1344] In every direction, with one thousand rays and one thousand eyes, he takes away water from rivers, oceans, wells, canals and mobile and immobile entities. From those one thousand rays, cold, rain and heat flow. Of those, four hundred rays, colourful in form, shower down. They are Chandragas, Gahas, Kanchanas and Shatanas.[1345]

[1341]The text says Sushumla, but uses Sushumna later. For consistency, we have made it Sushumna throughout.
[1342]That is, the moon.
[1343]Lohita, the red one, is Mars.
[1344]Based on *adana*, meaning to take, accept.
[1345]There are one hundred in each group.

All of these rays, named Amritas, create rain. There are
rays that originate from cold, and these rays also release
it. They are Reshya, Meshya, Vasya, Hradini and Sarjana.
All of these rays are tawny and are named Chandras.
Shukla, Kumkua, Go and Vishvabhrit—these are named
Shuklas. All of them create three different types of heat.
These sustain and nourish humans, ancestors and *devas*—
humans through herbs, ancestors through Svadha and the
gods through *amrita*. He satisfies all the three different
types through these three. In Vasanta and Grishma, the
lord heats through six rays.[1346] In Sharad and Varsha, he
showers down with four. In Hemanta and Shishira, he
creates cold with three. In the month of Magha, Varuna has
the form of Surya; it is Pushan in Phalguna; in the month of
Chaitra, it is Devesha; in Vaishakha, it is Dhatri Tapana; in
the month of Jyeshtha, it is Indra; Ravi heats in Ashadha; it
is Vivasvan in the month of Shravana; it is said to be Bhaga
in Proshthapada; it is Parjanya in the month of Ashvina,
Bhaskara in the month of Kartika; Mitra in Margashirsha
and the eternal Vishnu in Pousha. In performing his tasks
as Arka, Varuna has five thousand rays. Pushan has six
thousand, Devesha has seven thousand, Dhatri has eight

[1346] The six seasons (*ritu*) are Vasanta (spring), Grishma
(summer), Varsha (monsson), Sharad (autumn), Hemanta (late
fall, pre-winter) and Shishira (winter). Vasanta has the months of
Chaitra (March-April) and Vaishakha (April-May), Grishma the
months of Jyestha (May-June) and Ashadha (June-July), Varsha
has the months of Shravana (July-August) and Bhadrapada/
Proshthapada (August-September), Sharad has the months of
Ashvina (September-October) and Kartika (October-November),
Hemanta has the months of Margashirsha (November-December)
and Pousha (December-January) and Shishira has the months of
Magha (January-February) and Phalguna (February-March).

thousand and Shatakratu[1347] has nine thousand. Vivasvan
protects with ten thousand and Bhaga protects with eleven
thousand. Mitra heats with seven thousand and Tvashta
with eight thousand. Aryama protects with ten thousand
and Parjanya with nine thousand. Vishnu, who holds up
the universe, heats with six thousand rays. In Vasanta,
Surya is tawny; in Grishma, the complexion is golden; in
Varsha, he is known to be white; in Sharad, the lord is
pale; in Hemanta, the complexion is like copper; and in
Shishira, Ravi is red. Surya deposits parts in herbs, Svadha
in ancestors and *amrita* in immortals. He conveys these
three to the three different types.'

'O *dvijas*! It should be known that Surya presides over
eight other *grahas*—Chandrama, Soma's son, Shukra,
Brihaspati, Bhouma, Manda, Rahu and Ketu as the
eighth.[1348] All these *grahas* are tied to Dhruva by reins in
the form of the wind. They rotate in their places and as they
orbit, follow Divakara. The wheel of the wind makes them
move, like a circle of fire. The wind that bears them along
is said to be Pravaha. Soma's chariot has three wheels, and
the horses have the complexion of *kunda* flowers.[1349] They
are yoked to the maker of the night, ten on the left and ten
on the right. Like Ravi, he moves along the *vithi*s set by the
*nakshatra*s.[1350] O Indras among *brahmana*s! The increase
and the decrease are always dependent on Dhruva. In
shukla paksha, Soma is on the other side of Bhaskara. The
other side is constantly filled up with that radiance. When
the gods drink it, it diminishes.[1351] But Soma is constantly

---

[1347] One who has performed one hundred sacrifices, Indra.
[1348] Soma's son is Budha and Manda is Shanaishchara.
[1349] Jasmine.
[1350] *Vithi* means path and the ecliptic is divided into nine *vithi*s.
[1351] On each day, the gods drink a digit and the moon wanes.

nourished. O *brahmanas*! Bhaskara does this through the single ray, known as Sushumna. In this way, Soma's body is nourished through Surya's energy. This happens progressively, day by day, and on Pournamasi,[1352] the moon is seen to be complete. Soma is complete in half a month and is full of *amrita*. O *brahmanas*! *Deva*s, who subsist on *amrita*, drink this. In this way, out of the fifteen parts, only a single digit is left and, in the afternoon, the large number of ancestors resort to this last bit. For a period of two *lava*s,[1353] they drink the digit that is left. Indu[1354] is sacred and is full of the nectar of *amrita*, with *amrita* in its *atman*. On Amavasya,[1355] *amrita* is exuded through the rays in the form of Svadha. The ancestors are content and refrain for a month. Soma is not destroyed, it is only the nectar that is drunk. O excellent one! In this way, Surya is the cause behind the increase and the decrease. The chariot of Soma's son is yoked to eight horses that possess the speed of the wind. They arose from the water, and he moves everywhere on that chariot. Shukra's chariot is yoked to ten horses that were born on earth. Bhouma's beautiful and golden chariot has eight horses. Brihaspati's chariot is made from gold and is yoked to eight horses. Manda's chariot is made from silver and has eight horses. Svarbhanu and Bhaskarari's chariots are made from iron and each is yoked to eight horses.[1356] The chariots of the great *graha*s have been described. All these immensely fortunate ones are tied to Dhruva by reins made from the

[1352] Night of the full moon.
[1353] *Lava* is a small measure of time.
[1354] The moon.
[1355] Night of the new moon.
[1356] Svarbhanu is Rahu and Bhaskarari (Bhaskara's enemy) is Ketu.

wind. All the *graha*s, *nakshatra*s and their locations are bound to Dhruva. They revolve, and make others revolve, by reins made from the wind.'

Chapter 44(1)(44) (The *loka*s)

S uta said, 'Maharloka extends for one hundred thousand *yojana*s, above Dhruva. O bulls among *dvija*s! Those who have entitlements for a *kalpa* reside there. Janaloka is above Maharloka and extends for two crore *yojana*s. Brahma's sons, Sanaka and the others, are established there. Tapoloka is above Janaloka and extends for three crore *yojana*s. *Deva*s known as Vairajas are there and they are not burnt down by the fire.[1357] Satyaloka is above the world of the Prajapatis[1358] and extends for six crore *yojana*s. It is named Apunarmaraka[1359] and is described as Brahmaloka. Brahma, the creator of the universe and the *guru* of the worlds, with the universe in his *atman*, is there. Along with the *yogi*s, he constantly drinks the supreme *amrita* of *yoga*. Serene and devoted mendicants, *brahmachari*s, reside there. They are *siddha*s, *yogi*s and ascetics, who perform *japa* on Parameshthi. Using that single gate, *yogi*s proceed to the supreme destination. Having gone there, such a person becomes Vishnu and Shankara and does not grieve. His[1360] city is impossible to reach and resembles one crore suns. It is garlanded in flames. It is impossible for me to describe it. Narayana's residence is also there, in Brahma's

[1357] Of destruction.
[1358] Tapoloka.
[1359] A place where there is no death again.
[1360] Brahma's.

city. Hari, the glorious *yogi*, full of supreme *maya*, lies down there. This is described as Vishnu's world and there is no return from there. Great-souled ones who seek refuge with Janardana go there. Above Brahma's residence, there is an auspicious city that is full of radiance. There is fire all around it and Bhagavan Hara is there. Mahadeva is with Devi and learned ones think about him. He is surrounded by hundreds of thousands of *yogi*s, *bhuta*s and Rudras. *Brahmachari*s who are constant in their devotion go there. They are serene ascetics, truthful in speech, who are devoted to Mahadeva. They have no sense of "mine" and are devoid of *ahamkara*. They are devoid of desire and anger. O *brahmana*s! Those who are engaged in *yoga* see that place, described as Rudra's world. These are described as the seven great worlds, Prithvi[1361] and the others. O *dvija*s! Below, there are the nether regions, Mahatala and the others. Mahatala and Patala are decorated with every kind of jewel. There are many types of mansions and pure temples to *deva*s. Ananta is there and the intelligent Muchukunda. King Bali, earlier resident of heaven, is in Patala. O *brahmana*s! Rasatala has rocks and Talatala has gravel. Sutala is yellow and Vitala has the hue of coral. Vitala is said to be white,[1362] while Tala is said to be black. O best among sages! Because of Suparna and Vasuki, it is auspicious. The place known as Rasatala is inhabited by others, Virochana, Hiranyaksha, Taraka and others. The place known as Talatala possesses every kind of beauty. It is inhabited by Vinataa's descendants, Kalanemi being

---

[1361] The earth, Bhurloka.
[1362] Since Vitala has already been mentioned, this must be a typo for one of the other nether regions. There are many inconsistencies in these descriptions.

the foremost. Earlier, Sutala used to be full of *deva*s but is now inhabited by others. Vitala has Yavanas and others, like Taraka and Agnimukha. There are *naga*s, Jambhaka and others, and *asura*s like Prahlada. Vitala is famous because it is inhabited by Kambala, Indra among serpents. The brave Mahajambha and the intelligent Hayagriva, along with Shankukarna and Namuchi, are there. Like that, there are many other *naga*s in the extremely beautiful Tala. Below are the hells, described as Kurma and others. It is impossible to describe these. Sinners are cooked there. Below the nether regions, there is Vishnu's form, known as Shesha. This is Rudra, the fire of destruction, with *yoga* in his *atman*. He is Narasimha Madhava. One reads of the divinity Janardana as Ananta, in his form as a serpent. He is the support for everything, and he depends on the fire of destruction. Having entered him, the great *yogi*, Kala, resides in his mouth. Full of flaming poison, Isha himself destroys the world. With a thousand different kinds of *maya*, Shankara Bhava is the unmatched destroyer. This is Shambhu's *tamas* form as Kala, who destroys the worlds.'

Chapter 45(1)(45) (*Dvipa*s and mountains)

Suta said, 'I have described the cosmic egg, consisting of fourteen great worlds. After this, I will narrate the determination of Bhurloka. Jambudvipa is the most important. The others are Plaksha, Shalmali, Kusha, Krouncha, Shaka and Pushkara as the seventh. These are the seven great *dvipa*s, surrounded by seven oceans. A succeeding *dvipa* is said to be greater than a preceding one and a succeeding ocean is greater than a preceding one. The oceans are made of salt water, sugarcane juice, liquor, ghee, curds, milk and fresh water. With the oceans and the seven *dvipa*s, in every direction, the earth is said to extend for fifty crore *yojana*s. Jambudvipa is located in the centre of everything. In its centre, there is the famous and large Meru, golden in colour. It rises for eighty-four thousand *yojana*s. Downwards, it penetrates sixteen thousand *yojana*s. It extends for thirty-two thousand *yojana*s at the top. At the base, in every direction, it extends for sixteen thousand *yojana*s.[1363] This mountain is established as the pericarp of the lotus that is the earth. Himalaya, Hemakuta and Nishadha are to its south. Nila, Shveta and Shringi are the *varsha-parvata*s[1364] to the north. The two in the centre extend for one hundred thousand *yojana*s. Successively, the lengths are diminished by ten thousand *yojana*s. The heights are two thousand *yojana*s and the breadths are also described to be that much. Bharata is the first *varsha*, the next one is said to be Kimpurusha. Harivarsha is the next. O *dvija*s! All these are to the south of Meru. Ramyaka is the *varsha* to the north and Hiranmaya comes after that. Uttara Kuru is beyond this. O excellent *dvija*s! Just like Bharata, each of them extends for nine thousand *yojana*s. Ilavrita is in the middle and Meru rises in its centre. In the four directions of Meru, Ilavrita extends for nine thousand *yojana*s. O immensely fortunate ones! There are four mountains on all sides of Ilavrita. They rise for ten thousand *yojana*s and form supporting pillars for Meru. The one to the east is named Mandara and Gandhamadana is to the south. Vipula is on the western flank and Suparshva is said to be to the north. There is a *kadamba*, *jambu*, *pippala* and

---

[1363] Meru is in the form of an inverted cone.

[1364] *Varsha-parvata*s are mountains (mountain ranges) that separate the *varsha*s.

vata tree.[1365] O *maharshi*s! The *jambu* tree is responsible for the name Jambu-dvipa. The fruits are the size of large elephants. In every direction, they fall on the surface of the ground and are crushed. Because of the resultant juice, the famous Jambu River flows on the mountain. When the river flows, the residents drink from it. They do not suffer from perspiration, bad odour, old age or decay of the senses. There is no torment and the minds are pure. There is no unhappiness there. The juice mixes with the earth on the banks and is completely dried up by the wind. This results in the gold known as Jambunada, used by *siddha*s for their ornaments.'

'Bhadrashva is to the east of Meru and Ketumala is to the west. O best among sages! Ilavrita is located in between these two *varsha*s. The grove of Chaitraratha is to the east and that of Gandhamadana to the south. The one to the west is known as Vaibhraja and Savitar's grove is to the north. There are four lakes that are always worthy of being enjoyed by the gods—Arunoda, Mahabhadra, [1366] and Manasa. Sitanta, Kumuda, Kururi, Malyavan, Vaikanka, Manishaila, the excellent mountain Vrikshavan, Mahanila, Ruchaka, Sabindu, Mandara, Venuman, Megha, Nishadha and Mount Deva—these are said to have been constructed by *deva*s as habitations for *siddha*s. Mount Kesara is to the east of Lake Arunoda. Trikuta, Sashira, Patanga,

---

[1365]Respectively in Mandara, Gandhamadana, Vipula and Suparshva. *Kadamba* is *stephegyne parvifolia*, *jambu* is the rose apple tree and both *pippala* and *vata* are holy fig trees.

[1366]Each of the mountains, Mandara, Gandhamadana, Vipula and Suparshva, has a grove and a lake. This is usually stated as Chaitraratha and Arunoda in Mandara, Nandana and Manasa in Gandhamadana, Vaibhraja and Asitoda (or Sitoda) in Vipula and Savitra (Savitar's) and Mahabhadra in Suparshva.

Ruchaka, Nishadha, Vasudhara, Kalinga, the one named Trishikha, Samula, Vasuvedi, Kururu, Sanuman, Tamrata, Vishala, Kumuda, Venuparvata, Ekashringa, Mahashaila, Gajashaila, Pinjaka, Panchashaila, Kailasa and the excellent mountain of Himalaya are also there. These large and excellent mountains have been constructed by *deva*s. Mount Kesara is to the south of Lake Mahabhadra. Shikhivasa, Vaidurya, Kapila, Gandhamadana, Jarudhi, Surambhu, the excellent mountain of Sarvagandha, Suparshva, Supaksha, Kanka, Kapila, Viraja, Bhadrajala, Susaka, Mahabala, Anjana, Madhuman, Chitrashringa, Mahalaya, Kumuda, Mukuta, Pandura, Krishna, Parijata, Mahashaila, Kapilachala, Sushena, Pundarika and Mahamegha—these kings among mountains are frequented by *siddha*s and *gandharva*s. Mount Kesara is to the west of Lake Asitoda. Shankhakuta, Vrishabha, Hamsa, Naga, Kalanjana, Shukrashaila, Nila, Kamala, Parijata, Mahashaila, Mount Kanaka, Pushpaka, Sumegha, Varaha, Viraja, Mayura, Kapila and Mahakapila—these are frequented by *deva*s, *gandharva*s, *siddha*s and *yaksha*s. Mount Kesara is to the north of Lake Manasa. In the due order, these are the foremost mountains. Between them, there are valleys, lakes and groves. Sages and *siddha*s, who think about the *brahman*, reside there. They are serene, free of impurities and free from every kind of unhappiness.'

Chapter 46(1)(46) (Guardians of the worlds)

Suta said, 'On top of Meru, there is the great city of the creator, the lord of the *deva*s, extending for fourteen thousand *yojana*s. Bhagavan Brahma, the creator of the universe and whose *atman* is in the universe, is there.

He is worshipped by Indras among *yogi*s, Indras among sages, Upendra and Shankara. Bhagavan Ishana, lord of *deva*s and the Prajapati whose *atman* is in the universe, is there. He is constantly worshipped by Sanatkumara and worshipped by *siddha*s, *rishi*s, *gandharva*s and gods. With his *atman* immersed in *yoga*, he drinks the supreme *amrita*. The residence of Shambhu, the infinitely energetic lord of *deva*s, is located in front of Brahma's residence. It is dazzling and sparkling. It possesses a divine charm and is extremely beautiful, with four gates. There are large numbers of *maharshi*s and it is frequented by those who know about the *brahman*. Along with the *pramatha*s,[1367] Mahadeva, the lord of the universe and the lord of *pramatha*s, with the sun, the moon and the fire as his eyes, sports there, along with Devi. There are serene sages there, *brahmachari*s who know the Vedas. Truthful in speech, they use austerities to worship Mahadeva. Along with Parvati, Parameshvara Mahadeva directly accepts the worship of sages, who have cleansed their *atman*s, on his head.'

'On that excellent mountain, to the east, is Shakra's supreme city, which possesses every kind of beauty. It is named Amaravati. There, all the *apsara*s, *gandharva*s, *siddha*s and *charana*s, and thousands of *deva*s, worship the one with one thousand eyes. This supreme place is for those who are devoted to *dharma*, those who know the Vedas and are devoted to sacrifices and oblations. Even the *deva*s find it extremely difficult to reach there. In the southern direction,[1368] there is the city of the infinitely energetic

---

[1367] Literally, *pramatha*s are those who strike. They are Shiva's attendants and companions.
[1368] The south-eastern direction. The text means, to the south of the eastern direction.

Vahni, named Tejovati. It is full of divine wonders. There, the illustrious Vahni is resplendent in his own energy. This is a place for those who perform *japa* and offer oblations. *Danava*s find it extremely difficult to reach it. Yama's great city is to the south of the supreme mountain. It is named Samyamani. It is divine and possesses every kind of beauty. There, *deva*s and others worship the *deva* Vaivasvata.[1369] This is a world for those who are devoted to the truth, men who perform auspicious deeds. To its west,[1370] there is the great-souled Nirriti's city. It is named Rakshovati and is surrounded by *rakshasa*s. The *rakshasa*s worship *deva* Nirriti there. Those who are devoted to *dharma*, but those whose conduct is full of *tamas*, go there. To the west of the supreme mountain, there is Varuna's great city. This is named Shuddhavati. It is sacred and is full of every kind of desire and prosperity. There, large numbers of *apsara*s and *siddha*s serve the lord of immortals. King Varuna is there and those who offer water go there. To its north,[1371] there is Vayu's great city. It is named Gandhavati. It is sacred and Prabhanjana[1372] is there. Large numbers of *apsara*s and *gandharva*s serve the great lord there. *Brahmana*s who are devoted to *pranayama* go to that eternal place. Soma's supreme city is to the east of this. It is named Kantimati. It is sparkling and Soma is resplendent there. This is the appropriate place for those who are devoted to *dharma* and follow their own *dharma*. It has many objects of pleasure. To the east of this is Shankara's great city. It is named Yashovati. It is sacred and everyone finds it difficult

[1369] Yama is Surya's son.
[1370] That is, the south-western direction.
[1371] That is, the north-western direction.
[1372] Vayu.

to reach. There is Ishana's auspicious and extensive abode, presided over by Rudra, the lord of *gana*s. He is surrounded by *gana*s. Earlier, the lord of *deva*s, the wielder of the trident, had thought of habitations there, for those who are Parameshthi's devotees and desire objects of pleasure and other things.'

'Flowing from Vishnu's feet, Ganga floods the lunar disc and descends all around Brahma's city. O *dvija*s! Having descended, it is divided into four in the four directions—Sitaa, Alakanandaa, Suchakshu and Bhadraa. Sita travels from one mountain to another mountain, through the sky and towards the east. It flows through the eastern *varsha* of Bhadrashva and into the ocean. O excellent *dvija*s! Alakanandaa enters Bharata to the south[1373] and dividing itself into seven parts, proceeds to the ocean. Suchakshu passes over the western mountain and the western *varsha* of Ketumala, before entering the ocean. O *maharshi*s! Like that, Bhadraa passes over the northern mountain and Uttara Kuru, before entering the northern ocean. Between the two pairs of Nila and Nishadha and Malyavan and Gandhamadana, Meru is established like the pericarp of a lotus. Outside the mountains that set the boundaries, Bharata, Ketumala, Bhadrashva and Kuru are like the petals of the lotus that is the world. From the south to the north, Jathara and Devakuta are the boundary mountains, extending up to Nila and Nishadha. Gandhamadana and Kailasa extend from east to west, penetrating the ocean up to a distance of eighty *yojana*s. As was the case earlier, Nishadha and Pariyatra are the boundary mountains to the west of Meru. Trishringa and Jarudhi are *varsha-parvata*s to the north. They extend the same distance inside the

---

[1373] Of Meru.

oceans. O *dvija*s! I have spoken about the eight boundary mountains, Jathara and the others. O *maharshi*s! They are established in the four directions of Meru.'

Chapter 47(1)(47) (Ketumala and other *varsha*s)

Suta said, 'In Ketumala, all the men are like crows[1374] and eat jackfruit. The women possess the radiance of lotus petals and live for ten thousand years. In Bhadrashva, the men are fair, and the women resemble moonbeams. They live for ten thousand years and eat cooked food. In Ramyaka, men and women pleasure themselves and have the complexion of silver. They are full of *sattva* and live for eleven thousand and five hundred years. They eat *nyagrodha* fruit. In Hiranmaya, everyone has the complexion of gold. They eat *shriphala*.[1375] As if they are in the world of *deva*s, men and women live for twelve thousand and five hundred years. In Kuru *varsha*, they live for fourteen thousand and five hundred years. They are dark in complexion and subsist on milk. In Chandra-dvipa, they constantly worship Shiva Mahadeva. All of them are born through physical intercourse and enjoy happiness. O *brahmana*s! In Kimpurusha, men have the complexion of gold. Surviving on *plaksha*,[1376] they live for ten thousand years. They constantly worship the divinity with the four heads and four arms. Lovingly and full of devotion, they fix their minds in *dhyana* on him. In Hari *varsha*, they have the complexion of gold. They subsist on sugarcane

---

[1374]They are dark.
[1375]This can mean either coconut or *bilva* (wood apple).
[1376]A kind of fig.

juice and live for ten thousand years. The men there are
constantly devoted to the eternal divinity, Narayana, the
origin of the universe. They worship Vishnu. Vaasudeva's
vimana has the complexion of the moon. It is as white as
pure crystal and is located in a grove of *parijata* trees.[1377]
With four arches and four gates, it is unmatched. With ten
ramparts, it is impossible to assail and impossible to reach.
Like the residence of the king of *deva*s, there are pavilions
made of crystal. In every direction, it is decorated with
thousands of golden columns. There are golden stairs,
embellished with many kinds of jewels. There is a divine
throne, decorated with every kind of beauty. The place
is beautiful because of the lakes and rivers, full of tasty
water. The place is full of *yogi*s, who perform *dhyana* on
Hari Purusha. They are pure, devoted to Narayana and
intent on studying the *Veda*s. They constantly prostrate
themselves before Madhava and praise him with *mantra*s.
All the time, kings praise the greatness of the infinitely
energetic Vishnu, the lord of *deva*s. There are young
and charming women, always intent on beautifying
themselves. They sing and dance and amuse themselves. In
Ilavrita, they have the complexion of lotuses and survive
on the juice of *jambu* fruit. The lifespan is fixed at thirteen
thousand years.'

'It is said that in Bharata, men and women have many
kinds of complexion. They are engaged in worshipping
many kinds of *deva*s and performing many kinds of *karma*.
O ones excellent in vows! Their lifespan is said to be one
hundred years. The size of the *varsha* is said to be nine
thousand *yojana*s. O *brahmana*s! For men who possess the

[1377] A divine tree, the coral tree.

rights, this is *karma-bhumi*.[1378] The seven *kula-parvatas*[1379] are Mahendra, Malaya, Sahya, Shaktiman, Mount Riksha, Vindhya and Pariyatra. Indradvipa, Kaserukman, Tamraparna, Gabhastiman, Nagadvipa, Soumya Gandharva and Varuna—these are the others.[1380] But this *dvipa*, the ninth, is located along the ocean. From south to north, the *dvipa* extends for one thousand *yojana*s. The Kiratas are to the east and the Yavanas are to the west. In the centre, there are *brahmana*s, *kshatriya*s, *vaishya*s and *shudra*s. These men subsist through sacrifices, fighting and trade. Many purifying rivers emerge from mountains and flow there. Those that flow from the foothills of the Himalayas are Shatadru, Chandrabhaga, Sarayu, Yamuna, Iravati, Vitasta, Vipasha, Devika, Kuhu, Gomati, Dhutapapa, Bahudra, Drishadvati, Koushiki and Lohini. Those that emerge from Pariyatra are said to be Vedasmriti, Vedavati, Vrataghni, Tridiva, Varnasha, Chandana, Charmanyavati, Sura, Vidisha and Vetravati. The rivers which flow from the foothills of Rikshavan, and take away all the sins of men, are Narmada, Surasa, Shona, Dasharna, Mahanadi, Mandakini, Chitrakuta, Tamasi, Pishachika, Chitrotpala, Vishala, Manjula and Valuvahini. Those that flow from the foothills of Vindhya, and instantly take away the sins of men, are Tapi, Payoshni, Nirvindhya, Shighroda, Mahanadi, Vinna, Vaitarani, Balaka, Kumudvati, Mahagouri, Durga and Antahshila. O excellent *dvija*s! The rivers along *dakshinapatha*,[1381] flowing from the foothills of Sahya, are Godavari, Bhimarathi, Krishna, Vena, Vashyata,

[1378] Land where *karma* is performed.

[1379] A *kula-parvata* (also known as *kulachala*) is the principal mountain (mountain range) in a *varsha*. Usually, there are seven.

[1380] This sentence is inconsistent.

[1381] The southern road, the southern region.

Tungabhadra, Suprayoga and Kaveri. The rivers emerging from Malaya are Ritumala, Tampraparni, Punyavati and Utpalavati. It is said that they are always full of cool water. Rishikulya and Trisama flow from Gandhamadana. Kshipra, Palashini, Rishika and Vamshadharini flow from the foothills of Shuktiman and take away the sins of men. O bulls among *dvija*s! There are hundreds of rivers and smaller rivers. They are sacred, take away sins and are used for bathing, donations and other rites. The people in the central regions are Kurus and Panchalas. Those in the eastern region are inhabitants of Kamarupa. There are Pundras, Kalingas, Magadhas, all those from the southern parts, those to the west, Sourashtras, Shudras, Hinas, Arbudas, Malakas, Malapas, those who reside in Pariyatra, Souviras, Saindhavas, Hunas, Malyas, those who reside in Balya, Madras, Ramas, Andhras and Parasikas. They always live along the rivers and drink their water. The wise say that there are four *yuga*s in Bharatavarsha—*krita*, *treta*, *dvapara* and *kali*. These do not exist elsewhere. O *maharshi*s! There are the eight *varsha*s, Kimpurusha and the others. There is no sorrow or exertion there, no anxiety or hunger. The *praja*s are well, free of fear. They are devoid of every kind of misery. With constant youth, they amuse themselves in many kinds of ways.'

Chapter 48(1)(48) (Description of Jambudvipa)

Suta said, 'On the summit of Mount Hemakuta, there is the extremely sacred and extremely beautiful *vimana* of Parameshthi, the lord of *deva*s. It is made out of crystal. There, *deva*s, large numbers of *rishi*s and *siddha*s constantly worship the lord of *deva*s, the lord of *bhuta*s, the wielder of the trident. Girisha Mahadeva Maheshvara is there, along with Devi. Surrounded by *bhuta*s, the wielder of Pinaka is always resplendent. Mount Kailasa is there, with its separate and beautiful peaks. Crores of *yaksha*s and the intelligent Kubera reside there. The large residence of Bhava, the lord of *deva*s, is there. The beautiful and sacred Mandakini, with sparkling water, is there. There are many kinds of rivers, ornamented with many lotuses. *Deva*s, *danava*s, *gandharva*s, *yaksha*s, *rakshasa*s and *kinnara*s always touch the extremely holy and extremely beautiful water. There are hundreds of other rivers, ornamented with golden lotuses. The places of the divinity Parameshthi, large numbers of *deva*s and *rishi*s, and Narayana are there. On its white summit,[1382] there is an auspicious *parijata* grove. Shakra's large residence is there, studded with jewels. There are pillars made from crystal and it is adorned with golden gates. The beautiful and sacred residence of Vishnu, the lord of *deva*s, the lord whose *atman* is in the universe, is there. It is decorated with every kind of jewel. The glorious Narayana, the lord of the universe, is there, along with Lakshmi. He is the best and the lord of everything. He is eternal and is worshipped. Vasudhara of the Vasus is decorated with jewels. This is an excellent and sacred place, impossible for the enemies of the gods to reach. The habitation of the great-souled *saptarshi*s is on Ratnadhara, the excellent mountain. There are seven sacred hermitages there, along with the residences of the *siddha*s. The extremely sacred residence of Brahma, whose birth is not manifest, is there. It is made of gold, has four gates and is decorated with diamonds and blue sapphire. O *brahmana*s! *Deva*s, *rishi*s, *siddha*s and *brahmarshi*s are

---

[1382]Whose summit remains unclear.

there. They worship the grandfather, the supreme Aja, the lord of *deva*s. All of them constantly worship the one with the four faces, along with Devi.[1383] For the welfare of the worlds, he is the supreme destination for those who are serene. One of its summits is decorated with large lotuses. There is a sacred and extremely large lake, full of fragrant and clear water that is like *amrita*. Jaigishavya's sacred hermitage is there, and it is frequented by Indras among *yogi*s. The illustrious one is always there, surrounded by all his *shishya*s. They are great-souled and know about the *brahman*. They are serene, free from taints and inferior blemishes. They are Shankha, Manohara, Koushika, Krishna, Sumanas and Vedavada. Thanks to his favours, all these *shishya*s are devoted to *yoga*. They are tranquil and their bodies are covered with *bhasma*. Devoted to knowledge about the *brahman*, they worship the great *acharya*. To show his favours to mendicants who are serene in their minds, Maheshvara remains near them, along with Devi. There are many hermitages on that supreme and excellent mountain. These belong to sages whose minds are immersed in *yoga*. There are lakes and rivers. There are *brahmana*s there, engaged in *yoga*. They restrain their senses and perform *japa*. Their minds are fixed on the *brahman*, and they find pleasure in supreme *jnana*. Located on that summit, they fix their *atman*s on the *paramatman*. They perform *dhyana* on the divinity Ishana, whose residence, with its bejewelled turrets, is there. But he is actually everywhere. Bhagavati Durgaa, Maheshvari herself, is there. She is worshipped by many kinds of different Shaktis. She drinks the *amrita* of *yoga* and obtains that *amrita* from Ishvara himself. The summit of Mount

---

[1383] That is, Savitri.

Sunila shines with many kinds of minerals. O *dvijas*! The cities of *rakshasas* and hundreds of lakes are there. O *brahmanas*! Mahachala has one hundred peaks and there are one hundred cities there, with pillars made of crystal. The infinitely energetic *yakshas* live there. On the summit of Mount Shvetodara, there is the great-souled Suparna's city. It has ramparts and archways, gates ornamented with jewels. The glorious Garuda is himself there, like a second Vishnu. Within his own *atman*, he performs *dhyana* on the supreme and imperishable illumination. O bulls among sages! On Shrishringa, there is the residence of Shri Devi. It is excellent and is full of gold and every kind of gem, with bejewelled gates. Vishnu's extremely beautiful and supreme Shakti is there. She is infinite in her prosperity. She is Lakshmi, eager to delude the world. She is there, worshipped by *devas*, *gandharvas*, *siddhas* and *charanas*. One should think of the origin of the universe, blazing in his rays, in the form of his own Shakti. The large residence of Vishnu, the lord of the *devas*, is there. There are four lakes there, filled with colourful lotuses. On Sahasrashikhara, there are eight cities of the *vidyadharas*.[1384] The place is decorated with lakes and the stairs are made from jewels. The rivers are full of sparkling water and are covered with colourful blue lotuses. There is a grove of divine *karnikara* flowers there, where Shankara himself resides. Mahalakshmi's auspicious city is on Mount Paripatra. It has beautiful mansions, decorated with bells and whisks. Large numbers of *apsaras* adorn it and dance there. There are the sounds of *mridangas* and *panavas*, flutes and *veenas*.[1385] It is full of *gandharvas* and *kinnaras* and surrounded by bulls among

[1384] Semi-divine species.
[1385] *Mridangas* and *panavas* are different types of drums.

*siddha*s. It is full of great mansions that are extremely resplendent. It is full of large lords among *gana*s and those who are devoted to *dharma* find it charming to behold. Constantly devoted to *yoga*, Devi resides there. Mahalakshmi Mahadevi wields an excellent trident. She possesses three eyes. She is surrounded by all the Shaktis and she pervades them. Sages and *siddha*s who speak about the *brahman* see her there. Sarasvati's excellent city is on the northern side of Suparshva. O excellent ones! There are lakes and divine objects of pleasure, frequented by *siddha*s. The summit of Mount Pandura is covered with wonderful trees. There are hundreds of cities of *gandharva*s, full of divine women. The men and women there are constantly intoxicated. Intent on enjoyment and objects of pleasure, they are happy and constantly sport. On the summit of Mount Anjana, there is an excellent city for women. Rambha and other *apsara*s, eager to engage in intercourse, reside there. Chitrasena and the others always go there, to seek them out. That city possesses all the excellent jewels and has many waterfalls. O excellent ones! There are many cities on Koumuda. There are serene Rudras, who have no *rajas*, with their minds fixed on Ishvara. These Rudras are great *yogi*s, capable of reaching Mahesha's inner quarters. Astride a mass of radiance, they reach Ishvara's place in that city. On the summit of Mount Pinjara, there are the three cities of *ganesha*s. The city of the immensely intelligent Nandishvara, Kapila, is there. On the summit of Jarudhi, there is the sacred and blazing residence of the infinitely energetic Bhaskara, the intelligent lord of *deva*s. To its north, there is Chandra's excellent place. The illustrious one, with a serene and beautiful *atman*, lives there. O *maharshi*s! There is a divine residence on Mount Hamsa. It extends for one thousand *yojana*s and has gates made from gold and jewels. Bhagavan Brahma is there, surrounded by large numbers of *siddha*s. The one whose *atman* is in the universe is with Savitri. Vaasudeva and the others are with him. To its south, there is the excellent city of the *siddha*s. Bulls among sages, Sanandana and others, live there. There are three cities of *danava*s on the summit of Panchashaila. Their intelligent *acharya*[1386] lives close by. The summit of Mount Sugandha is adorned with beautiful rivers. The sacred hermitage of the illustrious *rishi*, Kardama, is there. To its east and a little to the south, lives the illustrious Sanatkumara, who knows about the *brahman*. O lords among sages! Similarly, on all the other mountains, there are lakes, sparkling rivers and residences of *deva*s. There are sacred *siddha-lingam*s,[1387] instated by sages. It is impossible to easily enumerate their dimensions and numbers. I have briefly spoke about Jambu-dvipa. Even if I try for one hundred years, I am incapable of describing it in detail.'

Chapter 49(1)(49) (Plaksha and other *dvipa*s)

Suta said, 'On every side, Jambu-dvipa is surrounded by an ocean of salty water[1388] that is double the size of Jambu-dvipa. Plaksha-dvipa surrounds this ocean. O Indras among *brahmana*s! There are seven *kula-parvata*s in Plaksha-dvipa. The mountains possess excellent ridges and are frequented by large numbers of *siddha*s. Gomeda

---

[1386] Shukracharya.

[1387] *Lingam*s instated by *siddha*s.

[1388] The text says ocean of milk, which is an error. We have corrected it.

is the first and Chandra is said to be the second. The others are Narada, Dundubhi, Maniman and Meghanisvana. Vaibhraja, extremely loved by Brahma, is the seventh. Bhagavan Aja's *atman* is in the universe. He looks at the universe and is a witness to everything. There, *deva*s, *rishi*s, *gandharva*s and *siddha*s worship him. There are sacred habitations, lacking physical ailments and mental ailments. Men who perform evil deeds can never go there. There are seven rivers in each *varsha* and they proceed to the ocean. There, *brahmarshi*s constantly worship the grandfather. The names of the rivers are said to be Anutapta, Shikha, Vipapa, Tridiva, Krita, Amrita and Sukrita. There are minor rivers that are famous and many lakes. No *yuga*s exist here and men live for a long period of time. They are Aryakas, Kururas, Videhas and Bhavins. In that *dvipa*, it is said that there are *brahmana*s, *kshatriya*s, *vaishya*s and *shudra*s. These *varna*s reside there and worship Bhagavan Isha. O bulls among sages! They are entitled to Soma's kingdom and obtain *sarupya* with him.[1389] All of them are constantly devoted to *dharma*. All of them are happy in their minds. Without any disease, they live for five thousand years.'

'In every direction, Plaksha-dvipa is surrounded by an ocean of sugarcane juice that is double the size of Plaksha-dvipa. Shalmali-dvipa surrounds this ocean. There are seven *varsha*s there and seven *kula-parvata*s that are straight, with excellent ridges. O ones excellent in vows! There are seven rivers. The mountains are Kumuda, Annada, Balahaka as the third, Drona, Kamsa, Mahisha

---

[1389]There are different levels of emancipation. *Sarupya* is to have the same form as the divinity. *Salokya* is to be in the same world as the divinity. *Sayujya* is to obtain identity with the divinity. *Samipya* is to be near the divinity.

and Kakudman as the seventh. The rivers, which take away the sins of men, are said to be Yoni, Toya, Vitrishna, Chandra, Shukla, Vimochini and Nivritti. O excellent *dvija*s! Greed and anger do not exist there. There are no *yuga*s there and people live free from disease. All the *varna*s there constantly worship the eternal Vayu. As a result of these means, they achieve *sarupya* and *salokya* with Vayu. The *brahmana*s are said to be tawny and the kings are red. O *dvija*s! In that *dvipa*, the *vaishya*s are said to be yellow and the *vrishala*s are dark.'[1390]

"In every direction, Shalmali-dvipa is surrounded by an ocean of liquor that is double the size of Shalmali-dvipa. Kusha-dvipa is all around this. The seven mountains are Vidruma, Homa, Dyutiman, Pushpavan, Kusheshaya, Hari and Mandara. The seven great rivers are Dhutapapa, Shiva, Pavitra, Sammita, Vidyut, Prabha and Rama. O *brahmana*s! There are hundreds of other pure rivers, with water that sparkles like jewels. *Deva*s and others worship Brahma and Ishana. O *brahmana*s! *Brahmana*s are known as Dravinas, *kshatriya*s as Shushmins, *vaishya*s as Stobhas and *shudra*s are said to be Mandehas. Men possess *jnana* and friendliness and other qualities. All of them do what they have been instructed to do. All of them are engaged in the welfare of beings. With many kinds of sacrifices, they worship Parameshthi Brahma. They achieve *sayujya*, *sarupya* and *salokya* with Brahma.'

'O *brahmana*s! In every direction, Kusha-dvipa is surrounded by an ocean of *ghee* that is double the size of Kusha-dvipa. Krouncha-dvipa is all around this. The seven mountains are said to be named Krouncha, Vamanaka, Adhikarika as the third, Devabda, Viveda, Pundarika

---

[1390] While *vrishala* means *shudra*, it also means outcast.

and Dundubhisvana. The main rivers are said to be Gouri, Kumudvati, Sandhya, Ratri, Manojava, Kobhi and Pundarikaksha. O excellent *dvijas*! *Brahmanas*, *kshatriyas*, *vaishyas* and *shudras* respectively are Prishkalas, Pushkaras, Dhanyas and Tishyas. These are the *varnas* in the due order. Through sacrifices, donations, self-control, vows, fasting, many kinds of oblations and performing rites for the ancestors, they worship Mahadeva. Because of his favours, they obtain *sayujya* with Rudra, the extremely rare *sarupya*, *salokya* and *samipya*.'

'O *brahmanas*! In every direction, Krouncha-dvipa is surrounded by an ocean of curds that is double the size of Krouncha-dvipa. Shaka-dvipa is all around this. The mountains are Udaya, Raivata, Shyama, Kashthagiri, Ambikeya, Ramya and Kesari. The rivers are Sukumari, Kumari, Nalini, Venuka, Ikshuka, Dhenuka and Gabhasti. The men there drink these waters and live, free from disease, grief, attachment and hatred. In the due order, *brahmanas*, *kshatriyas*, *vaishyas* and *shudras* are Mrigas, Magadhas, Manasas and Mandagas. Through vows, fasting and many other rites, they constantly worship the divinity Divakara, the lord of *devas* and a witness to all the worlds. O Indras among *brahmanas*! Through his favours, they achieve *sayujya*, *samipya*, *sarupya* and *salokya* with Surya.'

'In every direction, Shaka-dvipa is surrounded by an ocean of milk and Shveta-dvipa is in its centre. There are sacred habitations, full of many kinds of wonders. The men are devoted to Narayana. They are always born fair and are devoted to Vishnu. There are no physical or mental ailments there. There is no fear of old age or death. They are free from anger and greed. They are devoid of delusion and envy. They are always nourished and without fear. They always enjoy constant bliss. All of them are devoted to Narayana and are just like Narayana. Some of them are *yogi*s who have controlled their senses. They are constantly engaged in *dhyana*. Some perform *japa*. Others torment themselves through austerities. Others pursue *vijnana*. Others are permeated by thoughts about the *brahman* and engage in *nirbija yoga*. They perform *dhyana* on the supreme *brahman*, the eternal Vaasudeva. They worship him alone and require no other support. They are great devotees of Bhagavan. They perceive the supreme *brahman*, beyond darkness, known as Vishnu. All of them possess four arms and hold a conch shell a *chakra* and a mace. Their excellent garments are yellow and all of them have the Srivatsa mark on their chests. There are others devoted to Maheshvara, with *tripundraka* marks on their foreheads. Their excellent *yoga* leads to their prosperity and their mounts are giant Garudas. All of them possess Shaktis. All of them are sparkling, full of constant bliss. The men who reside there roam around in Vishnu's inner circle. Narayana's city is named Narayana. It is difficult to reach and difficult to assail. It is adorned with mansions. There are golden ramparts and crystal pavilions. It is impossible to assail and extremely beautiful. The radiance manifests itself in a thousand different ways. There are mansions and palaces and large houses. There are thousands of golden arches, decorated with many kinds of beautiful jewels. The place is ornamented with different types of white spreads. There are many kinds of pleasure gardens and beautiful rivers. There are lakes everywhere, resounding with the sounds of *veena*s and flutes. The place is decorated with many kinds of colourful flags. There are roads everywhere and the stairs are studded with jewels. There are hundreds and thousands of excellent rivers, resounding with divine songs. The place is full of swans, *karandava*s and

*chakravaka*s.[1391] There are four gates. It is unmatched and
the enemies of *deva*s cannot reach it. Large numbers of
extremely beautiful *apsara*s dance there. They know the
rules about many kinds of singing that are unknown even
to the *deva*s. They know many kinds of amorous gestures.
They are extremely delicate and full of lust. Their many
faces resemble the moon. There are the sounds of anklets.
They smile a little and their lips resemble the *bimba* fruit.
Their beautiful eyes resemble those of young fawns. Their
waists are slender and they possess every kind of prosperity.
Their gait resembles that of royal swans. Their garments
are excellent and their voices melodious. Adorned with
divine ornaments, they are accomplished in conversing.
The weight of their breasts makes them stoop and because
of liquor, their eyes roll around. Their wonderful limbs
have many kinds of hues, and they are addicted to objects
of pleasure and intercourse.'

'The city is decorated with hundreds of gardens, full
of blossoming flowers. Its qualities cannot be enumerated.
It is full of innumerable pure *deva*s. This is the glorious
and sacred city of the divinity, the infinitely energetic
Shripati.[1392] In its centre, there is a place full of energy,
with ramparts and gates. This is Vishnu's divine place, that
bestows *siddhi* on *yogi*s. In its centre is the one and only
Bhagavan, with a radiance resembling the petals of a lotus.
The origin of everything in the universe lies down. Hari lies
down, with Shesha as his couch. Indras among *yogi*s, with
Sanandana at the forefront, think about him. He drinks
the *amrita* of bliss from his own *atman*. He is beyond

[1391] *Karandava* is a kind of duck, *chakravaka* is the Brahminy
duck.
[1392] Shri's husband, Vishnu.

darkness. He is attired in yellow garments. His eyes are large. He is mighty-armed and full of great *maya*. His two feet are always clasped by the daughter of the ocean of milk.[1393] She is the Devi who is worshipped by the universe. Hari's beloved is always at his feet. Her mind is fixed on him and she constantly drinks Narayana's *amrita*. Those who are devoted to *adharma* do not go there, nor do those who are devoted to other *deva*s. The name of this place is Vaikuntha and it is worshipped even by the gods. I do not possess the wisdom, nor am I sufficiently well-versed in the sacred texts, to be able to describe Narayana's city. This much can be said. The eternal Vaasudeva is the supreme *brahman*. The glorious Narayana lies down, confounding the world with his *maya*. Everything is born from Narayana and is established in him. When the time is over, everything dissolves into him. He is the supreme destination.'

Chapter 50(1)(50) (Pushkara-dvipa)

Suta said, 'Shaka-dvipa is surrounded by an ocean of milk that is double the size of Shaka-dvipa. The place that depends on the ocean of milk is known as Pushkara-dvipa. O Indras among *brahmana*s! There is only a single mountain there, Manasottara. Its height is more than fifty thousand *yojana*s. In every direction, its circumference is also that much. Manasottara is established such that it divides the *dvipa* into two parts. That immensely fortunate region is divided into two parts. It is said that there are two sacred and auspicious countries in that *dvipa*. They are

---

[1393]When the ocean of milk was churned, Lakshmi manifested herself.

on two sides of Mount Manasottara. They are said to be
Mahavita *varsha* and Dhataki *khanda*. Pushkara-dvipa is
surrounded by an ocean of fresh water. In that *dvipa*, there
is a giant *nyagrodha* tree, worshipped by the immortals.
Brahma, the creator of the universe, whose *atman* is in the
universe, resides there. O tiger among sages![1394] The abodes
of Shiva and Narayana are there. Mahadeva Hara resides
in one half and the imperishable Hari resides in the other
half. Brahma and others, Kumara[1395] and others, and *yogis*
worship them. *Gandharvas*, *kinnaras* and *yakshas* worship
Ishvara, who is dark and tawny. All the *prajas* are healthy
and the *brahmanas* are a hundred times more energetic.
They are devoid of ailments and grief. They are devoid of
attachment and hatred. Truth and falsehood do not exist
there. Nor is there any notion of superior, middling and
inferior. The *dharma* of *varnas* and *ashramas* does not
exist. There are no rivers or mountains. O excellent *dvijas*!
In every direction, Pushkara is surrounded by a large ocean
of fresh water that extends beyond. The great region that is
beyond the world can be seen beyond this. There is a single
rock that extends everywhere. The ground is golden and is
double its size. Beyond this, there is a mountain that forms
the boundary for the solar circle. Part has illumination and
part lacks illumination. This is spoken of as Lokaloka.
It is said to rise for ten thousand *yojanas*. The expanse
of the great mountain of Lokaloka is also that much. In
every direction, that mountain is enveloped by darkness.
In turn, this is enveloped by the shell of the cosmic egg.
Thus, the seven great worlds and the nether regions have
been described. The cosmic egg is infinite in expanse. I

[1394] The singular is used.
[1395] Sanatkumara.

have described it briefly. It should be known that there are thousands of crores of such eggs. Since Pradhana is the cause, with an undecaying *atman*, it goes everywhere. In each of these eggs, there are fourteen worlds. In each of these, there are those with four faces, Rudras, Narayanas and others. In every direction, there are seven sheaths that cover the cosmic egg, each sheath ten times the size of the preceding one. O *brahmana*s! Only the learned can go there. Beyond all this, there is Mahat, infinite and unmanifest, without a beginning and without an end, and the undecaying Prakriti, the cause of the universe. This is infinite and endless and cannot be enumerated. It should be known that this is not manifest. This is the eternal and supreme *brahman*. One reads about this as infinite, which is everywhere, in every place. I have spoken about its excellent greatness earlier. It goes everywhere and is worshipped in every place, the earth, the nether regions, the firmament, the wind, the fire, all the oceans and heaven. There is no doubt about this. The immensely radiant one is also present in the *tattva* of *tamas*. Dividing himself into many bodies, Purushottama sports. Maheshvara is beyond the unmanifest. He is beyond the manifest, from which the cosmic egg originates. Brahma originates from the egg and creates this universe.'

Chapter 51(1)(51)
(*Manvantara*s and Vishnu's greatness)

The *rishi*s said, 'O *Suta*! Please tell us about past and future *manvantara*s, the Vyasas of every *dvapara yuga*, the intelligent lords of *deva*s who classified branches

of the *Veda*s. To propound *dharma, artha* and the others,
how many incarnations did Ishana have in *kali yuga*? How
many *shishya*s did the lord of *deva*s have in *kali yuga*? You
should briefly speak about all this.'

Suta answered, 'Six Manus belong to the past—
Svayambhuva Manu was the first. After that, there were
Svarochisha, Uttama, Tamasa, Raivata and Chakshusha.
Currently, it is the seventh and the seventh Manu is
Vaivasvata, Ravi's son. I have spoken about Svaymabhuva,
at the beginning of the *kalpa*. After this, hear about
Svarochisha Manu. The *deva*s in Svarochisha *manvantara*
were Paravatas and Tushitas. The Indra of the *deva*s was
named Vipashchit, and he crushed *asura*s. The seven
*saptarshi*s were Urja, Stambha, Prana, Danta, Rishabha,
Timira and Arvarivan. The sons of Svarochisha Manu
were Chaitra, Kimpurusha and others. I have spoken about
the second *manvantara*. Now hear about Uttama. In the
third *manvantara*, Manu's name was Uttama. The Indra
of *deva*s was Sushanti, and he crushed his enemies. There
are said to have been five categories of *deva*s, Sudhaman,
Satya, Shiva, Pratardana and Vashavartin. Each category
had twelve *deva*s. The seven *saptarshi*s were Rajas,
Gatra, Urddhabahu, Savana, Anagha, Sutapa and Shakra.
In Tamasa *manvantara*, the categories of *deva*s were
Surayasaharas, Satyas and Sudhis. There were twenty-
seven *deva*s in each category. Shibi was the Indra, and he
had the characteristic of having performed one hundred
sacrifices. He was devoted to Shankara and was engaged
in worshipping Mahadeva. The seven *saptarshi*s in that
manvantara were Jyoti, Dhama, Prithaka, Kalpa, Chaitra,
Agnivasana and Pivara. O Indras among *brahmana*s! In
the fifth *manvantara*, Manu's name was Raivata. The
Indra was Vibhu, who crushed *asura*s. The excellent gods

were Amitas, Bhutis and Vaikunthas. In each of these
categories, there were fourteen *deva*s. O brahmanas! In
Raivata *manvantara*, the *saptarshi*s were Hiranyaroma,
Vedashri, Urddhabahu, Vedabahu, Subahu, Saparjanya
and Mahamuni. These four Manus, Svarochisha, Uttama,
Tamasa and Raivata, are said to have belonged to
Priyavrata's lineage. O *dvija*s! In the sixth *manvantara*, the
Manu was Chakshusha. The Indra was Manojava. Now
hear about the *deva*s. There are said to have been five
categories of *deva*s—Adyas, Prabhutabhavyas, Prathanas,
Mahanubhavas and Lekhyas. The seven auspicious *rishi*s
are said to have been Viraja, Havishman, Soma, Manusama,
Avinama and Savishnu.'

'O *brahmana*s! Vivasvat's son was the immensely
radiant Shraddhadeva. O *brahmana*s! In the current seventh
manvantara, the Manu is Samvartana.[1396] The *deva*s are
Adityas, Vasus, Rudras and Maruts. Purandara is Indra
and he is a slayer of enemy heroes. The seven *saptarshi*s
are Vasishtha, Kashyapa, Atri, Jamadagni, Goutama,
Vishvamitra and Bharadvaja. For the sake of preservation,
Vishnu's unmatched Shakti is present with an excess of
sattva. All the kings and residents of heaven are born as his
portions. O *dvija*s! Earlier, in Svayambhuva *manvantara*,
his portion was born as the son of Prajapati Ruchi and
Prakriti,[1397] through their mental powers. Thereafter, when
Svarochisha *manvantara* arrived, the divinity was born
through Tushitaa, along with the Tushita *deva*s. In Uttama
manvantara, Vishnu Janardana, the excellent god whose
form is the truth, was born through Satyaa, along with the
*deva*s known as Satyas. When Tamasa *manvantara* arrived,

[1396] Meaning Vaivasvata Manu.
[1397] This is a typo and should read Akuti.

Hari was born through Haryaa. He was known as Hari, and he was born along with the gods known as Haris. In Raivata *manvantara*, the immensely radiant Hari was born to Samkalpaa, through her mental powers, along with the *deva*s known as Manasas. In Chakshusha *manvantara*, Purushottama was born as Vaikuntha, through Vikunthaa. He was born along with *deva*s known as Vaikunthas. When Vaivasvata *manvantara* arrived, Vishnu was born as Vamana, the son of Kashyapa and Aditi. In three strides, the great-souled one conquered the three worlds. He gave the three worlds back to Purandara, bereft of thorns. These are his incarnations in the seven *manvantara*s. O *brahmana*s! These are the seven forms in which he has drawn together *praja*s. The entire universe was protected by the great-souled Vamana. Indeed, in each form, *deva*s remember him as the one who slays *daitya*s. In this way, Keshava creates, preserves and destroys everything. The *shruti* texts say that Bhagavan Narayana is in the *atman*s of all beings. In one portion, Narayana is established, pervading the entire universe. He is established in four forms that pervade, *saguna* and *nirguna*. There is a single form of Bhagavan. It is auspicious and without blemish, in the form of *jnana*. This is known as Vaasudeva, *nishkala* and beyond *guna*s. The second form is known as Kala. It has *tamas* and is known as Shiva. In this supreme form, Vishnu destroys everything at the end. There is a third form, with an excess of *sattva*, known as Pradyumna. This is for establishing the universe. This is Vishnu's certain and natural form, in the universe. Vaasudeva's fourth form is known as Brahma. This is Aniruddha's *rajas* form, as the entity embarking on the act of creation. Having destroyed everything, the lord sleeps, along with his form of Pradyumna. As Brahma, known as Narayana, he embarks

on the task of creating *praja*s. Narayana's auspicious form
is described under the name of Pradyumna. He deludes
the universe, with *deva*s, *asura*s and humans. His form in
the universe is said to be Prakriti. Vaasudeva's *atman* is
infinite. Hari is absolute and *nirguna*. His three excellent
forms with *sattva* are Pradhana, Purusha and Kala. But all
this is always Vaasudeva's *atman*. When one knows this,
one is liberated. Achyuta Vaasudeva Pradyumna Bhagavan
Hari divided the single *Veda*, with four parts, into four
*Veda*s. Krishna Dvaipayana Vyasa was Vishnu Narayana
himself. As a result of his complete free will, Bhagavan
Hari assumed this *avatara*. He is without a beginning and
without an end. He is the supreme *brahman*. *Deva*s or *rishi*s
do not know him. The lord, Bhagavan Vyasa Narayana, is
the only one who knows. O excellent sages! I have thus
spoken about Vishnu's greatness. This is the truth. Let me
again say that if one knows the truth, one is not deluded.'

Chapter 52(1)(52) (Branches of *Veda*s)

Suta said, 'In the current *manvantara*, in the first
dvapara yuga, the great lord, Svayambhuva Manu, is
regarded as Vyasa. Urged by Brahma, the lord divided the
*Veda*s into many parts. In the second *dvapara*, Prajapati
was Vedavyasa. In the third, it was Ushanas. In the fourth,
Brihaspati was Vyasa. In the fifth, Savitar was Vyasa. In the
sixth, it is said to have been Mrityu. In the seventh, it was
Indra. It is held to have been Vasishtha in the eighth. It was
Sarasvata in the ninth. In the tenth, it is said to have been
Tridhama. In the eleventh, it was Rishabha. In the twelfth, it
is said to have been Suteja. In the thirteenth, it was Dharma.
In the fourteenth, it was Suchakshu. In the fifteenth, it

was Trayyaruni. In the sixteenth, it was Dhananjaya. It was Kritanjaya in the seventeenth and Ritanjaya in the eighteenth. The next Vyasa was Bharadvaja and the one after that was Goutama. In the twenty-first, it was Vachashrava. The next one was Narayana. In the twenty-third, it was Trinabindu. The next one is said to have been Valmiki. O *dvija*s! In the twenty-fifth, there was a Vyasa.[1398] In the twenty-seventh, the great sage, Jatukarna, was Vyas. Parashara's son, Krishna Dvaipayana, became Vyasa. He is the one who indicated the way for all the *Veda*s and the Puranas. Parashara's son, Hari Krishna Dvaipyana, was a great *yogi*. He worshipped the divinity Ishana. Having seen him, he praised the three-eyed one. Through his favours, the lord Vyasa classified the *Veda*s. After this, he accepted four *shishya*s who were accomplished in the *Veda*s—Jaimini, Sumantu, Vaishampayana and Paila as the fourth. The great sage accepted me as the fifth. The great sage accepted Paila for the recital of the *Rig Veda*. Vaishampayana was the propounded of the *Yajur Veda*. Jaimini was accepted as the one who would recite the *Sama Veda*. The excellent *rishi*, Sumantu, was accepted for the *Atharva Veda*. He engaged me for narrating Itihasa and Puranas. There was a single *Yajur Veda*, but this was divided into four. For undertaking sacrifices, there were four officiating priests. O excellent *dvija*s! In *agnihotra* sacrifices, *adhvaryu*s recited from the *Yajur Veda*, *udgatri*s from the *Sama Veda*, *brahmana*s from the *Atharva Veda* and *hotri*s from the *Rig Veda*. The lord composed *Rig Veda* after extracting it from a sacrifice. Yajur hymns are in *Yajur Veda* and Sama hymns in *Sama Veda*. Earlier, he divided *Rig Veda*

[1398]The text doesn't mention the name and skips the twenty-sixth.

into twenty-one branches. *Yajur Veda* was composed of
one hundred branches. He divided *Sama Veda* into one
thousand branches. Kushaketana[1399] divided *Atharva
Veda*. The lord Vyasa composed the Puranas with eighteen
divisions. Formerly, the ancient *Veda* was one. But it was
divided into four parts. OUMKARA was generated from
the *brahman*. It purifies all taints. The eternal Bhagavan
Vaasudeva can be known through the *Veda*s. The supreme
one is sung about in the *Veda*s. A person who knows him,
knows the *Veda*s. He is the *brahman*, greater than the
greatest. He is excellent illumination and bliss. The truth
uttered in the words of the *Veda*s is that Vaasudeva is the
supreme destination. He is known through the *Veda*s. A
person who knows him, knows the *Veda*s, and is a sage
who is devoted to the *Veda*s. He is the one who knows
the supreme. The *Veda*s emerged through his breath. He
is Bhagavan Maheshvara, who is known through the
*Veda*s. The *Veda*s are his form. He is the *Veda*s, the object
to be known. A person who seeks refuge with him, is
liberated. The great sage who was Parashara's son knew
the *akshara*.[1400] He knew the imperishable OUMKARA.
He knew everything that is not known.'

Chapter 53(1)(53) (Shiva's incarnations)

Suta said, 'I have spoken about the Vedavyasa *avatara*s
in *dvapara yuga*. O ones excellent in vows! Now hear
about Mahadeva's *avatara*s in *kali yuga*. In the first *kali yuga*
of Vaivasvata *manvantara*, for the welfare of *brahmana*s,

[1399] Kushaketana cannot be identified.
[1400] OUM.

the immensely radiant lord of *deva*s manifested himself under the name of Shveta. He was born on the beautiful slopes of the Himalayas, the best among all mountains. His *shishya*s and subsidiary *shishya*s[1401] were infinite in radiance. There were four great-souled *brahmana*s, accomplished in the *Veda*s—Shveta, Shvetashikha, Shvetasya and Shvetalohita.[1402] Shiva's incarnations were Sutara[1403] in the first *kali yuga*, Madana in the second, Suhotra in the third, Kankana in the fourth, Lokakshi in the fifth, Yogindra in the sixth and Jaigishavya in the seventh. The incarnations were Dadhivaha in the eighth, Lord Rishabha in the ninth, Bhrigu in the tenth, Ugra in the eleventh, Pura in the twelfth, the supreme devotee Bali in the thirteenth, Goutama in the fourteenth and Vedadarshi in the fifteenth. The subsequent ones were Gokarna, Guhavasa, Shikhandadhrik, Yajamalin, Attahasa, Daruka, Langali, Mahayama, Muni, Shulin, Dindamundishvara, Sahishnu, Somasharma and Nakulishvara. In Vaivasvata *manvantara*, the *avatara*s of Shambhu, the wielder of the trident, are said to number twenty-eight. At the end of *kali yuga*, the lord, the lord of *deva*s, will take an *avatara* as Nakulishvara, in the *tirtha* of Karyavatara. O bulls among sages! In each of these, the lord of *deva*s had four *shishya*s, who were excellent stores of austerities. Each of these had other *shishya*s who were controlled, pleasant in their minds and full of devotion towards Ishvara. In the due order, I will

[1401] *Shishya*s of *shishya*s. For twenty-eight *yuga*s, the names of twenty-eight *avatara*s are given.

[1402] Presumably Shveta's disciples.

[1403] This seemingly contradicts Shveta, because of the way the text states the numbering, starting with Sutara. However, the first two were Shveta and Sutara and all the names add up to twenty-eight, corresponding to twenty-eight *kali yuga*s.

describe these *yogi*s, who were excellent among those who knew about *yoga*.[1404] They were: (1) Shveta, Shvetashikha, Shvetasya and Shvetalohita; (2) Dundubhi, Shatarupa, Richika and Ketuman; (3) Vishoka, Vikesha, Vishakha and Shapanashana; (4) Sumukha, Durmukha, Durdama and Duratikrama; (5) Sanaka, Sanatana and Sanandana; (6) Dalabhya, Mahayogi, Dharmatmana and Mahoujasa; (7) Sudhama, Viraja, Shankhavani and Aja; (8) Sarasvata, Mogha, Dhanavaha and Suvahana; (9) Kapila, Asuri, Vodhu and sage Panchashikha; (10) Parashara, Garga, Bhargava and Angiras; (11) Chalabandhu, Niramitra, Ketushringa and Tapodhana; (12) Lambodara, Lamba, Vikrosha, Lambaka and Shuka; (13) Sarvajna, Samabuddhi, Sadhya and Asadhya; (14) Sudhama, Kashyapa, Vasishtha and Varija; (15) Atri, Ugra, Shravana and Suvaidyaka; (16) Kuni, Kunibahu, Kusharira and Kunetraka; (17) Kashyapa, Ushanas, Chyavana and Brihaspati; (18) Ucchasya, Vamadeva, Mahakala and Mahanili; (19) Vajashrava, Sukesha, Shyavashva and Supathishvara; (20) Hiranyanabha, Koushilya, Akakshu and Kuthubhitha; (21) Sumanta, Varchasa, the learned Kabandha and Kushikandhara; (22) Plaksha, Darvayani, Ketuman and Goutama; (23) Bhallachi, Madhupinga, Shvetaketu and Tapodhana; (24) Ushidha, Brihadraksha, Devala and Kavi; (25) Shalahotra, Agniveshya, Yuvanashva and Sharadvasu; (26) Chhagala, Kundakarna, Kunta and Pravahaka; (27) Uluka, Vidyuta, Shadraka and Ashvalayana; (28) Akshapada, Kumara, Uluka and Vasuvahana; and (29) Kunika, Garga, Mitraka and Ruru. In different *avatara*s,

---

[1404]The numbering doesn't exist in the text. There should be 28 sets of four names each. But there are twenty-nine sets. (5) only has three names, while (12) has five.

these were the great-souled *shishya*s who were *yogi*s. They were free from impurities, immersed in the *brahman* and devoted to *jnana* and *yoga*. For the welfare of *brahmana*s and to establish the *Veda*s, they follow the instructions of the lord of *yoga* and take *avatara*s. *Brahmana*s who always remember them and prostrate themselves before them, satisfying them and worshipping them, achieve knowledge about the *brahman*.'

'This Vaivasvata *manvantara* has been described in detail. The future *manvantara*s are Savarna as the eighth, Dakshasavarna as the ninth, Brahmasavarna as the tenth, Dharmasavarna as the eleventh, Rudrasavarna as the twelfth, the one named Rouchya as the thirteenth and Bhoutya as the fourteenth. In the due order, these are said to be the future Manus. I have told you the first part of what Narayana said. The extended accounts are about the past, the present and the future. If a person reads it, hears it, or makes it heard to excellent *dvija*s, he is freed from all sins and obtains greatness in Brahma's world. One should read it in a temple, or after bathing, on the banks of a river. Full of sentiments about Purushottama, one should prostrate oneself before Narayana. "I prostrate myself before the lord of *deva*s, the *paramatman* for *deva*s. He is the ancient Purusha, Vishnu, whose power pervades everything."'

This ends *Purvarddha* of Kurma Purana.

Uttararddha (the second part)

Chapter 54(2)(1) (Conversation between *rishis*—Ishvara Gita)

The *rishis* said, 'You have properly described the creation of Lord Svayambhu, the expanse of the cosmic egg and the determination of *manvantaras*. You have said that, for all *varnas* who are devoted to *dharma*, the divinity Ishvara, the lord of lords, must always be worshipped through *jnana* and *yoga*. This is the excellent truth that destroys all the miseries of *samsara*. This is *jnana* about the *brahman* alone. Through this, we can perceive the supreme. You have obtained all this *vijnana* from the lord Krishna Dvaipayana, who was Narayana himself. Therefore, we are asking you again.'

Hearing the words of the sages, Suta, who knew the Puranas and had heard them from the lord, Krishna Dvaipayana, started to speak. O best among sages! But at the time, Krishna Dvaipayana Vyasa himself arrived at the place where the assembly had gathered for the sacrifice. They saw the one who knew the *Vedas*, with a radiance resembling that of a cloud of destruction. The bulls among *dvijas* prostrated themselves before Vyasa, whose eyes were like the petals of a lotus. On seeing him, Lomaharshana

319

prostrated himself on the ground, like a rod. He lowered his head down on the ground and joined his hands in salutation. O *brahmanas*! He[1405] asked about the welfare of Shounaka and other great sages. He seated himself on an appropriate seat that had been devised for him. The lord who was Parashara's son addressed them in these words. 'I hope your austerities, studying and learning are not suffering.' Suta prostrated himself before his own *guru*, the great sage, and said, 'You should speak to the sages about *jnana* connected with the *brahman*. These sages are serene ascetics who are devoted to *dharma*. They are eager to hear. You should tell them the truth. This is divine *jnana* about liberation, that I have directly learnt from you. In the form of Kurma, Vishnu told the sages about this earlier.'

Hearing Suta's words, the sage who was Satyavati's son prostrated his head before Rudra and spoke these words, which bring happiness.

Vyasa said, 'I will tell you what the divinity Mahadeva was asked by the lords of *yoga*, Sanatkumara and others, earlier. He himself spoke to them. Sanatkumara, Sanaka, Sanandana, Angiras, Rudra, Bhrigu, who knew supreme dharma, Kanada, Kapila, Garga, the great sage Vamadeva, Shukra and the illustrious Vasishtha were those who were in control of their minds. With their minds controlled, they discussed with each other. In the sacred hermitage of Badarika, they tormented themselves through terrible austerities. They saw the great *yogi* and *rishi*, Narayana, the sage who was Dharma's son. Without a beginning and an end, at the time, he was with Nara. They praised him with many kinds of *stotram*s from all the *Veda*s. Full of devotion, the *yogi*s prostrated themselves before the

---

[1405] Vyasa.

excellent *yogi*. The illustrious one, who knew everything, determined what they wished for. He addressed them in deep words. '"Why are you tormenting yourselves through austerities?" Pleased in their minds, they replied to the eternal Narayana, the divinity whose *atman* was in the universe, and who had himself arrived, indicating their achievement of *siddhi*. "All of us are restrained and speak about the *brahman*. O Purushottama! You are the only refuge for us. We seek refuge with you. You are Bhagavan *rishi*. You know everything and the greatest mystery. You are Narayana himself. You are the ancient and unmanifest Purusha. O Parameshvara! Barring you, there is no one else who knows. You should dispel our firm doubts. What is the cause behind everything? What constantly moves in *samsara*? What is the *atman* and what is emancipation? What is the reason behind *samsara*? What is *samsara*? Who is Ishana, who sees everything? What is the *brahman*, greater than the greatest? You should tell us everything." When they said this, the sages saw that Purushottama had shed his garb as an ascetic and was standing there, in his own radiance. He was without blemish and radiant. He was ornamented by a circle of brilliance. The Shrivatsa mark was on his chest and his radiance was like that of molten gold. He held the conch shell *chakra* and mace in his hands. He held the Sharnga bow in his hand and was surrounded by prosperity. At that instant, because of his energy, Nara could not even be seen.'

'Meanwhile, intending to show them his favours, Rudra Maheshvara manifested himself. Mahadeva was marked by the moon on his crest. On seeing the three-eyed lord of the universe, ornamented by the moon, they were delighted in their minds. Devoutly, they praised Parameshvara. "Victory to Ishvara Mahadeva. Victory to

Bhutapati[1406] Shiva. Every kind of victory to Ishana, whom
the sages worship through their austerities. O one with a
thousand forms! O one whose *atman* is in the universe!
O one who makes the machine of the universe function!
Victory to the infinite one. O one who creates, preserves
and destroys the universe! O Ishana with the one thousand
feet! O Shambhu! O one who is worshipped by Indras
among *yogis*! Victory to the divinity who is Ambikaa's
lord! I prostrate myself before Parameshvara." Bhagavan
Isha Tryambaka is affectionate towards his devotees. Thus
praised, he embraced Hrishikesha and spoke in a deep
voice. "O Pundarikaksha! What is the reason why these
Indras among sages, who speak about the *brahman*, have
assembled in this spot? O Achyuta! What should I do
for them?" Hearing these words, Janardana, the lord of
*deva*s, spoke to the divinity Mahadeva, who was standing
there, willing to bestow his favours. "O divinity! These
sages are ascetics who have destroyed their sins. They have
come here and sought refuge, desiring proper insight. O
Bhagavan! If you are pleased with these sages, who have
cleansed their *atman*s, in my presence, you should speak to
them about divine *jnana*. O Shiva! Other than you, there
is no one else who knows your own *atman*. Speak about
your *atman* and reveal your *atman* to these Indras among
sages." Saying this, Hrishikesha glanced at Vrishadhvaja.
He displayed his own *siddhi* of *yoga* and spoke to the
bulls among sages. "You have seen Mahesha Shankara,
the wielder of the trident. You should regard yourselves
as successful and deserve to know. You should look at
the lord of *deva*s, standing directly in front of you. In my
presence, Ishvara will tell you the truth." Hearing Vishnu's

[1406] Lord of *bhuta*s.

words, Sanatkumara and the others prostrated themselves before Vrishadhvaja and asked Maheshvara. Meanwhile, a divine, sparkling and auspicious seat appeared. For Ishvara, it arose from the sky, in a manner that was unthinkable. Along with Vishnu, the creator of the universe, with *yoga* in his *atman*, sat down on it. The divinity Maheshvara was resplendent, and his energy filled up the universe. Those who spoke about the *brahman* saw Shankara, the lord of lords among the *deva*s. They saw him resplendent on that sparkling and excellent seat. They saw the lord of *bhuta*s seated on that seat. Everything is inside him and the universe is not different from him. They saw the supreme Ishana Isha, along with Vaasudeva. Asked, Bhagavan Parameshvara glanced at Pundarikaksha and spoke to the sages about his own excellent *yoga*. "O unblemished ones! With serene minds, all of you listen, as I properly speak about pure *jnana* about Ishvara."'

Chapter 55(2)(2) (Ishvara's *yoga*)[1407]

Ishvara said, 'My *vijnana* is an eternal mystery. It cannot be spoken about. O *dvijas*! Even though they try, *deva*s do not know. Depending on this *jnana*, excellent *dvija*s have become one with the *brahman*. Those who spoke about the *brahman* earlier, no longer had to experience *samsara*. This is the greatest secret among all secrets. One must make every effort to keep it a secret. Today, I will speak about it to you, since you are full of devotion and speak about the *brahman*. The *atman* is absolute and clear.

[1407]Throughout this Chapter, some liberties have been taken to make the meanings clear. These are also somewhat subjective.

It is pure, subtle and eternal. It directly exists inside everything. It is consciousness alone. It is beyond darkness. The *shruti* texts say that he is Antaryamin,[1408] Purusha, Prana, Maheshvara and Kala. He is the unmanifest one. He is the one who knows. The universe originated from him and dissolves into him. He is full of *maya*. Not bound by the *maya*, he assumes many kinds of bodies. He does not move in *samsara*. The lord is not identical with *samsara*. He is not earth, water, fire, wind or space. He is not *prana*, the mind or the unmanifest.[1409] He is not sound, touch, form, taste or smell. He is not the doer, nor speech. O excellent *dvija*s! He is not hands, feet, anus or genital organs. He is not the one who does, nor the one who enjoys. He is not Prakriti or Purusha. He is not *maya*, nor the different types of *prana*. He is not the supreme objective. No connection is possible between illumination and darkness. Like that, there is no union or association between *prapancha* and the *paramatman*. In this world, shadow and light exhibit traits that are distinct from each other. In that way, *prapancha* and Purusha are distinct. That is the supreme meaning. If the nature of the *atman* is such that it is dirty, created and subject to transformations, then it cannot be emancipated, even in hundreds of births. Emancipated sages perceive the supreme truth about their own *atman*s. It is without transformations. It is devoid of the opposite pair of sentiments. The *atman* is without change and is full of bliss. "I am the doer. I am happy. I am miserable. I am thin. I am stout." Such views are caused by a sense of *ahamkara*. People impose these on the *atman*. Those who know the *Veda*s speak of the *atman* as the

---

[1408] The one who dwells within.
[1409] Meaning Pradhana.

witness, beyond Prakriti. It enjoys and does not decay. It understands and is established everywhere. Thus, for all those with bodies, the cause behind *samsara* is ignorance. As a result of ignorance and incorrect understanding about the truth, there is association with Prakriti. Purusha is supreme, always arising in its own luminescence. It goes everywhere. As a result of *ahamkara* and lack of discrimination, a person thinks, "I am the doer." *Rishis* perceive the eternal and the unmanifest, consisting of existence and non-existence. A person takes Pradhana to be Purusha and speaks of the *brahman* as being the cause. But this is an association brought about for the *atman*, which is deep and without blemish. Thus, he does not understand the truth about his own *atman* being the imperishable *brahman*. Lacking knowledge about the *atman*, he takes it to be something else and thus, suffers from grief. All taints like attachment and hatred are bonds brought about through confusion. This has the great taint of *karma* and good deeds and bad deeds. This is the state for everyone and gives rise to every kind of body. The *atman* is everywhere and eternal. It is hidden deep and is devoid of taints. It is one. But it appears as many because of the strength of *maya*, not because of its own nature. Therefore, sages say that the supreme truth is that of non-duality. Differences are the nature of the unmanifest,[1410] which is dependent on *maya*. The sky does not become dirty because of its association with smoke. Like that, the *atman* is not touched by the inner organ of the mind. A sparkling piece of crystal shines because of its own radiance. Like that, the sparkling *atman* shines, without any defining attribute. Discriminating people say that this universe has

[1410] Meaning Prakriti.

the form of *jnana*. Others, whose vision is warped, consider
it as consisting of material objects. The *atman* is deep and
nirguna. Its nature is that of consciousness. But men, with
insight warped by ignorance, look at it in the form of a
material object. When pure crystal comes into contact with
a red *gunja* seed, people think it is red.[1411] In that way,
there is an imposition on the supreme Purusha. The *atman*
is imperishable, pure and eternal. It does not decay and
goes everywhere. Those who desire liberation should
worship it in this way, think about in this way and hear
about it in this way. When the consciousness shines
everywhere, and all the time, in the mind of a faithful *yogi*,
he achieves success. He sees all beings in his *atman* and his
atman in all beings. He then realizes the *brahman*. When
he is in a state of *samadhi*, he does not see other beings. He
becomes one with the supreme and the absolute alone
exists. He is then freed from all the desires in the heart.
Such a learned person then obtains immortal peace. He
sees all the separate beings as established in the one and as
expanding from the one. He then realizes the *brahman*. He
sees the supreme truth of the absolute *atman*. With
everything in the universe mere *maya*, he experiences
nivritti. The medication for birth, old age, misery and
ailment is *vijnana* about the *brahman* alone. When this
happens, he becomes Shiva. All major and minor rivers in
this world proceed towards the ocean and become one. In
that way, one proceeds towards unity with the imperishable
and the *nishkala*. Therefore, *vijnana* alone exists. *Prapancha*
has no base. In this world, *vijnana* is enveloped by

[1411] *Gunja* is the Indian licorice or rosary pea. *Gunja* can be red
or white. The text uses the word *raktika*, meaning *raktagunja* or red
gunja.

ignorance. That is the reason for delusion. *Vijnana* is sparkling and subtle. It does not change and is without an alternative. This is held to be *vijnana*. Everything else is ignorance. The excellent *jnana* spoken about in *samkhya* has been described. This is the essence of *Vedanta* and *yoga* is single-minded focus on this. *Jnana* results from *yoga*. From *jnana*, *yoga* functions. For a person who possesses both *yoga* and *jnana*, there is nothing that cannot be accomplished. *Yogis* proceed to the same destination that the followers of *samkhya* go to. A person who seeks *samkhya* and *yoga* as one, is a person who knows the truth.[1412] O *brahmana*s! There are other *yogis* whose minds are attached to prosperity. They are submerged because of this, and their intelligence suffers. There is the divine, sparkling and great prosperity, spoken about by everyone. When they give up their bodies, those with *jnana* and *yoga* obtain this. I am the unmanifest *atman*. I am Parameshvara, full of *maya*. I am described in all the *Vedas*. I am in all *atman*s and face every direction. I am every kind of form, every kind of taste and every kind of smell. I do not suffer from old age or death. My hands and feet are everywhere. I am the eternal Antaryamin. Even without hands and feet, I grasp swiftly. I am established in the heart. I have no eyes, but I see. I have no ears, but I hear. I know everything. But no one ever knows me. Those who possess insight about the truth speak of me as the one great Purusha. *Rishi*s, subtle in insight, see the cause behind the *atman*. They see the excellent glory of the *nirguna* form, which is without blemish. Deluded by my *maya*, *deva*s do not know this. O those who speak about the *brahman*! I will tell you about it. Control yourselves and listen. Since my nature transcends

[1412] This is *Bhagavat Gita* 5.5.

maya, no one is able to praise me. But the wise ones know me as the cause that urges the restrictions. Those who possess insight about the truth know my mysterious body as one that goes everywhere. Such *yogi*s enter and obtain *sayujya* with the imperishable. They cross over my *maya*, which has the universe as form. Along with me, they achieve the supreme and pure *nirvana*. As a result of my favours, they do not return, even in hundreds of crores of *kalpa*s. O Indras among *yogi*s! These are the instructions of the *Veda*s. This[1413] should be given to sons, *shishya*s and *yogi*s who speak about the *brahman*. I have spoken about the *vijnana* that is based on *samkhya* and *yoga*.'

Chapter 56(2)(3) (Purusha and Prakriti)

Ishvara said, 'Kala, Pradhana and the supreme Purusha originated from the unmanifest.[1414] Everything originated from it. Therefore, the universe is full of the *brahman*. The extremities of its hands and feet extend everywhere. The eyes, heads and mouths are everywhere. There are ears everywhere. It is established, pervading everything in the world. There are indications of the qualities of the senses everywhere. But everywhere, it is devoid of senses. It is the support for everything. It is unmanifest and constant bliss. It is devoid of duality.[1415] It cannot be compared with anything. It cannot be perceived and is beyond the norms of proof. It is without an alternative. It is without

---

[1413] The knowledge.

[1414] The *brahman*.

[1415] These *shloka*s are almost exactly those in *Bhagavat Gita* 13.13 and the first part of 13.14.

an indication. It is the abode for everything. It is supreme *amrita*. It is without distinctions but is based on distinctions. It is eternal, constant and without change. It is *nirguna*. It is supreme refulgence. This is the *jnana* wise ones know about. The *atman* is supreme and is inside about outside all beings. I am that. I go everywhere. I am tranquil. *Jnana* is in my *atman*. I am Parameshvara. I penetrate this entire universe, with its mobile and immobile entities. All beings exist in me. A person who knows this, knows the *Vedas*. This is spoken of as both Pradhana and Purusha. Kala, which results from their union, is said to be supreme and without a beginning. All three are without a beginning and without an end. They are established in the unmanifest. Those who know me know that my *atman* is in them, but my form is also distinct from them. The one spoken of as Prakriti confounds all those with bodies. Starting with Mahat and ending with Vishesha, everything in the universe originates from her. Established in Prakriti, Purusha enjoys the qualities of Prakriti. Since it is devoid of *ahamkara*, it is spoken of as the twenty-fifth.[1416] The first transformation of Prakriti is said to be Mahat, which possessed knowledge. From the power of knowledge, *ahamkara* evolved. Mahat, the *atman* and the one known as *ahamkara* are one. Those who have thought about the truth have sung that the one who is inside is the *jivatman*. In various births, it is this that experiences all the happiness and unhappiness. The *atman* possesses *vijnana* and *manas* is an aide. Permeated by this, Purusha is immersed in *samsara*. The lack of

---

[1416] The twenty-five *tattvas* of *samkhya* are five gross elements, five subtle elements, five organs of action, five senses of perception, *manas* (mind), *ahamkara*, Mahat/*buddhi* (intellect), Prakriti and Purusha.

discrimination occurs because of the association between
Prakriti and Kala. Kala creates beings and Kala withdraws
prajas. Everything is under the subjugation of Kala. But
Kala is not under the subjugation of anything. It is eternal
and controls everything from inside. It is spoken of as
Bhagavan, Prana, the omniscient one and Purushottama.
The learned say that *manas* is superior to all the senses.
Ahamkara is superior to *manas*, and Mahat is superior to
ahamkara. The unmanifest[1417] is superior to Mahat and
Purusha is superior to the unmanifest. Bhagavan Prana is
superior to Purusha and everything in the universe belongs
to him. Space is beyond *prana*[1418] and lord Agni is beyond
space. I am the serene and imperishable *brahman*, beyond
maya and this universe. There is no entity that is superior to
me. If one knows me, one is liberated. Beings, and mobile
and immobile entities in the universe, are not eternal. I,
the unmanifest one, am the exception. I am Maheshvara,
in the form of space. I create everything. I always destroy
the universe. I am the divinity who possesses *maya* and
is full of *maya*. I am associated with Kala. Because of my
presence, Kala undertakes everything in the universe. I,
the infinite *atman*, am the one who engages. This is the
instruction of the *Veda*s.'

Chapter 57(2)(4) (Greatness of Shiva)

Ishvara said, 'O ones who speak about the *brahman*! I
will speak about the greatness of the lord of *deva*s, who
makes everything function. Control yourselves and listen.

[1417]Prakriti.
[1418]Meaning wind.

Men are incapable of realising me through austerities, many kinds of donations and sacrifices. The only exception is excellent *bhakti*. I am established inside all beings and all around them. But lords among sages do not know me, the witness to everything in the world. Everything is inside me and I am the supreme destroyer of everything. I am Dhatri and Vidhatri. I am the fire of destruction, facing every direction. All the sages and the ancestors and residents of heaven do not see me. Nor do Brahma, the Manus, Shakra and others famous for their energy. The *Veda*s always sing about me alone, as the one Parameshvara. *Brahmana*s worship me through many kinds of sacrifices and sacrifices mentioned in the *Veda*s. All the worlds do not perceive me. Nor does Brahma, the grandfather of the worlds. *Yogi*s perform *dhyana* on the divinity, Ishvara, the lord of *bhuta*s. I am the one who enjoys all the oblations and bestows the fruits. I am in the bodies of all *deva*s. I am in all *atman*s and submerge everything. In this world, learned ones who speak about the *Veda*s and follow *dharma*, see me. For those who constantly worship me, I am always near their presence. There are *brahmana*s, *kshatriya*s and *vaishya*s who follow *dharma* and worship me. I grant them the supreme destination, the place that is full of bliss. There are others, *shudra*s and others of inferior birth, who follow their own *dharma*. Since they are devout, they are liberated, even though they are associated with Kala. My devotees are not destroyed. My devotees are devoid of sin. I promised right at the beginning that my devotee will not be destroyed. A foolish person who criticizes my devotees, criticizes the lord of *deva*s. If a person worships my devotee with devotion, he always worships me. To worship me, if a devotee always offers a leaf, a flower, a fruit, or water, that devotee is loved by me. At the beginning of the universe,

I created Brahma Parameshthi and gave him all the *Veda*s that emerged from me. I am the undecaying *guru* of all the *yogi*s. I am the one who protects those who follow *dharma*. I am the one who kills those who hate the *Veda*s. I am the one who liberates *yogi*s from everything in *samsara*. Though I am devoid of all connection with *samsara*, I am the cause behind *samsara*. I am the destroyer, the creator and the preserver. *Maya* is my Shakti and this *maya* deludes the worlds. It is my supreme Shakti that is spoken of as Vidya.[1419] Established in the hearts of *yogi*s, I destroy that *maya*. I am the one who makes all the Shaktis function and withdraws them. I am the support for all of them. I am the store of *amrita*. One of my Shaktis is inside everything and makes the universe function in different ways. O *brahmana*s who have resorted to supreme *yoga*! But I am not the one who urges. My Shakti assumes the form of Brahma. Full of me, it is established in me. I establish the world through another extensive Shakti. This is in the form of the infinite Jagannatha Narayana, who pervades the universe. A third great Shakti destroys the entire universe. This is said to be full of *tamas*. This is known as Kala, in the form of Rudra. Some perceive me through *dhyana*, others through *jnana*. Some follow *bhakti yoga*, others *karma yoga*. Among all my desired devotees, the one who constantly worships me through *jnana*, is the one I love the most. It is not otherwise. There are other devotees of Hari who worship me. They also obtain me and do not return again. Everything, with Pradhana and Purusha, is pervaded by me. Consciousness is established in me. I urge the universe. O *brahmana*s! But I am not the one who directly urges. Resorting to my supreme *yoga*, I urge the

---

[1419]Knowledge.

entire universe. A person who knows this, obtains *amrita*. I observe everything, seemingly existing because of its own nature. Bhagavan Kala, the great lord of *yoga*, is the one who himself does this. In the sacred texts, the learned ones speak of me as a *yogi*, as the one who possesses *maya*. I am Bhagavan, the lord of *yoga*. I am the great lord of *yoga* himself. The greatness of Parameshthi is because he is the best among all beings. He is spoken of as Bhagavan Brahma. He is without blemish and is full of the great *brahman*. If a person knows me as the lord who is the great lord of *yoga* and uses *yoga*, without resorting to anything else, there is no doubt that he is united with me. I am the divinity who urges. Depending on this supreme bliss, I am the *yogi* who constantly dances. A person who knows this, knows *yoga*. This is the secret *jnana* that has been determined in all the *Veda*s. It should be imparted to a person who is serene in mind, who is devoted to *dharma*, and who performs sacrificial rites to the fire.'

Chapter 58(2)(5) (The sages praise Shiva)

Vyasa said, 'Bhagavan Parameshvara told the *yogi*s this. Displaying his supreme sentiments, Ishvara started to dance. They saw Ishana, the store of supreme energy. Along with Vishnu, they saw Mahadeva dancing in the sparkling sky. Those who know the truth about *yoga*, *yogi*s who have restrained their minds, know him. They saw Isha, the lord of all beings, in the firmament. Everything in the universe is impelled by his *maya*. The *brahmana*s saw the lord of the universe himself dance. Remembering his lotus feet, a man gives up the fear that results from ignorance. They saw the lord of *bhuta*s dancing. There are some

who have conquered sleep and the breath of life. They are
serene and full of devotion. Such people see him as a *yogi*,
full of radiance. He is favourable and affectionate towards
his devotees and swiftly destroys their ignorance, liberating
them. They saw that supreme Rudra in the sky. The divinity
possessed one thousand heads. His form had one thousand
feet. He possessed one thousand arms. His hair was matted,
and he wore the half-moon on his crest. His garment was
made from tiger skin, and he held a mighty trident in his
hand. He held a staff in his hand and his three eyes were
the sun, the moon and the fire. He was established there,
enveloping the cosmic egg with his own radiance. His teeth
were cruel. With a radiance like that of one crore suns,
he was unassailable. The creator of everything blazed and
seemed to burn down the entire universe. They saw the
divinity Ishvara, the creator of the universe, dancing. This
was Mahadeva, the great *yogi*, the lord of *deva*s. He was
Pashupati. He was Ishana, the imperishable resplendence
and bliss. He held Pinaka. His eyes were large. He was the
medication against the disease of the world. Kala was in his
atman. He was the destroyer of Kala. He was Maheshvara,
the lord of *deva*s. He was Umaa's consort. He had large
eyes. He was full of supreme *yoga* and bliss. He was the
abode of *jnana* and non-attachment. He was eternal *jnana
yoga*. His glory and prosperity were eternal. He was the
support for *dharma* and was impossible to approach. He
was worshipped by the great Indra, Upendra and large
numbers of *maharshi*s. Covering himself with the *yoga* of
maya, he was established in the hearts of *yogi*s. He was
the origin of the universe and in an instant, he was united
with Narayana, who is free from ailments. Those who
spoke about the *brahman* saw the absolute Ishvara. They
saw Ishvara's form, with Rudra and Narayana combined.

Those who spoke about the *brahman* thought themselves to have been truly successful. Sanatkumara, Sanaka, Bhrigu, Sanatana, Sanandana, Raibhya, Angiras, Vamadeva, Shukra, *maharshi* Atri, Kapila and Marichi saw Rudra, the lord who saves from the world. The one seated on a lotus[1420] was to his left. They performed *dhyana* on him, in the heart. They prostrated their heads and repeatedly joined their hands in salutation. Uttering OUMKARA, they saw the divinity, inside their bodies, hidden inside the cavities of their hearts. Their minds were filled with delight. They praised him in words that were full of the *brahman*.'

The sages said, 'You are the sole Isha. You are the ancient Purusha. You are lord of *prana*. You are Rudra, whose *yoga* is infinite. We prostrate ourselves before the one who is established in our hearts. You are the sacred Prachetas, full of the *brahman*. Controlled and serene sages see you, Brahma's sparkling origin, golden in complexion. Inside their own bodies, they perform *dhyana* on the Kavi[1421] who does not move. He is supreme. He is greater than the greatest. The mother of the universe[1422] originated from you. Though you are as small as a *paramanu*, you experience everything.[1423] You are smaller than an *anu*. You are greater than the greatest. The virtuous say that you are everything. You are Hiranyagarbha, the *atman* inside the universe. It is from you that the ancient Purusha was born. Even as he was being born from you, you instructed him to follow the rules and immediately create everything. All the *Veda*s were born from you. In the end, it is in you

---

[1420] Vishnu.

[1421] The wise one.

[1422] Prakriti.

[1423] Both *paramanu* and *anu* are translated as atoms. But *paramanu* is smaller than *anu*.

that they find a place of rest. We see you, the cause behind
the universe. We see you inside our own hearts, dancing.
You are the one who makes Brahma's wheel revolve. You
are full of *maya*. You are the only lord of the universe. We
prostrate ourselves before you. We seek refuge with you.
Yoga is in your *atman*. You are dancing this divine dance.
As you dance in the middle of the supreme firmament, we
see you. We remember your greatness. In many ways, you
pervade every *atman*. You are the one who experiences,
and causes others to experience, the bliss of the *brahman*.
You are expressed in words as OUMKARA. You are the
seed of liberation. You are imperishable. Your mysterious
form is hidden in Prakriti. You are self-luminous. The
virtuous speak of your powers as the truth. All the *Veda*s
constantly praise you. The *rishi*s, whose taints have been
destroyed, prostrate themselves before you. Mendicants
who are devoted to the *brahman* are serene in their
*atman*s. They enter you, the greatest one, who is fixed to
the truth. You are the one who destroys the earth. With
the universe as your form, you have no beginning. You are
Brahma, Vishnu and Parameshthi. You are the greatest.
They experience bliss in their own *atman*s. They are always
liberated and enter you, the unwavering and self-luminous
one. Though you alone are Rudra, you create the universe.
With the universe as your form, you protect the entire
universe. At the end, everything obtains a refuge in you.
We prostrate ourselves before you. We seek refuge with
you. The *Veda*s are one and infinite, but they have many
branches. You are one and they convey an understanding
about your form alone. Those who seek refuge with you
are worthy of being worshipped. In this world, those
*brahmana*s cross over *maya*. You are spoken of as the only
Kavi. You alone are Rudra, but are praised as Brahma,

Hari, Agni and Isha. You are the eternal Rudra. You are Anila.[1424] You are Chekitana.[1425] You are Dhatri. You are Aditya, with many different forms. You are imperishable. You are supreme. You are the one who should be known. You are the supreme abode of the universe. You do not change. You are the eternal protector of *dharma*. You are the eternal Purushottama. You are Vishnu. You are the one with the four faces. You are Rudra Bhagavan Isha. You are the lord of the universe. You are Prakriti. You are the lord who provides establishment to everything. You are Parameshvara. You are spoken of as the eternal Purusha. With the complexion of Aditya, you are beyond darkness. You are consciousness alone. You are not manifest. You are infinite in form. You are the sky. You are Brahma. You are the void. You are the *guna*s of Prakriti. You are radiant inside everything. You are without transformation. You are sparkling, with a single form. Your truth is resplendent within you alone. Who can think of your form? You are the fortunate lord of *yoga*, infinite in powers. We are devoted to the ancient one, whose body is that of Brahma's. All of us seek refuge with you and prostrate ourselves before you. O lord of *bhuta*s! O Mahesha! Be pleased. When one remembers your lotus feet, all the seeds of *samsara* proceed towards dissolution. We control our bodies and restrain our minds. We seek to propitiate Isha alone. I prostrate myself before Bhava, the origin of the world, Kala, Sarva and Hara. I prostrate myself before Rudra Kapardi. I prostrate myself before the divinity who is Agni. I prostrate myself before Shiva.'

[1424] Vayu, the wind-god.
[1425] Shiva's name, the intelligent one.

Vyasa continued, 'Bhagavan Kapardi Vrishavahana[1426] was pleased. He withdrew his supreme form. Bhava showed himself in his natural form. They saw Bhava, the lord of the past and the future, in front, as had been the case earlier. They saw the divinity Narayana. Amazed, they spoke these words. "O Bhagavan! O lord of the past and the future! O one who is marked by the sign of the bull! We have seen your supreme and eternal form and are content. You are sparkling. You are supreme. You are Parameshvara. Thanks to your favours, unwavering devotion towards you has been generated in us. O Shankara! We now wish to hear about your greatness. We also wish to hear the eternal truth about Parameshthi again." The one who bestows the *siddhi* of *yoga* heard the worlds spoken by the *yogis*. He glanced towards Madhava and spoke in a deep voice.'

Chapter 59(2)(6) (Shiva's glory)

Ishvara said, 'O *rishi*s! All of you listen. I will tell you exactly about the greatness of Isha Parameshthi. Those who know the *Veda*s, know this. I am the sole creator of all the worlds. I am the sole protector of all the worlds. I am the sole destroyer of all the worlds. I am the eternal one, inside all *atman*s. I am Maheshvara, the Antaryamin inside all objects. Everything is established inside me and around me. But I am not established everywhere. You have witnessed my wonderful form. O *brahmana*s! I can only be compared to my own self. I have shown you my *maya*. I am established inside all beings. Through my Kriyashakti,[1427] I

[1426] Shiva, with the bull as a mount.
[1427] The Shakti of action.

urge the entire universe. Because of what I do, the universe follows my will and moves. I am Kala and I propel the entire universe, with its portions. O bulls among sages! With one of my portions, I create the entire universe. I destroy with another form. The state of stability is also because of me. I am devoid of any beginning, middle and end. I am the one who makes the principles of *maya* function. At the beginning of creation, I agitate both Pradhana and Purusha. When they are associated with each other, the universe originates from them, with Mahat and the others in the due order. It is my energy that spreads through this. Hiranyagarbha Martanda[1428] is a witness to all the worlds and makes the wheel of time function. He is also born from my body. O *dvija*s! At the beginning of the *kalpa*, I myself gave him the four *Veda*s, my own divine glory and eternal *jnana yoga*. The divinity Brahma was engaged by me and carried out my sentiments. Bestowed with my divine glory, he always knows. He knows everything. Urged by me, he creates all the worlds. The one with the four faces, who originates from his own self, embarks on the task of creation. All the worlds flow from the imperishable Ananta Narayana. As my other form, he undertakes the task of preservation. The lord Rudra, with Kala in his *atman*, is the one who destroys all beings. He is my body. Following my instructions, he constantly destroys. Vahni is urged by my Shakti. He bears *havya* to *deva*s, *kavya* to those who subsist on *kavya*, and also cooks.[1429] Urged by Bhagavan Ishvara, Vaishvanara Agni constantly cooks the food that has been eaten. Varuna, bull among *deva*s, is the source of all the waters. Urged by Ishvara, he imparts life to everyone.

[1428] Surya.
[1429] In the form of the digestive fire.

The *deva* Prabhanjana is inside and outside all beings.
Following my command, he maintains the bodies of beings.
Soma is made to rise because of my urging. He brings life
to men and is a store of *amrita* for *deva*s. Surya illuminates
the entire universe with his own radiance and uses his
rays to shower down rain. He does it on Svayambhuva's
instructions. Shakra, the lord of the immortals, rules
over the entire world and bestows the fruits of sacrifices.
This *deva* functions because of my command. The *deva*,
Vaivasvata Yama, is urged by the lord of *deva*s. He
chastises the wicked and ensures that rules are followed in
this world. Kubera always functions as a result of Ishvara's
bidding. He is the lord of all riches and bestows riches. The
deva Nirriti always follows my instructions. He is the lord
of all *rakshasa*s and bestows fruits on those who are full
of *tamas*. Ishana is the lord of large numbers of *vetalas*[1430]
and *bhuta*s, bestowing objects of pleasure and fruits on his
devotees. He too abides by my command. Vamadeva, the
shishya of Angiras, is foremost among large numbers of
Rudras. He constantly protects *yogis* and always abides by
my command. Vinayaka is devoted to *dharma* and follows
my words. He is worshipped by the entire world and is the
lord of impediments.[1431] The lord who is the commander of
the *deva* army is foremost among those who know about
the *brahman*. Skanda always functions on the basis of the
rules set by Svayambhu. Marichi and other *maharshi*s are
Prajapatis. Urged by the supreme, they create different
worlds. Shri bestows extensive prosperity on all beings. She
is Narayana's wife. She functions because of my favours.
Devi Sarasvati bestows extensive speech. She rises and

[1430]Evil spirits.
[1431]He removes impediments.

functions because Ishvara urges her. When remembered, Savitri saves all men from terrible hells. She too follows my bidding. Parvati is a supreme Devi. When one specially performs *dhyana* on her, she bestows knowledge about the *brahman*. She too follows my words. Ananta Shesha is infinite in greatness and is the lord of all the immortals. Urged by the divinity, he holds up the worlds on his hoods. The Samvartaka fire is always established in the form of a mare.[1432] On Ishvara's instructions, it drinks up all the oceans. There are fourteen Manus in the world, famous for their energy. Following his commands, they protect all the *praja*s. The Adityas, Vasus, Rudras, Maruts, the two Ashvins and all the other *deva*s are devised by me. It is Svayambhu who created and established the *gandharva*s, Garuda and the others, the *siddha*s, the Sadhyas, the *charana*s, the *yaksha*s, the *rakshasa*s and the *pishacha*s. *Kalaa*s, *kashtha*s, *nimesha*s, *muhurta*s, days, nights, seasons, fortnights and months are established because of Prajapati's instructions. *Yuga*s and *manvantara*s are based on my commands. This is also true of *para*s, *parardha*s and other divisions of time. It is through the instructions of the divinity *paramatman* that the four categories of beings,[1433] and mobile and immobile entities, exist. All the nether regions, all the worlds and all the cosmic eggs function according to Svayambhu's command. Following my command, there were innumerable cosmic eggs in the past. In every direction, they functioned with floods of objects. In the future too, cosmic eggs and their *atman*s,

---

[1432] The Samvartaka fire is the fire of destruction. It is located inside the oceans and is in the form of a mare's (*vadava*) head (*mukha*), thus known as the *vadavamukha* fire.

[1433] Those born from wombs, those born from eggs, those born from sweat (worms and insects) and plants and trees.

will follow my *atman*. They will act in accordance with the instructions of the supreme *paramatman*. The earth, water, fire, wind, space, *manas*, *buddhi*, *bhutadi* and primordial Prakriti function under my instructions. *Maya* is always transformed under Ishvara's command. It is the origin of the entire universe and deludes all those with bodies. One reads about the divinity Purusha, who assumes a body and is the *paramatman*. He constantly functions under Ishvara's instructions. Getting rid of delusion, *buddhi* perceives the objective and also functions under Mahesha's command. What is the need to speak a lot? The entire universe is my Shakti. Everything is urged by me and everything proceeds to dissolution within me. I am the eternal Bhagavan Isha, the self-luminous one. I am *paramatman* and the supreme *brahman*. There is no one other than me. I have described supreme *jnana* to you. Knowing this, a creature is liberated from the bonds of birth and *samsara*.'

Chapter 60(2)(7) (Shiva's powers)

Ishvara said, 'O *rishi*s! All of you listen to Parameshthi's powers.[1434] On knowing this, a man is liberated and does not fall into *samsara* again. This is my supreme abode, greater than the greatest, the eternal certain and imperishable *brahman*, without an alternative and full of constant bliss. Among those who know the *brahman*, I am Svayambhu Brahma, who faces every direction. Among those who possess *maya*, I am the ancient divinity, the imperishable Hari. Among *yogi*s, I am Shambhu. Among

[1434]There are similarities with Chapter 10 of *Bhagavat Gita*.

women, I am Devi, the mountain's daughter. Among
Adityas, I am Vishnu. Among Vasus, I am Pavaka. Among
Rudras, I am Shankara. Among birds, I am Garuda.
Among Indras among elephants, I am Airavata. Among
those who wield weapons, I am Rama.[1435] Among *rishi*s,
I am Vasishtha. Among *deva*s, I am Shatakratu. Among
artisans, I am Vishvakarma. Among those who hate the
gods, I am Prahlada. Among sages, I am Vyasa. Among
*gana*s, I am Vinayaka. Among those who are brave, I am
Virabhadra. Among *siddha*s, I am the sage Kapila. Among
mountains, I am Meru. Among *nakshatra*s, I am the moon.
Among those used to strike, I am the *vajra*. Among vows,
I am truthfulness. Among serpents, I am Ananta. Among
generals of the gods, I am Pavaki.[1436] Among *ashrama*s,
I am *garhashthya*. Among Ishvaras, I am Maheshvara.
Among *kalpa*s, I am the great *kalpa*. Among *yuga*s, I am
krita. Among all *yaksha*s, I am Kubera. Among all kinds
of grass, I am *virudha*.[1437] Among Prajapatis, I am Daksha.
Among all *rakshasa*s, I am Nirriti. Among all those that
are strong, I am Vayu. Among *dvipa*s, I am Pushkara.
Among lords of deer, I am the lion. Among mechanical
contrivances, I am the bow. Among *Veda*s, I am *Sama
Veda*. Among hymns of the *Yajur Veda*, I am Shatarudriya.
Among everything used to perform *japa*, I am Savitri.
Among everything that is secret, I am Pranava. Among
*suktam*s, I am Purusha *suktam*. Among *Sama* hymns, I am
Jyeshthasama. Among those who know the meanings of all
the *Veda*s, I am Svayambhuva Manu. Among regions, I am

[1435] Parashrama.
[1436] Pavaka's son, Skanda.
[1437] Shrub/plant that sprouts.

Brahmavarta.[1438] Among *kshetra*s, I am Avimuktaka.[1439] Among all kinds of knowledge, I am knowledge about the *atman*. Among all kinds of *jnana*, I am supreme *jnana* about Ishvara. Among elements, I am space. Among *tattva*s, I am Mrityu. Among all kinds of bonds, I am *maya*. Among those used to enumerate, I am Kala. Among objectives, I am liberation. Among all those who are supreme, I am Parameshvara. Among everything else in the worlds that possesses an excess of the energy and strength of *sattva*, know that all this is an expansion of my energy. All the *jivatman*s that follow *samsara* are said to be *pashu*s. The learned describe me as their lord, the divinity Pashupati.[1440] In my own pastimes, I bind these *pashu*s down in the noose of *maya*. Those who speak about the *Veda*s say that I am the one who liberates *pashu*s. Other than me, there is no one else who can liberate those who are bound by the noose of *maya*. Other than me, the *paramatman*, the imperishable lord of *bhuta*s, there is no one else. There are twenty-four *tattva*s—*maya*, *karma*, *guna*s and so on. These are the *pasha*s used by Pashupati to bind *pashu*s down in hardships. *Manas*, *buddhi*, *ahamkara*, space, wind, fire, water and earth—these are the eight transformations of Prakriti and there are others too. There are held to be ten—ears, skin, eyes, tongue, nostrils as the fifth, anus, genital organs, hands, feet and speech as the tenth. There are sound, touch, form, taste and smell. These are the twenty-three *tattva*s of Prakriti. The twenty-fourth is the unmanifest Pradhana, with *guna*s as attribute. This has no beginning,

---

[1438] The region around Kurukshetra, between the rivers Sarasvati and Drishadvati.

[1439] Kashi.

[1440] While *pashu* means animal, anyone bound by the noose (*pasha*) of *samsara* is *pashu*. Pashupati frees from this *pasha*.

middle or destruction. This is the supreme cause behind
the universe. The three *guna*s are *sattva*, *rajas* and *tamas*.
When these are in equilibrium, the learned know that this
is unmanifest Prakriti. *Sattva* is *jnana*. *Rajas* and *tamas* are
said to be lack of *jnana*. The wise know that disequilibrium
in *buddhi* causes disequilibrium in the *guna*s. *Dharma*
and *adharma* are described as the two *pasha*s of *karma*.
Without offering the *karma* to me, it is not possible to
free oneself of bondage. Ignorance, egotism, attachment,
hatred and desire—these are described as hardships.
They are said to bind the *atman* in *pasha*s. *Maya* is said
to be the cause behind these *pasha*s. The unmanifest and
primordial Prakriti is the Shakti that is established in me.
He is primordial Prakriti, Pradhana, Purusha, Mahat and
the other transformations. He is the eternal lord of *deva*s.
He is the bondage and the creator of the bond. He is *pasha*
and the one who supports *pashu*s. He knows everything,
but no one knows him. He is spoken of as the primordial
and eternal Purusha.'

Chapter 61(2)(8) (Crossing over *samsara*)

Ishvara said, 'O bulls among *brahmana*s! I will tell you
about another *jnana* that is most secret. Using this,
creatures can cross over this terrible ocean of *samsara*. I
am Brahma, serene, eternal, without blemish and without
decay. I alone am spoken of as Bhagavan. I alone am
Parameshvara. My womb is the great *brahman*.[1441] I
conceive in that womb. This is known as original *maya*

[1441] Meaning Prakriti.

and the entire universe is generated from that. Pradhana, Purusha, the *atman*, Mahat, *bhutadi*, the *tanmatras*, *manas*, the elements and the senses were generated from that. The golden egg resulted, with the radiance of one crore suns. Extended by my Shakti, the great Brahma was born from this. There are many other living beings, all permeated by me. Deluded by my *maya*, they do not perceive me, the father. All those wombs result from this and all the resultant forms in this world. That womb[1442] is their supreme mother and I am known as the father. If a person knows me, the lord, as the father who sows the seed, in all the worlds, such a brave person does not succumb to delusion. I am the lord of every kind of learning. For all beings, I am Parameshvara. I am Bhagavan, with a form as OUMKARA. I am Prajapati Brahma. I am the Parameshvara who is established equally in all beings. When they are destroyed, I am not destroyed. If a person perceives this, he truly sees. Such a person perceives me, Ishvara, as established equally everywhere. He does not make his *atman* suffer and proceeds to the supreme destination. He knows Maheshvara's seven subtle parts and six limbs. He knows what is assigned to Pradhana and proceeds to the supreme *brahman*. Omniscience, contentment, limitless understanding, self-dependence, constant Shakti that is never exhausted and infinite Shakti—for those who know, these are spoken of as Maheshvara's six limbs. The *tanmatras*, *manas* and the *atman*—these are spoken of as the seven *tattvas* in my *atman*. Prakriti is the cause. It is also spoken of as Pradhana, the bond that is applied. Prakriti's Shakti is latent in form. The *Vedas* speak of it as the cause, Brahma's womb. Parameshthi alone is in front

---

[1442] *Maya*.

of her. He is Purusha Maheshvara, with truth as his form. He is Brahma. He is a *yogi*. He is the *paramatman*. He is the greatest one, pervading space. He is the ancient one, who can be known through the *Veda*s. He alone is Rudra. He alone is Mrityu, not manifest. He alone is the seed of the universe. He is the divinity. Some say that he is one. Others say that he is many. Some say that he is the *atman*. Others speak of him as something else. He is smaller than the smallest. He is greater than the greatest. He is described as Mahadeva, with the universe as his form. He is the supreme and ancient lord, hidden in the cavity of the heart. He is the golden Purusha, with the universe as his form. A person who knows this, achieves the supreme destination for the intelligent. Such an intelligent person is established beyond *buddhi*.'

Chapter 62(2)(9) (Shiva's *nishkala* form)

The *rishi*s said, 'Parameshvara is *nishkala* and without blemish. He is eternal and does not act. O Mahadeva! Therefore, please tell us how the universe becomes your form.'

Ishvara replied, 'O *dvija*s! I am not the universe. But the universe does not exist without me. *Maya* alone is the cause and she seeks refuge in my *atman*. *Maya* is a Shakti that is without a beginning and without destruction. She finds support in a form that is manifest. She is the cause behind *prapancha*, which is indeed born from the unmanifest. The unmanifest is spoken of as the cause. It is bliss and radiance and is imperishable. I am the supreme *brahman*. Other than me, there is nothing else. Therefore, those who speak about the *brahman* have determined that I possess the attribute of having the universe as my form. They say that the instances exist in I being one, and being many. Thus, I am the supreme *brahman*. I am the eternal *paramatman*. O *dvijas*! Since I am not spoken of as the cause, there is no taint associated with my *atman*. The infinite Shaktis are eternal and not manifest. They are established by *maya*. That eternal and unmanifest one is established in the firmament, in the form of radiance alone. The eternal *brahman* is not manifest. It is constant and without destruction. It is one and without differences. But united with *maya*, it is described as possessing differences. One of Purusha's powers does not vanish because of the existence of another. He is established, without a beginning and a middle. He functions through knowledge alone. The supreme is not manifest and is ornamented by a circle of radiance. This is a supreme and imperishable resplendence. This is Vishnu's supreme abode. Like warp and woof, everything in the universe is woven into this. When one realizes that the entire universe is this, one is liberated. Speech cannot reach this. Thoughts cannot reach this. A person who knows the bliss of the *brahman* is never scared of anything. I know the great Purusha. This Purusha, with the complexion of the sun, is in front of me.[1443] Knowing this, a learned person is liberated. He is full of constant bliss and becomes one with the *brahman*. There is nothing else that is greater than this. This alone is the radiance of the luminous bodies established in the firmament. Realizing that his *atman* is this, a learned person is full of constant bliss and becomes one with the *brahman*. I cannot be penetrated. My body is subtle. I am the *amrita* and bliss of the *brahman*. I am the abode of the

[1443] This echoes the *Upanishads*.

universe. *Brahmana*s who are devoted to the *brahman* say this. Having reached there, there is no return again. There is a supreme and golden energy that seems to shine in the firmament in the form of the sky. In their own *vijnana*, those who are wise perceive this radiance as the sparkling abode of space. After this, those who are wise directly experience this *atman* within their own *atman*s. This is the lord Parameshthi himself, the greatest. This is Bhagavan Isha, the bliss of the *brahman*. This alone is the divinity hidden inside all beings. He pervades everything. He is inside the *atman*s of all beings. Wise ones, who perceive him alone, obtain eternal peace, not others. His heads and necks are on all sides. He is in the cavities of the hearts of all living beings. He is Bhagavan, who pervades everything. Other than him, there is nothing else. O bulls among sages! This *jnana* about Ishvara has been narrated to you. This is especially secret and is difficult for even *yogi*s to obtain.'

Chapter 63(2)(10) (Shiva as the supreme *brahman*)

Ishvara said, 'The absolute unmanifest has no *lingam*s. But it has been determined that the *brahman* has *lingam*s. It is self-luminous and the supreme truth. Thereafter, it is established in space. The imperishable unmanifest is the cause and the supreme destination. Through the *siddhi* of *vijnana*, the learned perceive it as *nirguna*. There are those who are constantly immersed in it. Thereby, all their resolutions are destroyed and come to an end. They perceive the supreme *brahman* and the *shruti* texts say that this is the *lingam*. O bulls among sages! It is impossible to see me through any other means. There is no other *jnana*

through which the supreme can be realized. This is the
supreme abode, only known by the wise. Since the universe
is full of *maya*, every other kind of *jnana* is the darkness
of ignorance. The sparkling *jnana* is pure. My *atman* is
without an alternative and is without blemish. Those who
are learned speak about me in this way. I am the supreme
objective. There are those who perceive me, the supreme,
as one or many. They resort to supreme devotion. I am
the imperishable truth and am understood according to
their understanding. There are those who perceive me, the
supreme, as the single truth. Others perceive Ishvara as
many. Devotees visualize me in this way. They understand
according to their own *atman*s. There are those who
directly perceive Parameshvara within their own *atman*s,
as constant bliss, without an alternative and established in
the form of truth. They worship this supreme bliss, which
is everywhere, with the universe in its *atman*. They are
serene, established in their own *atman*s. They perceive the
supreme as beyond the manifest. This is supreme liberation
and is excellent *sayujya* with me. This is *nirvana* and unity
with the *brahman*. The wise know this as *kaivalya*.[1444]
Thus, there is only one single, supreme and auspicious
entity without a beginning, a middle and an end. This is
Ishvara Mahadeva. Knowing him, one is liberated. The sun
does not shine there, or the moon, or the large number of
*nakshatra*s.[1445] There is no lightning there. Illuminated by
it, the entire universe shines. Everything is illuminated by
that great radiance, free of blemishes. This is the origin
of the universe, *nishkala*, pure and without an alternative.
This is the great and supreme refulgence. Inside this, those

[1444] The absolute state of becoming one with the *brahman*.
[1445] This echoes the *Upanishad*s.

who know the *brahman* constantly perceive the unwavering truth that is Isha. This is constant bliss and *amrita*. This is pure and the form of truth. All the *Veda*s speak of this as Purusha. Those who have determined the meanings of the *Veda*s perform *dhyana* on this as Pranava, the *prana* inside them. The earth, water, *manas*, fire, *prana*, wind, the sky, *buddhi* or consciousness does not shine inside that supreme firmament. It is the divinity Shiva alone. This supreme secret and *jnana* has been stated. All the *Veda*s sing about this. The *yogi* knows. In a solitary spot, one should make efforts to practice this *yoga* innumerable times.'

Chapter 64(2)(11) (The path of *yoga*)

Ishvara said, 'After this, I will speak about the *yoga* that is extremely difficult to achieve. Through this, one can see the *atman*, Ishvara, who is as radiant as the sun. The fire of *yoga* quickly burns down the cage of sins. Pure *jnana* is directly generated and it bestows the *siddhi* of *nirvana*. *Jnana* is generated through *yoga* and *yoga* functions through *jnana*. When *yoga* and *jnana* are united, Maheshvara is pleased. Those who practice this great *yoga* once a day, twice a day, thrice a day or constantly, are themselves known as Maheshvaras. *Yoga* is known to be of two types. The first is said to be *abhava yoga*. The second is *mahayoga* and this is best among every kind of *yoga*. When one thinks of one's own form as void, without any kind of reflection, this is known as *abhava yoga*.[1446] Through this, one perceives the *atman*. There is a *yoga* through which one

---

[1446] *Abhava* means the absence of any existence.

perceives the *atman* as constant bliss, without blemish and identical with me. I myself speak of this as supreme *yoga*. There are *yogis* who practice other kinds of *yoga*, heard about in extensive texts. All of these do not deserve to be a one-sixteenth part of *brahmayoga*.[1447] There is a *yoga* where those who are liberated directly perceive unity between the universe and Ishvara. Among every kind of *yoga*, this is held to be the best *yoga*. There are thousands of types of *yoga*s and many *yogis* who control their minds but exclude Ishvara. They do not see me as the only one. O best among sages! There are *pranayama*, *dhyana*, *pratyahara*, *dharana*, *samadhi*, *yama*, *niyama* and *asana*. *Yoga* is the restraint of everything ancillary, with the mind immersed in me alone. There are other *sadhana*s and I will describe them to you. Non-violence, truth, lack of theft, *brahmacharya* and non-acceptance of objects—briefly, these are spoken of as *yama*. These purify the minds of men. Never creating hardships to all beings, in thoughts, words and deeds— supreme *rishi*s describe this as non-violence. Non-violence is supreme *dharma*. Nothing yields greater happiness than non-violence. But violence that follows the rules is also stated to be non-violence.[1448] Everything is achieved through truth. Everything is established in truth. *Dvija*s say that truth is the conduct of stating what is accurate. Seizing another person's possessions through stealing or force is theft. One should refrain from theft. Refraining from theft is a *sadhana* for *dharma*. *Brahmacharya* is described as refraining from physical intercourse everywhere and in every possible situation, in thoughts, words and deeds. The voluntary avoidance of gifts, even in times of

---

[1447] *Yoga* that leads to the *brahman*.
[1448] Such as violence in the course of sacrifices.

hardship, is said to be non-acceptance of objects. One must make efforts to observe this. Austerities, self-studies, contentment, purity and worship of Ishvara—briefly, these are said to constitute *niyama*. They bestow the *siddhi* of *yoga*. Fasting, *paraka* and other kinds of hardship, *chandrayana* and other rites and the drying up of the body are described by ascetics to be excellent austerities.[1449] The learned say that self-studying involves *japa* with *Vedanta*, Shatarudriya or Pranava. This brings about the *siddhi* of *sattva* in men. There are three kinds of divisions in self-studying—*vachika*, *upamshu* and *manasa*.[1450] Those who know the meanings of the *Veda*s say that succeeding forms are superior to preceding ones. *Svadhyaya* is said to be *vachika* when the words are clearly stated and can be understood by others who hear them. The characteristic of *upamshu* is that the lips merely quiver, and the words cannot be understood by others. *Upamshu* is superior to one thousand rounds of *vachika japa*. When the syllables are properly articulated, without any quivering of the lips, and the words are merely thought of, this is known to be *manasa japa*. When a man regards any wealth obtained as sufficient, without striving for it, the *rishi*s describe this praiseworthy attribute as contentment. This is a sign of

[1449] Paraka involves fasting for twelve days. *Chandrayana* is a kind of fasting that follows the progress (*ayana*) of the moon (*chandra*). On the full moon night, one only eats fifteen mouthfuls of food. For the fifteen lunar days following the full moon, this is decreased by one mouthful per day. For the fifteen lunar days following the new moon, this is increased by one mouthful per day.

[1450] *Svadhyaya* has been translated as self-studying, but the three divisions refer to *japa*. *Vachika* is when the *japa* is done loudly, *upamshu* when it is virtually inaudible and *manasa* when it is completely in the mind.

happiness. O excellent *dvija*s! Purity is said to be of two types—external and internal. External purity uses clay and water.[1451] Internal purity relates to the mind. Praise, remembrance and worship, in thoughts, words and deeds, and unwavering devotion to Shiva constitute the worship of Ishvara.'

'*Yama* and *niyama* have been spoken about. Now, hear about *pranayama*. *Prana* is the air that circulates within one's own body and *ayama* is the act of restraining it. *Pranayama* is said to be of three types—superior, middling and inferior. It is also classified as belonging to two types—*sagarbha* and *agarbha*.[1452] For inferior *pranayama*, the duration is twelve *matra*s.[1453] For middling *pranayama*, it is twenty-four *matra*s. For the last type of superior *pranayama*, *prana* is restrained for thirty-six *matra*s. In the due order, perspiration, shivering and gasping are generated. The bliss this generates in men determines the degree of excellence. The learned say that the triumph of *sagarbha pranayama* is when there is *sunapha yoga*.[1454] *Yogi*s say that these are the characteristics of *pranayama*. Controlling *prana*, one should perform *japa* thrice with *gayatri mantra*, along with *vyahriti*[1455] and Pranava. This is known as *pranayama*. In all the sacred texts, *yogi*s who

[1451] For cleaning and ablutions.

[1452] *Sagarbha* is when a *mantra* is uttered in the process. *Agarbha* is without the use of a *mantra*.

[1453] *Matra* is a syllabic instant, the amount of time required to pronounce a short vowel. Duration refers to each act of inhalation, retention and exhalation.

[1454] *Sunapha yoga* is a configuration of planets when a planet, barring the sun, occupies a secondary position to the moon. This does not fit at all and there is an error difficult to determine.

[1455] *Vyahriti*s are sacred and mystical words. They are usually mentioned as three—*bhuh*, *bhuvah* and *svah*.

have controlled their minds have said that *pranayama* has components of *rechaka*, *puraka* and *kumbhaka*. *Rechaka* is external exhalation of the breath. *Puraka* is its retention. A state of equilibrium between the two is said to be *kumbhaka*.[1456] By nature, the senses wander around among material objects. O excellent ones! Virtuous ones say that restraining them is *pratyahara*. *Dharana* is fixing the mind in the lotus of the heart, the navel, the head, the joints, the forehead and other such places. Learned ones know that *dhyana* is being seated in one particular spot and fixing the mind, without allowing it to waver and without being distracted in any other way. In the case of *samadhi*, there is one form alone, without being conscious of the place. Only a single object is perceived. This is the excellent instruction of *yoga*. Twelve *pranayama*s constitute *dharana*. Twelve *dharana*s constitute *dhyana*. Twelve *dhyana*s are said to constitute *samadhi*. *Asana*s are said to be *svastika*, *padma* and *arddha*.[1457] Among every kind of *sadhana*, this is said to be excellent *sadhana*. O Indras among *brahmana*s! When the soles of both feet are duly placed over the thighs and one is seated in this way, this is said to be the excellent

[1456] *Pranayama* has three components—*puraka*, *rechaka* and *kumbhaka*. *Puraka* is when the inhaled *apana* air fills up the exhaled *prana* air and temporarily stops its exit. *Rechaka* is when the exhaled *prana* air stops the entry of the inhaled *apana* air. *Kumbhaka* is when *prana* and *apana* are both controlled and the air is restrained inside the body. The breath of life is *prana* and this has five actions—*prana* (exhalation), *apana* (downward inhalation), *vyana* (diffusion through the body), *udana* (upward inhalation) and *samana* (digestive breath).

[1457] *Padmasana* is the lotus posture. In *svastikasana*, the left leg is folded near the right thigh and vice-versa, so that the posture of the body is in the shape of a *svastika*. *Arddha* means *arddha padmasana*, where only one leg is locked in the lotus posture.

padmasana. When the soles of both feet are placed between the knees and the thighs and one is seated in this way, this is said to be the supreme *svastikasana*. O excellent ones! When one foot is placed on the other thigh and one is seated in this way, this is *arddhasana*. This is an excellent *sadhana* for *yoga*. *Yoga* is never seen in the wrong time or place. It is not practised near fire or water, or where there is a heap of dry leaves. It should not be practised where creatures abound, in cremation grounds, where there are destroyed cow-pens, at crossroads, where there are accumulations of sound, near *chaitya*s,[1458] near termite hills, in inauspicious places attacked by wicked men and where the place is full of mosquitoes. Nor should it be practised when the body is suffering or the mind is depressed. With the *atman* constantly fixed on him,[1459] one should engage in *yoga* in a well-protected place, in an auspicious spot, in a cave within a mountain, on the banks of a river, in a holy spot, in the temple of a *deva*, in an extremely auspicious spot within the house and in a desolate spot not frequented by creatures.'

'One should first prostrate oneself before Indras among *yogi*s and their *shishya*s, Vinayaka, the *guru* and me. Controlling oneself, one should then engage in *yoga*. One should bind oneself in *svastikasana*, *padmasana* or *arddhasana*. The eyes should be partly closed and the sight fixed in the centre of the tip of the nose. Fearless and serene, he should discard the world, full of *maya*. He must think of the divinity Parameshvara, located within his own *atman*. A lotus must be conceived above the tuft of hair and it must

[1458]The word *chaitya* has several meanings—sacrificial shed, temple, altar, sanctuary and a tree that grows along the road.
[1459]Shiva.

be twelve *angulas*[1460] in length. It arises from the tuber of *dharma*. It is extremely beautiful and *jnana* is the stalk. The eight powers are its petals.[1461] It is supremely white and non-attachment constitutes the pericarp. Within that pericarp, one should think of a supreme and golden *kosha*.[1462] There, one should think of the supreme, sparkling and imperishable radiance. This is said to be divine and without change. This directly possesses all the Shaktis. This is not manifest and is spoken of as OUMKARA. This is amid a blazing garland of rays. This is not different from me, and he must immerse himself in the bliss of this radiance. Within the *kosha*, he must perform *dhyana* on Isha, the supreme cause. Having become one with the *atman* that goes everywhere, he should not think of anything else. This is the most secret *jnana*. After this, another kind of *dhyana* is spoken about. As was the case earlier, one should think of an excellent lotus in the heart. There, the *atman* must be thought of as a doer, surrounded by fire. The twenty-fifth Purusha will be in the centre of this fire, in the form of a flame. He must think of the *paramatman* in its middle, in the form of the supreme firmament. OUMKARA kindles understanding about the eternal truth, spoken of as Shiva. This is the unmanifest, latent in Prakriti. This is the supreme and excellent resplendence. This is the ultimate and supreme truth, the support that is without blemish. Immersing oneself in this,

[1460] The length of a finger.
[1461] *Yoga* leads to eight major *siddhi*s or powers. These are *anima* (becoming as small as one desires), *mahima* (as large as one desires), *laghima* (as light as one wants), *garima* (as heavy as one wants), *prapti* (obtaining what one wants), *prakamya* (travelling where one wants), *vashitvam* (powers to control creatures) and *ishitvam* (obtaining divine powers).
[1462] Closed flower bud. The word also means sheath or vessel.

one should constantly perform *dhyana* on Maheshvara, single in form. All the principles should again be purified through Pranava. The *atman* must be established in me, the sparkling and supreme destination. One's body will be flooded with that water of *jnana*. The *atman* is in me. The mind is in me. *Bhasma* must be accepted from an *agnihotra* sacrifice. Using *mantra*s to Agni and Aditya, all the limbs must be smeared with this. One should think of Ishana, in the form of that supreme refulgence. This is *pashupata yoga*, which frees *pashu*s from *pasha*s. This is the path of all *Vedanta* and the *shruti* texts say that this is beyond the *ashrama*s. This is the greatest of secrets and bestows *sayujya* with me. I have spoken about *dvija* devotees who are *brahmachari*s. In particular, *brahmacharya*, non-violence, forgiveness, purity, austerities, self-control, contentment, truthfulness and belief are the components of *vrata*s.[1463] Even if one of these is missing, the *vrata* is not destroyed. Thus, those who possess excellent qualities of the *atman*, deserve to take up my *vrata*. Those devoid of attachment, fear and rage have sought refuge with me in this way. There are many who have purified themselves with this *yoga* and have immersed themselves in me. Whoever worships me, in whatever way, I entertain them in that way.[1464] Therefore, you should worship me, Parameshvara, through *jnana yoga*. Or, through supreme non-attachment, one can follow *bhakti yoga*. Always pure, one should worship me, the mind full of understanding. All *karma* should be renounced. One should not accept anything and should survive on the basis of alms. Thus, one obtains *sayujya* with me. I have stated a secret.'

[1463] Vows.
[1464] *Bhagavat Gita* 4.9-10 verbatim.

'He who has no hatred for all beings, is friendly and displays compassion and is without a sense of ownership and *ahamkara*, such a devotee is dear to me.[1465] If a *yogi* is always satisfied and controlled in mind, firm in resolution and with mind and intelligence immersed in me, such a devotee is dear to me. If a person is not agitated by other people and does not agitate other people, if he is free from delight, intolerance, fear and anxiety, such a devotee is dear to me. Without wishes, pure, skilled, indifferent, devoid of pain and one who has renounced all enterprise—such a devotee is dear to me. Indifferent to criticism and praise, restrained in speech, content with whatever is obtained, without habitation and steady in mind—such a devotee obtains me. When all *karma* is always performed with devotion to me, through my favours, he obtains the eternal and supreme destination. Through the mind, offering up all *karma* to me and devoted to me, without desires and without a sense of ownership, he seeks refuge in me alone. Renouncing attachment to the fruits of *karma*, always content and not dependent, one engages in *karma* and that *karma* kindles understanding. Without desires, controlled in mind and senses, having discarded all possessions, and performing *karma* with the body alone, he reaches that destination. Content with whatever has been obtained without efforts and beyond the opposite pair of sentiments, through my favours, that *karma* destroys *samsara*. Fix your mind on me. Prostrate yourself before me. Perform sacrifices to me. Be devoted to me. Knowing me as Parameshvara, the lord of *yogi*s, worship me. They call be the supreme refulgence and kindle understanding in each other. They constantly converse about me and obtain

[1465]These *shloka*s are paraphrases of *Bhagavat Gita* 12.13-19, 18.56-57 and 4.20-22.

sayujya with me. In this way, for those who are constantly
devoted to me and whose *karma* is driven by *sattva*, I use
the radiant lamp of *jnana* to destroy all darkness. There are
people in this world whose minds are immersed in me and
who constantly worship me. For those who are engaged in
this way, I preserve for them what has been attained and
what is yet to be attained.[1466] There are others who worship
other *deva*s for objects of pleasure, *karma* and *artha*. For
them, it should be known that the ultimate fruits are only
those under the control of that *deva*. In this world, there are
those who are devotees of other *deva*s and worship those
*deva*s. As long as they are immersed in sentiments about
me, such men are also liberated. Therefore, abandoning all
other *deva*s, one should resort to Ishvara alone. A person
who seeks refuge with me, Ishvara, proceeds to the supreme
destination. One should abandon affection towards sons
and others. One should cast aside grief and possessions.
Without any attachment, until death, one should worship
Parameshvara's *lingam*. If a person renounces all objects
of pleasure and constantly worships the *lingam*, in a single
birth, I grant them the supreme destination. Paramatman's
lingam is always absolute and is like silver in complexion.
With *jnana* as its *atman*, it is omnipresent and is established
in the hearts of *yogi*s. There are other controlled devotees.
Full of sentiments and in the proper way, they worship
Maheshvara's *lingam* in water, in the midst of fire, in the
sky, in the sun and elsewhere. Ishvara's *lingam* can be
conceived in jewels and other things and worshipped. The
lingam is everywhere and everything is established in the
lingam. Therefore, eternal Isha must be worshipped in the
lingam, anywhere. Those who perform rites visualize it in

[1466] Part of *Bhagavat Gita* 9.22. What is yet to be attained is
yoga and what has been attained is *kshema*.

the fire, learned ones in the sky and in the sun, while fools think of it in wood and other objects. However, for *yogis*, the *lingam* is in the heart. Even if *vijnana* has not been kindled, as long as one is full of non-attachment and love, as long as one is alive, one should perform *japa* with Pranava. It is Brahma's body. Or, until death, a *dvija* can perform *japa* with Shatarudriya. If a person is alone and has control over his mind, he proceeds to the supreme destination. Controlling himself, until death, a *brahmana* should reside in Varanasi. Through Ishvara's favours, such a person also proceeds to the supreme destination. There, at the time of passing, all those with bodies are bestowed supreme *jnana* and are thereby freed from bondage. Devoted to me, if a person observes all the rules of *varna*s and *ashrama*s, in that birth, such a person obtains *jnana* and proceeds to a destination with Shiva. O *dvija*s! Even if inferior ones and those with wicked births reside there, through Ishvara's favours, all of them cross over *samsara*. However, if the mind is overwhelmed by sin, there will be impediments. O *dvija*s! Hence, for the sake of liberation, one should always resort to *dharma*. This is the secret of the *Veda*s. It should never be revealed to everyone. It should only be revealed to those who are devoted to *dharma*, those who are devotees and *brahmachari*s.'

Vyasa continued, 'In this way, Bhagavan spoke about the eternal and excellent *yoga*. Narayana, free from ailments, was seated there and he told him, "For the welfare of those who speak about the *brahman*, I have spoken about this *jnana*. You should bestow this auspicious *jnana* on your *shishya*s, those with serene minds." After he said this, Bhagavan Aja spoke to the Indras among *yogis*.[1467] "O excellent *dvija*s! For the welfare of all devotees among

---

[1467] As will be evident, this is Shiva speaking again.

*dvija*s, you should follow the rules and impart this *jnana* to *shishya*s. Follow my words and instruct all devotees. This Narayana is Ishvara. There is no doubt about this. This supreme *jnana* must be bestowed on those who do not see a difference between the two. The one known as Narayana is my supreme form. He is tranquil and imperishable and is present in the *atman*s of all beings. There are other people who do not perceive it in this way and see a difference. Even if they are born repeatedly, they do not experience liberation. Those who see the unmanifest Vishnu and me, the divinity Maheshvara, as one, are those who do not return again to this world. Vishnu is the one with the imperishable *atman*, without a beginning and without an end. Therefore, see me in him and worship him. Those who perceive otherwise and see a difference between me and the divinity, go to terrible hells. I am not present there. If a person seeks refuge with me and is foolish, learned, a *brahmana* or a *shvapaka*,[1468] as long as he does not criticize Narayana, I liberate him. Purushottama is a great *yogi*. Hence, to generate pleasure in me, my devotees should prostrate themselves before him and worship him." Saying this, the wielder of Pinaka embraced Vaasudeva. While everyone looked on, he vanished. Bhagavan Narayana gave up his supreme body and assumed the excellent garb of an ascetic. He told all the *yogi*s, "Through Parameshthi's favours, you have obtained this sparkling *jnana* from the divinity Mahesha himself. This *jnana* destroys *samsara*. O lords among sages! Devoid of anxiety, leave. All of you propound Parameshvara's *vijnana* to *shishya*s and those who follow *dharma*. Ishvara's *vijnana* must be imparted to

---

[1468] *Shvapaka* means dog-eater or someone who cooks food for dogs. This is usually equated with *chandala* or outcaste.

devotees, those who are serene and follow *dharma*, those who offer oblations into the fire, especially *brahmana*s." Saying this, Narayana, the great *yogi*, whose *atman* is in the universe and who is supreme among *yogi*s who know about *yoga*, himself vanished. The *rishi*s prostrated themselves before Maheshvara, the lord of *deva*s, and Narayana, the origin of the elements. They returned to their own respective abodes.'

'The illustrious Sanatkumara bestowed this *jnana* about Ishvara to the great sage, Samvarta. He imparted it to Satyavrata. Sanandana, Indra among *yogi*s, passed it on to *maharshi* Pulaha. Prajapati Pulaha imparted it to Goutama. Angiras gave it to Bharadvaja, who was learned in the *Veda*s. Kapila passed it on to Jaigishavya and Panchashikha. My father Parashara, who could see everything, obtained this supreme *jnana* from Sanaka and Valmiki obtained it from him. *Deva* Vamadeva Rudra, who wields the Pinaka of destruction, originated from Sati's body and Bhava's limbs. Earlier, he spoke to me about this. Bhagavan Hari Narayana, Devaki's son, himself imparted this excellent knowledge to Arjuna. I obtained this excellent knowledge from Rudra Vamadeva and thus developed special devotion towards Girisha. I sought refuge with Girisha. In particular, I sought refuge with Rudra. Girisha Sthanu is the lord of *bhuta*s. The wielder of the trident is the lord of *deva*s. Along with your wives and sons, you should seek refuge with Shiva, the divinity Shambhu, whose mount is a bull. Through Shankara's favours, follow *karma yoga*. Worship Mahadeva, the lord of cattle, whose ornament is a serpent.'

Thus addressed, Shounka and the others prostrated themselves before the eternal Sthanu Maheshvara again. Delighted in their minds, they spoke to the lord Krishna

Dvaipayana Vyasa, Satyavati's son, who was the divinity
Hrishikesha and Shiva, the great lord of the worlds, himself.
"Through your favours, unwavering devotion has now
been generated towards the refuge, the one with the bull
on his banner. This is difficult for even the *deva*s to obtain.
O best among sages! Please tell us about excellent *karma
yoga*, through which, those who desire liberation worship
Bhagavan Isha. In your presence, let Suta hear Bhagavan's
words. In the form of Kurma, Vishnu, the lord of *deva*s,
spoke about this for the protection of all the worlds and
the accumulation of *dharma*. At the time of the churning
of the ocean, he was asked about this by all the sages
and Shakra." Hearing these words he, controlled himself
and told the sages everything about eternal *karma yoga*.
If a person constantly reads this conversation between
Krittivasa and Sanatkumara and other foremost sages, he
is freed from all sins. If a person makes pure *brahmana*s,
devoted to *brahmacharya*, hear this, and if he reflects
on the meaning, he proceeds to the supreme destination.
Full of devotion and firm in vows, if a person constantly
hears this, he is freed from all sins and obtains greatness in
Brahma's world. Therefore, learned ones must make every
effort to read this. In particular, along with *brahmana*s,
one should always hear this and acknowledge it.'

Chapter 65(2)(12) (Duties of *brahmachari*s)

Narration of Vyasa Gita[1469]
Vyasa said, 'O *rishi*s! All of you listen. I will narrate
eternal *karma yoga*, which bestows ultimate benefits

[1469]These chapters constitute Vyasa Gita.

on *brahmana*s. For *brahmana*s to obtain every kind of
success, this is the path that has been instructed. This
destroys all sins. Earlier, there was a sacred gathering of
*rishi*s. The *rishi*s heard what Prajapati Manu had spoken
about earlier. Control your minds and listen to my words.
O excellent *dvija*s! According to the rules followed in his
tradition, in the eighth year after birth or the eighth year
after conception, *upanayana* must be performed and he
must study the *Veda*s. The sage must hold a staff, wear a
girdle and sacred thread and be attired in black antelope
skin. He must subsist on alms and be a *brahmachari*.
He must happily dwell in his own hermitage. Earlier,
Brahma devised cotton for the sake of an *upavita*.[1470] For
*brahmana*s, the *upavita* must be made out of three strings,
with *kusha* grass or cotton. A *dvija* must always wear the
upavita and bind his tuft of hair. If he does not do this,
every rite he performs will be unsuccessful. His garment
should not be malformed. It should be made out of cotton
and ochre. A white piece of cloth, without holes, is also
regarded as an excellent garment. An upper garment made
out of black antelope skin is described as excellent. If this is
not available, the divine hide of *ruru* deer is recommended.
When the thread is placed over the left arm and under the
right arm, it is known as *upavita* and this is the way it
should always be worn. When it is wound around the neck,
it is known as *nivita*. O *dvija*s! If it is worn over the right
arm and under the left arm, it is known as *prachinavita*.
This should be used for rites concerning the ancestors. The
eternal rules for wearing *upavita* are that it must always be
worn in the chamber for the fire, in cow-pens, at the time
of oblations and *japa*, during self-studies, always when

[1470] The sacred thread.

eating, in the presence of *brahmana*s, when worshipping *guru*s, at the time of the two *sandhya*s and when one meets virtuous people. A *brahmana*'s girdle must be made out of three equal strands of *munja* grass and it must be smooth. O *brahmana*s! It can also be made out of three strands of *kusha* grass. A *dvija* must hold a staff made out of *bilva* or *palasha* and it should extend up to the tip of his hair. It can also be made out of any other tree fit to be used in sacrifices. It should be soft and without cracks. In the morning and in the evening, a *dvija* must control himself and perform the *sandhya* rites. If he abandons it out of desire, greed, fear or delusion, he falls down. In that way, following the rules, morning and evening, the fire rites must be performed. Having bathed, one should satisfy *devas*, *rishi*s and the large number of ancestors. *Deva*s must be worshipped with flowers, leaves and water. Following *dharma*, a person with good conduct must always honour the aged. First prostrating himself, he should properly state, "My name is such and such." This should be done to achieve a long lifespan and freedom from ailments, but without a desire for objects. In return, a *brahmana* will be greeted with the words, "O amiable one! May you have a long lifespan." When the name is spoken, अ must be pronounced at the end and the preceding *akshara* must be *pluta*.[1471] If a *dvija* does not greet back in return when he is greeted, the learned do not greet him and treat him like a *shudra*. When clasping the *guru*'s feet, the hands must be crossed in the following way. The left hand must be used to touch his left foot and the right hand to touch his right

---

[1471] A *pluta akshara* is pronounced over three *matra*s. A *hrasva akshara* is pronounced over one *matra*, while a *dirgha akshara* is pronounced over two *matra*s.

foot. The person from whom he has acquired *jnana* about worldly matters, about the *Veda*s and about *adhyatma*, must be honoured first. At the time of greeting, he should not hold water, food obtained through alms, flowers or kindling. Nor should he hold any other object used in rites for *deva*s. A *brahmana* will be asked about his *kushala*, a *kshatra-bandhu* about *anamaya*, a *vaishya* about *kshema* and a *shudra* about *arogya*.'[1472]

'The preceptor, the father, the elder brother, the king, the maternal uncle, the father-in-law, the maternal grandfather, the paternal grandfather, the paternal uncle and a person who belongs to a superior *varna*—all these are said to be *guru*s. The mother, the maternal grandmother, a female *guru*, sisters of the father or mother, the mother-in-law, the paternal grandmother, an elder brother's wife and the *guru*'s wife—all these belong to the category of *guru*s. These are the ones on the father's side and the mother's side. In thoughts, words and deeds, they must be followed. On seeing a *guru*, one should stand up, join one's hands in salutation and greet him. One should not sit alongside them. For the sake of wealth, one should not argue with them. Even for the sake of remaining alive, one should not display hatred towards *guru*s in speech. Even if a person has risen up because of his qualities, if he hates *guru*s, he falls downwards. All *guru*s must be worshipped. However, five are special. Among these, the three who are first and foremost are the mother, who is extremely revered, the biological father and the one who has imparted learning.

[1472] *Kshatra-bandhu* means inferior *kshatriya*, but is used here for *kshatriya*. The words are similar, with slightly different nuances. *Kushala* is welfare, *anamaya* is sound health, *kshema* is prosperity and *arogya* is freedom from disease.

With the brother and the husband[1473] added, these five are described as *guru*s. If a person desires his prosperity, he must make every possible effort to specially worship these five, even if this amounts to giving up his own life. As long as the mother and father are alive, a son must abandon everything else and be devoted to them. When the mother and father are extremely pleased with the son's qualities, that son will obtain everything in his rites connected with *dharma*. There is no *deva* equal to the mother. There is no *guru* equal to the father. It is impossible to repay them for what they have done. In thoughts, words and deeds, one should always do what is agreeable to them. Without their permission, one should not follow any other kind of *dharma*. The only exception is *nitya* and *naimittika* rites that yield fruits of liberation. The essence of *dharma* has been instructed and this bestows infinite fruits after death. Thereafter, one should properly take leave of the person who has expounded.[1474] The *shishya* then enjoys the fruits of the learning. After death, he is honoured in heaven. If a foolish person shows disrespect to an elder brother, who is like a father, as a result of that sin, after death, he descends into a terrible hell.'

'To follow the path, a man must always worship the *bharta*. Even if one serves the mother, one obtains honour in this world. Bhagavan Manu has said that if men offer up their own lives for the sake of the *bharta*, they obtain imperishable worlds. A younger person should stand up and greet a maternal and paternal uncle, a father-in-law, an officiating priest and a *guru* with the words, "I am so

---

[1473]The word *bharta* means husband. However, it also means the master, the one who supports.

[1474]Implicitly, the *guru*, who has spoken about *dharma*.

and so." If he has been initiated, even if he is younger, he should not be addressed by name. A person who knows about *dharma* will first use the words "*bho bhavan*"[1475] in his address. *Kshatriya*s and others, who desire their own prosperity, must always affectionately honour and respect a *brahmana* with the head lowered. Initially, a *brahmana* must never greet *kshatriya*s and others. Those who possess qualities of *jnana* and *karma* and are extremely learned perform such worship. The *shruti* texts say that a *brahmana* must always say "*svasti*"[1476] to all *varna*s. Those belonging to the same *varna* can greet each other according to whatever is desired for the *varna*. For *dvija*s, Agni is the *guru*. For all *varna*s, a *brahmana* is the *guru*. For women, the husband is the *guru*. For everyone, a guest is the *guru*. Learning, *karma*, austerities, friends and wealth as the fifth—these five are said to be revered. A preceding one is superior to a succeeding one. A person from the three *varna*s who possesses these, has a lot of strength, and deserves to be honoured. So does a *shudra* who is in the tenth decade of his life. Right of way must be granted to a *brahmana*, a woman, a king, a person who is blind, an aged person, a person who is bent down because of a burden and a diseased or weak person.'

'A person must control himself and collect alms from the homes of virtuous people. He must first offer it to his *guru*. After obtaining his permission, he must eat silently. An excellent *dvija*, who has been through *upanayana*, must roam around seeking alms, using the words "*bhavati*" first. A *kshatriya* should use the words "*bhavati*" in the middle, while a Vaishya will use the words "*bhavati*" at

---

[1475] Words signifying respect, a bit like, 'Honourable Sir'.
[1476] 'May all be well with you.'

the end.[1477] The first alms must be sought from a mother, a sister, a mother's sister, or someone who does not show him disrespect. It must be sought from a house that belongs to the same *jati*[1478] or the same *varna*. In roaming for alms, he should avoid the homes of those who have fallen down. Controlling himself, a *brahmachari* should accept alms from the homes of those who follow the *Vedas* and sacrifices and are devoted to their own *karma*. He should not beg from his *guru*'s family, or from the families of relatives and kin. If alms are not available, he can go to other houses, avoiding the ones that have been named earlier. If the ones mentioned earlier are not available, he can wander around in the entire village. He must control himself, be restrained in speech and not look around in different directions. Collecting the alms, without any deceit, he must cook the food. He must always eat while controlled, restrained in speech and attentive in mind. A person who is following the vow must survive on alms and eat once a day. It is said that surviving on alms is equal to fasting. The food must always be honoured and must not be criticized. He should not be delighted on seeing it and must eat while controlling his speech. Excessive eating is bad for health and reduces the lifespan. It does not lead to heaven. It is not sacred and is hated by the world. Therefore, one should avoid it.

[1477] *Bhavati* is the honourable way of addressing a woman, *bhavan* a man. Since the alms will typically be given by the lady of the household, the *brahmachari* will ask, '*Bhavati, bhiksham dehi.*' 'Please give me alms.' This is when the *brahmachari* is a *brahmana*. If the *brahmachari* is a *kshatriya*, he will say, '*Bhiksham bhavati dehi.*' If the *brahmachari* is a *vaishya*, he will say, '*Bhiksham dehi bhavati.*'

[1478] *Jati* is the class one has been born into. It is different from *varna*.

While eating, one should face the east or face the sun. It is the eternal rule that one should never eat while facing the north. After eating, the hands and the feet must be washed and *achamana* performed twice. One should eat while seated in a pure place. After eating, *achamana* should be performed twice.'

Chapter 66(2)(113)
(Virtuous conduct for *achamana*)

Vyasa said, 'After eating, drinking, sleeping, walking on the road, touching the part of the lips that have no hair, wearing a garment, discharging semen, urine or excrement, speaking improper words, spitting, before studying, hiccupping, returning from a cross-roads or cremation ground and at the time of the two *sandhya*s, an excellent *dvija* should perform *achamana*. In the last case, one should perform *achamana* yet again. After conversation with a *chandala*, *mleccha*, woman, *shudra* or someone who has touched *ucchishta*,[1479] or touching *ucchishtha*, a man should do the same. When one sheds tears or blood, after eating, at the time of the two *sandhya*s, after bathing and after passing urine or excrement, *achamana* should be performed twice. After sleeping, it can be done only once. After touching fire, cattle or women and after tying one's garment at the waist, *achamana* should be done. After touching one's hair or touching an unwashed cloth, after touching water, grass or earth must be touched. The water must be without froth and pure. At the time, one should be

[1479] Leftover and stale food.

silent. Desiring purity, one should always be seated facing the east or the north, while performing *achamana*. If the head or neck is covered, if the hem of the lower garment is not tucked in,[1480] if the tuft of hair is not knotted and if the feet are not washed, even after *achamana*, one remains impure. A learned person will not perform *achamana* with his footwear on, or while wearing a headdress. A learned person will not perform *achamana* with water that is poured down on his hand, or with water defiled with *ucchishta*. He should not use water with one hand alone. He should not be without his sacred thread. He should not be seated with his footwear on. Nor should they be placed just outside the knees. The water should not be poured by a *vaishya* or *shudra*, or by a person who has touched *ucchishta*. It is recommended that one should be attentive and not use the fingers to make a sound. There must be sufficient water. The water should not be stirred with the fingers and the act should not be performed outside the room. A *brahmana* is purified when the water touches the heart, a *kshatriya* is purified when the water touches the throat. A *vaishya* is purified on drinking the water. Touching the water purifies a woman or *shudra*."

"The *tirtha* on the line at the base of the thumb is known as *brahma-tirtha*.[1481] The base of the index finger is the excellent *pitri-tirtha*. The spot below the base of the little finger is known as *prajapatya-tirtha*. The tip of the fingers is described as *daiva-tirtha* and is said to be used for the *deva*s. Alternatively, the base of the middle finger is said to be *agneya-tirtha*, also known as *soumika-*

[1480]This tucking in is called *kaccha*. It should not be the case that there is no *kaccha*.

[1481]Base of the thumb with the palm facing upwards.

tirtha. If a person knows this, he is not deluded. A *dvija* must always perform *achamana* with *brahma-tirtha.* His body will also be purified if he performs *achamana* with *daiva-tirtha.* Initially, a *brahmana* must control himself and perform *achamana* thrice. He should touch his mouth and wipe it with the base of the thumb. Using the thumb and the ring finger, he should touch the two eyes. Using the thumb and the index finger, he should touch the two nostrils. Using the thumb and the little finger, he should touch the two ears. The arms must be touched with all the fingers and the heart with the palm. The navel and the head must be touched with all the fingers. Alternatively, both can be touched with the thumb. If water is drunk thrice, the *deva*s are extremely pleased. We have heard that this is for Brahma, Vishnu and Mahesha. When the mouth is wiped, Ganga and Yamuna are pleased. When the eyes are touched, the sun and the moon are pleased. When the two nostrils are touched, Nasatya and Dasra[1482] are pleased. When the two ears are touched, the wind and the fire are pleased. When the heart is touched, all the *deva*s are pleased. When the head is touched, Purusha is pleased. When one performs *achamana*, the *ucchishta* of sprays of water should not touch the limbs. If the tongue or the lips are used to touch the space between the teeth or the bottom of the teeth, one becomes impure. However, at the time of *achamana*, if drops of water touch the feet, there is no impurity. This is known as water meant for the earth and one need not be attentive about this.'

'Manu has said that one is not defiled if one has *madhuparka,*[1483] *soma,* betel leaves, fruits, roots or

---

[1482] The two Ashvins.
[1483] A mixture of honey and curds, typically offered to a guest.

sugarcane. If a *dvija* becomes *ucchishta* because of an excess of food or drink, he should place some of the objects on the ground and sprinkle water over what has been placed on the ground. If a *dvija* becomes *ucchishta* while carrying a shining metal vessel, he should place it on the ground, sprinkle water over it and then pick it up. If he picks something up without the requisite *mantra*, thereby becoming impure, he becomes pure through *achamana*, without placing the object down on the ground. If one touches cloth and similar objects, *achamana* is optional. In the forest, in a place without water, at night and in a place infested by thieves and tigers, if one passes urine or excrement while holding an object in the hand, one is not defiled. During the day, when passing urine or excrement, one should place the sacred thread on the right ear and face the north. At night, he should face the south. The ground must be covered with wood, leaves, stones or grass. Before passing urine or excrement, the head must be covered. Urine and excrement must not be passed in a place with shade, near wells, rivers, cow-pens and *chaitya*s, in the middle of the road, on ashes, in a fire, inside the house and in a cremation ground. Nor should it be done in a path used by cows, in a ploughed field, in a place with large trees or land covered with grass. On the summit of a mountain, one should not stand without any clothes. One should never pass urine or excrement in a dilapidated temple to *deva*s or a termite-hill. It should not be done in pits inhabited by creatures. It should not be done along a royal road or in a place with husks, coal and skulls. It should not be done in a pure *kshetra*, a *tirtha* or crossroads. Nor should it be done near a garden, in barren ground or a place that is impure. It should not be done while wearing footwear, or when travelling in a vehicle through the sky.

It should not be done in the direction of women, *guru*s and *brahmana*s. It should never be done in the direction of a *deva* or the temple to a *deva*. It should not be done while facing a river or luminous body, or against the wind. One should not do it in the direction of the sun, fire or the moon. Clay for wiping must be collected from the bank and must be free of stickiness and odour. Before the act of purification, pure water must be collected. A *brahmana* will never collect clay that is full of dirt and mud. He will not collect it from the road or barren ground, or a place that has become *ucchishta* because someone else has used the place for purification. He will not gather it from a temple to a *deva*, a well, a village or from inside the water. Achamana must always be performed following the rules mentioned earlier.'

Chapter 67(2)(14) (*Dharma* for *brahmachari*s)

Vyasa said, 'In this way, he[1484] must hold a staff and other things and be full of purity and good conduct. When summoned for studying, he should glance towards his *guru*'s face and do so. He must always keep his hands raised[1485] and follow good conduct at the time of *sandhya*. When he is asked to sit, he should sit, facing the *guru*. When he listens or converses, he should not lie down. When he is seated, standing or getting up, his face should not be turned away. In the *guru*'s presence, he should never be seated on a couch. As long as he is in the *guru*'s line of vision, he should not sit as he wills. The *guru*'s name

[1484] A *brahmachari*.
[1485] In salutation.

must never be uttered, even if he is not directly there. He
should not mimic his gait, speech or action. If someone
argues against the *guru* or criticizes him, he should cover
up his ears, or go somewhere else. If the *guru* is far away,
he need not be worshipped. In the presence of women,
anger should not be displayed towards him. He should
counter his arguments. When he is standing, he should not
be seated. Pots of water, *kusha* grass, flowers and kindling
must always be gathered. He should constantly smear and
massage his limbs. He should never step over the *guru*'s
garland, bed, footwear, seat, shadow or chair. Twigs for
cleaning the teeth must be collected and offered to him. He
should tell him about what he has done. Without taking
his leave, he should not go. He must always be engaged in
what is agreeable to him. In his *guru*'s presence, he should
never stretch out his legs. He should not yawn, laugh loudly
or cover the neck. In his *guru*'s presence, he should never
slap his arms and speak. Unless the *guru* is distracted, he
should study at the right time. When he is asked by the
guru, he can control himself and sit on a plank. He should
never be in the same seat, couch or vehicle with him. When
the *guru* runs, he should run and follow him. When he
walks, he should walk behind him. He should never be
seated with the *guru* in a vehicle drawn by a cow, a horse
or a camel, tops of mansions, on mats, rocky slabs and
boats. He should constantly conquer his senses. He should
restrain his rage and be pure. He should always use words
that are sweet and agreeable. He should not use fragrant
garlands made out of white flowers and juices. He should
not cause violence to creatures. He should not smear oil on
the limbs, apply collyrium or hold an umbrella. He must
take care to avoid desire, greed, fear, sleep, music, playing
of musical instruments and dancing, gambling, criticizing

people, glancing towards women and grasping them and attacking others with calumny. He must collect sufficient water in pots, flowers, cow dung, clay and *kusha* grass. Every day, he must roam around, seeking alms. He must avoid everything with salt and everything that is polluted. He should not witness dancing and he should be indifferent towards singing. While cleaning the teeth, he should not look at the sun. He should not be with impure women in private. He should not converse with *shudra*s and outcastes. He should do whatever brings pleasure to the *guru* and not what he desires. In whatever way, he must have a bath to clean the dirt. Even in his mind, a *brahmana* should never abandon the *guru*. If he abandons him out of delusion or greed, he will fall down. He should never hate the person from whom he has acquired *jnana*, of the world, about the *Veda*s or *adhyatmika*. However, Manu has said that a *guru* can be abandoned if he is arrogant, does not know what should be done and what should not be done or if he has resorted to a perverse path. When the *guru*'s *guru* is present, he should show the same devotion as towards the *guru*. Unless permitted by the *guru*, he should not greet his own seniors. This kind of conduct must always be shown towards a *guru* who imparts learning, towards a person who instructs about means of subsistence for his own class, towards a person who acts against *adharma* and towards a person who offers beneficial advice. It is best that he should always act towards a *guru*'s son and a *guru*'s wife and relatives the way he acts towards his *guru*. A young *shishya* should always honour those who perform rites at sacrifices. If he teaches, a *guru*'s son deserves to be honoured like a *guru*. He should not bathe the *guru*'s son or apply unguents on his limbs. He should not eat his *ucchishta* food or wash his feet. The *guru*'s wives must

always be worshipped like the *guru*, as long as they belong
to the same *varna*. If they do not belong to the same *varna*,
they should be honoured by getting up and greeting them.
He should never smear unguents, bathe, massage the limbs
or dress the hair of the *guru*'s wives. If the *guru*'s wife
is young, he need not bow down at her feet. She can be
honoured by touching the ground and saying, "I am so and
so." Every day, a *brahmana* must greet all the *guru*'s wives
by touching their feet. He must remember the *dharma*
followed by the virtuous. The mother's sister, the maternal
uncle's wife, the mother-in-law and the father's sister—all
of these are like the *guru*'s wife and must be honoured like
the *guru*'s wife. If the brother's wife is of the same *varna*,
her feet must be touched every day. Similarly, a *brahmana*
must touch the feet of wives of relatives and kin. He should
behave towards the father's sister, the mother's sister and
his own elder sister the way he behaves towards his mother.
However, the mother is superior to all of them.'

'If he possesses such good conduct, is in control of
himself and is not proud, he will always be taught the
*Veda*s, *dharma*, the Puranas and *Vedanga*s. If the *shishya*
resides with the *guru* for one year, but the *guru* fails to
instruct him about *jnana*, the *guru* takes all the *shishya*'s
wicked deeds upon himself. Following the *dharma* of the
place, the following people must be taught—a preceptor's
son, a person who serves for the sake of *jnana*, a person
who follows *dharma*, a pure person, a person who
expounds the meanings of the *suktam*s, a person not
interested in pleasure and a virtuous person. There are six
*dvija*s who must be taught in the proper way—a grateful
person, one who does not hate, an intelligent person, a
man who does what is good, a trustworthy person and one
who is loved. The *Veda*s must be imparted to them and

those mentioned earlier. One should always study after performing *achamana* and controlling oneself. One should face the north. He should clasp the *guru*'s feet and look towards his face. He should start with the words, "Please teach me." He should be seated comfortably, purified by purifying objects. He should purify himself by performing *pranayama* thrice and reciting OUMKARA. In the proper way, a *brahmana* must always pronounce OUM at the end. A *brahmana* must always study with his hands joined in salutation. The *Veda*s are the eternal eyes of all creatures. A *brahmana* must constantly study. Otherwise, he falls down. If a person constantly studies hymns from the *Rig Veda*, he offers oblations of milk to the *deva*s. As a result of these oblations, they are always pleased and content and grant him what he wishes for. If a person constantly studies hymns from the *Yajur Veda*, he pleases the *deva*s with offerings of curds. If he studies hymns from the *Sama Veda* every day, he pleases them with offerings of *ghee*. If he constantly studies hymns from *Atharva-Angirasa*[1486]   he pleases the *deva*s with offerings of honey. With *Vedanga*s and Puranas, the gods are satisfied with meat. He should approach a river, control himself and following the rules, perform the *nitya* rites. He should go to a forest and controlling himself, recite the *gayatri mantra*. Reciting it one thousand times is excellent, one hundred times is middling, and ten times is inferior. If one constantly performs *japa* with *Gayatri*, that is described as *japa-yajna*. The lord weighed *Gayatri* and the *Veda*s on a pair of scales. *Gayatri* on one side and the four *Veda*s on the other were equal. Having recited OUMKARA, he should follow it with *vyahriti*. After this, attentive and full

---

[1486] That is, *Atharva Veda*.

of devotion, he should recite Savitri. *"Bhuh bhuvah svah"* is eternal and originated in an earlier *kalpa*. These three constitute the great *vyahriti* and they ensure everything auspicious. In the due order, the three *vyahriti*s are said to be Pradhana, Purusha and Kala; Vishnu, Brahma and Maheshvara; and *sattva, rajas* and *tamas*. OUMKARA is supreme *brahman* and Savitri is imperishable. This *mantra* is great *yoga* and is said to be the essence of all essences. If a *brahmachari* understands the meaning and every day, recites Savitri, the mother of the *Veda*s, he proceeds to the supreme destination. *Gayatri* is the mother of the *Veda*s. *Gayatri* purifies the worlds. For *japa*, there is nothing superior to *Gayatri*. If a person knows this, he is liberated.'

'O excellent *dvija*s! Pournmasi in the month of Shravana, Ashadha or Proshthapada is said to be the time for *vedopakarana*.[1487] For two and a half months, the *brahmana* should abandon the city or the village. The *brahmachari* will control himself and study in a pure place. O *dvija*s! Studying the *chhanda*s should be suspended in the month of Pousha.[1488] It can also be done on the first day of *shukla paksha* in Magha, in the forenoon. O *dvija*s! The *chhanda*s must be pleased in their respective *nakshatra*s. A man should please the *Vedanga*s and Puranas during *krishna paksha*. But there are days when one should not study and those days, when one should not study, should be avoided. Prajapati has said that studying and teaching must be avoided if the sound of the wind can be heard at night, if the day is enveloped with dust, if there is lightning, thunder and incessant rain and if giant meteors

---

[1487]The start of studying the *Veda*s.
[1488]This is known as *utsarjana* and this temporary suspension is done twice a year.

descend. These are times when one should not study. If
there is a storm, if the earthquakes and if luminous bodies
are eclipsed—these are also times when there should be no
teaching or studying. After the fire has been kindled, if there
are omens like thunder and lightning, studying should be
stopped until there is light again. This is particularly true
if these are not seasonal. For those who study and desire
dharma and good merits, they should never do so on a
day when there is a foul stench in the city or the village. It
should not be done when there is a dead body in the village,
in the presence of a *vrishala* and when people collectively
gather to eat. One should not think of studying inside
water, at midnight, when releasing urine or excrement
and when one is *ucchishta* or has eaten at a *shraddha*. If a
learned *dvija* has accepted the invitation for an *ekoddishta
shraddha*,[1489] if the king is impure because of a birth in his
house and if Rahu causes an eclipse, he should not recite
the *Veda*s for three days. As long as attachment towards
an *ekoddishta shraddha* remains in the large body of a
brahmana, he should not recite the *Veda*s. He should not
study lying down, with his feet raised or when he has eaten
food in a house where there has been a childbirth. When
there is a snowfall, when there is a shower of arrows, at
the time of the two *sandhya*s, on *amavasya*, *chaturdashi*,
pournamasi and *ashtami* and at the time of impurity,
there should be no studies. After the annual rite of taking
up studies, it is said that there should be no studies for
three nights. At the time of *ashtaka*[1490] and at the end of
the season, they should be suspended for one night. The

[1489] *Shraddha* performed every year for a specific individual and
not for ancestors in general.
[1490] The eighth lunar *tithi* after the full moon.

learned say that there are three *ashtaka*s, in *krishna paksha*
in the months of Margashirsha, Pousha and Magha. One
should never study under the shade of *shleshmataka,
shalmali, madhuka, kovidara* and *kapittha*.[1491] When
a fellow *brahmachari* who is equal in learning, or the
preceptor dies, there should be cessation for three nights.
For *brahmana*s engaged in studies, these are said to be
holes. *Rakshasa*s cause violence at these times and they
must therefore be avoided. For *nitya* rites, worship at the
time of the *sandhya*s, at the annual initiation of studies
and when rites connected with *mantra*s for oblations are
over, there need be no cessation of studies. When there is
a strong wind at the time of *ashtaka*, a single hymn from
Rig Veda, Yajur Veda or *Sama Veda* can be recited. For
*Vedanga*s, Itihasas, Puranas and *dharmashastra*s, there are
no days for cessation of studies. However, auspicious days
must be avoided. In brief, the *dharma* for *brahmachari*s
has been described. Earlier, Brahma described this to *rishi*s
who had cleansed their souls. O *dvija*s! A person who does
not study the *shruti* texts, but studies something else, is
deluded. He is outside the pale of the *Veda*s and *dvija*s
do not talk to him. Excellent *dvija*s are not satisfied with
merely reading the *Veda*s. Those who do not follow the
conduct are like cows suffering in mud. If a person studies
the *Veda*s in the proper way but does not reflect on the
meaning of the *Veda*s, he is blind. He is like a *shudra* and
derives no substance. If a person wishes to reside with the
guru until the end and if he desires to serve him until his
body is destroyed, he can go to the forest and duly offer

[1491] *Shleshmataka* is fruit like a plum, *cordia myxa. shalmali* is
silk cotton, *madhuka* is the *ashoka* tree, *kovidara* is a kind of ebony
and *kapittha* is wood apple.

oblations into the fire.[1492] There, he controls himself and
devoted to the *brahman*, practices every day. In particular,
he studies Savitri, Shatarudriya and the *Vedanga*s. He
practices and is devoted to bathing with *bhasma*. These are
supreme and ancient rules, stated properly in the *agama*
texts of the *Veda*s. Earlier, asked by excellent *maharshi*s,
the lord Svayambhuva Manu stated them. If a person offers
himself up to Ishvara and follows the rules, as indicated,
his net of delusion is dispelled. He proceeds to immortality
and the auspicious destination that is free of ailments.'

Chapter 68(2)(15) (*Dharma* for householders)

Vyasa said, 'O *dvija*s! He should obtain knowledge
about one, two or four *Veda*s. O excellent *dvija*s!
Having studied and understood the meaning, he should
bathe. Having given the *guru* wealth, he should take his
permission and bathe.[1493] Controlled and having completed
the vow, he is capable of taking this bath. He must hold
a staff made of bamboo and wear an upper garment and
a lower garment. He should have two sacred threads
and a *kamandalu*[1494] filled with water. He must have an
umbrella, a spotless head-dress, sandals, footwear, golden
ear-rings and the *Veda*s. The nails must be clipped and he
must be pure. He must constantly study. He should not
wear a garland outside. A *brahmana* should not wear a red
garland, unless it is made out of *kanchana* flowers.[1495] He

---

[1492] He remains a *brahmachari* for life.
[1493] The concluding bath.
[1494] Water pot.
[1495] The *champaka* tree, yellow orpiment.

must always wear white clothes. He must use fragrances and be pleasant to behold. As long as he has wealth, he should not wear old and dirty garments. He must not wear clothes that are red or too gaudy. He should not wear a garment, water-pot, footwear, garlands or sandals used by someone else. Nor should he use an *upavita*, ornaments, *darbha* grass or black antelope skin used by another. The garment should not be worn in an *apasavya* way.[1496] Nor should it be disfigured. In the proper way, he should marry an auspicious woman who is similar to him. She should possess beauty and qualities and should not have any taints in the genitals. She should not have been born in his mother's *gotra*. She should have been born in a *gotra* that is different from the *rishi*'s *gotra*.[1497] A *brahmana* must marry a wife who possesses good conduct and purity. Until a son has been born, he must approach her at the time of her monthly period. But he must take care to avoid the prohibited days. A brahmana must always restrain his senses and be a *brahmachari* on *shashti, ashtami, dvadashi, chaturdashi* and *panchadashi*.[1498] He must maintain the *avasathya* fire[1499] and offer oblations to the fire. A *snataka*[1500] must always observe the vows of purification. Attentively, he must always perform his own *karma*, as indicated in the *Veda*s. If he doesn't do this, he will quickly descend into terrible hells. He must control himself and recite the *Veda*s, thinking of the great sacrifice. He must perform the rites

---

[1496] Over the right shoulder and below the left arm.

[1497] The *rishi* he traces his own *gotra* to.

[1498] Respectively the sixth, eighth, twelfth, fourteenth and fifteenth lunar *tithi*s.

[1499] The sacred fire maintained in the household, also known as *garhapatya*.

[1500] One who has graduated and has become a householder.

indicated in the *grihyasutras*[1501] and the *sandhya* rites.
His friends must be those who are equal or superior. He
must always worship Ishvara. If he has to go somewhere
else by chance, he must ornament his wife. He should not
proclaim his acts of *dharma*, nor hide his sins. He must
always do what is beneficial and be compassionate towards
all beings. He should always act in accordance with his
age, *karma*, wealth, learning, nobility, intelligence and the
words of the *Veda*s. Until death, he must properly follow
what has been stated in the *shruti* texts, that followed by
the virtuous. He must never act contrary to such conduct.
He must always follow the path traversed by his fathers
and grandfathers. That is the path of the virtuous and it
enables one to cross over. He must always be devoted to
studies. He must always wear the sacred thread. He must
be truthful in speech and conquer his rage. Such a person
deserves to become one with the *brahman*. He must always
bathe at the time of *sandhya*. He must always be devoted
to *brahma-yajna*. A householder who is without jealousy,
gentle and controlled flourishes after death. He must be
devoid of attachment, fear and anger. He must not possess
greed and delusion. He must be devoted to performing
japa with Savitri and observe the *shraddha* rites. Such
a person is said to be a true householder. He is engaged
in the welfare of his father and mother. He is engaged
in the welfare of cattle and *brahmana*s. He is controlled
and performs sacrifices. He is devoted to *deva*s. Such a
person obtains greatness in Brahma's world. He constantly
pursues the three objectives[1502] and worships *deva*s. Every
day, he controls himself and constantly prostrates himself

[1501] Texts that set out domestic rituals.
[1502] *Dharma*, *artha* and *kama*.

before the gods. He constantly follows the good conduct of
sharing. He is full of forgiveness and compassion. Such a
person is described as a householder. One does not become
a householder merely because one possesses a house. The
signs of a *brahmana* are forgiveness, compassion, *vijnana*,
truth, self-control, restraint of the senses and devotion
to *adhyatma jnana*. In particular, excellent *dvija*s do not
deviate from these. According to capacity, one should
perform these tasks, avoiding what is censured. All the
delusion will then be cleansed, and one will attain excellent
yoga. This is the way a householder is liberated from
bondage. There is no need to reflect about this. Forgiveness
is tolerance of taints that arise from the anger of others—
censure, transgressions, abuse, violence, imprisonment and
killing. Friendliness is when one is compassionate towards
the miseries of others, just as one is towards one's own
miseries. The sages have said that compassion is a direct
sadhana for *dharma*. *Vijnana* is the retention of the true
meanings of the fourteen kinds of knowledge. *Dharma* is
enhanced through such learning. Having studied the *Veda*s
in the proper way and understood their meanings, if one
refrains from acts of *dharma*, that is not said to be *vijnana*.
Truth conquers the worlds. Truth is the supreme objective.
The learned have said that truth is the exact statement of
what has occurred. *Dama* is supreme restraint of the body.
Shama results from pleasant intelligence.[1503] *Adhyatma* is
imperishable knowledge. Having obtained that, one no
longer grieves. *Jnana* is described as that through which
the divinity Mahadeva is directly known. The divinity,
Bhagavan, is the supreme object of knowledge and is known

[1503] *Dama* is restraint of the body, while *shama* is restraint of the
mind.

through such knowledge. A learned person is devoted to him. He is pure and always free from anger. Devoted to the great sacrifice, such a learned person becomes one with his excellent body. The body must be nurtured, since it is *dharma*'s abode. Without the body, men cannot know the supreme Rudra. A *dvija* should constantly engage himself in the pursuit of *dharma*, *artha* and *kama*. Even in his mind, he should not think of *kama* or *artha* that is devoid of *dharma*. Even if one suffers because of *dharma*, he should not resort to *adharma*. *Dharma* is the divinity, Bhagavan, and is the objective for all beings. A person should do what is agreeable to beings. Even in his mind, he should not think of acts that involve hatred towards others. He should not criticize the *Veda*s and *deva*s, or converse with those who do so. If a pure *brahmana* constantly reads this chapter on *dharma*, if he teaches it and makes others listen to it, he obtains greatness in Brahma's world.'

Chapter 69(2)(16)
(Good conduct for householders)

Vyasa said, 'He should not cause violence to any being. He should never utter a falsehood. He should never speak something harmful or disagreeable. He should never indulge in theft. If a being steals the possessions of others, even if it is a blade of grass, vegetables, clay or water, he goes to hell. One should not accept anything from a king, a *shudra* or a fallen person. A learned person should avoid seeking from a person who is condemned. One should not seek all the time. One should not seek from the same person again. An evil-minded person can rob the seeker of his life. In particular, an excellent *dvija* should never take away the possessions of *deva*s. He should never take away the possessions of a *brahmana*. It is said that poison is not as poisonous as the venom of taking away the possession of a *brahmana* or a *deva* Therefore, one should always make efforts to avoid this. Prajapati Manu has said that the taking of the following, even if they have not been given, do not constitute theft—flowers, vegetables, wood, roots, grass and fruits. *Dvija*s can take flowers for worshipping *deva*s in the proper way. If taken without permission, they should not be taken from one person alone. A learned person should take grass, wood, fruits and flowers openly. They should only be taken with the object of *dharma* in mind. Otherwise, one falls down. O *brahmanas*! When travelling, if one suffers from hunger, one can take a handful of sesamum, *mudga*,[1504] barley and similar articles, not otherwise. Those who know about *dharma* base themselves on this. On the pretext that it has been instructed by *dharma*, one should not observe a vow that involves the commission of a sin. If a *brahmana* hides his sin under the garb of a vow and depends on women and *shudra*s, those who speak about the *brahman* condemn him, in this world and after death. If a person uses deceit in observing a vow, he goes to *rakshasa*s. Without being a *lingi*, if a person earns his subsistence through the garb of a *lingi*, he takes away the sins of the *lingi* and is born as an inferior species.[1505] People who follow the vow of a cat are sinners.[1506] They destroy *dharma*. They instantly

---

[1504] Beans.

[1505] *Lingam* is a sign and *lingi* (*lingin*) is a person who bears the signs, such as of being an ascetic. The allusion is to those who bear false signs to earn a living.

[1506] They are deceitful and hypocrites.

suffer the fruits of their wicked deeds and fall down. One should never honour heretics and those who indulge in perverse *karma* and *vamachara*,[1507] such as those who follow *pancharatra* and *pashupata* only in words. Even in one's mind, one should not think of those who criticize the *Veda*s, mortals who criticize the *deva*s and those who criticize *dvija*s. A being who officiates at sacrifices for them, has intercourse with them, resides with them and converses with them, falls. Therefore, one should make efforts to avoid such people. Hatred of the *guru* is one crore times worse than hatred of *deva*s. Abuse of *jnana* and non-belief are one crore times worse than that. Families that trade in cows, *brahmana*s who earn a living through *deva*s, those who practise agriculture and those who earn a living by serving the king are families for whom *dharma* suffers. Bad marriages, non-performance of rites, not studying the *Veda*s and crossing *brahmana*s also makes families suffer. A family is swiftly destroyed through falsehood, intercourse with someone else's wife, eating what should not be eaten and not following the *dharma* indicated in the *shruti* texts. A family is swiftly destroyed through donations to those who do not follow the *shruti*s, *vrishala*s and those who are devoid of recommended conduct. One should not stay in a village full of people who follow *adharma*, or in a place that suffers a lot from disease. One should not reside in a kingdom where the king is a *shudra*, or in a place full of heretics. It is said that a *dvija* should reside in the auspicious region between the Himalayas and the Vindhyas, in the region between the eastern and western oceans, and not

---

[1507]The left-handed path, associated with *tantra*. *Pancharatra* (five nights) doctrines are usually associated with worship of Vishnu.

anywhere else. A *dvija* should reside in a place where black antelopes and deer are always naturally present, where there are sacred and famous rivers. An excellent *dvija* should not reside in a place that is a distance of more than half a *krosha*[1508] from the bank of a river. He should not dwell in an inauspicious place, nor in the vicinity of a village of *antyajas*.[1509] He should not reside with those who have fallen down, *chandalas* or *pukkasas*,[1510] the foolish, the condemned and other *antyajas* who reside in the extremities. There are eleven taints described as those that cause a mixture between the *varnas*—sharing the same bed, sharing the same seat, eating in the same row, eating from the same vessel, mixing up cooked food, officiating at sacrifices, teaching, physical intercourse, eating together, studying together as the tenth and officiating together at sacrifices. Even if one is in the vicinity, that sin is transmitted among men. Therefore, a learned person should make every effort to avoid any mixing up. If people are seated in the same row and do not touch each other and if *bhasma* is used to create a boundary between them, there is no mixing. The rows can be specially divided through six means—fire, *bhasma*, water, a door, a pillar and a path. One should not indulge in enmity that leads to grief, debating and calumny. One should never speak about a cow grazing in someone else's field. One should

---

[1508] Measure of distance, one-fourth of a *yojana*, distance from which a shout can be heard.

[1509] *Antyajas* are outcastes, those who live near the extremities of habitations.

[1510] These terms are often used as synonyms. Pedantically, a *chandala* is the son of a *brahmana* mother and a *shudra* father. A *pulkasa* (equivalently *pukkasa*) is the son of a *nishada* father and a *shudra* mother.

not dwell with someone who has had a childbirth in the house. One should not pierce the inner organs of others. A learned person should never speak to others about a solar eclipse, a rainbow, setting fire to a dead body or a lunar eclipse. One should never oppose many at the same time. If something causes harm to one's own person, one should not act in that way towards others. One should not speak about and indicate *tithi*s, *paksha*s and *nakshatra*s. An excellent *dvija* will not converse with a woman who is menstruating, or with an impure person. He will not prevent anything being given to *deva*s, *guru*s or *brahmana*s. He should never praise himself. He should avoid criticizing others. He must make every effort to avoid criticism of the *Veda*s or criticism of the *deva*s. O lords among sages! If a *dvija* criticizes *deva*s, *rishi*s, *brahmana*s or the *Veda*s, the sacred texts have not indicated any means of salvation for him. If a man criticizes *guru*s, *deva*s, the *Veda*s or the orthodox tradition, he is cooked in Rourava for more than one crore *kalpa*s. In the face of such criticism, it is better to keep quiet and not say anything in reply. He should cover his ears and go elsewhere. He should not even look at them. A learned person will avoid revealing the secrets of others. He should never engage in arguments with his own relatives. O excellent *dvija*s! He should not call a sinner a sinner. But nor should he say that he is devoid of sin. The sins are equal in either case and are equal to the sin of uttering a falsehood. When people who are falsely accused weep, the tears shed destroy the sons and animals of those who have indulged in false accusations. Means of purification have been indicated by the virtuous for killing a *brahmana*, drinking liquor, theft and having intercourse with the *guru*'s wife. But there is nothing like that for a false accusation.'

'Without reason, one should not look at the rising sun
or the moon. He should not look at them while they are
setting, at their reflections in the water, when they are at
the mid-point or when they are eclipsed. He should not
look at them through a piece of cloth, or at their reflections
inside a mirror. He should never look at a naked man or
woman. He should not look at a person passing urine or
excrement, or at someone in the act of sexual intercourse.
When impure, a learned person will not look at the sun,
the moon or the planets. He will not look at a fallen person,
a person who is maimed, a *chandala* or someone who is
ucchishta. He will not converse with someone who is
ucchishta. His words should not be filled with pride. He
should not touch a person who has touched a dead body.
When the *guru* is angry, he should not look towards his
face. He should not look at his reflection in oil or water.
While eating, he should not touch his wife. Nor should he
glance at her limbs when the knots of her garments are
loose. He should not look at a mad or intoxicated person.
He should not eat with his wife. He should not look at her
while she is urinating, sneezing or yawning, or when she is
comfortably seated. He should not look at his reflection in
the water. He should not jump over a bank or a pit. He
should never leap over urine or stand on it. He should not
impart intelligence to a *shudra*. Nor should he give him
krisara, *payasam*, curds, *ucchishta*, *ghee*, honey, the skin
of a black antelope or oblations.[1511] A learned person will
follow the vow of no giving food to a *shudra*. Nor will he
speak to him about *dharma*. He should not succumb to
rage. He must avoid hatred and attachment. He must avoid

[1511] *Krisara* is a dish of sesamum and grain, *payasam* is rice
mixed with milk and sugar.

greed and insolence. He should not abuse pilgrimages and
vijnana. He should shun pride, delusion, anger and hatred.
He should not cause suffering to anyone. However, a son
or a *shishya* can be struck. He should never serve those
who are inferior, or those who are sharp in intelligence. He
must not show disrespect towards his own self. He should
take care to avoid dejection. A learned person should not
praise himself but should honour anyone who is not a
shishya. He should not use his nails to etch the ground. He
should not dwell with a cow. He should not speak of other
rivers when he is bathing in a river, or other mountains
when he is on a mountain. Whether one has dwelt with
him or not, one should never abandon a fellow traveller.
He should not bathe naked in the water. He should not
place his foot on fire. After oil has been applied to the head,
the remaining oil should not be smeared on the limbs. He
should not play with weapons or snakes. He should not
touch his own limbs with these. He should not touch the
hair on his private parts. He should not travel with a person
who is wicked. He should not place his hands and feet in
the fire. He should never be fickle in touching his penis,
stomach or ears. He should not scratch his limbs with his
nails. He should not drink water from the cup of his hands.
He should never strike water with his hands or feet. He
should never bring down fruit by hurling bricks or other
fruit. He should never learn the language of *mleccha*s. He
should not drag a seat with his feet. He should not create
dissension. He should not crack the joints of his fingers,
nor snap his fingers. He should not etch with them. A
learned person will not indulge in futile acts of crushing
another. While eating, he should not place the food on his
lap. Nor should he move around unnecessarily. He should
not sing or dance, nor play musical instruments. He should

never scratch his head with both of his hands brought together. He should not praise *deva*s with worldly hymns or medications. He should not play with dice. He should not run. He should not release urine or excrement in water. When polluted by *ucchishta*, he should not have intercourse. He should not bathe naked. While walking, he should not read or touch his own head. He should not use his teeth to clip his nails. He should not wake up someone who is asleep. He should not warm himself in the morning sun. He should avoid the smoke from a dead body. He should not sleep alone in an empty house. He should not steal footwear. He should not spit without reason. He should not cross a river with the use of his arms. He should not use one leg to wash the other leg. A learned person will not warm his legs in the fire, nor wash his feet in a brass vessel. O *brahmana*s! He should not extend his feet towards *deva*s, *brahmana*s, a cow, the wind, the fire, the *guru*, the sun or the moon. When impure, he should never lie down in a bed, travel in a vehicle, study, bathe, eat or venture out. During the two *sandhyas* and midday, he must avoid sleeping, studying, travelling in a vehicle, bathing, eating and moving. Having become *ucchishta*, a *brahmana* should not touch a cow, a *brahmana* or a fire with the hand. Nor should he touch cooked food or the image of a *deva* with his feet. An impure person should not tend to the fire, or praise *deva*s and *rishi*s. He should not immerse himself in deep water, nor hold fire with a single hand. He should not drink water raised by the left hand, nor drink it directly with his mouth. He should not reply during *achamana*. He should not release semen in water. He should not cast anything foul, blood or poison into the water. He should not cross a flowing river. He should not have intercourse inside water. He should not cut down trees in a *chaitya*. He should not spit in water. He should never step on bones, ash, skulls, hair, thorns, burning coal or dry cow dung. A learned person will not cross a fire, nor will be place it below. He will not kick it with the feet or use his mouth to blow into it. He should not descend into a well. An impure person should never look at a well. He should not fling fire into fire, nor use water to extinguish it. He should not himself tell others about the death or affliction of a well wisher. He should not sell merchandise not fit to be traded. Nor should he use it. If he is impure, a learned person will not use the breath from his mouth to ignite a fire. He should not plough land near sacred water used for bathing, near water or near a boundary. He should never violate truth by going back on a pledge given earlier. He should not wake up animals, serpents and birds. Through channels for water, he should not create obstructions for others. He should not make artisans fashion excellent works of art and abandon them thereafter. In case people seek alms, the door to the house should not be bolted in the morning and the evening. He should avoid garlands from outside and fragrances from outside. He should not eat with his wife. He should shun arguments and avoid entering through an inferior door. A *brahmana* should not eat while standing. A learned person should not talk or laugh a lot. He should not touch fire with his own hand. He should not remain in water for a long time. He should not kindle a fire with a single feather, a winnowing basket or the hand. Nor should he blow with his mouth to light a fire. It is said that fire originated from the mouth. He should not converse with someone else's wife. A *dvija* should not officiate at the sacrifice of someone who is unworthy of a sacrifice. He should not enter an assembly hall alone but should avoid a multitude of *brahmana*s. Without *pradakshina*, he should

never go to a *deva*'s temple. He should not use a piece of
cloth as a fan. He should not sleep in the temple of a *deva*.
He should not travel alone, nor with people who follow
adharma. Nor should he travel with those who are diseased
and polluted, or with *shudra*s and those who have fallen
down. He should not travel without footwear, water and
other things. At night, he should not travel with an enemy.
He should not travel without a *kamandalu*. He should
never walk between fires, cows and *brahmana*s. O excellent
*dvija*s! He should not rebuff a woman who desires sexual
intercourse. He should not criticize *yogi*s, *siddha*s and
mendicants who possess qualities. In the temple of a *deva*
or in the vicinity of *deva*s, a wise person will not step on
the shadow of *brahmana*s or cows. He should not allow
those who have fallen and those who are diseased to step
on his own shadow. He should never stand on coal, ashes,
hair and such objects. He should avoid the drops of water
left after cleaning and bathing and those from a garment or
a pot. O *dvija*s! He should not eat what should not be
eaten, nor drink water not fit to be drunk.'

Chapter 70(2)(17)
(Permissible and prohibited food)

Vyasa said, 'Because of delusion or some other reason,
a *brahmana* should not accept cooked food from a
shudra. He who eats it, except at a time of a calamity, is
born as a *shudra*. If a *dvija* eats condemned food cooked
by a *shudra* for six months, he becomes a *shudra* while
alive and is born as one after death. O lords among sages!
A person is born as a *brahmana*, *kshatriya*, *vaishya* or

shudra depending on the food that is in his stomach when he dies. Food cooked by people from these six categories must be avoided— an actor, a dancer, a carpenter, a person who works with leather, a person who cooks for a multitude and a courtesan. Food cooked by a person who earns a living through the wheel, a washerman, a thief, a standard-maker, a musician, a blacksmith and a person with a birth in his house must be avoided. Food cooked by a potter, a painter, a moneylender and a fallen person must be avoided. So must that by a goldsmith, an actor, a hunter, an imprisoned person or one who is afflicted. He must avoid food cooked by a physician, a *pumshchali*,[1512] a person with a staff,[1513] a thief, a non-believer and a person who criticizes *deva*s. In particular, one should avoid food cooked by a person who sells *soma*, or a *shvapaka*. He must avoid food cooked by a person who is completely under the control of his wife and by someone who allows the wife's paramour to live in the house. Food cooked by those who are *ucchishta*, misers, those who eat *ucchishta*, those who are not fit to sit in the same row while eating, food cooked for a multitude and food cooked by someone who makes a living through weapons must be avoided. Food cooked by a eunuch, a *sannyasi*, a mad person, an intoxicated person, a scared person, a weeping person and food that is inferior and defiled must be avoided. Food cooked by a person who hates *brahmana*s, a person who has wicked inclinations, food offered at a *shraddha*, that cooked by a person who has had a birth in his house, food cooked in vain and that cooked by a deceitful and cunning person must be avoided. Food cooked by women without

[1512] A wanton woman.
[1513] *Dandaka*.

children, servants and artisans must be avoided, specially
avoiding that by those who sell weapons. One should
avoid food cooked by a drunkard, a murderer, a physician,
a person with pierced genitals and a *parivetri*.[1514] In that
way, one should make special efforts to avoid food cooked
by a woman who has married a second time, a person who
is despised and an *avadhuta*.[1515] Food offered with rage or
amazement must be avoided. If it has not been through a
process of cleansing, food from a *guru* must also be avoided.
All of a man's wicked deeds are established in his food. If
a person eats someone's food, he partakes of his sins too.
Learned people offer a little bit of money when they eat
food offered by the following—a cultivator who tills other
people's land, a friend of the family, a person who tends to
his own cows, a barber, an actor, a potter, a person who
works in the field and a *shudra*. *Payasam*, food cooked in
oil, milk, *saktu*,[1516] oilseeds and oil can be accepted from
a *shudra*. One should avoid brinjal, vegetables that grow
in the water,[1517] safflower, *ashmantaka*,[1518] onion, garlic,
fermented gruel, juices, mushrooms, village hogs that eat
excrement, stony food, nectar, anything dissolved, the
sumukha herb and mushrooms.[1519] Having eaten garlic,
kimshuka,[1520] a fowl, a fig or a gourd, a *dvija* falls down.

[1514] A younger brother who marries, though the elder brother is
not yet married.

[1515] An ascetic who has given up worldly attachments, but the
word also means someone who has been rejected and is discarded.

[1516] Ground and parched grain, *sattu*.

[1517] We have translated *jalika-shaka* in this way.

[1518] *Bauhinia*.

[1519] Two different words are used for mushroom, *chhatraka* and
kavaka.

[1520] Probably meaning the medicinal herb, *kalamegha*.

Krisara, samyava, payasam and *apupa* must not be eaten in vain.[1521] One must take care to avoid cooked meat that has not been purified, food for *deva*s, oblations, gruel, citron, cooked fish that has not been purified, *nipa*,[1522] *kapittha* and *plaksha*. During the day, he should not have oilcakes from which the oil has been extracted. At night, he should take care to avoid anything connected with sesamum and curds. Since one is like the seed on which the other is based, milk and buttermilk should not be had together. Anything tainted with action, tainted by wicked sentiments with which it is offered and tainted by association with the wicked must be avoided. One should always avoid food with hair and insects in it and food that has fallen down on the ground. Anything smelt by a dog must be cooked again. This is also true of something a *chandala* has looked at. He should always avoid food seen by a menstruating woman, a fallen person, something smelt by a cow, that not used for worship, that is tainted and full of mistakes, food touched by a crow or a fowl and that which is full of worms. If food has been smelt by men or touched by lepers, it should not be had. Food given by a menstruating woman or an angry *pumshchali* must be avoided, as must that offered while wearing a dirty garment, or that earned by someone else.'

'Manu has said the milk of a cow without a calf,[1523] that of a camel, that of sheep and that of a *sandhini* cow[1524] should not be drunk. The following should not be eaten—a

---

[1521] *Samyava* is a thin cake of unleavened bread, *apupa* is a small cake made of flour. These must be offered to *deva*s first.

[1522] The *kadamba* tree.

[1523] The calf has died.

[1524] A cow that yields milk only once a day, or a cow that has been milked unseasonably.

crane, a swan, a gallinule, a sparrow, a parrot, an osprey,
dry fish, a web-footed bird, a cuckoo, a blue jay, a wagtail,
a hawk, a vulture, an owl, a *chakravaka*, a bearded vulture,
a dove, a pigeon, a lapwing, a village fowl, a lion, a tiger, a
cat, a domestic dog, a wild dog,[1525] a jackal, a monkey and
a donkey. *Dvija*s should not eat any deer or animals that
roam around in the forest. Nor should they eat creatures
that are in the water or on land. That is the perception. O
excellent ones! Prajapati Manu has said that five nailed
animals can always be eaten—a lizard, a tortoise, a hare,
a large porcupine and a small porcupine. One can eat fish
with scales and the meat of *ruru* deer. But this must first be
offered to *deva*s and *brahmana*s, not otherwise. Prajapati
has said that a peacock, a partridge, a grey partridge, a
rhinoceros and a leopard can be eaten. O lords among
sages! It has been properly instructed that the following fish
can be eaten—*rajiva*, *simhatunda*, *pathina* and *rohita*.[1526] If
a *dvija* so wishes, the flesh must first be consecrated. When
there is a threat to life or there is a calamity, one should
eat according to the rules. Even if he eats the flesh last,
as medication, because he is incapacitated or because he
has been asked to, there is no taint. Invited to a *shraddha*
or the worship of a *deva*, if a person shuns the meat, he
goes to hell for as many years as the animal has body hair.
It is the case that *dvija*s must never discuss liquor. This
is prohibited and should not be drunk. It should not be
touched. Therefore, one must make every kind of effort
to avoid condemned liquor. Drinking leads to the loss of

[1525] We have distinguished two different words for dog, *shvana*
and *kukkura*, in this way.

[1526] Respectively mullet, lion-faced fish, a catfish and carp
(*rohu*).

his good *karma* and he falls down. *Dvija*s do not converse with him. If a *dvija* eats what should not be eaten and drinks what should not be drunk, he loses his rights and heads downwards. Therefore, one should always make efforts to avoid what should not be eaten. He alone will be responsible and will go to Rourava.'

Chapter 71(2)(18) (*Nitya* rites for a householder)

The *rishi*s said, 'O great sage! Please tell us about the daily tasks for *brahmana*s. Please tell us about all the *karma* that frees from bondage.'

Vyasa answered, 'I will tell you. Control yourselves and listen to my words. There are daily tasks for *brahmana*s, in accordance with the indicated order. He must get up at *brahma muhurta*[1527] and think about *dharma* and *artha*, the root cause behind physical efforts. In his mind, he must perform *dhyana* on Ishvara. When it is *usha*, a learned person will perform the necessary tasks. He will bathe in a river, purify himself and following the rules, undertake ablutions. Even people who have committed sins are purified by bathing in the morning. Therefore, every effort must be made to bathe in the morning. Since it brings visible and invisible benefits, bathing in the morning is praised. There is no doubt that *rishi*s become *rishi*s because they constantly bathe in the morning. When a person is asleep, saliva constantly drips from his mouth. Hence, no task should be undertaken without having a

---

[1527]The 14th *muhurta* of the night, the *muhurta* before dawn. *Usha* is dawn, before day-break.

bath first. Alakshmi,[1528] any adversity, nightmares and evil
thoughts—there is no doubt that all such sins are purified
by bathing in the morning. Therefore, without bathing, no
morning *karma* is recommended for men. This is especially
true of oblations and *japa*. Therefore, one should bathe. If
a person is incapable, a bath without wetting the head is
recommended. The head can be wiped with a wet piece of
cloth. This is described as a *kapila* bath. When a person is
incapacitated, this kind of bath should be performed. For
incapable people, the learned have spoken about Brahma
and other kinds of bath. In brief, six kinds of having a
bath have been laid down—Brahma, Agneya, Vayavya,
Divya, Varuna and Yougika. When the head is sprinkled
with drops of water from *kusha* grass, with *mantra*s being
recited, that is Brahma. From the head to the foot, when
the body is smeared with *bhasma*, that is Agneya. When
one bathes with dust raised by cattle, that is known as an
excellent Vayavya bath. When one bathes in the sun and
the rain, that is described as Divya. Immersing oneself in the
water is Varuna. In their minds, *yogi*s realize their *atman*s
and use *yoga* to think about the universe. This is known as
Yougika. This is known as *atma-tirtha* and is practised by
those who speak about the *brahman*. This always purifies
the minds of men and one should always undertake this
kind of bath. If a person is capable, along with Varuna, he
should perform *prayashchitta*. He should clean his teeth
with a twig and following the norms, chew it. Controlling
himself, he must perform *achamana* and always bathe
in the morning. The twig should be twice as thick as the
middle finger and should be twelve *angula*s long. The twig
for cleaning the teeth should have the bark intact and

[1528]The opposite of Lakshmi, misfortune.

one should use the tip to clean. Twigs from *kshiravriksha*
and *malati* are auspicious. In particular, *apamarga*, *bilva*
and *karavira* are recommended.[1529] He must avoid the
prohibited and choose the ones cited. Avoiding evil days,
following the rules, the twig must be chewed. The twig
for cleaning the teeth should not be broken, nor should
it be held with the tips of the fingers. After cleaning,
he should control himself and place it in a pure spot.
Having bathed, he should satisfy *deva*s, *rishi*s and the
large number of ancestors. He must always use *mantra*s
to perform *achamana*. He must then silently perform
achamana again. Using *mantra*s, he should use drops of
water from *kusha* grass to sprinkle himself. He should use
auspicious *mantra*s—"*apo hi shtha*",[1530] *vyahriti*s, Savitri
and *mantra*s to Varuna. Performing *japa* with OUMKARA
and the *vyahriti*s and Gayatri, mother of the *Veda*s, with
an attentive mind, he should offer oblations of water to
Bhaskara. Controlling himself, he should be seated on
darbha grass, on the bank. The *smriti* texts say that he
must perform *pranayama* thrice and meditate on *sandhya*.
Sandhya is the origin of the universe, *nishkala* and beyond
maya. Originating from the three *tattva*s,[1531] she is Ishvara's
Shakti alone. A learned person will meditate on her in the
solar disc and perform *japa* with Savitri. A *brahmana* will
always perform the *sandhya* rites while facing the east. A
person who does not perform the *sandhya* rites is always
impure. He is not worthy of performing all the rites. Even
if he does something else, he will not obtain the fruits from

---

[1529] *Kshiravriksha* is a tree that yields a milky sap, identified as
peepul. *Malati* is jasmine. *Apamarga* is the rough chaff tree and
karavira is oleander.

[1530] *Apah suktam* from *Rig Veda* 10.9.

[1531] *Sattva*, *rajas* and *tamas*.

those. Earlier, attentive in their minds, serene *brahmanas*,
accomplished in the *Vedas*, performed *sandhya* rites in the
proper way and obtained the supreme destination. If an
excellent *dvija* forsakes the worship of *sandhya* and makes
efforts to undertake other acts of *dharma*, he goes to hell
for ten thousand years. Therefore, every effort must be
made to undertake the worship of *sandhya*. In this way,
the supreme divinity, whose body is *yoga*, is worshipped.
A learned person must control himself, be seated facing
the east and perform *japa* with Savitri. One thousand
times is always the best, one hundred is middling and ten
is inferior. Seated, he must then control himself and use
many kinds of *mantras* to Surya, from the *Rig*, *Yajur* and
Sama Vedas, to worship the rising sun. With this great
yoga, he must present himself before Divakara, the lord of
devas. He must prostrate his head on the ground and recite
those *mantras*.'

'O infinite one who rises in the circle of the
firmament![1532] O infinite one! O root behind the three
kinds of causes![1533] I offer my *atman*. I prostrate myself
before the one whose form is the universe. I prostrate
myself before the compassionate one, Surya, who is a
form of the *brahman*. You are the supreme Brahma. You
are water, radiance, essence and *amrita*. You are *bhuh*,
bhuvah, *svah*. You are OUMKARA. You are the eternal
Sharva Rudra. You are the great Purusha who is inside.
I prostrate myself before Kapardi. You are the universe,
which originated and is originating, in many kinds of ways.

[1532]This is a *stotram* to Surya, known as the *Surya-hridaya
stotram*.
[1533]The three is interpreted in different ways. Thoughts, words
and action is one.

I prostrate myself before Rudra Surya. I seek refuge with you. I prostrate myself before Prachetas. I prostrate myself before the bountiful lord. I prostrate myself. I bow before Rudra. I seek refuge with you. I prostrate myself before Hiranyabahu, Hiranyapati. I prostrate myself before Ambikaa's lord, before Umaa's consort. I prostrate myself before Nilagriva. I prostrate myself before Pinaki. I prostrate myself before Bharga, the red one with one thousand eyes. I prostrate myself before the one who dispels darkness. I always prostrate myself before Aditya. I prostrate myself before the one who holds *vajra* in his hand. I prostrate myself before Tryambaka. I bow down. I seek refuge with the great Virupaksha Parameshvara. You are hidden in the golden abode that is inside the *atman*s of all those with bodies. I prostrate myself before the supreme brilliance, Brahma, the supreme *amrita*. You are the universe. You are the terrible Pashupati. You possess the bodies of man and woman. I prostrate myself before Surya Rudra, the radiant Parameshthi. You are Ugra, the one who destroys everything. I always seek refuge with you.'

Vyasa continued, 'In this way, he will perform *japa* with the excellent *Surya-hridaya stotram*. In the morning and at midday, one should prostrate oneself before Divakara. This *Surya-hridaya* was indicated by Brahma. It should be given to a son, a *shishya*, those who are devoted to *dharma* and *dvija*s. It originated from the essence of the *Veda*s and destroys all sins. It is sacred and brings welfare to *brahmana*s. Large numbers of *rishi*s have resorted to it. After this, the *brahmana* will return home and perform *achamana* in the proper way. He will kindle the fire in the proper way and offer oblations to Jataveda.[1534] After

[1534] Agni.

obtaining permission, the oblations can be offered by the
officiating priest's son, wife, *shishya* or brother. In the
proper way, so can the *adhvaryu*. With a *pavitra*[1535] on
his hand, clean in soul and purified, he should wear white
garments. With single-minded attention and restraining his
senses, he must always offer oblations. If a rite is conducted
without *darbha* grass or without the sacred thread,
everything goes to *rakshasa*s. No fruits are obtained in this
world or in the next. Prostrating himself before *deva*s, he
must submit the offerings, flowers and other things. He
should then greet the elders. He must worship his *guru*
and do whatever is beneficial for him. According to his
capacity, the *dvija* must then make efforts to study the
*Veda*s. He must perform *japa* and teach his *shishya*s. He
must retain everything and reflect on it. O excellent *dvija*s!
The sacred texts must be used to consider *dharma* and
other things. This includes the *Veda*s, the *nigama*s and all
the *Vedanga*s. For success in achieving *yoga* and *kshema*,
he should seek refuge with Ishvara. A *dvija* should then
gather together the various objects that are required for
the family. When it is midday, he must fetch clay for the
bath. He should gather flowers, *akshata*, *kusha*, sesamum
and pure cow dung. He must always take his bath in rivers,
natural ponds,[1536] tanks, rivers and hollows with flowing
water. One should never have a bath in a waterbody that
belongs to someone else. Before the bath, he must gather
five lumps of clay. The first lump is used to clean the
head, the second the region around the navel. The third
is used for the lower regions. The feet are cleaned with six

[1535] A ring of *kusha* grass worn on the fourth finger.
[1536] *Devakhata*, literally, those dug by *deva*s.

lumps.[1537] It is said that the clay must be wet and must be the size of an *amalaka* fruit.[1538] The size of cow dung is the same and it must be used to smear the limbs again. While standing on the bank, he must smear his limbs and recite the indicated *mantra*s. Washing and performing *achamana* in the proper way, he must then carefully have his bath. The *mantra* chanted over water is the auspicious Varuna *mantra*, which indicates water. He must hold the image of the imperishable Vishnu and purify his sentiments with the unmanifest. Water originated from Narayana and water is where he lies down.[1539] Therefore, at the time of having a bath, a learned person will remember the divinity Narayana. Reciting OUMKARA, he will look at the sun. He will then immerse himself in the water thrice. After performing *achamana* twice, a person who knows *mantra*s will recite the following *mantra*. "You are inside the cavities in the hearts of living beings. You face every direction. You are the sacrifice. You are *vashatkara*.[1540] O water! You are radiance. You are the essence. You are *amrita*." He should then chant the Drupada *mantra*,[1541] or *vyahriti* with Pranava, thrice. A learned person can perform *japa* with Savitri or *aghamarshana*.[1542] Having wiped himself, he will recite "*apo hi shtha mayobhuvas*"[1543] or "*idam apah pra*

[1537] The numbers don't add up.

[1538] A type of myrobalan.

[1539] *Nara* (water) + *ayana* (resting place). Thus, Narayana.

[1540] Exclamation made at the time of offering oblations.

[1541] The Drupada Savitri.

[1542] This is a reference to the Aghamarshana *suktam* (after the sage Aghamarshana) from the *Rig Veda*. This is used for consecration ceremonies, ablutions and at times of bathing.

[1543] *Rig Veda* 10.9.1. 'O water! You are the source of happiness' and so on.

vahata",[1544] with *vyahriti*. With the three *mantra*s "*apo hi shtha*" and so on,[1545] he will consecrate the water and submerge himself in it. He will then perform *japa* thrice with *aghamarshana*. He will recite Drupada and Savitri. Vishnu is the supreme destination. He will use Pranava to reflect on the divinity or remember Hari. The *mantra* "*drupadadiva*" is established in the *Yajur Veda*.[1546] Inside the water, if one recites this thrice, one is cleansed from all sins. He should take water in his hand, do *japa* and perform the rite of wiping. When that water is sprinkled over the head, he is freed from all sins. The horse sacrifice is the king of all sacrifices and takes away all sins. In that way, *aghamarshana* is said to take away all sins. He must then worship the sun above, using flowers and *akshata*. These must be flung up towards the divinity above, who is beyond darkness. Any of the following *mantra*s can be used—*udutyam*, *chitram*, *tach chakshur*, the one that ends with *hamsah shuchishad*, Savitri in particular and other *mantra*s to Surya from the *Veda*s that destroy sins.[1547] He must do *japa* with Savitri. This is said to be *japa-yajna*. There are many other bits to sacred and secret knowledge. There are Shatarudriya, *Atharvashirsha* and all the different *mantra*s to Surya.'

[1544] *Rig Veda* 1.23.22. 'O water! Take away whatever sin' and so on.

[1545] From *Apah suktam*.

[1546] *Vajasaneyi Samhita* 20.20. This requests water to cleanse oneself of sin.

[1547] *Udutyam* probably means *puru tva*, *Rig Veda* 1.150.1, addressed to Agni; *chitram* is *Rig Veda* 1.115.1, addressed to Surya; *tach chaksur* is *Rig Veda* 7.66.16, addressed to Surya; and *hamsah shuchishad* (the *mantra* actually begins with this) is *Rig Veda* 4.40.5, addressed to Surya.

'He must be pure and be seated on *kusha* grass, with the tips of the blades facing the east. He must face the east. Remaining there, he must control himself, glance at the sun and perform *japa*. The beads on the string can be made out of crystal, *indraksha*, *rudraksha* or *putrajiva*.[1548] Using *aksha*, one should make a string of beads. The succeeding ones are said to be superior to the preceding ones. At the time of *japa*, a learned person will not speak, jest, look at anything, shake his head or neck or display his teeth. Otherwise, *guhyaka*s,[1549] *rakshasa*s and *siddha*s forcibly take away the benefits. He must perform *japa* alone, in a pure spot. If he sees a *chandala*, an impure person or someone who has fallen down, he must perform the *japa* again. If he converses with them, he must bathe and then perform the *japa* again. If he sees anything impure, he must always control himself and do *achamana*. According to capacity, he should recite *mantra*s to Surya and according to his wishes, *pavamani*.[1550] If his clothes are wet, he can perform the *japa* inside the water. Otherwise, he can concentrate and perform it on *darbha* grass, on pure ground. He must do *pradakshina*, prostrate himself on the ground and perform *achamana* according to the sacred texts. Then, he should devoutly study. After this, he should satisfy *deva*s, *rishi*s and the large number of ancestors. Initially, he will recite OUMKARA and mention his name. At the end, he will say, "I hereby satisfy you."

[1548] *Aksha* is a seed and there are different types, *indraksha*, *somaksha*, *bhadraksha* and *rudraksha*. *Putrajiva* (*putranjiva*) is *roxburghii*. *Rudraksha* is *Elaco Carpus*.

[1549] Semi-divine species, companions of Kubera.

[1550] The *pavamana* (purifying) hymns from the ninth *mandala* of the *Rig Veda*.

The *tarpana*[1551] for *deva*s and *brahmarshi*s will be done with *akshata* and water. For ancestors, following the rules of one's own *grihyasutra*s, it must faithfully be done with sesamum and water. For *deva*s and *rishi*s, an intelligent person will perform the *tarpana* with the right hand, supported from below by the left hand. For ancestors, he will use water from the cups of his hands. For *deva*s, the sacred thread will be worn as *upavita*. For *tarpana* of *rishi*s, it will be worn as *nivita*. For ancestors, it will be worn as *prachinavita* and *pitri-tirtha* will be used. He will squeeze out water from the garment worn during the bath and silently perform *achamana*. *Deva*s will be worshipped with their own respective *mantra*s, using flowers, leaves and water. An excellent man, devout in conduct, will worship Brahma, Shankara, Surya, Madhusudana and other revered *deva*s. Using Purusha *suktam*, he will offer them flowers. All *deva*s are in water, and they are properly worshipped with water. First uttering Pranava, he must control himself and meditate on the *deva*s. Prostrating himself, he should separately offer them flowers. Through the worship of Vishnu, all the rites of the *Veda*s become sacred. Therefore, one should always worship Hari, who is without a beginning, a middle and an end. He must control himself and use Purusha *suktam*, or the *mantra* "*tad vishnoh*".[1552] There is no *mantra* in the *suktam*s of the four *Veda*s equal to these two. He must immerse his *atman* and mind. The *mantra* "*tad vishnoh*" will ensure serenity. Alternatively, purifying his sentiments, he can worship the eternal divinity, Bhagavan Ishana Mahadeva Maheshvara. He must control himself and can use Rudra

---

[1551] Offering of libations, such as of water.
[1552] *Rig Veda* 1.22.20, addressed to Vishnu.

gayatri mantra[1553] or Pranava. He can also use *mantra*s to Ishana, Rudra and Tryambaka. He should worship Maheshvara with flowers, leaves, water, sandalwood and such articles. Or he can do *japa* with the *mantra* "*Namah Shivaya.*" He should prostrate himself before Maheshvara, Ishvara, who conquers death. He should offer himself to Ishvara with "*yo brahmanam*".[1554] A learned *dvija* should do *pradakshina* with the *pancha brahman*.[1555] He will perform *dhyana* on the divinity Ishana, Shiva who is in the centre of the firmament. Or he will recite the *hamsah shuchishad* hymn from the Rig Veda and look at the sun.'

'He should go home, and controlling himself, perform the five great sacrifices. These five *yajna*s are said to be *deva-yajna*, *pitri-yajna*, *bhuta-yajna*, *manushya-yajna* and *brahma-yajna*.[1556] If there has been no *brahma-yajna* after *tarpana*, he should perform *manushya-yajna* and then study. At the end of *bhuta-yajna*, he should sit on a pile of *kusha* grass in a spot that is to the west of the fire, controlling himself and holding *kusha* in his hand. Rites to the Vishvadevas are described as *deva-yajna*. This must be performed in the sacrificial or ordinary fire, in the water or on the ground. If food has been cooked in an ordinary fire, oblations must be offered to that fire. If fire has been

[1553] OUM *tatpurushaya vidmahe mahadevaya dhimahi tanno rudrah prachodayat.*

[1554] *Shvetashvatara Upanishad* 6.38. '*yo brahmanam vidadhati purvam*' and so on, a *mantra* to seek refuge with the divinity.

[1555] The text states, for five years (*varshani*). This does not make sense. We have replaced it with *pancha brahman*, based on the *Pancha Brahma Upanishad*. This identifies Shiva's five facets of Sadyojata, Aghora, Vamadeva, Tatpurusha and Ishana as the five aspects of the *brahman*.

[1556] Respectively worshipping *deva*s, *tarpana* for ancestors, offering food to creatures (*bhuta*s), tending to guests and studying.

cooked in a sacrificial fire, it must be offered to that fire.
This is the eternal rule. After cooked food has been offered
as oblations to *deva*s, the remnants constitute offerings
for *bhuta*s. It should be known that *bhuta-yajna* brings
prosperity to all those with bodies. O excellent *dvija*s!
Food should be laid out on the ground outside for dogs,
*shvapaka*s, those who have fallen and birds. In the evening,
his wife will cook food and offer it, without using *mantra*s.
These are the rules for *bhuta-yajna*, every morning and
evening. With the ancestors in mind, one should feed one
brahmana every day. This is *nitya shraddha*. The remnants
constitute *pitri-yajna* and bestow the desired destination.
Alternatively, according to capacity, he can take some
food, control himself and offer it to a learned *dvija* who
knows the meanings of the *Veda*s. He must always worship
and prostrate himself before the *atithi*, who is like a lord.
Serene, in thoughts, words and deeds, he must welcome
him into his own house. According to capacity, a *dvija*
must offer *hantakara*, *agra* and *bhiksha* alms with his right
hand, supported from below by his left hand. It should be
known that giving this is like offering it to Parameshvara.
If one mouthful of alms is given, that is *bhiksha*. Four
times that is *agra*. Four times that is *hantakara* and that
is enough. It is only at the time of milking the cow that
the guest should be made to wait. According to capacity,
an *atithi* who has arrived must always be welcomed and
worshipped. In the proper way, *bhiksha* must be given
to mendicants and *brahmachari*s. One should offer food
according to one's capacity to all those who seek, bereft of
greed. If no one is available,[1557] the food must be offered
to cows. When one eats with many, one should not speak

[1557] Guests and those seeking alms.

while eating, nor criticize the food. O excellent *dvija*s! If a *dvija* eats without performing the five great *yajna*s, he is foolish in his mind and is born as an inferior species. Studying the *Veda*s and performing the five great sacrifices every day, according to capacity, lead to imperishable benefits. They swiftly destroy sins. Worship of *deva*s is also like that. Out of delusion or ignorance, if a person eats without worshipping the *deva*s, there is no doubt that he goes to the hell known as Sukara.[1558] O *dvija*s! Therefore, every effort must be made to perform these tasks. After this, if a person eats with his own relatives, he proceeds to the supreme destination.'

Chapter 72(2)(19) (Rules for eating)

Vyasa said, 'One should have food facing the east or facing the sun. He should be comfortably seated in a pure spot, with his feet placed on the ground. If one eats while facing the east, one obtains a long lifespan. If one eats while facing the south, one obtains fame. If one eats while facing the west, one obtains prosperity. If one eats while facing the north, one obtains truth. With the vessel placed on the ground, food must be had with five wet things. Prajapati Manu has said that this is equal to fasting. The spot must be pure and smeared. The hands and feet must be washed. He must perform *achamana* and the face must be wet. Food must be had with these five wet things. He should not be angry. He should recite the great *vyahriti*s and sprinkle the food with water. He must perform the rite

---

[1558] *Sukara* is pig, and the hell is full of pigs.

of sipping the water, reciting, "*amritopastaranamasi*".[1559]
He must use *svaha*, alone with Pranava. This is an oblation
to *prana*. This must be followed with oblations to *apana*,
vyana, *udana* and *samana* as the fifth. He will eat after
this. A *dvija* who knows the truth knows that these are
oblations to the *atman*. After this, he can eat the food
as he pleases, mixing it with the dishes. In his mind, he
should meditate on the divinity Prajapati, the *atman*. He
will then sip water, with the words, "*amritapidhanam
asi*."[1560] After *achamana*, he will again do *achamana* with
the "*ayam gouh*" *mantra*.[1561] He can also recite Drupada
mantra thrice. It destroys all sins. He will then stroke his
stomach with the words, "*prananam granthirasi*".[1562] After
achamana, he will control himself and use the thumb of
his right hand to drop some water on his right toe. With
the *mantra* "*shraddhayam*", he will complete the task of
offering oblations.[1563] Alternatively, he can unite his *atman*
with the imperishable *brahman*. Among all kinds of *yoga*,
atma-yoga is described as supreme. A *brahmana* who
follows the rules on his own is wise. He should eat with
the sacred thread worn as *upavita*. He should be pure and
should wear fragrant garlands. He should not eat between
morning and evening, especially at the time of the two
*sandhya*s. He should not eat immediately before a solar

[1559] A *mantra* for *achamana*. 'This water is the seat of *amrita*.
May it protect me' and so on.
[1560] 'You are the covering for the *amrita*.'
[1561] *Rig Veda* 10.189.1, a *mantra* to Agni and Surya.
[1562] 'You are the knot of *prana*.' From the eleventh *anuvaka* of
Shatarudriya.
[1563] There are serious errors in this *shloka* and we have amended
it. 'Shraddhayam' means with devotion, a reference to the *mantra*
in *Mahanarayana Upanishad*.

eclipse. If there is a lunar eclipse, he should not eat that evening. He should not eat at the time of the eclipse. When it is over, he should bathe and then eat. He can eat when the moon has been freed, unless it happens to be the middle of the night.[1564] However, if they set before being freed, he should only eat the next day, after seeing them. A person who eats without offering food to those who are looking, is evil-minded. The remnants of a sacrifice should be eaten, without being angry and without being distracted. If eating is only for one's own sake, if intercourse is only for the sake of pleasure and if studying is only for the sake of making a living, one's birth is futile. If one eats with the head covered, if one eats while facing the north or if he eats while wearing footwear, all his learning goes to *asura*s. He should not eat at midnight or mid-day. He should not eat when the earlier food has not been digested, or while wearing a wet garment. He should not eat when the seat is broken, or when he is in a vehicle. He should not eat from a broken vessel, from the ground or directly from the hands. If one is *ucchishta*, one should not have *ghee*. Nor should he touch his head with his hand. Until that state is over, he should not chant about the *brahman*. He should not eat with his wife. He should not eat in the dark, at the time of the *sandhya*s or in the temple of a *deva*. While wearing a single garment, while lying down and while in a vehicle, he should not eat. He should not eat without taking the footwear off. Nor should he laugh or lament at the time. After eating, one should be comfortable, so that the food is digested. The meanings of the *Veda*s have been

---

[1564] Known as *mahanisha*. A period of three hours is known as *yama* and there are eight *yama*s, four during the day and four during the night. The second and third *yama* of night constitute *mahanisha*.

expanded in Itihasa and the Puranas.[1565] Following the rules
stated earlier, he must be pure and perform the *sandhya*
worship. Seated facing the west, he must perform *japa* with
devi Gayatri. If a person does not observe the eastern or
the western *sandhya*, he is like a *shudra* in this world and
is barred from all rites. Having offered oblations into the
fire in the proper way, having recited *mantra*s and having
eaten the remnants of the sacrifice, along with servants and
relatives, he should sleep in the night, with his feet dry. He
should not sleep with his head facing the north. Nor should
it face the west. He should not sleep under the bare sky, or
when naked. He should never sleep on an impure seat. He
should not sleep on a broken bed, or in an empty house.
He should never sleep on a bed made out of bamboo or
palasha. I have thus spoken about everything *brahmana*s
must do every day. If a person follows this, he obtains
the fruits of liberation. Because of non-belief or laziness,
if a *brahmana* does not do this, he goes to a terrible hell
and is born as a crow. Except for the stated rules of one's
own *ashrama*, there is no other means of liberation. If one
performs these rites, Parameshthi is satisfied.'

Chapter 73(2)(20) (*Shraddha* rites)

Vyasa said, 'When it is *amavasya*, excellent *dvija*s must
faithfully perform the rite of *pindanvaharyaka*.[1566]
This yields objects of pleasure and liberation as fruits. A
pindanvaharyaka shraddha undertaken when the moon

[1565] This breaks the continuity and doesn't belong.
[1566] The monthly *shraddha*. Literally, after the *pinda*s (at the
time of the funeral) have been offered.

wanes, is praised. For *dvija*s, it is particularly praised if it is held in the afternoon and uses offerings of meat. During *krishna paksha*, starting with *pratipada*,[1567] all the *tithi*s are praised, but succeeding ones are superior to preceding ones. However, *chaturdashi* must be avoided. *Amavasya* and the three *ashtaka*s, in the three months, Pousha and others, are recommended. Other than the three *ashtaka*s, *panchadashi* in Magha is sacred. During the monsoon, *trayodashi*,[1568] when there is a conjunction with Magha *nakshatra* and when the crops have ripened, is a time for *shraddha*s. *Nitya shradda*s are said to be those that are undertaken every day. When there is an eclipse of the sun or the moon, along with relatives, an extensive *naimittika shraddha* must be undertaken. Otherwise, one goes to hell. *Kamya shraddha*s are praised at the time of eclipses, when *ayana*s change, at the time of the vernal or autumn equinox and at the time of *vyatipata*.[1569] These bestow infinite merits. *Shraddha*s performed at the time of *samkranti*,[1570] or on the date of birth, confer imperishable benefits. For all the *nakshatra*s, the *shraddha* must particularly be undertaken at the right time. If it is done during Krittika, the excellent *dvija* goes to heaven. During Rohini, he obtains offspring. During Soumya,[1571] he becomes as radiant as Brahma. During Roudra or Ardra, he obtains valour and success in deeds. During Punarvasu, he obtains land. During Pushya, he obtains prosperity. During the

[1567] The first lunar *tithi*.
[1568] The thirteenth lunar *tithi*.
[1569] When the sun and the moon are directly opposite each other.
[1570] When the sun enters a *rashi* (sign of the Zodiac), the first day of the solar month.
[1571] Mrigashira.

serpent's *nakshatra*,[1572] all desires are satisfied. During the
nakshatra of the ancestors,[1573] good fortune is obtained.
During Aryaman,[1574] one obtains wealth. During Uttara
Phalguni, sins are destroyed. During Hasta, one become
best among kin. During Chitra, one obtains many sons.
During Svati, there is success in trade. During Vishakha,
one obtains gold. During Mitra,[1575] one obtains many
friends. During Shakra's *nakshatra*,[1576] one obtains a
kingdom. During Mula, one is successful in agriculture.
During the *nakshatra* of water,[1577] there is success in
acquiring *jnana*. During Vishvadevas,[1578] all the wishes are
satisfied. During Shravana, one obtains superiority. During
Dhanishtha, all desires are met. During the *nakshatra* of
the lord of the water,[1579] one obtains supreme strength.
During Ajaikapada,[1580] one obtains metals. During
Ahirbudhnya,[1581] one obtains an auspicious house. During
Revati, one obtains many cows. During Ashvini, one obtains
horses. During Yama's *nakshatra*,[1582] the *shraddha* makes
one come alive. On Aditya's day, one obtains freedom from
disease. On the moon's day, one obtains good fortune. On
Kuja's day,[1583] there is victory in everything. On Budha, all

---

[1572] Ashlesha.
[1573] Magha.
[1574] Purva Phalguni.
[1575] Anuradha.
[1576] Jyeshtha.
[1577] Purva Ashadha.
[1578] Uttara Ashadha.
[1579] Shatabhisha.
[1580] Purva Bhadrapada.
[1581] Uttara Bhadrapada.
[1582] Bharani.
[1583] Tuesday. Kuja is another name for Mangala.

the objects of desire are met. On Guru,[1584] all the desired knowledge is obtained. On Bhargava,[1585] one obtains wealth. On Shanaishchara, one obtains a long lifespan. On *pratipada*, one obtains auspicious sons.[1586] On *dvitiya*, one obtains daughters. On *tritiya*, one obtains animals. On *chaturthi*, one obtains small animals. On *panchami*, one obtains beautiful sons. On *shashthi*, one obtains radiance and agriculture. On *saptami*, a man obtains wealth. Through a *shraddha* on *ashtami*, one always gains from trade. On *navami*, he obtains an animal with a single hoof. On *dashami*, he obtains many animals with two hooves. On *ekadashi*, he obtains silver and sons who are as radiant as Brahma. On *dvadashi*, he obtains gold, silver and base metals. On *trayodashi*, he become superior among kin. On *chaturdashi*, he obtains wicked sons. A person who offers *shraddha* on *panchadashi*, always obtains everything that he wishes for. Therefore, *dvija*s should not perform *shraddha*s on *chaturdashi*. *Shraddha*s on that day are conceived for those who are killed with weapons. If the *brahmana* is wealthy enough to get the objects, there are rules about the time. Therefore, for objects of pleasure and emancipation, *dvija*s must perform *shraddha*s.'

'A *shraddha* must always be performed before undertaking any task, when there is an increase in prosperity and when there is the birth of a son and similar things.

[1584] Thursday.

[1585] Friday.

[1586] The first lunar *tithi* is *pratipada*, the second *dvitiya*, the third *tritiya*, the fourth *chaturthi*, the fifth *panchami*, the sixth *shashthi*, the seventh *saptami*, the eighth *ashtami*, the ninth *navami*, the tenth *dashami*, the eleventh *ekadashi*, the twelfth *dvadashi*, the thirteenth *trayodashi*, the fourteenth *chaturdashi* and the fifteenth *panchadashi*.

One performed on *parva* days[1587] is known as *parvana shraddha*. One undertaken every day is *nitya shraddha*. That done for a desired object is *naimittika*. For one person, it is *ekoddishta*. There is *vriddhi shraddha*[1588] and finally, *parvana shraddha*. In this way, Manu has described five different types of *shraddhas*. A sixth kind of *shraddha* is mentioned at the time of undertaking a journey. Every effort must be made to perform it. For purity, Brahma has spoken about a seventh kind of *shraddha*. The eighth kind is *daivika shraddha*. If one performs this, one is freed from fear. Unless Rahu is seen, a *shraddha* should not be performed at the time of *sandhya*, or in the night. There are some places that are special and there, the good merits obtained are infinite. A *shraddha* along the Ganga, in Prayaga and in Amarakantaka yields imperishable benefits. The ancestors sing a song and learned ones dance to this song. "One desires many sons who possess good qualities and virtuous conduct. Out of them, perhaps one will go to Gaya. If he goes to Gaya and performs a *shraddha* will all the accompaniments, he saves his ancestors and proceeds to the supreme destination. Mount Varaha is special and so is Gaya. Varanasi is special. The divinity Hara is himself present there. There are Gangadvara, Prabhasa, Bilvaka, Mount Nila, Kurukshetra, Kubjamra, Bhrigutunga, Mahalaya, Kedara, the *tirtha* of Phalgu and Naimishiranya. Sarasvati is special and Pushkara is also special. Narmada, Kushvarata, Shrishaila, Bhadrakarnaka, Vetravati, Vishakha and Godavari are special. In addition, there are *tirtha*s along sandy beaches and the banks of

[1587] Sacred and auspicious days.
[1588] Performed on a prosperous occasion.

rivers. *Vrihi*,[1589] barley, black gram, water, roots and fruits, *shyamaka*,[1590] corn, *kasha* grass, *nivara*,[1591] *priyangu*,[1592] wheat, sesamum and *mudga* please the ancestors for a month. To please them, mangoes, sugarcane, grapes and pomegranates should be offered. At the time of a *shraddha*, *vidari* and *kuranda* must be offered.[1593] At the time of a *shraddha*, one must make efforts to offer parched grain with honey, *saktu* with sugar, *shringataka*[1594] and *kasheruka*.[1595] With fish, they are satisfied for two months. With the meat of deer, they are satisfied for three months. With the meat of sheep, they are satisfied for four months. With the meat of birds, they are satisfied for five months. With the meat of goats, they are satisfied for six months. With the meat of the spotted antelope, they are satisfied for seven months. With the meat of blackbuck, they are satisfied for eight months. With the meat of *ruru* deer, they are satisfied for nine months. With the meat of boar and buffaloes, they are satisfied for ten months. With the meat of rabbits and tortoises, they are satisfied for eleven months. With the milk of a cow and *payasam*, they are satisfied for one year. With the meat of a rhinoceros, they are satisfied for twelve years. With *kalashaka*, *mahashalka*, the meat of a horned and red goat, the food offered yields infinite satisfaction, lasting till

---

[1589] Type of paddy.
[1590] Millet, or grain in general.
[1591] Wild rice.
[1592] Millet.
[1593] *Vidari* is Indian kudzu, *kuranda* (*kuranta*) is probably the yellow amaranth.
[1594] With different meanings, such as *Trapa Bispinosa*.
[1595] A kind of grass or club-rush.

the end of a *kalpa*.[1596] A *dvija* must buy or obtain it himself.
He must bring the dead body and make every effort to offer
it at a *shraddha*. This brings him imperishable benefits. One
should avoid long pepper, citron, *masuraka*,[1597] pumpkin,
gourd, brinjal, succulent *bhutrina*,[1598] safflower, lumpy
roots and *tanduliyaka*.[1599] An excellent *dvija* will make
efforts to avoid seven items at the time of a *shraddha* -
kidney beans, milk from buffaloes, milk from goats, pigeon
peas, *kovidara*, *palaki*[1600] and chillies.'

Chapter 74(2)(21) (Rules for a *shraddha*)

Vyasa said, 'When the moon has vanished, in the
indicated way, a *dvija* will bathe and satisfy the
ancestors. With a pure and pleasant mind, he will perform
the *pindanvaharyaka shraddha*. Initially, he will look for a
brahmana who is accomplished in the *Veda*s. Such a person
is described as the *tirtha* for offering *havya* and *kavya*. Such
people should drink *soma* and be bereft of passion. They
should know *dharma* and be serene in their minds. They
should follow *vrata*s and *niyama*s and only approach their
wives at the time of their seasons. Such a *brahmana* must
maintain the five fires, study and know the *Yajur Veda*. He
should know many hymns from the *Rig Veda*, *Trisuparna*

[1596] *Kalashaka* is a kind of pot-herb, *mahashalka* is a large scaly
fish.
[1597] *Masur dal*.
[1598] A fragrant grass.
[1599] A medicinal herb.
[1600] A kind of medicinal herb.

and *Trimadhus*.[1601] He must know *Trinachiketa*. He must know *chhandas* and must know *Jyeshthasama*. He must have studied *Atharvashirsha*, especially the sections on Rudra. He must perform *agnihotra* sacrifices, be learned in *nyaya* and know the six *Vedangas*. He must know Mantrabrahmana and must have read the texts on *dharma*. He must be devoted to the vows of *rishis*. He must be a *rishi* who has conquered his senses and is serene in his mind. He must belong to a lineage of learned *brahmanas*. He must be pure in birth and must have given away thousands. He must be devoted to following the *chandrayana* vow. He must be truthful in speech and must know about the Puranas. He must be devoted to worshipping *gurus*, *devas* and the fire. He must be devoted to *jnana*. He must be free in every possible way. The excellent *dvija* must be persevering and immersed in the *brahman*. He must be devoted to worshipping Mahadeva and Vishnu. He must purify the *pankti*.[1602] He must be devoted to non-violence. He must be a person who never accepts gifts. He must be a person who performs sacrifices and is devoted to donating. Such a person is known as one who purifies the *pankti*. *Brahmanas* who are young, learned, healthy, devoted to great sacrifices and devoted to performing *japa* with Savitri are those who purify the *pankti*. A *brahmana* householder from a noble lineage, who is learned and possesses good

---

[1601] The *Yajur Veda* (*Taittiriya Aranyaka*) has three *mantras* that are recited together and these are known as *Trisuparna*. *Trimadhus* is the three verses in *Rig Veda* I.90.6-8. *Trinachiketa* is part of the *Yajur Veda*. *Jyeshthasama* is a hymn from the *Sama Veda*. *Mantrabrahmana* usually means the *Chhandogya Upanishad*.

[1602] *Pankti* is the row in which one sits down to eat. People from the same class sit in the same *pankti*.

conduct, is an ascetic and tends to the fire, is known as
someone who purifies the *pankti*. A *dvija* engaged in
the welfare of his mother and father, who bathes in the
morning and is controlled and is a sage pursuing *adhyatma*,
is known as someone who purifies the *pankti*. He is a great
yogi who is devoted to *jnana*. He thinks about the meaning
of *Vedanta*. He is faithful and devoted to *shraddha*s. Such
a *brahmana* purifies the *pankti*. He is engaged in the
knowledge of the *Veda*s. He bathes and is always devoted
to *brahmacharya*. He knows the *Atharva Veda* and desires
liberation. Such a *brahmana* purifies the *pankti*. He should
belong to a different *pravara* and a different *gotra*.[1603] He
should not be related. Such a *brahmana* is known as one
who purifies the *pankti*. A tranquil *yogi* engaged in the
truth about *jnana* should be fed. In his absence, it can
be a faithful and controlled *brahmachari* student. In his
absence, it can be a householder who desires liberation and
is devoid of attachment. If all these are lacking, a *sadhaka*
householder can be fed. If a mendicant who knows the
truth about Prakriti's *guna*s is fed, the fruits surpass those
from feeding one thousand who know *Vedanta*. Therefore,
efforts must be made to feed *havya* and *kavya* to an Indra
among *yogi*s who is devoted to *jnana* about Ishvara. In his
absence, other *dvija*s can be fed. This is the best mode for
offering *havya* and *kavya*. It should be known that there is
an alternative mode always followed by the virtuous. The
maternal grandfather, the maternal uncle, the sister's son,
the father-in-law, the *guru*, the daughter's son, the king,
relatives, the officiating priest and the person performing
the sacrifice can be fed. A friend should not be fed at a
shraddha. His task is to ensure the collection of wealth.

[1603] *Pravara* is a lineage of ancestors, distinct from *gotra*.

The expectation of *dakshina* is *pishacha* in nature. It does not yield fruits in this world or the next. If one desires, one can honour a friend at a *shraddha*. However, one should not act in a similar way towards an enemy. If an enemy partakes of the oblations, after death, the fruits are futile. A *brahmana* who has not studied is pacified, like grass with fire. *Havya* should not be given to him. Oblations are not offered into ashes. This is like sowing seeds on barren land. The person who sows does not reap any fruits from this. In that way, oblations should not be offered to a person who does not know the *Rig Veda* hymns. No fruits are obtained. If a person who does not know *mantra*s partakes of the *pinda*s of *havya* and *kavya*, after death, the performer of the *shraddha* is made to swallow thick and blazing iron balls, as many as the mouthfuls that were partaken. O *dvija*s! If the worst among men, inferior in conduct, partake of the *havya*, even if they possess learning and noble birth, the *shraddha* becomes *asura* in nature. If the *Veda*s and sacrificial platforms have not been in use for three generations, that person is a wicked *brahmana*. He is never worthy of a *shraddha* and similar rites. There are six types that are *brahma-bandhu*s[1604]—the servant of a *shudra*, the servant of a king, a person who officiates at the sacrifice of a *vrishala*, a person who survives by killing others and a person who survives by imprisoning others. They do not deserve to be given. Manu has said that they have fallen for the sake of material objects. Those who sell the *Veda*s are also barred from *shraddha*s and similar rites. Those who sell their sons, those who are the sons of widows who have remarried and those who

---

[1604]Inferior *brahmana*s, *brahmana*s only in name. Five types are listed. To this, one adds the wicked *brahmana* mentioned earlier.

officiate at sacrifices for the ordinary—these are described
as people who have fallen. Teachers who have not cleansed
themselves and those who teach as salaried servants—even
if they have studied the *Veda*s, they are described as those
who have fallen. There are evil-souled ones who are full of
tamas—aged *shravaka*s, *nirgrantha*s,[1605] those who know
about *pancharatra*, *kapalika*s, *pashupata*s and atheists.
If they eat the food offered at a *shraddha*, no fruits are
obtained, in this world and after death.'

'If a *dvija* does not follow any *ashrama*, if he does not
follow the rules of the *ashrama*, or if he falsely proclaims to
be in an *ashrama*—he should be known as one who defiles
the *pankti*. O *dvija*s! The following must be shunned in any
rites connected with a *shraddha*—those with malformed
skin, with malformed nails, a leper, with white leprosy, with
brown teeth, with mutilated genitals, a thief, a eunuch, a
non-believer, a drunkard, one attached to a *vrishali*,[1606] one
who kills a hero, one who has sexual intercourse with his
brother's widow, an arsonist, a pimp, one who sell *soma*, a
parivetri, a violent person, a *parivitti*,[1607] one who does not
perform the five sacrifices, the son of a remarried widow,
one who lives off usury, one who gazes at *nakshtara*s,[1608]
one addicted to singing and musical instruments, a
diseased person, a person with one eye, one deficient in
limbs, one with an excess limb, one who violates a vow of
brahmacharya, one who pollutes food, a widow's son, an
accused person, one who earns a living through *deva*s, a
person who harms a friend, one who indulges in calumny,

[1605] Respective reference to Buddhism and Jainism.
[1606] Feminine of *vrishala*.
[1607] An elder brother who is unmarried, despite his younger
brother having married.
[1608] Presumably meaning an astrologer.

one who always follows his wife, a person who abandons his father, mother and *guru*, a person who abandons his wife, one who harms the *gotra*, one who has deviated from purity, a vile person, one without offspring, one who bears false witness, a beggar, an actor, a person who travels the oceans, an ingrate, a person who breaks a contract, one who criticizes the *Veda*s, one who criticizes the *deva*s and one who criticizes *dvija*s. In particular, the following defile a *pankti*—an ungrateful person, one who indulges in calumny, a cruel person, a non-believer, one who criticizes the *Veda*s, one who harms friends and a deceitful person. All of them do not deserve to be given food. They are not worthy of rites. One should make efforts to avoid the slayer of a *brahmana* and an accused person. A *brahmana* who nourishes his limbs through food and drink obtained from a *shudra*, one who does not perform the *sandhya* worship and one who does not perform the great sacrifices is a defiler of the *pankti*. A *brahmana* who destroys what he has studied and is devoid of bathing and donations is full of *tamas* and *rajas*. He defiles the *pankti*. What is the need to speak a lot? Those who do not act according to what has been instructed and act according to what is reprimanded must carefully be avoided in *shraddha*s.'

Chapter 75(2)(22)
(Rules for a *shraddha* continued)

Vyasa said, 'One should control oneself and purify the ground with cow dung and water. Virtuous people must be engaged to invite all the *dvija*s on the preceding day. The invitation will say, "Tomorrow, there will be a *shraddha* at my place." If this is not possible on the preceding day, observing the requirements, it can be done on that day. His ancestors will hear that the time for the *shraddha* has arrived. In their minds, they will meditate and tell each other this. With the speed of thought, they will arrive there. Stationed in the firmament, the ancestors eat with the *brahmana*s. Remaining in this state in the air, they eat and proceed to the supreme destination. When the time for *shraddha* has arrived, the *brahmana*s who have been invited must control themselves. All of them must observe *brahmacharya*. The person performing the *shraddha* must certainly avoid anger, hurry and carelessness. He must be truthful in speech and controlled. He should not carry a load and should refrain from sexual intercourse and travelling. If a *brahmana* accepts the invitation meant for another, he goes to a terrible hell and becomes a pig. Having invited a *brahmana*, if a *dvija* invites someone else out of delusion, he becomes a greater sinner.[1609] He becomes a worm that subsists on excrement. Having been invited for a *shraddha*, if a *brahmana* indulges in sexual intercourse, he incurs the sin of killing a *brahmana*. He is born as an inferior species. Having been invited for a *shraddha*, if an evil-minded *brahmana* embarks on a journey, his ancestors subsist on wicked food for a month. Having been invited for a *shraddha*, if a *dvija* indulges in quarrelling, his ancestors survive on excrement for a month. Having been invited for a *shraddha*, a *dvija* must control himself. He must avoid anger and be intent on purity. The performer must control his senses.'

'On the next day,[1610] he must control himself. He must go to the southern direction and gather *darbha* grass, along

[1609] Than the one who has accepted the invitation.
[1610] The day of the *shraddha*.

with the roots. They must be extremely pure. Sprinkled with water, they must be placed, with their tips pointing to the south. He must select a soft spot that slopes to the south. It must be isolated and must possess all the qualities. Having searched out the pure spot, he must clean it and smear it with cow dung. The ancestors are always content when the *shraddha* is performed in an isolated spot on the banks of a river, a *tirtha* or on his own plot of land, but not when it is performed in water. The ancestors must never be offered a *shraddha* on a piece of land that belongs to someone else. Out of delusion, if a man tries to do this, the owner may obstruct this. Forests, mountains, sacred *tirtha*s and temples are said to be places without owners. No one can claim possession. Sesamum must be spread in everydirection butt must be prevented from germinating. Even if *asura*s take away the benefits of a *shraddha*, sesamum purifies it, as long as it does not germinate. Many different kinds of food must be cleaned and prepared. There should be many dishes, not just one. According to capacity, he should think of *choshya*, *peya* and other food items.[1611] When it is midday, he should approach the *dvija*s, who have shaved their hair and clipped their nails. He should indicate the way and offer them twigs for cleaning the teeth. "Come and please be seated separately." He must give them oil for smearing their limbs and for having a bath and everything else required for a bath. Uttering *mantra*s to Vishvadevas, they must be given vessels made of *udumbara*.[1612] When they have returned after having their baths, he must stand up and greet them, hands joined in salutation. In the due

---

[1611] The four types of food are those that are chewed (*charvya*), sucked (*choshya* or *chushya*), licked (*lehya*) and drunk (*peya*).

[1612] The fig tree.

order, he must offer them *padya* and *achamaniya*. There
are *dvija*s, representing Vishvadevas, who had been
invited earlier. Their seats must be covered with three
blades of *darbha* grass, the tips facing the east. The seats
of those representing the ancestors must be covered with
darbha grass, with the tips facing the south. These must
be sprinkled with sesamum and water. Touching the
seats, he should make them sit, saying, "Please be seated
separately." Two represent Vishvadevas and face the east.
Three represent the ancestors and face the south. One
represents that paternal grandfather, and one represents
the maternal grandfather. There are five things that can be
hampered if done extensively—proper honour, the time,
the place, purity and choice of a *brahmana*. Therefore,
the gathering should not be large. Alternatively, a single
brahmana, accomplished in the *Veda*s, can be fed. He must
possess learning and good conduct and should be devoid
of inauspicious traits. From all the food, he must gather a
bit in a vessel and offer it to the *brahmana* who represents
*deva*s in the temple. Some food will be offered to the fire or
given to a *brahmachari*. It is best that a single learned *dvija*
be fed. If a mendicant or *brahmachari* presents himself for
food and seats himself, it is desirable that he is also fed at
the *shraddha*. If an *atithi* is not fed, the *shraddha* is not
praised. Therefore, *dvija*s should carefully honour *atithi*s
at *shraddha*s. If *dvija*s eat at a *shraddha* that does not have
*atithi*s, they are born as crows. There is no doubt that this
also happens to the person performing the *shraddha*. The
following must be shunned and kept at a distance from a
shraddha—a person lacking a limb, a person who has fallen,
a leper, a person with wounds, a non-believer, a cock, a pig
and a dog. A loathsome person, an impure person, a naked
person, an intoxicated person, a crooked person, a woman

going through her periods, a person wearing blue or ochre garments and a heretic must be shunned.'

'Whenever rites for the ancestors are performed with *brahmana*s, it is necessary to first worship the Vishvadevas. When they are seated, all of them must be decorated with ornaments, garlands, headdresses, incense, garments and unguents. Taking the permission of the *brahmana*s, the *deva*s must be invoked. He will face the north and recite, "*vishve devasa*".[1613] He will wear two *pavitra*s and reciting "*sham no devir*",[1614] pour water into a clean vessel. With the words "*yavosi*",[1615] he will sprinkle barley into this. With "*ya divya*,"[1616] he will pour the *arghya* onto his hand. According to capacity, he will then offer fragrances, garlands, incense and similar items. A learned person will then turn to the left and face the south. Using the *mantra* "*ushantas tva*,"[1617] he will invoke the ancestors. Having invoked them and having taken permission of the *brahmana*s, he will perform *japa* with "*ayantu nah*".[1618] With the words "*shanno devih*",[1619] he will pour water into the vessel and with "*tilosi*",[1620] add sesamum to it. As was the case earlier, he will pour *arghya* onto his hand. Controlling himself, he will pour the remnants of the libations into all the vessels. In the place meant for the

---

[1613] *Rig Veda* 2.41.13, invoking the Vishvadevas.

[1614] *Rig Veda* 10.9.4, invoking the waters.

[1615] *Vajasaneyi Samhita* 5.26. Literally, 'You are barley.'

[1616] *Taittiriya Brahmana* 2.7.15.4.

[1617] *Rig Veda* 10.16.12. An offering made to the ancestors. 'We desire you' and so on.

[1618] *Vajasaneyi Samhita* 19.58. 'May our ancestors come' and so on.

[1619] *Yajur Veda* 36.12. 'May the divine waters be pleasing' and so on.

[1620] You are sesamum.

ancestors, the vessel should be placed, face downwards. He will take the cooked food, soaked in *ghee*. Desiring to offer it into the fire, he will seek the permission of the *brahmana*s. When they grant him permission to do so, wearing the sacred thread as *upavita*, he will render the oblations. Oblations must be offered with *kusha* in the hand and with the sacred thread worn as *upavita*. For the ancestors, the sacred thread must be worn as *prachinavita*. A person who knows about oblations will also offer it to the Vishvadevas. When worshipping the *deva*s, one should always kneel on the right knee. While worshipping the ancestors, one should kneel on the other knee. He should recite, "To Soma, to the ancestors, Svadha—I prostrate myself." Reciting, "To Agni, who bears the oblations, Svadha", he should offer the oblations. In case fire is not available, the right hand of the *brahmana* can be used. Or he can control himself and perform the rite near Mahadeva, or in a cow-pen. Taking their permission, he should then head in a southern direction. Smearing the place with cow dung, he should use sand to draw a square *mandala*.[1621] The place should be auspicious and should slope towards the south. With a single blade of *darbha* grass, he should etch the centre thrice. He should then spread *darbha* grass over the place, the tips pointing to the south. Controlling himself, with the remaining oblations, he should make and offer three *pinda*s. After offering the *pinda*s, he should wipe his hand with *darbha* grass, for those who feed on *lepa*.[1622] Thereafter, he should perform *achamana* thrice. A person

[1621] A mystical diagram, a *mandala* is usually circular.
[1622] The three *pinda*s are for the preceding three generations. Generations above that are entitled to *lepa*, the remnants left after the hand has been wiped.

who knows about *mantra*s will then slowly smell the food and prostrate himself before the ancestors. The remaining water will be gently poured near the *pinda*s. Controlling himself, he will smell the *pinda*s.'

'With the food left after offering the *pinda*s, in the proper way, he should feed the *dvija*s.[1623] In accordance with the rules for a *shraddha*, there should be many kinds of excellent meat and *apupa*s. When they have eaten, he should spread the remaining food on the ground in front of them and ask, "What will I do with this food?" Content, they will perform *achamana*. He will ask, "Are you satisfied?" The *brahmana*s will then reply, "Svadha to you."[1624] When they have eaten, he will offer them the remaining food. Permitted by the *dvija*s, he will do what they ask him to do. In rites for the ancestors, one should say, "May the food be tasty." In cow-pens, one should say, "May the food be cooked well." In rites for prosperity, one should say, "May this lead to prosperity." In rites for *deva*s, one should say, "May this serve well." Taking his leave of the *brahmana*s, he should silently stand before the ancestors, facing the southern direction. He should ask the ancestors for the desired boons. "May the donor flourish. May the *Veda*s and our offspring flourish. May my faith not leave. May I have lots to donate." The *pinda*s may be given to cows, goats or *brahmana*s, or cast into fire or water. A wife who desires a son may eat the *pinda* in the middle. He will wash his hands and perform *achamana*. With what is left, he should satisfy the kin.'

[1623] It is difficult to make sense of the text here and we have taken liberties.
[1624] In the sense of, 'Be comfortable.'

'The Indras among *dvija*s should be offered whatever they desire—soups, vegetables, fruits, sugarcane, milk, curds, *ghee*, honey, cooked food that is wished for and different kinds of food and drinks. A person who desires his prosperity should give *dvija*s many kinds of grain, sesamum and sugar. Except for fruits, roots and drinks, different kinds of hot food should be given. He should not rest his knees on the ground. He should not be angry. He should not utter a falsehood. He should not touch the food with his feet. He should not criticize it. If something is said in rage, if something said is against the norms, or if there is excessive talk, *yatudhana*s take away what is offered. If one is perspiring, one should not stand near the excellent *dvija*s. One should not look at crows and other such prohibited birds. Hungry, the ancestors arrive there in those forms. Salt must not be given directly into the hand. An iron vessel should not be used. There should not be a lack of faith. Food offered in gold, silver or *udumbara* vessels, or one made out of rhinoceros horn, yield imperishable benefits. At a *shraddha*, if a person feeds *dvija*s in vessels made of clay, he goes to a terrible hell. So do the person who eats, and the priest. There should be no differentiation in food served to those seated in the same *pankti*. One should not have to beg for food, nor pay for it. If a person has to beg or pay for food, the donor goes to terrible hells. It is best to eat the food silently, without speaking about its natural qualities. The ancestors eat only as long as the qualities of the oblations are not mentioned. The *dvija* who is seated in the chief seat should not eat first. If he does so, while many others look on, he appropriates the sins of all those who are in the *pankti*. An excellent *dvija*, engaged for a *shraddha*, should not refuse anything. There is no restriction on meat. He should not look at someone else eating. If a *dvija* engaged for rites connected with the ancestors does not eat meat, after death, he is born as an animal for twenty-one births. At the time of a *shraddha*, it is excellent if there is a recital of the *Veda*s, *dharmashastra*s, Itishasa and Purana. The person eating the food should spread some on the ground in front. He should ask, "Was the food tasty?" Satisfied, he should perform *achamana*. Once they have done *achamana*, he should take their permission and ask, "Are you pleased?" The *brahmana*s will then say, "Svadha to you." When they have eaten, he should ask them about the remaining food. Taking their permission, he should do what the *dvija*s ask him to do. In rites for the ancestors, one should say, "May the food be tasty."[1625] In cow pens, one should say, "May the food be cooked well." In rites for prosperity, one should say, "May this lead to prosperity." In rites for *deva*s, one should say, "May this serve well." Taking his leave of the *brahmana*s, he should silently stand before the ancestors, facing the southern direction. He should praise the ancestors and ask for the desired boons. "May the donor flourish. May the *Veda*s and our offspring flourish. May my faith not leave. May I have lots to donate." The *pinda*s may be given to cows, goats or *brahmana*s, or cast into fire or water. A wife who desires a son may eat the *pinda* in the middle. He will wash his hands and perform *achamana*. With what is left, he should feed the kin. After the kin, he should next feed his own servants. Subsequently, he will eat the remaining food, along with his wives. As long as the sun has not set, the leftovers should not be thrown away.'

'That night, the couple must observe *brahmacharya*. Having performed a *shraddha*, or eaten at it, if one engages

---

[1625]There is repetition of what has been said earlier.

in sexual intercourse, one goes to the hell of Maharourava.
Thereafter, one is born as a worm. He must be pure and
without anger. He must be serene, truthful in speech and
controlled. A person who performs a *shraddha*, and a
person who eats there, must avoid studying and travelling.
Having eaten at a *shraddha*, if *dvija*s subsequently eat at
another *shraddha*, they are like those who commit major
sins. They go to many hells. In brief, these are the proper
rules for performing a *shraddha*. If a *brahmana* faces
hardships, he will always prosper through this. If a person
performs an *amashraddha*,[1626] if he knows the rules, he
will devoutly offer oblations into the fire and then offer
*pinda*s. Serene in his mind, if a person follows these rules
and performs a *shraddha*, he always destroys his sins and
obtains the destination obtained by mendicants. Therefore,
an excellent *dvija* must make every effort to perform
a *shraddha*. In this way, the eternal Isha is properly
worshipped. A *dvija* without wealth can perform it with
roots and fruits. Controlling himself, he should bathe and
perform *tarpana* for the ancestors with sesamum and water.
If the father is alive, it is not recommended that he should
not perform a *shraddha*. However, some say that he can
perform a *shraddha* for those to whom his father offers a
shraddha. Or he can simply offer oblations. The *shraddha*
is performed for the father, the grandfather and the great
grandfather and for anyone else who is pleased by this, not
for anyone else. A person who is alive must be faithfully
fed, until he is content. A controlled and pure person does
not ignore those who are alive. A *dvyamushyayana* must
equally offer *shraddha* to both the fathers, the owner of the

[1626] A *shraddha* with uncooked food.

seed and the owner of the *kshetra*.[1627] A son born through *niyoga* also has those rights. If born without *niyoga*, a son can offer *pinda* to the owner of the seed and the owner of the *kshetra*. He should offer two *pinda*s, to the owner of the *kshetra* and the owner of the seed. He should separately mention the owner of the *kshetra* and the owner of the seed. Following the rules, *ekoddishta shraddha* must be performed on the day of death. When the period of impurity is over, he can perform any rite he wishes to. A person who performs a *shraddha* for prosperity should do so in the forenoon. Everything must be done just as it is done for the *deva*s, but there must be no rites with sesamum. The *darbha* grass must be straight and one should feed an even number of *dvija*s. In a *nandimukha shraddha*,[1628] he should say, "May the ancestors be pleased." *Shraddha* for the mother should be performed first, that for father thereafter. After this, for the maternal grandfather. It is said that, for a *shraddha* at a time of prosperity, these three must be performed. *Deva*s must be worshipped first, but there will be no *pradakshina*. A learned person will control himself, face the east, wear the sacred thread as *upavita* and perform it. The *matrika*s must be devoutly worshipped first, along with the *ganeshvara*s. This can be done in colourful ways on the ground, in images, or in *dvija*s. The worship must be done with flowers, incense, offerings of food and ornaments. Having worshipped the

---

[1627] *Dvyamushyayana* means the son of two fathers, the biological father and the father who has adopted him. But here, it is being used in a more specific sense. *Kshetra* (field) means the mother. The owner of the field means the mother's husband, who need not necessarily be the biological father. In a *niyoga* system, a married woman (or a widow) had a child through some other man.

[1628] Performed before a festive occasion, such as a marriage.

*matrika*s, a *dvija* must perform the three *shraddha*s. If a person performs a *shraddha* without worshipping the *matrika*s, the *matrika*s are overwhelmed with rage and cause violence to him.'

Chapter 76(2)(23) (Impurities of birth and death)

Vyasa said, 'O excellent *dvija*s! If it is a *sapinda*, it is said that the recommended period of impurity for *brahmana*s is ten days, for both birth and death.[1629] At the time, it is not recommended that *nitya*, and especially *kamya*, rites be performed. Nor should one study, not even in the mind. One should think of *dvija*s from the area who can offer oblations into the fire in the sacrificial pavilion. They should be pure and devoid of anger. Or he can use dry food and fruits to offer oblations into the fire. At the time of impurity, no one should touch them, or have food with them. The learned say that they can be touched on the fourth or fifth day. In cases of child-birth, there is no taint if *sapinda*s touch each other. However, men should avoid touching the infant and the mother who has given birth. If the father knows the *Veda*s and teaches the *Veda*s, he can touch all of them after having a bath. However, the mother is impure for ten days. If a person lacks qualities or completely lacks qualities, the

---

[1629] A *sapinda* is a relative who can offer a *pinda*, related either on the father's side or the mother's side. In some texts, *sapinda* extends for seven generations. In other texts, it is seven generations on the father's side and five generations on the mother's side. In others, it stops with the fourth generation. Lists are given of *sapinda*s. *Sapinda*s cannot marry.

period of impurity is said to be ten days. If a person possesses one, two or three qualities, he respectively becomes pure in four, two or one day.[1630] After four days, one can properly study and offer oblations. Prajapati Manu has said that he can be touched on the fourth day. For the following, impurity only ends with death—a person devoid of rites, a fool, a person suffering from a grave disease and a person who acts as he wills. For *brahmana*s, the period of impurity is for three nights or ten nights. If the person who has died is less than one year old, the impurity is for three nights. Otherwise, it is for ten nights. When the person who has died is less than two years old, for the mother and father, the period of impurity is ten nights. If the person who has died is extremely devoid of qualities, for others, the period of purification is three nights. If the child who has died has not yet cut the teeth, the parents are impure for one day. If the parents are devoid of qualities and the child who has died has cut the teeth, the impurity is for three nights. If the child has not cut the teeth, or if the tonsure ceremony has not been performed, for *sapinda*s, the period of impurity is one night. If the *upanayana* ceremony has not been performed, it is for three nights. If the child dies immediately after being born, the father and the mother who has given birth should not be touched. For uterine brothers and sisters, *sapinda*s must observe the rules of impurity. If the uterine brother or sister is devoid of qualities, the period of impurity is eleven days. After cutting of the teeth, if the *sapinda*s are devoid of qualities, the period of impurity is

---

[1630]It is not clear what these qualities refer to. In several parts of this chapter, the meanings are not clear and there are texts within brackets, which we have also translated.

one night. If the tonsure ceremony has been performed, it is three nights. O excellent ones! If the child dies before cutting of the teeth, if the *sapinda*s are extremely devoid of qualities, the period of impurity is one night. If there is abortion or miscarriage, it is instructed that *sapinda*s must observe *vrata*s. For those with qualities, the unfavourable period is more than that. If the miscarriage occurs before six months, for women, the period of impurity is said to be as many days as the number of months that have passed. If the miscarriage occurs after that, for women, the period of impurity is twelve nights. If there is abortion or miscarriage, *sapinda*s are instantly purified. If there is miscarriage and the *sapinda* is extremely devoid of qualities, the period of impurity is a day and a night. A kinsman can do as he wishes. But the determination is that it should be three nights. If there is an impurity due to another birth when there is impurity due to a preceding birth, or if there is impurity due to another death when there is impurity due to a preceding death, purification happens after the remaining period of purification is over. However, if less than a day is left, it is three nights. When birth and death happen to coincide, purity occurs when the impurity due to death is over. However, if the first impurity is due to birth, purification happens when the first period of impurity is over. In other cases, the impurity can last for five nights. If the person happens to be in some other country and happens to hear of the birth or death, his duration of impurity lasts for the remaining period of impurity. If the impurity due to birth is over, it is said that *sapinda*s must observe it for three nights. Alternatively, if the death occurs beyond one year of age, a bath is sufficient. In every situation, if a person knows the meanings of the *Veda*s and teaches the *Veda*s, if he maintains the sacrificial fire or if his subsistence has made him emaciated, he is always rendered instantly pure. If a woman has not been through the sacrament of being bestowed on someone else, *sapinda*s are impure for three nights. However, if she has been married, it is only the husband who is impure. It is also said that if maidens die, the period of impurity is for one day. If the girl who has died is less than two years old, it is said that purification is instantaneous. When the teeth have not been cut, the uterine brother or sister become instantly pure. If the tonsure ceremony has not been performed, the impurity is for one night. Until marriage, the impurity is for three nights. After being bestowed, it is for ten nights. On the death of a maternal grandfather, the impurity is for three nights. In the case of birth, the impurity is of the same duration. For relatives through marriage, for a *guru* and for a fellow *brahmachari*, it is two days and a night. When a king dies during the day, for everyone in the kingdom, the impurity is till the next sunrise. If he dies during the night, it is until the stars appear next night. For all daughters who die within the house, the father is impure for three days. If a wife who has previously been married dies, or if an adopted son dies, the impurity is for three nights. If the *acharya*'s wife dies, regardless of her *varna*, or if the preceptor's son dies, the impurity is said to be for a day and a night.[1631] If an *upadhyaya* or a learned *brahmana* from the same village dies, it is for one day. If a person who is not a *sapinda* dies in one's house, it is for three nights. If the father-in-law or the mother-in-law dies, it is for one day or one night. If the father-in-law or

---

[1631] An *acharya* is a preceptor, but is inferior to a *guru*. An *upadhyaya* is a teacher, but is inferior to an *acharya*.

the mother-in-law dies, the impurity is for three nights.[1632]
If someone from the same *gotra* dies, the instruction is
that purification is immediate. A *brahmana* is purified in
ten days, a king in twelve days and a *vaishya* in fifteen
days. A *shudra* is purified in a month. If a *brahmana* has
kshatriya, *vaishya* or *shudra* sons and relatives and if that
person dies, the period of impurity for that *brahmana* is
said to be ten days. There is no doubt that a *kshatriya* or
a *vaishya* should perform the rite of purification for a
person of inferior *varna* who is related by marriage. It is
said that everyone must observe the rite of purification
for a superior *varna*.[1633] For those of the same *varna*, the
period of purification is as indicated for that respective
varna. The period of purification for a *vaishya*, *kshatriya*
and *brahmana*, when a *shudra* relative dies, is respectively
six nights, three nights and one night. O bulls among
*dvija*s! When a *vaishya* relative dies, the impurity for a
shudra, a *kshatriya* and a *brahmana* is respectively half a
month, six nights and three nights. O bulls among *dvija*s!
If a *brahmana* relative dies, the period of impurity for a
vaishya or a *shudra* is respectively six nights and ten days.
Kamala's lord[1634] has said that if a *brahmana* relative dies,
the impurity for a *shudra*, *vaishya* or *kshatriya* lasts for
ten nights. If a *brahmana* carries the dead body of a *dvija*
who is not *sapinda*, like a relative, and stays and eats with
them,[1635] he is purified in ten nights. If he accepts their
food, he is purified in three nights. If he does not accept

[1632]In contradiction of the preceding sentence. There are several
such inconsistencies, indicating differing instructions in different
texts.

[1633]Presumably for those related by marriage.

[1634]Vishnu.

[1635]The relatives, carries to the cremation ground.

their food, he should not stay in their house. The rules for *sapinda*s and *samanodaka*s of a mother's close relatives are the same.[1636] If the dead body has been touched, the period of purification is ten days. Because of greed overcoming the mind, if a *brahmana* carries a dead body, he is purified in ten days. A similar *kshatriya* is purified in twelve days, a *vaishya* in half a month. A *shudra* is purified in a month. Alternatively, all of them are purified in six nights or three nights. If *brahmana*s and others carry the dead body of an orphan or poor *brahmana*, they are purified through bathing and drinking *ghee*. If, out of affection, a person from an inferior varna touches a superior *varna*, or a person from a superior *varna* touches an inferior *varna*, during a period of impurity, he is purified through the usual means of purification. If a *brahmana* voluntarily follows the dead body of a *brahmana* who has died, he is purified by bathing with his clothes on, touching fire and drinking ghee. If one follows the dead body of a *kshatriya*, the period of purification is one day. For the dead body of a *vaishya*, it is two days. For the dead body of a *shudra*, it is said to be three days. In addition, one hundred *pranayama*s must be done. If the bones[1637] of a *shudra* have not been collected and if a *brahmana* weeps, along with the dead person's relatives, the period of impurity is three nights. Alternatively, the period of purification is said to be one day. Similarly, if the bones of a *kshatriya* or *vaishya* have

---

[1636] *Samanodaka* is similar to *sapinda*, but is different. A *sapinda* is entitled to offer *pinda*s, a *samanodaka* can only offer libations of water. Usually, *samanodaka* goes up to the fourteenth generation. But sometimes, *sapinda*s are excluded and only the subsequent seven generations included in the definition.

[1637] After cremation, *asthi*.

not been collected, the period is one day, or till the next sunrise.[1638] For a *brahmana*, a bath suffices. If a *brahmana* weeps when the bones of a *brahmana* have not been collected, he is purified when he bathes with his clothes on. There is no doubt about this. If a person eats and sleeps with relatives who have gone to the cremation ground, even if he is not one, he is purified in ten days. When he voluntarily eats with them even once, once the period of impurity is over, he is purified through taking a bath. If a man suffers from famine and has food with them, his impurity lasts for as many days as he has eaten. After that, he must undertake *prayashchitta*.'

'For *dvija*s who observe *agnihotra* rites, the period of impurity starts from the moment of cremation. When a *sapinda* has died, it starts from the moment of death. It is similar for impurity due to birth. The *sapinda* relationship ends with the seventh generation. If names and birth are not known, there is no *samanodaka* relationship. It is known that three generations feed on *lepa*, the father, the grandfather and the great grandfather. *Sapinda* is up to the seventh generation. If women have not been bestowed in marriage, the *sapinda* relationship is up to the seventh generation. The divinity, the grandfather, has said that their *sapinda* relationship is that of their husbands. Among those born from the same biological father, but born in different *varna*s, the *sapinda* relationship is up to the third generation. For the following, purity is said to be instantaneous—artisans, craftsmen, physicians, male servants, female servants, donors, those who follow *niyama*s, those who know the *brahman*, *brahmachari*s, those who perform sacrifices and those who observe

---

[1638]If it is night, till the stars appear next night.

*vrata*s. Purity is also said to be instantaneous for a king who has been consecrated, for a person who distributes free food, at a sacrifice, at the time of a marriage and when there is divine intervention in the form of a famine or other calamity. Purity is also said to be instantaneous for those who die in petty warfare,[1639] death from snakebite and death of one's own kin. Instantaneous purification is also indicated if a person dies from fire or a violent storm, if a person dies while following the path of heroes, if a person dies for cows and *brahmana*s and for a *sannyasi*. The virtuous say there is no impurity for those who are lifelong *brahmachari*s, those in *vanaprastha*, mendicants and *brahmachari*s. Nor when a fallen person dies. For a fallen person, there is no cremation, no funeral rite, no collection of *asthi*, no shedding of tears, no *pinda* and no *shraddha* and other rites. If a person kills himself through fire or poison, no period of impurity is stipulated for him. There is no cremation and no offering of water. However, if a person involuntarily dies through fire or poison, impurity is recommended for him and libations of water must also be offered. When a son is born, if one wishes, one can accept the following as gifts—gold, grain, cows, garments, sesamum, molasses mixed with *ghee*, fruits, flowers, vegetables, salt, wood, buttermilk, curds, *ghee*, oil, medicines and milk. If a person is impure, dry food can always be accepted from his house. If a person duly maintains the three fires, he must be cremated with three fires. A person who does not maintain three fires will be cremated with the *garhapatya* fire. Inferior people will be cremated with ordinary fires.'

[1639] *Dimbahava*, a fight without use of weapons.

'If the dead body is not available, an image should
be made out of *palasha*. Faithfully, following the rules,
*sapinda*s will perform the cremation. Mentioning the name
and the *gotra*, the image will silently be sprinkled with
water. Controlling themselves, all the relatives will perform
a *shraddha* for ten days. Following the rules, every morning
and evening, *pinda* must be offered to the dead person at
the door of the house. *Dvija*s will be fed on the fourth
day. On the second day, along with relatives, the shaving
rite will be performed. On the fourth day, all the relatives
will collect the *asthi*.[1640] Earlier, devoutly, even numbers of
pure *brahmana*s must be engaged. O *dvija*s! Even numbers
of *brahmana*s must be fed on the fifth, ninth and eleventh
day. This is known as *nava-shraddha*. Thinking of the dead
person, this rite must be performed on the ninth, eleventh
or twelfth day. One *pavitra*, one *arghya* and one vessel for
*pinda*s must be used. On the day of death, this must be
done every month, for a year. When a year is complete,
*pinda*s must be offered, as was stated earlier. O excellent
*dvija*s! Four vessels mut be prepared for the dead person
and others.[1641] On behalf of the dead person, water will be
sprinkled in the vessels for the ancestors. After joining the
*pinda*s, the two *shloka*s "*ye samana*"[1642] are recited. It is
recommended that before performing the *shraddha* with
*pinda*s, the *deva*s should be worshipped. Having invoked
the ancestors there, the dead person must be indicated. If
*pinda*s have been offered, no separate rites are needed for
the deceased. If a person separates the *pinda*s, he is born as

---

[1640]In this case, there are no bones. So this is a symbolic
collection of the ashes.
[1641]The dead person and three preceding generations.
[1642]*Ye samanah samanasah*, *Vajasaneyi Samhita* 19.45-46.
'The ancestors who are equal' and so on.

a person who kills his father. When a father dies, the son must offer *pinda*s for a year. Following the *dharma* for the dead, food and pots full of water must be offered. Following the rules, a *parvana shraddha* must be performed every year. These are the eternal rules. *Pinda*s to the father and mother should be offered by sons. In the absence of a son, the wife can perform it. In the absence of a wife, the uterine brother or sister can perform it. The living must follow these rules and perform *shraddha*. Controlled and faithful, donations and every other rite must be observed. I have thus properly told you the rites and rules for householders. Wives must serve their husbands. In this world, it is said that there is no other *dharma* for them. They must always follow their own *dharma*, with their minds dedicated to Ishvara. Those who speak about the *Veda*s have said that this is the way they attain the supreme destination.'

Chapter 77(2)(24) (*Agnihotra* and other rites)

Vyasa said, 'In the morning and in the evening, following the rules, the *agnihotra* oblations must be offered. This must be done on the new moon day that follows a new harvest. When the season is over, following the rules, a *dvija* must perform sacrifices. When the *ayana* is over, he must perform an animal sacrifice. When the year is over, he should perform fire-sacrifices. If a *dvija* maintains the fire and desires to live for a long time, he should not have cooked food or meat without performing a sacrifice after a new harvest and without sacrificing an animal. If a person desires to eat fresh crops and meat but does not perform sacrifices with fresh crops or offer oblations of animals into the fire, it is as if he wants to eat his own *prana*. On *parva* days, he must always offer oblations of peace to Savitar. He must always worship the ancestors on *ashtaka* and *anvashtaka*.[1643] This is supreme *dharma* for the three *varna*s who reside in the *ashrama* of *garhasthya*. Everything else is spoken of as perverse *dharma*. Because of non-belief or laziness, if a person does not wish to maintain the sacrificial fire, if he does not perform sacrifices, he goes to many hells. They are Tamisra, Andhatamisra, Maharourava, Rourava, Kumbhipaka, Vaitarani and Asipatravana. The extremely evil-minded person goes to many other terrible hells. O *brahmana*s! He is born in the families of *antyaja*s and *shudra*s. Therefore, everyone, especially a *brahmana*, must make every effort to maintain the sacrificial fire. Pure in his *atman*, he must offer sacrifices to Parameshvara. In this world, for *dvija*s, there is no *dharma* that is superior to *agnihotra*. Therefore, through *agnihotra*, one should always worship the eternal. If a person maintains the sacrificial fire, but does not wish to perform sacrifices to *deva*s, he is foolish. One should not converse with him. He is a non-believer. What more needs to be said? If a person possesses enough to maintain his servants for three years and more, he deserves to drink *soma*. Among all sacrifices, a *soma* sacrifice is spoken of as the foremost. Through *soma*, the divinity Maheshvara, in Soma's world, is worshipped. In worshipping Mahesha, there is nothing superior to a *soma* sacrifice, with *soma*. Therefore, the supreme should be worshipped with *soma*. For *brahmana*s, the grandfather has earmarked *pashu*s. There are two kinds of *dharma* that directly ensure liberation— based on *shruti* texts and based on *smriti* texts. *Shruti dharma* is based on the three fires.

[1643]Ninth lunar *tithi* in *krishna paksha* in Margashirsha, Magha and Phalguna.

I have spoken about *smriti dharma* earlier. *Shruti dharma* is superior. Therefore, *shruti dharma* should be followed. Since they flow out of the words of the *Veda*s, both kinds of *dharma* are beneficial. In the absence of *shruti dharma* and *smriti dharma*, good conduct is the third kind of *dharma*. Those who have understood the *Veda*s and the accompanying works are spoken of as virtuous *brahmana*s. They always possess the qualities. Their minds are such that they are always revered. The *dharma* that the virtuous speak about is nurtured by others. The *Veda*s are amplified by the Puranas and *dharmashastra*s. One represents *vijnana* about the *brahman*. The other represents *jnana* about *dharma*. Those who have questions about *dharma* say that there is no greater proof than the *dharmashastra*s and Puranas. Those who seek *jnana* about the *brahman* resort to the *Veda*s. There is no other origin for *dharma*. Knowledge about the *brahman* is based on the *Veda*s. Therefore, the learned should have trust in the *dharma* of the Puranas.'

Chapter 78(2)(25) (A *dvija*'s subsistence)

Vyasa said, 'This is everything about the *ashrama* of *garhasthya* and supreme *dharma*. Now hear about the means of subsistence for *dvija*s. It should be known that there are two kinds of householders—those who are *sadhaka*s and those who are not *sadhaka*s.[1644] For *sadhaka*s, the means are said to be teaching, officiating at sacrifices and acceptance of gifts. He can himself, or

---

[1644]That is, they do not strive.

through others, engage in usury, agriculture and trade. In the absence of agriculture, it is trade. In the absence of trade, it is usury. These should be known as the means in times of calamity.[1645] The primary means are those that were mentioned earlier. He should engage in usury, agriculture or trade himself. Usury is a hard and wicked means of subsistence. It is best to avoid it. Some say that instead of directly engaging in agriculture, *dvija*s should adopt the means of livelihood used by *kshatriya*s. Even when there is no calamity, a *dvija* can adopt the means of livelihood of *kshatriya*s. If he does not maintain himself through that, he can adopt agriculture, the means of subsistence for a *vaishya*. However, under no circumstances should a *brahmana* till the land himself. Having obtained his gains through these means, he must worship ancestors, *deva*s and *brahmana*s. If they are satisfied, there is no doubt that all sins are pacified. If he practices agriculture, he should offer one-twentieth of the share to *deva*s and ancestors and one-thirtieth of the share to *brahmana*s. In that event, there are no sins. In the case of trade, double that amount must be given. In the case of usury, the amount given must be three times as much as what is given through agriculture. In that event, there is no doubt that there is no association with sin. A *sadhaka* householder can also subsist through *unchavritti*.[1646] There are also many other means of subsistence, like knowledge and artisanship. There are those who are in the *ashrama* of *garhasthya*, but are described as those who are not *sadhaka*s. The supreme *rishi*s have said that there are two means of subsistence

---

[1645]That is, usury, agriculture and trade.

[1646]Subsisting on left-overs (in the field) after the harvest of grain.

for them—*unchavritti* and others. They subsist through means that are *amrita* or *mrita*. *Mrita* means to beg for alms. *Amrita* means to subsist on whatever is obtained unsolicited. There are four kinds of *dvija* householders[1647]— those who stock sufficient grain for three years; those who stock sufficient grain for six days; those who stock sufficient grain for three days; and those who don't have enough for the next day. Of these, the succeeding ones are superior to the preceding ones. Through his *dharma*, the last one conquers the world. The first of these performs six tasks.[1648] The second performs three and the third performs two. The fourth subsists through studying the *Veda*s and teaching them. If a person subsists through *unchavritti* and performs *agnihotra*, he should only perform sacrifices at the end of a *parva*. A *brahmana* should not earn his living through ordinary means of subsistence. His reason for existence isn't the means of subsistence. He should live a pure and upright life, without deceit. He can beg for alms from the wealthy and use that food to satisfy the ancestors and *deva*s. He should seek from the pure and the controlled and use that to satisfy himself. After earning sufficient objects, if a householder does not follow the rules and satisfy *deva*s and ancestors, he heads downwards and is born as a dog. *Dharma*, *artha*, *kama* and *moksha*—these four are beneficial. For a brahmana, *kama* should not be against *dharma*, not the other way around. *Artha* that is for *dharma* and not for one's own self is true *artha*, not the other kind of *artha*. Therefore, having accumulated *artha*, a *dvija* should donate and offer oblations.'

[1647] Those who aren't *sadhaka*s.
[1648] Studying, teaching, performing sacrifices, officiating at sacrifices, donating and receiving gifts.

Chapter 79(2)(26) (*Danadharma*)

Vyasa said, 'After this, I will describe the excellent *danadharma*.[1649] Earlier, Brahma narrated this to *rishi*s who speak about the *brahman*. Full of faith, *artha* must be donated to a worthy recipient. This is said to be *dana*, and it bestows objects of pleasure and emancipation as fruits. When it is faithfully given to the virtuous, it is special, and I regard it as wonderful. Anything left can belong to anyone. *Dana* is said to be of three types—*nitya*, *naimittika* and *kamya*. The fourth is known as *vimala* and it is the best among all kinds of *dana*. When something is given every day to a *brahmana*, who doesn't give back anything in return, and no fruits are expected, that is *nitya*. If something is given to the learned to pacify sins, that is known as *naimittika dana*, and it is practised by the virtuous. When something is given for offspring, victory, wealth or heaven, the *rishi*s who have thought about *dharma* have described this as *kamya dana*. When something is given to a person who knows about the *brahman*, for the sake of pleasing Ishvara, with the mind immersed in *dharma*, that auspicious *dana* is *vimala*.[1650] According to capacity, one should find a worthy recipient and follow *danadharma*. If he finds such a recipient, he will be able to cross over everything. Anything left after giving the family and dependents, should be donated. Otherwise, no fruits are obtained from *dana*. Donations must faithfully be made to learned and noble *brahmana*s, humble ascetics, those who follow *vrata*s and to the poor. If one faithfully gives land to a *brahmana* who maintains the fire, one proceeds

---

[1649] The *dharma* of gifts and donations.
[1650] Meaning, bright and spotless.

to the supreme destination. Having gone there, one does not grieve. If one gives a person learned in the *Veda*s land with sugar-cane, barley and wheat, the donor is not born again. Even if one gives land that can be encompassed by a cow's hide to a poor *brahmana*, one is freed from all sins. There is no gift that is superior to the donation of land. The donation of cooked food is equal, and the donation of learning is superior. Following the rules, if learning is imparted to a pure *brahmana* who possesses good conduct and is devoted to *dharma*, the donor obtains greatness in Brahma's world. Full of faith, if a person donates cooked food to a *brahmachari* every day, he is freed from all sins and obtains Brahma's abode. A man obtains fruits by giving cooked food to a householder. It must be given as soon as he arrives. Having given, the donor obtains the supreme destination.'

'A person must follow the rules and fast on *pournamasi* in Vaishakha. He must then worship five or seven *brahmana*s who are serene, pure and controlled in their minds. He should particularly use black sesamum and honey. He should worship them with fragrances and make them pronounce benedictions over himself. "Let Dharmaraja be pleased." Whatever sins he may have committed in the course of his life, even if they are in the mind, are instantly destroyed. If a person gives a *brahmana* sesamum, gold, honey and *ghee* on a black antelope skin, he crosses over every kind of hardship. Especially in Vaishakha, a pot full of cooked food and water, meant for Dharmaraja, must be given to *brahmana*s. The donor is then freed from fear. If five or seven *brahmana*s are satisfied with gold, sesamum and pots full of water, the sin of killing a *brahmana* is dispelled. On *dvadashi* in the month of Magha, a *brahmana* must fast. He must wear

white garments and offer oblations of black sesamum to
the fire. Controlling himself well, he must then donate
to brahmanas. A dvija then passes over every sin he has
committed since birth. When it is amavasya, he must offer
something to an ascetic brahmana. This is directed towards
Shankara, the divinity who is the lord of devas. "Let the
eternal Ishvara Mahadeva be pleased, along with Umaa."
Sins committed in the course of seven births are instantly
destroyed. If a person bathes on chaturdashi in krishna
paksha and worships the divinity Pinaki in the form of a
foremost dvija, he is not born again. Especially on ashtami
in krishna paksha, a person must bathe and duly worship
a dvija who is devoted to dharma by washing his feet and
doing other things. "Let Mahadeva be pleased with me."
Saying this, he must hand over his possessions. He is then
freed from all sins and proceeds to the supreme destination.
Devoted dvijas especially worship the three-eyed one
on chaturdashi in krishna paksha, ashtami in krishna
paksha and amavasya. Dvadashi is for Purushottama.
Having fasted on ekadashi, one must worship a foremost
brahmana. He then proceeds to the supreme destination.
Dvadashi of shukla paksha is Vishnu's tithi. Therefore, one
must make every effort to worship the divinity Janardana.
If anything is directed towards Ishana or Vishnu and
offered to a pure brahmana, the gift yields infinite fruits. A
man may wish to worship any deva. If that learned person
worships a brahmana, that becomes a reason for the deva
to be satisfied. Devas are always present in the bodies of
dvijas. A person desiring prosperity must always worship
Purandara. A person desiring to be as radiant as Brahma
and desiring the brahman, should worship Brahma. A
person desiring freedom from disease should worship Ravi.
A person desiring cows should worship Hutashana. A

person desiring success in tasks should worship Vinayaka. A person desiring objects of pleasure should worship the moon. A person desiring strength should worship the wind god. A person desiring liberation from all *samsara* should make every effort to worship Hari. If a person desires *yoga*, *moksha* and *jnana* about Ishvara, he should make efforts to worship Virupaksha Maheshvara. If a person desires *jnana* through great *yoga*, he should worship Maheshvara. Those who worship the lord of *bhuta*s and Keshava obtain objects of pleasure.'

'A person who donates water obtains satisfaction. A person who donates cooked food obtains inexhaustible happiness. A person who donates sesamum obtains desired offspring. A person who donates lamps obtains excellent vision. A person who donates land obtains everything. A person who donates gold obtains a long lifespan. A person who donates a house obtains an excellent residence. A person who donates silver obtains excellent beauty. A person who donates garments obtains Chandra's world. A person who donates horses obtains the world of the Ashvins. A person who donates bulls obtains prosperity and nourishment. A person who donates cows obtains the world of the sun. A person who donates vehicles and beds obtains a wife. A person who grants freedom from fear obtains prosperity. A person who donates grain obtains eternal happiness. A person who donates the *Veda*s obtains equality with Brahma. According to capacity, one should give grain to *brahmana*s, especially those who know the *Veda*s. After death, one will then obtain heaven. If a person donates cows, he is freed from all sins. By donating kindling, a man becomes as radiant as a fire. If a person gives fruits, roots, vegetables and many kinds of foodstuff to *brahmana*s, he himself becomes full of joy. To pacify disease, if a person

gives medicines, oil and food to a sick person, he becomes
happy and free from disease, with a long lifespan. The
path to Asipatravana[1651] is as sharp as a razor's edge,
with terrible torments. A man who donates an umbrella,
crosses over that. Anything desired in the world, anything
loved in the house and anything that possesses qualities
should be given away by a person who desires infinite good
merits. Anything given when the *ayana* changes, at the
time of the equinoxes, when there is an eclipse of the sun
or the moon and at periods like *samkranti*, yields infinite
benefits. Infinite benefits are obtained if donations are made
at *tirtha*s like Prayaga, at sacred temples, along the banks
of rivers and in forests. For beings, there is no *dharma*
that is superior to *danadharma*. Therefore, *dvija*s must
donate to a learned *brahmana*. If a person desires heaven,
a long lifespan, prosperity, the pacification of sins and
liberation, every day, he should donate to *brahmana*s. Out
of delusion, if a person prevents offerings to *brahmana*s,
the fire and gods, he is evil-souled and is born as an inferior
species. After earning objects, if a person does not worship
*brahmana*s and gods, all his possessions should be taken
away and he should be exiled. A *brahmana* who does not
give food at the time of a famine, when creatures are dying,
is condemned. Nothing should be accepted from him, and
nothing should be given to him. The king should mark that
brahmana with his seal and exile him. If a man does not
give to virtuous people, as a means of achieving *dharma*,
he is a greater sinner and is cooked in hell. O excellent
*dvija*s! Donations must be made to learned *brahmana*s
who are intent on studies, those who have conquered their

[1651]The name of a hell where there are forests of trees, with
leaves like swords.

senses and are full of truth and restraint. Even if he has eaten, a learned *dvija* who is devoted to *dharma* must be fed. But a foolish person devoid of conduct must not be fed, even if he has fasted for ten nights. Overlooking a learned *brahmana* in the neighbourhood, if a person gives to someone else, as a consequence of that deed, he becomes a sinner and is burnt for seven generations. However, if the external *brahmana* is superior in conduct and learning, every effort must be made to donate to him, overlooking the one in the vicinity. If a person who is honoured accepts what is given to him and honours the donor in return, both of them go to heaven. If this is violated, both of them go to hell. But a person who knows about *dharma* must not give to those who are non-believers, sceptics, heretics and those who don't know the *Veda*s. If a person who is not learned accepts *apupa*s, gold, villages, land and sesamum, like wood, he is reduced to ashes. An excellent *dvija* should wish to receive wealth from praiseworthy *dvija*s, even from those who are born as *dvija*s, but never from *shudra*s. Even when the means of subsistence are constrained, one should not seek to expand wealth. If a person is addicted to greed about wealth, he diminishes his status of being a *brahmana*. Even if one studies all the *Veda*s and even if one performs all the sacrifices, one does not obtain the destination obtained when the means of subsistence are constrained.[1652] One should not be addicted to receiving. One should only accept as much wealth as is required for the journey. If a *brahmana* accepts more wealth than is required for subsistence, he heads downwards. A person who constantly begs is not worthy of heaven. He agitates

[1652]Presumably implying that *artha* should not be the primary pursuit.

beings and is like a thief. If a person desires to honour *guru*s, servants, *deva*s and *atithi*s, he can accept from everywhere. But this should never be for his own satisfaction. In this way, a householder's *atman* should be such that he worships *deva*s and *atithi*s. Controlled in his *atman*, he exists and proceeds to the supreme destination. Handing over everything to his son, a person who knows the truth should leave for the forest. He should roam around alone, indifferent and controlled. O excellent *dvija*s! I have thus described *dharma* for those who are in *garhasthya*. Knowing this, you should always base yourselves on this and make *dvija*s follow it. Thus, following the *dharma* of a householder, one should worship the primordial divinity, the one and only Isha. In this way, he transcends Prakriti and birth as every kind of creature. He proceeds to the supreme, from where, there is no rebirth.'

Chapter 80(2)(27) (*Dharma* of *vanaprastha*)

V yasa said, 'In this way, the second part of the lifespan must be spent following the *dharma* of a householder. After this, with his wife and with the sacrificial fire, he should proceed to the *ashrama* of *vanaprastha*. Or he can entrust his wife with his sons and proceed to the forest. By the time he sees the offspring of his children, his body will be decayed. The praised time for departure is *uttarayana*, in the forenoon of *shukla paksha*. Having gone to the forest, he should control himself, follow the *niyama*s and perform austerities. He should always collect pure food, in the form of fruits and roots. He should be restrained in his diet and worship ancestors and *deva*s. He should always honour *atithi*s. He should bathe and worship the gods. Controlling himself, he should only gather eight mouthfuls from homes. His hair should always be matted. He should not clip his nails or cut his body hair. He must always study. Otherwise, he should be restrained in speech. He should offer oblations into the *agnihotra* fire and perform the five sacrifices. For sages, different types of forest fare, roots and fruits, is appropriate. He should always wear garments made of bark. He should be pure and bathe thrice a day. He must be compassionate towards all beings and refrain from accepting gifts. A *dvija* must always perform sacrifices on the days of the new moon and the full moon, at the time of the appropriate *nakshatra*s and *agrayana* and *chaturmasya*.[1653] He should duly observe the rites of *uttarayana* and *dakshinayana*. In spring and autumn, himself collecting crops that are fit to be offered in sacrifices, he must prepare two types of *purodasha* and *charu*.[1654] Using wild fare fit to be offered in sacrifices, he must offer oblations to *deva*s. He will then eat the remainder, using salt he has himself prepared. He should avoid honey, meat, coverings strewn on the ground, mushrooms, *shishuka*[1655] and the fruit of *shleshmataka*. He should never eat anything that is the result of ploughing or is thus left over. Even when he is suffering, he should not use flowers and fruits that grow in villages. In Shravana, he should follow the rules and tend to the fire. He should not show hatred towards any creature. He should be devoid of fear and the opposite pair of sentiments. He should not eat

[1653] *Agrayana* is a sacrifice when a fresh crop is offered to gods and ancestors. *Chaturmasya* is a sacrifice performed every four months, beginning in Kartika, Phalguna and Ashadha.
[1654] *Purodasha* is a cake made from meal, *charu* is a mix of rice and barley, cooked in *ghee*.
[1655] Drumstick.

at night. At night, he should immerse himself in *dhyana*.
He must conquer his senses and conquer his rage. He must
think about the true meaning of *jnana*. He must always
be a *brahmachari* and must never approach his wife.
Having gone to the forest, if he falls prey to desire and
has intercourse with his wife, his vow is destroyed. Such a
dvija must undertake *prayashchitta*. If there is a resultant
conception, no *dvija* can touch that child. He will have no
right to the *Veda*s. Nor will anyone who takes birth

'He must sleep on the ground. He must always be intent
on performing *japa* with Savitri. He should be the refuge of
all beings and must always share. He should avoid slander,
false accusations, sleep and laziness. He should maintain
one single fire and have no abode. His refuge is the ground,
sprinkled with water. He should roam around with deer
and live with them. He should control himself and lie
down on rocks and gravel. He should instantly wash
off everything,[1656] or accumulate for one month. He can
accumulate for six months, or even for a year. But in the
month of Ashvayuja,[1657] he should throw away everything
he has collected earlier—old garments, vegetables, roots
and fruits. He should be a *dantaulukhalika*, or follow the
conduct of a pigeon.[1658] He should be an *ashmakutta* or
kalapakkabhuga. According to capacity, he should collect
food during the day and eat at night. He can miss three
meals and eat a fourth time. Or he can miss seven meals and
eat at the eighth time. During *shukla paksha* and *krishna*

[1656] Not collect and hoard.

[1657] Ashvina.

[1658] A *dantaulukhalika* uses his teeth like a mortar to grind
grain. A pigeon picks up grain from the ground. An *ashmakutta*
uses stones to grind grain. A *kalapakkabhuga* eats what has ripened
over time.

paksha, he should follow the rules of *chandrayana*. Once in every *paksha*, he should eat gruel made of barley. He should always maintain himself only on leaves, roots and fruits that have fallen down on their own. He should thus behave like a *vaikhanasa*. During the day, he should move around on the ground or stand on one foot. He should never lose his fortitude and give up either *asana*. During summer, he must expose himself to the five fires. During the monsoon, he must expose himself to showering clouds. During Hemanta, he must wear wet clothes. Thus, he must gradually increase the intensity of austerities. He must bathe thrice a day and satisfy the ancestors and *deva*s. He must stand on one foot and drink air. He must expose himself to the five fires and drink smoke, heat or *soma*. In *shukla paksha*, he should drink milk. In *krishna paksha*, he should eat cow dung. He should subsist on dry leaves and always follow a rite of hardship.[1659] He must always practice *yoga* and always perform *dhyana* on Rudra. He should always study *Atharvashirsha* and be intent on practising *Vedanta*. He must constantly practice *yama* and be attentive in practising *niyama*. His upper garment will be made out of black antelope skin. He will wear a white sacred thread. Alternatively, invoking the fire on his own *atman*, he will be intent on *dhyana*. He will not maintain the sacrificial fire and be without an abode. He will be a sage who is intent on *moksha*. He will be an ascetic who gathers alms from travelling *brahmana*s. He can also accept them from householders or other *dvija*s who reside in the forest. Residing in the forest, he should eat eight mouthfuls he gathers from villages. He should accept these

---

[1659]There were different such rites of hardship, known as *kriccha*. Extreme rites of hardship are *ati-kriccha*.

in the cup of his hands or in a potsherd. For his own *siddhi*, he must perform *japa* with various Upanishads and specific knowledge, Savitri and chapters on Rudra. He should leave on the great journey, or live there, fasting until death. Otherwise, offering himself up to the *brahman*, he can enter the fire. Those who resort properly to this auspicious *ashrama*, destroy everything inauspicious that has been accumulated. They enter Ishvara's abode. After departure, they remain established in that destination.'

Chapter 81(2)(28) (*Dharma* of *yatis*)

Vyasa said, 'Having spent the third part of the lifespan in the *ashrama* of *vanaprastha*, in the fourth part of the lifespan, one must duly progress to *sannyasa*. Invoking the fire on his own *atman*, a *dvija* becomes a mendicant. He is intent on practising *yoga*. He is tranquil, devoted to knowledge about the *brahman*. When the mind develops a lack of thirst towards all material objects, then one should desire to opt for *sannyasa*. Otherwise, there will be a calamity. He should first perform the sacrifices of Prajapatya or Agneya. He becomes controlled and desires are wiped off. He can then resort to the *ashrama* of the *brahman*. Some are *jnana-sannyasis*. Others are *Veda-sannyasis*. Still others are *karma-sannyasis*. Many different types are described. A *jnana-sannyasi* is said to be a person who has freed himself from all association. He is devoid of the opposite pair of sentiments and devoid of fear. He is established in his own *atman*. A person who studies the *Veda*s every day is said to be a *Veda-sannyasi*. He is without the opposite pair of sentiments and without possessions. He has conquered his senses and wishes for liberation. A *dvija* may absorb the fires into his *atman*, intent on offering himself up to the *brahman*. Devoted to the great sacrifice, he should be known as a *karma-sannyasi*. Among the three, the one who possesses *jnana* is held to be superior. He does not have any tasks or signs. He is learned. He is without a sense of ownership and has no fear. He is tranquil and without the opposite pair of sentiments. He has no possessions. His tattered garments are a loincloth. Or he is naked. He is devoted to *dhyana*. He is a *brahmachari*. Collecting his food from villages, he eats little. He is extremely intent on *adhyatma*. He is indifferent. He does not eat meat. He roams around in this world, searching for happiness, with only his *atman* as an aide. He is not delighted with death, nor is he delighted with remaining alive. Like a servant waiting for orders, he waits for the time. There is nothing for him to study, speak or hear. Knowing this, the supreme *yogi* is fit to be merged with the *brahman*. The learned one wears a single garment. Or he covers himself with a loincloth. He shaves his head or has a tuft of hair. He is a *tridandi*.[1660] He has no possessions. He wears ochre garments. He is always devoted to *dhyana* and *yoga*. He resides on the extremities of a village, under a tree, or in a temple. Friend and enemy are equal to him and so are honour and dishonour. He sustains himself through begging. Some eat only one meal a day. Out of delusion, if a *yati* eats more than one meal a day, the *dharmashastra*s do not speak of any salvation for him. He is free of attachment and hatred. Clay, stone and gold are the same to him. He refrains from causing violence to any being. He is silent and does not desire anything. Before stepping forward, he purifies the spot with his

---

[1660] His staff consists of three staffs bound together.

eyes.[1661] He drinks water purified and strained with a piece
of cloth. His words are purified by the sacred texts. His
mind is purified. Other than during the rains, a mendicant
does not live in the same place for more than a day. He is
always devoted to purifying himself through bathing. He
is pure and holds a *kamandalu* in his hand. He is always
devoted to *brahmacharya*. He is devoted to dwelling in the
forest. He is devoted to sacred texts on *moksha*. He is a
brahmachari who has conquered his senses. He is free of
insolence and *ahamkara*. He does not indulge in criticism
and calumny. Possessing the quality of *jnana* about the
atman, such a *yati* achieves *moksha*. He follows the rules
about bathing and *achamana*. Pure, in temples and in
other places, he always practices the eternal *Veda*s, known
as Pranava. He wears the sacred thread and is tranquil
in his *atman*. He is controlled and holds *kusha* grass in
his hand. He wears a washed ochre garment. His hair is
covered with *bhasma*. He performs *japa* on *brahman*, the
adhiyajna, the *adhidaiva*, *adhyatma* or the one who is
in all *Vedanta*.[1662] The *yati brahmachari*, who is a sage,
can also live with his sons. If he constantly studies the
*Veda*s, he reaches the supreme destination. In particular,
he should follow *vrata*s like non-violence, truth, avoidance
of theft, *brahmacharya*, supreme austerities, forgiveness,
compassion and contentment. He must be devoted to the
jnana of *Vedanta*. He must control himself and perform
the five sacrifices. He should devote himself to *jnana* and
dhyana, not to seeking alms alone. At the indicated times,

[1661] To ensure he doesn't step on any living creatures.

[1662] Here, *adhiyajna* means the supreme divinity who presides
over the sacrifice and *adhidaiva* means the divinity present in
material objects.

he must control himself and always offer oblations, chant *mantra*s and perform *japa*. Every day, he must study and at the time of *sandhya*, perform *japa* with Savitri. In solitude, he must perform *dhyana* on the divinity, Parameshvara. In solitude, he must always cast aside desire, anger and possessions. He will wear a single piece of cloth, or two garments. He will wear a tuft of hair and the sacred thread. He will hold a *kamandalu* in his hand. Such a learned *tridandi* achieves the supreme.'

Chapter 82(2)(29) (*Dharma* of *yati*s continued)

Vyasa said, 'In this way, *yati*s must always control their *atman*s and be established in their own *ashrama*. As has been said, such a person must subsist on the basis of alms, or fruits and roots. He must seek alms only once and not practice it extensively. A *yati* who is attached to alms becomes attached to material objects. He should roam around, seeking alms only in seven houses. If nothing is obtained, he can roam around again. He must wash the vessel and eat from it. Once he has eaten, it must again be washed with water. Alternatively, he can always use one vessel for alms and another for eating. After eating, the vessel must be cleaned. This is for the journey of life, not for any greed. A *yati* must always go and seek alms in a house where there is no smoke, where the mortar has been kept away, where the coal is not burning, where people have eaten and where the pots have been covered up. With his face facing downwards, he must only remain for as long as it takes to milk a cow. "Please give me alms." Saying this once, he should remain silent. When he eats, he must be pure, maintaining silence. In the proper way, he must

wash his hands and feet and perform *achamana*. Showing
the food to the sun, he must be pure and eat while facing
the east. Five mouthfuls are eaten as oblations to *prana*.
Controlling himself, he should only eat eight mouthfuls.
Having performed *achamana*, he should meditate on
Brahma Parameshvara. Prajapati Manu has said that he
can use four kinds of vessels—made out of gourd, a wooden
vessel, made out of clay or made out of bamboo. He must
always think of Ishvara, in the first half of the night, in the
second half of the night and at midnight. In particular, at
the time of the *sandhya*s, he must tend to the fire.'

'In the abode in the lotus of his heart, he must
establish the one known as the universe, the origin of
the universe. His *atman* is in all beings. He is established
beyond darkness. He is the support for all beings. He is
imperishable bliss and radiance. He is beyond Pradhana
and Purusha. He is the void in the firmament. He is Shiva.
He is inside every kind of sentiment. He is Ishvara, the
form of the *brahman*. He must perform *dhyana* on the
abode of qualities like bliss, without a beginning, a middle
and an end. He is the great Purusha. He is the *brahman*. He
is Brahma, the truth without decay. He resembles the rising
sun. He is Mahesha, with the universe as his form. Using
OUMKARA, he must establish the *paramatman* in his own
atman. The divinity Ishana is in the sky. He must meditate
on him, in the middle of the sky. He is the cause behind
every kind of existence. He is bliss, the only refuge. He is
the sparkling ancient Purusha. Performing *dhyana* on him,
he will be freed from all bondage. He is truly in the cavity
of the heart. He is the store of delusion in the universe. He
must think of the supreme space, the single cause behind
all beings. For all beings, he is live. The world is dissolved
into him. He is the subtle bliss of the *brahman*. Those who

desire liberation, see him. The *brahman* is hidden in the middle, the only attribute of *jnana*. Ishana is infinite and true. Controlling himself, he must be seated and think of him. What has been spoken about is the most secret of all kinds of *jnana* for *jati*s. It was related by Mahesha and a person who follows this, experiences Ishvara's *yoga*. Therefore, devoted to knowledge about the *atman,* one must always be engaged in *dhyana*. If one seeks refuge in *jnana* about the *brahman*, one is freed from all bondage. He realizes that his own *atman* is different from everything else. He meditates on the imperishable bliss that is *jnana* and meditates again on the supreme. All beings originate from him. Having gone there, one is not born in this world again. He is the divinity Ishvara, the supreme and the primordial, who presides over everything. The journey to him is described as eternal and auspicious. The one who is described as supreme is the divinity Maheshvara.'

'There are *vrata*s and subsidiary *vrata*s for mendicants. If any one of these is violated, *prayashchitta* is recommended. If he approaches a woman out of desire, he must control his mind and undertake hardships. He must perform *pranayama*. Purifying himself, he must torment himself. Controlling his mind, he must follow the rules of hardship. Returning to the *ashrama* again, the mendicant must follow it attentively. Learned ones say that a falsehood uttered in jest does not cause any harm. Nevertheless, one should not indulge in it, as it is terrible. If this is done, a *yati* who desires *dharma* and imperishable benefit should fast for one night and perform one hundred *pranayama*s. Even if one faces difficulties, one should not steal from others. The *smriti* texts say that there is no *adharma* worse than theft. This is said to be another form of violence and destroys *jnana* about the *atman*. What is known as wealth is another person's *prana*, wandering around outside. If a person takes away someone's wealth, it is like stealing that person's *prana*. If an extremely evil-souled person does this, he destroys his *vrata*, following contrary conduct. When he suffers from repentance, he should follow the *vrata* of *chandrayana*. The rules have been indicated in the sacred texts. The *shruti* texts say that this must be followed for a year. When he is filled with repentance again, the mendicant must attentively follow this. If the mendicant happens to suddenly indulge in violence, he must undertake rites of hardship and great hardship, such as *chandrayana*. On seeing a woman, out of his weakness, if a *yati* discharges his semen, he must perform sixteen *pranayama*s. If there is emission of semen during the day, for three nights, he must perform one hundred *pranayama*s. If he has liquor or meat in private, or if he directly has salt at the time of the first *shraddha* after death, it said that he is purified through a Prajapatya rite. If one is constantly engaged in *dhyana*, all sins are destroyed.'

'Knowing Maheshvara, one should meditate on the supreme. He is the supreme *brahman*, the resplendence that is established as the imperishable, without decay. The supreme *brahman* is inside everything and is known as Maheshvara. This is the divinity Mahadeva, absolute, supreme and auspicious. He is imperishable and non-dual. He is the supreme who is inside the sun. He is the greatest divinity, established in Svadha, the fire and *jnana*. Mahadeva is said to be established in the truth known as *yoga* of the *atman*. Those who see no divinity superior to Mahadeva and those who see his *atman* in their own *atman*s, proceed to the supreme destination. People who think their own *atman*s are distinct from Parameshvara, do not perceive the divinity. Their efforts are in vain. The supreme *brahman* is one. The *brahman* should be known as the imperishable truth. This is the divinity Mahadeva. If one knows this, one is not constrained. Controlled in his mind, if a *yati* constantly worships him, he is devoted to *jnana yoga*. He is tranquil and devoted to Mahadeva. O *brahmana*s! I have told you about the auspicious *ashrama* of *yati*s. Earlier, the lord, the grandfather, spoke about this to the sages. This excellent *jnana*, about the auspicious *dharma* of *yati*s, was narrated by Svayambhu. It should not be imparted to anyone other than sons, *shishya*s and *yogi*s. The rules and *niyama*s for *yati*s have been described. This satisfies Pashupati, the single and absolute cause. With attentive minds, if people constantly practice this, they are not born again in this world. Nor do they face destruction.'

Chapter 83(2)(30) (Rules of *prayashchitta*)

Vyasa said, 'After this, I will speak about the auspicious rules of *prayashchitta*. This is for the welfare of all *brahmana*s and for the destruction of taints. If a man does not perform ordained *karma* and does what is reprimanded, he commits sin and purification requires *prayashchitta*. No *brahmana* should refrain from undertaking *prayashchitta*. He should do what serene and learned *brahmana*s ask him to do. A serene and excellent *dvija*, who desires *dharma*, knows the meaning of the *Veda*s and maintains the fire, will act according to supreme *dharma*, even if he is the only one to do so. If three *brahmana*s who are accomplished in the meanings of the *Veda*s speak about *dharma* and *kama*, even if they do not maintain the sacrificial fire, that should be known as a means for achieving *dharma*. If seven *dvija*s know many *dharmashastra* texts and are

skilled in deliberations, they are said to have studied the
*Veda*s. If twenty-one famous *dvija*s know the truth about
critical reflections and are accomplished in *Vedanta*, they
can speak about *prayashchitta*. A person who kills a
brahmana, a drunkard, a thief and a person who violates
his *guru*'s bed, commits a grave sin. If a person resides with
and associates with such a person, he too falls down. If
he constantly shares their vehicles, beds or seats, he also
falls down. A *dvija* who officiates at their sacrifices, has
a matrimonial alliance, teaches them or eats with them,
instantly falls down. Out of delusion or ignorance, if a
dvija teaches them or studies with them, within a year, he
falls down. A person who kills a *brahmana* will construct
a cottage and live in the forest for twelve years. To purify
himself, he will beg for alms, holding the skull of a dead
body as a mark. He must avoid residing with *brahmana*s
and all temples to *deva*s. Remembering that *brahmana*,
he must criticize himself. Without considering their
worthiness, every day, he must softly enter seven homes,
when there is smoke, when the coal is not burning and when
the inhabitants have eaten. Proclaiming his sin to men, he
must beg for alms only once. Alternatively, he can sustain
himself on wild roots and fruits. He must hold a skull
and *khatvanga*[1663] in his hand and observe *brahmacharya*.
When twelve years are complete, the sin of killing a
brahmana will go away. If the sin has been committed
involuntarily, this is the auspicious means of *prayashchitta*.
If it has been committed voluntarily, it should be known
that purification is with death. There is no other means. He
can fast to death or fall down from a peak. He can himself
enter the blazing fire, or water. He can properly give up his

---

[1663] Ascetic's staff, with a skull affixed on top.

life for the sake or a *brahmana* or a cow. If death comes in this way, the sin of killing a *brahmana* is dispelled. If he cures a *brahmana* who has been ill for a very long time, or if he gives food to an extremely learned person, the sin of killing a *brahmana* goes away. The *avabhritha* bath[1664] after a horse sacrifice also purifies a *dvija*. At the confluence of Sarasvati and Varuna, famous in the three worlds, everything he possesses must be given away to a *brahmana* learned in the *Veda*s. After bathing there thrice a day and fasting for three nights, a *dvija* is purified. He should go to the sacred Rameshvara and bathe in the great ocean. Observing *brahmacharya*, he will be freed when he sees Rudra. There is the *tirtha* named Kapalamochana, which belongs to the divinity who wields the trident. If one bathes there and worships the ancestors and the *deva*s, the sin of killing a *brahmana* is destroyed. Earlier, the infinitely energetic Bhairava, the divinity who is the lord of *deva*s, deposited Brahma Parameshthi's skull there. One should worship Mahadeva, in the form of Bhairava, there. When one bathes and satisfies the ancestors, one is freed from the sin of killing a *brahmana*.'

Chapter 84(2)(31) (Kapalamochana *tirtha*)

The *rishi*s asked, 'Earlier, how did the divinity Rudra, the infinitely energetic Shankara, separate Brahma's skull from his body and set it down on the ground?'

Suta replied, 'O *rishi*s! Listen to this sacred account. It destroys all sins. This is about the greatness of the

---

[1664] Ceremonial bath at the end of a sacrifice.

intelligent Mahadeva, the lord of *deva*s. Earlier, on the
summit of Meru, the *maharshi*s prostrated themselves
and asked the divinity, the grandfather. "What is the
single imperishable truth?" The origin of the worlds was
deluded by Mahesha's *maya*. Not knowing the supreme
one's nature, he was arrogant enough to say that it was
he himself. "I am Dhatri, the origin of the universe. I am
Svayambhu, the single Ishvara. I am the supreme *brahman*,
without a beginning. By worshipping me, one is liberated. I
am the one who makes all the *deva*s function and withdraw.
In the worlds, there is no one else who is superior to me."
While he thought of himself in this way, a portion was
born from Narayana. He laughed and spoke these words.
"The three-eyed one is angry. O Brahma! For what reason
have you acted like this now? You have been overwhelmed
by ignorance. The truth does not exist in you. I am the
primordial creator. I am the lord Narayana and the worlds
originate in me. Without me, there can never be any life
in the universe. I am the supreme resplendence. I am the
supreme destination. Urged by me, you have created the
circle of the world." In this way, they were deluded and
debated, each wishing to be victorious over the other. The
four *Veda*s arrived at the place where the two divinities
were. They saw the divinity Brahma and the one whose
atman is established in sacrifices. Anxious in their hearts,
they spoke about Parameshthi's truth. *Rig Veda* said, "All
beings are inside him. Everything flows from him. He is
spoken of as supreme. He is the divinity Maheshvara."
Yajur Veda said, "Isha is worshipped through *yoga* and
all sacrifices. The divinity is spoken of as Ishvara. That
divinity is the wielder of Pinaka." *Sama Veda* said, "He
is the one who makes the universe revolve. He is Shiva,
inside the firmament. The *yogi*s know the truth about

Shankara Mahadeva." *Atharva Veda* said, "Mendicants see and worship the supreme lord of *deva*s. He is Mahesha Purusha Rudra. He is the divinity, Bhagavan Bhava." Bhagavan Brahma heard the auspicious words spoken by the *Veda*s. Hearing this, the one whose *atman* is in the universe laughed. Deluded, he replied. "The supreme *brahman* is devoid of all attachment. Extremely insolent, he amuses himself with his wife, along with the *pramatha*s." When this was said, the eternal Bhagavan, whose *atman* is Pranava and who does not have a form, manifested himself in a form and addressed the grandfather in these words. Pranava said, "Bhagavan Isha does not sport with anyone other than himself. Rudra Maheshvara sports with the one who is no different from him. Bhagavan Isha is eternal and self-luminous. The one who is described as Devi is his own bliss. Shivaa is not someone who has come from outside." Aja, whose form is the sacrifice, was addressed in this way. However, because of Ishvara's *maya*, understanding did not dawn on him.'

'At that time, Virinchi, the creator of the universe, saw a great radiance. This divine and wonderful sight manifested itself, filling up the space in the firmament. There was a luminous circle in the centre, blazing in energy. O excellent *dvija*s! This divine splendour appeared in the centre of the firmament. The grandfather of the worlds saw this divine face over his head. There was a terrible circle of radiance, without blemish. Brahma's fifth head blazed in great rage. In an instant, the great Purusha, Nilalohita, could be seen. The tawny divinity held a trident and a serpent was his sacred thread. Bhagavan Brahma spoke to Shankara Nilalohita. "O Shankara! Earlier, for the sake of *jnana*, you emerged from my forehead. You appeared in the form of Mahesha. Seek refuge with me." Ishvara heard

the proud words uttered by the one who originated from
a lotus. He sent the being Kalabhairava, who burns up
the worlds. Kalabhairava fought an extremely great battle
with Brahma. He severed Virinchi's fifth head. The divinity
Shambhu severed the divinity Brahma's head. The creator
of the universe lost his life. However, Isha's *yoga* made him
come back to life again. He then saw Ishana, established
inside the circle. The eternal Mahadeva was seated with
Mahadevi. His bracelet was a king of serpents. The body
of the moon was his ornament. He resembled one crore
suns. His matted hair was radiant. He wore a garment
made out of the hide of a tiger. He wore a divine garland.
With a trident in his hand, he was impossible to behold.
He was a *yogi*, with ashes as his ornaments. Those who
are devoted to *yoga* see Ishvara inside their hearts. They
see the one and only primordial Mahadeva, the *brahman*.
The supreme Devi, known as the firmament, is his Shakti.
He possesses infinite prosperity and *yoga* in his *atman*.
Mahesha could thus be seen. He is the seed of everything
in the universe. If one sees Rudra even for a single instant,
all delusion dissolves away. Those who do not follow good
conduct, but are only devoted to him, even those who are
freed by the one whose *atman* is in the worlds. Indeed,
the leader could be seen. Brahma and the other *deva*s and
*rishi*s who speak about the *brahman* constantly worship his
lingam. Indeed, Shiva could be seen. Ishvara's body is made
out of *vijnana* and the entire universe originates from him.
He never leaves Shankara's side and Shankara could be
seen. Vidyaa[1665] is Bhagavan's aide. The supreme Ishvara,
Hiranyagarbha's son, could be seen inside the circle. If a
flower, a leaf or water is offered at his feet, one can cross

---

[1665] The personified form of knowledge.

over *samsara*. Indeed, that Rudra could be seen. Because of his presence, the eternal Kala controls everything. His *atman* engages Kala and he could be seen. He is the life of all the worlds. He is the ornament of the three worlds. The divinity, whose ornament is the moon, could be seen, along with Umaa. His direct union with Devi is always natural. He is chanted about, as supreme liberation. That Mahadeva was seen. Though he is detached, *yogis* who know the truth about *yoga* meditate about union with him. The *yogi* was seen, along with Devi.'

'He saw the eternal Mahadeva, along with Mahadevi, seated on the supreme seat and got back his supreme memory. Bhagavan Aja regained the divine memory of Maheshvara. He placated the one who grants boons, who wore half the moon as his ornament and was with Umaa. Brahma said, "I prostrate myself before the great divinity. I prostrate myself before Mahadevi. I bow down. I prostrate myself before the tranquil Shiva. I always prostrate myself before Shivaa. OUM. I prostrate myself before the *brahman*. You are Vidyaa. I prostrate myself before you. I bow down. O Mahesha! I prostrate myself before you. O primordial Prakriti! I prostrate myself before you. I prostrate myself before the one whose body is *vijnana*. I prostrate myself before Chintaa.[1666] I bow down. I prostrate myself before Rudra. I bow down. I prostrate myself before Rudrani. I bow down. I prostrate myself before Kala. I bow down. I prostrate myself before Mayaa.[1667] I bow down. I prostrate myself before the one who controls all action. I prostrate myself before Kshobhikaa.[1668] I prostrate myself before

[1666] Devi, as the personified form of contemplation.
[1667] The personified form of *maya*.
[1668] Devi, as the personified form of the one who agitates.

Prakriti. I prostrate myself before Narayana. I prostrate myself before the one who bestows *yoga*. I prostrate myself before the *guru* of *yogis*. I prostrate myself before the one who resides in *samsara*. I prostrate myself before the origin of *samsara*. You are the lord who is constant happiness. I prostrate myself before the one whose form is bliss. I prostrate myself before the one who is devoid of action. I prostrate myself before the Prakriti behind the universe. Your form is OUMKARA and you are established inside it. I prostrate myself before the one who is established in the firmament. I prostrate myself before the Shakti of the firmament. I bow down." In this way, the grandfather prostrated himself and recited the eight verses to Isha and Umaa.[1669] Like a rod, he prostrated himself on the ground and chanted Shatarudriya. The divinity, Mahadeva Hara, is one who removes the afflictions of those who prostrate themselves. He raised him with his two hands and said, "I am pleased with you now." He gave him the unmatched and great prosperity of supreme *yoga*. He spoke to Ishvara Rudra Nilalohita, who was standing in front of him. "This Brahma will be established as the first one who will be worshipped in the universe. You should protect him. He is your father and superior in qualities. He is the ancient Purusha. O unblemished one! He should not be killed by you. Because of the great power of his *yoga*, he has sought refuge with me alone. He is proud that he is the sacrifice. O unblemished one! You should chasten him and carry Virinchi's pride, his head. To dispel the sin of killing a *brahmana*, follow this *vrata* and display it to the world. Roam around, seeking alms. Establish gods and *dvijas*." Bhagavan spoke these words to Parameshvara and

---

[1669] If one counts, there are eight verses within the quotes.

returned to his own natural and divine abode, the supreme destination.'

'Bhagavan Isha Kapardi Nilalohita made Kalabhairava accept Brahma's head. "To destroy the sin and to bring welfare to the worlds, roam around, observing the *vrata*. O Bhagavan! With the skull in your hand, accept alms everywhere." Saying this, he sent his daughter, famous as Brahmahatyaa.[1670] Her mouth possessed cruel teeth. She was adorned in garlands of flames. "Until he goes to the divine city of Varanasi, in this terrible form, follow the wielder of the trident." After this, Maheshvara, the lord of the worlds, spoke to Kalagni.[1671] "Instructed by me, roam around the entire world, seeking alms. When you see Narayana, the lord of *deva*s who is without ailments, he will clearly tell you the means of cleansing this sin." He heard the words spoken by Bhagavan Hara, the lord of *deva*s. With the skull in his hand, the one whose *atman* is in the universe wandered around the three worlds. He assumed a hideous garb and blazed in his own energy. But he was handsome, beautiful and sacred, with three eyes. He resembled one thousand suns and was surrounded by *siddha*s and bulls among *pramatha*s. Mahadeva's eyes were like the fire of destruction. Parameshthi[1672] drank the *amrita* of divine bliss. Ishvara was full of a great deal of sport and pastimes and he came down to the world. Shankara Kalabhairava's visage was dark and he possessed beauty and charm. Hordes of women started to follow him. They sang many kinds of songs and danced in front of the lord. They arched their eyebrows and glanced at his

[1670]The personified form of the sin of killing a *brahmana*.
[1671]The fire of destruction, another name for Kalabhairava.
[1672]Meaning Kalabhairava.

smiling face. The wielder of the trident passed through the lands of *deva*s, *danava*s and others. He went to Vishnu's abode, where Purushottama was. Shankara, who brings all that is auspicious to the worlds, reached that divine residence. With the best among *bhuta*s, he sought to enter. The extremely strong gatekeeper did not know about Parameshvara's supreme and divine nature and prevented the wielder of the trident. He was born from Vishnu's portion and was famous under the name of Vishvaksena. He was mighty-armed, attired in yellow garments, and held a conch shell, *chakra* and mace in his hands. Following Bhairava's command, Shankara's terrible *gana*, known as Kalavega, fought against the one who had originated from Vishnu. His eyes red with rage, he defeated Kalavega. Rushing towards Rudra, he hurled Sudarshana *chakra*. The divinity Mahadeva, wielder of the trident and destroyer of Tripura, saw that it was descending. However, the conqueror of enemies ignored it. There was a great *bhuta* who resembled the fire that comes at the end of a *yuga*. He struck the gatekeeper on the chest with his trident and brought him down on the ground. Struck severely by the trident in this way, he lost his great strength. He was seen to give up his life like a person afflicted by disease dies. Having killed Vishnu's being, along with the bulls among *pramatha*s, he gathered up the dead body and entered inside the residence.'

'Bhagavan Hari saw Ishvara, the cause behind the universe. He struck a vein in his forehead and allowed the blood to flow. "O Bhagavan! O immensely radiant one! Accept these alms. O crusher of Tripura! There is nothing else that is worthy of you." The blood flowed into the skull of Brahma Parameshthi for one thousand divine years. But it could still not fill it up. The lord Hari Narayana

spoke to Kalarudra.[1673] Showing a great deal of respect,
he first praised him with many kinds of hymns. "Why are
you holding Brahma's head?" Maheshvara, the lord of
*deva*s, told him everything that had happened. Achyuta
Hrishikesha summoned Brahmahatyaa. He entreated,
"Let go of Bhagavan, the wielder of the trident." Though
Murari requested this, she did not leave his side. The origin
of the universe, the one who knows everything, thought
for a long time and spoke to Shankara. "O Bhagavan!
Go to the divine and auspicious city of Varanasi. There,
Ishvara swiftly destroys all the sins of the universe." At
this, along with all the *bhuta*s, desiring the welfare of the
worlds, the divinity playfully went to the place that was
full of *tirtha*s and temples. Here and there, he was praised
by *pramatha*s and great *yogi*s. With the skull attached
to his hand, the great *yogi* danced. Desiring to witness
the dance, the lord, Bhagavan Hari Narayana, assumed
another form and followed him. On seeing Govinda, the
one marked by the sign of the bull smiled. With *yoga* in
his *atman*, he danced again and again. Hari, with *dharma*
as his mount, followed Rudra. He reached Mahadeva's
famous city of Varanasi. Kapardi, the lord of the universe,
entered. As soon as he did this, Brahmahatyaa lamented
loudly. Extremely miserable, she went to Patala. Having
entered that supreme place, the divinity, Hara Shankara,
placed Brahma's skull in front of the *gana*s. Mahadeva
laid it down and handed over the body to Vishnu, the
ocean of compassion. He said, "May this come back to
life. If people remember my excellent garb with the skull
here, their sins, in this world and in the next one, will be
swiftly destroyed. If one comes to this excellent *tirtha*,

[1673] Kalabhairava.

bathes according to the rules and satisfies the ancestors and *deva*s, one will be freed from the sin of killing a *brahmana*. Knowing that the world is transient, all of you go to that supreme city. After death, it will bestow supreme *jnana* and the supreme destination on you." Saying this, Bhagavan embraced Janardana. Along with the *pramatha*s, Ishana vanished instantly from the spot. Bhagavan Krishna got Vishvaksena back from the wielder of the trident. Accepting him, the extremely intelligent one silently returned to his own abode. Thus, the sacred account, which destroys great sins, has been narrated. It is about the auspicious *tirtha* of Kapalamochana, which brings pleasure to Sthanu. In the presence of *brahmana*s, if a person reads this chapter, he is freed from sins, of thoughts, words and deeds.'

Chapter 85(2)(32) (Description of *prayashchitta*)

Vyasa said, 'An excellent *dvija* who is a drunkard should drink liquor when it is hot, with the complexion of fire. When it burns his body, he will be freed. If he drinks cow's urine that has the complexion of the fire, or cow dung mixed in milk, *ghee* or water, he will be freed from the sin. In wet garments, he should control himself and meditate on Hari Narayana. If he does this, he will pacify the sin of killing a *brahmana*. A *brahmana* who has stolen gold should approach the king. He should confess his own deed and tell him, "Please punish me." The king will seize a bludgeon and strike him with him once. A thief is purified when he goes through the austerity of being killed by a *brahmana*. A thief must carry a bludgeon or mortar on his shoulders, made out of *khadira*[1674] wood. Or he can carry a spear, sharp at the tip, or an iron rod. With this, with dishevelled hair, he should rush to the king. He should say, "I have committed this sin. Please punish me." Through the punishment, a thief is freed from the sin of theft. If the king does not punish him, he accepts the sin of theft. A *dvija* who wishes to dispel the impurity of stealing gold should perform austerities. He should wear bark, roam around in the forest and perform the *vrata* of having killed a *brahmana*. Alternatively, the *dvija* is cleansed when he has the *avabhritha* bath after a horse sacrifice. Or he can give gold, equal to his own weight, to *brahmana*s. A *brahmana* who steals gold can perform a *vrata* of hardship for a year, observing *brahmacharya*. The sin will then be dispelled. Overcome by desire, if a *brahmana* mounts his *guru*'s wife, he should fashion an iron image of a woman and embrace it when it is hot and blazing. Or he can cut off his penis and testicles. Holding them in the cup of his hands, he should walk straight in a southern direction, until he falls dead. If a person has intercourse with his *guru*'s wife, to purify himself, he should observe the *vrata* of having killed a *brahmana*. For a year, he should control himself and lie down on the bare ground, embracing a thorny branch. A person who violates his *guru*'s bed will then be purified. Wearing bark and controlling himself, he can perform a rite of hardship for a year. A *dvija* is purified when he has the *avabhritha* bath after a horse sacrifice. Observing the vow, he should always be a *brahmachari* and eat the eighth meal, skipping the first seven. For three days, he should attentively stand or sit. He should sleep on the bare ground for three years. The sin will be dispelled.

[1674] Acacia.

Alternatively, he can perform four or five *chandrayana* vows. I will speak about cleansing for a *dvija* who is intimate with fallen people and associates with them. To destroy that sin, a *vrata* must be observed. For one year, he must attentively observe the austerity of hardship. This is the *prayashchitta* when the period of association is for six months. If these vows are observed, the impurity of committing great sins is destroyed. Alternatively, the atonement is by visiting the sacred *tirtha*s on earth. Killing a *brahmana*, drinking liquor, theft, intercourse with the *guru*'s wife and wilful association with such sinners are crimes. A *brahmana* who does these should fast and, controlling himself, visit a *tirtha*. Perform *dhyana* on the divinity Kapardi and enter the blazing fire. The sages who have spoken about *dharma* have not indicated any other means of atonement. Therefore, one should burn one's own body in a sacred *tirtha*.'

Chapter 86(2)(33)
(Description of *prayashchitta* continued)

Vyasa said, 'If a *brahmana* voluntarily has intercourse with his daughter, sister or daughter-in-law, he must enter a blazing fire. If he does this with his mother's sister, the maternal uncle's wife, the paternal uncle's wife or the niece, he must observe a vow of hardship or great hardship. To pacify the sin, he must observe the *chandrayana* vow. He must meditate on the divinity Hari, the origin of the universe, who is without a beginning and without an end. If he has intercourse with his brother's wife, to pacify the sin, he must control himself and perform four or five *chandrayana* vows. If he has intercourse with his father's niece, mother's niece or maternal uncle's daughter, he must observe a *chandrayana* vow. If he has intercourse with a friend's wife or wife's sister, he must fast for a day and a night and perform a rite of hardship. If a *brahmana* has intercourse with a woman who is going through her periods, he is purified in three nights. It is known that if one has intercourse with a *chandala* woman, three rites of hardship must be performed. If a person mounts someone belonging to the mother's *gotra* or belonging to the same *pravara*, it is said that he must control himself and observe *chandrayana*. Thus controlled, he will be purified. There is no other means of purification and atonement. If a *brahmana* has intercourse with a *brahmana* woman who is not his wife, he must perform one rite of hardship. Committing the sin of polluting a maiden, he must perform a *chandrayana vrata*. For pacification, a rite of hardship must be performed if the semen is released in a non-human entity, in a man, in the vagina of a woman going through her period or in the water. If a *brahmana* approaches an old woman, he is purified in three nights. If one unites with a cow, one must perform a *chandrayana vrata*. If a *dvija* has intercourse with a courtesan, he must perform Prajapatya. If he has intercourse with a fallen woman, he is purified with three rites of hardship. If he has intercourse with a *pulkasa* woman, he must observe the hardship of *chandrayana*. *Chandrayana* must be performed if one approaches a female dancer, an actress, a washerwoman, a woman who earns her living through bamboo or a woman who earns her living through hides. Deluded by desire, if a *brahmachari* approaches a woman, he must wear a donkey's hide and beg for alms in seven houses. He must bathe thrice a day and proclaim his sin. He will be freed from the sin after one year. If a *brahmachari* violates the vow of celibacy, for six months, he must observe the *vrata* meant for the killing of a *brahmana*. If he follows what is sanctioned by *brahmana*s, he will be freed. If he releases his semen, he must undertake an act of *prayashchitta*. For seven nights, he must not beg for alms or worship the fire. Reciting OUMKARA first, he must always chant the great *vyahriti*s. For one year, he must only eat at night. Pure, he should eat what he obtains as alms. Swiftly casting aside his rage, he must perform *japa* with Savitri on the banks of a river or in *tirtha*s. He will then be freed from the sin.'

'If a *brahmana* kills a *kshatriya* unintentionally, for six months, he must follow the *vrata* meant for the killing of a *brahmana*. Alternatively, he can donate five hundred cows. He can control himself and reside in the forest for one year, performing *dhyana*. Or he can torment himself through rites of hardship like Prajapatya. Voluntarily or involuntarily, if he happens to kill a *vaishya*, for three years, he must follow the *vrata* meant for the killing of a *brahmana*. Alternatively, he can donate one thousand two hundred and fifty cows. Involuntarily, if one kills a *shudra*, a *vrata* of hardship or great hardship, like *chandrayana*, must be observed for a year. Having killed a *kshatriya*, a *vaishya* or a *shudra*, one should respectively donate one thousand, five hundred or two hundred and fifty cows. That pacifies the sin. Alternatively, the vow meant for the killing of a *brahmana* can be observed for eight years or three years. If a *brahmana* kills a *brahmana* woman, he must follow the *vrata* for eight years. If he kills a *kshatriya* woman, it must be observed for six years. If he kills a *vaishya* woman, it must be observed for three years. Having killed a *shudra* woman, an excellent *dvija* is purified in one year. Having killed a *vaishya* woman, *dvija*s must donate something to *dvija*s. Having killed an *antyaja*, one must perform *chandrayana vrata*. Alternatively, Bhagavan Aja has said that one is purified after fasting for twelve days. Having killed a frog, a mongoose, a crow, a cat, a mule, a rat or a dog, a *dvija* must perform one-sixteenth of the great *vrata*. Inattentively, if he kills a dog, he must drink milk for three nights. If he kills a cat or a mongoose, he must walk for one *yojana*. If he kills a horse, a *dvija* must observe a rite of hardship for twelve nights. Having killed a snake, an excellent *dvija* must donate an iron image. Having killed a eunuch, he must donate a bundle of straw and a weight of lead.[1675] Having killed a boar, he must donate a pot full of *ghee*. Having killed a partridge, he must donate a *drona*[1676] of sesamum. Having killed a parrot, a two-year-old calf, a three-year-old curlew, a swan, a crane, a stork, a peacock, a monkey, a hawk or a vulture, he must touch a cow and give it away to a *brahmana*. Having killed a predatory animal, he should give away a milk-yielding cow. Having killed a non-predatory animal, he should give away a calf. Having killed a camel, he must give away a *gunja* plant. Having killed a creature with bones, he must give something to a *brahmana*. If violence is caused to a creature without bones, *pranayama* is enough to purify. If one cuts down a tree that yields fruit, one hundred *japa*s with hymns from the *Rig Veda* must be undertaken. Drinking of *ghee* purifies the cutting down of shrubs, creepers, winding plants, flowering plants and anything with flowers and fruits, in addition to the killing of creatures born from eggs and sweat. If an elephant is killed, the instruction is that purification occurs through a rite of hardship. If a cow is killed inadvertently,

[1675] *Mashaka*, a measure of weight.
[1676] Measure of weight.

one must perform *chandrayana* or fast for twelve days. If one does it voluntarily, there is no *prayashchitta.*'

Chapter 87(2)(34)
(Description of *prayashchitta* continued)

Vyasa said, 'For abducting a man or a woman, or seizing a house, well, tank or water-body, purification is through *chandrayana*. If objects of limited value are stolen from someone else's house, purification is through a rite of hardship, after returning the object to the owner. Because of desire, if an excellent *dvija* steals grain or wealth from the home of someone who belongs to the same *varna*, he is purified through a rite of hardship. If he steals food and edible items, a vehicle, a bed or a seat or roots, flowers and fruits, he is purified by drinking *panchagavya*.[1677] If he steals grass, wood, trees, dry food, molasses, oil, hides and meat, he must not eat for three nights. If he steals jewels, pearls, coral, copper, silver and lodestones, he must eat grain particles for twelve days. If he steals cotton, a two-hooved or one-hoofed animal, flowers, scents and herbs, he must drink milk for three days. If he eats human flesh, he must perform *chandrayana*. If he eats a crow, a dog, an elephant, a boar or a cock, he is purified through a rite of hardship. If he eats the flesh of a predatory creature or its urine or excrement, or if he eats a cow, jackal or monkey, the same *vrata* must be undertaken. If he eats a Gangetic porpoise, blue jay or the flesh of a fish, he must fast for twelve days and offer oblations with *ghee* and ash gourd.

[1677] Five products that come from a cow—cow's urine, cow dung, milk, curds and *ghee*.

If he eats a mongoose, an owl or a cat, he must undertake a rite of hardship. If he eats a predatory creature, camel or donkey, he is purified through a rite of hardship. Following the rules mentioned earlier, he must cleanse himself. If he eats a crane, a stork, a *karandava* or a *chakravaka*, he must not eat for twelve days. If he eats a dove, a sandpiper, a parrot, a *sarasa* crane, an owl or an aquatic bird with webbed feet, he must undertake the same *vrata*. If he eats a Gangetic porpoise, a blue jay, the flesh of a fish or a creature that feeds on dead bodies, he must undertake the same *vrata*. If he eats a cuckoo, a fish, a frog or a serpent, if he eats barley mixed with cow's urine, he will be purified in a month. If he eats an aquatic creature, something born in water, a pecker bird, a gallinaceous bird or a parrot with red feet, he must perform that rite for seven days. If he eats the flesh of a dog and dried meat he has prepared himself, that sin will be destroyed if he follows the vow for one month. If he eats brinjal, fragrant earth-grass, drumstick, a kingfisher, a sparrow, a rhinoceros or the trumpet flower, he must undertake the rite of Prajapatya. If he eats garlic or onion, he must perform *chandrayana*. If he eats the stalk of a lotus or the spiny amaranth, he is purified through Prajapatya. If he eats *ashmantaka* or a young shoot, he is purified when he torments himself through a rite of hardship. If he eats safflower, he is purified through Prajapatya. If he eats bottle-gourd or *kimshuka*, he must undertake the same *vrata*. Out of delusion, if he drinks such concoctions, he is purified if he has barley mixed with cow's urine for seven nights. If he voluntarily eats figs, he is purified by tormenting himself through a rite of hardship.'

'If he eats at the first *shraddha*, when there is impurity because of birth or death, a *brahmana* must control himself and purify himself through *chandrayana*. If a *dvija* eats the food of a person who offers oblations to the fire every day, but does not offer it to him first, he must properly undertake *chandrayana*. If he eats what should not be eaten, or eats food that is not clean or eats the food of an *antyaja*, he must purify himself through a rite of hardship. A *dvija* who eats a *chandala*'s food must properly undertake *chandrayana*. If he eats this voluntarily, he must undertake a rite of hardship for one year and then cleanse himself again. If he drinks liquor that is not *sura*,[1678] he must undertake a *vrata* of *chandrayana*. If he eats what should not be eaten, he is purified through Prajapatya. If he has urine, excrement or semen, he must perform the same rite. If there are no specific instructions, the rite must always be properly undertaken for one day. If a *dvija* has the urine or excrement of a village-pig, a donkey, a camel, a jackal, a monkey or a crow, he must perform *chandrayana*. If *dvija*s, the three *varna*s, unknowingly have urine or excrement or touch liquor, they must cleanse themselves again. Out of delusion, if an excellent *dvija* has the urine or excrement of a predatory bird, he must undertake a great rite of purification. If it happens to be that of a vulture, frog, cock or gallinaceous bird, he must perform a rite of hardship. If he eats the *ucchishta* of a *brahmana*, he is purified through Prajapatya. If it is the *ucchishta* of a *kshatriya*, he must torment himself through a rite of hardship. If it is the *ucchishta* of a *vaishya*, he must undertake a rite of great hardship. If a *dvija* eats the *ucchishta* of a *shudra*, he must observe *chandrayana vrata*. If he drinks water from a vessel meant for liquor, he must observe *chandrayana*. If a *dvija* eats *ucchishta*, he is purified in three nights. He

---

[1678] A specific kind of liquor.

must have barley mixed with cow's urine, or drink the water left after a cow has drunk. If he happens to have water polluted by urine or excrement, to cleanse that sin, he has to torment himself through a *vrata* of hardship. If a *brahmana* knowingly drinks water from a *chandala*'s well or vessel, to cleanse that sin, he has to torment himself through a rite of hardship. If an excellent *dvija* happens to drink water touched by a *chandala*, he is purified by the supreme *vrata* of having *panchagavya* for three nights. If a *dvija* knowingly touches a great sinner or eats with him, because of that delusion, he must bathe and perform a rite of hardship. In his delusion, if he touches a great sinner, a *chandala* or a woman going through her period, or happens to eat with one, he is purified in three nights. Bhagavan, born from the lotus, has said that if one knowingly eats with such a person, he should have a bath and after a rite of hardship, will be purified in a day and a night. If he eats polluted food, or food polluted by cattle, he must fast and undertake one-fourth of a rite of hardship. If a *brahmana* has eaten food unknowingly, at the end of every year, he must repeatedly perform the rite of hardship for purification. This is especially the case if this has been done knowingly. If he officiates at the sacrifices of *vratya*s,[1679] and performs extreme rites of *abhichara*[1680] for those unworthy of them, he is purified through three rites of hardship. If a *dvija* performs the cremation rites for *brahmana*s and others who have been killed, he is purified by having barley mixed with cow's urine and performing Prajapatya. If he has

[1679] A *vratya* belongs to the first three *varna*s and has become an outcaste.

[1680] Incantations and charms used for a malevolent purpose.

smeared himself with oil and vomit, or passes urine and excrement or if he shaves while indulging in intercourse, he is purified in a day and a night. If an excellent *dvija* abandons tending to the fire for a day, he is purified in three nights. If this abandoning is for three nights, he is purified in six days. In his distraction, if he abandons it for ten or twelve days, to pacify that sin, he must undertake *chandrayana* and a rite of hardship. If he accepts objects from a fallen person, he is purified when he gives it up. However, Bhagavan Manu has said that he must follow the rules and undertake rites of hardship. If a person residing in *sannyasa* violates a vow of fasting, he must perform three rites of hardship and three *chandrayanas*. *Dvijas* must again cleanse themselves through *jatakarma* and the other *samskaras*.[1681] For purification, those who have insight about *dharma* must follow this *vrata*. If he does not perform the *sandhya* rite, he must fast during the day. If he does not perform the *sandhya* rite at night, he must control himself and fast during the night. If a person does not perform the pure act of collecting kindling, for purification, he must control himself, bathe and perform *japa* with one thousand and eight Gayatri *mantras*. Distracted, if a householder does not perform

---

[1681] *Samskara* means cleansing, specifically done at certain periods of life. There are thirteen *samskaras* or sacraments. The list varies a bit. But one list is *vivaha* (marriage), *garbhalambhana* (conception), *pumshavana* (engendering a male child), *simantonnayana* (parting the hair, performed in the fourth month of pregnancy), *jatakarma* (birth rites), *namakarana* (naming), *chudakarma* (tonsure), *annaprashana* (first solid food), *keshanta* (first shaving of the head), *upanayana* (sacred thread), *vidyarambha* (commencement of studies), *samavartana* (graduation) and *antyeshti* (funeral rites). After *samavartana*, one ceases to be a student and becomes (usually) a householder.

the *sandhya* rite, even if he is exhausted, for purification, he must control himself and immediately bathe and fast. If a *snataka* ignores the *nitya* tasks mentioned in the *Veda*s, as a result of the violation of the *vrata*, he must fast that day. If an excellent *dvija* makes someone else violate it, he must observe a rite of hardship for a year. If the person is a *vratya*, he is purified by performing *chandrayana* and donating a cow. If a *dvija* acts like a non-believer, he must undertake Prajapatya. If he acts against *deva*s and *guru*s, he is purified by tormenting himself through a rite of hardship. If he willingly rides on a vehicle drawn by a camel or a donkey, or if he enters water nude, he is purified in three nights. If he eats with those who are not deserving of the same *pankti*, for a period of one month, he must skip five meals and have the sixth. To purify himself, he must always offer oblations and perform *japa* with Shakala Samhita.'[1682]

'If a *brahmana* wears a red or blue garment, he must fast for a day and a night. When he bathes and has *panchagavya*, he will be purified. If he speaks about the *Veda*s, *dharma* and the Puranas to a *chandala*, he is purified through *chandrayana*. There is no other means of atonement. If a *brahmana* happens to touch a person who has died through hanging, he is purified through *chandrayana* or Prajapatya. In his distraction, if a *dvija* touches the *ucchishta* of a *chandala* and does not perform *achamana*, he must bathe and perform *japa* with the *gayatri mantra* one thousand and eight times. Or the *brahmachari* can control himself and do it with the Drupada *mantra* one hundred times. He will be purified if he fasts properly for three nights and has *panchagavya*. If

[1682] A school of the *Rig Veda*.

a *dvija* willingly touches a *chandala* or a fallen person, he becomes *ucchishta*. He is purified through Prajapatya. If he touches a *chandala*, a person impure because of a birth in the household, a corpse, a woman going through her season or a fallen person, he is purified by taking a bath. If he touches or is touched by a *chandala*, a person impure because of a birth in the household or a corpse, he must control himself, bathe, perform *achamana* and perform *japa*. If an excellent *dvija* voluntarily touches them or is touched by them, to purify himself, he must bathe and perform *achamana*. The divinity, the grandfather, has said this. When he is eating, if a *brahmana* is touched in this way, he must bathe to purify himself. He must fast and offer oblations. This is the *vrata*. If he touches a *chandala* or a corpse, to purify himself, he must undertake a rite of hardship. If he touches someone who should not be touched, he is purified in a day and a night. If a *dvija* touches liquor, he becomes pure when he performs three *pranayama*s. If he touches onion or garlic, he becomes pure when he has *ghee*. If a *brahmana* is bitten by a dog, for three days, he must drink milk in the evening. If he is bitten above the navel, the purification required is double that. If he is bitten in the arms, the purification required is three times as much. If he is bitten on the head, it is four times. Bitten by a dog in this way, an excellent *dvija* will bathe and perform *japa* with the *savitri mantra*. Even though he is not suffering, if an excellent *dvija* eats without performing a great sacrifice, he is purified by performing half a rite of hardship. If a person who maintains the sacrificial fire does not worship them on *parva* days, or if he does not approach his wife when it is her season, he must perform half a rite of hardship. Though he is not suffering, if a person immerses himself in water, without using it for washing himself, he is purified when he submerges himself in water with his clothes on and touches a cow. If he knowingly commits a sin, when the sun rises, a *dvija* must perform *japa* in the water. A *dvija* must fast for three days and perform *japa* with *gayatri mantra* one thousand and eight times. If an excellent *dvija* willingly follows the dead body of a *shudra,* in a river, he must perform *japa* one thousand and eight times with the *gayatri mantra.* If a *brahmana* swears a pledge to another *brahmana*, but violates it, he must have barley as food and undertake a *chandrayana vrata*. If he differentially serves food to those in the same *pankti*, he is purified through a rite of hardship. When he steps on the shadow of a *shvapaka*, he must bathe and have *ghee*. When impure, if he looks at the sun, he must look at the fire or the moon. If he touches human *asthi*, he is purified when he bathes. If his studies are false, for a year, he must roam around, seeking alms. An ungrateful person should reside in a *brahmana*'s house and observe a *vrata* for five years. If a person utters *humkara* against a *brahmana* or uses "*tvam*" to address a person who is senior, he must bathe and not eat for the remaining part of the day. He must prostrate himself and placate them.[1683] If he strikes a senior, even with a blade of grass, he must tie a piece of cloth around his neck.[1684] If he defeats him in an argument, he must prostrate himself and placate him. If he threatens a *brahmana*, he must perform a rite of hardship. If he brings down a *brahmana*, he must

---

[1683] *Humkara* means to utter the sound 'hum', a sound believed to possess special powers. A person who is senior should be addressed as '*bhavan*', not as '*tvam*'. Both words mean 'you', but the former shows respect.

[1684] The cloth around the neck (*galavastra*) is a mark of humility and submission.

perform a rite of extreme hardship. If he sheds the blood of a *brahmana*, he must perform rites of both hardship and extreme hardship. If he abuses a *guru* or lies to him, for purification and cleansing of the sin, he must fast for one night. If he spits in the direction of *deva*s and *rishi*s, he must burn his tongue with a torch and donate gold. If a *dvija* passes urine in a garden of *deva*s even once, to purify himself, he must cut off his penis and undertake a *vrata* of *chandrayana*. In his delusion, if an excellent *dvija* passes urine in a *deva*'s temple, he must cut off his penis and perform *chandrayana*. If an excellent *dvija* reviles *deva*s and *rishi*s, he must undertake Prajapatya properly. If he converses with these sinners, he must bathe and worship the *deva*s. If he looks at them, he must glance at the sun. If he remembers them, he must remember Vishveshvara. If a person criticizes Ishana, the lord of the universe and of all beings, that person is incapable of being saved, even in one hundred years. He must first perform *chandrayana* and then undertake rites of hardship and extreme hardship. To free himself of the sin, he must then seek refuge with the divinity. Following the rules, if all of one's possessions are donated, all sins are cleansed. Following the rules, *chandrayana* must be performed, and also rites of hardship and extreme hardship. Visiting a sacred *tirtha* cleanses all sins.'

'If a person worships Bhava on the *tithi* of *amavasya* and honours *brahmana*s, he is freed from all sins. If Mahadeva is worshipped on *ashtami* or *chaturdashi* of *krishna paksha*, by worshipping a foremost *brahmana*, one is freed from all sins. On the night of *trayodashi,* in the first *yama*, if one has offerings and sees Isha, one is freed from all sins. Controlling himself, he must fast on *chaturdashi* of *krishna paksha*. With sesamum and water in the cup of his hands, he must offer seven libations to Yama, Dharmaraja, Mrityu, Antaka, Vaivasvata, Kala and Sarvapranahara.[1685] Having bathed, these must be offered in the forenoon. He will then be freed from all sins. A person who observes a *vrata* must control his mind and be serene. He must follow *brahmacharya*, sleep on the ground, fast and honour *dvija*s. Directed towards Brahma, the grandfather, on *amavasya*, he must worship three *brahmana*s. He will then be freed from all sins. Having fasted on *shashthi* of *shukla paksha*, a person must control himself and worship the *deva* Bhanu on *saptami*. He will then be freed from all sins. If a person worships Yama when Bharani is in the ascendant, on *chaturthi*, or on Saturday, he is freed from sins committed in the course of seven births. If a person fasts on *ekadashi* and worships Janardana on *dvadashi* of *shukla paksha*, he is cleansed of great sins. Austerities, *japa*, visiting *tirtha*s and worship of *deva*s and *brahmana*s at times like eclipses, cleanses great sins. If a man has committed every kind of sin but follows *niyama*s and gives up his life at a sacred *tirtha*, he is freed from all sins.'

'If a woman enters the fire with her husband, she saves him, even if he has killed a *brahmana*, is ungrateful or is polluted because of great sins. The learned know that this is supreme *prayashchitta* for women. If a woman is devoted to her husband and is engaged in serving her husband, she does not incur any sin, in this world or in the next one. She is freed from all sins. There is no need to reflect on this. If a woman is devoted to her husband and is eager to serve her husband, she does not have any sins, in this world or in the next one. If a woman is devoted to her husband and is devoted to *dharma*, she always obtains what is fortunate.

[1685]These are different names for Yama.

No one is ever capable of vanquishing her. This was the case with the extremely fortunate Sita, famous in the three worlds. She was the queen and wife of Rama, Dasharatha's son. She vanquished the lord of *rakshasa*s. The extremely fortunate one was Rama's wife. But, urged by destiny, Ravana, the lord of *rakshasa*s, desired the large-eyed Sita. While she was wandering around in the desolate forest, he made up his mind to resort to *maya*, assume the garb of an ascetic and abduct the beautiful lady. However, she got to know of his intentions and remembered her husband, Dasharatha's son. The one with the beautiful smiles sought refuge with Vahni, the *avasathya* fire. Joining her hands in salutation, Rama's wife worshipped the great *yogi* who burns up all the worlds, as if he was her husband Achyuta himself. "I prostrate myself before the great *yogi* Krishanu,[1686] the supreme and deep one. You are the one who burns all beings. You are Ishana, in the form of Kala. I seek refuge with the *deva* Pavaka, the eternal one whose form is the universe. You are the *yogi* who wears a hide as a garment. You are the lord of *bhuta*s. You are the supreme objective. Your *atman* is blazing in form and is established in the hearts of all beings. I seek refuge with the one whose form is the universe, the power behind every kind of energy. You are Ishvara, the great *yogi*. You are Vahni, Aditya, Parameshthi. I seek refuge with Rudra, the wielder of the trident, the great one who devours. You are the fire of destruction. You are the lord of *yogi*s. You are the one who bestows objects of pleasure and emancipation as fruits. I seek refuge with you, Virupaksha. *Bhuh*, *bhuvah* and *svah* are your own forms. You are hidden inside a golden abode. You are the great and infinitely energetic one. I seek

---

[1686]Krishanu is another name for Agni.

refuge with Vaishvanara, who is established in all beings. I seek refuge with Vahni Ishvara, the *deva* who bears *havya* and *kavya*. I seek refuge with the supreme truth, the one who should be worshipped, Savitar Shiva, the Agni who is in heaven, the supreme resplendence, the imperishable bearer of *havya*." Rama's illustrious wife used these eight verses[1687] to perform *japa* on Vahni. With her eyes closed, in her mind, she meditated on Rama. Bhagavan Maheshvara, the *avasathya* fire, is the bearer of *havya*. Blazing in his *atman*, as if to burn down with his energy, he manifested himself. Wishing to slay Ravana, he created a Sita made out of *maya*.[1688] Taking the Sita loved by Rama, Pavaka vanished. Ravana, the lord of *rakshasa*s, saw that kind of Sita. Taking her, he went to Lanka, located inside the ocean. Along with Lakshmana, Rama killed Ravana and got Sita back. But his mind was agitated by doubts. To bring trust among beings, the Sita made of *maya* again entered the fire and Pavaka burnt her down. When the Sita made of *maya* was burnt down, Pavaka, the illustrious one with the hot rays, loved by the gods, showed Sita to Rama. The slender-waisted one clasped her husband's feet with her hands. Before Rama, Janaka's daughter prostrated herself on the ground. On seeing her, Rama's mind was delighted, and his eyes were filled with wonder. Raghava bowed his head down before Vahni and satisfied him. The illustrious one asked Vahni, "Who is this, with the beautiful complexion? I saw that you had burnt one earlier, but she has arrived by my side." In the presence of beings, the *deva* who bears

---

[1687]There are eight *shloka*s in the prayer within quotes.

[1688]In some versions of the Ramayana, the *maya* or illusory Sita was abducted, not the real one. The real Sita reappeared later, from the fire.

havya and burns the worlds told Dasharatha's son what had happened. "This is your beloved. She is extremely virtuous, like Parvati. She is loved greatly by Devi, whom she obtained after worshipping her with austerities. This one is intent on serving her husband. She possesses good conduct and is devoted to her husband, just as Bhavani is to Ishvara. Since Ravana desired her, I used my *maya* to protect her. Desiring to ensure Ravana's death, I used *maya* to create a Sita and that illustrious one was abducted by the lord of *rakshasa*s. Ravana, the lord of *rakshasa*s and destroyer of the worlds, has been killed by you. On seeing this, the *maya* has been withdrawn. Listen to my words and accept this sparkling Janaki. Behold the divinity Narayana, the imperishable origin of everything, within your own *atman*." The illustrious one, who faces every direction and whose rays are everywhere in the universe, said this. Honoured by Raghava and the other beings, Agni vanished.'

'I have thus spoken about the origin and greatness of *vrata*s. This is described as *prayashchitta* for women. It destroys all sins. Even if a man is full of every kind of sin, if he gives up his own body at a sacred *tirtha*, he is freed from sins. If a *dvija* bathes at all the sacred *tirtha*s on earth, that man is freed from all accumulated sins. I have thus spoken about Manu's *dharma* to you and the eternal path of *jnana yoga*, for worshipping Mahesha. Using the rules of *yoga*, one should practice *jnana yoga*. One will then see Mahadeva. Even if one tries for one hundred *kalpa*s, there is no other means. If a person establishes this supreme *dharma* and *jnana* about Parameshvara, he is held to be supreme. There is no *yogi* superior to him in the world. If a person is capable of establishing it, but does not do so because of delusion, even if he is a sage who practices *yoga*, he is not greatly loved by Bhagavan. Full of devotion, donations must be made, especially to *brahmana*s who are serene and full of *dharma*. If a person constantly reads this conversation between you and me, he is freed from all sins and goes to the supreme destination. In the presence of *brahmana*s, it must always be read at *shraddha*s and rites for the *deva*s. With intent minds, *dvija*s must hear it. If a person reflects on this in his mind and makes pure *dvija*s listen to it, he casts aside his covering of sins and goes to the divinity Maheshvara.'

Saying this, the illustrious Vyasa, Satyavati's son, assured the sages and Suta and returned to wherever he had come from.

Chapter 88(2)(35) (Gaya and other *tirthas*)

The *rishi*s said, 'There are famous and great *tirtha*s in the world. O Romaharshana! Please tell us about those now.'

Romaharshana replied, 'Listen. I will describe various *tirtha*s. Sages, who speak about the *brahman*, have narrated these in the Puranas. O best among sages! In each of these, if one bathes, performs *japa*, offers oblations and undertakes *shraddha* and other rites, one purifies seven generations. Brahma Parameshthis's famous *tirtha* of Prayaga extends for five *yojana*s. I have spoken about its greatness.[1689] Among others, there is the supreme *tirtha* of the Kurus,[1690] worshipped by *deva*s. It is full of hermitages of *rishi*s and it cleanses all sins. Devoid of insolence and jealousy and pure

---

[1689] Chapter 36(1)(36).
[1690] Kurukshetra.

in *atman*, if one bathes and donates something there, one purifies both lineages.'[1691]

"The supreme *tirtha* of Gaya is secret. It is for the ancestors and is extremely rare. If a man offers *pinda*s there, he is not born again. If a person goes there and offers *pinda*s even once, he saves his ancestors and goes to the supreme destination. For the welfare of the worlds, *paramatman* Rudra placed his foot on a slab of rock there. One should placate the ancestors there. Though capable, if a person does not go to Gaya, the ancestors grieve about him. His exertions are in vain. The ancestors sing a song that the *maharshi*s describe. "Anyone who goes to Gaya, saves us. Even if he has committed sins and does not follow his own *dharma*, if he goes to Gaya, he will save us. One should desire many sons who possess good conduct and are full of qualities. Among all of them, at least one will go to Gaya." Therefore, a person, especially if he is a *brahmana*, must make every effort to go to Gaya, control himself and following the rules, offer *pinda*s there. Indeed, a mortal who offers *pinda*s in Gaya is blessed. He saves seven generations on both sides and proceeds to the supreme objective. There is another supreme *tirtha*, said to be the abode of *siddha*s. This is famous as Prabhasa and Bhagavan Bhava is there. If a *brahmana* bathes there, performs a *shraddha* and honours *brahmana*s, he obtains excellent and imperishable worlds. There is a *tirtha* named Traimbaka, honoured by all *deva*s. If one worships Rudra there, one obtains the fruits of a *jyotishtoma* sacrifice.[1692] If a person worships the golden-eyed Mahadeva Kapardi and

---

[1691] The father's side and the mother's side.

[1692] *Jyotishtoma* is a great *soma* sacrifice, at which sixteen officiating priests are required. Traimbaka probably means the Tryambakeshvara *jyotirlingam* and Prabhasa probably means the Somanatha *jyotirlingam*.

honours *brahmana*s, one becomes a *ganapati*. There is Rudra Parameshthi's supreme and sacred *tirtha* of Someshvara. If one sees Rudra, the cause, there, all ailments are dispelled. Among all *tirtha*s, there is a supreme and beautiful one named Vijaya. There, Mahesha's *lingam* is famous under the name of Vijaya. O Indras among *brahmana*s! If a person goes there, controls himself, is a *brahmachari* with restrained diet and resides there for six months, he goes to the supreme destination. There is another supreme and beautiful *tirtha* in the eastern region. This is for the lord of *deva*s alone and yields the fruits of becoming a *ganapati*. If a king gives Shiva's devotees a little bit of auspicious land there, he becomes an emperor. A person desiring emancipation obtains *moksha*. Mahanadi's waters are sacred and destroy all sins. If one touches those waters at the time of an eclipse, one is freed from all sins. There is another river named Virajaa, famous in the three worlds. If a *brahmana* has a bath there, that man obtains greatness in Brahma's world. There is another *tirtha*, Narayana's Purushottama. The prosperous and supreme Purusha, Narayana, is there. If an excellent *dvija* bathes and worships the supreme Vishnu there and honours *brahmana*s, he obtains Vishnu's world. Among *tirtha*s, there is a supreme one, famous under the name of Gokarna. This is the abode of Parameshthi Shambhu and it dispels all sins. If one sees the divinity's supreme and excellent *lingam* in Gokarna, one obtains everything that one wishes for and becomes dear to Rudra. To the north of Gokarna, there is a *lingam* of the divinity who wields the trident. If a person worships Mahadeva there, he obtains *sayujya* with Shiva. There, the divinity Mahadeva is famous as Sthanu. If a man sees him there, he is instantly freed from all sins. There is another place, the sacred Kubjashrama, the abode of the great-souled Vishnu. If one worships the Purusha, Vishnu, there, one obtains greatness in Shvetadvipa. There, the divinity Rudra, Tripura's enemy, crushed Daksha's sacrifice and released Narayana. All around this, for one *yojana*, is a *kshetra* frequented by large numbers of *siddha*s and *rishi*s. This is Vishnu's sacred residence. Purushottama is there. There is another one, Kokamukha *tirtha*, belonging to Vishnu, wonderful in deeds. If a mortal dies there, he is freed from sins and obtains *sarupya* with Vishnu. Shaligrama is a great *tirtha* and enhances Vishnu's pleasure. If a man gives up his life there, he sees Hrishikesha. There is the extremely beautiful Ashvatirtha, the residence of *siddha*s. Brahma Parameshthi's *tirtha* is there and it bestows the auspicious. Pushkara destroys all sins. For those who die there, it bestows Brahma's world. If an excellent *dvija* remembers Pushkara in his mind, he is cleansed of all sins and rejoices with Shakra. There, *deva*s, *yaksha*s, *uraga*s, *rakshasa*s and large numbers of *siddha*s worship Brahma, who originated from the lotus. If a supreme *dvija* goes there, is pure and bathes there, worshipping Brahma Parameshthi, he sees Brahma. If a mortal person approaches the unblemished Puruhuta,[1693] lord of *deva*s, he assumes his form and obtains everything that he desires.'

'There is the supreme *tirtha* of Saptasarasvata,[1694] frequented by Brahma and others. If one worships Rudra there, one obtains the fruits of a horse sacrifice. Mankanaka sought refuge with Rudra Parameshvara there.[1695] With his

[1693] Puruhuta is one of Indra's names.
[1694] Near Kurukshetra.
[1695] Mankanaka (Mankana) was a *rishi*. His story is narrated in the Mahabharata and Vamana Purana. He lived in Saptasarasvata *tirtha*. His hand was cut by *kusha* grass and because of his austerities, instead of blood, the juices of herbs started to flow. That was the reason for his pride.

austerities he worshipped Shiva, who has the bull on his
standard. As a result of his austerities, the sage Mankanaka
blazed. On knowing that Rudra had arrived, he danced
energetically. Bhagavan Rudra asked him, "Why did you
dance?" Even after seeing the divinity Ishana, he continued
to dance repeatedly. On seeing that he was full of pride,
Bhagavan Rudra wished to quell the pride. He split his
own body and showed him a heap of ashes. "O excellent
dvija! Behold this pile of *bhasma* that has emerged from my
body. There is clearly another person who is equal to you
in the greatness of austerities. O bull among sages! In your
pride, you danced. In truth, this is not worthy of an ascetic.
I am superior to you." Having told the best among sages
this, Rudra, who witnesses everything in the universe, told
him about the supreme nature of the universe. After this,
Hara danced. He had one thousand heads, one thousand
eyes and one thousand feet. There were cruel teeth in his
mouth. With garlands of flames, he was terrible. Next to
Isha, the wielder of the trident, he[1696] then saw the beautiful
and charming Devi. Her eyes were large. This was Shivaa,
pleasant in face and resembling a million suns. He saw
the infinitely radiant lord of the universe standing there,
smiling. Seeing this, the lord among sages was scared and
his heart trembled. He prostrated his head before Rudra
and controlling himself, performed *japa* with hymns about
Rudra. Bhagavan Isha Tryambaka, affectionate towards
his devotees, was pleased. He assumed his earlier form
and Devi vanished. The lord of devas, Shiva himself,
embraced the devotee, prostrate before him. He said, "O
child! Do not be scared. What will I give you?" The sage
was delighted in his mind. He prostrated his head before

[1696] Mankanaka.

Girisha Hara, the destroyer of Tripura, and told him what
he desired. "O Mahadeva! I prostrate myself before you.
O Maheshvara! I prostrate myself before you. What is this
extremely terrible form of yours, that faces every direction?
Who was the radiant one who was standing next to you?
She vanished suddenly. I wish to know everything." Thus
asked, Isha Hara spoke to Mankanaka. Mahesha, the
fire that destroyed Tripura, told him about his own *yoga*
and about Devi. "I am the one with one thousand eyes. I
am in all *atman*s. My face is in every direction. I am the
one who burns down all bonds. I am Kala. I am Hara,
the cause behind Kala. I urge everything, with the nature
of the sentient and insentient. I am the Purusha who is
inside. I am Purushottama. She is supreme *maya*. She is
Prakriti, with the three *guna*s. The sages describe her as
the eternal Shakti, the womb of the universe. The creator
of the universe deludes the universe with this *maya*. The
shruti texts say that Narayana, supreme and unmanifest,
has the form of *maya*. In this way, I always establish the
entire universe. I am Purusha, the twenty-fifth, and unite
with Prakriti. The divinity is hidden and without blemish,
going everywhere. He unites with her. With Prakriti, the
one without birth creates everything, which is nothing
but his own form. That divinity is Bhagavan Brahma, the
grandfather, with the universe as his form. I have properly
described the *paramatman* and creation to you. I am
Bhagavan Kala, without a beginning and without an end,
the lord who brings an end to the universe. I assume that
supreme nature. The learned speak of me as Rudra. Devi
is my supreme Shakti, famous under the name of Vidyaa.
Indeed, you yourself have seen Vidyaa and the *tattva*s of
Pradhana, Purusha and Ishvara. The *shruti* texts speak of
Vishnu, Brahma, Bhagavan Rudra and Kala. The three are

without beginning and without end and are established in the *brahman*. The *shruti* texts say that this is the unmanifest and imperishable *atman*. The *atman* is the supreme *tattva* and bliss. The supreme objective consists of consciousness alone. The firmament is nothing other than the *nishkala brahman*. Realizing this, you must seek refuge in *bhakti yoga* and worship the one who should be worshipped. You will then see Ishvara." Saying this, Bhagavan Hara vanished. Using *bhakti yoga*, the sage worshipped Rudra. This sacred *tirtha* is unmatched and is frequented by *brahmarshi*s. If he seeks refuge here, a learned *brahmana* is freed from all sins.'

Chapter 89(2)(36) (Destruction of Kala)

Suta said, 'There is another sacred and extensive *tirtha*, famous in the three worlds. This is known as Rudrakoti and it belongs to Rudra Parameshthi. Earlier, during a time period that was sacred, one crore controlled *brahmarshi*s came to that supreme place, wishing to see the supreme divinity. "I will be the first one to see Girisha, the wielder of Pinaka." Full of devotion, they spoke to each other in this way and there was a dispute. Girisha, the *guru* of *yogi*s, witnessed their devotion. Rudra assumed one crore forms and Ishvara's Rudrakoti was the result. All of them saw Mahadeva Hara, Parvati's lord, who lies down in a cave in the mountain. Their minds were nourished and delighted. They said, "I was the first one to see Mahadeva Ishvara, without a beginning and without an end." Their minds were filled with devotion towards Rudra. Desiring the supreme objective, all of them then saw a larger mass of sparkling radiance in the firmament. The divinity manifested himself there, in that auspicious and most sacred of *tirtha*s. Having witnessed this, they worshipped Rudra and obtained *samipya* with Rudra. There is another foremost and auspicious *tirtha*, named Madhuvana. A person who goes there and follows the *niyama*s, obtains Indra's seat. There is also the region of Padmanagari, auspicious and most sacred. If one goes there and worships the ancestors, one saves one hundred generations of the family.'

'Kalanjara[1697] is a great *tirtha*. The great lord in that world is Rudra. Hara loves devotees who worship the divinity in Kalanjara. In ancient times, there was a foremost *rajarshi*. He was Shiva's devotee and his named was Shveta. He worshipped Isha, the wielder of the trident, by prostrating himself before him. Placing *bhakti yoga* at the forefront, he followed the rules and instated Rudra. Fixing his mind, he constantly performed *japa* on Rudra. Kala came to the spot where the king was, wishing to take him away. He seized a terrible and blazing trident and was clad in black antelope skin. On seeing that he was advancing, with the trident in his hand, the king was filled with fear. He was terrible and fierce, dreadful in his radiance, the bringer of destruction. With both hands, the king touched the excellent *lingam*. He lowered his head before Rudra and performed *japa* with Shatarudriya. The king was performing *japa* in his mind, prostrate before Bhava. Standing in front of him, Kritanta[1698] seemed to laugh as he said, "Come. Come." Overwhelmed by fear

---

[1697]In Banda district of Uttar Pradesh. There is a Nilakantha temple and a sculpture of Kala Bhairava there.

[1698]The one who brings about the end, the Destroyer, Kala/Yama.

and full of devotion towards Rudra, the king told him, "Ignore the one who is engaged in worshipping Isha and kill the others." Thus addressed, the illustrious one replied to the one whose mind was full of fear. "Whether engaged in the worship of Rudra or not, who is not under my subjugation?" Saying this, Kala, who destroys the worlds, bound the king up in nooses, while the king continued to perform *japa* with Shatarudriya. At this, an extensive and blazing mass of energy appeared in the firmament. This was the ancient lord of *bhuta*s. He was enveloped in garlands of flames and pervaded the universe. He[1699] saw him manifest himself and remain established in this way. In the centre, there was the divinity with blazing limbs, marked by the sign of the moon and golden in complexion. Devi was with him. On seeing this form, full of energy, he thought that this was advancing towards him. The divinity, Rudra Mahesha, was advancing, not very far away, and Devi was with him. On seeing the absolute lord of everything, his fear was dispelled. However, Kala advanced, to take the *rajarshi* away. Bhagavan Rudra, fierce in deeds, the ancient divinity who is the lord of *bhuta*s, saw this. He told Kala, who was nothing but his form, "This is my devotee and he is remembering me. Quickly give him to me." Though he heard Gopati's words[1700] and though he was but a form of Rudra, Kala was proud of his own nature. He again bound the devotee with nooses. Assuming a terrible form, he rushed forward towards Rudra with great force. Isha, who knows the modes about *maya* in the universe, saw him advance and glanced towards the mountain's daughter. While Shveta looked on, he contemptuously struck Kala

---

[1699] Shveta.
[1700] Gopati is also one of Shiva's names.

with his left foot. Struck by Mahesha's extremely terrible
kick, he died. Maheshvara, the wielder of Pinaka, was
resplendent, along with Umaa. On seeing the divinity
Ishvara, the imperishable Hara, the bull among kings was
delighted in his mind and prostrated himself. "I prostrate
myself before Bhava, the cause, before Hara, the creator of
the universe. I prostrate myself before the intelligent Shiva.
I prostrate myself before the one who grants liberation. I
prostrate myself. I bow down. I prostrate myself. I bow
down. I prostrate myself before the great potency. Your
form is devoid of divisions. I prostrate myself before the
lord of men. I prostrate myself before the lord of *gana*s.
You are the one who dispels the miseries of those who seek
refuge. You are without a beginning and an end. You are
eternal prosperity. You are the one who holds Varaha's
horn.[1701] I prostrate myself before the one who has a bull
on his standard. I prostrate myself before the one who
wears a garland of skulls. I prostrate myself before the
great mountain, Shiva Shankara." As the king prostrated
himself, Shankara showed him his favours. He made him
his own imperishable *ganapati* and bestowed *sarupya* on
him. Worshipped by lords among sages and *siddha*s, Hara
vanished in an instant, along with Umaa, his attendants
and the bull among kings. When Kala was killed by
Mahesha, the grandfather, the lord of the worlds, sought a
boon from Rudra, "May he come back to life. O Ishana! O
Vrishadhvaja! He did not commit the least bit of sin. You
appointed him as Kritanta and he was performing the task
you asked him to do." Hearing the words of the lord of
*deva*s, Ishvara Hara, the lord of *deva*s and the *atman* of the

---

[1701]Varahashringa is one of Shiva's names, a reference to Shiva,
in the form of Sharabha, killing Varaha.

universe, agreed. That is what happened. This is a supreme *tirtha*, famous as Kalanjara. If one goes there and worships Mahadeva, one obtains the status of being a *ganapati*.'

Chapter 90(2)(37) (Description of *tirtha*s)

Suta said, 'There is another supreme and great place, the greatest secret among all secrets. This belongs to the divinity Mahadeva and is famous as Mahalaya. To establish a proof for non-believers, the primordial lord of *deva*s, Rudra, Tripura's enemy, placed his foot on a slab of rock there. There, there are serene ones who follow the *pashupata* vow, their bodies smeared with *bhasma*. They are devoted to studying the *Veda*s and worshipping Mahadeva. If one bathes there, and full of devotion, sees the mark of Sharva's foot, prostrating one's head, one obtains *samipya* with Rudra. There is another place of the great-souled Shambhu, the lord of *deva*s. This is famous as Kedara and is an auspicious abode for *siddha*s. If one bathes there and worships Mahadeva, who has the bull on his standard, and drinks the pure water, one obtains the status of being a *ganapati*. If one performs *shraddha*s, donations and other rites, the fruits obtained are imperishable. It is inhabited by the best among *dvija*s and *yogi*s who have conquered their minds. The *tirtha* of Plakshavatarana destroys all sins. If one worships Shrinivasa[1702] there, one obtains greatness in Vishnu's world. There is also the place Magadharanya. For all people, it bestows the destination. Having gone there, an excellent *dvija* obtains eternal

---

[1702] Vishnu.

heaven. The sacred *tirtha* of Kanakhala destroys great sins. The divinity Rudra destroyed Daksha's sacrifice there. Full of pure sentiments, if a man touches the waters of Ganga there, he is freed from all sins and resides in Brahma's world. There is the sacred place known as Mahatirtha, loved by Narayana. If one worships Hrishikesha there, one goes to Shvetadvipa. There is another foremost and auspicious *tirtha*, named Shriparvata. If one gives up one's life there, one becomes dear to Rudra. Rudra Maheshvara is present there, along with Devi. Bathing, offering *pinda*s and other things bestow excellent and imperishable fruits. The sacred river of Godavari destroys all sins. If one bathes there and following the rules, satisfies ancestors and *deva*s, one is cleansed of all sins. Pure in *atman*, one obtains the fruits of donating one thousand cows. The large and sacred river of Kaveri has holy waters. If one bathes and performs the water-rites there, one is freed from all sins. One should fast there for three nights, or fast for one night. The modes followed by *dvija*s when visiting *tirtha*s will now be described. The hands and feet must be steady and one must be pure in thoughts and words. One should not be greedy and should be a *brahmachari*. One then reaps the fruits of visiting *tirtha*s. Svamitirtha is a great *tirtha*, famous in the three worlds. Skanda, honoured by the immortals, is always present there. If one bathes in Kumaradhara, offers libations to *deva*s and others and worships *deva* Shanmukha,[1703] one rejoices with Skanda. The river named Tamraparni is famous in the three worlds. If one bathes there and following the rules, devoutly satisfies the ancestors, there is no doubt that the ancestors are saved, even if they have committed sins. The place known as Chandratirtha

[1703] One with six faces, Skanda/Kumara.

is at the source of Kaveri. Whatever is donated at that *tirtha* brings imperishable benefits. It bestows a virtuous destination on those who die there. O *dvija*s! Those devotees who see Sadashiva, the lord of *deva*s, at the feet of the Vindhyas, do not see Yama's face. In Devikaa, there is the *tirtha* named Vrisha, frequented by *siddha*s. If one bathes there and offers libations, one obtains *siddhi* in *yoga*. The *tirtha* of Dashashvamedhika destroys all sins. There, a man obtains the fruits of ten horse sacrifices. The *tirtha* of Pundarika is beautiful because it is ornamented by *brahmana*s. If one goes there and controls oneself, one obtains the fruits of a Pundarika sacrifice. Among all *tirtha*s, the supreme *tirtha* is said to be Brahmatirtha. If one worships Brahma there, one obtains greatness in Brahma's world. There is Vinashana in Sarasvati,[1704] the auspicious Plaksha-prasravana, the famous Vyasatirtha and the excellent mountain of Mainaka. The origin of Yamuna destroys all sins. The *devi* who is the daughter of the ancestors is famous as Gandhakali. If one bathes there, after death, one goes to heaven. When one is born, one can remember the past life. Kuberatunga destroys sins and is frequented by *siddha*s and *charana*s. If one gives up one's life there, one becomes Kubera's follower. Umatunga is famous and Rudra's beloved is present there. If one worships Mahadevi there, one obtains the fruits of donating one thousand cows. If one torments oneself through austerities in Bhrigutunga, performs *shraddha* and donates, it is my view that both sides of the family are saved for seven generations. Kashyapa's great *tirtha* is known as Kalasarpi. Desiring the destruction of sins,

[1704] Where the river Sarasvati disappears in sand. Plaksha-prasravana is the source of Sarasvati.

one should always perform *shraddha*s there. Donations, *shraddha*, oblations, austerities and *japa* undertaken in Dasharna are always eternal and imperishable. The *tirtha* named Kurujangala is full of *dvija*s. Following the rules, if one donates there, one obtains greatness in Brahma's world. Vaitarani is a great *tirtha* and so is Svarnavedi. Dharmaprishtha and Brahmashira are greatly auspicious. Bharata's hermitage is sacred. The auspicious Gridhravana is also sacred. So are Mahahrada and Koushiki. Anything donated in these places becomes eternal.'

'For the welfare of all beings and as proof to non-believers, the intelligent Mahadeva placed his foot in Mundaprishtha. Like a snake shedding off old skin, in a short period of time, a man devoted to *dharma* quickly gets rids of his sins. The *tirtha* named Kanakananda is famous in the three worlds. It is to the north of Brahmaprishtha and is frequented by large numbers of *brahmarshi*s. If *dvija*s bathe there, they go to heaven in their physical bodies. It is said that anything donated there, or a *shraddha* performed there, always brings eternal benefits. Bathing there, a man is freed from his sins and from his three debts.[1705] If one bathes in Lake Manasa, one obtains half of Shakra's seat. If one goes to the north of Manasa, one obtains excellent *siddhi*. According to capacity and strength, one should perform *shraddha*s there. Divine wishes are then satisfied and one obtains means of *moksha*. The mountain named Himalaya is decorated with many minerals. That mountain extends for eighty thousand *yojana*s. It is full of *siddha*s and *charana*s and is frequented by *deva*s and *rishi*s. There is a beautiful lake there, known by the name of Sushumna. If a learned *dvija* goes there, he is freed

---

[1705] To *deva*s, *rishi*s and ancestors.

from the sin of killing a *brahmana*. A *shraddha* performed there is eternal and anything donated becomes extensive. Ten generations of ancestors and ten generations of descendants are thereby saved. The Himalayas are sacred everywhere. Ganga is sacred everywhere. Rivers that flow into oceans are sacred. Oceans are especially sacred. If one reaches Badarikashrama, one is freed from all sins. The divinity Narayana and the eternal Nara are there. Anything donated there becomes eternal and this is also true of *shraddha*s and other rites. There is a *tirtha* loved by Mahadeva and it is particularly purifying. If one controls oneself and donates and performs *shraddha*s there, one saves all the ancestors. Devadaru-vana is sacred and is frequented by *siddha*s and *gandharva*s and also by Maheshvara, lord of *deva*s. Anything donated there becomes great. After deluding all the sages and after being worshipped by them, Bhagavan Isha was pleased. He spoke to the Indras among sages, who had been cleansed. "Always reside in this beautiful and excellent hermitage. Be immersed in me and you will achieve *siddhi*. In this world, those who are devoted to *dharma* worship me there. I bestow on them the supreme and eternal state of being a *ganapati*. Along with Narayana, I always reside here. If a man gives up his life here, he is not born again. O excellent *dvija*s! If people go to other countries, but remember this *tirtha*, I destroy all their sins. Anything performed there—*shraddha*s, donations, austerities, oblations, offering of *pinda*s, *dhyana*, *japa* and *niyama*— become ever-lasting. Therefore, *dvija*s must make every effort to see the sacred Devadaru-vana, inhabited by Mahadeva." Wherever Ishvara Mahadeva and Vishnu Purushottama are present, Ganga, other *tirtha*s and all temples assemble there.'

Chapter 91(2)(38) (Devadaru-vana)

The *rishi*s asked, 'How did Bhagavan, with the bull on his banner, reach Daruvana?[1706] How did he delude the Indras among *brahmana*s? O Suta! You should tell us this.'

Suta answered, 'Earlier, the beautiful Daruvana was frequented by *deva*s and *siddha*s. There were thousand of them performing austerities there, along with their sons and wives. Following the rules, they engaged in many different kinds of *karma*. Those *maharshi*s tormented themselves and performed many kinds of sacrifices. Their minds were engaged in *pravritti*. The wielder of the trident wished to explain that this always has taints. Therefore, Hara went to Daruvana. The divinity Maheshvara had Vishnu, the *guru* of the universe, by his side. Shankara went there, to establish *vijnana* about *nivritti*. He assumed the form of a tall person who was twenty years old. He was charming in his playfulness and mighty-armed. His limbs were thick and his eyes were beautiful. His body was golden. He was handsome and his face was like the full moon. His gait was like that of a mad elephant. The lord of the universe was naked. He wore a garland made of gold, decorated with every kind of jewel. Assuming this disguise, Bhagavan Isha arrived there, smiling. The imperishable Hari is the origin of the worlds. He is Ananta Purusha. Vishnu assumed the garb of a woman and followed the wielder of the trident. His face was like the full moon. The thick breasts were upraised. There was a sweet smile on the pleasant face. Anklets tinkled on the two legs. The divine garment was yellow. He

---

[1706]The same as Devadaru-vana. Devadaru-vana means a forest (*vana*) of *devadaru* (cedar) trees.

was dark, with beautiful eyes. His noble gait was like that
of a swan. He was extremely beautiful and charming. In
this way, deluding the world with his *maya*, Bhagavan Isha
Hara roamed around in Devadaru-vana, along with Hari.
Wherever they saw the lord of the universe, the wielder of
Pinaka, roaming around, the women were deluded by his
maya and followed the lord of *deva*s. They scattered their
ornaments around. Although they were devoted to their
husbands, all of them gave up any sense of shame. Afflicted
by desire, they wandered around with him, with amorous
gestures. The sons of the *rishi*s were young and had not yet
conquered their minds. Suffering from desire, all of them
followed Hrishikesha. Seeking to entice, the large numbers
of women sang and danced. The sole hero was Isha. They
saw this handsome person, who was with his wife, and
desired him. They embraced him and acted in similar ways.
The sons of the lords among sages were also there. They
smiled, sang songs and acted in similar ways. They glanced
at the primordial lord, Padma's[1707] consort and acted so
as to follow the one with the beautiful limbs. Their wishes
were excited by Vasudeva Murari, who used his *maya* to
enter their minds. They experienced this *maya* completely
and their minds towards *pravritti* and acting for enjoyment.
The creator of the universe and the lord of the universe was
radiant. Along with Madhava, he was amid many women.
Although the lord of *deva*s is only with one Shakti, at the
time, he seemed to be with innumerable Shaktis. He again
regained his supreme nature and started to dance.[1708] Like
that, Hari also assumed his normal nature and followed
the primordial *deva*.'

[1707] Lakshmi's.
[1708] There are typos in this *shloka* and we have taken liberties.

'On seeing the many women deluded by Rudra and the
sons by Keshava, the best among sages were filled with great
rage. They addressed Kapardi in very harsh words. Deluded
by his *maya*, they cursed him in different types of sentences.
When the sun rises in the sky, the stars in the firmament
lose their brightness. Like that, Shankara's presence made
them lose their austerities. After reprimanding him with
their austerities, the *brahmana*s approached Vrishadhvaja.
Deluded, they asked the lord of *deva*s, "Who are you?"
Bhagavan Isha replied, "O ones excellent in vows! With
my wife, I have come to this country of yours to perform
austerities." Hearing his words, Bhrigu and the other
bulls among sages said, "Perform austerities after wearing
clothes and forsaking your wife." Isha Pinaki Nilalohita
laughed. He glanced towards Janardana, the origin of the
universe, who was by his side, and said, "How is it that
you are eager to maintain your own wives but are asking
me to forsake my wife? You are serene in your minds and
know about *dharma*." The *rishi*s responded, "It is said
that husbands must abandon wives who are wanton. Our
extremely fortunate wives are devoted to us and are not
like this. They need not be abandoned." Mahadeva said,
"O *brahmana*s! This one does not desire anyone else, not
even in her mind. Nor do I ever let go of her." The *rishi*s
said, "O worst among men! We have witnessed her wanton
ways. You have lied. Quickly leave this place." Mahadeva
said, "I did speak the truth. It only appears to you to be
like that." Leaving them, he wandered away.'

'Along with Hari, seeking alms, Parameshvara went
to the sacred hermitage of the great-souled Vasishtha,
Indra among sages. Arundhati was Vasishtha's beloved.
On seeing the divinity arrive, seeking alms, she devoutly
welcomed him and prostrated herself. She washed his feet

and gave him a spotless and excellent seat. She saw that his body was weak because the *dvija*s had struck him. Distress on her face, the virtuous lady sought out and applied medicines. After performing this great worship, she asked, "Who are you? With your wife, where have you come from? What kind of conduct do you possess?" Bhagavan replied, "I am the best among *siddha*s. There is that radiant and sparkling disc,[1709] always full of the *brahman*. That is the divinity always nurtured by me." Saying this, taking his leave of the chaste lady, he departed.'

'The *dvija*s saw that Girisha was wandering around naked. This was a loathsome indication. They beat him with staffs, stones and fists. They said, "O extremely evil-minded one! Uproot this *lingam*."[1710] Shankara, the great *yogi*, told them, "If my *lingam* generates hatred in you, that is what I will do." Saying this, Bhagavan, who had uprooted Bhaga's eyes, uprooted it. At that very instant, Isha, Keshava and the *lingam* could no longer be seen. There were many evil omens, signifying fear to the worlds. The one with the thousand rays did not shine. The earth trembled. The planets lost their lustre and all the oceans were agitated. Anasuya, Atri's virtuous wife, saw a dream. With her senses agitated by fear, she spoke to the *brahmana*s. "With Narayana as his aide, he illuminated everything with his energy. It was indeed Shiva who was seen in our houses, seeking alms." Hearing her words, the *maharshi*s were alarmed. All of them went to the great *yogi* Brahma, the creator of the universe. The lord was being worshipped by spotless *yogi*s, supreme among those who knew about the *brahman*. In personified form, the four *Veda*s and

[1709]The sun.
[1710]The penis.

Savitri were with him. He was seated on a beautiful seat,
with many kinds of prosperity. Thousands of rays, full of
jnana and prosperity, emanated. His body was radiant.
He smiled and his eyes dazzled. He was four-faced and
mighty-armed. This was supreme Aja, full of *chhanda*s.
They looked at the body of the divinity and his pleasant
and pure face. Lowering their heads on the ground, they
placated the lord. The divinity with the four forms and four
faces was pleased in his mind. He asked, "O best among
sages! What is the reason for your arrival?" All of them
joined their hands in salutation above their heads and told
Brahma, the *paramatman*, everything that had happened.
The *rishi*s said, "An extremely beautiful man entered holy
Daruvana. He was naked. He was with his wife, who was
beautiful in all her limbs. With his body, the lord deluded
the women and maidens in our families. His wife did that
to our sons. We pronounced many kinds of curses on him,
but they were repelled. We struck him a lot and brought
down his *lingam*. Along with his wife and the *lingam*, the
illustrious one vanished. Terrible portents resulted, causing
fear to beings. O divinity! O Purushottama! We are terrified.
Who is this man? O Achyuta! We have sought refuge with
you. You know about everything that is attempted in this
universe. Show us your favours and protect us." The large
number of sages informed the *atman* of the universe, the
one who originated from the lotus.'

'Joining his hands in salutation, he meditated on
the divinity who has the trident as a mark and spoke.
Brahma said, "Alas! What a great calamity has come
over you today. Everything has been destroyed. Shame
on your strength. Shame on your austerities and powers.
All of them have been rendered futile. Because of your
good merits and cleansing, you obtained a treasure, the

most supreme of treasures. But you ignored him. You
were deluded and all your good conduct is in vain. This
is the treasure *yogis* always desire and mendicants strive
for. You obtained it. But alas! You ignored him. Those
who speak about the *Veda*s obtain him after worshipping
him with many kinds of sacrifices. Having obtained that
great treasure, you neglected him. I became the lord of the
universe after constantly worshipping him. After seeing
the divinity, who is a treasure, you ignored him, like
people devoid of good fortune. All the divine potencies
have been gathered together in him. He is the imperishable
one. You did obtain that treasure, the *brahman*. But you
acted so as to render it futile. He is the divinity Mahadeva
Maheshvara, the one who should be known. There is no
other supreme objective one can strive for. Among *devas*,
rishis and ancestors, he is eternal. There is dissolution at
the end of one thousand *mahayuga*s. Assuming the form
of Bhagavan Kala, Maheshvara withdraws all those with
bodies. With his own energy, it is he who creates all *prajas*.
He is the one with the *chakra*. He is the *chakravarti*.[1711]
He is marked by the sign of Shrivatsa. This divinity is a
yogi in *krita yuga*, the sacrifice in *treta yuga*, Bhagavan
Kala in *dvapara* and the banner of *dharma* in *kali yuga*.
In three forms, Rudra pervades the entire universe. The
smriti texts say that Agni is *tamas*, Brahma is *rajas* and
Vishnu is *sattva*. It is said that he has another certain
and auspicious form that is naked. The *brahman*, full of
yoga, is established there. You spoke to his wife, who was
by his side. That was the divinity Narayana, the eternal
paramatman. Everything originates in him. Everything

[1711]Universal emperor, one whose wheel moves everywhere,
unimpeded.

proceeds to dissolution in him. He frees from everything.
He is the supreme objective. He is Purusha, with one
thousand heads, one thousand eyes and one thousand
feet. The *shruti* texts say that Narayana is the great *atman*,
with a single horn.[1712] The seed is in Bhagavan's womb.
The lord's body is full of *maya*. *Brahmana*s who desire
liberation praise him with many kinds of *mantra*s. At
the end of the *kalpa*, Purushottama withdraws the entire
universe. Drinking the *amrita* of *yoga*, he lies down in the
place that is Vishnu's supreme abode. He sees the entire
universe. He is not born, and he does not die. He does
not grow. Those who follow the *Veda*s sing of him as the
unmanifest and primordial Prakriti, without birth. When
night is over, Maheshvara desires to create the entire
universe. He flings the seed in the navel of the one who is
without birth. Know me to be the great *atman*, Brahma,
with a face in every direction. I am the great Purusha, the
water in the universe, the excellent womb. Deluded by his
maya, you did not recognize the father. He is Mahadeva,
the lord of *deva*s. He is Ishvara, the lord of beings. This
is the divinity Mahadeva. He is Bhagavan Hara, without
a beginning. Along with Vishnu, he creates and destroys.
He has no task to perform. There is no one superior to
him. With his body, full of *yoga* and *maya*, he bestowed
the *Veda*s on me earlier. He is full of *maya*. With his
maya, he creates and destroys. Knowing that he is the
source for liberation, go and seek refuge with Shiva." The
lord, Bhagavan, spoke in this way to them, Marichi being
the foremost. Prostrating themselves before the divinity
Brahma, they controlled themselves and asked.'

[1712]Ekashringa, Vishnu's name.

Chapter 92(2)(39) (Entry into Devadaru-vana)

The sages asked, 'How can we again see the divinity Pinaki? O lord of the universe and immortals! You are the one who saves those who seek refuge.'

Brahma answered, 'When it fell down on the ground, you saw his *lingam*. Imitating that *lingam* of Isha's, makes an excellent *lingam*. Lovingly, along with your wives and sons, worship it. Be *brahmachari*s and follow the various *niyama*s indicated in the *Veda*s. Instate it, with Shankara's *mantra*s from *Rig*, *Yajur* and *Sama Veda*. Resort to supreme austerities and chant Shatarudriya. Control yourselves and worship him, along with your sons and relatives. All of you join your hands in salutation and seek refuge with the wielder of the trident. You will then see the lord of *deva*s. Those who have not cleansed their *atman*s find it impossible to see him. On seeing him, every kind of ignorance and *adharma* are destroyed.'

Suta continued, 'At this, they prostrated themselves before the infinitely energetic Brahma, the bestower of boons. Delighted in their minds, they again went to Devadaru-vana. Though they did not know his supreme nature, they wished to worship him, as Brahma had suggested. They were devoid of attachment and devoid of malice. They based themselves in many kinds of flat ground, caves in mountains and deserted and auspicious banks of rivers. Some ate moss. Others lay down inside the water. Some exposed themselves to the sky, with clouds in it. Some stood on their big toes. Some were *dantaulukhalika*s. Others were *ashmakutta*s. Some ate vegetables and leaves. Some only washed themselves, while others fed on air. Some made their habitations under the roots of trees. Others lay down on rocky ground. In this way, they spent

their time in austerities, worshipping Maheshvara. Hara
is one who removes the afflictions of those who seek
refuge and he wished to show them his favours. Bhagavan
Vrishadhvaja decided to kindle understanding in them. The
divinity, Parameshvara, was pleased. In *krita yuga*, on that
auspicious summit of Himalaya, he reached Devadaru-
vana. His limbs were smeared with pale *bhasma*. He was
naked, hideous in form. He grasped blazing brands in
his hands. His eyes were red and tawny. Sometimes, he
laughed in a terrible voice. Sometimes, surprised, he sang.
Sometimes, he danced, in the throes of passion. Sometimes,
he repeatedly wept. He repeatedly roamed around in the
hermitages, begging for alms. Using his own *maya* to
create this form, the divinity arrived in the forest. The
divinity, wielder of Pinaka, created the form of Gouri, the
mountain's daughter, by his side. As was the case earlier,
Devi went to Devadaru-vana. They saw that the divinity
Kapardi had arrived, along with Devi. They prostrated
themselves, with their heads on the ground, and satisfied
Ishvara. They used many kinds of auspicious *mantra*s
and *stotram*s, dedicated to Maheshvara, from the *Veda*s.
Others worshipped Bhava Rudra with *Atharvashirsha*.'

'I prostrate myself before the divinity who is the
lord of *deva*s. I prostrate myself before Mahadeva. O
Tryambaka! I prostrate myself before you, the wielder of
the excellent trident. I prostrate myself before you, with
the directions as your garment. O malformed Pinaki! You
are the divinity before whom everyone bows down. But
you do not bow down before anyone. You are the one
who brought destruction to Death. You are the one who
destroys everything. I prostrate myself before the one who
is devoted to dancing. I prostrate myself before the one who
has the form of Bhairava. You possess the body of a man

and a woman. I prostrate myself before the *guru* of *yogi*s. I prostrate myself before the controlled and serene one. You are Hara, the ascetic. I prostrate myself before the terrible Rudra Krittivasa. I prostrate myself before the one who licks his tongue. I prostate myself before the one with the handsome throat. I prostrate myself before the one who has the forms of Aghora and Ghora, before Vamadeva.[1713] I prostrate myself before the one with the golden garland, the one who does what brings pleasure to Devi. You hold the waters of Ganga. You are Shambhu Parameshthi. I prostrate myself before the lord of *yoga*. I prostrate myself before the lord of *bhuta*s. I prostrate myself before the one who is *prana*. I prostrate myself before the one who smears his limbs with *bhasma*. I prostrate myself before the one who bears *havya*. You are the fanged one, with *havya* as your seed. You are the one who cut off Brahma's head. You possess the form of Kala. We do not know about your arrival. Nor do we know about your departure. O Vishveshvara Mahadeva! You are who you are. I prostrate myself before you. I prostrate myself before the lord of *pramatha*s, the one who bestows auspicious prosperity. I prostrate myself before the one who has the skull in his hand, the one who is most desired. I prostrate myself before the one who is golden and tawny. I prostrate myself before the one whose *lingam* is the water. I prostrate myself before the one whose *lingam* is the fire and the sun. I prostrate myself before the one whose *lingam* is *jnana*. I prostrate myself before the one whose garland is a serpent, the one who loves *karnikara* flowers. I prostrate myself before the destroyer of Kala, before the one with a diadem and

---

[1713] Literally, Aghora is the one who does not terrify, while Ghora is the one who terrifies.

ear-rings. O Mahadeva! O great *deva*! O lord of *deva*s! O three-eyed one! Please pardon what we did in our delusion. We seek refuge with you. Your conduct is wonderful, secret and mysterious. O Shankara! Brahma and all the others find it impossible to comprehend. Whatever a man does, voluntarily or involuntarily, is actually done by Bhagavan, using his *yoga* and *maya*.'

Suta continued, 'Praised in this way, Mahadeva entered inside their *atman*s. They prostrated themselves and told Girisha, "Let us see you, as was the case earlier." Along with Umaa, the one who has Soma as an ornament heard their words of praise. Shankara displayed his own supreme form. They saw Girisha Pinaki, along with Devi, standing before them, as was the case earlier. Delighted in their minds, the *brahmana*s prostrated themselves. All the sages praised Maheshvara—Bhrigu, Angiras, Vasishtha, Vishvamitra, Goutama, Atri, Sukesha, Pulastya, Pulaha, Kratu, Marichi, Kashyapa and the great ascetic, Samvartaka. They prostrated themselves before Isha, the lord of *deva*s, and addressed him in these words. "O Isha! O lord of *deva*s! O lord! How must you always be worshipped, through *karma yoga* or *jnana yoga*? O divinity! Through what path should Bhagavan be worshipped in this world? What should be practiced and what should not be practiced? Please tell us everything."'

Shri Shiva replied, 'O *maharshi*s! I will describe this. This is secret, mysterious and excellent. Earlier, Brahma narrated this about Mahadeva. It should be known that there are two types of *sadhana* for men—*samkhya* and *yoga*. *Samkhya*, along with *yoga*, bestows liberation on men. Through *yoga* alone, a man is incapable of seeing the supreme. However, *jnana* alone is capable of properly bestowing the fruit of liberation. For the sake of liberation, you only sought refuge in *yoga*. You made your exertions without resorting to sparkling *samkhya*. O *brahmana*s! That is the reason I arrived at this place, to explain that if men only resort to *karma*, delusion can be generated. Therefore, you should make efforts to know, hear and see that sparkling *jnana* is the only possible *sadhana* for *kaivalya*. The *atman* is one and goes everywhere. It consists of consciousness alone. It is always sparkling bliss. This is the *darshana* of *samkhya*. For liberation, this is sung about as supreme *jnana*. This is described as sparkling *kaivalya* and the state of the *brahman*. Great-souled mendicants resort to that which is supreme and are devoted to it. Thereby, they see me, the lord of the universe. This is supreme, unsullied and absolute *jnana*. I, Bhagavan, am the one who should be known and Shivaa is my form. For *siddhi*, many kinds of *sadhana*s have been spoken about. O bulls among *dvija*s! Among all those, *jnana* about me is the best. There are those who are serene, devoted to *jnana yoga*. They seek refuge in me. They use my *bhasma* and always meditate on me in their hearts. Always full of devotion towards me, these mendicants destroy their sins. For them, within a short period of time, I destroy this terrible cavity that is *samsara*. Earlier, I devised the auspicious Pashupata *vrata*. This is subtle and is the greatest secret among all secrets. For the sake of liberation, this has the essence of the *Veda*s. A person who practices Pashupata *vrata* must be serene and controlled in mind, his limbs smeared with *bhasma*. He must follow *brahmacharya* and be naked. The sage can also wear a loin-cloth, or a single piece of cloth as garment. He must be devoted to studying the *Veda*s. Such a learned person must perform *dhyana* on Pashupati Shiva. Those who desire liberation must practice this Pashupata *yoga*. One also reads and hears that those

who based themselves on this must be free from desire.
They are free from attachment, fear and anger. Absorbed
in me, they seek refuge in me. There are many who have
purified themselves with his *yoga* and have attained me.[1714]
In this world, there are other sacred texts that are meant to
confound. I am the one who propounded them, but they
are contrary to the *Veda*s. They are Vama, Pashupata,
Soma, Lakura, Bhairava and others that are spoken about.
These are outside the pale of the *Veda*s and must not be
followed. O *brahmana*s! I am the form of the *Veda*s. Those
who know the truth about other sacred texts do not know
about my nature. They do not speak of me as the eternal
divinity. Establish this path and worship Maheshvara.
Thus, within a short period of time, there is no doubt that
you will attain excellent *jnana*. O excellent ones! May
your devotion towards me be extensive. O excellent sages!
As soon as you perform *dhyana* on me, I will grant you
my presence.'

Suta continued, 'Saying this, along with Umaa,
Bhagavan vanished from that spot. They remained in
Daruvana and worshipped Shankara. They were serene
and practiced *brahmacharya*. They were devoted to *jnana
yoga*. Those great-souled sages assembled there and spoke
about the *brahman*. Resorting to *jnana* about their own
*atman*s, they held many kinds of discussions. "What is
the root cause behind this universe? Our *atman*s. Who is
the cause behind every kind of sentiment? Ishvara." Thus,
following the path of *dhyana*, they thought in this way.
Mahadevi, the daughter of the excellent mountain, arrived
there. She resembled one crore suns. She was enveloped in
garlands of flames. She filled up the entire firmament with

[1714]This is almost exactly Bhagavat Gita 4.10.

her own sparkling radiance. They saw the immeasurable daughter of the mountain, established inside one thousand flames. They prostrated themselves before the wife of the one who is the lord of everything. They knew that she is the supreme seed. "This is the wife of our supreme lord. She is our destination and our *atman*. She is spoken of as the firmament." They saw her within their own *atman*s and all the sages were delighted. They glanced at Paramesha's wife and the divinity who is the cause behind everything. They saw the wise Shambhu Isha, the saviour, Rudra, the great and ancient Purusha. On seeing Devi and the divinity Isha, they prostrated themselves and were overwhelmed with bliss. Through Bhagavan Isha's favours, the *jnana* that destroys the cause behind birth developed in them. "This is the single womb of the universe. She is in all *atman*s. She is the one who controls everything. She is Maheshvara's Shakti. She is without a beginning and possesses the *siddhi*. Known as the firmament, she shines in heaven. Greater than her is the supreme Parameshthi Maheshvara Shiva, the absolute Rudra. Ascending this *maya* and established in the supreme Shakti, the lord of *deva*s created the universe. The single divinity is in all beings. Rudra is hidden and is full of *maya*. He is *sakala* and *nishkala*. He and Devi are not distinct. If one knows this, one proceeds towards immortality." Along with Devi, Bhagavan Mahesha, the lord of *deva*s, vanished. The residents of the forest again worshipped Rudra, the primordial divinity. I have thus told you everything that the lord of *deva*s did in Devadaru-vana earlier. I have heard about it in the Puranas. If a person constantly reads or hears it, he is freed from all sins. If he makes serene *dvijas* listen to this, he proceeds to the supreme destination.'

Chapter 93(2)(40) (Greatness of Narmada)

Suta said, 'River Narmada is famous in the worlds and is an excellent *tirtha*. This *devi* is most sacred and is frequented by *deva*s and *gandharva*s. Hear about its greatness, as narrated by Markandeya to Yudhishthira. This is auspicious and destroys all sins.'

Yudhishthira said, 'O great sage! Because of your favours, I have heard about many kinds of *dharma*, about the greatness of Prayaga and many kinds of *tirtha*s. You have said that Narmada is foremost among *tirtha*s. O excellent one! You should now tell me about its greatness.'

Markandeya replied, 'Narmada, best among rivers, emerged from Rudra's body. It saves all entities, mobile and immobile. In the Puranas, I have heard about Narmada's greatness. I will now tell you about that auspicious account. Listen attentively. Ganga is sacred in Kanakhala and Sarasvati in Kurukshetra. But whether in the village or in the forest, Narmada is sacred everywhere. The waters of Sarasvati purify in three days, the waters of Yamuna in seven days. Ganga's waters purify instantly. But the sight of Narmada alone purifies. To the western side of the country of Kalinga, there is Mount Amarakantaka. It is beautiful and charming. It is the most sacred in the three worlds. It is always frequented by *deva*s, *asura*s and *gandharva*s. O Indra among kings! Tormenting themselves through austerities there, *rishi*s, stores of austerities, have achieved supreme *siddhi*. O king! If a man bathes there, follows the *niyama*s and conquers his senses, fasting for a single night, he saves one hundred generations of his lineage. O Indra among kings! It is heard that this excellent river extends for more than one hundred *yojana*s and is two *yojana*s in width. All around the mountain of Amarakantaka, there are sixty crore and sixty thousand *tirtha*s. O king! O unblemished one! Listen attentively to the sacred fruits obtained by a man who is a *brahmachari*, who has purified himself, conquering his rage and restraining his senses. He refrains from every kind of violence and is engaged in the welfare of all beings. O Pandava! If such a person, pure in conduct, gives up his life there, he enjoys himself in heaven for a hundred thousand years. That place is full of large numbers of *apsara*s and he is surrounded by divine women. He is smeared with divine fragrances and is ornamented with celestial flowers. He sports in the world of heaven and rejoices with the gods. When he is dislodged from heaven, he becomes a king who is devoted to *dharma*. He obtains a house that is full of many kinds of jewels. There are bejewelled pillars, decorated with divine diamonds and lapis lazuli. There are paintings, shining mounts and hundreds of female servants. He becomes a lord who is a king of kings. He is handsome and is loved by all the women. With objects of pleasure, he lives for more than one hundred years.'

'If a person ends his life by entering the fire or water, or by fasting to death, like the wind absorbed in the sky, there is no return for him. On the western slope of the mountain, there is a lake named Jaleshvara. It is famous in the three worlds and destroys all sins. If one offers *pinda*s there and worships with the *sandhya* rites, there is no doubt that the ancestors are satisfied for ten thousand years. On the southern bank of Narmada, there is a great river, known as Kapilaa. It is not very far and is covered by *sarala* and *arjuna* trees.[1715] It is sacred and extremely fortunate and is famous in the three worlds. O Yudhishthira! There are

---

[1715] *Sarala* is a type of pine and *arjuna* is a tall tree.

more than one hundred crore *tirtha*s there. In the course of time, there are trees that fall down in that *tirtha*. Because they touch Narmada's waters, they proceed to the supreme destination. There is a second immensely fortunate and auspicious river, Vishalyakarani. If a man bathes in that *tirtha*, he is instantly freed from distress.[1716] One hears about two excellent rivers, Kapilaa and Vishalyaa. Earlier, desiring the welfare of the worlds, Ishvara spoke about them. O lord of men! If a man gives up his life in that *tirtha*, he is freed from all sins and he goes to Rudra's world. O king! If he bathes there, a man obtains the fruits of a horse sacrifice. Those who reside on its northern bank reside in Rudra's world. O Yudhishthira! Shankara told me that bathing and donations in Sarasvati, Ganga and Narmada are equal in merits. If a person gives up his life in Mount Amarakantaka, he obtains greatness in Rudra's world for more than a hundred crore years. If a person sprinkles his head with sacred water and foam from Narmada, he is purified and freed from all sins. Narmada is sacred everywhere. It destroys the sin of killing a *brahmana*. If one fasts for a day and a night, one is freed from the sin of killing a *brahmana*. Jaleshvara is an excellent *tirtha* and destroys all sins. If a man goes there and follows the *niyama*s, he obtains everything desired. If a man goes to Amarakantaka during a solar or lunar eclipse, he obtains good merits that are ten times those of a horse sacrifice. This sacred and excellent mountain is frequented by *deva*s and *gandharva*s. There are many trees and creepers. It is adorned with many

---

[1716]The word *shalya* means thorn, pain, distress, defamation. Anything without this is *vishalya* and since the river does this, it is Vishalyakarani. Vishalyakarani and Vishalyaa are clearly the same river.

kinds of flowers. O king! Along with Devi, Maheshvara is present there. Brahma, Vishnu and Rudra are also there, along with large numbers of *vidyadhara*s. If a man does a *pradakshina* of Mount Amarakantaka, he obtains the fruits of a Poundarika sacrifice. There is the famous river named Kaveri. It destroys sins. If a person bathes there and worships Mahadeva Vrishadhvaja, at its confluence with Narmada,[1717] one obtains greatness in Rudra's world.'

Chapter 94(2)(41)
(Greatness of Narmada continued)

Markandeya said, 'Narmada is the best among rivers and destroys all sins. The sages said this earlier and so did Ishvara Svayambhu. The sages praised the excellent river, Narmada. For the welfare of the worlds, it emerged from Rudra's body. It destroys all sins and is always revered by all the *deva*s. *Deva*s, *gandharva*s and *apsara*s praise it. On its northern bank, there is a *tirtha* that is famous in the three worlds. It is named Bhadreshvara. It is sacred and auspicious and destroys all sins. O king! If a man bathes there, he rejoices with the *deva*s. O Indra among kings! After that, one should go to the excellent Vimaleshvara. O king! If a man bathes there, he obtains the fruits of donating one thousand cows. After this, controlling oneself and with restraint in diet, one should go to Angareshvara. It frees from all sins and pure in *atman*, one obtains greatness in Rudra's world. O Indra among kings! After this, one should go to the place named Kedara,

---

[1717]This confluence is near Omkareshvara.

which bestows the auspicious. If a person bathes in the waters there and drinks it, he obtains everything he wishes for. Then, one should go to Nishphalesha, which destroys all sins. O great king! If a man bathes there, he obtains greatness in Rudra's world. O Indra among kings! After this, one should go to the excellent Banatirtha. If a person gives up his life there, he obtains Rudra's world. After this, one should go to Pushkarini and bathe there. O king! If a man bathes there, he obtains lordship over a throne. After this, one should go to Shakratirtha, on the southern bank. As soon as a man bathes there, he obtains half of Indra's seat. O Indra among kings! The *shruti* texts say that after this, one should go to Shulabheda. If a person bathes and drinks the water there, he obtains the fruits of donating one thousand cows. An unblemished man should fast for a night and bathe, following the rules. He should worship the lord of *deva*s, the great *yogi*. He will then obtain the fruits of donating one thousand cows and go to Vishnu's world. After this, one should go to Rishitirtha, which destroys all sins of men. As soon as a man bathes there, he obtains greatness in Shiva's world. Narada's *tirtha* is there and it is extremely beautiful. As soon as a man bathes there, he obtains the fruits of donating one thousand cows. Earlier, Narada, the celestial *rishi*, tormented himself through austerities there. Pleased, Maheshvara, the lord of *deva*s, bestowed *yoga* on him. The *lingam* fashioned by Brahma is famous as Brahmeshvara. O king! If a man bathes there, he obtains greatness in Brahma's world. After this, a man should go to Rinatirtha. He will certainly be freed of debts. After this, he should go to Vateshvara, which bestows sufficient fruits for this birth. After this, he should go to Bhimeshvara, which destroys every kind of ailment. As soon as a man bathes there, he is freed from all miseries.

O Indra among kings! After this, one should go to the excellent Pingaleshvara. If one fasts for a day and a night there, one obtains the fruits of a *triratra* sacrifice.[1718] O Indra among kings! If a man donates a *kapila* cow there, he obtains greatness in Rudra's world for as many thousand of years as there are body hair on the cow or its calves. O lord of men! If a person gives up his life there, he rejoices for an eternal period of time, as long as the sun and the moon last. There are men who seek out Narmada's banks and live there. When they die, they go to heaven, like virtuous people who have performed good deeds. After this, one should go to Dipteshvara and the hermitage of Vyasatirtha. Earlier, sacred of Vyasa, the great river retreated from that place. When Vyasa uttered his *humkara*, it immediately started to flow south. O Yudhishthira! If a man does *pradakshina* in that *tirtha*, Vyasa is pleased and he obtains the desired fruits. O Indra among kings! After this, one should go to the confluence of the river Ikshu. This is sacred and famous in the three worlds. Shiva is present there. O king! If a man bathes there, he obtains the status of being a *ganapati*. After this, one should go to Rinatirtha. One will certainly be freed from debts. If one bathes there, all the sins committed since birth are destroyed. There,[1719] *deva*s and *gandharva*s worship Bharga's excellent son, the great-souled lord Skanda, who wields the spear. After this, one should go to Angiras-tirtha and bathe there. One obtains the fruits of donating one thousand cows and goes to Rudra's world. Angiras, Brahma's son, used his austerities to worship Vrishadhvaja, the lord of *deva*s, there. From the lord of the universe, he obtained

---

[1718] A sacrifice that lasts for three nights.

[1719] At Skandatirtha. Bharga is one of Shiva's names.

excellent *yoga*. After this, one should go to Kushatirtha,
which destroys all sins. If one bathes there, one obtains
the fruits of a horse sacrifice. After this, one should go to
Kotitirtha, which destroys all sins. If one bathes there, all
the sins committed since birth are dispelled. After this, one
should go to Chandrabhaga and bathe there. As soon as a
man bathes there, he obtains greatness in Soma's world.
The excellent Sangameshvara is on Narmada's southern
bank. O king! If a man bathes there, he obtains the fruits
of performing all sacrifices. On Narmada's northern
bank, there is an extremely beautiful *tirtha*. The beautiful
Adityayatana, spoken about by Ishvara, is there. O Indra
among kings! If a man bathes there and donates according
to his capacity, because of the powers of that *tirtha*, he
obtains imperishable fruits. The poor and diseased, those
who have committed wicked deeds, are freed from all their
sins and go to Surya's world. After this, one should go to
Matritirtha and bathe there. As soon as a man bathes there,
he obtains the world of heaven. After this, one should go
to the west, to the excellent Marutashaya. O Indra among
kings! A man should bathe there and control and purify
himself. According to the extent of his wealth, he should
donate gold to a mendicant. In Pushpaka *vimana*, he will
then go to Vayu's world. O Indra among kings! After this,
one should go to the excellent Ahalyatirtha. As soon as one
bathes there, one rejoices with *apsara*s for an infinite period
of time. When it is the month of Chaitra, *trayodashi* in
shukla paksha is Kamadeva's day. At the time, one should
worship Ahalya. Wherever he is born, a man will then be
greatly loved. He will be the darling of women. He will
be handsome, like another Kamadeva. After reaching the
excellent river, one should go to the famous Shakratirtha.
As soon as a man bathes there, he obtains the fruits of

donating one thousand cows. Having gone to Somatirtha, one should bathe there. As soon as a man bathes there, he is freed from all sins. O Indra among kings! During a lunar eclipse, this destroys sins. O king! Somatirtha is famous in the three worlds and bestows great fruits. If a person controls himself and undertakes *chandrayana* there, he is freed from all sins. Pure in *atman*, he goes to Soma's world. O lord of men! If a man enters the fire there, or does by immersing himself in water or fasting, he is no longer born as a mortal. After this, one should go to Stambhatirtha and bathe there. As soon as a man bathes there, he obtains greatness in Soma's world.'

'O Indra among kings! After this, one should go to the excellent Vishnutirtha. This is famous as Yodhanipura and is Vishnu's excellent place. Vasudeva fought against crores of *asura*s there and the *tirtha* came into being.[1720] If one bathes there, one becomes as handsome as Vishnu. If one fasts for a day and a night, the sin of killing a *brahmana* is dispelled. There is an extremely beautiful *tirtha* on Narmada's southern bank. This is famous as Kamatirtha and Kama worshipped Hari there. If a man bathes in that *tirtha*, intent on fasting, in the form of the one who has flowers as a weapon,[1721] he obtains greatness in Rudra's world. O Indra among kings! After this, one should go to the excellent Brahmatirtha. This is famous as Amogha and one should satisfy the ancestors there. Following the rules, one should perform *shraddha*s on *pournamasi* and *amavasya*. In the midst of the water there, there is a rock in the form of an elephant. In the month of Vaishakha, controlled, one should offer *pinda*s there. Controlling his mind, a person

---

[1720] *Yodhana* means fighting.
[1721] That is, Kamadeva.

should bathe. He should be free of insolence and envy. His ancestors will then be satisfied for as long as the earth exists. After this, one should go to Vishveshvara and bathe there. As soon as a man bathes there, he obtains the status of being a *ganapati*. O Indra among kings! After this, one should go to the place where Janardana exists in the form of a *lingam*. If a man bathes there devoutly, he obtains greatness in Vishnu's world. There, the divinity Narayana showed sages who had cleansed their *atman*s his own self, in the form of a *lingam*, the supreme objective. After this, one should go to Akolla, which destroys all sins. If one bathes, donates, feeds *brahmana*s and offers *pinda*s there, after death, one obtains infinite fruits. If a *dvija* makes *charu* with water from Tryambaka and following the rules, offers *pinda*s at the root of an *akolla* plant,[1722] he saves his ancestors for as long as the moon and stars exist. O Indra among kings! After this, one should go to the excellent Tapaseshvara. O Indra among kings! If one bathes there, one obtains the fruits of austerities. After this, one should go to Shuklatirtha, which destroys all sins. O Yudhishthira! Along Narmada, there is no other *tirtha* that is its equal. Seeing and touching the waters, bathing, donations, austerities, *japa*, oblations and fasting yield great fruits in Shuklatirtha. This *kshetra* is said to extend for one *yojana* and is frequented by *deva*s and *gandharva*s. It is famous as Shuklatirtha and destroys all sins. Even if one sees it from the top of a tree, the sin of killing a *brahmana* is destroyed. Along with Devi, Bharga Shankara is always present there. O one excellent in vows! On *chaturdashi* in *krishna paksha* in the month of Vaishakha, Hara emerges from his own world and is present there. *Deva*s, *danava*s, *gandharva*s, *siddha*s, *vidyadhara*s, *gana*s,

---

[1722] Meaning *ankola, Alangium salvifolium*.

*apsara*s and bulls among *naga*s are present there. Just as a coloured piece of cloth becomes white after being washed in water, all the sins committed since birth are cleaned in Shuklatirtha. Bathing, donations, austerities and *shraddha*s are seen to yield infinite fruits there. There is no *tirtha* that is more purifying than Shuklatirtha. If a man has committed sins in the earlier part of his life, they are destroyed if he fasts for a day and a night in Shuklatirtha. On *chaturdashi* in *krishna paksha* in the month of Kartika, one should bathe the divinity Parameshvara with *ghee* and fast. With twenty-one generations, he will then not be dislodged from Ishvara's abode. The destination obtained through Shuklatirtha is not obtained through austerities, *brahmacharya*, sacrifices and donations. Shuklatirtha is a great *tirtha*, frequented by *rishi*s and *siddha*s. O king! If a man bathes there, he does not take birth again. When the *ayana* changes, on *chaturdashi* and on *vishuva sankranti*, one should bathe and fast, controlling oneself and restraining the mind. One should donate according to capacity. Hari and Shankara are then pleased. The power of this *tirtha* makes everything infinite. Hear about the sacred fruits obtained by a person who supports a helpless and distressed *brahmana* in this *tirtha*, acting like a protector. He obtains greatness in Rudra's world for as many thousands of years as there are body hairs on his own body or those of his offspring. O Indra among kings! After this, one should go to the excellent Yamatirtha. O Yudhishthira. On *chaturdashi* in *krishna paksha* in the month of Magha, if a man bathes there, fasting in the night, he does not have to experience the hardship in a womb. O Indra among kings! After this, one should go to the excellent Eranditirtha. Intent on fasting, a man should bathe at that confluence.[1723] Even

---

[1723] Of the rivers Erandi and Narmada.

if one feeds a single *brahmana* there, that is like feeding one crore. Tinged with sentiments of devotion, one should bathe at the confluence of Erandi. One should immerse oneself in the water and apply the clay on the head. When he is touched by this mix of Narmada's waters, he is freed from all sins. O Indra among kings! After this, one should go to the *tirtha* of Kallolakeshvara. There is no doubt that on sacred days, Ganga descends here. If a person bathes and drinks the water there, donating according to the rules, he is freed from all sins and obtains greatness in Brahma's world. After this, one should go to Nanditirtha and bathe there. The lord Nandi is pleased there, and one obtains greatness in Soma's world. O Indra among kings! After this, one should go to the auspicious *tirtha* of Anaraka. O king! A man who bathes there, does not see *naraka*.[1724] O Indra among kings! If a man flings away his *asthi* in that *tirtha*, he is born in the world as handsome person, with wealth and objects of pleasure. O Indra among kings! After this, one should go to the excellent Kapilatirtha. O king! If a man bathes there, he obtains the fruits of donating one thousand cows. When it is the month of Jyeshtha, especially on *chaturdashi*, a man should fast, devoutly donating lamps and *ghee*. He should bathe Rudra with *ghee*. He will then obtain the fruit of being prosperous. He should donate a *kapila* cow, adorned with bells and ornaments. He will then be covered with every kind of ornament and be revered by all the *deva*s. He will then be as strong as Shiva and will always sport with Shiva. When it is Angaraka's day,[1725] especially if it happens to be *chaturthi*, one should bathe Shiva and give food to *brahmana*s. On a *vimana* that has everything desired, and with all the *deva*s,

---

[1724] *Naraka* is hell. Anaraka is negation of hell.
[1725] Tuesday, Angaraka is Mangala.

he will then go to Shakra's abode and rejoice with Shakra.
When he is dislodged from heaven, he will possess fortitude
and objects of pleasure. On Angaraka's day and on *navami*
and *amavasya*, one must make efforts to bathe Shiva. One
will then be handsome and extremely fortunate. O Indra
among kings! After this, one should go to the excellent
Ganeshvara. When it is *chaturdashi* of *krishna paksha* in
the month of Shravana, as soon as a man bathes there,
he obtains greatness in Rudra's world. When he performs
tarpana for the ancestors, he is freed from the three debts.
Near Gangeshvara[1726] is the excellent Gangavadana. Without
desires, or with desires, if a man bathes there, he is freed
from all sins that he has committed since birth. There is no
doubt about this. On its western side and not too far away,
there is the *tirtha* of Dashashvamedhika, famous in the three
worlds. One should fast for a single night in the auspicious
month of Bhadrapada, bathing Hara on *amavasya* and
worshipping Vrishadhvaja. On a golden *vimana* garlanded
with nets of bells, one will then go to Rudra's beautiful city
and rejoice with Rudra. He should bathe everywhere, on
all the days, and perform *tarpana* for the ancestors. He will
then obtain the fruits of a horse sacrifice.'

Chapter 95(2)(42)
(Greatness of Narmada continued)

Markandeya said, 'O Indra among kings! From there,
one should go to the excellent Bhrigutirtha. Earlier, in
ancient times, Bhrigu worshipped the divinity Rudra there.
If one sees the divinity there, one is instantly freed from

[1726]Perhaps Ganeshvara is intended.

sins. This *kshetra* is extremely large and destroys every sin.
Having bathed there, one goes to heaven. Those who die
there, are not born again. According to capacity, a pair of
footwear, gold and food should be given there. The fruits
are said to be imperishable. The fruits of all donations,
sacrifices, austerities and rites perish. O Yudhishthira!
However, if one torments oneself through austerities in
Bhrigutirtha, the fruits are imperishable. O Yudhishthira!
It is said that because of his fierce austerities, Rudra,
Tripura's enemy, is always present in Bhrigutirtha. O Indra
among kings! After this, one should go to the excellent
Goutameshvara. Having worshipped the one who bears
the mark of the trident, Goutama obtained *siddhi* there.
O king! If a man is intent on fasting and bathes there, he
goes to Brahma's world on a golden *vimana* and obtains
greatness there. *Vrishotsarga*[1727] undertaken there, ensures
progress to the eternal destination. Deluded by Vishnu's
maya, foolish men do not know this. One should then
go to Dhoutapapa, where Vrisha washes away sins.[1728] O
king! It is on the Narmada and it destroys all sins. If a
man bathes in that *tirtha*, the sin of killing a *brahmana*
is dispelled. O Indra among kings! If a person gives up
his life in that *tirtha*, he has four arms and three eyes and
a strength that is equal to that of Hara's. Like Shiva in
valour, he resides there[1729] for more than ten thousand
years. After a long period of time, he is born on earth and
becomes a universal emperor. O Indra among kings! After
this, one should go to the excellent Hastatirtha. O king!

[1727]Offering a bull, or setting the bull free, at the time of a
shraddha.
[1728]Vrisha is one of Shiva's names. Literally, Dhoutapapa
means—sins washed away.
[1729]It is implied that this is Shiva's world.

A man who bathes there, obtains greatness in Brahma's world.[1730] O Indra among kings! From there, one should go to the place where Janardana is present. This is known as Varahatirtha and bestows Vishnu's world as a destination. O Indra among kings! After this, one should go to the excellent Chandratirtha. One should have a bath there, especially on *pournamasi*. As soon as a man bathes there, he becomes a universal emperor on earth. From there, one should go to Devatirtha, revered by all the *tirtha*s. O Indra among kings! Having bathed there, a person rejoices with *deva*s. O Indra among kings! From there, one should go to the excellent Shankhatirtha. Anything donated there is multiplied by one crore in qualities. O Indra among kings! After this, one should go to the auspicious Paitamaha-tirtha. Anything donated at a *tirtha* there, brings imperishable benefits. If a person reaches Savitri-tirtha and gives up his life there, he is cleansed of all his sins and he obtains greatness in Brahma's world. Manohara-tirtha is extremely beautiful. O king! If a man bathes there, he obtains greatness in Rudra's world. O Indra among kings! From there, one should go to the excellent Kanyatirtha. O king! Having bathed there, a man is freed from all sins. On *tritiya* of *shukla paksha*, one should merely have one's bath there. As soon as a man bathes there, he becomes a universal emperor on earth. From there, one should go to the *tirtha* of Sargabindu, revered by *deva*s. O king! Having bathed there, a man never has to witness any hardship. From there, one should go to Apsaresha and bathe there. In the vault of heaven, one will then sport and rejoice with *aspara*s. O Indra among kings! From there, one should go

---

[1730] The reference to Brahma suggests this might be Hamsatirtha rather than Hastatirtha.

to the excellent Bharabhuti. If one fasts there and performs a sacrifice to Isha, one obtains greatness in Rudra's world. O king! If one dies in that *tirtha*, one obtains the status of being a *ganapati*. The learned say that if one worships the lord of *deva*s, Parvati's husband, in the month of Kartika, the fruits obtained are ten times those of a horse sacrifice. There, if one donates a bull, with the hue of a *kunda* flower or the moon, on a vehicle yoked to a bull, one goes to Rudra's world. Having reached this *tirtha*, if a person gives up his life, he is freed from all sins and goes to Rudra's world. O lord of men! If a person enters the water in this *tirtha*,[1731] he goes to the world of heaven in a vehicle yoked to swans. The confluence of Erandi and Narmada is famous in the world. That *tirtha* is extremely sacred and destroys all sins. One should fast there, constantly devoted to *vratas*. O Indra among kings! If a person bathes there, he is freed from the sin of killing a *brahmana*. O Indra among kings! After this, one should go to the confluence of Narmada and the ocean. This is famous as Jamadagni and Janardana is established there. O king! If a man bathes at the confluence of Narmada and the ocean, that man obtains fruits that are three times those of a horse sacrifice. O Indra among kings! From there, one should go to the excellent Pingaleshvara. O king! Having bathed there, a man obtains greatness in Brahma's world. If a person sees Vimaleshvara and fasts there, he discards sins committed across seven births and goes to Shiva's abode. O Indra among kings! From there, one should go to the excellent Alitirtha. One should fast for one night and be controlled and restrained in diet. As a result of the greatness of the *tirtha*, one is freed from the sin of killing a *brahmana*. I have briefly described

---

[1731]Killing himself in the process.

the foremost ones to you. O Pandava! One is incapable of enumerating the *tirtha*s in detail. This sacred and extensive river is famous in the three worlds. Narmada is best among rivers and is loved by Mahadeva. O Yudhishithira! Even if one remembers Narmada in the mind, the fruits obtained are more than those of one hundred *chandrayana*s. There is no doubt about this. But this should not be divulged to men who lack faith and are terrible non-believers.[1732] They will descend into a terrible hell. Parameshvara has said this. The divinity Maheshvara himself frequents Narmada all the time. It should be known that this sacred river takes away the sin of killing a *brahmana*.'

Chapter 96(2)(43) (Greatness of Japyeshvara)

Suta said, 'This excellent *tirtha* of Naimisha is famous in the three worlds. It is most loved by Mahadeva and destroys great sins. O excellent *dvija*s! Parameshthi Brahma constructed this place. Desiring to see Mahadeva, the *rishi*s tormented themselves through austerities here. *Brahmana*s from the families of Marichi, Atri, Vasishtha, Kratu, Bhrigu and Angiras had earlier approached Brahma, the one who originated from the lotus, the one with four forms and four faces. Prostrating themselves, they asked the imperishable creator of the universe.'

The six families asked, 'O divinity! I prostrate myself before you. How can I see the divinity, Bhagavan Ishana, the absolute one who is Kapardi? Please describe the means.'

[1732] As stated in the text, the sentence was incomplete. To make the meaning clear, we have expanded.

Brahma replied, 'Without any taints in words and thoughts, perform a sacrifice for one thousand years. I will tell you about a region. You should undertake the sacrifice in that place.'

Suta continued, 'Saying this, he touched the wheel that was in his mind. He told them, "I have released this wheel. Without any delay, follow it. The place where the rim is shattered is an auspicious place for austerities." Having said this, he released the wheel and they followed it. They quickly followed it to the place where the rim shattered. That sacred place came to be known as Naimisha[1733] and it is worshipped everywhere. It is full of *siddha*s and *charana*s and is frequented by *yaksha*s and *gandharva*s. This is Bhagavan Shambhu's excellent place of Naimisha. Earlier, *deva*s, *gandharva*s, *yaksha*s, *uraga*s and *rakshasa*s tormented themselves through austerities and obtained the best of boons from the divinity. Those from the six families resorted to this region. They controlled themselves and worshipped the lord of *deva*s through a sacrifice. They saw Maheshvara. Donations of food, torments through austerities, *shraddha*s and sacrifices—each of these, when undertaken here, destroys sins committed across seven births. Earlier, when the *rishi*s cleansed themselves through a sacrifice here, Bhagavan Brahma narrated Brahmanda Purana to them. It is here that the divinity Bhagavan Mahadeva, witness to the universe, sports even now with Rudrani, surrounded by *pramatha*s. If *dvija*s follow *niyama*s and give up their lives here, they go to Brahma's world. Having gone there, they are not born again.'

'There is another extremely famous *tirtha*, known as Japyeshvara. Nandi, the great *gana*, constantly performed

---

[1733] Derived from *nemi*, the rim/felly of a wheel.

japa on Rudra here. Along with Devi, Mahadeva, the
wielder of Pinaka, was pleased. He granted him equality
with himself and the ability to deceive death. There was a
rishi named Shilada. He had *dharma* in his soul and knew
about *dharma*. To please Vrishadhvaja, he worshipped
Mahadeva. He tormented himself through austerities for
one thousand years. Sharva, the witness to the universe,
arrived there, surrounded by *gana*s and with Umaa. He
said, "I am the one who grants boons." He asked for a
boon from Ishana, Girijaa's husband, the one who should
be worshipped. "Let me have a son just like you. He
should not be born from a womb and he should not suffer
death." Along with Devi, Bhagavan Maheshvara agreed to
this. While the *brahmana rishi* looked on, Hara vanished.
Shilada, excellent in following *dharma*, used that land. He
tilled the earth with a plough. When he broke it open,
he saw a beautiful son who seemed to be smiling. He
resembled the Samvartaka fire. He possessed beauty and
charm and his energy illuminated the directions. He was
unmatched, resembling Kumara. In a voice that rumbled
like the clouds, Nandi repeatedly addressed Shilada as
"Father! O father!" Seeing that the son had been born,
Shilada embraced him, as the sages who resided in that
hermitage looked on. He performed *jatakarma* and all
the other rites. Following the sacred texts, he invested
the sacred texts and taught him the *Veda*s himself.
Possessing excellent intelligence, the illustrious Nandi
studied the *Veda*s. He made up his mind, "I will see the
Lord Maheshvara and then conquer death". Attentive
and full of single-minded devotion, he went to the sacred
ocean. With his mind fixed on Mahesha, he constantly
performed *japa* on Rudra. When one crore *japa*s were
over, Shankara, affectionate towards his devotees, arrived

there with all his *gana*s and said, "I am the one who grants
boons." He asked Isha for the boon, "Let me able to do
one crore *japa*s again. Please grant me that." The divinity,
Mahadeva Parameshvara agreed to this and vanished. With
an attentive mind, the illustrious one again performed one
crore *japa*s. When the second lot of one crore *japa*s was
over, Vrishadhvaja arrived there and said, "I am the one
who grants boons." He was surrounded by a large number
of *bhuta*s. He said, "O Shankara! I desire to undertake a
third one crore of *japa*s." Agreeing to this, the *atman* of
the universe disappeared, along with Devi. When the third
one crore *japa*s was over, pleased in his mind, the divinity
arrived, surrounded by a large number of *bhuta*s. He said,
"I am the one who grants boons." He replied, "With your
energy, I wish to perform another one crore *japa*s." Thus
addressed, Bhagavan answered, "You will not do *japa*
anymore. You will be devoid of old age and death and
will always be at my side. You will be the lord of the great
*gana*s and Devi's son. Become a great lord. Be a great *yogi*
and a lord of *yoga*. Be a lord who is a lord of *gana*s. Be
handsome and the lord of all the worlds. Be engaged in
what is beneficial and be present in all sacrifices. Like an
amalaka in the palm of your hand, divine *jnana* about
me will be known to you. You will remain established
until the onset of the deluge. After that, you will go to my
destination." Saying this, Mahadeva Shankara summoned
the *gana*s and duly instated Nandishvara. The wielder of
Pinaka himself got him married to the auspicious daughter
of the Maruts and he obtained a status as Vishnu. This
place is Japyeshvara, belonging to the lord of *deva*s who
wields the trident. A mortal person who dies here, obtains
greatness in Rudra's world.'

Chapter 97(2)(44) (Greatness of *tirtha*s)

Suta said, 'Near Japyeshvara, there is another excellent *tirtha*. It is named Panchanada.[1734] It is sacred and destroys all sins. If a person fasts there for three nights and worships Maheshvara, purified of all sins, he obtains greatness in Rudra's world. There is another supreme *tirtha*, belonging to the infinitely energetic Shakra. It is known as Mahabhairava and it destroys great sins. Among *tirtha*s, the supreme *tirtha* is the supreme river of Vitasta.[1735] It is sacred and destroys all sins. It is itself the daughter of an Indra among mountains. There is the *tirtha* named Panchatapa, belonging to the infinitely energetic Shambhu. Here, the lord of *deva*s worshipped Bhava, so that he could become Shakra.[1736] *Pinda*s, donations and other things undertaken there bring bliss and happiness after death. If a person follows *niyama*s and dies there, he obtains greatness in Brahma's world. There is Mahadeva's auspicious abode, named Kayavarohana. The sages propounded Maheshvara's *dharma* there. *Shraddha*s, donations, austerities, oblations and fasting undertaken there, yield imperishable benefits. If a person gives up his life there, he goes to Rudra's world. There is another supreme and excellent *tirtha*, Kanyatirtha. Having gone there, if a person gives up his life, he obtains the eternal worlds. There is the place belonging to Rama, Jamadagni's son, the performer of unblemished deeds. If one bathes in that supreme *tirtha*, one obtains the fruits of donating one thousand cows. There is the *tirtha* known as Mahakala,

[1734]Literally, five rivers.
[1735]Jhelum.
[1736]That is, become Indra.

famous in the worlds. Having gone there, if a person gives up his life, he obtains the status of being a *ganapati*. The excellent Nakulishvara is the most secret among all *tirtha*s. The glorious Bhagavan Nakulishvara is present there. On a beautiful summit of Himalaya, there is the extremely beautiful Gangadvara. Along with Devi, Mahadeva is always there and his *shishya*s also gather there. If one bathes there and worships Mahadeva Vrishadhvaja, one is cleansed of all sins. After death, one obtains *jnana*. There is another place that belongs to the lord of *deva*s. It is auspicious and most sacred. It is known as Bhimeshvara. If one goes there, one is freed from sins. There is also the confluence of Chandavegaa, which destroys sins. If a person bathes and drinks the water there, he is freed from the sin of killing a *brahmana*. There is a supreme and divine city, named Varanasi. This is superior to crores and crores of all these *tirtha*s. I have spoken to you about the greatness of this city. Even if one resorts to *yoga*, there is no other place where one can be liberated in a single birth. Thus, the prominent places that take away the sins of men have been mentioned. By going there, one should wash away sins committed in hundreds of births. However, if a person gives up his own *dharma* and visits *tirtha*s, the *tirtha*s do not bring him any fruits, in this world, or in the next world. A person undergoing *prayashchitta*, a widower, a nomad and a householder should visit *tirtha*s, as should other similar people. One should make efforts to visit a *tirtha* along with the sacrificial fire, and along with one's wife. One will then be freed from all sins and obtain the destination mentioned earlier. A person intending to visit *tirtha*s must first clear the three debts. He must ensure a means of subsistence for his sons and entrust his wife to them. In connection with *prayashchitta*, the greatness of *tirtha*s has been described. If a person reads this, or hears it, he is freed from all sins.'

Chapter 98(2)(45) (Types of *pralaya*)

Suta said, 'The sages heard *vijnana*, as stated by the divinity Narayana, who had assumed the form of Kurma. They asked the lord.'

The sages said, 'You have narrated *jnana* about *moksha dharma* in detail. You have also spoken in detail about the creation of the worlds, the lineages and *manvantaras*. O divinity! O lord of *deva*s! O lord of the past and the future! You should now tell us about the *pralaya*[1737] of beings. You have spoken about it earlier.'

Suta continued, 'Hearing their words, Bhagavan, the great *yogi* who had assumed the form of Kurma, told them about the withdrawal of beings.'

Kurma said, 'In this Purana, four kinds of withdrawal are spoken about—*nitya*, *naimittika*, *prakrita* and *atyantika*. In this world, daily destruction of beings is witnessed. The sages describe this withdrawal under the name of *nitya*. At the end of a *kalpa*, Brahma brings about the destruction of the three worlds.[1738] The learned describe this under the name of *naimittika*. Starting with Mahat and ending with Vishesha, when all this heads towards destruction, those who have thought about time describe that destruction as *prakrita*.[1739] Other *dvija*s who have thought about time speak about a destruction resulting from *jnana*, when the

---

[1737] Dissolution, destruction.

[1738] At the end of Brahma's day, when Brahma goes to sleep.

[1739] At the end of Brahma's lifespan.

yogi dissolves into the *paramatman*. This is described as *atyantika*. *Atyantika* dissolution, with *jnana* as *sadhana*, has been described.'

'I will now briefly tell you about *naimittika*. This withdrawal results at the end of one thousand *mahayuga*s. Prajapati decides to establish *praja*s within his own *atman*. For one hundred years, there is a terrible drought. This is terrible and brings about a destruction of creatures. Thereby, all beings are destroyed. O lord of the earth! There are beings with limited substance. Those are first dissolved and merge with the earth. The sun rises, astride his chariot with the seven rays. These rays are intolerable and with these rays, he drinks up the water. His seven rays drink up the water from the great ocean. Having imbibed this, they blaze and become seven suns. Those seven rays dry up the four directions.[1740] Like fires, they burn up everything in the four worlds.[1741] With the flaming fire that comes at the end of a *yuga*, those seven suns blaze and their own fiery rays spread upwards and downwards. The water makes the thousands of rays of the suns blaze even more. They remain established, covering the sky and burn up the earth. The earth is scorched by their heat and the mountains, rivers, oceans and *dvipa*s are emptied of moisture. The blazing rays spread out in every direction, upwards, downwards and diagonally, so that everything is covered by a single fire. This fire and the fire from the sun mix with each other and reinforce each other. In this way, a single blaze results. The circle of the resultant fire

[1740] Meaning, the seven suns. Alternatively, each of the seven suns possesses seven rays.

[1741] Bhuloka, Bhuvarloka, Svarloka and Maharloka. Janaloka, Tapoloka and Satyaloka are not destroyed during *naimittika* dissolution.

destroys all the worlds. That energy swiftly burns down
these four worlds. All mobile and immobile objects are
dissolved into this. Without trees and without grass, the
earth looks like the back of a tortoise. The entire universe
is filled up and resembles a frying pan. Those rays fill up
everything and repeatedly burn them. Beings in Patala and
in the depths of the ocean are dissolved and merge into
the earth. The lordly fire, with seven parts in its *atman*,
reduces everything, *dvipa*s, mountains, *varsha*s and large
oceans, to ashes. The fire dries up all the water in oceans
and rivers. Drinking this water, it is kindled, and resting
on earth, blazes. As the winds expand and yawn, the
Samvartaka fire crosses over the great mountains, blazes,
burns the worlds. Having burnt earth, the *deva* dries up
Rasatala. Having burnt earth, below, it burns heaven,
above. The flames of the Samvartaka fire rise, hundreds,
thousands and tens of thousands of *yojana*s. Urged
by Kalarudra, the blaze burns *gandharva*s, *pishacha*s,
*yaksha*s, *uraga*s and *rakshasa*s. The body of the fire of
destruction is permeated by Kala himself and it burns
down everything, Bhulok, Bhuvarloka and Maharloka.[1742]
The fire envelopes these worlds, sideways and from above.
That energy gradually reaches everything in the universe.
Everything else is hidden. It alone remains illuminated. At
that time, terrible Samvartaka clouds rise in the firmament.
They resemble gigantic elephants and are ornamented with
lightning. Some are as dark as blue lotuses, others are like
waterlilies. Some possess the complexion of smoke, other
clouds are yellow. Some have the complexion of donkeys,
others have the hue of lac. Some are as white as conch-
shells and *kunda* flowers, others are like fine collyrium.

[1742] Including Svarloka.

Some possess the complexion of rocks, others are like pigeons. Some have the complexion of *indragopas*,[1743] others possess the complexion of yellow orpiment. Some clouds that rise up in the firmament resemble rainbows. Some are like mountains, others are like gigantic elephants. Some are like burning coal, others are like shoals of fish. They have many forms and terrible forms. They thunder in terrible tones. In this way, the clouds fill up the entire firmament. Those clouds, born from the seven suns, roar in terrible tones. They cover up and pacify the fire. After this, the clouds shower down in huge torrents. That extremely terrible and inauspicious rain quenches the fire. Flooded by copious amounts of water, the universe is filled up. Thus, the energy of the fire is subdued by the fire and the fire enters the water. As the clouds shower down for hundreds of years, the fire is destroyed. When it is destroyed, the entire universe is flooded with large torrents of water. Urged by Svayambhu, these flows fill up everything. Like the tide flowing in from the large ocean, there are large torrents of water. Gradually, the water covers the mountains, the *dvipa*s and earth. The water drunk up by the rays of the sun remains in the clouds. It showers down on the ground and the oceans are filled up again. At this, the oceans transgress all their shore-lines. The mountains are destroyed and the earth merges into water. All mobile and immobile entities are destroyed in that single and terrible ocean.'

'The divinity, Prajapati, lies down, immersed in *yoganidra*.[1744] The learned say that a *kalpa* consists of one thousand *mahayuga*s. The present one is Varaha *kalpa*

[1743] A reddish insect, sometimes identified with a fire-fly, also known as *shakragopa*.
[1744] The deep sleep of *yoga*.

and its dimensions have been spoken about. There are
innumerable *kalpa*s, with Brahma, Vishnu and Shiva in
their *atman*s. Sages, who have thought about time, have
spoken about them in the Puranas. In *sattvika kalpa*s,
Hari's importance is greater. Hara's is said to be more in
*tamas kalpa*s and Prajapati's in *rajas kalpa*s. The present
kalpa of Varaha is held to be *sattvika*. There are other
*sattvika kalpa*s and they belong to me. Through *dhyana*
and austerities, *yogi*s obtain *jnana*. They worship the
supreme Girish and proceed to the supreme destination. I
am the truth. I am myself full of *maya* and resort to *maya*.
When the universe is reduced to a single ocean, I proceed
to *yoganidra*. When it is time for sleep, great-souled ascetic
*maharashi*s from Janaloka see me, using the insight of
yoga. I am the ancient Purusha. I am the lord who is the
origin of *bhuh* and *bhuvah*.[1745] I am the glorious one, with
one thousand feet, one thousand eyes and one thousand
legs. I am *mantra*, *brahmana*s, cows and *kusha*. I am the
kindling. I am what is sprinkled. I am myself Soma. I am
vrata. I am Samvartaka, the great *atman*. I am sacred and
supreme fame. I am intellect. I am the lord who protects.
I am the lord of cows. I am Brahma's mouth. I am the
infinite saviour. I am *yogi*. I am the destination. I am
supreme among those who reach the destination. I am
Hamsa. I am *prana*. I am Kapila. I am the eternal one,
with the universe as form. I am *kshetrajna* and Prakriti.
I am Kala, the seed of the universe. I am *amrita*. I am the
mother and the father. I am Mahadeva. There is no one
other than me. I possess the complexion of the sun. I am
the protector of the world. I am Narayana. I am Purusha,
with *yoga* as form. Mendicants who are devoted to *yoga*

[1745] Bhuloka and Bhuvarloka.

see me. Knowing the truth about my *atman,* they proceed to my truth.'

Chapter 99(2)(46)
(Prakrita *pralaya* and subsidiary creation)

Kurma said, 'After this, I will briefly tell you about Prakrita *pralaya* and the excellent *pratisarga*. Listen attentively to me. When the second *parardha* is over, it is time for the destruction of the worlds. To reduce the entire universe to ashes, Kalagni roams around. Entering its *atman* with his own *atman*, the divinity becomes Maheshvara. He burns down the entire cosmic egg, with its *deva*s, *asura*s and humans. Bhagavan Mahadeva Nilalohita enters the fire. Assuming a terrible form, he destroys the worlds. He enters the solar disc and repeatedly manifests himself in many forms. Assuming forty-nine of his own forms,[1746] he burns down all the worlds. He unleashes the great Brahmashiras weapon and burns down everything in the universe. The fire that burns everything is flung onto the bodies of *deva*s. All the *deva*s are burnt down. Devi, the daughter of the excellent mountain, remains by Shambhu's side, as a witness. The *shruti* texts of the *Veda*s say this. Ishvara, the divinity, fashions his ornament, a garland made out of the heads and skulls of *deva*s. He fills up the circle of the firmament with large numbers of suns and moons. He has one thousand eyes and one thousand eye-lids. He possesses one thousand hands and feet. He is mighty-armed, with one thousand rays. There are fangs in his cruel mouth and his eyes are blazing fires. He wields a trident and his garment

[1746] Seven suns, each multiplied by seven.

is made of hide. He is established as the Ishvara of *yoga*. In his supreme bliss, he himself drinks copious quantities of *amrita*. Glancing towards Devi, Parameshvara performs the *tandava* dance. Devi drinks up the *amrita* from her husband's extremely auspicious dance. Resorting to *yoga*, her body merges with the body of the wielder of the trident. Out of his own will, the wielder of Pinaka enjoys the essence of *tandava*. With his own nature consisting of resplendence, Bhagavan burns down the circle of *brahmanda*. All the *deva*s are established in Brahma, Vishnu and the wielder of Pinaka. Earth and all its *guna*s are dissolved in water. Fire devours the *tattva* of water and its *guna*s. Fire, and all its own *guna*s, then head towards dissolution in wind. The wind, which holds up everything in the universe, and its *guna*s proceed towards dissolution in space. Space and its *guna*s dissolve in *bhutadi*. All the senses proceed towards destruction in *taijasa ahamkara*. O excellent one! *Vaikarika ahamkara* is also dissolved, along with groups of deities who preside over it. The three times of *ahamkara* head towards dissolution in Mahat. Along with these, Mahat is dissolved in the infinitely energetic Brahma. The origin of the universe is not manifest. It is single and imperishable and it destroys. In this way, Maheshvara withdraws the *tattva*s of the elements. He separates Pradhana and the supreme Purusha from each other. This is described as the destruction of the unborn Purusha and Pradhana. This dissolution does not exist on its own. It occurs because of Maheshvara. When there is a state of equilibrium of the *guna*s, this is described as unmanifest Prakriti. Pradhana is the womb of the universe. It is without consciousness and its *tattva* is that of *maya*. The *atman* is hidden and consists of consciousness alone. It is the twenty-fifth. The sages sing about it as the witness, and as the great grandfather.'

'In this way, the Shakti of destruction is certainly Maheshvara's Shakti. The *shruti* texts say that, starting with Pradhana and ending with Vishesha, everything is present in Rudra's body. Shankara arranges for *atyantika laya* for all the *yogi*s whose minds are immersed in *jnana*. Thus, the self-controlled Bhagavan Rudra brings about destruction. The *shruti* texts say that the Shakti which sleeps and confounds belongs to Narayana. Bhagavan Hiranyagarbha has existence and non-existence in his *atman*. As the twenty-fifth, after identifying himself with Prakriti, he creates everything. The Shaktis of Brahma, Vishnu and Isha are relatively weak and tranquil, established within their own *atman*s. Going everywhere, they bestow objects of pleasure and emancipation. They are the lords of everything. They are the bonds of everything. They are eternal, providing infinite objects of pleasure. Thus, the single imperishable *tattva* is that of Purusha, the Ishvara, with Pradhana in its *atman*.[1747] There are thousands of other divine Shaktis. Thus, Shaktis, Adityas and immortals are worshipped through many kinds of sacrifices. Each one of these possesses hundreds and thousands of bodies. However, the greatness of a single *nirguna* Shakti is spoken about. The divinity Maheshvara himself resorts to this Shakti. Using that Shakti, in his pastimes, he is seen to create many kinds of bodies. *Brahmana*s, who speak about the *Veda*s, worship him in all sacrifices. The *shruti* texts of the *Veda*s say that Rudra is the one who bestows everything wished for. Among all the Shaktis, the Shaktis of Brahma, Vishnu and Maheshvara are described as the most important, since the Shaktis of these divinities are those of the *paramatman*.

[1747]These *shloka*s are confusing, with possible typos. We have taken liberties.

It is sung that the eternal Bhagavan, the *paramatman*, is beyond all these. Every kind of *maya* is in his *atman*. He is Maheshvara, with the trident in his hand. Some speak of him as Agni, others as Narayana. Some speak of him as Indra, others as *prana*. There are others who describe him as Brahma. Brahma, Vishnu, Agni, Varuna and all the *deva*s and *rishi*s are said to be different aspects of the single Rudra alone. In whatever form Parameshvara is worshipped, Shiva assumes that particular form and grants the fruits. Therefore, one should resort to the eternal form, without differences. If one worships Mahadeva in this way, one proceeds to the supreme destination. The divinity Mahadeva is eternal and possesses all the Shaktis. Girisha can be worshipped in *saguna* or *nirguna* forms. I have already told you about the *nirguna* form of *yoga*. A devotee wishing to ascend can worship Parameshvara in *saguna* form, with Pinaka, three-eyes, matted hair and wearing a hide. As stated in the *shruti* texts of the *Veda*s, he can be thought of as golden in complexion, resembling one thousand suns. O bulls among sages! It has been instructed that this is *sabija yoga*. If a person is incapable of doing this, he should worship Hara as the universe, or as Brahma. O bulls among sages! However, if one is incapable of doing even this, he should devoutly worship Vayu, Agni, Shakra and the others. Hence, one should really give up all the *deva*s, with Brahma at the forefront. One should worship Virupaksha, present in the beginning, the middle and the end. Pure, devoted to one's own *dharma*, one should resort to *bhakti yoga*. That is the ultimate form of Shiva one should seek to approach. This is instructed as the ultimate sentiment of *sabija yoga*. If one follows these rules, one will reach Ishvara as a destination. I have spoken about two other pure sentiments to you earlier. I have now

spoken about *nirbija* and *sabija yoga*. I have already spoken
to you about *nirbija jnana*. A learned person uses *sabija*
to strive for Vishnu, Rudra and Virinchi. Alternatively,
controlling himself, he can intently worship Vayu and the
other *deva*s. He should worship Purusha Vishnu Hari, who
assumes four forms. He is the divinity eternal Vasudeva,
without a beginning and without an end. Narayana is the
origin of the universe. He is the greatest destination in the
firmament. One should be controlled, wearing his signs.
As has been stated, one should be devoted to him. It is held
that, in the ultimate, one should use these means or one's
own sentiments. I have thus spoken about *jnana*, which
depends on the supreme sentiments. Earlier, I spoke about
this to the sage Indradyumna. This universe, consisting of
the sentient and the insentient, should be known to have the
unmanifest in its *atman*. Ishvara is the supreme *brahman*.
Therefore, the universe is full of the *brahman*.'

Suta continued, 'After saying this, Bhagavan Janardana
stopped. Along with Shukra,[1748] the sages praised Vishnu
Madhava.'

The sages said, 'I bow before Vishnu *paramatman*, with
the form of Kurma. I prostrate myself before Narayana,
Vasudeva and the universe. I prostrate myself before
Krishna. I bow down. I prostrate myself before Govinda. I
bow down. I prostrate myself before Madhava, the eternal
lord of sacrifices. I prostrate myself before the one with
one thousand heads, the one with one thousand eyes. I
prostrate myself before the one with one thousand hands
and one thousand feet. OUM! I prostrate myself before
Vishnu *paramatman*, whose form is *jnana*. I prostrate
myself before the one who is bliss. I prostrate myself before

---

[1748]This might be a typo for Shakra.

the one who is beyond *maya*. I prostrate myself before the one whose body is hidden. I prostrate myself before the one who is *nirguna*. You are the ancient Purusha, whose own form is only that of existence. I prostrate myself before *sankhya* and *yoga*. I prostrate myself before the absolute one. I prostrate myself before the one who is *nishkala*, the one who can be reached through the *jnana* of *dharma*. I prostrate myself before the truth of *yoga*, the great lord of *yoga*. I prostrate myself before the one who is the source behind the superior and the inferior, the one who is known through the *Vedas*. I prostrate myself before the pure and enlightened one. I prostrate myself before the one who is united with the cause. I prostrate myself. I bow down. I prostrate myself before the one with *maya*. I prostrate myself before the creator. I prostrate myself before Varaha. I prostrate myself before Narasimha. I prostrate myself before Vamana. I prostrate myself before Hrishikesha. I prostrate myself before the one whose *atman* is not impeded, the one who bestows heaven and emancipation. I prostrate myself before the one who can be reached through *yoga*, the *yogi*, the one who bestows *yoga*. You are the lord of *deva*s. You pacify the afflictions of *deva*s. Through the favours of Bhagavan, everything in *samsara* is destroyed. We have obtained *jnana*. By obtaining this, one attains *amrita*. We have heard in detail about many types of *dharma*, *vamsha*, *manvantara*, *sarga*, *pratisarga* and *brahmanda*. You are the witness to the entire world. You are the universe. You are the supreme Narayana. You are the infinite *atman*. You should save us. We have sought refuge with you.'

Suta continued, 'O *brahmanas*! Gadadhara[1749] narrated this Kurma Purana and I have described all of it. It bestows objects of pleasure and emancipation. In this Purana, the origin of Lakshmi, in earlier times, has been narrated. Vasudeva arranged this, so as to confound all beings. There is a narration of the creations of Prajapati, the conduct of *varna*s and *dharma*, and the auspicious signs of *dharma*, *artha*, *kama* and *moksha*. The identity and separate and special features of the grandfather, Vishnu and the intelligent Mahesha have been described and the signs, conduct and food of devotees. The attributes of *varna*s and *ashrama*s have been accurately described. O bulls among sages! After this, there is a narration of the original creation, the seven sheaths that cover the cosmic egg and Hiranyagarbha's creation. There is a description of the enumeration of time and Ishvara's greatness, Brahma's lying down in the water, the determination of names and the raising of the earth in the form of Varaha. There is a narration of Mukhya and other creations and after that, the creation of sages. There is explanation of Rudra's creation, the creation of *rishi*s and ascetics. After describing Dharma's creation of *praja*s, there is a description of *tamas* creation. There is the dispute between Brahma and Vishnu, Brahma's entry into Vishnu's body, the intelligent one's delusion, his origin from the divinity's lotus, the sight of Mahesha and Vishnu's description of his greatness. Brahma Parameshthi was granted divine vision and Brahma Parameshthi praised the lord of *deva*s. Girisha was pleased and bestowed boons. There is a conversation between Vishnu and the great-souled Shankara. Having first bestowed boons, Pinaki vanished.

[1749]Wielder of the mace, Vishnu.

O *brahmanas*! The earlier slaying of Madhu and Kaitabha has been described. Brahma assumed an *avatara* from the lotus in the divinity's navel. The former identity between the divinity and Brahma has been described. Brahma was deluded and obtained *jnana* about Hara. There is a narration of how the intelligent lord of *deva*s undertook austerities. There is a description of how Mahesha appeared from the forehead, the creation by Rudra and its prohibition by Brahma. The glory of the lord of *deva*s, his bestowing of boons and instructions, the divinity's disappearance and the performance of austerities by the one born from the egg are described. There is the vision of the lord of *deva*s, with a body that is half-man and half-woman. There is a narration of the separation of Devi from Pinaki, the lord of *deva*s. After this, there is a description of Devi being born as Daksha's daughter and the truth about Devi being born as a daughter of the Himalayas. There is a vision of her divine form and a vision of her form as the universe. Her father, Himalaya, himself enumerated her one thousand names. There is the instruction by Mahadeva and the granting of boons. There is a detailed description of the creation of *prajas* by Bhrigu and others and the lineage of kings. Daksha was born as the son of the Prachetas and Daksha's sacrifice was crushed. In connection with the sacrifice, there was a debate between Daksha and Dadhicha. O bulls among sages! After this, there is a description of the curse levied on sages. Rudra arrived. Pinaki showed his favours and vanished. For the fight, there is a narration of the grandfather's instruction. There is Daksha's creation of *prajas* and that of the great-souled Kashyapa. There is the destruction of Hiranyakashipu and the slaying of Hiranyaksha. After this, there is a narration of the curse on

the residents of Devadaru-vana. There is the chastisement
of Andhaka and his becoming an excellent *ganapati*.
There is the chastisement of Prahlada and the restraint of
Bali. There is the chastisement of Bana and the favours
shown by the wielder of the trident. There is a detailed
narration of the lineages of *rishi*s and the lineages of
kings. Of his own free will, Hari Vishnu was born through
Vasudeva. He went and saw Upamanyu and performed
austerities. After seeing the three-eyed Mahadeva, along
with Ambaa, he obtained a boon. The wielder of the
Sharnga bow went to Kailasa and stayed there. After
this, the fear of the residents of Dvaravati is described.
After the immensely strong enemies were vanquished,
they were protected by Garuda, their protector. Narada
arrived and Garuda undertook his journey. Thereafter,
Krishna arrived in the hermitage of the sages. Vasudeva
worshipped Shiva's *lingam* every day. After this, there is
mention of the questions asked by the sage Markandeya.
There is an accurate description of the reason why the
lingam is worshipped, the signs of the *lingam* and the
fear caused by the *lingam*. O bulls among sages! When
it appeared in the middle, there is a description of the
delusion caused to Brahma and Vishnu and a narration of
their travels, upwards and downwards. The lord of *deva*s
praised and obtained Parameshthi's favours. The *lingam*
vanished and Samba's birth is described thereafter. O
excellent *dvija*s! Aniruddha's birth is described. At the
time of Krishna's departure, the *rishi*s arrived. The great-
souled Krishna instructed them and granted them a boon.
After Krishna left, Partha saw Krishna Dvaipayana and
he spoke to him about the eternal *dharma* of *yuga*s. He
showed his favours to Partha and left for Varanasi. Vyasa,
the sage who was Parashara's son, was extraordinary

in his deeds. There is a description of the greatness of
Varanasi and of *tirtha*s. Vyasa went on a visit to *tirtha*s
and saw Devi. There is a narration of his exile and the
granting of a boon. There is a description of Prayaga's
greatness and of *kshetra*s and their extensive fruits. O
*brahmana*s! Markandeya left. The nature of the worlds
and the position of luminous bodies is described. There is
the determination of *varsha*s, rivers and mountains. The
positions of the residents of heaven are described. There
is a description of the division of *dvipa*s and Shvetadvipa,
the lying down of Keshava and the great-souled one's
greatness. The *manvantara*s and Vishnu's greatness are
described. After this, there is a narration of the Vyasas
and their propounding of branches of the *Veda*s. O bulls
among sages! The *Veda*s, and those that are not the
*Veda*s, are described. There is an account of the lords
of *yoga* and description of their *shishya*s. Many secret
Gitas are narrated by Ishvara. There is conduct for *varna*s
and *ashrama*s and the rules for *prayashchitta*. Rudra
was reduced to holding a skull and begged for alms.
There is an account of women who are devoted to their
husbands and the determination of *tirtha*s. O *dvija*s! The
restraint of Mankanaka is also described. O *brahmana*s!
Kala's death has been narrated briefly. Shambhu entered
Devadaru-vana and so did Madhava. The intelligent lord
of *deva*s saw those from the six families. He granted them
a boon and Nandana is described. After this, there is a
description of *naimittika pratisarga*. Thereafter, there is a
description of *prakrita pralaya* and *sabija yoga*.'

'This is a brief description of what is in the Purana.
If a person knows this, he is freed from all sins and
obtains greatness in Brahma's world. Having said this,
Purushottama took Devi Shri with him. Hari gave up his

form as Kurma and departed. O *dvija*s! After prostrating
themselves before Purusha Vishnu and accepting the
amrita, all the *deva*s and sages also went to their own
respective places. In his form as Kurma, this entire
Purana was narrated by the lord and divinity Vishnu,
the origin of the universe, himself. O *brahmana*s! If
a person follows the rules and always reads it, even
briefly, he is freed from all sins and obtains greatness in
Brahma's world. Understand the good merits of a person
who writes it, or donates it to a *brahmana*, learned in
the *Veda*s, in Vaishakha or Kartika. He is freed from
all sins and possesses every kind of prosperity. Having
enjoyed extensive objects of pleasure, a mortal goes to
the extremely beautiful heaven. When he is dislodged
from heaven, he is born in a lineage of *brahmana*s. As
a consequence of his earlier purification, he comes to
obtain knowledge about the *brahman*. Even if a person
reads a single chapter, he is freed from all sins. If a
person reflects on this properly, he obtains the supreme
destination. From one *parva* day to another *parva* day,
*brahmana*s should study this sacred account. O best
among *dvija*s! If it is heard, it destroys great sins. If
all the Puranas and Itihasa are placed on one side of a
scale and the supreme *Veda*s on another side, the former
are heavier. If this Purana is kept aside, there no other
supreme *sadhana*. O ones excellent in vows! The divinity,
Bhagavan Narayana Hari, is accurately described here.
There is no one else like Vishnu. In this Purana, the
Samhita on the *brahman* destroys sins. The nature of
the supreme *brahman* is accurately described here. This
is the supreme *tirtha* among *tirtha*s and the greatest
austerity among austerities. This is supreme *jnana* among
everything with *jnana* and the supreme *vrata* among

*vrata*s. This sacred text should not be studied in the presence of a *vrishala*. Deluded in his mind, if a person studies it in this way, he goes to many hells. It must be heard by *dvija*s, at *shraddha*s and in rites associated with *deva*s, particularly at the end of sacrifices. It cleanses all taints. Those who desire liberation must especially study this sacred text. Those who wish to expand the meanings of the *Veda*s should hear it and comment on it. After knowing, full of faith, one should make Indras among *brahmana*s hear it. One is then freed from all sins and obtains *sayujya* with Brahma. If a person gives this to an unfaithful person, or to a person who follows *adharma*, after death, he goes to hell. He heads downwards and is born as a dog. This sacred text must be studied after prostrating oneself before Hari Vishnu, the eternal origin of the universe, and before Krishna Dvaipayana. This is the instruction of Vishnu, the infinitely energetic lord of *deva*s, and of the great-souled *brahmarshi*, Vyasa, Parashara's son. The illustrious *rishi*, Narada, heard it from the divinity Narayana. Earlier, he gave it to Goutama and Parashara obtained it from him. O lords among sages! This bestows *dharma*, *kama*, *artha* and *moksha*. At Gangadvara, the illustrious Parashara narrated it to the sages. Earlier, Brahma narrated it to the intelligent Sanaka and Sanatkumara. It destroys all sins. Devala, supreme among those who knew about *yoga*, obtained it from the illustrious Sanaka himself. Panchashikha obtained this excellent text from Devala. Satyavati's illustrious son obtained it from the sage Sanatkumara. In this supreme Purana, Vyasa gathered together every kind of meaning. I heard this from Vyasa. It will destroy your sins. It is appropriate that you should give this to all the people who follow *dharma*. I prostrate myself before the sage Vyasa, the omniscient *maharshi*, Parashara's serene son, with Narayana in his *atman*. Everything originates in him, and everything dissolves into him. I prostrate myself before Vishnu, the lord of gods, with the form of Kurma.'

This ends *Uttararddha*, the second part.

This ends Kurma Purana.

Acknowledgements

The corpus of the Puranas is huge—in scope and size. The Mahabharata is believed to contain 1,00,000 *shloka*s. The Critical Edition of the Mahabharata, edited and published by the Bhandarkar Oriental Research Institute, Pune, doesn't quite contain that many *shloka*s. But this still gives us some idea about the size of the epic. To comprehend what 1,00,000 *shloka*s means in a standard word count, the ten-volume unabridged translation I did of the Mahabharata (published by Penguin) amounts to a staggering 2.5 million words. After composing the Mahabharata, Krishna Dvaipayana Vedavyas composed the eighteen *mahapurana*s, or major Puranas. Or so it is believed. (There are *upapurana*s, or minor Puranas too.). Collectively, these eighteen Puranas amount to 4,00,000 *shloka*s, meaning a disconcerting and daunting number of 10 million words.

After translating the Bhagavat Gita, the Mahabharata, the *Harivamsha* (1,60,000 words) and the Valmiki Ramayana (5,00,000 words), it was but natural to turn one's attention towards translating the Puranas, that is, the major Puranas. This is the daunting Purana Project, so to speak. (All these translations have been, and will be, published by Penguin Random House India.) As the most popular and most read Purana, the Bhagavata Purana was the first to be translated (three volumes, 5,00,000 words). The *Markandeya Purana*, another popular Purana (one volume, 1,75,000 words) came next. This was followed by the *Brahma Purana* (two volumes, 3,90,000 words), the *Vishnu Purana* (one volume, 1,75,000 words), the *Shiva Purana* (three volumes, 6,75,000 words) and the *Brahmanda Purana* (two volumes, 3,76,000 words). A relatively slim Purana, the *Kurma Purana* (one volume, 1,65,000 words) is the seventh in the series. That these translations were well-received was encouragement along the intimidating journey of translating the remaining Puranas, and I am indebted to the reviewers and readers of these various translations. Two obvious points that are sometimes missed: First, the quality of the texts, on the basis of which these translations are being done, varies from one Purana to another. If a Purana has been read a lot, such as the *Bhagavata Purana*, *Markandeya Purana* or *Vishnu Purana*, the text tends to be clean and not characterized by typos. Clearly, the *Kurma Purana* isn't one of these, and there are typos in the text. Second, the structure of the text varies, depending on the subject. Parts of the *Kurma Purana* are quite esoteric.

The journey of translating hasn't been an intimidating one only for me. Penguin Random House India must also have thought about it several times, before going ahead with the Purana translations. Most people have some idea about the Ramayana and the Mahabharata, but the Puranas are typically rendered in such dumbed-down versions that the readership for unabridged translations had to be created, particularly for the lesser-known Puranas. However, Penguin also believed in the Purana Project, which still stretches into some interminable horizon in the future, more than one and a half decades down the line. For both author and publisher, this is a long-term commitment. But seven have been completed and *Matsya Purana* is eighth in the line. I am indebted to Penguin Random House India, in particular, Milee Ashwarya, Moutushi Mukherjee and Yash Daiv. The exceptional editing has ensured that the final product is superior to what I delivered. These Purana translations have been brought alive by the wonderful illustrations by Shamanthi Rajasingham and *Kurma Purana* is no different. I also thank the cover designers.

On 21 January 2024, I had a brush with death. Since my heart had stopped for a while, this was more than a mere brush. The near-death experience deserves to be written about, but not here, and not now. That I am alive is because of three contributory factors: First, destiny, which clearly believes in the Purana Project, too and blesses it, with *Kurma Purana* marking a threshold of sorts. Second, as I have traversed the route of the Purana Project, my wife, Suparna Banerjee Debroy, has been a constant source of support and encouragement, providing the conductive environment for the translation work to continue unimpeded. On 21 January 2024, it was much more than that. An acquaintance, privy to the details of what transpired, used the Savitri–Satyavan analogy, comparing her to Savitri. (The story occurs in the Mahabharata and will also feature in the forthcoming *Matsya Purana*.) Had it not been for her promptness and efficiency in rushing me to AIIMS, there would have been no *Kurma Purana* translation. The AIIMS (Delhi) logo has the expression शरीरमाद्यं खलु धर्म साधनम्. Every visitor to AIIMS will have passed it, without paying much attention to it. 'In the pursuit of *dharma*, the body is the foremost instrument.' The original is from Kalidasa's *Kumarasambhavam* (the fifth canto) and was stated by Shiva to Parvati, to dissuade her from austerities and emaciating herself. Third, Dr Rajiv Narang and the doctors at the Department of Cardiology, AIIMS, ensured that I had a renaissance and *prana pratishtha* on 22 January 2024. *Kurma Purana* is accordingly dedicated to Dr Rajiv Narang and the doctors in AIIMS.

Scan QR code to access the
Penguin Random House India website